MARK ELLIOTT is a writer and travel consultant who has specialized in Azerbaijan since 1995. In over a dozen visits he has driven, hiked and ridden into virtually every corner of the country. He has contributed to conferences on Azeri tourism and culture and advised journalists and prospective film crews on Azerbaijan projects. He also offers pre-departure cultural briefings to Baku-bound expats from the UK and Europe.

Mark's first guidebook was *Asia Overland*, also for Trailblazer. He is co-author of Lonely Planet guides to neighbouring *Iran* and *Russia* amongst numerous other books. When not travelling he lives a blissfully quiet life in suburban Belgium.

Azerbaijan

Azerbaijan – with excursions to Georgia
First edition: 1999; this fourth edition: 2010

Publisher
Trailblazer Publications
The Old Manse, Tower Rd, Hindhead, Surrey, GU26 6SU, UK
Fax (+44) 01428-607571, info@trailblazer-guides.com
www.trailblazer-guides.com

British Library Cataloguing in Publication Data
A catalogue record for this book is available from the British Library

ISBN 978-1-905864-23-2

Editor: Anna Jacomb-Hood
Series editor: Patricia Major
Typesetting: Nicky Slade
Layout: Nick Hill
Cartography: Mark Elliott
Index: Mark Elliott

Front cover photograph: Niyazi (1912-1984) conducting from the statue-filled
arches of the Axundov (National) Library, Baku (see p96). (Photo © Mark Elliott)

Every effort has been made by the author and publisher to ensure that the information
contained herein is as accurate and up to date as possible. However, they are unable to
accept responsibility for any inconvenience, loss or injury sustained by anyone as a
result of the advice and information given in this guide.

Printed on chlorine-free paper by
D2Print (☎ +65-6295 5598), Singapore

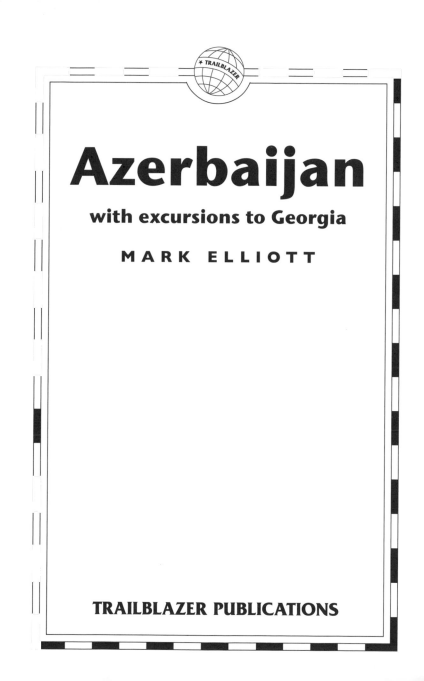

Azerbaijan

with excursions to Georgia

MARK ELLIOTT

TRAILBLAZER PUBLICATIONS

Acknowledgements

This book is dedicated to my long-suffering, unflinchingly supportive wife (Dani Systermans), 'the kids' (my unbeatable parents) and my adopted 'Baku family' (Saadat, Narmin and Ian Peart) without whom Azerbaijan would be so much less like home. Continuing gratitude to misunderstood philosopher Vasif Sadikhov who showed me so much, to the charming Serdar Koleli who gave us the wheels, to Cedric Philp at Mobil who made the original edition of this book possible, to Jane Elliott who opened my eyes to the humorous side of Caucasian travel and to Inga Goguadze whose hospitality inspired the project in the first place.

Amongst the uncountable others who have made crucial contributions large or small, thank you to Abulfaz Qarayev, Adam German, Adelia Efendieva, Akhshin and Samir Mehtiyev, Alex Burnett, Aliheydar Pashayev, Alison Logan, Aliya and Farid, Andrew Barnard and Rebecca Weaver, Andrew and Judith Tucker, Andy Hill, Angus Hay, Anna Jacomb-Hood and her Jaffa Cakes, Araz Azimov, Aspasia Drosopoulou, Bachar Alchahin, Badal Lalayev, Bahram Khalilov, Balchik and family in Alpan, Bayram Balci, Benjamyn Damazer, Betty Blair, Bohdan Nahajlo, Brian Coulson and colleagues, Brigid Keenan & AW, Bruce Dolby, Bryn Oilbasher, Carl Hawkings, fellow ethical hedonist Carlo Castoro, Donny and Josh in Zaqatala, Carly Edgington, Charles Van Der Leeuw, Charlie, Chris Gotch, Chung Wah Erinyes, Claire Doyle, Damir Bağirov Amrah and the welcoming committee in Qäbälä, Dave Askeland, Dave Puls, Dave Watson, David Zaridze, Deanna Ricketts, Derek Lavery, Elchin Amirbekov, Elchin Rzaev, Elchin Sultanov, Eldar, Elnara Zakiri, Elhan Bagirov, Elvin at the Old City Inn, Eran and Nergiz, the lovely Esmira Rahimova and family, Farkhad, Frank Müller, Fuad Orujov, Gabil Kocharli, Galib at Samur, Gila Altmann, the inspiring Guntakin, Guy Jacobs, Habib Abasquliev in Nakhchivan, Hartmut Müller at Shirvan NP, Hassan from Yengija, Hilary and Colin Munro, Husein Hağarverdiyev, Huub Delahaye Ibragim at the Europa, Igor Issayev, Iman Gasanov, Intiqam Ismayilov and family, Jacob Nell, Javanshir Salayev in Pensar, Jean François Daganeaud, Jean-Pierre Guinhut, Jenn in Goranboy, Jim and Ginny, Joel Robbins, Joe Valles, John Boit, Jonathan Shiland, Jorn Eide, Judith Patten, Julian Coulter, Justin Odum in Mingachevir, Justyna Hellebrand, Jyoti Pande, Karen Wrightsman, Katherine Meunier, Khaled Evasov, Khanoğlan Malim, Koidezha Mexmanov and family in Priship, Larry and Uschka Dunbar, Laurent Ruseckas, Lesley Ataker, Lewis Dorman, Leyla Aliyeva, Lutful Kabir, Marc Noguera, Marc Spurling, Mahir Gahramanov, Margaret Jack, Maria Baez, Mark Trier, Markus Hochuli, Mary in Bärdä Fatma and family, Maryam Abassova, Maura and James Martin, Minai Massimova, Mishel in Göylar, Mohammad Gassanov in Mamrux, Mukhtar at the Görush, Naira and family, Napier Shelton, Natasha and Max, Nazia Nabi, Nazim Machano, Nicole de Lalouviére, Oktay and Elmar at the ministry, Pål Eitrheim, Paul and Stuart at MAG, Phil and Julia Prestridge, Philip Bragdon and family, Rachel Alxasova, Rachel, Rahim, Ronnie Gallagher, Rövsan Shirinov, Rövshan Äliyev, Rufat in Bideyiz, Rustam Mustafayev in Gädäbäy, Sabina Shukhlinskaya, Sachin Dalal, Saraf Abdurahmanonov, Sarah Riddle, Sarita Vaid, Scott Richardson, Sebastian Schmidt, Sheila, Dave and Don Churchman, Stein Iversen, Steinar Gil and family, Stephanie Furness, Suad and Sada, Suzanne for the Altı Ağach insights, Tanya Bowen, Tarlan Zahidov, Thomas Humer, Tim Ong in Lankaran, Tim Wall and Seville, Tofiq Verdiyev for rescuing us en route to Allar, Tonie and Kristian Steffensen, Ulvi Ismayil, Wieland de Hoon, Wolfgang Bekstein, Xeyraddin Cabbarov, Yusif Mirza, Zaza Makharadze, Zhora Kechari, and many, many more whose names I may have missed (sorry!) or never known.

A request

The author and publisher have tried to ensure that this guide is as accurate and up to date as possible. Nevertheless things change amazingly rapidly in Azerbaijan. If you notice any changes or omissions or can suggest improvements for the next edition of this book, I'd be delighted if you'd let me know. Please write to Mark Elliott at Trailblazer (address on p2) or email me at mark.elliott@trailblazer-guides.com. Many thanks in advance.

Updated information will shortly be available on the internet at
www.trailblazer-guides.com

CONTENTS

INTRODUCTION

Fascinating Azerbaijan offers an incredible wealth of scenic contrasts, is famous for caviar and carpets and has curiosities from bizarre mud volcanoes to mysterious medieval fire temples. Baku, the cosmopolitan capital, is one of the world's fastest-changing cities, its medieval-walled Old City ringed by century-old 'oil boom' architecture and an ever grow-ing platoon of shiny new tower blocks. Its hospitable people are highly cultured, there's a vibrant art and music scene, several colourful markets and an ever-expanding choice of din-ing and entertainment possibilities.

Just an hour or two's drive beyond the city amazingly varied landscapes encompass painted deserts, vineyards, orchards, oak woodlands, snow-capped peaks, iron-wood forests, hilltop castles and magnificent canyons. While few foreigners come specifically to enjoy these delights, their discovery can transform one's experience of Baku life. And in many areas you may still be among the first foreign visitors locals have seen in generations. The recent economic boom means that changes even in the countryside are accelerating with new roads to provincial centres under construction and an ever wider range of rural getaway 'rest zones' offering accommodation to richer Baku weekenders. But to explore Azerbaijan's most spectacular regions in and around the soaring High-Caucasus mountains, you'll still need hiking boots, a horse or a strong four-wheel-drive vehicle.

This guide, now in its fourth fully updated edition, gives you an unparalleled depth of background information and all the practical tips necessary to appreciate and make the most of this beautiful, varied and under-estimated land.

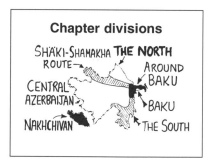

Chapter divisions

❏ **Baku map-symbol key**
To locate any site in Baku simply reference the code symbol for the relevant Baku map (key below) then use the grid reference to pinpoint the exact position.

Ψ Around Central Baku p77	Σ Old City p83	∂ Central Baku pp92-3
φ Around the Old Town p86	α Station Area p99	π Western Baku p101
β North-Central Baku p106	τ Hyatt Area p105	ϑ Gänclik p107

❏ Essential information for visitors

● **Visa** Required by all (see p9). Invitation or hotel bookings are usually required but not when applying on arrival by air at Baku.

● **Currency** New Manat (1AZN) = 100 qäpiq (q). One 'Shirvan' = 2AZN.

● **Exchange rates** US$1 = 0.80AZN, £1 = AZN1.28. ATMs for MasterCard/Visa cash advances are widespread in Baku and available in all main towns, typically at Kapital Bank or IBA. Rate-splits are excellent for US$, good for euros but poor for pounds sterling and other currencies. Re-exchanging $ and € is no problem. Travellers' cheques are awkward to cash, especially outside Baku.

● **Hotel prices** Top hotel (Baku) AZN200-1000. Mid-range Baku hotel AZN80-200. Rural en suite bungalow AZN50. Rural motel AZN25-50. Homestay or basic Soviet-style room AZN10-25.

● **Food prices** Cheap local meals AZN3, typical shashlyk meal AZN5-15, mid-market Baku restaurant meal AZN20-40.

● **Drink prices** Bottled water from 40q per litre. Draft beer from AZN0.50 (NZS), bottled lager from AZN1 (Xırdalan in cheap bars) to AZN7 (imports in hotels etc).

● **Transport prices** Short taxi hop AZN1 in most provincial towns, AZN2 in Gänjä, AZN3-5 in central Baku. Cross the country for AZN9 (by bus) or AZN7 (by sleeper train).

● **Time zone** 4hrs ahead of GMT (+5 in summer); 2hrs ahead of Turkey; 30 minutes ahead of Iran (90 minutes in summer).

● **Religion** Very tolerant form of Shi'ite Islam with animist undertones, see p47.

● **Dress code** Unlike most Islamic places, it's men not women who would cause a stir if they wore shorts. In the countryside women should also cover their legs but, in Baku, fashion allows remarkably risqué outfits. No need to cover hair.

● **Language** Azeri (Azerbaijani). Russian is also spoken widely in Baku and among older folks across the country, Turkish is similar enough to Azeri to be useful. English is widely understood by younger people in Baku, but by few in the provinces. See p53 for an overview, p372 for Azeri phrases, pp21-7 for food terms, and pp374-5 for geographical terminology.

● **Best seasons** Spring is ideal for the lowlands, summer for the mountains, May for the deep south. Beware that during the Annual Oil and Gas Show (early June), flights and Baku's better-quality accommodation will be full.

● **Telephone codes** Azerbaijan is +994, dial out code (from Azerbaijan) is now 00 as from most other countries. Remove the zero of the city code if calling from abroad.

● **Health factors** Little to worry about. Avoid drinking tap water except in mountain villages. A good repellent avoids annoying mosquitoes but malaria risk is minimal (and what little there is is mostly limited to marsh areas around Imishli where few travellers venture anyway).

● **Safety** Generally safe and hospitable. Occasional hassles from suspicious police. Violence and crime is minimal though do beware late at night around Sahil Garden in Baku where there have been muggings.

● **Problems** Unresolved Nagorno-Karabagh war (around 15% of Azerbaijani territory remains occupied by Armenian forces), many refugees. Ecological problems in the Caspian Sea and post-Soviet pollution legacies.

● **Shopping** Most international goods are available in Baku but the choice is vastly more limited in the provinces. Export certificates are required for carpets (pp60-1), art (pp58-9) and antiques. There's a 200g limit on exporting caviar (p21). Copperware is a popular souvenir from Lahic.

PART 1: AZERBAIJAN OVERVIEW

Practical information

VISAS

Most Western nationals require a visa. Two photos are usually required. Visa fees vary by nationality: Brits pay US$100, Schengen-Europeans pay €60, Americans $131. A few embassies give a double-entry visa at no extra cost. A multiple-entry visa costs $250 regardless of nationality, but requires fairly lengthy approval procedure from Baku. Approved Azerbaijani tourist companies can provide their customers with a 'tourist-voucher' which halves the cost of single-entry visas.

You can download visa application forms on 🖥 www.mfa.gov.az/eng/images/stories/downloads/applicationforvisa.pdf.

If you're just changing planes in Baku airport (eg using the AZAL connections from Europe to Kabul) you're allowed to wait visa-free for up to 24 hours BUT only if you stay within the airport (ie even though it's barely 200m away you can't access the Holiday Inn unless you have a visa).

● **Visas on arrival** For the same fees you can get a (single-entry) visa on arrival but ONLY arriving by air at Baku, NOT if you arrive overland. An invitation letter isn't usually necessary but you will need two visa photos: if you don't have the latter a photographer is on hand to snap polaroids for €10.

The bizarre procedure requires that you get stamped in at immigration BEFORE you apply for the visa! The only apparent purpose for this is to double everyone's queuing time.

Note that the foreign ministry website says visas are available at Nakhchivan and Ganja airports as well as at Baku. However, I've yet to meet anyone who dared test this and according to people working at Nakhchivan airport this is definitely NOT possible.

Beware: there are rumours that by 2010 the visa on arrival might be dropped so dou-

ble check carefully with an Azerbaijani embassy before assuming anything...

● **Tourist/entry visas** To arrive overland you need a visa in advance, which almost always takes five days to process. And that's not including however long it takes to get the required letter of invitation (LOI) from an Azeri friend, tour agency or business contact that must be approved by the Ministry of Foreign Affairs. In previous years it was easy to get around this annoyance by presenting instead a proof of a Baku hotel booking. However, as of 2009, the rules appear to be tightening. There remains a degree of confusion and as we go to press it's still possible to get a visa on arrival at Baku airport without such LOIs. But you should check carefully for the latest information before making any assumptions.

In recent years Tbilisi (Georgia), Tashkent (Uzbekistan), Tabriz (Iran) and Istanbul (Turkey) have proved good places to get visas (ie without any supporting documents). Ankara (Turkey) and Tehran (Iran) have proved comparatively awkward demanding expensive extra paperwork from your 'home' embassy.

When applying for the visa, almost inevitably you'll have to pay the fee into a specific bank branch (not to the consul). Annoyingly the bank might be way across town and afterwards you'll have to return to the consulate with the payment slip, so start your application process early in the day.

● **Transit visas** Transit visas cost only US$20 but generally require the same application formalities as tourist visas. They aren't usually available at the airport.

Azerbaijan embassies abroad

The foreign ministry usually lists embassy addresses under Azerbaijan Missions Abroad on 🖥 www.mfa.gov.az/eng/index.php.

Many Azeri consular departments only work Mon, Wed & Fri 10am-noon.
● **Austria** Hügelgasse 2, Vienna A-1130 (☎ 1-403 1322, 🖥 www.azembvienna.at).

● **Belgium** 464 Ave Molière, Brussels, but enter from the side (☎ 02-345 2660; 🖳 www.azembassy.be). If you have Bancontact/MisterCash (ie a Belgian debit card) you avoid trekking off to make the visa payment in a Brussels bank.

● **Bulgaria** 6 Charles Darvin St, Iztok district, 1113 Sofia (☎ 2-817 0070; 🖳 www. azerembsof.com).

● **Canada** Suite 904, 275 Slater St, Ottawa KP1 5H9 (☎ 613-288 0497 🖳 www.az embassy.ca).

● **China** Qijiayuan Diplomatic Compound, Villa B-3, Beijing 100600 (☎ 10-6532 4614, 🗎 1 6532 4615; 🖳 www.azerb embassy.org.cn).

● **Czech Republic** Na Mícánce 32, Prague 6 (☎ 24-603 2422; 🖳 www.azembassy prague.az)

● **Egypt** 10 Maadi St, Villa 16/24, 11431 Cairo (☎ 2358 3761; 🖳 www.azembassy .org.eg).

● **France** 209 rue de l'Université, Paris 75007 (☎ 01 44 18 92 20; 🖳 paris@ mission.mfa.gov.az.

● **Georgia** (see p323) 🖳 www.azembassy.ge

● **Germany** Hubertsallee 43, Berlin 14193 (☎ 30-219 1613; 🖳 www.azembassy.de).

● **Greece** Consulate 23 Vasilissis Sofias, 10674 Kolonaki-Athens (☎ 210-724 8236; 🖳 www.azembassy.gr).

● **Hungary** Eötvös utca 14, Budapest 1067 (☎ 1-374 6070; 🖳 www.azerembassy.hu).

● **India** E-70, Vasant Marg, Vasant Vihar, Delhi 110057 (☎ 011-2615 2228).

● **Indonesia** Jalan Mas Putih, Blok D, Persil 29, Grogol Utara Kebayoran Lama, Jakarta (☎ 021-549 1939).

● **Iran: Tehran:** Nader Sq, 15 Golbarg St, Chizar (☎ 021-2224 8770) Applications Tue, Thu & Sun 9am-noon; **Tabriz**: Mohabarat St, Valiasr (☎ 0411-333 4802).

● **Italy** 1 Viale Regina Margherita, Piano 2, 00198 Rome (☎ 068-530 5557; 🖳 www .azembassy.it)

● **Japan** Higashigaoka 1-19-15, Meguro-ku, Tokyo (☎ 03-5486 4744; 🖳 www. azembassy.jp).

● **Jordan** Mohammad Ali Bdair St, Abdoun, 11185 Amman (☎ 6 593 55 25; 🖳 www.azembassyjo.org)

● **Kazakhstan** Diplomatic City, C-14 (☎

3172-241 581, 🖳 www.azembassy.kz).

● **Kuwait** Al-Yarmuk block 2, Street 1, Building 15 (☎ 5355247; 🖳 www.azer embassy-kuwait.org).

● **Latvia** 2-5, Rainas Blvd, Riga LV1050 (☎ 6-714 2889; 🖳 www.azembassy.lv).

● **Malaysia** Wisma Chinese Chamber, 2nd fl, 258 Jalan Ampang, KL 50450 (☎ 603-4252 6800; 🖳 www.azembassy.com.my).

● **Netherlands** 127 Laan Copes van Catenburch, 2585EZ The Hague (☎ 070-364 8546; 🖳 www.azembassy.nl).

● **Pakistan** Atatürk Ave, House 14, Street 87, Sector G-6/3, Islamabad (☎ 282-3455, consular 🗎 282-0898; 🖳 www.az embassy.com.pk).

● **Poland** 12 ul Zwyciezcow, Warsaw 03941 (☎ 22-616 2188; 🖳 www.azer-embassy.pl).

● **Romania** 10 Grigore Gafencu St, Sector 1, Bucharest 014132 (☎ 21-233 2466; 🖳 www.azembassy.ro/eng/contacts.htm) Website gives map of embassy location.

● **Russia** 16 Leontiyevski (Stanislavsky) per, **Moscow** (☎ 629 4332/5546; 🖳 www .azembassy.msk.ru). Metro Tverskaya. **St Petersburg:** 2 Sovetskaya (☎ 12-717 3991).

● **Saudi Arabia** Al Worood Guarter St, Amir Feysal Bin Saud Abdul Alrahman 59, Aloroba Road, Riyadh (☎ 1-419 2382; 🖳 www.azembassy.org.sa).

● **Spain** 38 Ronda Avutarda, Madrid 28043 (759 6010; 🖳 www.azembajada.es) To apply for a visa first call the consulate for an appointment.

● **Switzerland** 27 Dalmaziquai, **Berne**, CH3005 (☎ 31-350 5040; 🖳 www.az embassy.ch) and 67 rue de Lausanne, 1202 **Geneva** (☎ 22-901 18 15).

● **Turkey** 1 Bakü Sok, Or-An, **Ankara** (☎ 312-491 1681/2/3, 🗎 492 0403) It's on the very far edge of the city; bus #189 from Kizlay, #188 from Çankaya – 15 stops. **Istanbul** (see map opposite): Sümbül Sok 17, 1-Levent (☎ 212-325 8045, 🖳 www.az consulateistanbul.org.tr; metro Levent from Taksim), Mon-Fri 10-13.00 & 15-17.00. **Kars**: Sukapi mahallesi, Eski Erzrum caddesi, 123, (☎ 474-223 6475; 🖳 www.az consulatekars.org.tr).

● **Turkmenistan** 44, ul 2062, Ashgabat

AZERBAIJAN – OVERVIEW

744020 (☎ 364608, 🖳 www.azembassy
ashg.com), Mon-Fri 09-13.00 & 14-18.00.
• **UAE** PO Box 45766, Al-Bateen area,
sector W/16, Plot N-297 Abu Dhabi (☎ 666
28 48; 🖳 www.azembassy.ae).
• **UK** 4 Kensington Court, London W8
(High St Kensington tubc) (☎ 020-7938
5482; 🖳 www.azembassy.org.uk).
• **Ukraine** 24 Glibochitska St, Kiev (☎
484 6932; 🖳 www.azembassy.org.ua/site/).
• **USA** 2741 34th Street NW, **Washington
DC** 20008 (☎ 202-337-5912; 🖳 http:/
/azembassy.us); 11766 Wilshire Blvd, **Los
Angeles**, CA 90025 (☎ 310 444 9101;
🖳 www.azconsulatela.org).
• **Uzbekistan** 25 Sharq Tongi St, Tashkent
700043 (☎ 71-789 304; 🖳 www.az
embassy.uz). Next door to UzCom head
office, south of Metro Yoshliq on Halqar
Dustligi. Travellers report getting tourist
visas without invitation.

For foreign embassies in Baku see box p132.

Extending a visa
Take a new invitation letter, passport and
passport photocopies to the Ministry of
Foreign Affairs Consular Department
(p101, πT9; ☎ 492 3410, 492 9692, 🖳
www.mfa.gov.az), at 4 Shikhali Gurbanov
St. If an extension is possible you'll have
to pay the relevant fee into a nearby bank
then return with the receipt. Applications
are accepted between 10.00 and 13.00
Monday to Friday.

Police registration If you're intending
to stay over a month, or if you have a one-
year multiple-entry visa, you are expected
to register within three days at the main
police station of the *rayon* in which you're
resident. You'll be required to show some
proof of where you are staying/living ie
your residential address. As landlords
aren't always keen to oblige with such
written proof, the theoretically minor act
of registration can end up becoming an
oddly frustrating ordeal. Some rayons are
notoriously uncooperative at issuing registrations even with all the correct paperwork. For years that mattered little since
nobody ever checked registrations anyway. However, in early 2007, a series of
random checks landed several unregis-
tered expats with $1000 fines.
    If you stay less than a month, police
registration is technically unnecessary.
Technically. However, some provincial
policemen seem to think otherwise. I've
twice been 'pulled in' for lack of a
Müvaqqati Qeydiyat (temporary registration) which they claim I needed. But even
they seemed to have no idea how I could
actually obtain such a document given that
I was travelling with no residential address
in Azerbaijan. Very frustrating.

Work permits
Expatriate residents are now expected to get
a work permit, though employers will usually take care of this for you. Officially the
cost is AZN45 though I've heard instances
of vastly higher fees being requested and as
of February 2009 the press reports that the
official fee will soar to AZN1000.

Border zones Any *rayon* which has a
border zone with Armenia or Armenian-
occupied Azerbaijan may choose to find
your presence undesirable. In the mountain-
ous regions such as Gädäbäy and
Xanlar–Göygöl there are manned army
roadblocks so it's easy to know how far
you're allowed to go. In other areas there is
no such demarcation but that does not mean
you're entirely at liberty to explore. I found
myself in uncomfortable situations in
Ordubad, Qazax and Ağstafa where my

photography was considered very suspicious. The latter two provinces seem to require tourists to have clearance from the Ministry of Defence should they wish to do more than transit en route to/from Georgia. If you're travelling in a group or by car you're much less liable to arouse the curiosity and suspicion of the authorities.

GETTING THERE

There are no direct flights from the Americas, Africa or Australasia. Western travel agents may not immediately remember the codes for Azerbaijan's international airports: Baku GYD, Gänjä KVD, Nakhchivan NAJ. The website 🖳 www .alternativeairlines.com is a useful guide for less immediately obvious international routes, though I haven't tried booking a flight through them.

From Europe

AZAL (🖳 www.azal.az; the Azeri national carrier) has Boeing 757 flights from London Gatwick (☎ UK 020-7629 3722), London Heathrow (Sat, AZN470/555 one-way/return), Paris (☎ France 1 40 15 61 34, AZN345/460) and Milan (AZN327/420). There are also scheduled flights from London Heathrow (daily, BMI, 🖳 www.fly bmi.com), Frankfurt (Lufthansa), Riga (Air Baltic), Vienna (Austrian), Istanbul (THY, AZAL), and several other Turkish and CIS cities. Planes are most likely to be full in early June at the time of the Oil Show with fares usually lowest in mid-summer.

Booked online (🖳 www.airbaltic. com), low-cost Air Baltic's flights can be especially good value for reaching Brussels (from €150 one way), Oslo (from US$270), Stockholm (from US$275) and much of Scandinavia. Their flights to Dublin and London Gatwick are also a relative bargain. Like all no-frills airlines fares fluctuate wildly according to demand and seasonal service stoppages can be annoying. All require connecting in Riga, some connections giving you transit times of just half an hour which incredibly IS just enough given Riga's tiny but modern terminal (though not if you've got check-in baggage). Otherwise building in a day's

stopover (no extra cost) is a great pleasure as Riga is a delightful place to explore with wonderful art nouveau cafés and decent-value accommodation.

If money is more important than time you may save a little by flying from Europe to Turkey, using budget airlines to Istanbul (EasyJet, Corendon etc) or charter airlines (Thomas Cook, Tui, Jetair etc) to Antalya, Izmir or Dalaman, and then continuing overland. One-way charter flights are especially cheap at the end of the season (ie October **to** Turkey, March **from** Turkey). Dozens of agencies in the Sultanahmet area of Istanbul offer one-way fares to Europe in the €80-120 range. From Istanbul trotting across to Georgia is a pleasure now that Georgian visas aren't required and police corruption has been largely eradicated.

From Asia

An intriguing AZAL flight links Baku to Ürümqi in western China (Tue, Thur, AZN228, AZN302 return). Otherwise, connections to east Asia require transfers, typically starting with the Thursday flight to Tashkent on Uzbekistan Airways. Their Baku–Tashkent–Delhi (US$462, return $660) has only a two-hour wait outbound, to Bangkok ($560/790) the wait is four hours, to Kuala Lumpur ($560/780) it's eight hours. You might need to overnight in Tashkent (and get a visa) for the Beijing ($570/730), Seoul ($575/800), Tokyo ($685/1000) and Osaka ($685/1000) connections. Another alternative is flying to Dubai on AZAL (AZN285, return AZN390) then buying an onward ticket or using a major carrier via Europe. Beware of flying via Moscow (Aeroflot) or Tehran (Iran Air) as you'll almost inevitably need a Russian or Iranian transit visa which can prove an annoying fiddle.

From/to Turkey

By air THY (Turkish Airlines, 🖳 www .thy.com) is a reliable carrier offering competitive fares between European cities and Baku via Istanbul (daily). AZAL (🖳 www .azal.az) is often slightly cheaper with Baku–Istanbul (daily) costing AZN225/340

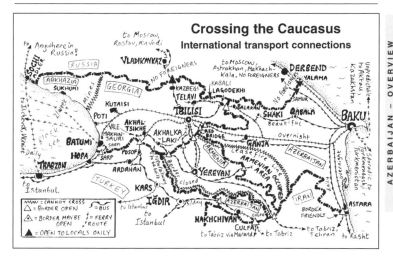

Crossing the Caucasus
International transport connections

(map labels) to Moscow, Rostov, Min Vody · to Anywhere in Russia? · SOCHI · RUSSIA · VLADIKAVKAZ · NO FOREIGNERS · to Moscow, Astrakhan, Makhach-Kala, NO FOREIGNERS · DERBEND · YALAMA · Unpredictable? to Kraus, Kazakhstan · ABKHAZIA · SUKHUMI · GEORGIA · KABALI · KAZBEGI · TELAVI · LAGODEKHI · SAMUR · KUTAISI · POTI · TBILISI · BALAKAN · SHAKI · QABALA · BAKU! · AKHAL-TSIKHE · Beautiful · AKHALKA-LAKI · RED BRIDGE · GANJA · overnight · BATUMI · MAKHIN-JAURI · SARPI · Black Sea · daily · HOPA · PSOF · SARP · CEASEFIRE · AZERBAIJAN · ARMENIA · ARMENIAN AREA · overnight · Sporadic to Turkmenbashi, Turkmenistan · TRABZON · ARDAHAN · YEREVAN · closed · overnight · to Istanbul · TURKEY · KARS · IGDIR · 8/day · to Istanbul · AZERBAIJAN · IRAN · BORDER FRIENDLY · ASTARA · NAKHCHIVAN · CULFA · to Tabriz, Tehran · to Rasht · to Tabriz via Maraud · to Tabriz

(legend) ∼∼∼ = CANNOT CROSS · △ = BORDER OPEN · ⧩ = BUS · ⚠ = BORDER MAYBE OPEN · ⧫ = FERRY · ‚ = ROUTE · ▲ = OPEN TO LOCALS ONLY

AZERBAIJAN – OVERVIEW

one-way/return and Baku–Ankara (Tue, Fri) at the same prices). Turan Air flies Ganja–Istanbul and operates summer-only Baku–Kars hops twice weekly. AZAL flies Nakhchivan–Istanbul.

By road Three times weekly a convoy of buses drive between Baku and Istanbul via Georgia. It's a 48-hour ordeal costing US$60 whichever company you use plus an additional AZN10 paid to the driver. Most company offices are based around Sahil Gardens (p93, ∂K10) in Baku (see Listings p131). In Istanbul they're huddled around the Laleli tram stop.

It is much more enjoyable to do this fascinating trip in stages via Eastern Turkey and Georgia. And because the through buses get stuck for hours at each frontier, doing it yourself is not necessarily that much slower. Buses (around US$30, 17 hours) and low-cost flights link Istanbul to Trabzon with remarkable frequency. Trabzon–Hopa buses run hourly or more (three hours) and from there dolmuş minibuses depart for the Georgian border post, Sarp, from the Petrol Ofisi fuel station on Hopa's waterfront main road (500m from the bus station). It's a short walk from Sarp (Turkey) to Sarpi

(Georgia) whence regular minibuses shuttle into Batumi. Cheap, comfy overnight trains run from Batumi to Tbilisi but note that Batumi's train station is 5km northeast of the centre at Makhinjauri by minibus 101 or 122.

A second alternative is to travel via Kars to which there are flights plus a very slow but enjoyable train ride from Istanbul taking 36 hours. The railway line is being extended to Tbilisi so one day you should be able to stay on the train all the way. For now you'll need to take a bus between Kars and Ardahan (itself with direct bus connections from Istanbul) and then on to delightfully alpine Posof through very attractive and varied sub-mountainous scenery. From Posof taxi-hop across to Vale and Akhaltsikhe in Georgia from where there are overnight trains to Tbilisi at 21.00 (see map on p347).

For locals the cheapest way to Turkey is via Nakhchivan using one of eight daily Nakhchivan–Istanbul direct buses (approx 27 hours, from AZN38) via Igdır. However, getting to Nakhchivan from Baku requires flying and while locals pay a pittance for that flight, foreigners pay $100 making the whole fiddle unattractive.

From/to Georgia
AZAL flies daily between Baku and Tbilisi for US$123-161 (US$208 for a two-week return).

The overnight train departing daily at 20.00 ex Baku, costs around AZN26 kupe and is reasonably comfortable but timing can be erratic thanks to laborious immigration/border procedures. Tbilisi-bound many locals hop off the train at the border (Böyük Käsik) and do the last section by taxi. As a foreigner DON'T try this. Wait until you have crossed onto Georgian territory as the road border here is designated 'local only' and foreigners can only cross by train.

A bus to Tbilisi's Ortajala bus station (12 hours, AZN20) supposedly runs nightly from Baku's main terminal at 21.00. There's also a 21.45 bus to the ethnic Azeri Georgian town of Marneuli which is cheaper (AZN10) but uncomfortable and terribly slow.

There are morning services between Tbilisi (Ortajala) and Qax but these tend to be organized privately amongst Qax's ethnic Georgian community so can be hard to find especially westbound.

If you have time it's preferable to take a leisurely drive through Kaheti (p324), cross the Lagodekhi border (easy enough by public transport hops plus a short taxi ride) and arrive in Azerbaijan near Balakän (p238). If you're driving a car to Georgia you'll have to pay around $45 in insurance and short-stay road tax payments at the Customs department. See p18 for Azerbaijan's car rules.

From/to Central Asia
Turkmenistan The only air connection is the Lufthansa (AZAL codeshare) thrice-weekly flight Baku–Ashgabat costing a whopping US$386 ($538 return). The alternative is an overnight Caspian ferry. This sounds like a romantic idea but the reality can be overwhelmingly frustrating. It's essential to realize that these ferries are primarily transporters of railway wagons and that the 11 passengers taken by each ship are little more than an afterthought. Tickets (AZN58) are 'sold' from a small window in a laughably poorly

marked hut on the access road to the port. However, the system keeps changing: you might be put on a list, or you might simply be waved away altogether. Call ☎ 447 7314 or ☎ 447 2258 to check if they're open before setting out. Even if you manage to buy a ticket you'll still have little idea of when the boat will actually depart. Give the ticket office your local mobile telephone number and they'll (hopefully) call you when you need to get to the boat. Be packed and ready as this can be very sudden! If you don't have a mobile phone get one, or risk days of missed boats. Better still keep calling yourself.

Once aboard the tribulations aren't over. The first conundrum is getting a cabin: usually $10 or $15 extra paid to crew members. It's well worth the money for a bed and shower as although the crossing itself takes only about 16 hours when the boat arrives at Turkmenbashi it needs to wait for a berth to come free. This in turn requires that previous boats have loaded their train trucks. The result can be an appallingly frustrating wait just off the coast. I waited 40 hours but I've heard of others stranded for five days! Bring plenty of food and water in case. For a blogger's-eye view of the boat ride, read the well-titled 'Floating Vomitorium' section of 🖳 http://carpetblog.blogspot.com/2005_0 4_01_archive.html.

On the Turkmen side the port is 6km by road from Turkmenbashi station (from where there are cheap overnight trains to Ashgabat). On foot, an obvious short-cut descends by the second overhead pipe across the main Ashgabat road so you could walk from the station in around 30 minutes.

Other 'stans'
AZAL has direct flights to Kabul, Afghanistan (Wed, Fri, Sat, AZN250, AZN355 return). Uzbekistan Airlines flies to Tashkent (Mon, Thur, $246, one-month return $384) where with a short (visa-free) transfer you can use the Monday flight to connect to Bishkek, Kyrgyzstan ($310 from Baku) or Almaty ($320). Alternatively for Almaty, ImAir flies on Saturdays for US$330 (also via Tashkent, $245).

For other Kazakh destinations, Scat (🖥 www.scat.kz, 135 Nizami St, ☎ 498 1918) flies Baku–Atirau (Mon, Wed, Fri, AZN220) and Baku–Astana (Tue, Thu, Sat, Sun, AZN355) via Aktau (AZN200). AZAL also flies to Aktau five times weekly but charges US$301 ($553 return). Alternatively there's a very irregular Baku–Aktau ferry charging $60 one way for foot passengers. Vehicles are charged at $55 per metre length, or $130 for a motorbike. The same frustrations that apply to the Turkmen ferries (see opposite) are even worse for the Aktau ferry. With rather more available spaces it's more likely to be able to buy last-minute tickets but it's easy to wait around for a week or three for a departure. This is too unreliable an option if you have limited visa time. Cyclists note that a bicycle can be taken aboard for free but that if you mention the bike at the time you buy the ticket they'll charge around $15 extra.

If you make it to Aktau, daily trains link to Aktöbe/Aktyubinsk and Atirau on the main Kazakh–Russian rail network.

From/to Russia, Ukraine and Belarus

AZAL and many ex-Soviet 'babyflots' fly to a wide variety of Russian and CIS cities. Prices have risen steadily in recent years and you're now looking at around AZN260 to fly to Moscow (on various carriers), slightly more to St Petersburg (on Imair or Pulkovo). Belavia flies to Minsk, AeroSvit and AZAL fly to Kiev and you can reach virtually any major city in Russia for US$200 to $400 from one of a dozen aerokassas around Zorge St and Vurgun Gardens. A good variety of Siberian and Urals cities are served by S7 Airlines (☎ 498 3077, 🖥 www.s7.ru), UtAir (🖥 www.Utair.ru) and what ever becomes of Air Union (a former alliance which had combined KrasAir, Samara and Domodedovo airlines before collapsing in late 2008).

Russian land borders with both Azerbaijan and Georgia remain closed to foreigners so only locals can take the trains that run from Baku to Moscow, Kiev and various other destinations via Makhachkala.

There are similar problems with assorted Russia–Azerbaijan bus services.

From/to Iran

There are flights to Tehran with IranAir or AZAL (Mon, Wed, Thu, Sat, Sun, AZN124, AZN160 return). The direct bus, Baku–Tabriz can take as much as 24 hours thanks to long border waits so it's generally quicker and more comfortable to make the overland trip in hops, heading to Astara,

---

❏ Getting an Iranian visa

Iran is conveniently close to Azerbaijan and, contrary to all the negative Western media images, is an astonishingly friendly and hospitable place to visit. Don't miss the chance to see for yourself! Once you're in Iran, travel is cheap and as a tourist destination it's probably one of the safest places anywhere apart from the suicidally manic driving. The main hurdle is getting a tourist visa. That will almost always require you to pre-arrange visa clearance through a reputable agency like 🖥 www.persianvoyages.com (£70). Allow at least two weeks for that to be arranged (vastly more for US citizens who'll also need to pre-book a tour guide). Normally with this visa clearance the Iranian visa should be available almost instantly, though in Baku there's the annoyance of having to trek across to Black Town to pay the fee into Bank Melli.

In recent years some British travellers have been randomly refused a visa in Baku, while in other cases I've heard of French, Polish and Japanese travellers even managing to get visas without the visa clearance (taking two days). There seems to be a significant element of luck.

Note that the Iranian consulate (p132) in Baku is NOT at the embassy. There's also an Iranian consulate in Nakhchivan (p307).

walking across the border (easy and friendly), then continuing to Rasht or Ardabil. From Nakhchivan there's a crossing point at Poldasht but most traffic uses Culfa where you can cross to Iranian Jolfa, a fascinating starting point for visiting little-known Iranian Azarbaycan.

Plans for a new railway line to link Qazvin (Iran) to Russia via Azerbaijan have been under discussion since 2005, but as of 2009 the connector line (300km in Iran, 8km in Azerbaijan) has yet to be built. Passenger ferry services from Baku to Iran ceased many years ago.

If you're Baku based and considering driving to Iran, bear in mind that Iran's cities utterly dwarf anything in Azerbaijan. Tehran is a bewildering sprawl of some 15 million people all driving with a fervour that makes Baku driving look tame and on expressways that allow speed to add danger to the chaos. Even 'small' cities such as Ardabil (400,000) and Tabriz (1.6 million) are very confusing for the uninitiated. I'd recommend leaving your vehicle in Baku, starting with the train to Astara and then using a mixture of taxis (around US$35 for a full-day charter) and long-distance overnight buses (ultra cheap and pretty comfy if you buy two adjacent seats).

GETTING AROUND
By air
The vast majority of internal flights are between Baku and Nakhchivan (6/day, local/foreigner AZN16/US$100). Accredited journalists and humanitarian workers pay the ludicrously tiny local fares. AZAL also flies Baku–Gänjä flights (3/week, local/foreigner AZN7/US$50) and Baku–Zaqatala (twice weekly, AZN52 all nationalities) but the useful Gänjä–Nakhchivan flight is currently suspended. Baku–Länkäran flights should start during 2009. Naftalan (NFT), Shäki (SKI) and Yevlax (EVL) airports are all currently disused.

Domestic tickets are not sold by agencies: you'll have to go to the relevant AZAL office or to the airport sales counter. In some seasons queues can be extremely long and confusing with tickets often sold out over a week in advance. However, 'contacts' can sometimes get you on a 'full' plane at short notice.

SW Business Aviation (☎ 012 437 4784, 🖳 www.businessaviation.az/en) offers domestic charter flights.

By train
For around AZN7 you can cross Azerbaijan in reasonable overnight comfort including a reserved sleeping berth and clean sheets. The wide-gauge trains give fairly good leg room and the relatively slow progress means you can get a full night's sleep even on shorter trips such as Baku–Gänjä. Trains are safe (quite contrary to some odd misapprehensions about train travel in the ex-USSR). The only real problem is that carriages can be unbearably hot and, ridiculously, few of the compartments have opening windows. Air-conditioning only becomes effective an hour or two after leaving the terminus station. Another petty annoyance is that the train lighting is rarely switched on until the train is ready to depart which can make finding your berth rather awkward at night. This does not result in panic or mass thievery, just the need for a torch.

Unlike trains in Russia the on-board samovar rarely seems to work so don't count on boiling water for tea-making and pot noodles. The cleanliness and orderliness of the carriage is very much dependent on the personality and integrity of the *provodnik* (*provodnitsa* if female). With at least one per carriage these ticket collector-guards are at best guardian angels, at worst mini mafiosi to their passengers. Fortunately the former is much more common.

Classes Worth avoiding except for the 'experience' *electrichka* local/suburban trains have bare, wooden benches and stop at every halt. However, standard inter-city trains are relatively comfortable all-sleeper overnight expresses. These have three main classes. The best is '*S/V*' (pronounced 'essvay') in which a special closable compartment holds just two passengers in relative luxury. These carriages are normally very clean (except for the separate toilets) and you have your own reading light, fold-out mirror and (for the better lower bunk) a small desk with a powerpoint. Roughly half the price are the most popular *Kupe* berths which have four beds in a larger, sparser compartment. Open *Platskart* class squeezes in a further two people by removing the compartment dividers and adding two berths along the walkway/corridor. These open carriages are clearly less secure than closed kupe compartments but I have used them many times without incident.

● **Berth numbers** If you have luggage it can be stowed in a large box beneath the lower seats. Thus, for security, it is reassuring to have an (odd-numbered) lower (▲ *ashağı*) berth and sleep on top of your stowed bags. In platskart or kupe the best berths are probably #17, #19 or #21 as they're in the middle of the carriage, well away from the smelly toilets. Avoid berth numbers over #33 in platskart since they are shorter, have no luggage box and, being alongside the passageway, are prone to frequent disturbance by other passengers wandering by.

● **Bed sheets** There's a mattress roll and pillow to add comfort to each berth. Before you use these, however, you're supposed to make up the bed using sheets (*yatag*) provided by the provodnik. The 60q cost is usually included in the ticket price in Azerbaijan. In Georgia, sheet rental usually costs 2Lari extra, or you can use your own sleeping bag.

Buying tickets Ever since petrol prices (and thus bus fares) doubled in 2006, train travel has come back into vogue so it's now advisable to book tickets at least a day or two before you plan to travel. If the train is reported full but you're desperate to get aboard you might be able to get an ○ *obshchii*, ▲ *umumi* (unreserved) ticket or go direct to the provodnik on the train itself and pay your way aboard. But don't count on it.

To purchase any train ticket you'll need to present a passport (or local ID card) and you'll need to show it again when you board the train (except on *elektrichka*s).

From a station that is not the train's departure point only a limited quota of tickets are available. Once this has been reached further bookings are impossible until about half an hour before the train's arrival or whenever it has signalled ahead the number of berths remaining. This explains why you might occasionally see a small mêlée at the ticket office that never seems to diminish.

When you have the ticket in your hand it's worth checking that the details are what you expected. On the most common computerized ticket there are four lines of printout: the first gives the train (*qatar*) number, departure date/time (*getmä tarixi*), carriage number (*vaqon*) with a code for class (Kp = kupe, Pl = Platskart), base price (before the compulsory insurance – separate blue receipt) and your passport number (bring that ID!). Hidden away on the second line between the routing and your name is the all-important berth number (*yer*). The third line lists any surcharges – including the small *yataq* fee for bed-sheets. The last line records the cashier and date of purchase. Ticket vendors are usually most obliging and will often underline the key points without being asked.

On boarding the train the provodnik initially examines the ticket to make sure you have the correct carriage and returns it. Once the train has departed he walks up the carriage collecting tickets in a numbered wallet. Being left ticketless is unnerving for first-time passengers but is quite normal. Still, for my own peace of mind, I make a photocopy of the ticket before boarding.

By bus, minibus and shared taxi

There are (mini)bus services on most roads. They run at least hourly on major roads (Baku–Quba, Baku–Länkäran, Qazax–Gänja) and at least once per day to most villages as long as there's a way through the potholes. Even roadless villages still manage a 6-wheel Ural truck-bus every week or so. On certain routes, shared taxis (*yoltaksi*, *paputni-taksi*) fill up quicker and cover the routes slightly faster charging roughly double the minibus fare. Chartering one of these will cost around half the full-price taxi fare as long as the driver can expect to find a return ride.

AZERBAIJAN – OVERVIEW

Car, car hire and taxi

Own car Bringing a car or motorbike into Azerbaijan requires paying a hefty cash deposit at the border calculated according to the book value of the vehicle. This is repaid when you leave whether at the same or a different crossing. Understandably many drivers find it very nerve-racking to hand over $1500 or so for a mere paper receipt, though in cases I've followed the sums have indeed been reliably repaid on exit. Note that if you transit for less than three days en route to a third country the deposit is not payable (some visitors have been given 20 days without deposit).

Car rental Several specialists as well as many travel agents offer car hire. Reliable Avis (map p107, Husein Cavid 528A, ☎ 497 5455, 🖳 www.avis.az) has Ford Focus cars from US$80 per day (with US$100 returnable deposit). If you don't have an international licence they can make a temporary permit using driving documents issued by your home country. Other possibilities include Hertz (Hyatt Regency, p105 ∂G3, ☎ 497 8757), Magic Life (Caspian Plaza, ☎ 497 3347, from AZN40) and Yusif Co (528 A Aleskerov, ☎ 447 7173, from AZN55). Add around AZN10 for a driver. Should you need a stretch Hummer limo with internet, DVD player, bar and disco-interior contact Exotico (☎ 012-436 9778, 🖳 www.baku exoticlimo.com).

Licences and driving problems

Driving styles are somewhat chaotic and there are several unexpected highway codes. Overtaking and pulling onto major roads are subject to some bizarre and confusing laws that seem designed to get motorists into trouble. Crossing a bridge (even an insignificant one on a main highway) you're generally meant to slow to 40km/hr. And some complex junctions are officially considered a 'roundabout'. Faded signage often makes it very hard to see what the rule really is but that doesn't mean the cops will be sympathetic as they write up your fine! And it seems there's almost always a YPX (Yol Polis Xidmeti) traffic cop lurking ready to spring out of nowhere

❏ Approximate driving times from Baku	
Astara	6hrs
Besh Barmaq	1½hrs
Länkaran	5hrs
Minare (Cloudcatcher)	4hrs
Qäbälä	3½hrs
Quba	3½hrs
Red Bridge (Georgian border)	8hrs
Shamakha	1¾hrs
Shäki	6hrs
Xinalıq	4½hrs

and wave you down with his little baton. Typically you'll pay an on-the-spot fine (these days you'll get a receipt). Should your licence be confiscated it will usually be sent to the YPX HQ in Xirdalan where you'll need to show up in person to pay the fine and retrieve it. In such cases you should get a document to explain this which still allows you to drive for a day or two in the interim. Some cunning expats have hit on the idea of applying for numerous international licences in their home country before arriving in Azerbaijan so that they're not concerned at having one or two confiscated during a road trip.

Taxi/chauffeured vehicles Driving can be stressful. Fortunately, taxi-chartering is often no more expensive. You'll get the best deals if you locate a share-taxi which is already heading where you're going – offer to pay five times the single-person fare and in return request a few photo stops and side excursions en route. Make sure you explain these ahead of time – if you add them later the price may rise substantially. Just don't leave things too late in the day: if the driver thinks he won't be able to find passengers for the return journey he'll probably want to charge you double.

A great way to weekend in the deep south or around Shäki is to take the night train out on Friday night, walk around or use a taxi to explore on Saturday, then get a share taxi to drive you back to Baku on the

Sunday via a few rural points of interest. That's much less tiring than driving there AND back, whoever's at the wheel!

Despite new roads to Xinaliq and Lahic, reaching several of the more interesting mountain villages still requires a 4WD vehicle. If you're interested in the mountains for the views rather than the automotive challenge, consider engaging a local driver with a Niva (easy to find around the bus stations or bazaars of Quba, Ismayıllı, Qusar and other hub towns).

Prices vary substantially but will usually be cheaper and less stressful than renting a 4WD and driving it yourself. For harder routes eg to Allar (p291) or Xinaliq via Rük (p178) even a Niva may struggle: finding a driver with a high-clearance, virtually indestructible UAZ jeep is the solution.

Petrol (*Yanarcaq* ▲, *Benzin* ◐) Most hire cars and expat vehicles take 95-octane petrol, unlike Ladas which seem to run on vodka when necessary.

Petrol stations along almost all the main roads might advertise 95 ('*doksan-besh*') but not all actually stock any. The green-and-white AzPetrol stations are usually most reliable and there's one near virtually every regional town. Deep in the mountains only fuel comes in old Coca Cola bottles and is of highly uncertain provenance.

Buying a car If you plan to stay a while and do a lot of exploring, it may be worth purchasing a Niva. These Russian-made 4WDs don't have the best reputation for reliability but are easy to repair – spare parts are available throughout the country – and are remarkably tough. Ask local friends to help you select from the car markets at Sumgayit or out near Baku airport.

The biggest headache (unless you have a fixer and pay some 'extras') is getting the car registration which must be renewed annually. Initially you'll need the seller to come with you to the YPX office in Xırdalan and have the car inspected by a series of different officials, each requiring a stamp and payment. You'll also need to take with your passport, visa and police registration document (p11).

An alternative to transferring the full ownership of the car into your name is to establish power of attorney over the car (*Etibar namä*) through a notary in the Rayon in which you live.

Travelling by horse
Up in the mountains where roads are awful or non-existent the easiest way to travel is often by horse. Finding a guide and a mount is not as hard as you might think, though ideally allow a spare day or two to make the arrangements. Don't expect a thoroughbred. Indeed donkeys and some local horses are more suited as pack animals to carry your bags while you hike.

Finding horses for a group of people will be harder as few owners have more than a couple of mounts available. Locals ride sitting upon cushions and kilims draped over the horse's back; this is photogenic and easier for an equestrian novice than using a Western-style saddle. The frequent lack of stirrups is OK if you're happy with the docile animals sauntering along at tortoise pace.

There are no set rates but AZN20/40 seems typical for renting a donkey/horse. For longer trips try fixing a price that includes guide, accommodation and food en route.

The word for horse is *loshad* in Russian, *at* in Azeri, *palkan* in Lezghian and *pshii* in Xınalıqi.

MONEY
Azerbaijan's currency is the new *Manat*, usually abbreviated to AZN (or YAM). That's to differentiate it from the old manat (AZM or simply M) which was phased out in 2006, 1AZN=5000M. In the old money locals never used the term Manat, counting instead in *Shirvan* (10,000M) and *Mammad* or min (1000M). Very confusingly for first-time visitors prices are still sometimes quoted in the old money, particularly in the provinces. So, if someone quotes you a price of 'six' without stating six what, triple check whether they mean new manats or shirvan.

The name mammad comes from Mammad Rasulzade, the 1918 democrat who used to grace the 1000M note. Shirvan was for the Shirvanshahs palace in Baku which featured on the 10,000M note.

There is no black market and it is very easy to reconvert manats to dollars or euros with minimal loss, given the very competitive rates in Baku exchange booths (no commission). There's sometimes a marginally better rate for high denomination US$ and euro bills. Russian roubles and pounds sterling are fairly easy to exchange in Baku but at slightly worse rates. Other currencies get relatively poor rates. Rates for Georgian Laris and Iranian Rials are generally atrocious and nobody wants Turkmen manats at all.

There's at least one ATM for withdrawals on MasterCard, Visa or major debit cards in any regional centre and ATMs are ubiquitous in Baku. Travellers' cheques are sold (0.5-1% commission) and cashed (2% commission) by IBA bank in Baku.

On entering Azerbaijan, if you're carrying more than around US$1000 in currency or have any sophisticated electronics you are expected to declare this formally on a customs declaration form (*deklaratsi*) but you'll usually have to ask for one. Having that form when you leave is theoretically very important: without it the customs officer could confiscate all your money claiming you'd made it by illegally profiteering in Azerbaijan. At the time of writing most customs officers have stopped bothering to request or issue these forms but once in a while someone might try and ask you for

one when leaving. Simply saying you weren't issued with one on arrival seems to work just fine, even at the land borders. Technically manats cannot be imported or exported, but again, in recent years, enforcement of this rule appears to have become lax.

ACCOMMODATION
Hotels
In Baku there are hundreds of new hotels but prices are high for what you get with anything under AZN50 reckoned budget. Beyond the capital, most towns now have one or two new or decently refurbished hotels for AZN30-50 while a few provincial centres still maintain an ugly old Soviet-era hotel with cheap but spirit-sappingly dismal rooms for around AZN10 per night. I often carry a roll-mat and sleeping bag to lay over less salubrious beds in such places.

If you can't find a decent hotel room, it's worth trying the local sports complex as many have accommodation facilities for visiting sportsmen. Some of the new Olympic centres have comparatively plush full-blown hotels and guests might be allowed to use the sports facilities and/or swimming pool.

Rest zones, turbazas, sanatoria
In popular country getaways (Nabran, around Quba, the Laza road, Pirguli, beyond Masallı) there are scatterings of rest zones (variously translated *Zona istrahat*, *Istraha zonasi*, *Zona odikha* or, for the simplest places, *Turbaza*.) Many of these offer fully equipped (if often gerry-built) bungalows with several rooms designed for extended family groups (AZN50-150). However, there are also a few pretty squalid older rural sheds – think of the latter as camping without the tent.

A *sanatorium* (*kurort*) is primarily designed for curative retreats, though in the Soviet system this often came to mean de facto family holidays. These days some still require a *putiovka* (typically government-issued voucher from your 'work unit', doctor etc) and stays should be pre-booked and pre-paid. A few are open to casual visitors but you may need to discuss at some length

---

❏ Exchange rates
At the time of going to press a Manat was worth a little more than a US$1, a little less than a euro. Rates (🖥 www.oanda.com/convert/classic) as of October 2009 were:

US$1	AZN0.80
UK£1	AZN1.28
€1	AZN1.17
Aus $1	AZN0.70
Can $1	AZN0.75
NZ$1	AZN0.56
RussianR1	AZN0.03

as to how much (and to whom) money should be paid. Prices quoted as *yemek daxil olmaqla* (✪ *s'pitaniyem*) will include meals.

Motels

A few rural AzPetrol stations have neat, inexpensive motel rooms attached. Some country restaurants also have motel-style rooms. In some cases, however, these will be suites with a big private dining area, a much smaller double-bedded room and no bathroom at all: they are generally rented by the hour and guests are presumably expected to go home to wash afterwards!

Homestays

Homestays make a pleasant alternative to hotels and give a real insight into local life. Sadly the homestay idea hasn't yet become widespread but it's possible and recommended in Shäki and Lahic.

Members of 🖳 www.couchsurfing .com will find several potential Peace Corps Volunteers (PCVs) hosting in rural Azerbaijan. As Americans speaking decent Azeri PCVs can be particularly helpful at introducing sensitive travellers to Azeri communities but do remember that they are paid minimal (local) wages so be a generous guest if invited!

FOOD

This section includes an overview of Azeri cuisine, an extensive dictionary of English–Azeri/Russian food translations and a description and guide to drinks. For a menu decoder to translate from Azeri/ Russian/Turkish/Georgian into English, see pp351-6.

Azeri cuisine

As you might expect from a glance at the map, Azerbaijani cuisine falls stylistically somewhere between Turkish and central Asian. Glossy trilingual recipe books sold in Baku show the tangy gourmet touches that are possible in a land so rich with fruit, saffron, nuts and fish. But there's no escaping the overwhelming accent on mutton.

The great stalwarts of everyday cuisine are mostly variants on the *tava äti* lamb, vegetable and potato stew/soup theme.

❏ Caviar (▲ kürü ✪ ikra)

The lugubrious grey eggs of the sturgeon fish are nowadays a byword for luxury. Yet Caspian caviar was once so plentiful that British troops occupying Baku in 1919 were force-fed the stuff as cheap rations. Bechoffer quotes one soldier complaining that 'this 'ere jam do taste of fish'. Today, over-fishing and pollution have drastically reduced sturgeon populations and the fish is now considered 'endangered'. Since 2001 CITES has attempted to impose a quota system for caviar exports (🖳 www.cites .org/eng/resources/quotas/sturgeon_ intro.shtml) designed to help the populations regenerate but this is no easy task given the fish's slow reproductive cycle along with widespread poaching.

There are five main sub-species of Caspian sturgeon. The three commonest collectively known as Aseterine/Osetra (*Acipenser persicus/gueldenstaedtil/nudiventris*) produce the cheapest caviar as well as commonly eaten fish steaks. Much more soughtafter for their caviar are Sevruga (*Acipenser stellatus*) and especially Beluga (*Huso huso*). The biggest Beluga ever recorded weighed well over a ton and was 9m long. As Beluga can live as long as humans and don't reach reproductive age till around 20 years old, many are fished before they can even produce any caviar. No surprise then that Beluga caviar is now one of the world's most expensive delicacies. As of 2009 Azerbaijan's Beluga export quota is a mere 300kg (3000kg for other types). That is currently translated at customs as meaning a per person limit of two small officially sealed 113g pots. In late 2008 such pots of Beluga cost around AZN50-70 in the markets, roughly 12 times more than in 1998 but still less than a quarter of the price in European airport duty-free shops.

AZERBAIJAN – OVERVIEW

Typical examples are *bozbash*, *peritme* (with a little sour cream) and *köfte bozbash* (where the meat is minced and wrapped in a ball around a cherry). An Azeri classic is *piti*: fatty mutton, potatoes and chick peas in a rich tomato broth served in its own little pot. To eat it, first soak up the soup in bread then mash the solids. It's known across the Iranian border as *abgusht* or *dizi*. Also popular is *dushbara* – a sort of tiny *manti* ravioli served in stock.

If you prefer a less soupy consistency try *bozartma*, *jizbiz* (tripe fried with potato) or *qovurma* (often fruity). Meals are typically served with bread but rice (*duyus*), mashed potato (*pure*) or boiled split wheat (*qreçki*) are alternatives. If you don't want to pay for the bread, salad or green garnishes which turn up along side any such meal, send them back promptly.

Dovğa and *doğrama* (**○** *okroshka*) are both soupy starters made with sour milk, spring onions and cucumber. Doğrama is lighter and served cold – refreshing on a hot summer's day but not always good for sensitive stomachs. Dovğa is safer as it has to be heated and laboriously stirred to gain its thicker consistency.

Ash, also widely known by its Russian name *plov*, is a meat and rice pilaff. There are numerous varieties of which the classic, *shirin plov* is loaded with nuts and dried fruit. Though hailed as a typical national dish, ash is generally reserved for special occasions and appears relatively rarely on restaurant menus. If presented traditionally it should arrive on an *ash-gazan* tray covered with an engraved metal *särpush* which looks rather like a Prussian helmet. Note that *syudli plov* is more like rice pudding.

The best poultry dish in Azerbaijan, *chicken Lävängi*, hails from the Talysh/Länkäran region but is increasingly popular in Baku too. *Cholpan* is a fruity chicken dish served with fried onion and potatoes. *Tabaka*-grilled chicken seems to have been pounded flat! Spit-roast chicken is sold fresh from the rotisserie (*qril*) in ever-more numerous Baku takeaways; the most renowned is opposite the Landmark building. In rural restaurants where custom is limited, beware of ordering chicken if you're

❏ Meat

	Azeri ▲	Russian ○
beef	*mal äti*	*govyadina*
chicken	*jücha/toyug*	*kuri/kuritsa*
kidney	*böyrek*	*pochki*
horse meat	*at äti*	*kanina*
lamb's tail	*guyrug*	*guyrug*
liver	*chiari*	*pechen*
meat	*ät*	*myasa*
mutton	*qoyun*	*baranina*
salami	*kalbasa*	*kalbasa*
rams'	*goch*	*ptichyi*
testicles	*yumurta*	*yaitza*
steak	*biftek*	*bifshteks*
tongue	*dil*	*yazik*

in a hurry: the plucking can take a while!

Though *balıq* is the general term for fish, used unqualified on an Azeri menu it's likely to mean sturgeon of which there are five varieties and various qualities. To make the most of sturgeon steak don't overlook the tart *nasharab* sauce. Where there's sturgeon there's also caviar – and Azerbaijan produces some of the world's best (see box p21).

Dolma are leaves or vegetables filled with a mixture of spiced lamb, rice and herbs; delicious but certainly not vegetarian. Indeed, there is supposedly more lamb per ball in Azeri *dolmasi* than in Greek or Turkish equivalents. A gourmet *yarpag dolmasi* comes wrapped in vine leaves, the meat studded with pine nuts and raisins. Cabbage-wrapped *kelem domasi* can be fatty, tasteless and over-boiled in cheap restaurants but home-made Baku versions sometimes come delightfully transformed by including a succulent chestnut in the middle. A mixed plate of dolma will typically be a trio of stuffed vegetables, a tomato, a baby aubergine and a sweet green pepper.

● **Shashlyk and kebab** All the above fade into insignificance against the mighty *shashlyk*. The national passion for barbecued lamb is insatiable, whether skewered in chunks as *tika* (Azeri shish-kebab), minced and barbecued in strips as *lüle*, or simply roasted in hunks. A trap for the unwary foreigner is white *guyrug* ('fatty kebab') cut from the characteristic wobbly rear of a fat-tailed sheep. It looks like a cardiovascular death wish. And you might assume that people leave it to last as everyone's trying to avoid it. On the contrary – it's considered the finest morsel and if it's being shunted in your direction you're supposed to feel honoured, whatever its life-shortening effect.

Nice as shashlyk often is, even quirky touches like drizzling it with fresh pomegranate juice or smearing it in plum sauce (*alcha turshusu*) doesn't disguise the fact that many rural restaurants have virtually nothing else. The standard accompaniment to kebabs/shashlyk is sliced cucumbers and tomatoes, a plate of *göy* (herbs and spring onions to eat as salad) and hunks of bread. Locals eat in such places only on special occasions and tend not to ask the price. So extras tend to pop up regularly and pricing can be rather random. Kebabs might cost only AZN2 in the provinces but AZN3 is reasonable in Baku and you'll generally need to budget around three to five times that for a whole kebab meal once you've included all the trimmings.

As people get wealthier it's becoming commoner to find chops (*entrekot*) and *dana bastirma* (beef strips) and despite Islamic mores pork has made something of a reappearance in Baku in recent years.

● **Day-to-day favourites** Many typical menu items are of Russian origin eg *borshch* (beetroot soup; usually lunch-time only), *Kiyevsayağı/kievski kotlet* (chicken Kiev), *langet* (minute steak), *pashtet* (roulade of ground fried liver and onion) and *escalop* (similar to Wiener schnitzel). Ever popular *monastirsky* is meat topped with sauce and melted cheese. A variety of fancifully named salads (*salatlar*) are eaten as a starter but don't expect fresh green leaves (for that request *göy*). Salads here are Russian-style affairs, typically based on boiled potato cubes in mayonnaise with various additions eg *stalichni salat* (with diced vegetables) and *mimosa salat* (with grated cheese).

● **Menus** In Baku most better restaurants have menus, often with translations into English. Unless you've double checked when ordering you can't necessarily assume that the prices on the menu are what you'll be charged as prices rise rapidly and most locals seem to accept that the menu is only a rough guide. These days few restaurants continue the quaint communist-era habit of stocking only one item on a very extensive but entirely redundant menu. Don't, however, expect everything to be available.

In rural restaurants there'll rarely be any written menu whatever so be prepared to suggest what you'd like to eat (prepared to be told, of course, that they only have shashlyk anyway).

● **Breakfast (Sahar Yemeyi)** A typical Azeri breakfast features bread, butter (*yağ*), cheese (*pendir*), honey (*bal*) and maybe some cream (*khama*) all washed down with very sweet, weak tea. Alternatively you can get *pomidor yumurta/gayanag pomidorla*, a kind of tomato omelette. Or join the real men for the great hangover-cure delicacy of *xash/kalpacha*, a garlic-supercharged soup of sheep's heads and trotters. And always served with a vodka chaser. Lovely!

● **Vegetarian** Meat fills the star role in the daily drama of Azeri meals but the supporting cast of salads, cheese, bread and fruit should be able to fill you up, albeit without particular panache. If you eat dairy products there's almost always cheese and varieties of egg/tomato (*yumurta/pomidor*) dishes, often tastily spiked with garlic and onion. Georgian cuisine has some rather more inspired fleshless options, notably *khajapuri* and *badrizhan nizgit*.

Georgian food

Ubiquitous *khajapuri*, the 'pizza of the Caucasus', has various forms. The most commonly sold on street stalls in Tbilisi and Baku is a cheese-filled flaky pastry square – best straight from the oven. In restaurants you're more likely to be served *Imeruli khajapuri*, a bready circle filled with melting sulguni cheese that's the staple diet of Georgian mountain families. Another popular alternative originally from the Batumi region is *ajaruli khajapuri* – a volcano of hot, fresh bread whose crater is filled with melted butter and a raw egg, added at the moment of serving. Quickly stir the egg into the hot dough to cook it.

Georgian *khingkale* are large lamb-and-herb-filled ravioli dumplings, markedly different from the Azeri lasagne-style *xingkal*, though suburban restaurants in Baku often serve both (calling the Georgian version *Gruzinski xinğal*). *Kharcho* (spicy lamb hot pot/stew-soup) is also served by some Azeri restaurants (as *Xarço*) but the full Mingrelian Kharcho is hard to beat.

As in Azerbaijan, Georgian celebrations call for fresh meat. This is normally *mtsvadi* (shashlyk-barbecued mutton), though being non-Muslim, Georgians are also partial to pork. More refined Georgian delicacies employ garlic and walnuts to great effect as in *satsivi*, a garlic, walnut and creamy herb sauce chicken dish usually served cold. It's somewhat reminiscent of Iranian *fesenjan*. For less adventurous palates an ideal choice is *arabuli*, a cheese-topped meat fillet with creamy sauce, similar to beef monastirsky.

As well as khajapuri (see p23), cheap, delicious meatless dishes include spicy beans (*lobio*), fried sulguni cheese (often very salty) and heavenly *badrizhan nizgit*. The latter are thin, marinated strips of eggplant spread with a tangy paste of garlic, crushed walnuts and pomegranate. Darra Goldstein's *The Georgian Feast* gives recipes and culinary insight.

Turkish meals
Many mid-market Turkish restaurants are set up like cafeterias so you can point-and-pick from a considerable selection of pre-cooked meals displayed in heated cabinets with no need to decipher a menu. More upmarket places specialize in kebabs. As well as the ubiquitous *shish* (various types of skewered meat) and *döner* (slices cut from a rotisserie of mixed chicken or lamb and served in bread) the most common kebab varieties are *köfte* (meatballs); *Adana* and *Urfa* kebabs are spicy variations of lüle. The very filling *Iskender kebab* consists of bread cubes fried in butter and draped in döner meat, tomato sauce and yogurt.

For starters choose from a wide choice of salads and dips or fill up cheaply with *mercimek chorba* (lentil soup), hunks of bread and a sizeable squeeze of fresh lemon. *Manti* are tiny dushbara-style ravioli balls served on a bed of garlic-yoghurt. In better places the freshly crushed garlic may be served on the side in case you have to protect your breath for a business meeting in the afternoon.

Lahmacun are sometimes nicknamed 'Turkish Pizza' but don't be fooled by the name; lahmacun are thin with barely any topping and not meant to be eaten alone. Wrapped around a bundle of salad herbs (ordered separately) or filled with aubergine paste and a squeeze of lemon, they're transformed.

Snacks
In any rural spot that people have to wait around you'll probably find someone selling little newspaper cones of black roasted sunflower seeds (▲ *tum*/ ✪ *semichki*). Spat-out *tum* husks threaten to swamp buses by the end of a long journey.

A typical beer snack, also sold occasionally by wandering vendors on trains, is *nohud* – boiled chick peas. On street corners and in railway stations the most common snacks are *pirozhki* – Russian-style cold doughnuts usually stuffed with peppered potato. Less common, but more typically Azeri, is the *qutab* – a very thin pancake turnover lightly filled with meat or spinach. Baku street vendors and bakeries have discovered the delights of Georgian khajapuri (cheese pastry).

Bread (▲ *Chörek*, ✪ *Kleb*)
In Islam, bread is quietly holy and Azeri respect for bread is real and heartfelt. There are several bread-related customs:

● *Duz chörek kasmak* – the power of bread and salt – a traditional belief that sharing bread with someone opens your souls to a bond of mutual friendship which can't be easily broken. Refusing bread when offered could thus cause offence – at the very least break off and nibble a symbolic corner.

● If locals drop a crust on the floor they kiss it and put it to one side.

• Bread is never thrown away with the normal household rubbish but is fed to birds or animals or put in a special place (notice the bags of crusts hanging from trees in Baku courtyards).

• To swear on bread is considered more binding even than to swear on the Koran. 'After all' said one respondent, 'bread has been around longer'. He didn't appear to be joking.

• During a round of toasts if someone dunks a crust of bread in vodka they are toasting the dead, symbolically offering the deceased a sip for themselves. Not all locals approve of this gesture.

Bread is served with almost every dish. Note that even in cheaper restaurants there's normally a small charge whether you eat it or not.

The standard circular *chörek* loaves are bought daily by the sackful. However, traditional hand-baked *tandir* bread has more flavour and is increasingly making a resurgence in the cities. Wafer-thin *lavash* is good for making wrap-sandwiches. A *karpiç* (literally 'brick') loaf is Western-style bread ideal for toasting.

Cakes and pastries
Azerbaijan's most archetypal pastries are sweet forms of baklava (*paxlava*) and halva for which Shäki is especially famous. Especially in Baku there are many new bakery-patisseries selling wide varieties of cakes and pastries. *Bulki* – fruit buns – are sold fresh off the baking pallet for breakfast. *Qorabiyyasi* cookies are rather dry, as are many of the spiced, speciality pastries like *ovma*, *kölchasi*, *tikhmasi* and the various nut rolls/roulades (*borujuq/dörmayi*): they are best eaten with a good big pot of tea.

Egg and dairy products
Yumurta (eggs) are among the few standby options for vegetarians: *kuku*, *gayğanag* and *chıxırtma* are all forms of omelette or scrambled egg which usually incorporate vegetables – often crushed tomato. Plain scrambled eggs are *çalınmış qayqanaq*, hard-boiled eggs are *bişmis bärk yumurta*, soft-boiled eggs *bişmis ılıtma yumurta*, fried ('sunny-side-up') eggs are *[qayqanaq] qlazok*.

❑ Egg and dairy products

	Azeri ▲	Russian ✪
butter	*yağ*	*maslo*
cheese	*pendir*	*syr*
eggs	*yumurta*	*yaitsa*
ice cream	*dondurma*	*marozhna*
milk	*süd*	*malako*
omelette	*gayğanag/ kuku*	*omlet*
rice pudding	*yaima*	*yayma*
sour milk	*qatiq*	*matsonye*
sour cream	*xama*	*smetana*

Sour cream is popular with many dishes, notably ✪ *borshch* beetroot soup.

Fruit, nuts, vegetables and spices (see box p26)
Absheron saffron, Quba apples, Qax chestnuts, Göychay pomegranates, Bäläkan persimons, Nakhchivan watermelons, Shamakha grapes, Länkäran tea, Astara lemons, Bärdä strawberries, Zaqatala hazelnuts, Beylaqan okra... Azerbaijan produces a truly phenomenal range of fresh regional produce. And Azerbaijani fruit comes filled with sunshine, packed with an intensity of flavour that puts to shame the industrially perfect yet tasteless Western equivalents. Delightful.

DRINK
Non-alcoholic
• **Water** (♠/▲ *su*, ✪ *voda*, ✣ *tskhali*) The tap water supply is not constant and particularly in Baku even poorer locals never drink it without boiling it first, usually for tea. Old photos show vendors selling *jujums* full of spring water at Baku bazaars. Today's plastic bottles are rather less cumbersome. There are many brands of purified water on the market of which Shollar and Zam Zam are usually the cheapest, though Aquavita and the Coca Cola-bottled BonAqua are arguably worth the slight premium. Şirab and Badamlı (both in Nakhchivan) and Qax are well known for their springs but the most famous Caucasian mineral water is from Borjomi (p346; ✣), in

FRUIT, NUTS, VEGETABLES AND SPICES

	Azeri ▲	Russian ✺		Azeri ▲	Russian ✺
Almond	badam	mindal	Mulberry	tut	shchelkovitsi
Apple	alma	yablaka	Mushrooms	göbäläk	gribi
Apricot	arik	abrikos	Onion	soğan	luk
Aubergine	badımcan	baklazhani	Orange	portağal	apelsin
Banana	banan	banan	Quince	heyva	aivi
Basil	reyhan	basilik	Parsley	cafari	petrushka
Beans	lobya	fazola	Peach	shaftali	persiki
Beetroot	chuğundur	svyokla	Pear	armud	grusha
Cabbage	kelem	kapusta	Pea	gorokh	
Caraway	darchin	tmin	Pepper (black)	qara istiot	pepets chorni
Carrot	kök	morkov			
Cherries	albali	vishnya	Pepper (capsicum)	bibar	pepets sladki
Chestnut	shabalid	kashtan			
Chick peas	nohut	garbanzo	Plum	alcha	sliva
Coriander	kishnish	kinza	Pomegranate	nar	granat
Cucumber	xiyar	ogurtsi	Potato	kartof	kartofel/ kartozhki
Dill	shüyud	ukrop			
Garlic	sarimsaq	chesnok	Pumpkin	qabaq/borani	tikva
Grapes	üzüm	vinograd	Raisins	kishmish	kishmish
Hazelnuts	fındıq	funduk	Saffron	zafaran	shafran
Kaki/	xurma (the same term is		Salt	duz	sol
Persimmon	also used for dates)		Sorrel	avalik/ turshang	shchavel
Lemon	limon	limon			
Lentils	marci	chechevitsa	Spinach	ispanaq	shpinat
Mandarin	naringi	mandarin	Tomatoes	pomidor	pomidor
Melon	qovun/yemish	dinya	Walnut	qoz	orekhi
Mint	nana	myata	Watermelon	qarpiz	arbuz

Georgia. The heavily mineralized, sulphurous qualities of the latter make it more like a rehydration drink than a spring water.

When travelling in the countryside it's worth carrying an empty bottle to fill at local roadside springs.

● **Sodas** ▲ *Gazli su*/✺ *Gaz voda* In some kiosks and small window booths you may notice upturned glass cones containing liquids of various colours. They look medicinal but are in fact syrups for classic soda fountains: a *stakan* (small glass) gives you a shot of one or two flavours with chilled soda. That's made from filtered tap water. Despite drinking these frequently I didn't suffer any stomach upsets.

● **Soft drinks and juices** (✺ *sok*) A cheap refreshing alternative to the global-brand soft drinks is *ayran*, a type of watered-down drinking yoghurt. A traditional Azeri

summer favourite *shabat* – sherbet – is an iced fruit or herb infusion. *Compot* is fruit steeped in sugar solution. Both are common in local homes but rarely available commercially.

In glaring contrast to neighbouring Iran, **fruit juices** are very rarely fresh squeezed. In most restaurants the term 'Natural Juice' means it's sweetened fruit 'nectar' straight from the carton. The Saf brand is at least locally made. Rose water goes by two names: *Kyzyl gul sok* (literally 'golden flower juice') is for drinking,

❏ **Language codes**

Azeri	▲	Russian	✺
Georgian	✤	Turkish	♠

but *gulab* is to anoint the faces of the dead.

In the summer you may spot the odd yellow mini-tanker trailer from which a man appears to be serving jam jars full of beer. In fact the liquid is likely to be *kvas* – an odd, lightly fermented but non-alcoholic drink made from old bread. It tastes vaguely like watery ginger ale.

Hot drinks
● **Tea** (♠♥❖▲ *chai/çay*) is a symbol of hospitality and remains the predominant social drink in Azerbaijan. It is drunk from pinch-waist armudi ('pear') glasses and sweetened with sugar lumps or jam (... *murabbasi* served in *rosetka* saucers). The sugar lumps are traditionally sucked separately, Persian style, after briefly dipping them in the cup. Such sugar dipping is said to date from the Middle Ages when tea was an exclusive, aristocratic drink. Such aristocrats were the constant target for assassination attempts but could detect poison in their tea by examining a dunked sugar lump for greenish discolouration.

At breakfast, tea is drunk a little weaker and piled spoonfuls of granulated sugar are typically heaped into each steaming glass. If you want your tea weak specify *achiğ*, for strong tea ask for it *tünt*. Herbal teas are available in some places; one worth trying is the refreshing *kaklik-oto chai* flavoured with delicate mountain grasses.

Although a few places will serve a single glass, restaurants and *chaikhana* (*çayxana*, tea houses), usually served tea by the pot (*chaynik*); this makes it easy to linger and meet people. Some chaikhanas are smoky indoor nard parlours, others are sprawling terraces or simply tables in public parks. Almost all are traditionally all-male domains where single women are simply not expected. Tea prices vary radically. The cheapest I've found was 30q a pot but AZN1 is more typical in a simple çayxana while it's quite possible to be charged AZN20 in fancy Baku tea houses where you'll get a samovar of boiling water and a selection of jams and fruits thrown in.

In a rural chaikhana, the teapots seem to have more lives than a proverbial cat – handles and spouts once broken are ingeniously refashioned from beaten aluminium cans.

● **Coffee** (❖ *kofe* ♠▲ *khave*) is predominantly a drink for the rich. Baku is the only town to have blossomed with trendy coffee houses which are often delightful but where an espresso will typically cost AZN3 or more. Passable Turkish coffees are available in many restaurants, but good filter coffee remains relatively rare. Even cafés that have the machine, don't always seem able to make a good cappuccino, while in cheaper cafés and in any provincial town, the term cappuccino simply means an instant drink made from a Nestlé sachet of that name. In small towns coffee, even 'Neskafé' (ie instant coffee), is pretty rare.

Alcoholic drinks
● **Beer** (▲❖ *Pivo* – *piva/pivasi*) Baku's main domestic beer is **Xırdalan**, a perfectly acceptable lager whose cost on a menu is a good benchmark for quickly judging the overall price-scale of a restaurant. AZN1 is cheap, AZN1.50-3 is typical in a better local restaurant, AZN3-5 is possible in a nightclub or hotel. Essentially similar is the **33 Lager**, branded like the French equivalent but brewed in Azerbaijan under licence. In contrast unpasteurized **draft NZS** typically costs 50q-AZN1/pint. If a nicer-looking local restaurant advertises NZS it's generally a safe bet that the food will be good value. **Napoleon Beer** is as flat and watery as NZS but much better than **Solomon Beer** which is acidic and tastes like gingery cider.

Increasingly hard to find are the various regional beers of which **Naxçivan Pivasi** is probably the best but available only in Nakhchivan and only in summer. **Xachmaz Pivasi** tastes like home-made ginger beer and **Yevlax pivasi** is slightly reminiscent of a German weissbier. The wonderfully named Ganja Beer was sadly abysmal and no longer seems to be sold at all.

Georgian beers are excellent especially on draft, but rarely sold in Azerbaijan. **Natakhtari** and **Kazbegi** are the commonest of which *belaya* is a full-bodied lager and *barkhot* a deeper ale.

Numerous **imported beers** offer restaurants a chance to push up profit margins, though Turkish **Efes** is usually good value.

AZERBAIJAN – OVERVIEW

AZERBAIJAN – OVERVIEW

Note that in Georgia it is considered inappropriate, even rude, to make a toast using beer. Stick to wine or vodka there.

● **Wine** (✪/▲ *vino*, ✦ *kvino*) was once a major industry in the Shamakha and Gänjä areas while Nakhchivan was famous for its unique variety of perfumed muscat. In the late 1980s thousands of hectares of vineyard were neglected or ripped up, victims of Gorbachev's anti-alcohol campaign. The 1990s departure of the Armenians (who were major wine growers) didn't help and a botched privatization almost finished things off when it left in state hands the grape-buying wholesaler who consistently failed to pay private growers.

Recently the industry is rebounding although some **Azeri wines** are now fermented from imported Moldovan and Ukrainian grape extract. One cheap local plonk (around AZN2.50) that is approximately drinkable is the Ivanovka Red. It's thin and hardly an oenologist's dream come true but it's better than Ribena-flavoured Sevinc, unreliable Xan Qizi, woody Koroğlu or Çinar, which would be at home in car batteries. Somewhat better are the drinkable but unexciting Seven Beauties, Maiden's Tower and other 'culture theme' reds. Naznazi and Qaragile are darker and richer.

Georgian wines are much more enticing and you'll often be served by the flagon at Georgian restaurants. Rich Saparavi reds at their best are powerful and full of character, category-defying Kinzmarauli has an indecently sweet start but a strangely dry finish. Georgian whites come in two types. New 'Europuli' wines are crisp French-style vintages that contrast strikingly with the traditional home-made varieties that are the mainstay of a supra (toast-filled 'feast'). These have a quite distinctive, acquired taste and a straw-colour-like apple juice, but they're 100% ecological and remarkably rarely seem to cause hangovers.

Imported **European wines** are typically over priced.

✪ ✦ *Shampanski*, the local sparkling wine, suffers from a certain unpredictability and tends to be too sugary for many Western palates. But it's generally more palatable AND less expensive than cheap white wine. The Azeri XXI ÄSR brand tastes more like peach spritzer than champagne.

● **Vodka** (▲ *Arak*, ✪ *Vodka*) **and other spirits** In the Soviet Union, vodka was traditionally sold in standardized half-litre bottles with foil-sealed cardboard caps. These were not resealable, giving anyone the perfect excuse to say 'well it's open now, better finish it'. The methanol-tainted 1990s saw consumers moving towards more trustworthy brands and as a result, distinctive bottle designs have been emerging as trademarks, notably the respected Karat brand vaguely shaped like Hong Kong's Bank of China building. Other designs are mere gimmicks like Goldfinger (containing a glitter of goldleaf) or Ladywolf (with a red cap that flashes insanely when opened). As drinkers get more wealthy so ever-finer vodkas appear in the lengthy addenda to many a restaurant menu.

Toasts are important especially in Georgia (box p327) where you may be asked to choose between vodka and wine. The choice is a tough one. OK so the vodka is strong. However, downing numerous large glasses of wine can be even more taxing thanks to the sheer volume. In Azerbaijan hosts are generally a lot more restrained and may even be content to stop after a single shared bottle of vodka: they're Muslim after all.

Vodka is a soft drink in comparison to certain lethal forms of local home-made hooch like *chacha* (local grappa) or *tutovka* (*tut arağı*), an 80% alcohol distilled from mulberries.

Georgian brandy is not VSOP but it can be surprisingly drinkable. However, be careful about telling local friends if you do like it; social 'down-in-one shots' are bad enough performed in vodka or wine but brandy hangovers are even worse. Azerbaijani brandy is gaining an ever improving reputation, enough so that the industry chose in 2009 to officially change the Azeri term (formerly *konjak*) to allow exports without incurring the legal wrath of French Cognac producers. Most of the better brandies are frighteningly expensive but bargain value Göy Göl offers the warm, caramel tones of a Spanish Veterano at under AZN5 a bottle.

HEALTH

Despite the prevalence of mosquitoes, malaria is almost unknown in Azerbaijan, except in remote marshy areas towards the Iranian border. Even there, the few cases (at worst a few thousand per year) are non-fatal and are limited to the rainier seasons. Baku's ubiquitous mosquitoes are mostly *Aedes aegypti*, which are not capable of carrying malaria's *Plasmodium vivax* parasite which does the damage. The mosquitoes to be scared of are the female *Anopheles genus*. Since they don't usually introduce themselves formally, note that these are relatively large and tend to rest at a 45° angle. As always, check carefully with your doctor for formal medical advice before departing. It is worth bringing a good repellent with you.

Medical facilities

Local doctors are mostly very well qualified but some hospitals are short of supplies. 'Tell everyone – never go to hospital here' pleaded one expat. Apparently once you're part of the local health-care system you simply can't check-out till you're either better – or dead. So the standard advice is, if you can afford it, stick with one of the expat medical services. If you're not covered by insurance, basic consultation costs start from AZN24 with Medi Club & Ambulance which has local English-speaking doctors and clinics in Baku (☎ 012-497 0911), Gänjä, Şirvan (Ali Bayramli) and Tbilisi. Baku offers lots of alternative choices along with Folk, Chinese and Korean Medical Centres (see p135).

Certain doctors perform an unusual 'blood cleaning' filtration process. This requires a great deal of trust from the patient but apparently has very favourable results.

Locals put a lot of faith in mud and spa cures as you'll gather from the dozens of sanatoria dotted about the country offering thalassotherapy, salt caves, mud baths, sulphur showers etc. Traditionally garlic is good for headaches. Childağ is for people who are feeling jumpy (see Mäshtağa p150

and Märdäkän p149). Website 🖳 http://alakbarli.aamh.az/index.files/64.htm has more on traditional Azeri folk cures.

HIV/AIDS and sexually transmitted diseases

The Institute of Epidemiology (☎ 012-494 7353/494 8518), 34 Cäfär Cäbarly, Baku performs HIV/AIDS tests and is open 24 hours. The procedure should take no more than 40 minutes and some staff speak English.

ANNOYANCES AND SAFETY

Like the whole region, Azerbaijan is prone to earthquakes. Seismic wobbles damaged Ağdash in 1999 and worried Baku in November 2000, though graciously without substantial loss of life. Many worry that the next earthquake will be vastly more destructive as construction standards of Baku's endless new tower blocks are suspected to be inadequate. Such fears were chillingly underlined in August 2007 when an unfinished 16-storey apartment block collapsed... and that was **without** a quake.

Baku's infamous winds can cause injuries when roofing gets dislodged. Many accidents are caused by reckless driving with young men speeding carelessly about in their expensive new vehicles seeming to think that a fancy imported motor makes them immune from traffic rules. While roads have been repaved, pedestrian facilities remain abysmal in many places with uneven pavements and uncovered manholes which are easy to fall into if you walk along the unlit streets at night.

In human terms Azerbaijan is very hospitable and much safer than most Western countries. The biggest annoyance is likely to be meddlesome police, over-inquisitive intrusions and a surfeit of hospitality. Violent crime is largely confined to domestic disputes, some jilted husbands having a disturbing tendency to avenge a wife should she stray or even seek divorce. The gangs of 'munchkins' (street kids) who annoyed and occasionally mobbed lone foreigners a few years ago have been largely swept off the streets. However, it's

AZERBAIJAN – OVERVIEW

worth avoiding Sahil Gardens late at night where there have been several muggings.

CLIMATE

Like Chicago and Wellington, Baku is famous for its winds which bluster a few times a month mitigating the unpleasantly humid, summer heat, disrupting Caspian shipping or adding a bite to the slight winter chill. Snow is rare in Baku but common inland where winters are very much colder. Lows under -20° are possible in mountain villages such as Xınalıq where you'll need good woollens even in summer if you stay overnight. The flat centre of the country is typically dry with the irrigated farmland veering on semi desert. Here too summers are roasting while winters can be colder than one might expect.

The southern forests get heavy rains especially in October, November and March. The area is best for hiking in May; May is also ideal for visiting the west with fields full of flowers and a good chance of clear skies. Only in July does the snow clear sufficiently to allow trekking across the high passes around Xınalıq. In August people escape unbearably sweaty Baku for the cool hills of Pirguli or Altı Ağach, or the beaches of Nabran or the Absheron. Autumn arrives suddenly in mid-September often bringing with it low clouds and drizzle that can obscure the views for two or three weeks.

WHAT TO WEAR, THINGS TO TAKE

An eccentric 19th-century traveller advised tourists: 'In summer a helmet should be taken not omitting some pipeclay to clean it for helmets rapidly soil and Russians in the south are very particular about the spruceness of their headgear.' These days it's only 'white-beards' who still regularly wear hats (see box p134 for typical designs) with baseball caps more the norm amongst the Westernized Baku youth.

In most of the country modest dress is appropriate but in total contrast to neighbouring Iran, women are **not** required (nor expected) to hide wrists, ankles, hair or smiles. Veils were ceremoniously discarded following a 1920s Soviet *hujum* (attack) on Islamic female-fashion restrictions and a mass unveiling on March 8th (International Women's Day) 1928. That's commemorated by a fine statue (see p100) near Nizami Metro, Baku. In modern Baku, dress codes are specially liberal and girls can get away with the skimpiest of outfits. Don't assume an ultra-short mini-skirt means a girl is 'naughty': only if she smokes will Bakuvians think she's a bit of a tart. Curiously, even in Baku, it is men who provoke raised eyebrows if they walk around in shorts. A cultural equivalent would be strolling through London in Y-fronts.

For shopping, Baku is a great place to stock up with almost any conceivable Western item, though slide film and good mosquito repellent can still be hard to track down. Outside Baku the situation is very patchy, but apart from ubiquitous Pepsi and Snickers bars, don't assume you'll find Western products in most villages. Travellers are advised to carry a torch (provincial back streets are unlit and power cuts still occur) and keep a stash of toilet paper handy for rural emergencies.

Photos of yourself and your family are very useful conversational aids and make popular gifts, as do small curiosities (coins, souvenirs, badges etc). Giving these to the children of a local friend is nice. However, giving them randomly to villagers or Baku street urchins is strongly discouraged.

SOURCES OF INFORMATION

For Baku-based tour-guides and information offices see p134 and p137, for books see p348, and for internet info see p33.

Tourist information centres

TICs are a new concept in Azerbaijan. While several offices have opened, others are semi-dormant and of limited use but things are improving steadily as they gain experience. Baku's office gives away some glossy brochures and listings 'guide books'. In other TICs you might be given (or sold) a pamphlet but don't expect local maps of any great accuracy nor too much advice that involves critical assessment. Online the tourist ministry gives many similar listings on websites 🖳 **www.tourism.az** and 🖳 **www.mct.gov.az**.

Maps

For printed maps it's generally worth waiting till you arrive in Baku and buy maps there. If you're prepared to pay between three and ten times the local prices 🖳 www.omnimap and other online retailers can help.

Country maps

Great, one-sheet 1:500,000 scale country maps sell in better Baku bookshops for 5.70AZN. There are two versions, one slightly clearer topographically, the other has major roads more obviously marked. It is highly recommended that you travel with at least one of these. Both are more accurate than the confusingly transliterated 1:650,000 **ITMB** Azerbaijan & Armenia map or the **Freytag & Berndt** Caucasus map (also available as the cheaper Hungarian **Gizi** imprint).

Local bookshops also stock cheap Azeri language atlas-pamphlets showing the country's geography, mineralogy, flora, fauna patterns etc.

Note that no commercial map shows the front-line nor the area which is inaccessible thanks to the Armenian occupation! Ageing but highly detailed Soviet-era maps exist (in Cyrillic) at 1:100,000, 1:50,000, 1:25:000 and 1:10,000. These remain 'classified' and if you don't have specific permission to buy (at over $70 per sheet!) and use them you could be in trouble. Nonetheless, you can currently down load the 1:100,000 sheets as .gif files free from 🖳 http://maps.poehali.org/. Or pay US$12 and get the whole set at once from 🖳 http://mapstor.com/map-sets/country maps/azerbaijan.html. Other interesting if less-detailed maps can be viewed on 🖳 www.azerbaijan24.com (click 'About Azerbaijan', then 'Azerbaijan Maps') and 🖳 www.dtxk.gov.az/maps/maps_r.html (links in Russian).

The State Cartographic Committee (Dövlät Torpaq vä Xäritäcäkmä Komitäsi, ☎ 432 8959, 🖳 www.dtxk.gov.az) produces most of the maps listed above and has redrawn the 1:100,000 series to reflect alphabet and place-name changes but they remain reluctant to sell anything too detailed. Call before visiting.

City maps

Accurate Baku city maps are available locally (see p135) but maps of any other towns are almost impossible to find and where available are generally schematic rather than to any scale. Probably maps will eventually be created based on Google Earth images as has happened in most other poorly mapped countries but that has yet to happen for Azerbaijan. For now the best available printed town maps are in the hard-to-find *Informative Cartographic Reference Book* (AZN30) but scales can be very unreliable at the edges and in some places there is no differentiation between footpaths and major roads.

GPS points and maps

With GPS ownership increasingly common amongst visitors and expats, I have added a fair number of location coordinates for out-of-the-way places and road junctions. If you find my points to be inaccurate or have extra points to be included for the next edition, please drop me a line on 🖳 mark .elliott@trailblazer-guides.com. The website 🖳 www.trailblazer-guides.com will occasionally post an updated list of useful coordinates.

For those with Garmin GPS devices a limited selection of .img file vector maps of Azerbaijan (ie scaleable, line format) can be downloaded from 🖳 http://mapcenter2 .cgpsmapper.com with more at the older site, 🖳 http://mapcenter.cgpsmapper.com/ maplist.php?cnt=17&rgn=&cat=4.

Companies such as 🖳 http://www.ozi explorer.com offer software allowing you to use scanned maps (ie Raster/image maps like those downloaded from 🖳 http:// maps.poehali.org/en/) with your GPS. Many Garmin receivers can upload third-party vector maps and free software is available at 🖳 http://code.google.com/ p/gpsvp for PC and smartphones with inbuilt GPS that can read and navigate the Garmin format maps. To be really clever you can download the map source code from these sites and update/edit them (eg adding the new Baku bypasses or personal places of interest) then recompile them for upload to your GPS. For map editing the free GPSMapedit at 🖳 http://www

.geopainting.com/en/ is recommended, though the optional paid-for version has the valuable ability to draw directly on top of Google maps. Uploading a new or revised map from GPSMapedit to Mapcenter2 will result in it being compiled for Garmin receivers and available to all. For help on making your own maps see ▭ http://tech.groups.yahoo.com/group/map_authors/.

Press and media

For in-depth analytical articles read or subscribe to **Caucasian Review of International Affairs** (▭ http://cria-online.org/) and **IWPR** (▭ www.iwpr.gn.apc.org). With reporters in all the countries of the region, the latter is particularly good at giving a range of viewpoints.

Soros-funded **OSI-Eurasianet** (▭ www.eurasianet.org/resource/azerbaijan/) has useful annual reports. The quarterly journal *Caucasus and Globalisation* is available as pdfs for €20 per edition on ▭ www.ca-c.org.

Azerbaijan International (▭ www.azer.com) thematically covers various cultural and historical issues in a glossy, professionally produced quarterly themed magazine all reproduced on their brilliantly comprehensive website. Their Baku office (☎ 012-492 8701) is on the alley behind the Brewery and is curiously unmarked except for the cryptic numbers '27-18' over the door.

● **Free weeklies** Baku has several free weekly papers in English offering mainly agency newsfeeds sandwiched between lashings of advertising for restaurants, apartment-rentals and other useful alerts for what's new in the fast-changing city. *Caspian Business News* (▭ www.caspianbusinessnews.com) is generally best for news; *Baku Sun* (▭ www.bakusun.baku.az), *AzerNews* and others are sometimes inadvertently comical and worth reading for their curious expressions of patriotism.

● **News agencies** The following online agencies have locally relevant news in English: ANS (▭ www.anspress.com); APA (▭ http://en.apa.az); AzärTac (▭ www.azertag.com) state agency; Trends (▭

http://news.trendaz.com); Turan (▭ www.turan.az); Today (▭ http://today.az).

● **Local press** Most local press seems to view events from an undisguised viewpoint of staunch 'patriotism' while defamation laws make outspoken investigative journalism potentially risky and a number of such journalists have found themselves in jail. Popular mainstream newspapers include *Zerkalo* and *Exo*. *The Monitor* was a harder-hitting local magazine but its aggressive approach to uncovering political scandals led to its closure and legal claims. The murder of its editor, Elmar Huseynov, gunned down in 2005, remains a sensitive issue.

● **TV** The main stations are AzTV, Space, Ichtimai, INS, Lider, ATV and ANS. Popular Russian channels Rossiya (ex-RTR) and ORT were re-broadcast locally until 2007. Now they are only available on cable or satellite but with two competing cable providers, and an increasing proliferation of satellite receivers (especially in the provinces), it is not uncommon to find CNN, BBC World and many more English-language channels especially in upmarket hotels. In cheaper accommodation a uselessly crackly TV blaring in the corner of the room will often be the excuse for a big price hike.

● **Radio** There are dozens of stations but in any Baku minibus or taxi you're likely to hear 106FM or Burch FM (100.5FM) pumping out their 24hr mix of Turkish and Azeri pop music. Until December 2008 the BBC and Voice of America were broadcast locally but they fell foul of the new law against foreign broadcasters.

POST AND TELECOMMUNICATIONS
Post

For sending mail I have found smaller post offices to be more reliable than major ones. For receiving mail, be sure to get the addressee's postal box and 'Indeks' (post code). Mail is rarely delivered to the door. In villages it simply arrives at the nearest post office for collection. In Baku various courier companies offer an alternative (see Post and parcel services p136).

Telephone

Calling Azerbaijan from abroad use the country code ☎ +994 and drop the first 0 from the city code. To call internationally from Azerbaijan start with 00 but note that some phones can still only call local city numbers.

• **Mobile phones** For Azeris there's a great social cache in the brand and model of mobile phone they carry. Being without a phone is virtually unthinkable and an endless parade of shops pander to the seemingly unquenchable demand.

More prosaically note that Azerbaijan's system is GSM standard. A SIM card with an initial 1000 'kontor' (credit units) costs as little as AZN5, making the number effectively free. Typically sending SMS texts costs 11 units whether local or international.

Buying a local SIM card is quick and easy if you have a local address and Azerbaijani residency ID. If you don't, the easiest solution is asking a local friend to get the SIM card for you.

There are three competing networks: Azercell ('SimSim' cards, code 050),

❏ **Emergency numbers**
Fire: ☎ 01
Police: ☎ 02
Ambulance: ☎ 03/113
  (or ☎ 012-497 0911,
  Medi Club, see p29)
Gas leaks: ☎ 04

Bakcell ('Cin Kart', code 55) and cut-price newcomer NarMobile (code 070).

Calling a mobile phone from a terrestrial one is effectively like calling a long-distance number. From mobile phone to landline dial ☎ 0 then the city code.

• **Pay phones** Now that mobile phones are so ubiquitous, it's increasingly hard to find a pay-phone. A few do still operate. Most are simple, rotary phones under blue metal hoods operated using a ribbed metal *jeton* token the size of a small coin. Jetons cost 20q when bought from phone offices, more when resold by kiosks but finding anyone to sell them is getting tough these days. The

❏ **Useful websites**
⌨ http://azenviron.aznet.org Environmental contacts and projects. See also ⌨ www.ecotourism.aznet .org

⌨ www.azer.com Brilliant wide-ranging *Azerbaijan International* site. Books, CDs and an Azeri course are available for sale

⌨ www.azerb.com An A-Z of things Azeri, albeit with much travel information suspiciously similarly worded to older editions of this book

⌨ www.azerbaijan.az Professional official information site with links to the websites of top politicians

⌨ www.azeris.org/travel Has a particularly useful series of links

⌨ www.azerbaijan.az Useful general information collated by the Heydar Aliyev Foundation

⌨ www.bakucity.az City Administration

⌨ www.bakuguide.az Listings of events, hotels etc. Less dated than most.

⌨ http://carpetblog.typepad.com/carpetblogger/azerbaijan Offbeat, amusingly irreverent, articles

⌨ www.peacecorpsjournals.com/?showcountryinfo,aj Links to a series of blogs by US volunteers who live and work in Azerbaijani towns and villages, giving you a great view of local life from the inside.

⌨ www.si-travel.com Baku's top travel agency, flight deals

⌨ www.traveler.az Professionally designed commercial tour site

⌨ www.tourism.az and www.mct.gov.az Extensive tourism ministry sites.

⌨ www.window2baku.com Baku historical photos

jeton only works for calls within the city: you cannot reach a mobile or long-distance number. For these lines you'll need a call office or one of Baku's handful of new card phones. Cards (AZN13.60) are available from the central post and telephone boxes in Fountains Square, though generally people pay an attendant on a per-call basis to use part of a card.

Alternatively use a phone office. These are usually inside or attached to post offices. Write down the number required, give it to the supervisor who will usher you to a dingy cubicle to take the call.

Internet connection

Almost every major town now has a few internet Klubs (numerous in Baku) where you can check your emails for as little as 60q per hour. Connection is very variable: one place in Göychay was super fast and cheap, while another in Ağdash was appallingly slow and AZN1 per hour. Shop around.

Facts about the country

HISTORY
Overview

Azerbaijan was the original paradise. But since the fall of Eden and the crashing of Noah's Ark through the peak of Ilan Dağ (p304), it has ridden a historical and political roller-coaster. Always at the edge of somebody else's patch, overlordship has been dragged to and fro between empires whether Roman, Parthian, Persian, Arab, Georgian, Mongol, Turkish or Russian. Conquerors not only conquered but in medieval tradition, often killed or moved whole populations, carrying women and craftsmen back to the imperial capitals and substituting their own herdsmen to exploit the land. The most significant influx was the various waves of Turkic nomads who have come to form the main ethnic element in today's Azeri population.

As no explicitly Azerbaijani state existed until 1918, getting a feel for the phenomenally rich and complex historical background requires one to grapple with a melting pot of peoples, religions and several poorly defined mini states which have come and gone over time. Confusingly the most abiding of these was known as **Albania**, though it has nothing to do with today's European Albania (Shqiperia). Another key entity was Shirvan ruled by the Shirvanshahs and based mostly at Shamakha and Baku.

Further confusion arises in that the most historically important Azeri cities are not in the Azerbaijan Republic at all but outside its borders – Tabriz and Ardebil in Iran, Derbend in Russia. Inevitably much Azeri historical source material is focused on those towns and on the great area of Southern Azerbaijan that remained within Persia/Iran after 1828 when today's Azerbaijan Republic was chipped off by Russia.

Another key point to note is that the ethnic 'Turks', waves of whom progressively came to populate Azerbaijan, came from Central Asia not from 'Turkey'. Indeed it was via Azerbaijan that some Turks may have reached Anatolia (Turkey) eventually pushing out or assimilating the Greek-Byzantine population. Persians (Iranians) and Turks who we now associate with Islam were not necessarily Muslims earlier in history and certainly not before the 7th century (Mohammad didn't start preaching till 610). However, after Mohammad's death in 632, the Arabs led by a combined politico-spiritual leader ('Caliph') are indeed largely synonymous with Islam which they spread systematically in the vast empire they rapidly built up (finally toppled by the Seljuk Turks in 1055).

A most confusing aspect is the way that empires come and go, yet for centuries the little principalities, and petty nobles wielding regional power, continually pop up again apparently relatively unaffected by years or even centuries of foreign overlordship. Historians have suggested that the inability of these lords to agree or for one to out do all the rest explains why they were so frequently subservient to others and also why Azerbaijan was so rarely an aggressive empire-building state.

Beware of the term '**Tatar**' in historical sources. Today the term refers to the descendants of Mongol-Turkic Golden

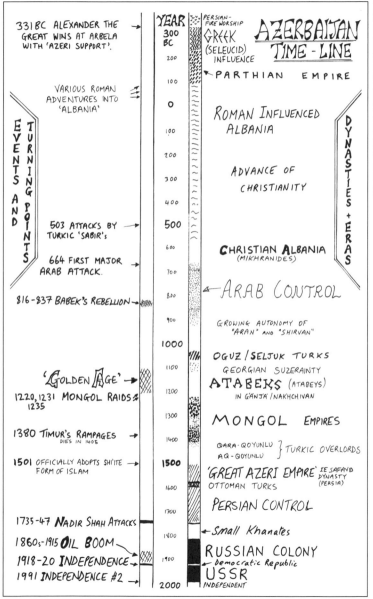

AZERBAIJAN TIME-LINE

EVENTS AND TURNING POINTS

DYNASTIES + ERAS

YEAR		
300 BC	PERSIAN-FIRE WORSHIP	
200	GREEK (SELEUCID) INFLUENCE	
100	PARTHIAN EMPIRE	
0	ROMAN INFLUENCED ALBANIA	
100		
200	ADVANCE OF CHRISTIANITY	
300		
400		
500		
600	CHRISTIAN ALBANIA (MIKHRANIDES)	
700	ARAB CONTROL	
800		
900	GROWING AUTONOMY OF "ARAN" AND "SHIRVAN"	
1000		
1100	OGUZ/SELJUK TURKS — GEORGIAN SUZERAINTY — ATABEKS (ATABEYS) IN GANJA/NAKHCHIVAN	
1200		
1300	MONGOL EMPIRES	
1400	QARA-QOYUNLU AQ-QOYUNLU } TURKIC OVERLORDS	
1500	'GREAT AZERI EMPIRE' IE SAFAVID DYNASTY (PERSIA)	
1600	OTTOMAN TURKS	
1700	PERSIAN CONTROL	
1800	Small Khanates	
1900	RUSSIAN COLONY — Democratic Republic — USSR	
2000	INDEPENDENT	

331BC ALEXANDER THE GREAT WINS AT ARBELA WITH 'AZERI SUPPORT'.

VARIOUS ROMAN ADVENTURES INTO 'ALBANIA'

503 ATTACKS BY TURKIC 'SABIR's

664 FIRST MAJOR ARAB ATTACK.

816-837 BABEK'S REBELLION

'GOLDEN AGE'

1220, 1231 MONGOL RAIDS 1235

1380 TIMUR'S RAMPAGES DIES IN 1405

1501 OFFICIALLY ADOPTS SHI'ITE FORM OF ISLAM

1735-47 NADIR SHAH ATTACKS

1860s-1915 OIL BOOM

1918-20 INDEPENDENCE

1991 INDEPENDENCE #2

Horde, now settled mostly around Kazan in the Russian Federation (Tataristan). However, in the 19th century the term Tatar was widely if inaccurately applied to the Muslim-Turkic population of the east Caucasus – today's Azeris.

Prehistory

The Caucasus region is one of the great cradles of humanity. Remarkable recent research suggests that the Biblical **Garden of Eden** was less metaphorical than previously assumed. Archaeologist David Rohl has traced numerous geographical references in the book of *Genesis* to real places in southern Azerbaijan, postulating the vale of 'Eden' as the Aji Chai Valley around modern Tabriz and placing the Land of Nod around Ardebil. There were, however, many other communities of proto-humans, notably around Mingächevir, in Karabagh (where some especially ancient remains have been recovered at the Azikh Cave, p276) and on the Caspian coast at **Qobustan**. The famous Qobustan rock carvings (see p140) span millennia from early Stone Age until well into the Iron Age as recorded by the changing nature of tools used to scratch animal and shamanist designs on the cave walls.

On the Absheron peninsula, archaeologists suggest that 6000 years ago, remarkably advanced men were building conical homes around a hollow central pillar that acted as fireplace and chimney for flaming gas vents which they harnessed for cooking and heat. From the ancient rocky grooves of wheel-less 'cart' tracks found near **Türkan** (map p144) it seems they did some pretty heavy moving too.

Early kingdoms

Until well into the first millennium BC, most recorded regional history focuses on southern Azerbaijan (now Iran). Here the state of Zamoa, centred near Lake Urumiyeh, fought periodic battles with the Assyrian empire to whose rule it capitulated around 815BC. Other kingdoms – Manae, Uratu and Medea – came and went and Azerbaijan was eventually incorporated into Akhaemenid dynasty Persia. During the 6th century BC, this empire grew extremely powerful, fortified by the first great monotheistic religion, Zoroastrianism.

Alexander the Great

Aged only 21, Alexander of Macedonia (▲ Iskender) had already once defeated the magnificent army of Persian Emperor Darius III. Darius escaped, but rather than chasing immediately across Asia, Alex wandered off to take Egypt and found Alexandria. Three years later, in 331BC, he returned and faced Darius a second time at the battle of Arbela. That he won was thanks, in part, to the *satarap* (governor) of Persian Azerbaijan who changed sides just before the battle to support the Greeks. Alexander went on to vandalize the beautiful city of Persepolis, but rewarded the turncoat with de facto rule over his province which he called Atropatena (or in Persian Aturpatkan – 'protected by fire'), from which the name Azerbaijan is possibly derived.

Albania and Atropatena

Alexander died in Babylon nine years later having built an empire stretching as far as India. In the squabbles which followed, Atropatena became a peripheral part of the Greek Seleucid empire. A century later it swapped allegiance to the Parthian Empire along with 'Albania' to the north (which has nothing whatever to do with today's Albania in the Balkans). By 100BC the Parths were enjoying a long jousting match with the Romans' Eastern Empire, which resulted eventually in three Roman incursions into the Caucasus, notably under Pompey in 67-66BC. One Roman soldier thoughtfully left a little souvenir graffiti on a rock at Qobustan (p140) – the furthest east any such inscription has been found. Despite several reverses in imperial fortune, the Arshakid dynasty installed by the Romans to run Albania and much of the Caucasus, survived till the 4th century AD during which the region became at least nominally converted to Christianity.

The centralized Albanian government finally broke down in the 6th century with the arrival of a nomadic, Turkic warrior tribe called the Sabir around AD503. The state was divided into several small, long-

AZERBAIJAN – OVERVIEW

lasting principalities including Shirvan and Shäki. Nonetheless, Albania was to reform twice thereafter. The most notable leader was King Javanshir (Joanshir) who managed to survive the whirlwind invasion of the Arabs in 664 and boot them out of Derbend before accepting vassal status to the Caliphate in 667. He was mysteriously stabbed to death in 680. The very same year, the Arab civil war was reaching a climax in distant Kerbala (Iraq) with the death of Hussein, grandson of the prophet Mohammad. His 'martyrdom' is still mourned today in the Shi'ite masochistic self whippings of Mohtarram (in Iran and, much less widely, in Azerbaijan).

Arab conquest

By the 8th century the Arabs had already built the Dome of the Rock in Jerusalem and conquered most of North Africa, so definitively grabbing Albania in 705 proved to be a pretty straightforward excursion. The pragmatic Albanian king was understandably happy to swap certain death and loss of his kingdom for a nominal conversion to Islam, and the promise to guard his northern borders against Khazar raiders – something he'd been doing anyway. Despite the official switch to Islam, the Albanian church was allowed to keep functioning. All in all, nothing much seemed to change for several decades. Then in 750 almost the entire Arab ruling family was massacred by the usurping new Caliph Abu Abbas. His aggressive new 'Abbasid' dynasty increased taxes to pay for a new capital (Baghdad), turned the screws on non-Muslims and generally started making itself unpopular. In Azerbaijan the result was a series of rebellions, of which by far the most sustained and celebrated was

---

❏ Geo-political facts

● **GDP per capita, 2008**: US$9500, a truly incredible increase since 2003 ($917). Previous figures: 1997 ($509), 1995 ($318), (1987) $3350.

● **Major exports/economy**: Oil, gas. Azerbaijan is the world's fifth largest producer of hazelnuts. Silk, caviar, cotton and wine production have all declined considerably since independence.

● **Leader**: President Ilham Aliyev (since 2003, replacing his father Heydar).

● **National flag**: Blue (for the sky) represents God in ancient Turkic symbolism, red represents the blood shed for freedom. Green, the colour of Islam, is tellingly relegated to the bottom stripe. A central white crescent clasps an archetypally Azeri eight-pointed star (compare with a Turkish five-pointed star).

● **Population**: 8,676,000 (2008 official figure), 8,177,000 (CIA estimate). Wildly varying estimates put the ethnic Azeri population of Iran at anywhere between 10 and 24 million according to definition. Around 400,000 ethnic Azeris live in the USA, up to a million work in Turkey and over 2 million work in Russia (albeit some seasonally).

● **Capital**: Baku

● **Area**: 86,600 sq km (slightly smaller than Portugal).

● **Geography**: Elevation ranges from -27m on the Caspian coast to 4466m on the Russian border in the Greater Caucasus and 3724m in the Lesser Caucasus. Woodlands are in a narrow band between 2000 and 2300m. A little lower things are scrubby and dry except for the forests around Nabran and Länkäran. At greater elevations the mountains are bald and grassy.

● **Ethnic groups**: Azeris (91%), Russians, Lezghians (north-east), Talysh (south-east), Avars, Georgians and Tssakhur (north-west), Udi (in Nic), Tat Mountain Jews (at Krasnaya Sloboda) and many tiny populations of 'other nationalities' (supposedly 26 in Zaqatala district alone!). Official figures say that Armenians form around 1.5% of the population. That's misleading but technically true since occupied Nagorno Karabagh where almost all of them live remains legally part of Azerbaijan.

Babek's Khuramid Movement. Today Babek (see p297) is hailed with romantic nostalgia as a Robin Hood-style crusader for the oppressed. Though Babek was eventually executed in 838, low-key struggles continued for most of the century.

Seljuks and Atabeks

By the late 10th century Arab power was finally waning and Albania had fizzled out into a series of disparate fiefdoms – notably 'Aran' (based on Tärtär), Shirvan (at Shamakha) and the Shaddedid dynasty of Gänjä. The 11th century saw a large-scale influx of the Muslim Oguz Turks under the powerful Seljuk dynasty who rapidly came to control most of the Middle East, eclipsing the Arabs.

The foremost Seljuk leader was Alp Arslan whose interest in the Caucasus was widened by his favourite Georgian wife. Under his enlightened rule Azerbaijan benefited from strong but decentralized government which permitted a degree of free trade beyond feudal tribute while allowing the continued autonomy of the regional principalities. Later Seljuk leaders were less adept and a newly self-confident Georgia helped to fracture their empire at the decisive battle of Didgori (August 1121). Georgia was entering her Golden Age and under Georgian protection the multi-racial, cultural and artistic boom extended to the Azeri principalities too, notably in Shirvan under Shirvanshah Manuchehr III. This continued after the 1150s when the principalities formed a confederation under Shamseddin and his 'Atabek' dynasty, though later rulers fell out with the Georgians who marched back into Azerbaijan a few times between 1185 and 1211 to 'maintain order'. During this period many great artists and poets gained prominence notably Nizami Gänjävi, the national literary icon whose statue today adorns almost every Azeri town.

Mongols and Turks

Unwashed, unshaven and drunk, the Mongols were about as welcome as a busload of football supporters at The Ritz. And they did even more damage. Thanks to two revolutionary inventions – stirrups and trousers – Mongols were able to ride their horses across huge distances without genital discomfort. They used this new-found freedom to smash and grab anything they found from Samarkand to Budapest. Azerbaijan was just one of many places utterly devastated by several waves of Mongol and related nomads starting in 1225. Cities were razed, crops burnt, populations massacred and irrigation systems destroyed where leaders refused to surrender quickly.

The Mongols' barbaric phase was enough to completely kill the Caucasus's Golden Age. But within a few decades they had mellowed noticeably. Genghis Khan's sons maintained and expanded his empire but thereafter it was split among the likes of Kublai Khan who moved to China where he'd rather build pleasure domes than go to the office for a hard day's massacring. The Iranian chunk of the Mongol empire (including Azerbaijan) fell to Hulugu Khan's Il Khanid dynasty after 1250, though Hulugu himself was too busy in Iraq to care much about what happened in Baku. The Azeri lords had periods of recovery in which to bicker amongst themselves before renewed attacks from different Mongol-related groups (Golden Horde in 1319 and 1382, Timur in 1380 and 1386). Timur, known also as Tamerlane (Timur-the-lame), ransacked even places such as Nakhchivan and Qazax which had survived the earlier raids. On returning to central Asia he scared away much of that region's nomadic Turkic-Turkmen population who drifted west into Anatolia (Turkey) and Azerbaijan.

Black sheep, white sheep and the great Azeri Empire

Following Timur's death in 1404, one of these Turkmen groups (the Shi'ite Qarakoyunlu 'Black Sheep') fought a coalition of 'traditional' lords for control of southern Azerbaijan, only to be ousted by another (the Sunni Aqkoyunlu 'White Sheep') in the late 1460s. The Aqkoyunlu then spent much of the century squabbling with the Ottoman Turks who by this stage had occupied Anatolia and were growing increasingly into a regional power.

Throughout this period the smaller Azeri sub-khanates continued to fight amongst themselves, notably Shirvan versus Ardebil. In 1456 there was a major battle at Häzrä (p191) on the Samur River, where amongst the Ardebil leaders to die was a certain Sheikh Juneid. In 1500-1, Juneid's grandson Ismail set out to avenge his death, as the improbable 14-year-old leader of the Ardebil army. Following a remarkable run of success, he found himself rapidly propelled to ruler of all Azerbaijan eventually becoming Shah Ismail I of Persia (Iran).

In Azerbaijan, Ismail is generally remembered by his poetic pen name Xatai under which he popularized Azeri as a written language of arts and letters. He wrote everything from love ballads and seasonal odes to works on philosophy and morals, but perhaps most interesting are the surprisingly self-deprecating little verses he wrote to himself as apparent reminders of good government or behaviour:

Xatai looking pensive as the Baku road around him gets widened

Xatai's of a pedant's school
Sufi by heart and should know much
Yet tell the truth I'm but a fool
With all that business puts in train
Remember Xatai, to be restrained:
Bite off more than you can chew
And little of friendship will remain.

Xatai's Safavid dynasty is remembered for forcing the Persian empire to definitively embrace Shi'ite rather than Sunni Muslim traditions (see p47).

Later Safavids

The Shirvanshahs, who had fled to their isolated mountain strongholds in the face of Xatai, were finally wiped out once and for all at the 1538 seige of Qalabugurt (p201).

Nonetheless, wars continued throughout the 16th century, notably between Safavid Persia and Ottoman Turkey. This encouraged the later Safavid shahs to lose touch with their Azeri roots as they moved their capital ever eastwards from Tabriz via Qazvin to the safety of Isfahan, a glorious new city in central Iran, far from the ravages of interminable wars with the Ottomans.

To provide the necessary skilled expertise for this, Shah Abbas I simply dragged away the entire artisan population of Old Julfa (Culfa, see p311) and resettled them outside Isfahan. Shirvan (centred on Shamakha), Karabagh (administered from Gänjä) and Nakhchivan (aka Shukur-Saada) retained some identity as *beklerbeklik* regions within Safavid Persia.

In 1580 the Ottoman Turks occupied Shirvan in an unlikely coalition with Crimean Tatars and Caucasian mountain tribes. This was an economic disaster for Azerbaijan which had been rebuilding itself as a north–south trade route. A splendid if long out-of-print account of the period (Morgan, p350) was written by a group of swashbuckling Elizabethan English wool traders who got caught in the middle, see box p40.

The Khanates

From 1708 Iran's Safavid Shahs were increasingly distracted by infighting and were overthrown altogether in 1722. Peter the Great of newly expanding Russia took the opportunity to occupy much of Azerbaijan and the Caspian coast but was chased out by a new breed of Persian ruler – the Afghan-descended Nadir Shah.

As his name aptly suggests, Nadir's brutal arrival was the lowest ebb for some Caucasian fortunes since the rampages of Timur. Nadir devastated Azerbaijan all over again and utterly depopulated Shamakha, forcing its population to an entirely new spot near Aqsu. They swiftly rebuilt Shamakha once Nadir had been assassinated in 1747. Indeed Nadir's death proved the cue for a confederation of Azeri khans to drive out the Persian governors altogether. The result was a renewed blossoming of Azeri culture, notably in Gänjä and under Panakh Khan in

❏ Stiff upper lip

The British Muscovy Company's experience of Azerbaijan was not a brilliant one. William Turnbull, Matthew Talboys et al had hoped to repeat the moderate success of five previous expeditions down the Volga and across the Caspian to trade at Shabran or Shamakha. But despite heroic derring-do, the traders' 1579 trip was a catalogue of disasters. Prevented from landing at Gil Gil (the port for Shabran, p166), they had to continue south. Narrowly avoiding pirates, they moored off Bildigh (Bilgah) 'on ye Apsherone only one day's walk from Baku'. But on arriving they were told that Shamakha, the great trade entrepôt, had been destroyed by the Turks, and that Shabran market was empty.

At the time Baku was little more than a secure port for Shamakha so, with the latter destabilized, nobody in Baku was at all anxious to buy British woollens. The Brits therefore decided to march north to flog their wares in Derbend, itself under a Turkish Pasha. But, in the meantime, the Turks occupying central Shirvan had been defeated by the 'Persian widow of blind King Khodabendeh' so to reach Derbend, still under Turkish control, meant sneaking along forest tracks across the zone retaken by the Persians. This was so dangerous that one of the crew had to offer himself as a hostage to guarantee the safe return of the local guide. The coastal road was considered far too dangerous. But their wool proved unsellable in Derbend too – hardly surprising given all the shepherds in the region – so increasingly desperate they attempted, nearly fatally, to reach Shamakha.

By the time they got back to Bildigh their moored boat was leaking dangerously. The ship they purchased to replace it was dashed to pieces just as they prepared to leave, resulting in the loss of a chest of gold and the soaking of their modest purchases in Caspian brine. Finally the Pasha expelled them, but the season was late and they got caught in the ice on the way back to Astrakhan. Miraculously the party finally made it back to England in 1581 but, not surprisingly, few British businessmen were destined to return until the oil boom 300 years later.

Karabagh where Shusha became Azerbaijan's cultural capital par excellence. There was the usual cycle of jostling for superiority between the several regional power centres (see Khanates map opposite), with Shäki under Haci Saleb an initial front runner. Latterly Fatali Khan of Quba attempted to unite the regions into a single Azeri state. The enterprise was inevitably interrupted by incursions from Persia and Russia.

In 1795, the last year of Catherine the Great's rule, Russian expeditionary troops marched into Azerbaijan, took Shamakha and might have gone further but for the simultaneous northward march of a great Persian army. Iran was newly rampant under the vicious Qajar dynasty of the 'eunuch-king' Aga Mohammad, while for the next few years Russia was governed by mad Tsar Paul. However, once Paul had been conveniently murdered in 1801, the Russians returned to the Caucasus in force, initially occupying Georgia then whittling away at the Azeri khanates (1804-06).

Great games and Russian rule

By 1807, only Nakhchivan remained an independent khanate. However, weakened by the Napoleonic wars, the Russian grip on the Caucasus took a long time to tighten. The British, initial tacit supporters of Russia as a counterbalance to France and their Ottoman allies, started getting nervous at Russia's expanded empire and possible threats to India. Britain began helping the Ottomans to arm bands of Caucasus mountain resistance fighters such as Shamil (see p237). Meanwhile Persia used the opportunity to try grabbing Azerbaijan back again. However, after initial successes aided by popular support (eg in Gänjä), the Persians were unceremoniously ejected again and

AZERBAIJAN – OVERVIEW

were forced to sign the 1828 Treaty of Turkmenchay which formally recognized the division of Azerbaijan into Russian and Iranian zones along the Araz/Arax River which remains the borderline to this day.

The consolidation of Russian rule caused some important demographic changes – notably the mass influx of Armenians into Azeri lands such as Karabagh and Zangezaur, where they felt safer than in the Muslim Ottoman or Persian empires. This was eventually to sow the seeds of the Karabagh war. Russian colonization took off relatively slowly as the region was seen as a hardship posting and place of exile. The economy was

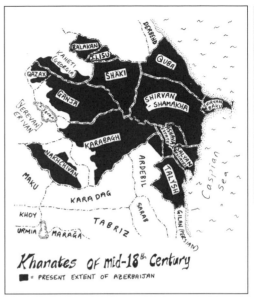

Khanates of mid-18th Century

■ = PRESENT EXTENT OF AZERBAIJAN

not aided by redistributing many of the feudal lands to Russian military officers and disinterested nobles so, to improve matters, hard-working German migrants from impoverished states such as Würtemburg were bribed to settle the area (see box p262). Nonetheless, the Europeanization of Azerbaijan had an important effect in tempering local Islam, and making the Azeris an important cultural bridge for an interchange of ideas between the West, Ottoman Turkey and Iran.

Oil

Russia took several decades to stabilize the region militarily and even then was slow to appreciate the potential of Baku oil. A state monopoly did little to garner investment as private individuals were at best allowed to lease land for two-year periods which was rarely sufficient to repay investment in refining or transportation infrastructure.

Everything changed in 1872 when the industry was denationalized. The invention of the motor car and development of refining methods meant that in 30 years produc-

tion soared from 63 to 32,000 tons per day. In the first years of the 20th century half the entire world's production was supplied from Baku. Famous names including Rothschild, the Nobel brothers and HZ Tağiyev contributed to harnessing the profits into a major economic boom and transforming Baku from a sleepy port town of 5000 souls into a burgeoning metropolis. Many of the traders, investors and workers who arrived to swell the population were not native Azeris at all but Russians, Europeans, Persians, Armenians and Jews. By the turn of the 20th century Baku was a highly cosmopolitan city but despite several rags to riches tales of Azeris striking oil, most of the wealth remained in the hands of foreign companies and investors.

While Baku's elite were attending the new opera house or giving musical soirées in their grand new stone mansions (that still beautify the city centre), workers suffered appalling conditions. Not only did labourers have to wallow in poisonous petroleum while hand digging wells but the powerful companies could and did interfere in their personal lives. The Caspian Oil Co even forbade marriage without company permission. Thus Baku became a hotbed for Bolshevik agitators and oilfield strikes set the scene for the abortive first Russian revolution of 1905.

Massacres and provocation

The ethnic mixture of Baku at the turn of the 20th century was very complex. The Azeri population ('Tatars' according to the disdainful appellation of the day) had become a minority in their own land and did many of the worst manual jobs. Tensions especially between poor Tatars and nouveau-riche Armenians were simmering even then, but the massacres on 'Black/ Bloody Sunday' (Jan 22nd 1905) were deliberately provoked.

To prevent a united revolutionary movement emerging in the notoriously independent-minded Caucasus, the Russian government set out to confuse and destabilize the region. They were prepared to burn the oilfields rather than allow them to fund an opposition movement. The 'Black Hundreds', a series of government-recruited gangs, deliberately killed Armenians and blamed Tatars, killed Tatars blaming Armenians and set children of one community against one another inciting their parents to fight. This successfully ignited one of the worst inter-racial massacres ever recorded. The blatant use of *agents provocateurs* was to prove a useful lesson to Russian governments in future moments of crisis at home – in 1918 and 1988-90. On both occasions the Caucasus dissolved into civil war and popular opinion was persuaded to blame the maligned Muslims.

Once the ash had settled and the corpses had been buried, Baku still managed to retain a degree of revolutionary fervour out of proportion with the waning revolution elsewhere. Russian communists had been effectively defeated (for now) by a 1907 coup d'état. But at this time in Baku, the workers continued to elect Bolshevik representatives. These efforts led to very little at the time, but proved historically pivotal in hindsight: leading the Baku movement was a shadowy figure using the pseudonym Gayoz Nisharadze. Nisharadze's

tenacity caught the eye of an almost-despairing Lenin and thus began the long rise to infamy of the man who later rebranded himself as Stalin.

World War I

The events leading to Azerbaijan's independence in 1918 are fascinatingly complex. In 1917 Russia collapsed into civil war. Lenin dashed back to St Petersburg passing secretly through enemy German territory on a sealed train from Paris, and once in control of Russia simply gave up on WWI (Brest Litovsk Treaty, 3 March 1918). Azerbaijan, Armenia and Georgia initially formed the short-lived Trans-Caucasian Federation.

Revolutionary Russia sent a team of commissars under the much-reviled Stepan Shaumian, to newly 'liberated' Baku where they were to nationalize the oil industry on behalf of the Bolsheviks. The Baku 'commune' fearing ethnic Azeris to be 'anti-revolutionary' did little to stop street fights which snowballed into wide-scale inter-ethnic conflict resulting in the massacre of an estimated 12,000 Azeris. The so-called 'March Days' saw the burning of much of the city and brought the oil business to a virtual standstill (see pp96-7, '26 Commissars').

Meanwhile WWI was reaching a climax. Enver Pasha's Turkish army was advancing towards the Caucasus, ostensibly promising aid to their ethnic Azeri kin, but doubtless also hoping to press home their own territorial ambitions. However, they ended up squabbling with their supposed allies (the Germans) who the Georgians had invited in as the better of two evils. Georgia feared an Armenian-style massacre if the Turks arrived first.

Thus the Turks fought their way towards Azerbaijan through northern Iran, harried by a pathetically small force of British troops working secretly in the pay of the Shah of Persia.

The ethnic Azeris welcomed the arrival of the Turks wholeheartedly. Azerbaijan had declared its independence from the Trans-Caucasian Federation on 28 May 1918 and set up an independent Azeri Parliament in Gänjä (the building still stands). The Turks reached Gänjä on 20 June and many Azeri patriots joined an 'Army of Islam' to march on Baku. Meanwhile, in Baku, a bizarre coalition of mutually loathing forces put aside their differences to prepare the city's 'defence': Communists, Armenian Dashnak nationalists, pro-Tsarist Russian Cossacks under General Bichkarov and, arriving right at the last minute, the British 'Dunsterforce'.

The climax, as if written by a hammy movie mogul, came melodramatically slowly. As if waiting for the director's cue, the Turks delayed their final assault just long enough to allow numerous additional defenders to arrive in the nick of time. Nonetheless the city fell on 15 September. The 'brave' British defenders had requisitioned a steamer and quietly slipped out of port the night before. For three days much of the Armenian population was massacred in belated revenge for the March Days.

The Turks had over-reached themselves, however. Their supply lines were cut by Allenby and his British Palestine force and on 30 October they were forced to sign a humiliating armistice, handing back Batumi (Georgia) and Baku to Allied (but in practice British) peacekeeping troops.

Azeri independence

The Azerbaijan Democratic Republic (ADR) had a breathing space in which to prove itself to its people and to the world powers. Initially Westerners were very sceptical of Azeri self government and most were fundamentally anti-Turkic. However, General Thompson, the British commander in Baku was slowly won over to the educated and principled new Azeri leadership, of whom the best remembered is Mammad Rasulzade. At the 1919 Paris Peace Conference, US President Woodrow Wilson apparently remarked upon the 'very dignified and interesting gentlemen from Azerbaijan ... who talked the same language that I did in respect of ideals, conceptions of liberty and conceptions of right and justice'. However, the Muslim-socialist Musuvat government was slow to deal with land reform, allowing the initially discredited Bolsheviks to regroup as a champion of the rural poor.

Meanwhile, Lenin was starting to gain the upper hand in Russia. He had never forgotten the rest of the Russian empire – merely sacrificed it in the short term to install his revolutionary regime. Increasingly secure in Moscow, he turned his attention to stirring up trouble in the 'lost areas' starting with the sponsorship of a Länkäran-based Talysh Mugam Soviet Republic which survived three months, 25 April-28 July 1919. In August 1919 the Versailles agreement demanded British troops be withdrawn from Baku.

The Bolsheviks stepped up anti-Azeri propaganda, with false or exaggerated claims. By March 1920 visitors to Baku reported prices spiralling out of control as people prepared for a Russian invasion which finally arrived in Baku on 28 April, and Länkäran on 3 May. Battles raged in Gänjä and Zaqatala in June, but Turkey was in no position to help as it was itself on the verge of extinction following the carve up of the imploded Ottoman empire. Attaturk who would doubtless have lent a hand later, at the time needed all the support he could get to hold onto Turkey itself. By turning a blind eye to Moscow's invasion of the Caucasus he was able to secure the arms he desperately needed to reclaim Istanbul and Anatolia. Turkey thus acquiesed to the Soviet takeover in Azerbaijan and signed a friendship treaty with the new Baku regime in 1921.

In 1922 Azerbaijan was shuffled first into the TransCaucasian SSR (12 March) then, on 30 December, into a newly formed 'voluntary union' called the USSR.

Soviet era

One of the remarkable things about the early Soviet period is the persisting popularity of Azerbaijan's first long-term Communist leader, Nariman Narimanov, whose gigantic statue still towers above Baku, if increasingly obscured by apartment blocks. He used brutal force to snuff out anti-communist rebellions in Gänjä, Sabirabad and Zaqatala, but is remembered as a writer, doctor and leader of genuine principle. Despite being a committed Bolshevik he bravely (if unsuccessfully) stood up against Lenin's plans to amalgamate the Caucasian countries. And he managed to persuade Stalin at the last minute to stop a planned transfer of Karabagh to Armenia in the early 1920s. But, having proved too independent minded, Narimanov was assassinated by poisoning in 1925. Similarly Stalin killed off Kirov, the once vastly popular but now disgraced Caucasian communist pioneer. In both cases the deed was covered up by developing an overblown posthumous personality cult. As Stalin had found with Lenin, dead men make very safe heroes. Stalin's redrawing of Azerbaijan's borders set the scene for future conflict by giving away much of the country's western flank (Zangezaur) to Armenia and resulted in Nakhchivan's total severance from the rest of the republic. This was a deliberate ploy, aimed to ensure that nationalists in Azerbaijan proper remained disconnected from any possible help from Turkey.

The 1930s were particularly harsh as the atheist USSR instituted a severe crackdown on religion bringing a series of persecutions and demolitions. Collectivization resulted in famine as peasants killed their animals rather than hand them over to *kolkhoz* committees and whole villages that refused to co-operate were simply burnt! Between 1936 and 1938 Stalin's paranoia reached intense proportions. With the apparently enthusiastic co-operation of Mir Jafar Bağirov in Azerbaijan, he reacted by killing or exiling much of the nation's elite whether communist party officials, WWI heroes, old democrats or simply distant relatives of the old khans. A glance at the dozens of memorial plaques on many buildings on Baku's Istiqlaliyyat St gives an idea of just how many fine fellows happened to fall in front of passing cars between those years: by one estimate 120,000 from a population of 3 million! Of course the army was equally purged, leaving the USSR dreadfully ill-prepared for WWII. And sending Azerbaijan's long-term ethnic German population into exile in Kazakhstan (October 1941) didn't help a bit.

World War II

In a famous home-movie clip, Hitler is pictured at his birthday party being served a cake in the shape of the Caspian Sea. With very intentional symbolism he bites into the slice marked Baku and removes the confectionery oil derrick. Following Stalin's purges, the Russian military had lost most of its best commanders and was not at all prepared for Hitler to tear up the August 1939 non-aggression treaty and send the Panzers east. The Führer saw his chance.

Once it was clear that Hitler had set his sights on Azerbaijan's oilfields, Stalin summoned his commissioner of energy, Baibakov, with the following stark choice: 'If Hitler gets a single drop of oil you'll be shot. If you destroy the oil wells unnecessarily we'll be left without oil. In which case you'll be shot. Now go to the Caucasus and save the war.' As it happens, Baibakov survived to tell the story to the BBC. The Germans never reached Azerbaijan proper, thanks to Hitler's obsession with Stalingrad.

Passing so close to Stalingrad (now Volgagrad), Hitler thought it would be a shame not to drop by. He reckoned that taking the city that held Stalin's name would be a psychological victory way beyond the mere military value of the place. However, the defenders saw it the same way and fought to the last bullet. The Germans' little detour got bogged down for months in the smouldering ruins of the city. Meanwhile, having divided the troops, Hitler lacked the force to reach Azerbaijan so Baku went uncaptured.

In an ironic twist, captured German prisoners of war were later brought to Azerbaijan to work on the expansion of the railway system and to build several of the fine stone Stalinist buildings in Baku. Quite how many is uncertain: amateur historians claim almost every building one sees was so constructed. Some prisoners didn't get home to Germany till 1950.

Azerbaijan didn't fare too well after the war. Although its oil facilities survived, their geographical vulnerability led the Soviet Union to develop more secure sources in Siberia. Baku's production dropped from 70% to 2% of the national total between 1940 and 1970.

The republic's prestige was salvaged in great part by Heydar Aliyev who rose through the ranks of the KGB to become the first Turkic member of the Politburo, the council ruling the USSR.

Karabagh conflict and independence

In 1991 the USSR collapsed and Azerbaijan regained her independence. Incredibly important as this may have been, the whole 1988-93 era is completely overshadowed by the Nagorno Karabagh dispute and war with Armenia. To get a real grasp of the issues and the underlying web of political intrigues you really need to read a small library of books, though a great start are the titles listed in the reading section on pp348-51. Bear in mind that no book is free from conscious or subconscious bias. With the conflict still unresolved there is no such thing as a 'balanced view'.

The early history of Nagorno Karabagh (Mountain/Upper Karabakh) is too complex and controversial to examine in detail here. In the 18th century the area was predominantly Azeri and site of the Azeri 'cultural capital' at Shusha. However, during the Tsarist Russian era it became increasingly populated with Christian Armenians fleeing Turkish control. By the 1980s the Armenian population formed a majority though substantial numbers of Azeris and some Kurds remained. It still legally remained (and remains) part of Azerbaijan. In February 1988, Armenians started demanding a transfer of Nagorno Karabagh from Azerbaijani to Armenian control. This was seen in Baku as a deliberately provocative demand. One convincing theory suggests that Gorbachev had intended to stir up trouble in Karabagh as a smoke screen for humiliating troop withdrawals from Afghanistan. Perestroika or not, how else would an issue so contentious have received major press attention in the notoriously secretive USSR? Tragically things spiralled out of anyone's control. Frightened by the apparent arming of Armenian nationalists (again, unlikely without tacit Russian support), long-term ethnic Azeri residents of Armenia fled to Azerbaijan. Their plight resulted in tit for tat attacks on Armenians in Azerbaijan, possibly by refugees, possibly by agents provocateurs. However, even in the worst violence in Sumgayit, stories abound of Azeri and Armenian friends sheltering one another from the violence. Nonetheless, as ethnic Armenians started fleeing to Armenia the conflict steadily ratcheted itself up to a higher pitch, exacerbated by propaganda in which the Armenians had an unquestionably stronger hand thanks to a well-organized Armenian diaspora in Western countries and better access to and relations with the Soviet leadership.

The last straw for Azerbaijan's faith in the USSR came on 20 January 1990 when Gorbachev sent the Red Army into Baku. This was ostensibly to restore order following severe disturbances in which several Armenians had died. But the killings had been in Sumgayit, not Baku. And they had been over a week before. On arrival the Red Army massacred (by the lowest estimate) 130 unarmed civilians, almost certainly more. Horrified citizens blockaded the port to prevent the corpses being taken out and dumped at sea.

But worse was still to come. Over the following three years, Armenian forces progressively advanced into and beyond Nagorno Karabagh. Before each advance there would be a propaganda barrage about how the poor population in this or that village was being subjected to 'Azeri terror'. Then lo and behold, the Armenian troops would march in a few days later to the 'rescue'. Azeri citizens were infamously massacred at Hojali. The Lachin Corridor separating Nagorno Karabagh from Armenia was also invaded and the population of Kelbajar, boxed in on three sides, was forced to flee across frozen mountain passes to the north. To add insult to injury, once Armenians had occupied a huge swath of Azerbaijan, the USA decided to impose sanctions against Azerbaijan for blockading the Baku–Yerevan railway line. That the Armenians had previously blockaded the railway line to Nakhchivan went apparently unnoticed.

Deal of the century

In the meantime, Azerbaijan had been through two changes of government. The original communist 'left over' president,

Mutalibov, was forced out and replaced by an elected president, Abulfaz Elchibey, who fled a year later in the face of a military rebellion. His place was filled by the recently drafted parliamentary speaker, none other than Heydar Aliyev the ex-Politburo member who was later confirmed in the presidential role by an overwhelming referendum followed later by an election. Aliyev turned the tide, preventing further Armenian advances, retaking Horadiz and organizing a lasting ceasefire. The first really good news in a while was the so-called 'Deal of the Century' signed in September 1994, promising a $7.4 billion oil investment programme. Baku began to swarm with expats and there was a minor building boom. When oil prices briefly plummeted to around $12/barrel in 1998-9 things suddenly looked pretty bleak. Oil companies merged frenetically and the whole Caspian oil project was questioned. But a year later optimism had soberly rebounded with the price of crude.

The 21st century

After years of prevarication and politico-economic wrangling, work finally began on the multi-billion dollar Baku–Tbilisi–Ceyhan (BTC) Azerbaijan–Turkey oil pipeline in 2003 resulting in another major investment spree. The year 2003 also marked the end of an era, with the death of long-term president Heydar Aliyev. Having passed the baton of presidency to his son Ilham through summer elections at best described as opaque, his death was announced on December 12th. Though criticized abroad, Heydar had been a dominating figure, a strong, wily diplomat who the vast majority of Azeris respected as the father of the nation. He's still widely beloved though since his death the cultivation of a Heydar personality cult has reached rather absurd proportions with virtually every town now sporting a Heydar Aliyev statue, park and museum.

Rising global oil prices arrived at a great time for Azerbaijan coinciding with the first major feeds from new Caspian fields and the completion of the BTC pipeline to Turkey. A vast cycle of infra-structure projects is now in full swing with buildings everywhere getting major facelifts, airports and major roads being upgraded and a new rail-project planned to link Azerbaijan to Turkey via Georgia. A concerted move to distance Azerbaijan from its Soviet past has seen all Cyrillic signage removed and foreign broadcasting (on terrestrial radio and TV) has been stopped. Some names of towns and regions have been changed to more historically resonant ones, causing a degree of confusion for cartographers and travellers. However, while Baku enjoys an especially astonishing period of growth, the occupation of Nagorno Karabagh continues to weigh prominently on people's minds. The UNHCR estimates over 575,000 Azeris are still IDPs (internally displaced persons) from the conflict while the government put the figure at 686,586 in March 2007. Sporadic fighting continues to break out from time to time along the front line but any sabre rattling towards an escalation is less likely following the sobering shock of the Russia-Georgia war in summer 2008.

ECONOMICS

Astonishingly in the last decade Azerbaijan's GDP has risen around 1000% with particularly spectacular growth since 2004. However, some 95% of the economy is oil and gas based. While Sofaz (🖥 www.oilfund.az/en) helps ensure that the windfall profits are used for long-term national regeneration, the oil industry itself employs only a tiny fraction of the workforce. The 2008-9 slump in oil prices threatens to bust the economic bubble but for now vast infrastructure projects and the incredible Baku building boom have been creating large numbers of short-term jobs. These have been tempting home some of the labourers who had spent many years working abroad (mostly in Russia and Turkey) and whose remittances kept afloat many families earlier in the decade. However, it will be a tricky job balancing the oil-boom city wealth with rural development in villages where around 40% of the population are still employed in mostly small-scale farming (10% more than in Soviet days).

RELIGION

Iran and Azerbaijan are both dominantly **Shi'ite Muslim** countries but the two states could not be more different. As the first Muslim country to be subjected to full European colonialism (1813), Azerbaijan has a long history of making liberal interpretations of Islam. During the atheistic Soviet era, Islam was as much a badge of national identity as a religion. Following independence Azerbaijan did experience a few months of stricter Islam during which women became a little nervous to walk alone without scarves. This lasted barely a year and today some Baku beauties unselfconsciously expose bare midriffs and wear miniskirts that would turn heads in Rio de Janeiro. Today's Azerbaijan is proud of its cross-religious tolerance and local Islam is laissez-faire: as one local put it 'The Koran told us not to drink wine. So let's drink vodka'.

Another feature of Azeri Islam are the strong undercurrents of **animism** reflected in numerous superstitions (pp50-1), holy places (*pir*s) and ceremonies with pre-Islamic and Zoroastrian influences.

Religious history

Long part of the Persian world, it's not surprising that Azerbaijan would have picked up elements of the first great monotheistic religion, **Zoroastrianism**. And the miraculous gas-fires of the Absheron must have lent credence to the ancient Persian reverence for fire, a reverence later incorporated into Zoroastrianism despite being somewhat contrary to the original ideas of that religion's prophet Zarathustra.

Christianity first arrived in Azerbaijan within a century of Christ's death. The Araz Valley (Nakhchivan) was a major conduit for ideas and Jesus's disciple, St Bartholemew (aka Nathaniel), is said to have founded a church near Culfa around AD62. He was later captured and crucified in Baku by the King of Albania's brother Astiagus. Chronicles record that around the same time St Elisius founded a church at 'Gis', a place that many identify as Kish (p227). By the 4th century, like Georgia and Armenia, Albania (as the region was then

known) had been heavily Christianized. Unlike its neighbours, however, Albania adopted a Nestorian-Assyrian-style faith with a spiritual centre at Nic (p218) monastic settlements throughout the northwest (there are 6th-century church remnants at Bideyiz, Orta Zeyzit, Läkit etc).

Arab attacks in the 8th century began the conversion of the plains-folk to **Islam**. Contrary to popular Western stereotype, the Arabs didn't force Albanians to become Muslims, though a high tax on 'infidels' encouraged voluntary conversion. And a steady influx of Muslim-Turkic settlers tended to push the Christian populations into the hills. Nonetheless, with certain changes, the Albanian church survived up until 1836 when Russian authorities forced the minimal remnants of the creed to accept Armenian and Georgian priests.

Azerbaijan was a crucible in the complex development of Persian Islam. The rebellions led by Babek (p297) were a crucial element in 'Persianizing' local Islam and today Babek's image is still commonly seen alongside Imam Ali in Azerbaijani mosques. From 1501, ethnic Azeris largely followed the Shi'ite form of Islam following the example of Shah Ismail, the Azeri-Persian emperor, though Lezghians and other Dagestani-Muslim groups tended to retain a Sunni creed (as they do today).

A few mountain tribes had meanwhile decided that they'd rather not be either Christian nor Muslim and converted to Judaism! These Tat 'mountain Jews' were respected by Muslim *khans* who took a conscious policy of religious tolerance and even today Azerbaijan has one all-Jewish village (at Krasnaya Sloboda, p175, near Quba).

Back on the plains, Gänjä, Nakhchivan and certain Absheron towns became leading Islamic centres and 18th-century pilgrims travelled great distances to the Muslim shrines in Bärdä, Nardaran and Bibi Heybat.

During the Russian era there was a colonial influx of Russian Orthodox Christians as well as strict Protestant sects such as the Molokans (who don't believe in building churches or using crosses). Armenian Christians also arrived from the Ottoman Empire, notably into Karabagh.

They simply felt safer under the Christian rule of Russia than in an Islamic empire showing increasing signs of religious intolerance. Armenians co-opted some of the by-then disused old Albanian churches while building many of their own.

Stalin's anti-religious crusade of the 1930s was harsh on all religions. Azerbaijan's most sacred Islamic shrine at Bibi Heybat was demolished for road widening and the splendid Alexander Nevsky Cathedral was replaced by a dumpy concrete school. Throughout the country fine mosques disappeared, most notably in Islamic strongholds such as the Absheron peninsula, though fortunately a few were preserved as cultural exhibits, 'museums of atheism' or occasionally as state-licensed places of worship. Stalin was also hard on the small Jewish communities which were later depleted by emigration so that only 17,300 Jews remained by 1993.

Since independence, new mosques have been built in many towns and old ones de-mothballed including the 100-year-old grand mosque at Shamakha, once claimed to be one of the world's three biggest. In 1998 Bibi Heybat shrine became the first Stalin-demolished mosque in the former Soviet Union to be fully rebuilt. The dramatic new religious constructions at Shuvälän (p154) and Nardaran (p151) reflect a very curious Azeri spiritual revival.

Meanwhile numerous deserted church ruins lie across the country. Many are historic Albanian structures that have been abandoned for over a century. Others were deliberately desecrated as an outpouring of frustrated anger by ethnic Azeri refugees driven out of Armenia or Armenian-occupied Azerbaijan during the 1988-93 conflict. Orthodox and German churches were not attacked, though lacking congregations many have decayed or were converted into cafés and sports halls. However, several have since been renovated and remain active. Azerbaijan has such a miniscule congregation of Catholics that some wondered whether Pope John Paul had got on the wrong plane when he arrived in Baku in May 2002. But as well as blessing the first stone of a new Catholic church on land donated by the Government (map p77, ΨH13), he delivered a powerful message, that 'people of Azerbaijan should be proud of the climate of tolerance in their country'. And indeed they are.

CULTURE AND ATTITUDES
Birth
Traditionally the umbilical cord is cut with a *gabir kendere* which is then thrown into the air. The place it lands is read as a sign of the baby's future.

Marriage
● Weddings are inappropriate during Ramadan (the Islamic fasting month, dates p52) and Moharram (the Shi'ite month of mourning for Imam Hussein) so just before and after those months there are 'rushes'.

● Weddings are big business: although no gifts are given, wedding guests are expected to present an envelope of cash on arrival at the bash. The appropriate sum varies according to the couple's social status: the type of wedding hall (shadliq sarayi) they have hired gives a fair indication. In Baku AZN50 is a likely minimum: a very signif-

---

❏ **Lending a hand**
One of the most typical and ubiquitous Shi'ite Islamic symbols in Azerbaijan is the 'hand of Fatima' (see photo C11, left) considered both lucky and representative of faith/loyalty – Fatima, daughter of the prophet Mohammad, was the wife of Imam Ali. Some local mollahs alternatively call this the 'hand of Allah', claiming a finger each for Mohammad, Fatima, Imam Ali, and Ali's brothers/successors, Hussein and Hassan. In a third variant it's the 'hand of Abbas'. Abbas was Imam Hussein's heroically faithful standard bearer at the battle of Kerbala whose doomed, swordless mission to collect water for Hussein's camp resulted in both of his arms being fatally severed.

icant expenditure especially for poorer Azeris who, with large, extended families, must often attend numerous such bankrupting events each year.

• Traditionally brides wore a red dress to symbolize long life together. This has been replaced by a fashion for Western-style white gowns, though the tradition is often maintained by a red sash. A red ribbon is also worn in the bride's hair until symbolically removed three days later in part of a ceremony known as *duvag gampa*.

• A beheaded sheep on the path to the wedding is a sign of good luck, not a threat from a jilted former boyfriend.

• The wedding entourage goes on a noisy tour of the town/village, often in overloaded cars, supposedly 'chasing good fortune'.

• On reaching the groom's home the bride is led three times around the stove and crushes a plate with her heel. This is not explicitly meant to show that she is angry about spending the rest of her life tied to the kitchen.

• Ideally the groom (or his family) is expected to provide the couple with a home, then the bride's family should pay for furniture to fill it.

Sex

Summer strolls on Fountains Square, Baku, can trigger a hormonal overload for the less-controlled male observer. Watching the *passeggiata* of Baku's tanned beauties, all mini-skirts and gaping midriffs, one expat rolled in his tongue long enough to describe this as 'the best sight in Azerbaijan'.

However, this gives a somewhat misleading view of Azerbaijan's women. Outside central Baku and one or two of the rich datcha towns (Märdäkän, Kirovka etc where the same people go for weekends), women are much more influenced by Islamic mores. Even the raunchily dressed Baku beauties are usually much less liberated than they may appear, typically living with the extended family and expected home before dark. Curiously, while wearing short mini skirts and meretricious make-up is not considered a sign of loose living for Baku women, smoking in public generally is. Good girls generally won't go to a pub or

nightclub alone so the ladies you meet in such places (especially downstairs dive bars) are most likely to be seeking paid companionship. Given the difficulties of maintaining licit sexual relationships in a land still swayed by predominantly 'marry-first' religious strictures, many frustrated men seem to accept that the 'use' of a prostitute is a necessary evil.

The prostitute predominance in many nightclubs means that any single male tourist that thinks he's 'struck lucky' is probably in for an expensive shock. Nonetheless, there is a cadre of students and educated 'good girls' who are in the chase for Western husbands so if you're serious, there is always the chance of falling in reciprocated love.

Homosexuality

Despite having been officially decriminalized in September 2000, homosexuality remains deep in the closet. Being openly gay even in Baku has its dangers, but in private there is nonetheless a well-organized local community which reportedly organizes private parties at which photography is banned for discretion and where free AIDS tests are sometimes available. Meanwhile **Gender and Development** (🖳 www.lgbt.az) raises awareness over sex education, AIDS prevention and gender issues and also offers legal and psychological support. They have forums in several languages (including English and German) and their website has a (largely empty) 'events' calendar.

There are no specifically gay hangouts but in certain Baku bars and discos 'doctors' cruise in search of 'patients' using pseudo-medical euphemisms to prevent disclosure. Before its 2007 demolition, the Capitol Club had a reputation for mixed clientele and transvestites have been spotted at the Bermuda Bar (p86, ◑R2). Places currently popular with the 'lbgt' crowd include Domino and Lea.

Note that 'blue man' is a perjorative term for a male homosexual so don't wear your favourite old Blues Brothers T shirt if you're afraid of being misconstrued!

Death

● When a family member dies, tents are erected in the yard or street outside the family home for three to seven days. Here friends, neighbours or even passers-by can come and pay respects. Female family members serve all comers with *ehsan* (food and tea) having first washed their hands with water from a ceremonial *kilab* jug (picture p208). Tent-blocked roads can cause serious traffic problems.

● Muslim corpses are buried, where possible, on the day they died and with their heads facing Mecca.

● For mourning use an even number of flowers.

● Only men may visit the burial site during the interment, women relatives mourn outside the home of the deceased.

● Women's graves are deeper than men's.

● On the third, seventh and fortieth day after somebody dies and at each anniversary relatives should give gifts (usually meat) to friends and neighbours on behalf of the deceased.

● Men in mourning should not shave for 40 days after the death of a loved one.

● By Muslim tradition, halva should be prepared and served each Thursday for an undefined mourning period after the death of a loved one, and on the anniversary of his/her death.

● To show respect at a funeral (and indeed any time) after Islamic prayers, pass the palms of both hands vertically downwards across one's face then bring them together

(the *salavat*) – you'll know when – everyone else will be doing the same.

● A car on a gravestone or memorial probably means that the deceased died in a motor accident.

Presents

● Taking a gift is good manners when visiting any home. Flowers are appreciated but always bring an odd number (see Death column opposite).

● If you give a wrapped present the recipient is unlikely to unwrap it in front of you – this is a great way of avoiding embarrassment if it turns out to be something they loathe. However, the fact that you never know whether it was appreciated or not can be disconcerting to the Western giver.

● A common practice is to refuse gifts twice before accepting them. This doesn't necessarily mean that the recipient doesn't want what you offer. The same two-refusal rule often applies to drinks at the pub, invitations etc.

Superstitions

● Spitting three times (or at least pretending to do so) is the local equivalent of touching wood/knocking on wood.

● A sprig of camel thorn (eg placed behind the rear view mirror of a car) is supposed to ward off jealousy.

● Stopping to make a *nazir* (donation) at a roadside shrine (*pir*) ensures a safe journey. Several other pirs bring help with personal problems and for certain medical condi-

---

❑ **Business tips**
● Print business cards double-sided with both Azeri and English transliterations. The Azeri version will even transliterate your name (eg Andrew > Andrü, Jean > Cin etc)!
● Be careful to check any map in your promotional material with a sensitivity to Karabagh etc.
● Positive words or even a mention of Armenia in a company report may cause trouble.
● Don't eat while a speech is being delivered and beware of the importance of protocol – a strict hierarchy in speaking order.
● Toasting is important, though less so than in Georgia. Some schools of thought consider it better not to drink at all (giving a medical excuse) than to have two or three vodkas and then decline to finish the bottle.
● Whilst it is a Muslim country, there is no problem for women to conduct business, though some hosts might seem over-protective.

tions (particularly mental health and fertility). Many people would visit a suitable pir before calling a doctor.

● Cleaning a table with a paper napkin is liable to cause discontent, so use a cloth.

● If you spill salt you should put a little sugar on top, or dribble water on it rather than simply wiping it up.

● If you accidentally step on a friend's foot they should briefly take your hand. Otherwise the superstition says you'll be in for a quarrel later.

● *Jadu* witchcraft and the evil eye can be deflected by bundles of *uzarlik* (special dried flower stems that you see hanging in many windows) or increasingly with the Turkish *Nazir Boncuk*, a blue glass 'eye' with white, blue and black pupil. Mini *gozmuncuğu* beads are also used.

● Traditionally camels were considered to be very wise and receptive to good and bad vibes. They might be brought to inspect

plots of land on which a house was to be built. Ethnic Russians saw cats as similarly receptive and traditionally chose to place their beds where puss liked to lie down.

FESTIVALS AND HOLIDAYS

NOTE The symbol * means it's an official national holiday, ☭ shows an event formerly celebrated in the Communist era – included for reference. C denotes the predicted date of a Muslim festival that follows the lunar calendar for 2009-2013 ie AH1431-1436.

● **1, 2 Jan*** New Year (*Yeni Il*) Previously Soviet Christmas with Father Frost instead of Santa Claus

● **20 January*** 'Martyrs' Day' (Matäm Günü) Anniversary of the Red Army's massacre of Baku civilians in 1990, now also commemorating victims of the Karabagh war. Bakuvians in their thousands take flowers to the Shähidlär

---

❏ Calendars

Unlike neighbouring Iran, Azerbaijan uses the Western (Gregorian) calendar. However, like Russia it used the **Julian calendar** until WWI. Other European countries changed on 15 October 1582, with Britain staying on the Julian system till 1752. This creates a slight confusion over precise historical dates according to who was counting. European- and Russian-quoted dates had been very gradually diverging and were 12 days apart by 1918. To catch up, 18 January 1918 was followed by 1 February in Azerbaijan and a fair few Azeris missed a birthday.

To add further complications Islamic holidays are calculated according to the **Muslim calendar** and many older mosques and monuments are inscribed in Arabic with Muslim dates. The Islamic year has 12 lunar months giving a total of 354 or 355 days. That's about 11 days short of a solar year. So every 32-33 years the Islamic 'AH' year gets one year closer to the Western 'AD' year and Muslim months occur in different seasons each year getting progressively earlier. AH1 (*al hijrah*) officially marks the year of the prophet Mohammad's flight from Mecca to Medina though in fact the calendar starts from 16 July AD622 (in the Julian calendar, July 19th Gregorian) while the historical event was 20 September. Note that Islamic days start at sunset, not at midnight and that the exact date of Eid al Fitr, the end of the Ramadan fast, can only be announced following an official sighting of the new moon – a virtual impossibility which can result in the day varying slightly from 'predictions' according to one's exact location. AH1431 should start at sunset on 17 Dec 2009, AH1432 on 6 Dec 2010, AH1433 on 25 Nov 2011 and AH1434 on 14 Nov 2012. The first month of the Islamic year is Muharram, a month of mourning amongst Shi'ites for the death of Imam Hussein at Karbala.

Website 🖳 www.islamicfinder.org/dateConversion.php converts Hijri (Islamic) dates to Gregorian (Western) ones while 🖳 www.calendarhome.com/converter interconverts a whole range of calendars.

Xiyabanı graveyard (Martyr's Alley, p102).

● **2 February (approx)** *Kichik Chil* – the run-up to Novruz – begins with gifts of melons (to women as a sign of fertility). The number of pips inside are read superstitiously like tea leaves. Ten days later is *Khydyr Nabi*, feast of the spirit of benevolence.

● **Islamic New Year** ☾ 17 Dec 2009, 6 Dec 2010, 25 Nov 2011, 14 Nov 2012, 4 Nov 2013.

● **Ashura** ☾ 16 Dec 2010, 5 Dec 2011, 24 Nov 2012, 13 Nov 2013 In Iran Shi'ites flagellate themselves to commemorate the death of Imam Hussein at the battle of Kerbala (AD680). In Azerbaijan only a few of the most pious Absheron towns such as Mäshtağa take this seriously.

● **26 February*** Anniversary of the 1992 Hojali massacre

● **8 March** International Women's Day (*Qadınlar günü*) It's not a holiday but woe betide any man who forgets to buy presents and/or flowers for female friends and colleagues on this day.

● **20-24 March*** Novruz Bayramı – Azerbaijan's biggest festival (see below).

● **Birthday of the Prophet** ☾ 3 Mar 2010, 20 Feb 2011, 9 Feb 2012, 29 Jan 2013

● **28 April** ☾ The day in 1920 when Azerbaijan's independence was crushed by the entry of Soviet troops into Baku.

● **1 May** ☾ Labour Day

● **9 May*** Victory Day (*Qäläbä Günü*) of the USSR over Germany in 1945

● **10 May*** Holiday of Flowers Anniversary of Heydar Aliyev's birth celebrated with colourful floral decorations in many parks.

● **28 May*** Republic Day Declaration of the first independent Azerbaijani state in 1918 following the overthrow of the brief first Bolshevik regime.

● **1 June** ☾ USSR Children's Day

● **15 June*** National Salvation Day (*Milli Qurtulush Günü*) Celebrates former president Heydar Aliyev's return to power at the invitation of the parliament in 1993.

● **26 June*** Army day (*Ordu Günü*) Commemorating the founding of the Azeri army in 1918; previously observed 9 October.

● **Ramazan (Ramadan)** The month of day-time fasting has little effect on day-to-

day life in Azerbaijan. One 'pious' Muslim told me he was giving up alcohol for the month! **Ramazan Bayramı (Eid al Fitr)**, the two days after Ramazan, are national holidays*. Approximate Ramazan dates: 12 Aug-10 Sep 2010, 1-30 Aug 2011, 20 Jul-19 Aug 2012, 9 Jul-8 Aug 2013.

● **18 September** Music day (*Musiqi Günü*) Start of the theatre season; commemorates the birthday of composer Üzeyir Hacibäyov.

● **5 October** Teachers' Day Children bring their teachers hideous plastic flowers as a sign of appreciation.

● **18 October*** Freedom Day (*Istiqlaliyyat Günü*) commemorating independence from the USSR in 1991.

● **26 Oct 2012, 6 Nov 2011*** Qurban Bayramı (Eid al-Adha) Muslim festival involving sheep sacrifices to remember the Koranic/Biblical test of faith in which Isaac gets a last-minute divine reprieve from daddy-Abraham's desire to impress God.

● **12 November*** Constitution Day (*Konstitusiya günü*) Anniversary of voter ratification of the fourth constitution in 1995.

● **16 November 2010*** Qurban Bayramı (see above)

● **17 November*** National Revival Day (*Milli Dirchalish Günü*) commemorating the 1988 anti-Soviet uprising fighting Moscow's policy on Nagorno Karabagh.

● **12 December** Anniversary of Heydar Aliyev's death. Laying a wreath shows how much you miss him.

● **25 December*** Christmas Day

● **31 December*** Solidarity Day Celebrates the tearing down of border fences with Iran in 1989 and is intended to focus attention on the bonds with Azerbaijanis in that country and around the world.

Novruz Bayramı Novruz, Azerbaijan's main festival, is an ancient 'new year' festival celebrated at the spring equinox. Officially it starts after sunset on 20th March but the days before this are also important.

Novruz translates from the Persian meaning 'new day', though in Iran the Ayatollahs have tried to play down the festival's significance which long pre-dates Islam. Indeed it was already celebrated before Zoroastrianism which, like Islam, adopted the festival adding elements of its own.

Each Tuesday night before Novruz has a special significance initially with *Yalanchi* and *Khabarchy*, 'the herald days of spring', then celebrating in turn the four elements (earth, water, air and fire). On the evening of the final Tuesday (*Chershänbä*), local kids jump to and fro across street bonfires; a tradition which anthropologists link to an ancient Zoroastrian rite.

Two weeks before Novruz families (literally) spring clean their houses and start to grow wheat (*bugda*) and barley (*arpa*) seeds on special plates called *sämäni*. These should have grown into a healthy mass of vividly green grass by the time of the festival, a potent symbol of rebirth.

The celebration itself lasts three days. There are processions, shows, and a play fight between a goat and the dressed-up figure of winter (the *kossa*) who is symbolically killed. Special rice dishes are cooked with milk and raisins, these are best eaten while standing in the Caspian!

● Putting 10 apple seeds under a girl's pillow at Novruz means she'll dream of her future husband.

● Rain can be invoked at Novruz by throwing into a river a stone that was gathered on a holy mountain.

● Unlike NoRuz in Iran, Azeris don't generally lay out '*seven s*' tables (displaying seven items spelt with an 's' in Farsi).

LANGUAGE

In Baku many younger people speak surprisingly good English. In the rest of the country it can prove very difficult indeed to get by without at least rudimentary Azeri or Russian.

The Azeri language is closely related to older Ottoman Turkish and is reasonably intelligible to speakers of modern Turkish. However, many of the most fundamental words (eg bread) are utterly different, there's a certain Persian influence and technical terms tend to be borrowed from Russian. Some nuances make Azeri sound comical to Turkish speakers and vice versa.

Travelling for the first time on an Azeri plane, Turks are liable to get alarmed. When the pilot says in Azeri that the plane is about to land (*düşmek*), the same phrase in Turkish means it's about to crash!

Russian, the colonial language, was widely spoken in the Soviet era so most educated people over 40 years old are likely to speak it (some are a little rusty but get nostalgic once they start speaking it). In Baku, Russian remains relatively common as a day-to-day means of communication and some middle-class Baku parents still prefer to have their children educated in Russian medium schools since these are considered to have higher standards. Contrastingly the majority of rural youths, particularly in Nakhchivan, have never learnt a word of Russian and will be totally bemused if you try to speak it.

Azerbaijan has several local regional languages. In the far south Talysh (see p279) is the mother tongue, while around Qusar and dotted about the northern regions there's a fair proportion of Lezghian speakers (p188). Lezghian along with Udi (p219), Avar (p238), and Tssakhur (see Mamrux, p233) may be related to ancient Caucasian Albanian which was the region's *lingua franca* during the 5th century. Albanian started to fall out of use in the 8th century, initially overwhelmed by Arabic. Since the 15th century that language has been lost entirely, leaving only a dead alphabet. The approximate pronunciations of the Caucasian Albanian letters have since been reconstructed 'Rosetta Stone' style, from a linguistic puzzle of bilingual inscriptions and of biblical parchments found on Mt Sinai. Some remarkable villages have maintained their own distinct languages (Xınalıqi p182, Qriz p186, Buduq, p179) while in Lahıc people speak a special Azero-Persian dialect (p206).

See ▢ www.minorities.aznet.org for a little more on minority language groups.

Writing Azerbaijani

Azerbaijani as a written language has been through tremendous convulsions with three alphabet changes in the 20th century:

Arabic to Latin in 1929 (followed up with ruthless mass book burning), to modified Cyrillic in 1939, then back to Latin on Christmas Day 1991. Azeri Cyrillic had several non-standard letters absent from Russian but since 2003 Cyrillic script has virtually disappeared from all signage. The present alphabet is a specially modified Turkish Latin in which a typical McDonald's order might be Biq Mak, Dabl Çizburger and Şeyk. That's still pronounced Big Mac, Double Cheeseburger and Shake! Only the writing system has changed. The main differences from English pronunciations are:

● **The three 'Gs'** To write a hard 'G' (as in Big) use the letter Q. The Azeri 'G' is softer, somewhere between 'Gy' and 'J' depending on regional accents. In Turkish 'Ğ' (often transliterated 'gh') extends the vowel before and is effectively silent, but in Azerbaijani it's quietly gargled.

● **C, S and X**: 'C' is pronounced like an English 'J', but 'Ç' is 'Ch'. Similarly 'S' = S but Ş = Sh. 'X' is pronounced as a throaty Russian 'Kh', like 'ch' in a Scottish lo*ch*.

● **Vowels** As in Turkish, Azeri vowels are divided into hard and soft. Both languages maintain a phonetic balance which ensures that word endings resonate with the vowel before: hard with hard, soft with soft etc. If the vowel group is 'mixed' (ie doesn't harmonize) the word is probably of foreign (typically Persian) origin.

Hard vowels are 'a', 'o', 'u' and undotted 'ı'. Soft vowels are 'ə', 'ö', 'ü', 'i'. The undotted ı is 'grunted' like a short 'uh', while 'i' sounds like 'ee' in meet. The ə (ä) sounds like the short 'a', in b*a*t pronounced with a South African accent, while 'a' is longer, more like 'a' in c*a*r (British accent). To the untrained ear this important difference can be pretty hard to hear. In 1991 the 'ə' was briefly replaced by ä in the official alphabet. In 1992 it changed back again. The 'ä' was more logical linguistically, would have been easier for international computers and is mostly used in this book for clarity of reading. The sound 'ey' is like the 'ay' in bay, while 'ay' is more like the 'y' in by.

Learning Azeri

Many locals offer private lessons in Russian or Azeri for around AZN8-10/hr. Check the *Baku Sun* or *Azeri Times*.

Elementary Azerbaijani by Kurtulush Oztopchu, published in 2000 and available through 🖳 www.azer.com (US$35) is a 400-page course book for English speakers to learn Azerbaijani, though some of the exercises are in the now defunct Cyrillic alphabet. A US$30 set of CDs to accompany the book helps with pronunciation.

❏ Names and spellings

At the request of readers my spellings of place names diverges somewhat from standard Azeri-Latin to make the text more easily pronounceable to short-term visitors. Notably I have used 'ä' in many cases rather than the daunting 'shwa' (ə) and have substituted sh and ch for ş and ç which are all too easy to confuse with s and c especially on maps where those all-important cedillas don't show up well. Thus Şəki is rendered Shäki. Where there is a commonly used English version of a name (eg Baku for Bakı, Nakhchivan for Naxçivan and Azerbaijan for Azärbaycan) I have used the English form.

Sometimes you'll find alternative spellings that have come from being transliterated from the Russian rather than the Azeri form. A tell-tale sign is a heavy 'g' replacing an 'h', or a 'ch' replacing a 'j' thus rendering Lahıc as Lagich (h and j are absent in Russian). Then there's the constant tinkering with names for historical or political purposes. The Milli Majlis (parliament) has a special Toponymy Commission which seems unable to resist changing names. In 2008 it officially renamed Xanlar region as Göygöl and Ali Bayramlı as Şirvan.

ENTERTAINMENT AND THE ARTS

Azerbaijan is fiercely proud of its musical, literary and artistic achievements. Baku has a vibrant arts scene, a great variety of theatre and live music and dozens of galleries. However, especially in the provinces, entertainment for impoverished locals typically involves hanging out with friends, drinking tea and maybe shooting a few rounds of billiards. Even these activities are usually restricted to men – 'respectable' women are expected home by early evening. In Baku, like modern cities anywhere, this conservatism has broken down somewhat, though by no means all the women you see in the Baku bars and clubs are 'respectable'.

Literature

Azerbaijan traces its rich literary heritage back to the classic pan-Turkic epic *Dädä Qorqud* (Dede Korkut) though before **Füzuli** (16th century) most early poets wrote in Persian. *Khamza*, by the Azeri Shakespeare, **Nizami Gänjävi** (1141-1209) gives you five classic tales for the price of one. Popularly rendered as operas and ballets, these include *The Seven Beauties*, *Iskander Nameh* (loosely based on the adventures of Alexander the Great), and *Leylı and Majnun*. The latter is an ancient tale of forbidden love, from which, it's claimed, Eric Clapton found the 'Layla' of his Derek and the Dominoes song.

A visit to the statue-fronted Literature Museum in Baku introduces you to the succession of poets and playwrights who have shaped the culture and given their names to half the city's streets (see the Who's who section pp362-71).

Available to read at the Axundov Library, a Soviet-era compendium of *Azerbaijanian Poetry* offers considerable excerpts from dozens of classic and modern writers in stolid English. Old English translations of **Nasimi**'s *Gazels* and *Rubaiyats* have recently appeared on Baku street bookstalls and seem to capture his romantic, pantheistic mysticism rather well. Also available is a colourful trilingual picturebook of miniatures illustrating Nizami's *Khamsa* and a collection of his aphorisms.

A classic must-read is the disarmingly poignant *Ali and Nino* by mysterious author **Kurban Said**. According to who you believe this may have been the pen name of Essad Bey aka Lev Nussimbaum or of Elfriede Ehrenels the Austrian baroness who copyrighted it. Perhaps it was all along the plagiarized work of Yusif Vezirov. It doesn't really matter. The book remains a stunning collection of cultural observations wrapped up in a low-key love story between a Georgian girl and an Azeri boy, painting a vivid picture of Caucasian life to the backdrop of World War I: a must. Essad Bey's *Oil and Blood in the Orient* is arguably even better and if you're intrigued by the author's story and don't mind long digressions into the history of the Jews in Europe, you could read Tom Reiss's *The Orientalist*.

Music

For more on Azeri music see 💻 http://azworld.org/music.

Muğam Azerbaijan's traditional music, is the oldest form of 'rap' – part poem, part song with seven possible scales each offering a different mood. To the uninitiated, all tend to sound rather similar – wailing chants accompanied by plinking strums at the Sass or Tar and possibly a drum or clarinet to add body. But without speaking the language, it's impossible to appreciate the often inventive, witty and sarcastic lyrics. In 2003 UNESCO declared Azerbaijani Muğam to be a masterpiece of intangible world heritage.

The quintessential muğam performer is a wandering *ashug* (aşıq) minstrel topped with a *papax* hat. You may see such fellows strolling the rural lanes heading for a village wedding or popping up from nowhere at a popular country restaurant. They will expect reasonable payment from the tables they serenade and should be able to sing any subject you propose; the beauty of Shusha is a common favourite. The greatest ashugs (*khanendes*) come from western Azerbaijan and many are memorialized in statues and remembered as poets. In 1977, muğam went universal: a 140-second snippet was amongst the 27 tracks on Voyager

AZERBAIJAN – OVERVIEW

❏ Traditional musical instruments

▲ **Arum** A copper/tin standing drum; ▲ **Balaban** A reed instrument, visually similar to a descant recorder. Balaban duets can achieve a sound like bagpipes, one of the instruments creating the drone through the player's cyclical breathing; ✣ **Changi** Onomatopoeic name for a small, right-angled harp, usually seven stringed; ✣ **Chonguri** Essentially the same as a panduri. A bass chonguri is the size of a cello; ✣ **Daira** Tambourine with the bells on the inside circumference; ◑ **Garmon** Accordion; ▲ **Goshan Nagara** Tom-tom-like pair of mini drums, usually played with sticks; ▲ **Kermancha** Banjo-like instrument with cello-style spike: played with a bow (✣ Tchianuri); ▲ **Nagara** Drum on a tubular frame played with the hands; ✣ **Panduri** Three-stringed lute that's the most ubiquitous popular Georgian folk instrument (🖳 www.hangebi.ge/panduri-chonguri.htm describes numerous forms); ▲ **Sindj**

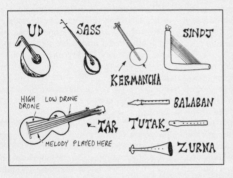

Nineteen-string harp-like instrument similar to a Changi; ▲ **Sass** The classic long-necked Azeri lute; **Tambur** Long, thin, two-stringed Avar instrument; ▲ **Tar/**✣ **Tari** Derives from *vatar* which simply means stringed instrument. Today's tars are most famously made in Shäki and have distinctive figure of eight double sound boxes. They may have 5, 11 or 13 mostly paired strings. The tune is played mainly on the lower strings, the shorter upper ones adding drone; ▲ **Tutak** Basic flute; ▲ **Ud** Variety of Turkic lute with a short, bent-back neck and a body wider than a sass. The plectrum should be made from the flattened shaft of an eagle's feather; ▲ **Zurna** Simple conical 'trumpet'.

Baku has a small museum of folk-musical instruments (☎ 494 6062: Tue-Sun 10.00-18.00; map p101, A4) at 119 Zargarpalan St, a workshop for repairing them beneath the Music Academy (98 Badalbeyli, ☎ 498 6972) and a **State Museum of Azerbaijani Musical Culture** (5 Behbudov, ☎ 598 4479; map p93 F12) where you can sometimes hear an ensemble of traditional instruments played live.

spacecraft's 'Hi this is earth' tape for curious aliens.

Alim Qasimov is probably the foremost pop-Muğam singer of the present generation. And his incredibly talented daughter **Ferghana Qasimova** seems set to continue and enhance the family reputation. Other top names include **Aşaxhan Abdullayev**, **Sekina Ismayilova**, **Gadir Rustamov** and **Aşıg Pari**.

A fun variant on Muğam is **Meyxana**. Literally translated as 'drinking den' from

its disreputable origins, the art pairs two singers who must improvise a rhyming, poetic tirade of insults against the other to a steadily chugging orchestral beat. The result can be hilarious – even when you don't understand the words, the crowd's hysterical laughter at the best lines is infectious.

A grand new Muğam Evi building opened in early 2009 but as yet shows no signs of hosting any regular performances or even a museum.

Classical music Azerbaijan's 'best loved' composer is **Üzeyir Hacibäyov** (Hajibayli, Gajibekov), composer of the national anthem and all-round star of every genre. He is hailed for combining mugam and operatic genres, though some find his classic operas such as *Laylı and Majnun*, less of a blend than a stylistic switchback. Other greats include **Qara Qaraev** (Kara Karayev) who penned ballets, symphonies and the patriotic opera *Vatan* (Motherland); and **Fikrat Ämirov** whose *Gülüstan Bayati Shiraz* was used by US figure-skating champion Michelle Kwan.

Several opera singers are national heroes, eg **Muslim Magomayev** (1885-1937, also a composer), **Shövkat Mammadova** (1897-1981) whose uncomfortable silver shoes, jewellery and make-up are preserved in Baku's Theatre Museum; and **Rashid Behbutov** (1915-88). Behbutov's voice was 'so captivating that the Communists could not bear to banish him from the stage even when he refused to sing the mandatory praise songs for the regime'. Best loved was **Murtuza Rza Mammadov**, unanimously remembered as 'Bül Bül' (the 'nightingale'). Before his four years at La Scala, Milan, he had trained as a *khanende* (ie mugam master) and painstakingly recorded ageing ashug greats on his Edison phonograph. The original machine is still on display in Bül Bül Museum, Baku. His son, **Polad Bülbüloğlu**, was a major Soviet pop star of the late 1960s who spent some time as minister of culture after 2000.

Internationally, the most famous Azeri musician was probably cellist and conductor **Mstislav Rostropovich** who actually spent most of his youth in Moscow and defected to the West in 1974. Nonetheless, the Baku street where his family lived has been renamed in his honour and their house is now a Rostropovich museum (p101, πO7).

Jazz Jazz was played in Azerbaijan when frowned upon elsewhere in the USSR, though even here some suffered for their 'decadence' including 'Baku's Benny Goodman', clarinetist **Parvis Rustam-**

The passageway to Vagif Mustafazadeh's house museum in Baku (marked VM on map p83, I7) sports this expressive Mustafazadeh bust by master sculptor Omar Eldarov.

beyov, who died in KGB detention on Christmas Eve 1949.

The nation's most celebrated artist was **Vagif Mustafazadeh** who blended jazz with traditional mugam wailing. His daughter **Aziza** is a phenomenally talented pianist and 'scat'-jazz singer of international repute. Her live performance at the 2007 Baku Jazz festival culminated in an astonishing rendition of *Shamans* in which she managed to harmonize with her own echo.

Other names to watch out for include pianists **Shahin Novrashı** and the young **Isfar Sarabsky**, bassist **Ruslan Huseynov** and saxophonist **Rain Sultanov** ex-Syndicate. Sultanov is now the producer of many interesting projects including the remastering of classic **Rafiq Babayev** recordings as well as his own broadening range of music, including the 2008 *Tale of My Land* CD/DVD/ photo album. The 1998 mugam/jazz/pop fusion album of **Rast** is worth seeking out. The truly international five-day Baku Jazz Festival was a highlight of early summer but at present the festival has an uncertain future. The best website is 🖥 www.jazz.az.

Azeri pop Baku's CD shops still stock plenty by Western and Russian artists but as production improves, Azeri and Turkish artists get increasing attention. There's a blurred line where mugam music crosses into Azeri popular dance music. The latter still commonly uses droning, wailing voices but often has the counterpoint of an upbeat hip-waggling rhythm that's infectious once you get used to the style.

Among the most polished female stars is **Aygün Kazimova**; rated 'best singer' by a randomly sampled group of male Azeri students largely because they considered her buxom figure 'very very beautifuls'. Her repertoire swings from strong blues-rock songs such as *Mäni Sevirsän* through wailing dirges, painfully MOR Russo-pop (eg *Ötän Illär*) to zippy Turkish disco (*Üräyim od tutub*). More recently **Röya** has proved a major crowd pleaser helped by a certain notoriety for bad language, scanty clothing and her appearance on a local real-ity TV show.

A distant descendant of 19th-century humanist Hasanbey Zardabi, **Aysel Teymurzadä** landed Azerbaijan a very creditable third-place at the 2009 Eurovision Song Contest performing with popular Swedish-Iranian star Arash.

Other long-term female favourites include the lithe, adaptable **Manana** (fre-quently topping the bill at expensive restau-rants), **Zulfiya Hanbabayeva**, **Metanet Iskenderli**, the matronly **Ilhama** (Guliyeva) and the remarkably dull yet widely popular **Nazperi Dostaliyeva**.

Of the male stars, little **Faiq Ağayev** is a powerfully voiced bundle of energy, given to frenetically dancing himself into the audience. **Samir Bagirov** is also popular despite a camp flamboyance that makes some question his masculinity. For a perfect encapsulation of the whirling dance-music you're likely to encounter at any local restaurant or wedding, it's hard to beat *Mister Alibaba*, by **Eyyub Yaqubov**.

Anar Nağilbaz is considered the father of modern Azeri Rap, an up-and-coming genre whose present stars include **Mone**, the curiously lispy **Elshad Hose**, and **Deyirman**. The latter's hard hitting *Yol Yox!* (No choice!) sampled sound bites by martyred war-reporter Chingis Mustafayev in a song whose frighteningly stark mes-sage is 'Karabagh or death'.

Azeri pop music websites Before buy-ing it's worth listening to a wide selection. That's easy since hundreds of computer-stored samples are available in virtually any internet club. Or listen to samples on 💻 http://zeng.open.az, or 💻 www.mp3-az.com which also offers (very slow) down-loads. For lyrics try 💻 http://mp3.azeri.net.

You can listen to a limited selection on 💻 www.azeroo.com/mp3_index.php but you'll need to sign up as a member to download.

A very extensive if rather dry source of information of Azeri music is 💻 www .yusif.org/music.html.

Theatre

Some opera and ballet productions are par-ticularly lavish albeit often recycling the same basic repertoire of global classics plus a few Hacibäyov compositions. Should you understand enough of the language, the Baku theatre scene (see p122) can be inspiring.

There are also theatres in Nakh-chivan, Shäki and Gänjä plus a Lezghian theatre in Qusar.

Cinema

The Azeri film industry is modest but Baku has been the backdrop to several Soviet movies not to mention the James Bond film *The World is Not Enough*. Locally made *Yarasa* (The Bat) by **Ayaz Salayev** won a couple of international awards in 1995 and **Rustam Ibrahimbäyov** (pp365-6) has worked on three Oscar-nominated movies.

Renovations are finally starting to improve some cinemas notably Baku's classic Nizami Cinema which is due for total refurbishment by 2011. However, many other venues remain tatty places showing mostly Russian, Turkish and Bollywood Indian movies. Western films are so dreadfully dubbed (into Azeri or Russian) as to be funny; a single voice often reads all the parts in a perversely deliberate monotone. An example: during a fight scene a man is thrown off a cliff screaming 'Nooooooooooooooooo'. Silence. Two seconds later the translator yawns, rus-tles his script and reads: 'nyet'. Once is usually enough to get the idea.

Art (Rəsm)

Pre independence Before the Russian era (19th century), Azeri artists busied themselves predominantly with stone carv-ing, engraving, metal work and carpet mak-ing. In the Tsarist era Azeris produced plenty of stolidly realist portraiture, which only really started to develop with the satirical art of **Azim Azimzade** (Baku house museum ∂S5, statue ∂S10, pp92-3) some of which is displayed in Baku's National Gallery (p85).

The best-known 20th-century Azeri painter was **Sattar Bahlulzade**, an archetypal artist whose camp, skeletal appearance looked like Dali and Serge Gainsbourg rolled into one. With a blatant disregard for the requirements of Soviet Social Realism he painted huge, distinctive canvases of streaked colours. These do for finger-painting what Seurat did for dots. Though virtually abstract, the overall effect in his most successful canvases is a remarkable evocation of the Azeri landscapes – quite an achievement when painting the subtle landscapes of pan-flat Shirvan. There's an original Bahlulzade in the foyer of Landmark Tower III (p99 αM16 and p100) and wonderful Bahlulzade statue at his grave-site in Ämircan, see p146.

Other 20th-century greats include **Mikhael Abdullayev** (whose works, like those of Bahluzade are considered national treasures so may not be exported) and **Xalida Safarova** (mixing colourful impressionism with Soviet Realism with very variable degrees of success). Other artists with a keen knack for using strong colour and bold lines to great effect include wonderfully expressive **Togrul Narimanbekov** and **Javad Mirjavad** whose portraits are like vivid tribal icons, though they remained sadly under-estimated until the 1990s. If you like Soviet Realism you'll love the pure, stark works of **Tahir Salakhov**. His 1959 classic *Neftyanik* (Oilworker) showing Baku workers battling against the wind has been mimicked by contemporary stars.

For sculptors the late Soviet period was a fine time. There were enough Lenins already made and not yet any major demand for carved Heydar Aliyevs. This allowed Azeri sculpture to come of age in the masterworks of **Omar Eldarov**. His passion and superb allegorical eye for detail are most clearly seen in the Huseyn Cavid statue (Cavid Sq, p103) and Vahid bust (p82) but also in many unsigned memorial statues in Faxri Xiyabani (p103).

Post independence Don't be put off by the awful, trashy paintings on sale along Baku's *passaj* (p91 and p92 ∂K5) and displayed in so many mid-range hotels. In fact Azerbaijan's art scene is dynamic and has seen a particularly brilliant period in the post-independence years. And with good reason. In the Soviet era artists were classically trained to exacting standards yet would face a career in which they would be mainly employed in prescriptive, limiting state-commissioned works. However, when the USSR abruptly collapsed, these highly skilled artists suddenly found themselves with unprecedented freedom of expression. The result was an explosion of creativity in the 1990s, somewhat helped by expat collectors and oil companies whose bargain purchases and commissions (partly) made up for the artists' lost state salaries.

Of the present generation, paintings by incredibly versatile **Yusuf Mirza** (p94) and the intricate etchings of **Ismayil Mammadov** have been especially popular. Highly talented artists including **Sabina Shikhlinskaya**, **Elchin Nadirov**, **Huseyn Hagverdi**, **Eybat Babayev** and **Bähram Khälilov** form a loose collective called the United Artists' Club (Labyrinth group) whose works can be seen at Baku's Centre of Contemporary Art (p82) and on 🖥 www .ussr-remix.az. Many of these inspiring folk work at the 'secret studios' at 31 Istiglalyat St (p87) and cooperate on exhibitions and large-scale installation art projects.

Many other Old City galleries (see p82) along with building 2 of the National Gallery (p85, ϕL2) display a good range of modern Azerbaijani art while 🖥 www.az gallery.org has a truly magnificent range, putting online around 4000 works by 170 artists. Though not commercial, the artist's contact details are given in case you should want to negotiate a purchase. Note that exporting an artwork requires a certificate. If you want to get that yourself you'll have to visit the Artists' Union (19 Xaqani St; p96 and p93 ∂K10) on a Wednesday. If the work is over 25 years old and liable to be considered a 'work of cultural importance', you'll need to take the painting to the National Gallery to be assessed (Tuesdays only!).

CARPETS

Some of the world's most sought-after carpets were made in the area of greater Azerbaijan. Cottage-industry carpet-making diminished considerably during the Soviet era as the process was mechanized and carpets were churned out of big factories using inferior dyes and little imagination. The Azerbaijan State Art Institute, however, maintains a faculty of 'Carpet Skills' and Baku now has at least one excellent private carpet workshop.

Motifs and shapes

Certain carpet-design styles and motifs are traditionally associated with a specific town or region of Azerbaijan. The issue becomes confused as regions later copied the popular designs of another. Thus you might for example get a Baku-style carpet which was actually made in Gänjä. The Carpet Museum in Baku uses **Latif Karimov**'s classification system giving the name of the village first and the motif-style second. For example, Xille Buta would mean a carpet employing buta (Paisley-arabesque) motifs made either in Xille (now Ämircan) or at least in the accepted style of that village.

Other classic motifs include the Zeyva and Gol ('hands') both typical of Quba carpets and the small multiple rhomboid flowers of Qobustan carpets.

A small namazlığ prayer carpet (especially common from the Shirvan region) is easy to identify by the arrow device that points the supplicant towards Mecca. Thin strip carpets around 5m long but barely a metre wide were not necessarily designed for a long hallway. Most started life as part of a matching five-part set called a Dastkheli Gebe, traditionally presented by the bride at her own wedding. These come from the greater Karabagh and Talysh areas.

Many villages in the Qazax sultanate (mostly now in Armenia/ Georgia) were high in the cold mountains so it's not surprising that the 'Qazax'-style carpets are coarser with extra-deep-pile.

From a collector's point of view, the finest carpets are usually those with the greatest knotting density, counted by examining the underside.

Azeri flat weaves are divided into seven main categories. The best-known types are kilim and sumakh, the latter having an embroidered quality. If you're interested in telling a kilim from a palas etc, Baku's Carpet Museum guides can talk you through all the subtleties.

Buying and exporting carpets

In 1861 Azeri carpets were so cheap that British tourist John Osmaston carelessly picked up a rug in a Baku market to use as a makeshift bed. Today, a carpet is no giveaway so unless you know exactly what you're looking at, purchases should be seen as souvenirs not as investments. Beware of older items: any carpet considered antique (over 30 years) cannot be legally exported and may anyway be 'forged' (ie artificially aged).

Even new carpets need an export certificate. Start the application procedure at least two weeks before you leave by visiting the Carpet Museum. Theoretically you could go on your own to apply at 19 Boyuk Gala (p83, ΣN9) (entrance around the corner, red bell) but it opens only once a week (Thursday at 10am at the time of writing but previously on Monday and before that Fridays just to keep you guessing!). Some dealers will do the paperwork and shipping for you, and in the case I followed up the carpet really did arrive albeit after a nail-biting wait.

The old city in Baku has a handful of dealerships which cater to visiting collectors. To get a better deal at such places it may well be worth employing the help of Asya (mobile ☎ 50 328 0985), the English-speaking lady who guides tours of Baku's Carpet Museum. She can also help with the certification procedure.

Novelty carpets

Portrait carpets are something of an Azeri speciality with foreign heads of state liable to receive their likeness in thread during any official gift-giving. Ex-president

Heydar Aliyev graces many a carpet including little AZN25 souvenir versions commonly sold in Baku curio shops. Should you want to see your own face in wool there are several workshops that can oblige, eg in Yardımlı (p290) and at the Baku Scientific and Restoration Centre for Carpets (p83, ΣK6; ☎ 492 4306, door marked 'Oguz') who can also run you off promotional carpet coasters with your name or company logo.

SPORTS AND GAMES
Olympic sports
Before becoming President, Ilham Aliyev ran Azerbaijan's Olympic Committee and amongst the first signs of the nation's regeneration were the swish modern Olympic sports centres that appeared across most of the regions. In 2008 Baku presented itself unsucessfully as a candidate host for the 2016 games (see 💻 www.2016baku .org for the pitch).

Combat arts are the sports at which Azerbaijanis most regularly excel internationally. Of seven medals won at the Beijing Olympics three each were for **judo** and **wrestling**. An Azeri **weightlifter** took gold and a world record in the 2000 Sydney para-Olympics only to lose it on a doping charge.

Football
As in most of the world, soccer is Azerbaijan's most popular spectator sport. For years the nation's top soccer team was Gänjä Kyapaz but more recent champions have been Neftchi (Baku) and Xazar Länkoran (💻 www.lankaranfc.com). See 💻 www.affa.az for fixtures and league standings. The Azeri national side is not renowned for storming successes but they did manage to beat Finland in 2006 causing such delight that fans set fire to their programmes en masse to create celebratory makeshift candles. The police were horrified. Programmes have been noticeably absent at matches ever since.

There are Baku **expat teams** for a variety of sports including **rugby** (the Baku Barbarians) and **soccer** (Bailov Rovers). See pp123-4 for more about participatory sport.

Indoor games and sports
Billiards (though rarely pool or snooker) is a passion with younger Azeri men. In the 1990s tables could be found in most parks across the country, but the gentrification of parks has shunted cue-pushers into cellar rooms and smoky halls.

Older men tend to prefer chess, dominoes or **nard**. A guide at Baku's Historical Museum was once trying to explain the fundamentals of market design. 'What every market place needs is space for trade, somewhere for animals and a place to play nard!' Also spelt 'nart', this ever popular ancient game is similar to backgammon but with different starting positions and two key rule changes:
i) only one starting *dash* (playing piece) may be moved per dice throw (except with doubles)
ii) single dash are safe and cannot be sent to the centre bar as in backgammon.

At teahouses and on park benches across the country, pieces are slammed down with a passion that seems to be a psychological projection of the player's machismo. Or is it gamesmanship designed to give the opponent a headache?

Chess is very competitive with special chess schools in most Azeri towns. Grandmaster Garry Kasparov, now a prominent Russian opposition politician, was born in Baku and honed his game at the chess club on Husi Haciev St (now pr Azerbaijan, δR1). One of the first people to beat him in twenty years was Azeri prodigy Teymur Rajabov, one of the world's top ten current players.

This relief graces the wall of the Electricity Dept (formerly a chess club)

What to see, where to go

GEOGRAPHICAL OVERVIEW

Baku has pretty much everything you would expect of a historic city with a million plus inhabitants. Its medieval walled old-city area is a UNESCO World Heritage site and the surrounding central area is delightfully cosmopolitan with attractive turn of the 20th-century buildings. The **Absheron peninsula** (p143) lacks scenic appeal but offers beaches and assorted curiosities (castles, religious sites and fire phenomena) plus a fascinating array of cultural discoveries: superstitious practices jarringly co-exist with Islam here in the nation's most self-conscious pious Muslim communities. Also within day-trip range of Baku are the world-renowned Qobustan petroglyphs (p140) and some of the most delightful mud volcanoes (p142) anywhere. **North** of Baku are the wildly colourful geology of the 'Candy Cane' mountains (p161) and the quaint twin towns of Quba and Krasnaya Sloboda (pp172-6) can be visited en route to one of numerous woodland getaway resorts but harder to reach in the dramatic mountains is a fabulous patchwork of canyons and timeless villages of which Xınalıq (p181) and Laza (p189) are the most spectacular.

The **Shamakha–Shäki route** (pp192-239) skirting just south of the High Caucasus foothills gives a fabulous snapshot of Azerbaijan's extraordinary diversity with desert, farmland, forests and high mountains all within a few hours' drive. Lahıc makes a great side trip and Shäki's palaces and caravanserai hotel make it Azerbaijan's foremost provincial attraction. This route is the recommended way to head for Georgia.

Central Azerbaijan (pp240-278) offers much less in the way of scenery and many of its historic sites are underwhelming, though if you can make it to Lake Göy Göl (unlikely, see p263) the scenery makes up for it all. Beautiful but Armenian-occupied **Nagorno Karabagh** (p275) is still tragically out of bounds to visits from the rest of Azerbaijan.

The **south** (pp279-303) is lushly fertile with thick woodlands and delightful hidden teahouses in the charmingly peaceful Talysh mountain foothills. The disconnected **Nakhchivan** enclave (pp304-316) has several important historical monuments scattered across a dramatically rocky semi-desert landscape but due to the closed borders with Armenia you'll have to fly (or drive via Iran or Georgia/Turkey) to get there.

LAND OF FIRE

Tourists and Zoroastrians alike are fascinated to see fire emerging spontaneously from the earth. The classic '*ateshgah*' is the **Suraxanı Fire Temple** (p154) but some visitors prefer the spooky naturalism of **Yanar Dağ** (pp155-6). The small natural ateshgah beyond **Xınalıq** (p182) is in a fabulously scenic amphitheatre of mountains. There are Yanar Bulaq **burning springs** at Archivan (p302) and near Qäsämänlı (p272) while west of Masallı there's a remarkable section of river that catches fire when lit (pp288-9).

BEACHES

Azerbaijan isn't a beach paradise. Still, Baku weekenders can cool off with a dip at Shix(ov) (p138) or on the north Absheron coast (p150, p159). Much harder to reach and virtually unknown are the narrow shell/sand beaches around Shurabad (p161), Xachmaz (p168) and Narimanabad (p292). There's a fairly decent grey-sand beach at Astara (p302) though the town isn't Azerbaijan's most welcoming. In summer locals rush off en masse to Nabran (p169), Azerbaijan's top seaside strip, but those with time and money prefer Turkey, Spain or Dubai.

MUD VOLCANOES (▲ Palchik Volkane, ✪ Gryazevye Vulkan)

Like cows, mud volcanoes constantly fart flammable gasses. They also like throwing gobs of mud and streaming forth watery flows with a vigour that varies seasonally. This behaviour is gently amusing rather than life threatening. Unlike 'normal' volcanoes, mud volcanoes are cold and have mul-

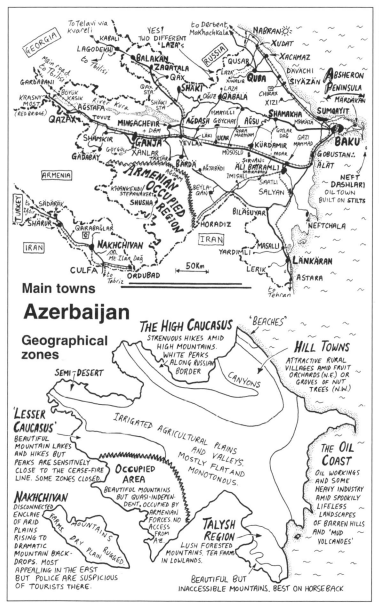

Main towns

Azerbaijan

Geographical zones

tiple vents (*gainarja*) through which they exhale. These come in two types: *gryphons* (distinctive, abrupt conical nozzles) and *salses* (bubbling watery pools). Each has its own rather lovable character and when gathered in groups they almost appear to converse. Though not unique, Azerbaijan has more of these odd 'creatures' than any other country in the world, around 300 groups on land plus hundreds more offshore where they sometimes rise to form islands in the shallow coastal waters.

Where to see them?
Classic giants such as Turaguy are impressive from a distance but smaller volcano hills often have a better collection of active gryphons and salses. From Baku the most accessible group is right beside the road to Shamakha (see p193). Less dramatic but even nearer there are some extinct gryphons along the Baku bypass. However, the most interesting active groups are between Älät and Qobustan at 'Clangerland' (p142) and Bahar near

---

❏ Mud volcanoes

● **Why are they cold?** 'Normal' volcanoes spew lava, molten rock that comes from deep within the earth or that has been melted by massive geological friction. In comparison, mud volcanos emanate from much shallower depths. Natural gas generated by pressure on organic materials produces the volcano's flatulence (94% methane, 3% carbon dioxide) and forces pressurized mud through fissures and weak points in the sediment above. Like cold air rushing from an inflated tyre, the expanding gas cools as it emerges, making the mud that it carries unexpectedly chilly.

Mud volcanoes are a product of the same geological system responsible for Azerbaijan's rich oil and gas fields and can be used as clues by explorers seeking additional reserves.

● **Mud-batan** At times a volcano goes into overdrive and spews forth a considerable volume of mud. The effect can be quite impressive but inconvenient. In Azeri, the suffix *-batan* refers to what would happen to animals and people trying to cross such a mud field. It's derived from ▲ *batmag* to get stuck; ie Lökbatan and Ceyranbatan – *Lök* = camel, *Ceyran* = gazelle.

● **Using the mud volcanoes** Pliny noted mud's medicinal qualities in Roman times. Local scientists baldly admit that the mud of the volcano fields is not as rich in key minerals as certain silts. But that doesn't stop sanatoria at Märdäkän and Qala Altı (p164) using it for mud baths and mud massages which they claim aid spinal maladies, slipped discs and arterial clogging. 'Mud collars' are also supposed to aid blood flow to the brain and Sharq-Qarb Enterprises will sell you packaged dry mud if you want to make your own!

In the Soviet era some volcano craters were used as handy disposal sites and simply filled with assorted refuse. Recently geologists have proposed a 'volcano reserve' to protect the remaining examples of these weirdly fascinating phenomena for future generations. But for now you can simply wander freely amongst the little fellows. Please don't drive onto the mud field nor stand too close to the caldera lips.

● **Are they safe?** On very rare occasions, extreme gas pressure blows out the whole crater throwing masses of rock and mud into the air and showering a wide area. In such events, the methane can ignite creating a dramatic flare several hundred metres high as happened in 2001 at Lökbatan (pp138-9). The flames were visible from Baku and burnt for weeks. On another occasion six unlucky shepherds and their flock were blown clean out of a remote crater in the Xızı region. But such violent eruptions are very rare and usually preceded by discernible warning rumblings and movements of the whole crater surface. The more accessible crater fields generally gurgle away safely and make very intriguing places to explore. Tourists are more of a danger to the fragile gryphons than vice versa.

Dashgil (see map p141) where a recent giant mud flow is particularly impressive. Deep in the desert between Ceyrankachmas and Pir Hussein are yet more.

POST-SOVIET CURIOSITIES
In its wake, the Soviet system left a legacy of appalling pollution and ecological misman-agement (especially on the Absheron Peninsula) which will take years and billions of manats for Azerbaijan to clear up. Stacks of junked vehicles, despoiled oilfields and satanic-ruined factories are not obvious tourist attractions. Yet perversely, some such places are so awesomely dreadful that they are compulsively photogenic. Seeking out the isolated last statues of Communist icons also appeals to certain tastes.

Oilfield landscapes
The greatest views of massed derricks were once between Bayil and Bibi Heybat but this 'James Bond Oilfield' (p104) is being reclaimed. For other remarkable vistas of antiquated nodding donkeys and gruesome-coloured run-off pools look down (west) from Ramana Castle (p153). Or climb Lök-batan's blown-out mud volcano (p138) for fantastic all-encompassing views of oil-fields, building yards and offshore installa-tions. Assuming you can't get to Neft Dashlari (p152) the next best thing is the network of roads heading miles out to sea south of Sangachal (p140) and best surveyed from the terrace of the Qobustan petroglyphs museum. For oil-field archae-ologists the 1880s' hand-dug well remnants south of Yanar Dağ (pp155-6) are an incredible discovery – almost certainly unique anywhere in the world.

Other sad scenes Fascinatingly disturb-ing landscapes include the huge aluminium smelter and associated 'red mess' on the eastern edge of Gänjä, the vast quarry at Dashkäsän (p264), and the vast rusting post-industrial nightmare that was once Sumgayit's chemical works (p157) – wow! Depending on the wind direction, the bil-lowing chimneys of Qaradagh cement works can produce a peculiar, photogenic grey curtain or simply smother everything in a filthy dust cloud (p139). Moving for altogether different reasons are the Shafaq graveyard (p252), post-holocaust Ashağı Ağcakänd (p253) and the village of Narimanabad which seems idyllic until you walk down Narimanov St (p292).

Lenin
On 20th Jan 1990 the Red Army massacred hundreds of innocent civilians in Baku. Spontaneously people began to discard their Communist Party membership cards as a sign of defiance to the perpetrators of the outrage. As the country became inde-pendent, Lenin statues disappeared from virtually every town square, village office and factory gate. But not quite all of them.

Vladimir Ilich still stands proudly near Puta (p139), there are two minuscule busts on the summit of Mt Shahdağ and a brilliant giant Lenin in Yevlax, sawn in half (see photo C11 and p248).

For years locals couldn't imagine the attraction of the old Soviet symbols. However, a certain comic-nostalgia is creeping in. There's now a handful of places that sell Lenin heads (eg Baku ∂G4) plus a couple of cafés with Soviet nostalgia themes – the USSR in Baku (Tagiyev St) and the Retro at Amburan (p146).

In Georgia there's still a big statue of Stalin in his home-town, Gori (pp344-5).

ARCHITECTURE
Thanks to the multitude of earthquakes and invasions, relatively little of Azerbaijan's truly ancient architecture remains. The most notable medieval exceptions are Baku's unique Maiden's Tower and the Momine Khatun mausoleum tower in Nakhchivan.

Surviving buildings from the 12th to 19th centuries are predominantly religious, though several caravanserais (Baku, Shäki, Sangachal, Ağdash), brick bath-houses, and many castle ruins (best at Chirax, Gädäbäy/Rustam Aliev, Perigala/Muxax) remain. There are khans' palaces in Baku, Shäki and Nakhchivan.

Architectural styles
● **Tomb tower design** There are three main types: a polygonal cross-section with pointed polyhedral roof comes from ancient Hittite design and was also the most popu-

lar throughout eastern Turkey and Armenia. The best examples are at Häzrä (p211), Kalaxana (p202) and Göylar Dağ (p202). Taller Persian-influenced polygonal or cylindrical towers are often decorated with blue majolica tiles, most impressively at Nakhchivan (p307), Qarabağlar (p315) and Bärdä (pp248-50). Stubby cubic or cuboidal bases with a dome are taken from stylized miniaturizations of local mosque designs and are relatively common.

● **Mosque design** The most visually appealing old mosques are in Baku, Gänjä (Imamzade shrine), Ordubad and Bärdä, with several more in Shäki. Traditional designs vary considerably from area to area. Shamakha's mosque (p197), misleadingly dubbed the 'second oldest in the Caucasus', has a unique temple-like appearance. A flat-roofed stone cube with a simple central dome is particularly common on the Absheron Peninsula, while a simple wooden-house-style box with a tim-

ber-pillared entrance area is more common in the foothills above Ismayıllı (Lahıc, Damırchı). Around Zaqatala, large multi-arched structures are favoured (Tala, Muxax, Balakän) while in the far south several follow a quite distinct style with a small central chimney-like turret and arched stained-glass windows (Pensar, Qumbashi, Alasha). Baku's old stone mosques are relatively ornate by Azeri standards.

Many square-plan Lezghian village mosques (Qächräsh, Alpan, Qusar Laza etc) have spaceship metallic towers and steep-pitched corrugated roofs belying their often considerable age. A few dramatic Turkish-style new stone mosques with big dome and associated minarets have been built in recent years, notably in Qusar, Zaqatala, Mingächevir, Nakhchivan and Nardaran.

● **Mosque and tomb ornamentation** Pre-14th-century builders mostly used geometrical patterns and stalactite vaulting. Where tiled, the predominance of blue decoration

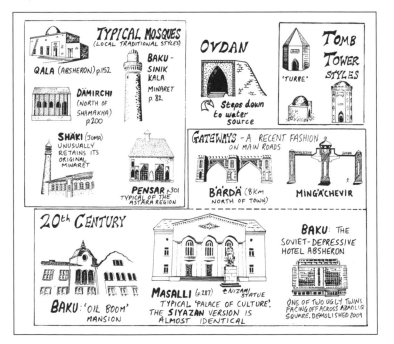

TYPICAL MOSQUES (LOCAL TRADITIONAL STYLES)

QALA (ABSHERON) p.152

DÄMIRCHI (NORTH OF SHAMAKHA) p200

SHÄKI (JUMA) UNUSUALLY RETAINS ITS ORIGINAL MINARET

PENSAR p301 TYPICAL OF THE ASTARA REGION

BAKU - SINIK KALA MINARET p.82

OYDAN

Steps down to water source

'TURBE'

TOMB TOWER STYLES

GATEWAYS - A RECENT FASHION ON MAIN ROADS

BÄRDÄ (8 KM NORTH OF TOWN)

MINGÄCHEVIR

20th CENTURY

BAKU: 'OIL BOOM' MANSION

MASALLI (p287) NIZAMI STATUE TYPICAL 'PALACE OF CULTURE'. THE SIYAZAN VERSION IS ALMOST IDENTICAL

BAKU: THE SOVIET-DEPRESSIVE HOTEL ABSHERON

ONE OF TWO UGLY TWINS FACING OFF ACROSS AZADLIQ SQUARE. DEMOLISHED 2009

was due to the durability of available dye stuffs. More often carved or smoothed stone was left bare. A more recent fashion for shrine interiors are the dazzling mosaics of mirrored mini tiles like the *Imamzadeh*s of neighbouring Iran.

● **Hamams** Bath-houses (*hamams*) were a great leap forward for public sanitation, especially in desert towns where there was little fresh water or firewood to heat it. Usually multi-domed, brick-built low buildings, many century-old examples are still functioning (Baku, Ağdash, Qazax). Indeed the idea of a hamam party as a sort of Azeri stag-night is re-emerging and some classic historic bath-houses have been suitably gentrified to fill the demand (eg Baku's Tazabäy hamam, p102, p101 πM8). Even ruined hamams remain interesting architectural monuments, as with Quba's strange single-domed bee-hive design, p172.

● **Caravanserais** Caravanserais were the truckers' motels of the Silk Route: a place to sleep, eat and park the camel. While each design has its own peculiarities, the essential feature is a series of small basic rooms around a lockable courtyard, all very solidly built to keep out thieves and bandits.

While the term now seems deeply antiquated, in fact caravanserais were still being built until the beginning of the 20th century.

● **City gates** When city walls were demolished in the 19th century, there remained little need for the traditional town gates. However, a recent fashion has led several provincial towns to erect imposing new gateways at their nominal city limits, often several kilometres from the town centre.

Oil-boom architecture
Styles started to change radically from the latter half of the 19th century. The initial division of oil-prospecting land into very small, affordable plots meant that even the poorest peasant or worker had a lottery chance of digging out a 'gusher'.

Dozens of illiterate overnight millionaires spent the years between 1880 and WWI vying to outdo one another with displays of new-found opulence and 'good taste' with typical nouveau-riche zeal. Teams of architects were brought to Baku

from Europe and Russia, while local architects and the oil magnates themselves toured Europe looking for designs and motifs which caught their fancy.

The resulting 'oil-boom style' is thus an unabashed mélange with an immediate appeal to anyone except po-faced architectural purists. Though neglected and subdivided during the Soviet era, the basic fabric of most of these mansions survives.

20th- and 21st-century architecture
Inspirational guide Fuad Akhundov succinctly sums up the three main phases of 20th-century design:

    1900-1915 Impressive
    1920-1955 Oppressive
    1955-1990 Depressive

He sees the cycle reversing now. Although there's no new Stalin trying to daunt people with massive stone edifices as in the '40s and '50s, the almost endless growth of independence-era tower blocks do indeed seem to characterize a new oppressiveness – of rich over poor. But if extraordinary new plans are ever built, by 2020 Baku might be really architecturally impressive – assuming you like sci-fi glass grandeur (see 'Baku – The New Dubai?' box, p78).

The original oppressive phase was not only a political gesture but a real need to provide decent housing for some 10,000 families working in appalling conditions in the Absheron oilfields. Thus 380 apartment blocks were rushed to completion between 1925 and 1929. Initially apartment design tried to incorporate a few traditional features of local architecture such as pointed arched entrances, windows on wooden frames in 5x7-pane Shäbäkä patterns and, most practically, steps up to the doors to prevent dust collecting.

The remarkable post-WWII construction boom and the return to high-quality stone buildings with a surprising level of carved detail was possible in large part to the free labour of relatively skilled German prisoners of war who, in a little-known postscript to WWII, were not allowed to return till 1949-50 or even 1951. They were also put to work on the construction of railways.

MUSEUMS

Except in Baku, Azerbaijan has really only three types of museum, all with predictable format and content that, after a couple of visits, you'll start to find cosily familiar (or crashingly monotonous). Fortunately few charge entry fees so there's no need to fear stepping inside except for the embarrassment of waking up the slumbering attendants. Even if you don't understand the language, you may be treated to a guided tour in Russian or Azeri if only because you're the first visitor that week. There's also the comical formality of signing the guest book: somehow visitors manage to fill acres of paper with their reflections. Occasionally guest books started in the 1970s have not yet been filled up and the communist-era entries can make intriguing reading as you'll see at the Narimanov Apartment (p87) in Baku.

House museums

House museums are the mothballed homes of the great and the good and filled with their personal effects. While fascinating for fans of the individual concerned, such places are rarely a big draw for the average foreign tourist except perhaps for giving a taste of Soviet-era living conditions. The most compulsive such museum is Stalin's father's hovel in Gori (pp344-5), Georgia.

Historical (aka 'Local Studies') museums

Almost every mid-sized town and provincial capital has one, often situated in a building of local historic importance. Displays will almost inevitably start with some neolithic spearheads, a papier-maché tableau of cavemen and a tatty troop of stuffed animals. Then there'll be a very cursory blast through 7000 years of history depicted in one or two rooms with a few copper pots (see diagram p208), carpets and old banknotes. This will be followed by a room dedicated to 20th-century horrors: WW2 ('Great Patriotic War'), 20 January 1990, the Hojali massacre, and Karabagh with martyrs' photos and medals.

The most interesting part of such museums is usually the fading photo-board depicting local scenes of architectural or archaeological interest. Sadly, the wardens who trail behind you like vultures don't always know exactly where to find half the sites depicted. Instead you're likely to be hurried on to give due honour to the last room which is almost inevitably filled with books by Heydar Aliyev.

Heydar Aliyev museums

Since his death in 2003, the Heydar personality cult has gone into overdrive. Today virtually every town has a Heydar Aliyev Park sporting a Heydar Aliyev statue and a swish new Heydar Aliyev museum. Curiously these museums' mainly photographic exhibitions are often without labels but there's usually an obliging guide at hand to talk you through if you don't yet know the scenes by heart. You'll soon start to recognize the same family photos from Heydar's youth, his Moscow era and his handshakes with other world leaders including a pixie-faced Tony Blair. And you can bet there'll be that classic 'first oil' photo of him smearing son (now president) Ilham's face with crude oil. Heydar's many books are lovingly encased and there's usually one board of photos from the time that the great leader deigned to visit the town in question.

INTO THE MOUNTAINS

Azerbaijan's hills and mountains offer unparalleled opportunities for summer off-road adventures by four-wheel drive vehicle, horse or foot. Alpine wild flowers will delight botanists while zoologists, ornithologists and hunters vie with one-another in the search for Caucasian black grouse, *ceyran* gazelles and *tür* mountain goats.

4WD adventures

Land was communal under the Soviet system and mostly remains unfenced. So, when the contours and terrain allow, you can go pretty much where you please on the wide sheep-grazed slopes. There's a fine choice of routes around Altı Ağach, Chirax, Qonaqkänd, Söhub and Xınalıq, all approached from the Baku–Quba road. A fabulous variety of landscapes hide barely passable canyons and a web of challenging inter-village tracks on which you'll stumble into timeless stone hamlets that rarely, if ever, see visitors.

The map on p70 shows a compilation of routes and average levels of difficulty (very subjective). On harder routes it's best to go in a convoy of vehicles with a winch to pull each other out of muddy sections. After rain and especially as the snows melt, the mountain tracks can be treacherously slippery. Take spare fuel and tyres.

Approached from the south, the same mountains are harder to penetrate so there is a lower wow-per-ouch factor. Nonetheless, there are some challenging excursions behind Lahıc and Pirguli and attempting to find the route between the two (via Damirchi) is something of an offroader's holy grail. The Talysh mountains in the far south offer some interesting possibilities too, but with a greater population density, more arable agriculture, wetter conditions and fewer dramatic peaks to discover it is something of a secondary choice. The Allar (p291) and Sım (p302) trips are interesting but punishingly tough.

In the lesser Caucasus there are some exciting routes south of Gänjä (Todan), Dashkasan (Mt Qoshqar) and Gädäbäy (via Rustam Aliev) but proximity to the ceasefire line reduces one's options at present.

In the north-west a 4WD is handy to reach the forgotten Albanian churches in mountain villages such as Läkit and Bideyiz. These are a series of out and back trips, however, and even the toughest vehicles will struggle to ascend the upper river valleys where slopes are too steep and tree cover too thick for much off-roading.

Hiking

The off-roading areas mentioned above are perfect for hiking, as are the high mountains of the north-west. On foot, or with a horse (p19), you can climb into some magical ridge-top scenery with relatively minimal effort. Free camping, particularly in the north-east, is relatively safe though keep away from flocks of sheep – the shepherd dogs are trained to be extremely fierce. There are a few wolves and bears in the forests of the north-west.

Laza (p189), Kish (p227), Ilisu (p231), Vändam (p212), Lahıc (p206) and Car (p236) all make excellent bases for day hikes into the very best scenery and have handy places to stay. Xınalıq (p181) is probably best of all and makes a great starting point for longer hikes as guides and horses are comparatively easy to arrange there. Mondigar, Qalacık, Durja and Xoshbulaq are other tempting potential trailheads if you have a tent or a local friend to put you up.

Mountain biking

There's lots of scope for off-road biking and Azerbaijan's minor roads are generally very quiet (if often very bumpy). The Quba–Baku, Qazax–Älät, Baku–Länkäran and Baku–Ağsu roads are dangerously busy but other routes including Qäbälä–Balakän are pleasant for longer distance pedalling. Don't expect to find many spares in Azerbaijan, though you might be able to get help at the Cycling Club beside the Velotrek Hotel in Baku. There's also an active expat mountain bike club which organizes weekend rides and has put together some great off-road route suggestions, see 💻 www.baku bicycleclub.com.

Climbing and mountaineering

Baku rock climbers practise on a cliff near Bilgah/Amburan on the Absheron and occasionally venture to (holy) Besh Barmaq (p163) which makes for curious culture clashes. Baltagaya and Qizilqaya (between Xınalıq and north Laza) have spectacular mountain-top cliffs that offer particularly exciting climbing possibilities. In winter a frozen waterfall on Shahdağ makes an interesting ice-climb when access allows.

If you want to climb any of the highest mountains, a guide is pretty much essential. In Baku you could approach the Extreme Sports Federation (91 Neftchilar, Baku, ☎ 012-437 3129, 💻 www.fairex.az) or Baku's Alpinist Klub (c/o Salydan, mob ☎ 050 320 9936). Various travel agencies can also arrange guides. Informal guides are also possible to find in Laza if you have all your own equipment.

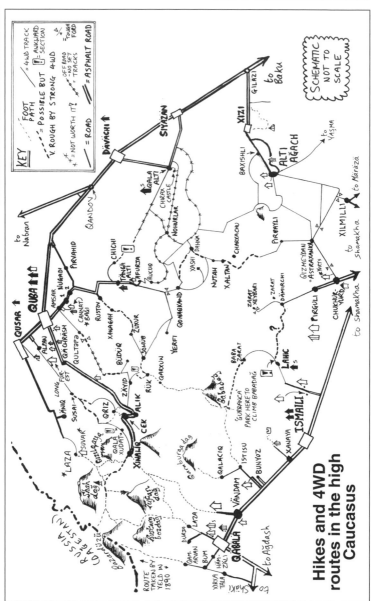

Hikes and 4WD routes in the high Caucasus

Three of the big four Azeri mountains (Tufan, Bazardüzü, Shahdağ) are approached by walking up the valley from Laza (Qusari Laza, p189) or by driving the extremely rough river-bed route by 4WD via Xınalıq to the very foot of Shahdağ (see p185).

The fourth great mountain of Azerbaijan is 3629m Babadağ. Somewhat away from the group described above, it can be approached from the north by following the Qarachay river south from Rük (p178), or from the south via Sumagalle/Istisu (tough) or Lahıc/Zarat Baba following a rough pilgrims' trail. On the top, prayer ribbons and cairns mark Häzrät Baba pir, honouring a mysterious Albanian-era holy man who climbed the mountain and then disappeared, advancing directly to heaven without passing 'Go'.

Skiing
At the time of writing Azerbaijan's first ski-resort was under construction between Aladasht and Laza (p189). Snow is rare in Baku but when the city whitens free-lancers rent skis for an informal schlep along the Bulvar.

FLORA AND FAUNA
Flowers
The wild flowers are particularly impressive in late spring with massed poppies giving emerald green young cornfields a surreal blush (eg along the Shäki–Oğuz road). The mountain flora is especially delightful in June. Look out for the delicate deep-blue Alpine Squill (Zhükh), in the foothills at around 1500m (eg Laza). The common cream-yellow Neked Chük (Milk Flowers) are reminiscent of Auricula but with finer leaves. Cheme Chük (literally 'butter flower') is a kind of buttercup. Note that the names given above are in Lezghiar.

In September the shrubs of the alpine foothills are awash with berries, notably rosehips, barberries and tiny red zirinj which have a slightly sour taste like a grape-paste confection – watch out for the thorns.

Cultivated flowers are very important socially and any evening at the theatre ends submerged in bouquets. In a florist make sure you buy an odd number of blooms unless you're planning to put them on a grave (see p50). Shuvälän and Mäshtaga on the Absheron peninsula supply most of the capital's cut flowers and once did so for large parts of the Soviet Union.

Trees
The main tree species are reassuringly familiar. Chestnut and oak are common in the forests of the north-west, juniper bushes climb exposed sub-Alpine slopes, white-barked plane trees and brush constitute the Turgay riverbank habitat that lines the Kura. Mulberry trees on Baku's streets annually dump their gooey black berries to get trampled messily underfoot. In the deep south look for the remarkable Iron-wood trees (see box p298).

Birds
Buzzards float above many of the bald grassy hills. White-tailed eagles have been spotted over the Biläsuvar marshes and Lammergeyers have been seen in the high mountains behind Zaqatala. The eastern edge of Turyanchay Nature Reserve is also good raptor-watching country and Imperial eagles have been spotted where dry hills with some juniper forest meet the turgay. Native Sapsan/Falcon (Falconidae peregrinus Tunstall) numbers have dwindled to under two dozen pairs. A collection of rare birds of prey is easy to see but cruelly caged at Däshtvänd Hotel (Masallı) and Cännät Bağı (Altı Ağach).

Present in the higher alpine zones are the very rare Caucasian snowcock, great rose finch and Güldenstadt redstart. In Zaqatala Forest Reserve (restricted entry) there are black woodpeckers and Caucasian black grouse. The latter are found virtually nowhere else and are counted annually by energetic enthusiasts in early September.

Talysh pheasants (phasianus colchicus talisophensis lorenz), found below 1200m in the southern mountain foothills, have also been hunted to the edge of extinction. Rare white pelicans (Pelecanus onocratalus L.) may occasionally be seen in winter at Mingächevir, Nakhchivan and Xanbulaq reservoirs and along with flamingos (Phoenicopterus roseus pallas) on marshy Kızılagach Bay (Oct/Nov till Feb/Mar). Waterfowl can be found on many of Azerbaijan's shallow lakes with little bustards plentiful on the coastal flats northwest of Dävächi. In these areas ornithologists are less common than hunters.

A superb new resource for ornithologists is *Birdwatching in Azerbaijan* by Sebastian Schmidt, Kai Gauger and Nigar Agayeva. The splendid 224-page full-colour guide comes with species-list, numerous maps and excellent photos plus a CD of referenced bird-calls. As well as exhaustive coverage of local birdlife, spotting tips are given for a range of other wildlife and trees. Copies can be purchased online at 🖳 www.nhbs.com or contact the authors (who also offer birding tours) via 🖳 www.succow-sif tung.de.

Animals

Tür mountain goats have long curly horns that make all too popular hunting trophies. Tür are increasingly hard to see but there have been recent sightings above the Ilisu road (p231). In the forests above Zaqatala one can hear the calls of red deer and roe deer. There are doubtless wolves and bears in the mountains too, as cubs have been brought back to several restaurants to be caged in menageries.

Delightful Ceyran, Caucasian gazelles *(Gazella subgutturosa Guldenstaedt)*, once common in Azerbaijan, were hunted almost to oblivion but are making a very visible comeback within Shirvan National Park (p281).

Caspian seals *(Phoca caspica Gmelin)*, amongst the world's smallest, are found seasonally (spring/summer) on the Caspian islands and at the extremities of Absheron Peninsula. The total population is now estimated at around 300,000 but is dwindling rapidly due to pollution in the Caspian. Snakes are all too common. Gurza *(Vipera lebetina)* are found across the country. A gang of them was milked for venom at Zira snake farm (p146) till the critters escaped.

❏ **Caspian Sea**

According to a tale in the ancient classic *Derbend Nameh*, the creation of the Caspian Sea was an impulsive act of retribution by God to punish the founder of Baku for mistreating his sister. Another version credits a Persian wizard called Arestoon who had been called upon to protect his ruler from the attacks of tribal Gogs and Magogs. Using a 'spirit formula' spell, he transformed the land between the Terek and Volga rivers from solid to liquid form, instantaneously drowning the territories of many an enemy and creating a natural defence.

The Caspian is relatively shallow and its volume varies significantly according to water inflows and evaporation. The result is a very substantial fluctuation in the water level. This is potentially disastrous for Azerbaijan which has lost most of its beaches to the rising waters since 1951. The most outlandish conspiracy theorists have absurdly tried to claim that Russia has been pumping water into the sea to destabilize Azerbaijan (and its own Caspian shore presumably). Of the many lost coastal buildings and facilities, perhaps most poignant is the drowning town of Narimanabad.

The great oil wealth beneath the Caspian sometimes produces natural gas and oil bubbles but commercial exploitation has added greatly to this pollution. A 1960 painting by Bakhlulzade in Baku's main art gallery depicts a smoggy, Turner-esque coastal haze through which loom ranks of ugly black derricks. It's sarcastically named 'Caspian Beauty'. Pollution today threatens the sea's other great source of wealth, the sturgeon; 90% of the world's caviar comes from the Caspian.

The five littoral states – Turkmenistan, Russia, Kazakhstan, Iran and Azerbaijan – have a long-running disagreement over whether the Caspian is a sea or the world's biggest lake. This apparently trivial semantic dispute is taken very seriously. In international law, a lake's mineral resources are shared between littoral countries while for a sea, each has its own territorial claims, some much richer than others.

PART 2: BAKU

INTRODUCTION

Azerbaijan's cosmopolitan capital forms a low sweeping amphitheatre curling gently around a south-facing bay of the Caspian Sea. Historic but tiny till the 19th century, it suddenly blossomed into the world's most important petro-town a century ago and was graced by many fine European-style buildings. Later, as one of the five biggest cities in the USSR, its architecture added a thick outer concrete mantle. The remarkable visual result is a 'post Soviet lovechild of Paris and Cumbernauld' (as described by Caucasus scholar Jonathon Shiland) that is once again being transfomed month by month as a renewed oil boom throws up ever more shiny glass towers. If all the dramatic city plans are realized, Baku will look like a sci-fi Dubai (see box p78) within a decade.

ORIENTATION

Close to the Caspian shore, the city's atmospheric, ancient core (Icheri Shähär/İçəri Şəhər, see p80) is a UNESCO World Heritage site, a warren of lanes surrounded on three sides by sturdy crenellated walls. Directly beyond those walls, a wealth of fine stone mansions date from the first oil boom (1880-1915). These extend into the commercial/entertainment district, notably 'Fountains Square' and pedestrianized Nizami St, along which one can admire the scanty summer costumes of local fashion victims doing their nightly passeggiata.

In the lanes behind, a 21st-century building boom is throwing out high-rises at an incredible rate while in the more distant mikro-rayons the towers form soulless ranks of predominantly late-Soviet vintage. Here

and there are the flares of the refineries and extraordinary wasteland patches of former oil workings. Then suddenly there's desert.

NAMING CONFUSIONS
Street names

Around 1920 Baku's streets were given good old communist names. In 1991 virtually all the street names changed again, with a preference this time for honouring artists and writers or at least 'translating' Russian names (eg Neftyanikov to Neftchilar [both mean Oil Worker] and Stroitel to Inshaatchilar [both mean Construction Worker]). For those street names that didn't change, it sometimes took years for signage to fully reflect the new Azeri Latin spellings which, in certain cases, can appear startlingly different to foreigners (eg Qoqol = Gogol, Azizbäyov = Azizbekov). Ever since, piecemeal renaming has continued as a way to honour national heroes. The results have at times been very confusing. Notably the vast eastern Märdäkan-bound thoroughfare, formerly known as Moskovskaya, was renamed Heydar Aliyev pr after the beloved leader's death but in a politically savvy gesture towards Russia another major road (formerly Tbilisi pr) was chosen to be Moskovskaya (Moscow pr). And so on. In 2008 a similarly bewildering change saw Azerbaijan pr renamed after Zärifä Äliyeva (the president's mum) while Hüsi Häciyev [Gusa Gajiyev] became the new Azerbaijan pr. So if you're given an address on Moskovskaya or Azerbaijan prospekts be sure to check if the address is 'new' or 'old'. And if the address is H Aliyev pr double check whether the H is for Heydar or Häsan (ie the former Inglab St).

Note that in a few cases locals continue to use the pre-independence street names, notably Basina for Füzuli St, Qorki (Gorki) for Mardanov Qardashlari and Torgovaya (a nickname simply meaning shopping street) for Nizami's central section.

The box below gives major road-name changes but for a fuller listing see 🖥 www .window2baku.com/eng/9Streets.htm.

City districts
By official definition, Baku City actually encompasses the whole Absheron peninsula, thus sprawling for over 50km. The inner-city districts are divided against what might seem conventional wisdom: the

seafront and old town fall within the mainly oil-suburb **Sabail district**; the rest of the central area is split between **Yasamal** and **Nasimi** districts.

Nasimi district is not the same as **Nizami district** and the latter contains neither the main Nizami St nor Nizami Park.

In reality knowing the name of a city district is only of relevance to most foreigners when it comes to finding the correct police station at which to register residency. In other respects the terms are unimportant as district names don't feature when people give directions or addresses.

HISTORY
Baku is perhaps the 'city of God' or the 'place of fire'. But the most popular deriva-

---

❏ Old and new street names

Present name	Communist era	Pre-communist
28th May	28 April	Telefonnaya
D Äliyev	Pervomaiskaya (1 May)	Surakhanaskaya
Alärbekov	Myasnikova	Milyutin
Saladin Askerovoi	Sverdlov	Kanni-Tepinskaya
Azadlyq Pr	Lenin Pr	Stanislavskogo
Ak Shamil Azizbekov	Khetskhoveli	Verhnaya Priyutskaya
Zärifä Äliyeva*	Shaumaniya	Merkuryevskaya
Shamil Badalbäyli	Dimitrova	Bondarnaya
Rashid Behbutov	Leitenata Schmidt	Kaspikaya
Bül-Bül	Kirova	Bolshaya Morskaya
Akhmed Cavid	Karayeva	Vrangelskaya
Füzuli	Basina	Balakhanskaya
Istiglaliyat	Kommunisticheskaya	Nikolayevskaya
Mardanov Qardashlari	Gorki	
Murtuz Muxtarov	Polukhina	Persia
Nariman	Narimanov	Sovetskaya
Neftchilar	Neftyanikov (Stalin)	Alexander Embankment
Nizami (Torgovaya)	Gubernskaya	
Niyazi (into Azneft Sq)	Chkalova	Sadovaya
Rasul Rza	Korganova	Mariinskaya
Rasulzade	Aparidze	Oliginskaya
Suleiman Rahimov	Kamo	Nizhnaya Priyutskaya
Prof K Safaraliboi	Rosa Luxemburg	
Bashir Safaroğlı	Shors	Kamenistaya
Tağiyev	Malygina	Gorchakovskaya
Tağizade	Ostroskova	Pochtovaya
Tabriz	Chapaeva	
Topchubashev	Krupskoi	Tatarskaya

*was pr Azerbaijan 1991-2008

tion is from Bad Kube meaning 'blustering wind'. Certainly Baku rates up there with Chicago or Wellington for gale-force gusts, see box p78.

Baku is a very ancient fortress and port town whose petroleum wealth has been exploited since pre-history. Marco Polo, who never actually bothered to visit, described how people came from 'vast distances' to collect an oil which 'is not good to use with food but is good to burn and is also used to anoint camels that have the mange'.

Despite the needs of lamps and mangy camels, however, the real value of this commodity was not to be fully appreciated until the late 19th century. In commercial terms the city's medieval importance was rarely equal to the great metropolises of the era – Shamakha, Gänjä and Derbend. Baku was a minor specialist in north–south shipments but the much-celebrated transcontinental 'Silk Route' usually took a more southerly course.

In the 12th century an earthquake flattened Shamakha and the Shirvanshah, Ahistan I, took the opportunity to move his capital to Baku – as far as possible away from his then nominal imperial overlords (the Georgians). This gave Baku a period of exceptional growth. Ahistan graced Baku with several mosques, remodelled the mysterious Maiden's Tower and built the first stage of the Shirvanshah palace complex which still stands today. Almost unique in the region, Baku's city fathers managed to talk the Mongols out of barbecuing the population in 1235 and the town remained reasonably intact. The city's next period of importance was the reign of Shirvanshah Ibrahim I (1382-1417), who rebuilt the city's double walls. (Today only the inner one still stands.)

Baku's importance dwindled as Shirvan's rulers returned to Shamakha and various attackers took occasional swipes at the city. The great 'Azeri empire' was ruled from Tabriz, not Baku which retained its fundamentally 14th-century layout right up until the start of the 19th century.

Although its population grew thereafter, the continued threat of attack meant that few people were prepared to risk life beyond the protective shelter of the old walls. With space so limited growing families simply enlarged existing homes. The result was the tight maze of alleyways that one can still observe in parts of the Old City.

The Russian era

After the 1828 peace treaty with Persia, Baku dared to spill outwards, albeit only cautiously before the 1870s. Then the privatization of the oil industry changed everything. Oilfields were so bountiful that one could become a millionaire just by digging up one's backyard. And many people did just that. Landowners who struck

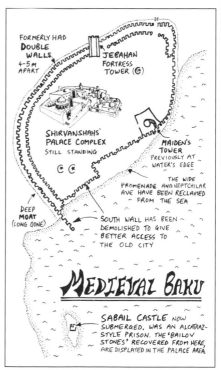

FORMERLY HAD DOUBLE WALLS 4-5m APART

JEBAHAN FORTRESS TOWER (G)

SHIRVANSHAHS' PALACE COMPLEX
STILL STANDING

MAIDEN'S TOWER
PREVIOUSLY AT WATER'S EDGE

THE WIDE PROMENADE AND NEPTCHILAR AVE HAVE BEEN RECLAIMED FROM THE SEA

DEEP MOAT (LONG GONE)

SOUTH WALL HAS BEEN DEMOLISHED TO GIVE BETTER ACCESS TO THE OLD CITY

MEDIEVAL BAKU

SABAIL CASTLE NOW SUBMERGED, WAS AN ALCATRAZ-STYLE PRISON. THE 'BAILOV STONES' RECOVERED FROM HERE, ARE DISPLAYED IN THE PALACE AREA.

BAKU

BAKU

'gushers' became the 'oil barons' if they managed to trap enough of the oil which poured out, sometimes all too rapidly. Black-gold rush fever and booming support industries attracted tens of thousands of workers, investors and adventurers to the rapidly expanding city. At one point the population doubled in three years.

By 1910 Baku produced more than half the world's petroleum. Oil profits funded grand public buildings, mosques, churches, the dozens of grand mansions and, indirectly, the Nobel Prize. The prize's founder Alfred Nobel made a fortune from his shares in the powerful oil company of his brothers Robert and Ludvig. Curiously Robert had originally come to Azerbaijan seeking a shipment of quality walnut timber for rifle butts. He ended up buying a refinery instead.

While landowners and entrepreneurs made huge fortunes, conditions for oil workers were appalling resulting in communist agitation and strikes. Meanwhile the rapid influx of 'outsiders' made Baku an easy place to stir up ethnic unrest. The first terrible massacres in 1905 led British commentator JD Henry to call it the 'greatest blood spot on the mysterious, rebellious

❏ **Baku population figures**	
1850	7000
1874	16,000
1905[1]	206,751
1930	310,000
1935	660,000
1967	780,000
1970	1,000,000
1985	1,700,000
1999	1,708,300
2007	2,745,000 est

[1] Only six women per 10 men in 1905: no wonder there were a lot of disturbances! The population plummeted immediately after the 1905 and 1918 massacres but rapidly started to climb again.

blood stained Caucasus'. For more detail on the provocateurs, on Stalin's time in Baku and on the complex history of the WWI era, see p42 then box pp96-7.

By the time the Azerbaijan Democratic Republic had installed its parliament in a former Baku school (now the Institute of

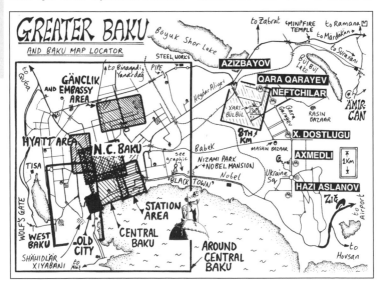

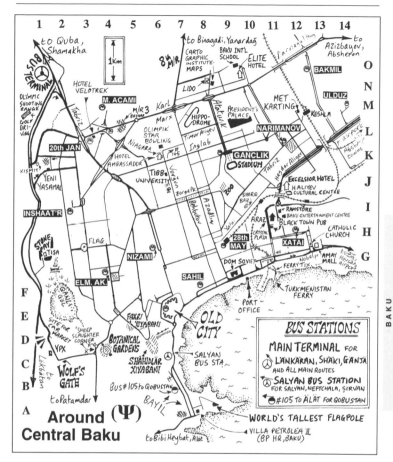

Around (Ψ) Central Baku

BAKU

Manuscripts, p89), much of the city lay in ashes. Then on 28 April the Red Army marched in. The date was later celebrated with all intended irony as a national holiday and given to a metro station and major street (now renamed 28th May St after the 1918 independence day). After an initial period of reprisals, Communist rule settled for a while into a period of reform led by the intriguingly ambivalent figure of Nariman Narimanov (giant statue πN6, house museum φT3, p87).

In the 1930s, however, Stalin's purges were extremely harsh on people and on monuments. There was even a plan to replace the historic heart of the city with 'appropriately modern blocks'. Fortunately, this never proceeded beyond the Azadlyq Sq area. Indeed, the Old City was later consecrated as a historical preserve.

Recent history

Baku survived WWII (only just, see p44) and grew into one of the five biggest cities

❑ Wind

In Baku the 'air is fine except for the fierce winds which often blow man or beast clean into the sea' – Abdar Rashi ibn Salih, 15th-century historian.

Baku is the 'Chicago of the Caspian' but the gusts and gales for which it is renowned are by no means constant. Maybe two or three times a month, after a cruelly humid lull of some three days (almost unbearable in summer), one can reasonably predict a veritable hurricane to knock loose any carelessly attached debris from roofs and balconies.

The winds take different names according to their direction. A *khazri* blows off the Caspian Sea, while a *gilavar* blows from inland but locals quip that the worst is a north wind, which brings political rather than climatic danger. Thank you big brother Russia.

in the Union but the oil industry was subsequently allowed to run down, for geo-political reasons as well as for lack of capital. Once-great mansions were carelessly divided into cheap apartments and similarly neglected. Much of this was reversed in a new post-independence oil-boom. In the late 1990s a flurry of spendthrift foreign oil execs and businessmen stimulated a rash of flashy new restaurants and bars, but while rents skyrocketed enriching landlords, ordinary citizens were increasingly pushed out into the distant suburbs. Since the completion of the Baku–Ceyhan pipeline in 2004, soaring oil revenues have allowed the city to go into a sudden overdrive of development. Most positively the city's century-old oil-boom mansions have received a long-overdue clean-up and now look especially gorgeous at night thanks to artful lighting that accentuates their mouldings. Meanwhile, many of the city's biggest thoroughfares have sprouted overpasses and pseudo-classical lighting. Parks have lost precious trees but gained ever-more fanciful fountains, several of which perform musical turns. Ugly carbuncles including the Absheron and Azerbaijan hotels have been demolished. Pedestrian underpasses have been lavished with (very slippery) marble and (poorly maintained) escalators. And virtually everywhere shiny new tower blocks have been rising, albeit with little apparent thought given to their location, nor their parking requirements. If planners have their way all this is just the start of a truly astonishing transformation (see box below).

❑ Baku – The new Dubai?

If all the mooted monster-projects go ahead Baku Bay could eventually be bracketed at either end by curvaceous sci-fi worthy 'Moon' buildings (🖥 www.heerim.com) and traversed by an astounding Zig to Bailov causeway. Heerim has also designed a twisting glass spike for the new SOCAR building. Meanwhile Dia (🖥 www.diaholding.com) has already started the wave-formed Heydar Aliyev Cultural Center (near Hotel Excelsior) and a remarkable triple-towered complex designed to look like three flames near Mili Majlis, the Parliament building. And in Bayil, a gigantic flagpole (156m) on imaginatively named National Flag Square was the world's tallest when built (2009).

How many of these projects survive the global economic meltdown and tumbling oil prices that started in late 2008 remains to be seen.

See 🖥 www.skyscrapercity.com/showthread.php?t=533733 to gawp at many of the proposed skyscraper designs.

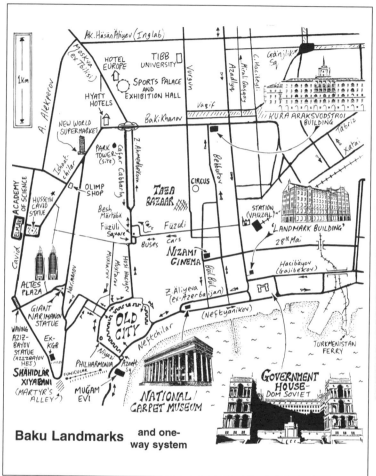

Baku Landmarks and one-way system

❑ **Great viewpoints (see map above)**

* From the 17th floor cocktail-bar and restaurant of the ISR Plaza.
* The site of the former Kirov monument and the new eternal flame dome in Martyr's Alley (Shähidlär Xiyabanı).
* The Old City from restaurants of Museum Inn and Sultan's Inn.

What to see and do

EXPLORING THE OLD CITY
(Icheri Shähär/İçəri Səhər,
Map Σ p83)

Narrow alleys, dozens of small, forgotten little mosques some barely distinguishable from the houses that surround them, a handful of old caravanserais and plenty of quirky, overhanging balconies. This delightful and evocative pastiche nestles in the long, powerful curve of the restored Old City wall, bristling with towers and battlements, but you'd better hurry to see it while any of its antique character remains. During the mid-1990s the mini oil boom seemed in danger of turning every building into an oil company HQ. This trend reversed noticeably for a while after the area was declared a UNESCO World Heritage site, and as bigger companies moved out. Sadly in the last couple of years the builders have returned once more. While most new structures have been very carefully designed and stone-clad to fit tastefully within the city's stylistic cocktail, some of the most recent constructions are unforgivable travesties and the 2007 demolition of the whole south-western corner for a big (if tastefully designed) new hotel caused considerable dismay. Still, there remain homely 'lived-in' corners to discover and it's worth simply launching yourself into the alleys and wandering aimlessly. The map on p83 shows every path and thoroughfare but occasionally some routes are blocked by building work.

Maiden's Tower (see box below; Qız Qalası; Map ΣM14)

Unique in world architecture, this ancient, almost windowless, eight-storey, 29m-high fortress was reconstructed in the 12th century but may have started life as a fire beacon and lookout post as long ago as 500BC. There are some far-fetched suggestions for its cross-sectional shape: that it represents one half of the Yin-Yang oriental symbol of balance, that it's based on the Paisley-arabesque 'buta' motif (a Zoroastrian religious symbol of fire) or that it's inspired by the number 6, the base number of the Babylonian (world's first) counting system.

The name Qız Qalası translates literally as 'Virgin tower', leading to a host of Rapunzel-style, distressed-princess tales.

The most imaginative is of a warped city ruler who fell in love with his own beautiful daughter and asked to marry her. The poor girl was trapped between the obvious revulsion and illegality of her father's incestuous proposal and her duty of paternal loyalty. As a stalling manoeuvre she demanded that he build her a tower that would allow her to view her father/husband's entire domain. Each time the builders announced it was finished she would demand yet another storey be added. Finally when it reached its full height, she climbed to the top to examine the view and threw herself off.

❏ **Some facts and figures about Maiden's Tower**
● Walls 5m thick, an estimated 2900m³ of rock was used.
● The tower originally had seven storeys. The top one was added later as a gun emplacement.
● There were no steps to the first floor – a ladder which could be removed for added defence was used instead.
● Despite its size the 'buttress' pillar doesn't contain any rooms.
● An 'Operion' aperture (hole in the centre) allowed rapid descent between floors and surprisingly good light. This was lost due to remodelling in the early 20th century.
● The mysterious opening on the fifth floor appears to have been a door. Lock and hinge points are visible but nobody knows where the door would have led.

An alternative version accuses Khunsar, the legendary founder of Baku, of locking his guiltless sister in the tower. She threw herself to her death and as retribution God drowned Khunsar's great pastures and created the Caspian Sea.

In fact the term Qız Qalası has nothing whatever to do with young, abused female relatives. It is a name quite commonly applied to fortress towers – 'virginity' referring to the fact that it was never 'penetrated' by the various attackers who besieged it throughout history. True or not, the name gave defenders of such towers a certain feeling of invincibility.

Entry to the tower (AZN2, 11.00-18.00, closed Monday) allows you to climb to the top for good views though the interior exhibits are limited.

On the pedestrianized square outside is a rotunda seat and a useful **pictorial map** of the old city for further exploration. Behind that are the **excavations** of a medieval bazaar along with several interesting carved stones discovered in the area.

Shirvanshah's Palace (ΣP4)

(46 Böyük Qala St; 10.00-19.00 daily; entry AZN2, camera AZN2). The palace site was chosen for its five valuable wells in what was then a forbidding desert. The oldest surviving remnants are 15th century but considerable renovations have been made throughout history. Defensive slits were added to the outer walls during the Russian period.

In 1905, JD Henry reported that plans to turn the palace into a museum had been shelved. Initially it was declared that the space was needed as a hospital for wounded Russian soldiers returning from the war in Manchuria. Ironically, following the appalling massacre within Baku itself, the hospital idea was dropped and the palace became an ammunition store. The complex was finally reconstructed in 1920 and opened to the public. Renovations in 2006 were so extensive that parts of the complex feel virtually new.

At the back of the courtyard area is the *turbe* of court astronomer Seyd Yahya and the Bailov Stones, dozens of carved fragments recovered in 1951 from **Sabail Castle**. Azerbaijan's Alcatraz, Sabail prison island in Baku Bay was originally built in 1235 as Bandar Gala ('port castle'). The whole structure disappeared under the rising Caspian, perhaps with the help of an earthquake, and was only rediscovered when the water level started dropping rapidly in the 1930s and '40s. It is now hidden again.

The Bailov stones of greatest interest to experts are the sections showing bison and somewhat Mongoloid human faces. These elements show the carvers had either a wide

BAKU

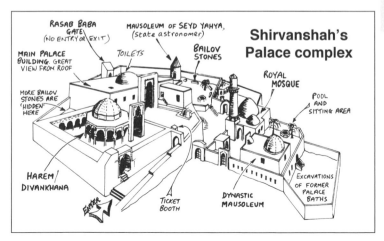

RASAB BABA GATE (NO ENTRY OR EXIT)

MAUSOLEUM OF SEYD YAHYA, (State astronomer)

Shirvanshah's Palace complex

MAIN PALACE BUILDING. GREAT VIEW FROM ROOF

TOILETS

BAILOV STONES

MORE BAILOV STONES ARE 'HIDDEN' HERE

ROYAL MOSQUE

POOL AND SITTING AREA

HAREM / DIVANKHANA

ENTER

TICKET BOOTH

DYNASTIC MAUSOLEUM

EXCAVATIONS OF FORMER PALACE BATHS

international understanding or a pretty poor standard of representation. Whichever is the case, they were certainly not inhibited by the mores of strict Islam which discourages representation of living creatures.

There are photogenic sunset views of the Shirvanshah complex from the rooftop terraces of some neighbouring hotels, notably the Icheri Shähär, though access may be limited to guests only.

Bust of Vahid (ΣN2)

Recently moved to a small garden behind Içəri Səhər metro is a thoughtfully impressive giant **bust of Vahid**. There is rich symbolism in the many contrasting scenes which have been carved into what initially looks like his hair. The overall point is to show the balance between optimism and realism, humour and tragedy for which the poet (who died relatively unknown in 1965) has come to be valued.

Double gates (ΣU12)

It was outside the old city's photogenic Double Gates that the Russian army's Caucasian commander Tsitsianov came in 1806 to receive the keys to the city from the Baku khan. Instead he received an assassin's bullet from the khan's cousin, much to general public delight! The Russian troops fled but returned in force within the year. The area was known as Tsitsanov garden until 1918, its fountain being an important early source of drinking water.

Mosques

The Old City is polka-dotted with tiny mosques. Although few are actually open to visitors or worth a special detour, some are intriguing for their very invisibility – often indistinguishable from neighbouring houses except for the little 'historic monument' plaque rusting quietly on a wall. The most visible mosques have old stone minarets topped with rounded, fluted mini-domes. Baku's oldest is the active little **Mohammad Mosque** (ΣL6) whose 1079 Sinik-kala minaret has a typical stalactite-vaulted parapet support and is encircled by kufic Koranic quotations. The minaret's

staircase was built so small that an apocryphally rotund muezzin once got stuck on the way up and couldn't call the faithful to pray. The **Juma Mechid** (ΣK9), originally 11th century too, was totally re-worked in the early 20th century and now has the most ornately carved façade, best appreciated by walking around the back and into the surrounding courtyard.

Other Old City mosques include: **Bäylär** (19th century but with an old-style minaret, ΣN7), **Gajibani** (16th century, now a house, ΣQ5), **Gileyi** (1309, ΣK2, active), **Haci Heybat** (1791, also a house ΣR5), **Lezghi** (1169, Sunni, ΣL11), **Mäktäb Mosque** (1646, ΣM11), **Molla Ahmed** (ΣR10), **Sheikh Ibrahim** (1415, ΣI6) and **Xıdır** (1301, ΣK5).

Caravanserais

Half a dozen historic caravanserai buildings are crammed within Icheri Shähär. The atmospheric *Karavansara Restaurant* (see p115) occupies both the 14th-century Bukhara Caravanserai and the cavernous 15th-century Multan Caravanserai just across the passage. In the latter a 'secret' swing door leads through into a private dining cavern which was supposedly once the tethering place for camels (notice the holes in wall-stones for tying the ropes). Other caravanserais hold the Mediterranea and Muğam Club restaurants (better food, pp114-15) and the Old City museum offices (ΣI9).

Galleries

The **Center of Contemporary Art** ([CCA], ΣP12, ☎ 492 5906, 11:00-20:00, closed Mon) is run by the talented United Artists' Club. Standards are excellent and this is the place to make contacts if you hope to visit the 'secret' **art studio** loft (φQ2, p87) or the **artists' apartments** (τC1, rear entry door 6) at Inshaatchilar 28.

The CCA's subterranean *café* hosts occasional film nights, writers' group meetings and parties. Outside look up to see some curious carved façade details including a trio of sandstone **cats** (graphic p84) in a faux window.

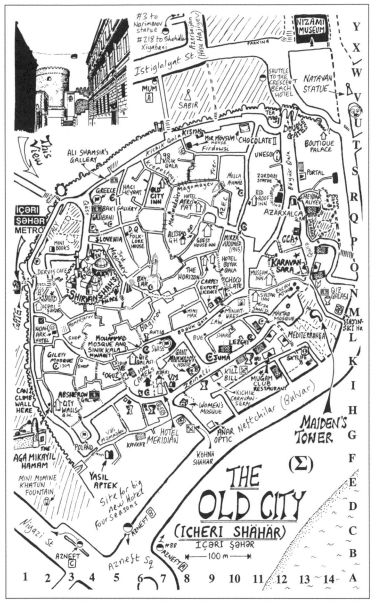

BAKU

The commercial but ever-inspiring **Qız Qalası Gallery** (ΣN14; Qüllä 6, 🖳 www.Qgallery.net, daily 10:30-19:00) has regularly changing exhibitions and an impressive stock of

works by classic Azeri artists. The latter aren't always displayed so ask. Other commercial galleries include **Absheron** (ΣI4), **Bakı** (ΣQ4) and **Ali Shamsir**'s atmospheric little Studio-Gallery (ΣS5, ☎ 497 7136) displaying his impressionistic poppies and women in red. There's a **Miniatures Gallery** (ΣN9) on Böyük Qala.

Oil-boom mansions
Both within and beyond the Old City walls are some superb turn-of-the-20th-century mansions.

Perhaps the most eye-catching exterior is the ornate 1912 Hajinski Mansion (ΣM14) decorated with a selection of stone-vines, gargoyles and animal heads, as well as distinctive overhanging corner windows. It was here that Charles de Gaulle (then an outspoken, independent-minded resistance leader) stayed on 26 November 1944. He was en route to see Stalin in Moscow to discuss the anticipated post-war carve-up of Europe. He'd flown via Tehran to avoid crossing enemy airspace and for reasons unexplained, decided to stay on an extra night in Baku for a performance of Hacibayov's classic Azeri opera *Koroğlu*.

Before merging with Exxon, Mobil spent millions recreating the Pre-Raphaelite/art nouveau interiors of the Gani Mammadov residence (ΣK8), but that's now a private residence not open to visitors. It was built on the site of a 1646 madrassa of which only one stone portal remains, now used as the diminutive Ticmä souvenir shop.

The attractive building at ΣR12 topped off with a statuette (once part of a trio) was once the Ethnographic Museum but is being repurposed as a Heydar Aliyev museum. Baku was much in need of one of those.

Yasil Aptek (ΣF5)
Qasimbey's Hamam was an elegant multi-domed 15th-century bath-house, renovated in the 19th century. Today it houses a small herbal pharmacy (Yasil Aptek, Mon-Sat 10-18:00) beneath the flaking ceiling-domes which had once been colourfully painted with Azeri literary themes. The whole area behind here all the way to Neftchilar was brutally demolished in 2007 to build the new Four Seasons Hotel.

Mir Mövsüm's house
Sit for a few minutes beside the little fountain in the stone patio area opposite 3 Firdowsi St and watch the people passing that house (ΣT8). At least one in three will touch the stone doorway as they pass. Coincidence? Not really. Though there is absolutely no sign this was the Baku residence of Mir Mövsüm, the 'Meat Lord' (see p154), and in the deeply superstitious Azeri form of Islam, his spirit remains a powerful source of good luck. Though a private house, you will be quite welcome to go into the recently gentrified room where the 'boneless one' used to sit. Make a prayer (and a token donation) at the makeshift shrine and feel free to kiss the door on the way out!

Other Old City attractions
For real 'local flavour' there's no beating a good rub down at the 18th-century **Aga Mikayil hamam** (ΣH2, AZN2.50, 8-22.00 women only Mon & Fri, men only other days), though don't expect the big communal pools or majestic vaulting of Istanbul equivalents. A passingly curious private museum displays a room full of **miniature books** (ΣP3, free entry, 11:00-17:00, closed Mon & Thu, ☎ 492 9464), the smallest of which is just 2mm across – remarkable, though still over double the size of the world record holder (0.9mm by 0.9mm). Jazz fans might appreciate the appealing **house museum of Vagif Mustafazade** (ΣI8). It's in the alley beside hotel Meridian, marked by an expressive bust-plaque (see graphic p57).

Carpet and souvenir shops
Icheri Shähär has various interesting carpet, 'antique' and souvenir **shops**, often tucked away in stone nooks and corners. Browsing

can be fun but before you buy read pp60-1 (Carpets) or pp58-9 (Art), and leave plenty of time (preferably two weeks) to certify your purchases for export.

AROUND THE OLD CITY – SUGGESTED WALK (Map p86)

The suggested walking route arcs clockwise arc around the northern side of the Old City ramparts where you'll find much of Baku's finest century-old architecture. The starting point, Azneft, is easy to reach by bus (#88, #20 etc). Or take the funicular down from Shähidlär Xiyabani (p102) then walk past the heroic fountain-statue of dragon-slaying **Bahram [1]**, a character from Nizami's Seven Beauties (and Firdowsi's Khamsa). Although sights on both sides of busy Niyazi and Istyglalyat streets are covered, beware that the only safe crossing point between Azneft and Fountains Sq is the underpass at Metro Içäri Şähär.

Azneft Square

Azneft Square (Azärneft Meydani, φH5) is known to many expats as 'SOCAR circle' since **SOCAR** (State Oil Company of the Azerbaijan Republic) has its HQ here in a solid 1896 stone mansion decorated with leaf and lion motifs. That building was originally constructed for folk singer Mir Babayev who turned tycoon when he just happened to hit oil on a piece of land that he'd received as a gift to thank him for giving a particularly fine performance.

Next door the new but classically styled, stone-clad tower is the **Heydar Aliyev Foundation [2]** (💻 www.heydar-aliyev-foundation.org). There's reputedly a museum within but only invited guests get shown around.

National Art Gallery

The National Art Gallery **[3]** (☎ 492 4196, 10-17.00 Tue-Sun, last entry 16.30 or earlier) is housed in two fine oil-boom mansions; the entry fee (local/foreigner AZN1/2.40) should include both buildings but if one is closed there are no reductions.

Enter via the lower building, built in 1891 for the Dutch representative of

Rothschilds. In the early Soviet era the building was an official residence of party leaders including Nariman Narimanov. There are a couple of minor works by Canaletto and Raphael along with cabinets of chinaware, a haggard bust of Seneca and a range of 19th century European landscapes. Azeri items include 3000-year-old pottery, copies of some Shäki palace murals and Azim Azimzade's satirical sketches depicting 1930s village life. Don't miss the upper floor Oriental Room. Here Cupid gets too busy to shoot his arrows leaving a 2000-year-old Apollo immune to the charms of a swooning Bartolini maiden.

The upper building was formerly St Mary's School for Girls but now houses an impressive collection of Azeri modern art. In pride of place are many splendid works by Sattar Bahlulzade. Don't miss Zeinalov's entrancing *Muza*, Nariman-bekov's *Muğam* nor the near-kissing pair of wooden sculptures called *Friendship* (G Abdullayev). The quality is a little diluted by the inevitable inclusion of dull, portrait-carpets of Ataturk, Rasulzade et al but is rescued with Rashid Heidarzade's evocative *Wrestling Match*.

Around the gallery In the courtyard behind gallery building #2 you'll find **bullet-riddled busts** of Hacibayov, Natavan and Bül Bül **[4]**. These originally stood in Shusha, Nagorno Karabagh, but were dismantled by the invading Armenians and sold to a Tbilisi scrap-metal dealer whence by chance they were rescued.

The dour, 14-storey marble-faced block directly north was built during the 1980s as offices for the Communist Party and is now the **President's Office** (aparat) **[5]**. Beware that police manning roadblocks in front don't appreciate photographs or even the sight of a camera.

Philharmonia

The splendid gilt-roofed building across Niyazi St is the **Philharmonia [6]** concert hall. Originally conceived as a casino, it was vaguely based on the Monte Carlo equivalent with a dome slightly

BAKU

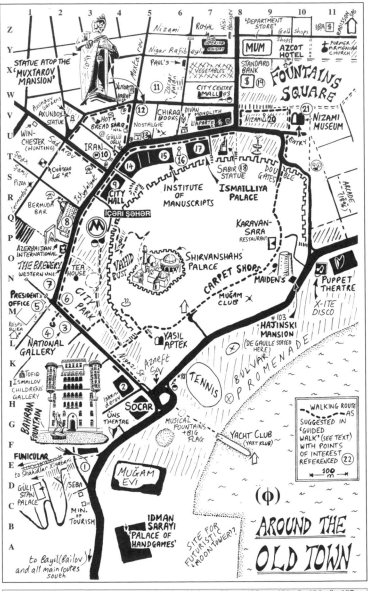

'Islamicized' by an architect who reputedly sketched the outline with a cigar stub during a moment of inspiration. Its construction in 1910 caused storms of protests because of the need to fell 300 precious trees from City Park to make the space. Every tree and all the necessary soil in which to grow them had been laboriously imported and nurtured (see box p90). The open-air stage, added later, became the subject of further controversy when it was claimed that the new owners of the Rothschild Mansion (now the Art Gallery) had bribed the builders to orientate it such that they could watch performances from home.

Istyglalyat St

When the outer wall of the Old City was torn down in the 19th century, Istyglalyat (Independence) St had room to develop its fine apartment houses and grand governmental offices amid the meticulously watered trees. Originally known as Nikolevskaya (after Tsar Nikolai I) and later Komunistischeskaya, only traffic has diminished the charm of this great crescent and almost every building has a tale to tell.

With its splendidly restored pseudo-Safavid mouldings and overhanging window-boxes, the **Sadıxov Mansion [7]** was built by merchant **brothers** and housed prominent 1918 democrat Fatalixan Xoyski. Beyond the prominent privately run **Western University**, the building at 31 Istyglalyat was the biggest building in Baku when completed back in 1915. Hidden away on the uppermost attic-floor is a series of over 20 **artists' studios [8]**. These are private and totally unadvertised, reached by several long flights of steps from the westernmost entry door, then by a locked spiral metal staircase. To get in you'll need to make a rendezvous with one of the artists, easiest by going first to the Center for Contemporary Art (p82).

Içäri Şähär ('Old City') **metro** has been recently redesigned with a striking if discordant Louvre-style glass pyramid roof. From its first month of operation the glass was found to let the rain through. The builders told the press that it wasn't their fault as the weather had been fine during construction so they weren't to have

known! A pedestrian arched-gate in the sturdy wall behind leads handily into the Old City near Shirvanshah's Palace (p81) and the brilliant **bust of Vahid** (p82).

Içäri Şähär metro was known till 2008 as Bakı Soveti, the Communist-era name for the sturdy 1870 **city hall [9]**. That's an iconic structure attractively mixing red brick and mansard stonework and topped with a clock tower. Notice the 'three fire-balls', Baku's city symbol.

Narimanov apartment Doctor, revolutionary and 1920s political leader, Narimanov was instrumental in consolidating a Soviet grip on post-independence Azerbaijan, but daringly stood up to Lenin and Stalin over territorial questions re Nakhchivan and Nagorno Karabagh. His gigantic statue still stands at πN6. But the man himself seems to have had a pretty modest life if his simple apartment-museum (over the sub-post office at #35 Istyglalyat St **[10]**, ☎ 492 0515, 10-17:00 Mon-Sat) is anything to go by. A green baize desk. An ink blotter. A tiny single bed that hints at a pretty monastic love life. Perhaps the most fascinating thing here is the guest-book which charts the astoundingly few visitors that have passed through since 1978. Most were awe-struck international communists hailing Narimanov as a 'great, inspirational revolutionary' in a plethora of exotic scripts.

Diversion from Istyglalyat St

Walking up past the attractive **Iranian embassy** building brings you to **Axundov Bağı/Akhundov Gardens**, a triangular handkerchief of park surrounded by several fine mansions. In the park sits a statue of **Misr-Fatali Axundov**, a great Azeri writer and critic known as the 'Muslim Molière' and reportedly first driven to the quill by the shock news of Pushkin's death. Perhaps Akhundov's most poignant work is *Monsieur Jordan and Shah Mastali*, which depicts the growing awareness of the dullness of local life stemming from meeting a privileged foreigner. It's a theme to which many educated young Baku folk can easily relate today.

The dumpy, concrete **music school** [11] is a dispiriting victory for mediocrity over style. On this spot from 1888 until the 1930s stood the fabulous Alexander Nevski Cathedral. A vast wedding-cake fantasy in the St Basil's mould, it was built with public donations from those of various faiths. It would have been one of the world's most iconic monumental churches today had it survived Stalin's campaign of anti-religious destruction. When it was dynamited in 1936, Muslims and Christians were said to have wept side by side at the loss of their city's most recognizable landmark.

The 1912 **Muxtarov Mansion [12]** is one of Baku's most beautiful oil-boom mansions with a glorious penchant for spires and pseudo-Gothic details echoing many a university building from

Cambridge to Cornell. Notice the Arthurian-carved **sandstone knight** on the gable high above the doorway. Adding this statuette was the building's final finishing touch, a moment of glory and recompense for master builder Imran Gasimov who was to cement it into place personally. However, as he finished the task, Gasimov slipped and fell to his death. To cap off the tragedy, Gasimov's wife killed herself too, unable to face the sudden transition from fashionable flapper to widow in permanent black chador. Muxtarov himself came to a sticky end here too in 1920 (see box below). Despite all these misfortunes the building was used till 2007 as Baku's foremost **Palace of Happiness** (ie wedding hall). Ever since it has been undergoing wholesale redecoration. Rumours suggest

❏ The Muxtarov mansion
This neo-Gothic masterpiece was the home of the millionaire Murtuza Muxtarov (1855-1920) who built it as a surprise Valentine's Day gift for his (second) wife, Liza Taghinova. She is supposed to have adored a similar building that she'd noticed while doing the 'grand tour' in Italy, so Muxtarov simply paid the renowned Qasumov brothers to build a copy. This was the topping to a relationship which reads straight from the pages of fairy-tale legend: lowly born Muxtarov, son of a Märdäkän carter, was a self-educated technician who became a major supplier of support equipment to the burgeoning oil industry. He fell in love with the daughter of his Ossetian aristocrat host while on business in Vladikavkaz, but his lack of pedigree resulted in the blank refusal of all his petitions to marry her. Realizing that even with his immense wealth, straightforward bribery couldn't buy him the woman of his dreams he adopted lateral thinking and funded instead the construction of two beautiful mosques, one in Ämircan (p146), the other more tactically in Vladikavkaz (looking curiously reminiscent of Baku's philharmonia, see 🖳 www.prok.uniyar.ac.ru/img/n/11641.jpg). Won over by his apparent piety, her father changed his mind and sanctioned the marriage. Mrs Muxtarov's education and cultured upbringing brought a strong new element to the Baku social scene. The new mansion became the venue for daily receptions and fundraisers for Mrs M's good deeds with orphans and the Muslim Women's Philanthropic Association. Curiously Muxtarov's spurned first wife is generally omitted from the whole jolly tale.

Muxtarov, as a ruthless industrialist, despised the Bolshevik troublemakers who led damaging strikes during much of the period. He is said to have personally threatened Stalin with 'a whipping or worse' if he came near any of Muxtarov's factories. Yet the old man was too stubborn to flee during 1920 when the Red Army was marching to overthrow the Azerbaijan Democratic Republic, convinced that no 'worker' would dare cross the threshold of his palace. However, two Bolshevik horsemen rode straight in. Without dismounting they demanded his surrender to the new communist authorities. 'Get off my bloody carpet' bawled Muxtarov and shot them dead. He shot himself straight after, though his wife somehow escaped out the back door.

that when renovations are complete it will become an exclusive guesthouse reserved for government guests and visiting heads of state.

Institute of Manuscripts area

Judging by the number of '.... lived here' memorial plaques, the building at the next corner **[13]** was clearly an apartment block for the great and the good. These are of no special interest until you look at the dates – chillingly, almost all died between 1936 and 1938 – the years of the Stalin-Bağirov purges. Across the road the **Institute of Economics building [14]** was originally a 1904 boys school while the building next door, **[15]**, was built as the Empress Alexandra Girls' School. It was the first modern girls' school in the Islamic world. Oil baron Tağıyev footed the bill on the premise that 'educating a boy educates one man, while educating a girl educates a whole future family'. The powerful Muslim 'clergy' of the day were initially against female education but fortunately proved eminently bribeable. And presumably the sycophantic name (for the Russian Tsar's wife) helped with the secular authorities. From 1918 to 1921 the building was used as the national parliament of the Azerbaijan Democratic Republic which moved here from its initial site in Gänjä once Turkish troops had scared away the Dunsterforce.

The **former parliamentary chamber** with its ornate interior, gilded mouldings, Moorish windows and large chandelier has been colourfully renovated and is used to display old miniatures, documents and beautifully illuminated books of the **Füzuli Institute of Manuscripts**. The star exhibits include some majestic 18th- and 19th-century Korans, a 1649 copy of Nizami's *Xamsa* (illustrated in Samarkand) and an especially intricate illuminated divan of the Persian poet Hafez. The

octagonal cabinet at the far end contains the personally embroidered album of the Karabagh princess-poet Natavan. The director noted that older, arguably finer examples of many books are held in the British Library/Museum in London. Far from calling for their prompt return, he pointed out the great good fortune that they had been so kept: most of the original Azeri collection was burnt during one of Stalin's bad moods in the 1930s. The exhibition is open to those with a special interest but you'll need to make an appointment (☎ 492 3197, 🖳 manuscript@dcacs.ab.az) at least one day in advance. Across the hallway within the same building is the **Hussein Cavid Apartment Museum** (☎ 492 7049). It's of very limited interest to the casual visitor and his house museum in Nakhchivan city (p309) is more appealing.

Ismayıllı Palace

Beyond a **Yusif Mammadaliyev statue [16]** the gorgeous mosaic-fronted **Ismayıllı Palace [17]** was built by infamously tight-fisted millionaire Nağiyev (not Tağiyev), loosely based on the design of the Doge's Palace in Venice. The reason for his lavish expenditure on this building was to memorialize his son, Ismail, who had died of TB. Nonetheless, it was so tough for him to spend the money that he asked his accountant to hide the costs from his eyes when he signed the authorization. Initially the building served as the HQ of the Ismaili Co and of the Muslim Philanthropic Organization but it was gutted by arsonists during the inter-ethnic riots of the 1918 'March Days'. The rebuilt version has retained most of the flavour of the original but incorporates Soviet stars instead of Koranic calligraphy as a design motif. Today it is the administrative office of the Academy of Sciences (the Academy itself has its main building in the great Stalinist block at metro Elmar Akadamesi, p103).

Ismayıllı Palace – façade

Towards Fountains Square

A **statue [18]** of the Shamakha-born poet Sabir has stood on its present spot since the 1920s. Sabir famously decried the backwardness of Islamic institutions. Quotes like 'I'm not afraid of ghosts or devils, but I fear a country where Mollahs rule' would have had CIA recruiters drooling. However, his anti-authoritarian views probably wouldn't have gone down so well with Stalin. Sabir's death in 1911 meant that this theory was never tested. But in 1958 when the old statue was replaced by a new Sabir sitting in a chair, the authorities had the last laugh: to have someone 'sit down' is a local euphemism for sending them to jail.

The powerful 'double gates' (p82) lead back into the old city. Alternatively descend the stairway near the archetypal 1930s **Standard Bank building** (ATM,

exchange) **[19]**. Halfway down a proud **Nizami statue [20]** surveys a particularly brilliant view of the statue-studded **Nizami Literature Museum [21]**. Second only to the Maiden's Tower as Baku's most photographed building, its façade looks especially appealing at night when the statue-filled arches are delightfully back-lit. The figures depict great Azeri writers from Füzuli (15th century) to Cäfär Cabbarly (20th), getting younger north to south. The building was originally the Metropole, Baku's top hotel, but was remodelled into a museum in 1940 preserving only the ground floor. The interior was visually disappointing on my last visit but has recently been under reconstruction. Exhibits rehash great historical themes stressing the importance of literary figures in defining a national identity.

❏ Parks, soil and water

Today Baku is a green oasis of parks and tree-lined avenues despite its desolate surroundings but the whole verdant character of the city is artificial. Before the oil boom there was barely a tree. Fifteenth-century Arab writer Abdar Rashid ibn Salih observed: 'The soil in the town is infertile and there is only one small part where gardens of figs and pomegranates can be seen'. Arriving here in the 1860s/70s the Nobel brothers, along with other homesick European entrepreneurs, set out to change all that. They had the novel idea of importing soil using their newly designed oil tankers. These would otherwise have returned empty from delivering exported crude. The city elders agreed to help by placing a tax on all returning tanker ships which did not bring soil or tree saplings to plant in it. Within a few years the city began to sprout the parks and avenues which are today its landmarks but these had to be watered. Before the 19th century Baku's only supply of fresh water would have come from underground streams, accessed by *ovdans* (sketch p66).

At first, the Nobels watered their new park with water produced ingeniously from condensed steam (a by-product of the oil cracking process). But, as with other desert cities, such as Las Vegas, the sudden economic boom required dramatic engineering solutions to ensure that the exploding population had something to drink. An extraordinary canal was cut all the way from the Russian border to carry the cool, fresh mountain water of the Samur river all the way to Baku where today, as then, it is stored in a great reservoir in the suburb of Xırdalan. A vast engineering project that started in 2007 is underway to supplement this supply with fresh mountain water piped in from near Qäbälä.

Meanwhile, laborious care is taken to maintain the city's parks which are often watered from tanker lorries while trees receive manicures from men wielding axes. Water remains a valuable resource which one cannot take for granted. Homes without large tanks can still be without supply for part of the day and there's at least one filling station in the city which on closer inspection proves to be dispensing not petrol but water.

CENTRAL BAKU (map pp92-3)
Fountains Square (▲ Fәvvarälör Meydani, ✪ Ploshad Fontanka)

Fountains Sq is the hub of Baku's strolling and shopping district. Originally the site of a military encampment, the then much smaller square was known a century ago as Parapet and was hemmed in by tram lines. These days it is a spacious, tree-dappled pedestrian area of sporadically operating fountains ringed by boutiques, mobile phone shops and a slowly increasing scattering of terrace cafés.

Along the diagonal eastern edge of the not-very-square square are a series of metal statuettes (a peacock, a perfume bottle etc) which were designed to hint artistically at the nature of the facing shops. The images worked well in the Soviet era when a shop stayed the same for decades. Such certainties are lost in today's commercial environment and the creations now appeal as random pure art.

At the eastern 'nose' of the 'square', **Passaj** ('Art Alley') follows the boutique-filled arches of a former Nağiyev Mansion. It is a great place to rummage through tourist bric-a-brac, old Soviet coins and stamps, not-really-so-rare Russian edition Rolling Stones 33rpms etc. You can get a portrait drawn or silhouette cut while you wait but the paintings on sale are trashy.

The rooftop *café terrace* of the Nargiz Mall (above McDonald's) is a good place to watch the world go by (though the café interior is disappointing).

'Boomland'

There is a very approximate parallelogram of central Baku to the south and east of Fountains Square on whose narrow, mainly quiet, tree-shaded streets you will find most of the expat bars and better cafés plus a gaggle of brilliant old oil-boom mansions. For the want of a better name I've labelled the area 'Boomland' – better suggestions are welcome!

The city's **Historical Museum** (∂E5, 4 Tağiyev St, ☎ 493 3648) occupies the splendid 1896 mansion of Zeinalabdin Tağiyev, once the richest of all the oil barons. The upper floor's oriental rooms have magnificently exotic décor and the exhibitions have

greatly benefited from a 2008 renovation but the entry fee (AZN10 for foreigners) is steep considering locals/Turks pay only AZN2/5.

Despite the fame of poet **Samed Vurğun**, his **House Museum** (∂C4, ☎ 493 5652, 4 Tarlan Aliyarbayov St, top floor) is looking pretty worn these days with sickly green paint peeling from the walls and an interior that's rather characterless except for the great man's hat and coat left on the peg by the door.

Built on the site of a 1909 original, the 1998 **Musical Comedy Theatre** (∂B5, ☎ 493 5101, 🖳 http://muzkomediya.az) was one of the first Baku theatres to be rebuilt post-independence. The intricate façade is attractive though being fashioned from unplastered concrete its longevity is questionable. Tickets cost around AZN20.

Carpet Museum (∂C5, Muzeyi Märkäzi)

The imposing, former Lenin Museum is a pseudo-Greek acropolis facing Baku's waterfront and built on the site of a 19th-century circus. While most of the space

 appears to be used as stairways and atrium, the building still finds room for three museums of which by far the biggest draw is the **Carpet Museum** (☎ 493 2019, 09.30-17.00, closed Mon). At any one time it displays around 1300 of the 6000 carpets of the permanent Lätif Kärimov Collection, named after the scholar who catalogued and categorized Azerbaijani carpets into 144 styles and types.

The exhibits are divided between flat weave and knotted carpet sections and displayed by style and geographical area. The definition of Azerbaijani for this purpose includes Tabriz and areas now in northern Iran, plus Borchali (now Marneuli, Georgia) and other Azeri villages that Stalin gave to Georgia/Armenia. The collection also houses 600 carpets which were rescued from the museum's Shusha branch days before the Armenian takeover in 1992.

Entry costs AZN5. Add AZN3 for some useful explanations by Asya, the English-speaking guide (day off on Thur).

BAKU

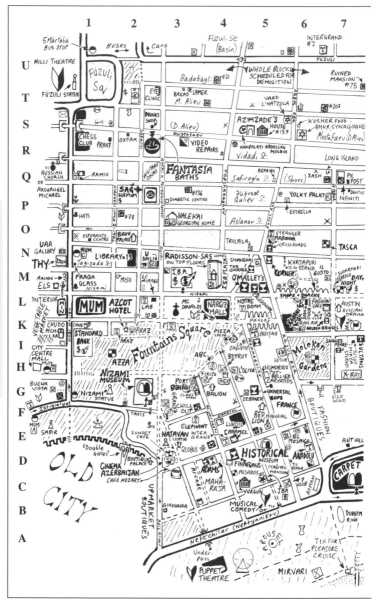

BAKU

Central Baku (ə)

Asya is also willing to help you through the minefield of carpet buying and certification and does city tours as well.

Upstairs, the **Theatre Museum** (10.30-18.00 Tue to Sun but not Fri) requires a separate ticket (AZN3). Its collection of programmes, costumes and photographs of Azeri thespian greats is of limited appeal to a foreigner with little knowledge of the personalities. Nonetheless, its mere existence reinforces the importance of theatre in the national psyche. A young Heydar Aliyev manages to show up in several photos.

The **Museum of Independence** (Istiqlal Muzeyi) across the hall displays a small collection of old photographs and the odd banknote. Despite the more hopeful new 'oil' room, the depressing theme is suffering and there's little to warrant the AZN3 entry fee.

Molokan Gardens A century ago this little park was awash with people of various nationalities as it was the only reliable place to find moneychangers. These days it remains cosmopolitan, if economically stratified. Veterans dawdle on park benches showing off their Soviet medals while expats congregate at a popular bar-restaurant perched in the middle of a little pond. Well that was true until late 2008 when the park was closed for unspecified renovations.

Behind the gardens, the **Russian Drama Theatre** (💻 www.rusdrama-az.com) has a bold façade with a series of stylized off-white arches nestling above a Vurğun bust. Renovated in 2008, this is the third incarnation of what was originally the pagoda-domed 'Mikado Theatre', a wonderfully idiosyncratic turn of the 20th-century palace of mock chinoiserie.

**Russian Drama
Theatre (∂K7)**

Artist **Yusuf Mirza** (☎ 493 5285, mobile ☎ 50 347 8543, 💻 yusif@torba.com) adds philosophical good humour to his brilliantly varied portfolio. He welcomes visitors to his evocatively cramped studio above 4 Xaqani St (∂I7) but do phone ahead. To enter take the passage beneath the building opposite the Russian Drama Theatre's ticket office then take the steps immediately to your left.

Stretching from ∂B4 to D4 is Baku's original 19th-century **shopping arcade**. Started in 1896 it was commissioned by the oil baron Tağiyev, conveniently close to his own mansion in case his wife should need to dash out for a bit of retail therapy. It's still attractive though some of the character has been lost in renovation and the shops aren't as suave as many of Baku's more exclusive boutiques.

**The city centre
(Map pp92-3; L5–M12)**
Baku's youthful passageiata continues east from Fountains Square along pedestrianized **Nizami St** (Torgovaya). Shops here are moving slowly upmarket if less dauntingly so than the boutiques of Rasul Rza. However, opposite an arched arcade is one exception, the heartwarmingly naive **Ivanovka shop** (∂L6). Here, uncompromising old babooshkas in blue overalls sell cheese from barrels and unwashed fresh produce direct from the Molokan-Russian village of the same name in the Ismayıllı region (see p209).

Across Vurğun St is a small park, till recently surveyed by a graceful **statue of Nasimi**. Not to be confused with Nizami, Nasimi was a 15th-century poet, mystic and heretic who got himself skinned alive for being a little too progressive minded.

**Nasimi –
AWOL from ∂M8**

BAKU

However his statue went AWOL during 2007.

Above the park soars one of Baku's oddest architectural mongrels, a new apartment looking as though a late-1940s stone edifice has had a chunk of 1990s tower-block implanted in its midriff.

Nizami cinema

Nizami cinema The massive 1934 Nizami Cinema (∂P10) has a certain art-deco appeal with pink walls and stained-glass-backed statuettes tempering its great Stalinist bulk. It was designed by Dadashev and Useynov who also master-minded the Axundov Library and Nizami Museum. As well as a cinema, it currently hosts video game salons and the long-lasting Black Jack disco bar, but the whole building is due to be totally renovated in the coming years.

Niyazi Museum The house museum of orchestral conductor **Niyazi** (∂O10, ☎ 493 1836, 10-18:00, AZN1) is entered from the rear of 21 Bül Bül, accessed via Hazi Aslanov St. Find a stairway in the far corner, ring the bell, then punch the code (6-7 at the time of writing) to get into the block. You get to see Niyazi's workroom with stubbed-out cigarette, specs and French thesis on the development of Koroğlu as a narrative theme. Then there is his touchingly ordinary bedroom and dining room looking much like any better Azeri home of the 1980s. CDs of Niyazi's work are available and on the first Wednesday of each month there is a free (but unadvertised) mini-concert here.

The opera-ballet (∂M12) In 1909 the wealthy Manilov brothers set off to tour Europe. En route they were captivated by an Argentinean opera star and tried to persuade her to visit them in Baku. 'Is there somewhere for me to perform?' she demanded having little idea what sort of place Baku might be. There wasn't. But the brothers brushed over this detail and assured her that there would be by the time she arrived. The beautiful opera-ballet was thus planned, designed, and completed within a year. Although ravaged by fire in 1985, the building was rebuilt three years later with its original gilded décor, torso columns, rounded proscenium and elegant galleries.

Tickets for a full ballet/opera typically cost AZN20-70. Standards are generally high but even lesser productions have lavishly captivating sets that make up for occasionally static performances. Try to avoid the cheapest gallery seating where annoying student-spectators chat endlessly throughout the show.

Sahil Gardens
Until recently this park hosted a large white figure who appeared to have exhausted himself burrowing out of the ground. However, he and his massive concrete 'halo' were dug up in January 2009 and with him the communal grave of the historically ambivalent **26 Commissars** which the statue had honoured (see box pp96-7). Initially the plan was to build a car park on the site. Now it's rumoured that the park will be preserved but with a new statue celebrating Nuri Pasha (1881-1949) who led the 1918 Army of Islam, the very

force whose march on Baku caused the Commissars to flee.

Around the square are several appealing buildings. The eyecatching **Axundov Library** is punctuated with statues in the style of the Nizami Museum albeit without the Nizami's blue majolica-tiled mosaic backing. It's the national book repository and is open to readers and researchers by request. Entrance is free and there's a modest English-language section but, just as at London's British Library, the signing-in process requires ID checks and a verifiable scholarly purpose.

The similarly grand building next door was previously the Turkish Embassy and Istanbul-bound buses still tend to start their 36-hour journeys from nearby.

Around the corner to the north-east, the stone-pillared **Behbutov Song Theatre** (∂L12, ☎ 493 9460) started life as a synagogue. Its cubic interior space has a cosy glamour but the variety of off-beat events staged here are rarely well publicized.

Across the north-west corner of the square, the grey building at 15 Bulbul Av (∂K10) hosts the **Artists' Union Gallery** ('Rässamlar Ittifaq', ☎ 498 6426) which stages imaginative, oft-changing art exhibits in a variety of media. Upstairs are two house museums but to reach them you'll have to go around the back via Panchos Lane, then ring the buzzer to get the entry code for the corner door of the courtyard (the courtyard guard can show you which one). The apartment of historical novelist **Mammad Said Ordubadi** is yet another attraction that's under renovation. Just across the landing is the **Bül Bül Memorial Museum**. Literally translated as

---

❏ The 26 Commissars

In March 1918 a gang of Bolshevik commissars seized power in Baku. Their 'Baku Commune' was an immediate disaster; during the 'March Days' which followed thousands of ethnic Azeris died in the worst inter-communal violence since 1905. And even their allies soon turned against them as they proceeded to give away Baku oil to Russia.

By the summer they'd been ousted and the 26 leaders were languishing in jail when 'liberating' Turkish troops finally reached Baku and started a siege. The new Menshvik 'People's Dictatorship' (also communists), who had taken control invited in British troops. But instead of the rescue force they had hoped for only the tiny Dunsterforce arrived. The Brits patently failed to add any fighting spirit to the mutually loathing coalition of defenders (Menshviks, Bolsheviks, White Russians and Dashnak Armenians), and managed to slip quietly out of port just before it was too late. In the chaos the 26 Bolshevik commissars escaped from jail and somehow got aboard the good ship *Turkmen*. Full of evacuating Russians and Armenians fleeing the coming bloodbath, the *Turkmen* was supposedly bound for 'red'-controlled Astrakhan. However, the hated commissars' faces were recognized and once the captain discovered their presence aboard, he changed course. The ship headed instead for Krasnovodsk (now Turkmenbashi in Turkmenistan), tenuously controlled by anti-Bolshevik Transcaspia.

The 26 discovered the new course and an eminently cinematic struggle ensued. They finally overpowered the crew and, with a gun to his head, the captain was forced to change course for Astrakhan once again. Commissars, however, aren't always good at reading quadrants and by a series of navigational tricks the ship arrived before dawn in Krasnovodsk, not Astrakhan after all. By the time they realized they'd been fooled the commissars had been arrested. Within a few days their bullet-riddled corpses lay gathering flies in an isolated spot in the Turkmen desert. Summarily executed. But by whom? We may never know.

The commissars' arrival was certainly a headache for the authorities in Krasnovodsk who had reason to fear Bolsheviks stirring up trouble against them.

nightingale, Bül Bül was the unanimously accepted pseudonym of Murtuza Rza Mammadov (1897-1961), Azerbaijan's most celebrated singer and musicologist. His lovingly maintained apartment almost feels lived in despite the many cases of exhibits, posters and photographs. And in a sense it is. The greatest delight of my first visit here was to sit down for a glass of tea with the cultured elderly lady-manager who turned out to be none other than Mrs Adilya Mammadova, the great Bül Bül's widow. She had been 25 years his junior when they married. An obliging, English-speaking guide who sometimes helps out is their granddaughter.

The museum has several points of quirky interest. Note the malevolent sprites carved into the bedhead and the old Edison phonograph with which Bül Bül

began the work of recording traditional folk music for cataloguing and transcription. Notice the Arabic script on Bül Bül's Soviet passport with which he travelled to Milan to study at La Scala. Leninist books still grace the shelves, there are photos of a young Heydar Aliyev at Bül Bül's funeral. Most intriguing of all is the curt telegram from Stalin offering personal thanks for Bül Bül's wartime donation of some 200,000 roubles to the Red Army. How a good Socialist came to have such a disposable fortune is not explained.

The Bulvar (Caspian Waterfront)

Gardens, fountains and a wide promenade sweep attractively around Baku's Caspian shore from the gigantic **Dom Soviet/ Government House** (see p100) to the **Idman Sarayi** (dubiously known in

Their arrival was reported to Ashgabat where the Transcaspian government was working with Reginald Teague-Jones of the British secret service. A real-life 007, Teague-Jones was a shadowy gentleman spy who had spent much of the past few years flitting about central Asia single-handedly trying to prevent the region falling under Bolshevik influence.

Ostensibly the British wanted to get hold of the Commissars as bargaining chips for dealing with Moscow. However, the Bolsheviks later blamed Teague-Jones himself for ordering their execution. Once Bolshevik power had taken a firm grip over Russia and its empire the 26 Commissars' atrocious management record in Baku was forgotten. They became heroes of the communist cause, celebrated right across the USSR until its demise in 1991.

Meanwhile, Teague-Jones became the Salman Rushdie of his day, hounded with death threats till he was forced to assume a new name and altogether new life – the spy who quite literally disappeared. Given the years of propaganda, as well as some discrepancies in Teague-Jones's various accounts of events, it is unlikely that the truth will ever be known. The commissars' bodies were returned to Baku for burial, curiously in Sahil Garden. Above their graves a powerful memorial was built along with an not-quite-eternal flame.

After Azerbaijan's independence in 1991 statues of some commissars (mostly the Armenian ones) were toppled and roads bearing their names changed. Others, including Djaparidze, a 'waving' Azizbekov (at Azizbayov Heyk, лK3) and the Sahil Gardens memorial, survived until early 2009.

When the latter was demolished a minor controversy erupted when it was discovered that three of the bodies beneath were 'missing'. Old rumours started recirculating that the much-despised commune leader, Stepen Shaumian had escaped death in Turkmenistan with help of sympathisers on the Caspian ship. The rumour was promptly quashed by Shaumian's granddaughter who reminded the press that her grandmother had been present at the reburial.

English translation as the 'palace of Handgames', by which they mean basketball, volleyball etc). The reclaimed land behind the latter is slated to become one of Baku's incredible, futuristic new towers if the funding doesn't dry up (see box p78).

Incredibly, the Maiden's Tower (see p80) was, till the 19th century, just metres from the water's edge. In 1884 the Old City's south walls were demolished to create the road that's now Neftchilär and over subsequent years a much wider strip of waterfront was laboriously reclaimed from the Caspian Sea. In 1910 this was further beautified and extended in a project instigated by businessman-politician Mammad Hasan Hajinski. As with other parks in Baku the soil, trees and even the water to maintain them have been transported hundreds of kilometres. Neglected in the 1990s the parks were once again spruced up in recent years, a Geneva-style water-spurt installed offshore and musical fountains created beneath a vast waving Azeri flag between Azneft Sq and the Yacht Club.

Amid the trees are several new **carousel roundabouts** along with some older Soviet-era fairground rides. A turn on the slow-moving **ferris wheel** (1M) offers pleasant views. Out of several park and boulevard cafés and tea spots, most notable is the archetypally 60s-Soviet style *Mirvari* (Pearl, ∂A6), an open-sided structure with a wonderful clam-shell roof that would be stylishly retro if it were not genuine.

When the weather and sea conditions oblige, it's possible to take half-hour **pleasure cruises** in Baku Bay for AZN1.50. This gives an interesting alternative view of Dom Soviet and the Bulvar, but rides can prove noisy with distorted piped music. Certainly you can't expect the excitement of equivalent trips back in the 1860s. One 19th-century group, after 90 minutes in a rowing boat, rounded a promontory into another bay where bubbles were rising so that the sea 'looked as if it were boiling'. By throwing out some burning tow the waves caught fire and 'flames could be seen dancing up and down with the waves' (*Old Ali*, John Osmaston).

North of Fountains Square

Unbridled construction has left the once-attractive back streets north of Nizami St claustrophobically overpowered by numerous new towers. Still, in between many half-forgotten oil-boom mansions remain along with a couple of classic 19th-century hamams. Most notable is the 1887 **Fantasia bath-house** (∂Q2). The lion gargoyles and fine stone façade are grimy and the interior is refreshingly 'real', so far largely untouched by the whirlwind of heavy-handed renovation that has transformed most of Baku in recent years. The bathing suites are simply tiled and unexotic but the tea room retains its late 19th-century picture tiles, mirrors and chandeliers.

The city **Chess Club** (∂S1) is where Baku-born grandmaster Garry Kasparov cut his teeth. Hidden nearby is the silver onion dome of the **Archangel Michael Orthodox church** (∂Q1/πQ9) entered from 38 Zargarpalan St.

Busy Füzuli Sq is overlooked by a statue of poet **Füzuli** (∂T1), the columned athenaeum of the **Milli Theatre** (∂T1, p123) and an ageing five-floor housing block that gives this corner its common nickname 'Besh Märtäbä' (five storeys). If plans go ahead, busy Füzuli St to the west will have its whole southern flank demolished in a vast urban-development plan to create a long central park stretching almost to the railway station. The eastern section is already a meticulously manicured park where a large 21st-century **Heydar Aliyev statue** (∂U12) stretches forth an arm towards the copper-glass National (Milli) Bank tower. Irreverent locals joke that he's gesturing 'Give me the money'!

STATION AREA

In 1883, British tourist Charles Marvin went to Charing Cross station (London), paid £35 and jumped on a first-class train to Baku. Second class would have saved him a tenner. He was not excited with his arrival in the city of wind: 'The train dropped us at a wretched little shanty station, a perfect curiosity of bad roads – alternate sand and rock, full of ruts and undulating like the sea.' He describes gloomy streets of low,

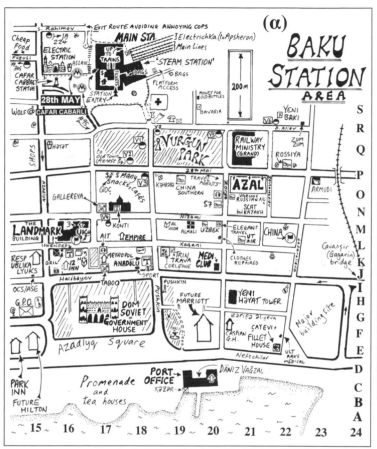

❏ Vurğun Park (Vurğun Bağı) bus stops (see map above)

V1 (αQ18) – #240 (via Keshla), 332 (via Xatai) to Neftchilar

V2 (αP18) – #20 to Azneft Sq and Bayil, #59 to bus station, #90 to Bilǎcari via Milli Bank and 20th Jan metro, #95 to ElmAk

V3 (αP18) – #17, 20 to Azneft Sq

V4 (αM17) – #124 to Lökbatan via Shikh(ov) beach

V5 (αR20) – #175 to Hovsan

V6 (αR22) – #1 to Araz Hotel, Ramstore etc

V7 (αR18) – #36 to Märdäkän

MAP SYMBOL KEY   Ψ p77; Σ p83; φ p86; ∂ pp92-3; α p99; τ p105; π p101; β p106; ϑ p107

forbidding houses and Hotel London – 'a villainous *café chantant* and as dirty a *gostinitsa* as it has been my fortune or misfortune to put up at'.

The next day, Marvin realized that he had treated Baku to the unfair first impression of 'an Italian arriving in London in dense fog and putting up in Wapping'. The exotically oriental 'Steam Railway' station was completed soon after Marvin's arrival, and he gushed: 'For beauty of design and excellence of accommodation it is one of the finest in Russia'. Today its appealing neo-Moorish features are picked out at night by coloured lights that give it a Disneyesque look. That building was superseded in 1926 by the now-disused 'Electric Railway' station whose Persian portals and Central Asian cupolas show that the early Soviet years had not yet cramped architectural creativity. Indeed the architect was the very same NG Bayev who had designed the Opera House 20 years earlier. See pp128-30 for practical station details.

Vurğun Park (αQ19)
Named after the Soviet-era poet whose sizeable statue stands proudly amongst restored fountains, Vurğun Park is overlooked at its eastern end by the very imposing, Stalin-era **Railway Ministry building** (αQ21).

The Landmark (αM16)
Based originally on a classic, redeveloped warehouse, the prestigious Landmark Building now comprises three art-filled buildings and hosts many international companies, the British and EU embassies, a hotel (Tower 3), smooth *café Hazz* and the virtually unmarked *Old Mill Café*, still offering one of Baku's best lunch buffets.

Azadlyq Square and Dom Soviet (αG17)
Looking like a gigantic MC Escher engraving, Government House is a Stalinist masterpiece. **Dom Soviet** (as it is still commonly known) took 20 years to build (1934-54) and originally hosted a Godzilla-sized Lenin statue on the focal plinth. Yet for all its imposing bulk, the interior is crushingly utilitarian and the warren of antiquated offices seem drawn straight from a Kafka-esque nightmare.

WESTERN BAKU
New high-rise blocks are slowly encroaching on the steep-stacked grid of the quietly appealing streets climbing above Muxtarov St with plenty of loveably tumbledown older homes that the Soviets fortunately never got round to demolishing. The area is punctuated with occasional religious buildings and oil-boom mansions, including the splendid **Union of Architects' building** (πP8-9) on Muxtarov St at Tolstoy St. The most interesting section is along Abdulla Shaiq St and around the twin-minareted **Taza Pir Mechid** (πP8). That's Baku's grandest stone mosque, laboriously built between 1905 and 1914 in honour of Nabut Khanum Ashurbekova who had died before it was completed. It is now the centre of Islam in the Caucasus.

Further west the slopes flatten out and the architecture changes to a mixture of bland and triumphant Soviet designs around ElmAk, the lively university area.

Around Nizami metro (πT-U/8-9)
The main road north divides in front of the brilliant **Free Woman statue** (πT9) a bronze beauty on a high plinth, symbolically throwing off her veil. Veils need to be put back on, however, if you visit the nearby Iran consulate. Right beside that the **Yasamal Rayon building** (12 Cäfär Cabbarly) occupies one of Baku's more sensuous oil-boom mansions though its façade detail seems to have suffered in recent heavy-handed cleaning.

The **Haji Sultanli Mosque** nearby has a gilded minaret and the mollah welcomes visitors. It's beside **Nizami Metro** whose platforms are graced with the best mosaic-

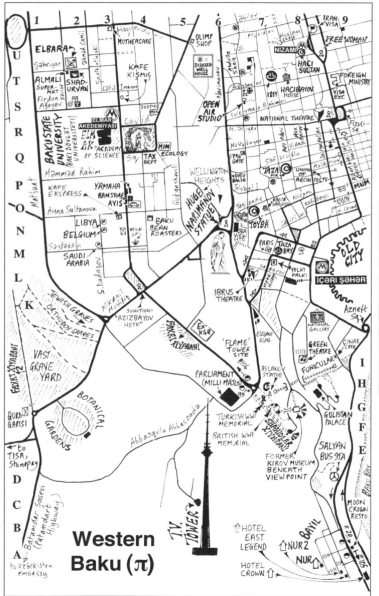

Western Baku (π)

work of any Baku underground station (but don't take photos if you value your camera).

At 67-9 Shamil Azizbekov is the well-maintained house museum of great composer **Üzeyir Hacibäyov** (πT8, ☎ 495 3061). Packed with original furniture, exhibits and a table set for dinner, it is unusually appealing and personal. Exit through the garden of trumpeting terracotta faces.

A new series of business tower blocks line upper Cäfär Cabbarly where, across from the Caspian Plaza, the new Park Tower will look like a 40-storey peanut if built as currently designed.

Abdulla Shaiq (Nagornaya) St and around

This quiet, partially tree-lined street retains numerous 'typical' if unsophisticated old-Baku homes, three disused well towers and an amusing 1901 stone house (at 22 Azizbayov, πS7) with fierce pigs rampant. At #140A (πS7) Zeinal Abdin's **Open-air Studio** is the artist's vine-shaded garden full of partly finished sculptures. Sadly it's not very 'living' these days and the once-colourful mural representing the history of religion is fading into invisibility. The attractive, late 19th-century **Töybä (Imam Hussein) Mechid** is a crenellated stone fortress of a mosque with a great low-hanging chandelier inside. **Abdullah Shaiq** after whom the street is named, was an early socialist who used poetry to highlight the suffering of the oil workers during the boom years, later becoming better known for children's verse. In a sturdy, subdivided stone house, the **apartment museum** (πN7, Mon-Fri 10-18.00) is entered by metal stairs at the back.

A block west is the awesomely immense statue of Azerbaijan's first Communist leader **Nariman Narimanov** (see p87). A block the other way the house-museum of world-famous cellist **Mstislav Rostropovich** (πN7, Tue-Sun 10-17.00, AZN2) has no English explanations. The beautifully renovated **Tazäbäy Hamam** (πL8, ☎ 492 6440) is an 1886 stone structure with three styles of sauna (AZN17) guarded

by doormen wearing gold-edged Dağestani satin cloaks.

Shähidlär Xiyabani
(Martyrs' Alley, former Kirov Park)

A large green area beautifully surveys the bay at **Shähidlär Xiyabani** (entrance πH7). This is and was a cemetery, but during the 1930s the area was used as a pleasure park and funfair. At its heart was a huge 20m-high bronze statue of Kirov, the man who had been a key player in bringing Communist power to Azerbaijan. Kirov had finally proved too popular for Stalin's liking, and was killed. But the deed was disguised by launching a full-scale personality cult and the giant statue survived till 1991 when it was toppled and cut into pieces. However, for now the large concrete square on which he once stood remains and beneath lie the fascinating if utterly vandalized remnants of what was once the Kirov Museum (πG8).

In the early 1990s the park was rededicated as 'Martyrs' Alley' in honour of the Baku citizens massacred by the Red Army on Jan 20th 1990. They are commemorated by a movingly understated row of marble slabs. Thousands of more recent graves are mostly those of heroes of the Nagorno Karabagh conflict. It's a moving sight. There's a small but attractive **mosque** (πH7) and an eternal flame within a tower on a dramatic overlook with sweeping **city views** (πH8). On 20 January every year the site is crowded with mourners commemorating the 1990 massacre.

In the same area are memorials to 1130 Turkish soldiers killed in the WW1 Caucasus campaign. In 2003 a small but highly controversial memorial was added commemorating the 92 British 'Dunsterforce' troops who were killed fighting against them. Given that the Brits were fighting on the 'wrong side' from the Azeri viewpoint, many consider it needlessly provocative that the British monument was placed here in the nation's most hallowed spot. After all, Dunsterville, the British commander at the time, was under orders to destroy the Baku oilfields rather than let them fall to the Turks – an order which he thankfully failed to achieve in his haste to escape. The **memorial** (πG7) has been defaced more than once and is now permanently guarded by a little police box.

Getting there The Funikyulor (**funicular railway**, 20q) runs up from the seafront every ten minutes between 11.00 and 18.30. It's also possible to climb a parallel stairway but don't take photos while you're doing so: several buildings are considered sensitive and guards lurking in the greenery can get aggressive. By minibus take #39 or 177 from near Içäri Şähär (Bakı Soveti) metro, 218 from City Centre Mall (ΣY7/∂H1, φW8), or 106 from near the Hyatt.

Faxri Xiyabanı
Beyond the big ex-KGB complex is Faxri Xiyabanı (πJ5) the ceremonial cemetery of great Azeri artists, sportsmen and politicians including the late president Heydar Aliyev. Most visiting international dignitaries are rounded up here to lay flowers at Heydar's grave as the first stop of their Baku motorcade tour. Some of the memorials are veritable works of art, many by great local sculptor Omar Eldarov. For a full list of who's buried in Faxri Xiyabani see 💻 www.azerbaijan.az/_Sosiety/_Honorary Cemetery/cemetery_02_e.html.

In fact there are two Faxri Xiyabanis, **Faxri Xiyabanı II** (πI1) is at the top end of a vast graveyard with big **Orthodox Christian** (πJ2) and **Jewish** (πJ2) sections. That's near the somewhat scraggy **Botanical Gardens** and **Wolf's Gate** (**Janavar Qapisi**, ΨC2) where an alternative road to Lökbatan (currently being rebuilt) dives suddenly down the side of a long, windswept cliff. This was the site of a classic WWI battle on 14 September 1918 when, despite the difficult terrain, the Turkish army finally broke through into Baku having launched diversionary attacks on Balakhani and Sabunchi. The fate of Dunsterforce (see p43) was sealed. The name Wolf's Gate might come from the Grey Wolf, ancestral symbol of the Turkic people. Or from more literal roaming wolves who scavenged bodies, dumped here back in the harsher era of duelling and traditional blood feuds.

ElmAk
There's a preening commercial area in some fine Stalin-era buildings along Huseyn Cavid pr at whose heart is ElmAk, the bulky **Academy of Sciences Building** (💻 www.science.az). The grandeur of that edifice loses a certain je ne sais quoi from being essentially unfinished but apart from the thundering traffic, the setting is pleasant facing across Huseyn Cavid square towards one of Omar Eldarov's finest sculptures depicting, surprise surprise, **Huseyn Cavid** (πQ4). The square is ringed by various ministry buildings while set behind is the State University (Bakı Dövlät Universiteti, πR1) and a bustling district of internet cafés, cheap eateries and mobile phone shops. A little further north there's also a little scattering of better restaurants and drinking places that are not necessarily worth a long trek from the centre but offer a decent alternative for the increasing number of expat residents living nearby or up in **Stonepay** (ΨH2).

Intriguing **Elbara** (πU2, ☎ 510 3787, 💻 www.elbara.az) has a pirate-ship-themed pub (Efes AZN3) and a variety of dining environments including curious little golden-walled cabins over the pub, a large tastefully spacious party room and a more modest downstairs restaurant where Muğam players serenade diners from a kilim-draped divan (from 8pm).

Shadurvan (πT2, ☎ 437 4533) is a wonderfully evocative exotic tea parlour with embroidered cushions and drapes, stylized bedouin 'tent' sections and a little eight pointed star pool. Tea costs AZN5, qalyan water-pipe AZN20.

For something vastly cheaper try the AZN1.20 lahmacuns at **Buyükfirat**, Turkish meals at AZN4 from **Antalya** or AZN6.50 pastas from the neat if smoky **Fellini**. An unnamed cellar **internet club** (80q/hr) shares its stairway with a particularly inexpensive chaykhana (tea 20q per cup). All are closely huddled together at the Xälilov/ Ağayev junction, πS2. **Kafe Kişmis** (πS3) is unusually attractive for an 80q beer joint.

Somewhat further south near a gaggle of embassies, **Kafe Ekspress** (πN3) has var-

BAKU

ious fast-food offerings in an abstract cubist-style new building while **Baku Bean Roasters** (πN4) serves decent coffee.

TV Tower
Visible from most parts of Baku, the 310m-high ball-and-spike **TV tower** (πC5) is Azerbaijan's tallest man-made structure. While not open to visitors, from afar it becomes a mesmerizing sight every evening when illuminated by a constantly changing cycle of coloured lights.

BAYIL
The southern end of Baku Bay is home to the BP HQ, nicknamed **Villa Petrolea II** (ΨA8) in what was once a Soviet workers' palace with a splendid ballroom. The building was named in honour of an original Villa Petrolea, a mansion built for the Nobel Brothers out in what is now Nizami Park (Greater Baku map p76). Near Villa Petrolea II is (for now) the **world's tallest flagmast** (ΨA9), at 156m. The steeply sloped suburb behind has no tourist sights but offers several accommodation options with reasonable bay views.

BIBI HEYBAT (see map p139)
One of Azerbaijan's holiest Muslim sites, **Bibi Heybat Mosque** was founded 1257 enshrining the simple grave of 'Bibi' (ie 'Aunty') Okuma Khanum, sister of Shi'ite Islam's controversial seventh Imam. She had fled to Baku with her sisters in the late 8th century to escape fallout from the schism which would eventually divide mainstream Shia Islam from the Ismaili branch. The name Heybat is said to be that of her faithful servant who is buried nearby. The sturdy if relatively modest shrine here originally resembled many an Old City mosque with typical stubby minaret as shown in a 1907 painting displayed in the National Gallery. However, it was totally demolished in the anti-religious campaigns of 1936, ostensibly for road widening! The current structure was built to a new design and re-dedicated in July 1998 making it the first Stalin-destroyed mosque in the former USSR to have been totally rebuilt.

Bibi Heybat surveys a compelling if far from beautiful city panorama across the bay.

In the foreground, directly beneath the cliff-edge road, is a dismal area of reclaimed land known colloquially as **James Bond Oil Field** after a scene from *The World Is Not Enough* was filmed there. However, most of the archaic Selimkhanov nodding donkeys that gave it its special fascination were swept away during 2008 and a major job is underway to clean up the decades of environmental damage before the land can be re-used. Had Baku's Olympic 2016 bid been successful this was to have been the site of the proposed Olympic Park.

Out in the middle of the bay, **Nargin Island** (see map p144) is a scrappy hummock of a former Soviet naval base. Till recently there was little to see here except for a graveyard of half-sunken old boats (at 40°17'49"N, 49°55'31-50"E). However, if plans go ahead, the island will be transformed into a futuristic 'eco' resort. See 🖳 http://photos.day.az/images/145875/2.jpg for a photo of how it's meant to look!

THE HYATT AREA
For guests at the Hyatt hotels there's now a fair selection of handy restaurants within five minutes' walk but sights are few and far between. Near the big Bakixanov roundabout a statue shows **Mehdi Husseinzade** (τG4) throwing a hand grenade. Hussein-zade was a WWII Soviet secret agent who earned medals for blowing up Hitler's army canteen in Trieste, exploding a major fuel depot and wandering around an enemy prison camp dressed as a German officer to almost single-handedly lead the rescue of some 850 partisans, agitators and collected anti-Nazis. The German guards later claimed, Falstaff-like, that there had been more like a thousand attackers.

Tucked away amid uninteresting housing blocks, the attractive **Cathedral of Holy Myrrh-Bearers** (τI1, ▲ *Jenmironosits kilesi*, ✪ *Sobor Svyatakh Zhen Mironsits*) was built in 1907-9 but stayed closed for most of its history. In the Soviet era it was used as an ammunition dump of the Sälyan Kazarma military compound and eventually lost its roof. Muslim Azeris (including Taǧiyev) donated significant sums towards its original construction costs and did so again with the 2002 restoration. Savvy

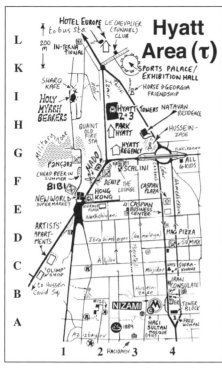

Hyatt Area (τ)

'BLUE' MOSQUE

minute acquaintanceship with the Persians ... One could examine forever and they would never be huffed or annoyed by one's not buying' (John Osmaston, 1861).

While today it's real Azerbaijanis in the markets, their atmosphere remains congenial and photogenic especially the herbs, nuts and colourful fruit polished and piled up in perfectly arranged pyramids. This is easiest to see at **Taza Bazaar** (βC3-4) which remains intriguing despite the oppressive encroachment of ever more tower blocks around it. Salesmen are unaggressive and generally very keen to be photographed amid their boxes of nuts or dangling hooks of meat. The covered lower meat-and-fish market was for years a place where hissed invitations would lure visitors to taste illicit caviar in an amusingly cloak-and-dagger caper. These days the caviar (see box p21) is openly on display and while it remains cheaper than in supermarkets, prices in the €50 range for a 113g pot make it far from the impulse purchase it was in the 1990s.

North of the bazaar the **Haji Ajarbek Mechid** (βF4) is pleasant enough but the nickname **Blue Mosque** (see graphic above) should not have you dreaming of Istanbul or Samarkand.

then-president Heydar Aliyev was quick to hail the reconsecration by the Patriach of Moscow as a sign of Azerbai-jan's religious tolerance and a 'big step in the further development of state relations between Azerbaijan and Russia'. The new interior has a lavish Christmas tree of gilt chandeliers, attractive icons and fine ceiling murals. The fluted spire has been gilded though some bullet holes remain in the south-east side of the tower. Some believe that the church retains a relic of Jesus's disciple, St Bartholomew. In some myths Bartholomew is claimed to have been crucified in Baku but there's no proof that he drank at Finnegans.

NORTH-CENTRAL BAKU
Taza Bazaar
Baku's bazaars 'were my favourite resort, enjoying their coolness and making a

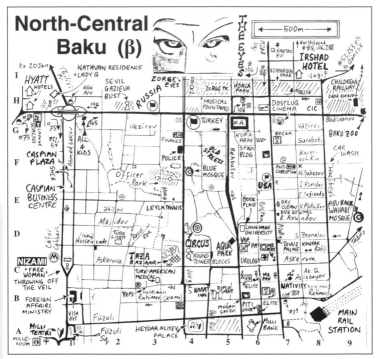

Zorge and Djaparidze parks

Zorge Park is a long strip running parallel to Bakixanov St, becoming Djaparidze Park (see column opposite) where it continues across Azadlyq Ave. Zorge Park is a popular place to stroll and play billiards. The main attraction is the powerful **'eyes' sculpture** (βI4) which commemorates very symbolically the spy work which ethnic-German Azerbaijani, Richard Zorge, did for the Soviet Union during WWII (he was eventually caught and executed by the Japanese). The sculpture is especially spooky at night with faint lamps glowing behind the hollow pupils. But try to avoid passing this spot around 9am when surrounding streets are blocked to allow the President's son painless access to his school.

At the top of Behbutov St is a new **musical fountain** (βH5) that plays around

8pm on summer evenings. Across Bakixanov St from there is the archetypal 1950 Soviet-inspired apartment block **'Kura Araksvodstroi'** (βG6)… at least for now: in late 2008 the Minister of Emergency Situations announced that all Stalin- and Krushchev-era apartment buildings would eventually be demolished. Quite why that's necessary remains unclear though it would certainly be one way to encourage reluctant tenants into the numerous new tower-apartments.

Just beyond the cosy if expensive **Koala Park** (amusement rides for toddlers), **Djaparidze Park** is named after Prokopius Djaparidze, a Georgian revolutionary who was one of the (in)famous 26 Commissars (see box pp96-7). At the far end of the park there's a little old steam loco to peruse while you wait for the summer-only

Children's Railway (βH9). Nearby **Baku Zoo** (βG9; Baki Heyvanet Parki, adult/child AZN1/AZN60q) is a rather maudlin little place with cramped cages for the rather under-fed big-cats. It's been slated for eventual relocation.

GÄNCLIK & MILLIONAIRES' MILE

North of the zoo, set back from giant Gänclik Square is the **national stadium**. Though now 'filled in', the stadium was originally shaped as a 'C', the Cyrillic first letter of Stalin. It retains Soviet insignia on the towers but these days it's named after Tofiq Bahramov who became the most loved Azeri in England during 1966 (see box). A statue of Tofiq was unveiled here in 2004 when England played Azerbaijan. Appropriately Geoff Hurst made a speech. When there's a major football match, crowds swarm the paved expanse in front of the stadium entrance yet surprisingly few ever seem to get in even though the stands are frequently half empty.

Although far from spectacular at first glance, the area north of the stadium has been nicknamed Millionaires' Mile due to the numerous grandiose new mansions of the second oil boom (ie post 1998) which have been built on a grid of narrow back

---

❏ **Sir Tofiq**

Tofiq Bahramov is possibly the most famous linesman in footballing history. Azeri (not Russian as he is often misremembered), it was his controversial decision which gave England a turning-point goal during extra time in the 1966 World Cup final. Geoff Hurst's shot had hit the underside of the bar then bounced down and out again. Tofiq decided that it had, in fact, crossed the line. Goal!! They thought it was all over ... And it soon was.

Along with the referee and other linesman, Bahramov received a souvenir golden whistle from the queen at the end of the game. For many fans he more deserved a knighthood.

---

streets hereabouts. Many of the mansions have carved or porticoed stone façades and a vast new presidential palace is under construction behind the Old Gänclik tennis courts (ϑE8).

For visitors the area's most interesting attraction is **AzerIlme carpet factory** (ϑB4;

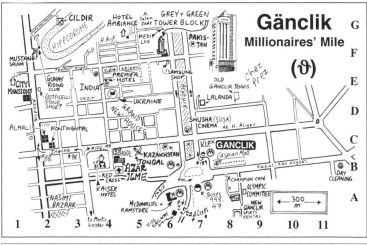

☎ 465 9036, 💻 www.magicalknots.com) at 2 Shamsi Rahimov St [NOT Suleyman Rahimov St]. Behind a fine new stone façade, as well as an inevitable sales room there's an attractive open courtyard decked with Azeri craftwork and a samovar-side seat to sip tea while awaiting a tour of the workshops. Tours (free) are best arranged in advance but often possible even for drop-in visitors. The guide/sales-lady Sevinc speaks English. Highlights include the dyeing room with its centrifuges and exhibit of dye ingredients including pomegranate rind and red-onion peelings. And, of course, the weaving room where their biggest project is 're-weaving' a copy of the world-famous 1539 Ardabil Carpet, all 29,014,040 knots of it. AzerIlme considers that the original, now in London's Victoria & Albert Museum, is the '8th Wonder of the World'.

Bus #106 and the rarer #99 pass nearby. Get off at Kral Wedding Palace and walk a block south.

Practical information

ACCOMMODATION
Overview
In 2001 Baku had barely 20 hotels. By 2009 there were nearly 300 with several major upmarket giants (Hilton, Marriott, Four Seasons) all constructing hotels on the Bulvar. Still, for now, the availability of full-scale business standard rooms is limited and several of the better options (Hyatt, Excelsior, Ramada, Holiday Inn) are well out of the centre. Many other hotels which consider themselves 'business standard' are self-deluding. Some of the boutique mini-hotels are worth the cash, but others are hopelessly overpriced. There's a growing rash of small (10 to 20 room) mid-priced hotels (AZN80-150). The standards in these are acceptable but the rooms are rarely anything luxurious and commonly feature poorly chosen curtains, functional G-plan style furniture and

BAKU PHONE CODE: 012

a lacklustre 'art' (if anything) on stark bare walls. Although occupancy remains high, particularly during the Oil and Gas Show in early June, supply is just starting to overtake demand for lower- to mid-range accommodation and there are sometimes opportunities for (polite) bargaining, something that's previously been virtually impossible. Note that most hotels offer corporate rates (around 20% discount) while internet discounters can often offer prices far better than the walk-in rack rates at many upper market places. During the quiet summer season cheaper rates are likely to be available both direct from the hotel and through agencies such as SI Travel/Amex (see p137, 💻 www.si-travel.com).

However, here I've quoted rack rates. If paying by credit card you'll generally need to add 18% tax and AZN1.20 local tax. Informally, smaller places might waive these taxes when guests pay in cash.

Listings are by area and then by subjective appreciation level. However, all **budget options** (ie under AZN50) are listed together on pp113-14.

Within the Old City
The perfectly located *Sultan Inn* (ΣN11, ☎ 437 2305, 💻 www.sultaninn.com, sgl AZN230-250, dbl AZN250-270) is the Old City's most sought-after address. There are just 11 stylishly luxurious rooms each with a fireplace and rainforest shower. The lounge is inviting and the rooftop restaurant is the perfect Old City perch.

The brand-new *Atropat Hotel* (ΣQ8, ☎ 497 8950, 💻 www.atropathotel.com, sgl/dbl AZN150/180) seems to be a good notch above most similarly priced hotels with a lift, underground parking, private rooftop restaurant and unusually professional management. LCD TV screens are set into dark wood desk units. The golden bedspreads are a little too glitzy.

Better appointed than many Old City options, *Hotel Meridian* (ΣI7, 39 Zeynalli, ☎ 497 0809, 💻 www.meridianhotel.az, AZN180-280) has big beds, stylish rooms and trendy bathrooms behind a new stone neo-classical façade. The sauna costs AZN20 per person per hour. Do poke your nose into the 17th-century cavern that forms the hotel's underground billiard room.

Built right onto an exterior section of old-city rampart, the 11-room *Boutique Palace* (ΣT14/∂D2, ☎ 492 2288, 🖳 www .boutique-palace.com, dbl AZN295) is characterful and amusingly over-the-top. It's packed with innovative décor ideas and pseudo historical paintings but the many gadgets don't always work perfectly and, while comfy, its claims of five-star luxury are very much wishful thinking.

Tucked behind and above a 13th-century *takiya* (dervish house) the 8-room *Museum Inn* (ΣO11, ☎ 497 1522, 🖳 www .museum-inn.az) is architecturally somewhat out of place, but its vine-shaded terrace is a delight and its summer restaurant offers Maiden's Tower views equivalent to those from the Sultan's Inn's at considerably lower prices (Xirdalan beer AZN3). Rooms (sgl/dbl from AZN160/180) are designer-style with cork floors, flat screen TVs and somewhat narrow queen beds.

Hotel Kiçik Gala 98 (ΣS6, ☎ 437 1950, 🖳 www.hotelgef.com/98.html) is brighter and more spacious than most in the AZN100 price-range and looks pretty at night with its twinkling lights.

Brand-new *Noah's Ark Hotel* (ΣL2, ☎ 497 0982, 🖳 www.noahsark-hotel.com, sgl/dbl AZN120/140) overlooks one of the Old City's most 'lived-in' squares. Flowers embroidered on pillows but dowdy blankets, good shower booths, flat-screen wall TVs, free WiFi and fabulous 360° views from the glass-walled roof-top dining room. No lift.

Eight-room *Icheri Shähär Hotel* (ΣM2, ☎ 492 5315, 🖳 www.icherisheher .net, dbl AZN120) is a little ordinary though the roof-top terrace has fine Shirvanshah's Palace views.

Icheri Shahar's original boutique hotel, *Old City Inn* (ΣS7, ☎ 497 4369, 🖳 www.oldcityinn.com) is not especially luxurious but the fireplaces and sepia photos add a little character. There are brilliant views from some rooms and especially from the roof-café. The friendly staff are mostly tourism-faculty students and Elvin,

the charming manager, can help organize trips to the mountain villages of his native region beyond Quba. They co-manage the pleasant if slightly dark *City Walls Guesthouse* (ΣH2).

The Horizon (ΣO9, ☎ 492 6786, 🖳 www.thehorizonhotel.biz, dbl AZN120) has pleasant floral paintings, a generator and a lift. It claims to be a 'full service hotel with 14 staff' though I only saw two. Be aware that the hotel has moved from its 2006 location where all the buildings have since been demolished.

The friendly 12-room *Red Roof Inn (Red Roof Old City Guest House* (ΣR11, 12 Sibir, ☎ 437 2115, dbl AZN85) has clean if fairly functional rooms with decent showers, kettle, multi-channel TV and minibar. There's a small British-style pub in the basement.

Altstadt Guesthouse (ΣP8, Mammed yarov 3/2A, ☎ 493 3492 or 492 6402, 🖳 aae@box.az) is about the cheapest hotel in the Old City (dbl from AZN50). The rooms are by no means sophisticated but all have air-con and basic bathrooms while the family atmosphere and congenial little bar (full of footballs and beersteins) makes a stay here more personal than at many alternatives.

Less interesting Old City options *Qiz Qalasi Hotel* (ΣK6, ☎ 497 1785) has a lift, plastic ivy, awful paintings and a tiny (2x4m) pool. The good sized if unexceptional rooms cost AZN100 on the ground floor, AZN120 upstairs. Sauna use is included.

Tucked behind the Meridian, 11-room *Azäri Hotel* (ΣI7, ☎ 497 0228, sgl/dbl AZN83/106) has unremarkable rooms around an open courtyard: bright with cream-tones but a little musty. Some have kitchenettes. I was very swiftly offered a 25% discount making the price more sensible.

The rather tatty *Hotel Böyük Qala* (ΣO9, ☎ 497 2583, sgl/dbl AZN80/100) welcomes guests with a fuzzy Ilham portrait on custard-yellow walls. The carpets are getting ragged and there's no lift to reach the bland breakfast room which could make more of its fine Old City views.

BAKU

Guesthouse Inn (ΣP9, ☎ 437 1263, 🖳 guesthouseinn@mail.ru; AZN60-75) is inexpensive but lacks character and two of the rooms are windowless. Roma speaks English.

Central Baku

The *Radisson SAS* (∂M4, 17th floor, ISR Plaza, ☎ 498 2402, 🖳 www.baku.radis sonsas.com, dbl from AZN299) has a perfect location high above Fountains Square and great views especially from the stylish rooms numbered XX02. However, the professionally appointed rooms are accessed directly from the business-tower elevator and reaching the gym/swimming pool requires crossing a public atrium so the whole atmosphere doesn't really feel like a hotel at all.

With a superb position almost on Fountains Sq, the Western-managed *Azcot Hotel* (∂K2, ☎ 492 2507, 🖳 www.azcot hotel.com) occupies several floors of an oil-boom mansion. The rooms (from AZN110) are well equipped and the corridors have more character than in most equivalent places.

Hotel Austin (∂L7, ☎ 598 0812, 499 0811, 🖳 http://austinhotel.az, AZN177-210, B&B) goes for a boutiquey, fashionably modern choco-retro feel within a historic older building.

The welcoming American-run *Hale Kai* (∂O3, ☎ 596 5056, 🖳 www.hotel halekai.com, dbl AZN130-160) has an imaginative fixation with Frank Lloyd-Wright that's clearest in the '30s-retro lobby bar and occasional stained-glass panels. The location is quiet yet central and the attached Georgian restaurant is Baku's best but is viciously pricey.

Baku Palace Guesthouse (∂O2, ☎ 497 6271, 🖳 www.bakupalace.az) is an oil-boom-era house with high ceilings where a sweep of marble stairs leads up to a stylistic mish-mash with rounded arches, plastic trees and bits of jade-effect. In the better rooms (AZN100-120) the wardrobes retain old, heavily carved doors. The plain AZN70 room has its bathroom across the hallway.

BAKU PHONE CODE: 012

With sepia photos and a brilliant old clock on the stairs, the very homely *Red Lion Hotel* (∂F5, 7 Mammadaliyev, ☎ 598 3358, 🖳 www.redlion.az, AZN90-110, B&B) has retained a little more of their building's oil-boom personality than some competitors. There are large rooms and a DVD library but no lift despite the four floors.

Hotel Balion (∂G4, 12 Tarlan Äliyarbeyov, ☎ 418 4329, 🖳 elcinruf@yahoo.com) lacks pzazz but the reasonably large rooms are very handy for Fountains Sq.

The obliging *Karat Inn* (βB5, 175 Suleyman Rahimov ☎ 596 1223, 🖳 www .karatinnhotel.com, sgl/dbl AZN90/110) has only 12 rooms in its five-storey stone-clad building that's dwarfed by a neighbouring tower. It uses many gilt fixtures as befits its name and seems somewhat better appointed than many in the price range but there's no lift.

Behind a pseudo-classical stone façade, the 9-storey *Hotel Diplomat* (βB5, 185 Suleyman Rahimov, ☎ 596 1127, 🖳 www.diplomathotelbaku.com) has high ceilinged standard rooms (sgl/dbl AZN95/105) with a desk and fairly neutral décor plus somewhat sparse suites (AZN150-180) but there's a cute little ground floor bar, imaginative top-floor restaurant and the helpful staff look good in their tie-and-jeans combo.

The *Yacht Club Hotel* (φF9, ☎ 598 1895, 🖳 yclub@caspar.baku.az, sgl/dbl AZN100/120) sits on stilts above Baku Bay. Even-numbered rooms are sea-facing, but some toilets smell a little musty. Little golf-cart buggies run guests along the jetty.

For many years the exclusive reserve of party cadres and international dignitaries, by the Millennium the *Hotel Respublika* (φL1, ☎ 498 7191) had become a fascinating timewarp of 1970s Soviet retro-design. Not surprisingly given its potential (central location and magnificent views), the huge chintzy rooms are being totally rebuilt and the humorous commie-kitsch elements will soon be history.

Station/Landmark area

The once-vast Absheron Hotel has been demolished like its former identical twin,

Se

r rt

the Azerbaijan across Azadliq Sq (being rebuilt as the **Baku Hilton**). Rather than imploding the structure a bizarre demolition technique was used, crane-lifting JCB diggers onto the building's roof and slowly bulldozing the building bit by bit into history. Curiously the new **Marriott Baku Hotel** planned to replace the Absheron (αF20, 🖥 www.skyscrapercity.com/showthread .php? t=604868) looks rather similar to the old one, albeit predominantly in 21st-century glass instead of 1970s concrete.

The Landmark Hotel (☎ 465 2000, 🖥 www.thelandmark.az) in Landmark Tower 3 (αM16) has spacious rooms (dbl/ste AZN150/180) with fashionably retro chocolate-and-cream colours and soaring rainforest showers. A great feature is the 10th-floor swimming pool with wrap-around view windows.

New but designed to look like a grand oil-boom mansion, the government-owned *Hotel Respublika Lyuks* (αK15, ☎ 598 1048, 🖥 www.hotelrespublika.com) makes little attempt to lure guests – there's not even a sign. But the 27 large, classically suave rooms (AZN150) and vast plush suites (AZN180-300) are well worth investigating when not full of official guests.

Although lacking a swimming pool, the *Park Inn* (αE15, ☎ 490 6000; 🖥 www .baku.rezidorparkinn.com; dbl from AZN 235) is a popular option offering small but fully modernized business-quality rooms. Caspian Sea view rooms cost AZN11 extra, bigger 'Business Rooms' (AZN306) include free WiFi.

12 Inn (αJ16, ☎ 498 1203, 🖥 www .12inn.az, sgl/dbl/'oriental' AZN160/170/ 270) goes overboard with a palate of strong colours and modernist décor searching for that design-book look. The basins are trendy and some walls stunningly purple but the queen beds are narrow and first-floor ceilings are annoyingly low. In a similar genre the nearby *Metropol Hotel* (αK17, ☎ 499 9910; 🖥 http://metropol baku.com) has an angular, twinkle-ceiling foyer and 15 almost-fashionable rooms from AZN145/175. It's hidden behind pointedly hip Taboo Restaurant.

The four-floor, late 1990s *Caspian Guest House* (αF21, ☎ 498 6581, sgl/dbl AZN80/90) is characterless but adequate with silly-frilly sofa-covers, slightly worn carpets and 1990s bathrooms. A largely pointless new lift stops in between floors.

An off-beat but central waterside option is the *Deniz Vaqzal* (αC20, ☎ 498 1013, AZN120-140) with 14 motel-style guest rooms recently rebuilt above the oddly functionless Marine Station. Seems overpriced.

Hyatt area

Baku's two Hyatt hotels (☎ 496 1234, 🖥 www.baku.hyatt.com) and related office buildings form a virtual expat town within a town. They were Baku's original international business hotels and remain (for now) about the best on offer. The *Hyatt Regency* (τG3, dbl AZN260+) **was** the city's original international business hotel adding modern conveniences and stylish interiors to the appealing Stalinist architecture of the former Hotel Nakhchivan. Turn right on entering to enjoy a little-used but appealing sitting room. Turn left to reach the sprawling lobby of the *Park Hyatt* (τH3) next door whose rooms are a little larger if less fashionably decorated. There's a big pool and gym and some houselets for long-stay guests.

Caspian Palace Hotel (τE4, Caspian Plaza, upper floors, ☎ 436 7100, 🖥 www .caspianpalace.com) is one of Baku's better deals in the AZN90 range. There's no sign and getting past the Caspian Plaza building's security guards takes a bit of energy, but the rooms are very spacious, albeit stylistically neutral, and come with marble basins, kettle and free WiFi.

When Baku had minimal choice the once 'Grand' *Hotel Europe* (τL2, ☎ 490 7090, dbl from US$200) was one of the best hotels. However, on my last visit many rooms and even the best US$600 suites seemed severely in need of TLC. Its main plus is its location right by the main Exhibition Center along with a decent nightclub, gym and indoor and outdoor swimming pools.

BAKU

Gänclik (Millionaires' Mile) area

Hotel Ambiance (ϑG5, 52 E Salamzadeh, ☎ 436 4980, 💻 www.hotelambiance.az, rooms AZN80-130) is probably the cheapest Baku accommodation to have its own swimming pool but its 'gym' is just two running machines. Tucked down an unlikely suburban road it's an architectural oddity fashioned from two very different-looking town houses. There's a businesslike foyer-bar behind blood-red revolving doors, just one of the quirky décor touches. Minibus 116 to Teymur Äliyev St gets you close.

In a calm garden setting, *City Mansions* (ϑE1, 153 Azadliq, ☎ 436 1041, 💻 www.felsbaku.com/citymansion) is part-hotel part-residence where fair-value apartments (AZN90-120) with kitchen, bathtub and sitting room share a 20m indoor swimming pool and gym. There's no lift and reception only works 08-21:00 Mon-Fri, 09-17:30 Sat-Sun. Buses #88 and #288 pass outside.

The 19-room, six-storey *Premier Hotel* (ϑE4, ☎ 447 5700, 💻 www.premierhotel.az, sgl/dbl AZN128/148) feels a little better constructed than many competitors, there's a nicer choice of art and heavy old doors albeit on a late 20th-century façade. Note that while it is as it claims in Millionaires' Mile, that's NOT the 'heart of the city' at least as far as tourists are concerned.

Hidden away on the 5th and 6th floors of a metallic-fronted courtyard tower the odd *Kaiser Hotel* (ϑB4, ☎ 564 4354, sgl/dbl US$70/90) is cheap by Baku standards and the wooden-floored, golden-bedded rooms are decent value but it's mainly used by sports teams and just getting to reception past the confused door-guard can be a challenge.

Irshad Hotel (βI7, Vaqif pr 11, ☎ 441 0132, 💻 www.irshad.az) was the extraordinary choice of lodging for Pope John Paul II who used room 62 on his May 2002 Baku visit. Never luxurious the Irshad is looking a little tired these days though its Djaparidze Park location is surprisingly good for bus links to anywhere in town. Rooms from AZN70.

Bayil

Bayil has a few options which are comparatively handy if you have business at BP.

The area is also not too far from central Baku though the heavy traffic and one-way system can slow things down more than you might expect.

Crown Hotel (πA9, 💻 www.crownhotelbaku.com, ☎ 491 0227, corporate/walk-in rates from AZN140/180) is the one fully business-standard hotel. Highlights are the excellent indoor swimming pool and remarkably obliging service but the largely pleasant décor does succumb occasionally to glittery tassels and crass apologies for 'art'. Beware of traffic noise in the east-facing rooms. The 7th-floor Vista Restaurant (meals from AZN10, beer AZN3) serves quail lavangi and has harbour views.

East Legend (πA9, ☎ 499 7717, 💻 www.eastlegendhotel.com, sgl/dbl AZN 100/110) has much more character than most smaller Baku hotels with a vine-draped courtyard, mini 3x6m pool and loads of Azeri copperwork adornments. The rooftop terrace restaurant has bay views, the shower booths are good, there's sturdy wooden furniture and even a seven-machine fitness room.

Hotel Nur (πA9, 48 A Mammedov ☎ 491 5000) is a homely place where a central lounge and nice view-terrace are shared by nine en suite rooms whose décor is frilly rather than fashionable. Co-owned *Nur 2* (πA9, 9 Alibeyovlar, ☎ 491 1100) is newer but lacks views and doesn't have a restaurant.

Around Central Baku

Excelsior Hotel (ΨJ12, Heydar Aliyev pr 2, ☎ 496 8000, 💻 www.excelsiorhotelbaku.az) has a Las Vegas style taste in OTT pseudo-classical grandeur. The suites (AZN850-3500) are vast and full of gadgets, Heritage Rooms (AZN350) are fair sized but Duke Rooms (AZN270) are surprisingly small. Service is very professional and the location will be less annoying once the big new Heydar Aliyev Cultural Center opens nearby.

West of Gänclik, *Ambassador Hotel* (ΨK6, ☎ 449 4930, www.hotelambassador.az, 934 Vurğun) advertises widely but seems overpriced and the corridors weave some strange meanders.

In a former taxi-park way out off ugly Darnagul Highway (Karl Marx Ave) *Elite*

BAKU PHONE CODE: 012

Hotel (ΨO10, ☎ 563 5205, 🖳 www.elite
hotel.az, 40°25'12"N, 49°51'16"E) gives
itself an over-generous four stars for what
are fairly average motel standard rooms.
The occasional concerts in the car park can
be disturbing. Take bus #253 from Metro
Nizami or #122 from Metro Gänclik.

Shix(ov) Beach (see map p139)
If you don't mind being 10km out of town,
there are two decent choices on Shix(ov)
Beach, a curious stretch of sand with surreal views of offshore oil rigs. Locals swim in
the oily sea here but the hotel pools are a
much safer choice.

The *Ramada Baku* (☎ 491 7303, 🖳
www.ramadabaku.com, dbl AZN220+) is
one of the city's better-value upscale choices. It has a sinuous glass façade, an ostenta-
tiously luxurious interior and a superb in-
and-outdoor pair of imaginatively linked
swimming pools. The sea-view rooms have
good-sized balconies.

Right next door is the long-standing
Crescent Beach Hotel (☎ 497 4777).
Architecturally it has all the charm of a pre-
fabricated open prison, but in fact the
Crescent Beach is a business-standard hotel
with a good range of facilities (squash,
swimming pool, wind surfing etc). There's
a free guest-shuttle bus from just outside
Baku's Old City double gates (ΣW11)
seven times daily.

Airport
Opened by President Aliyev in June 2007,
the remarkably plush *Holiday Inn* (☎ 437
4949, 🖳 www.ichotelsgroup.com/h/d/hi/1/
en/hotel/bakap) has standards well above a
typical Holiday Inn, with great pools and
stylish spacious rooms at sensible prices
(dbl/twin AZN150; AZN115 possible if pre-
booked two weeks ahead via 🖳 www.holi
dayinn.com); this would be one of Baku's
top hotels were it downtown. Shuttle buses
will whisk you into town for free but the
half-hour commute is offputting. Amongst
the helpful staff is a rare Geordi-Azeri!
There is no visa-free waiver for transit guests
staying here so if you're just changing planes
in Baku overnight you'll still need to go

through full entry procedures if you want to
sleep here. The International terminal is a
ten-minute walk away.

Out of town
There are a number of motels within an
hour's drive of Baku, including the increasingly grand *Hotel Neapol* (map p162; ☎
448 3100, 🖳 www.neapolbaku.com) 10km
from the 20th January metro station
between Xırdalan and Sarai as well as several options out on the Absheron beaches at
Märdäkän (p150), Novxanı (p159),
Pirshağı (p152) and Zagulba (p148) that
can prove good-value off season.

Delfin Hotel (☎ 499 6101, 🖳 www
.delfinhotel.az, map p162) is an odd concept, a sort of beach resort but without a
beach – instead it's 3km beyond 20th Jan
metro on the very unglamorous Sumqayit
Highway. Rooms ($106+) are ranged round
an attractive swimming pool with a swim-
up bar, occasionally host to loud live music.

BUDGET ACCOMMODATION
Less than AZN50/night
Baku's a tough place for budget travellers.
Classic Baku cheapies including the
Circus Hostel and Hotels AnBa, Baku,
Absheron and Azerbaijan have all been
demolished while the infamous Kompas
Boatel has sailed off into history. If none
of the possibilities listed below appeals
there are some comparatively modest-
priced guesthouses in the Old City (eg
Altstadt Inn, see p109).

Hotel Cänub ('Janub', ∂F10, ☎ 598
1152, 🖳 www.canub-hotel.com) is downtown Baku's last-surviving budget hotel.
The building is ageing and standards are
notoriously variable but refurbishments in
2007 gave many rooms (dbl AZN40) air-
conditioning and OK bathrooms where the
water should run warm eventually. The old
dezhurnaya (floor lady) system remains,
however, and the front desk can be erratic.

Hotel Velotrek (ΨL3, ☎ 431 5187,
Cycling stadium) is the neatest budget hotel
with plain but newish rooms with good private bathrooms. Good value for single travellers at AZN15 per person. Nagi speaks

BAKU

OK English and the nearby cycle club can help with bicycle repairs. Receptionists are sometimes hard to find and remember to double check whether the doors will be locked at night. Beware that visiting sports teams get priority over tourists even if you've been staying a while. The site is very near metro 20th Jan but is not signed. Turn right as you exit the station then right again through (hopefully open) gates between some market-style shops.

For now *Hotel Araz* (ΨI11; Yusif Safarov St 30, ☎ 490 5063) still offers some dorms (AZN10) and functional twin rooms (AZN20) with fans and shared semi-clean squat toilets. These are OK for male travellers and Turkish truck drivers. However, the (good, hot) showers are in a single communal bathroom without cubicle doors so washing would be a potentially hazardous cultural challenge for women! The hotel is gradually upgrading its rooms, adding bathrooms and charging AZN40-80 for newer rooms. That seems ill-considered given that the only reason to head this far out on the noisy airport road (minibus 1 from Vurğun Gdns, 4 from Bulvar) is for the rock bottom prices.

1000 Camels Hostel (ΣI6; Zeinalli first alley, ☎ mob 55-677 8175 Samir, 💻 www .thousandcamels-az.com) is Baku's first backpacker place with two rooms of (rather uncomfortable) bunks in an unmarked old-city house. The welcome is friendly, there's internet and a little cooking space and it's great for meeting other travellers. Don't be deterred by older reviews – the original, appallingly crushed hostel site has been bulldozed and this venue is considerably better. Take the second doorway to the left walking up from the Meridian Hotel, then head for the pink-painted area through the small courtyard. Dorm beds cost US$20 a night, or $22 if booked via various hostelling websites. *Caspian Hostel* (☎ 492 1995, ☎ mob 050-377 8444 [Aika], 💻 seyf@box.az, beds US$20) in apartment 9 of the same little courtyard house as the 1000 Camels is effectively a one-bed apartment that has been turned into an 8-bed dorm by a friendly family. It's not unduly cramped but there's minimal storage space.

The **cheapest beds** in Baku (dorm from AZN4) are in the old Soviet tower above the train station (αT17) but nobody speaks English and to get past the guards to access the relevant lift you'll need to get a payment paper from the little kiosk-booth within the ticket concourse marked Istirahät Otaqlqrinen Inzilbatchisi. For several years they seemed to refuse foreigners here. More recently I did manage to get a very plain but warm single room (AZN8) though these are often in great demand.

Apartment rental

Apartment rental is often a decent option if you're hoping to pay less than AZN70 per night, especially if you have a group of friends to share the cost. The cheapest (from AZN40) that are bareably centrally located tend to be a little dowdy though perfectly clean with a kitchen and maybe a washing machine. However, many have minimal rental periods (3 or 7 days). Useful contacts include: 💻 www.travelazerbaijan.land.ru, 💻 www.bakurealestate.net, 💻 www.baku services.com and 💻 www.prant.az. Companies that have regular relationships with agencies can get better deals.

RESTAURANTS

Baku's restaurants change with such alarming regularity that within a year it's common to find that around half have closed, changed style or moved to a new address. Nonetheless, the reviews here should still give a feel for what you're likely to find and I've concentrated particularly on the already longer-lasting operations.

There's a wide selection of international cuisines if you're prepared to spend as much as in any Western European capital. Azeri and Turkish meals can still be found for as little as AZN3-6 though for the special atmosphere it's worth dining at least once in one of the caravanserai restaurants below. And if you're not likely to make it to Georgia, take the opportunity to sample the unique, wonderful tastes of Georgian cuisine while you're in Baku.

❑ Meal options

● **Breakfast** Cheap if mediocre all-night cafés on the south side of Vurğun Gardens (eg *Qoç*, αP18) serve a typical Azeri breakfast of *yağ pendir* (butter and cheese) with a pot of tea for around AZN2. *Anadolu* (∂E6 or αK18, from 07.30) and *Mozart Café* (∂C3 from 09.00) do Turkish breakfast buffets. Some expat pubs serve Western breakfasts but rarely before 10.30.

● **Lunch deals** Most expat-orientated restaurants offer great-value 'Bizlunch' specials (AZN6-12) on weekdays from 12.00 to 15.00. To see what's new stroll along the lanes around the History Museum and look at the various menu boards or consult the weekly free newspapers. Places with reliable good deals include *Maharaja* (see p119), *L'Oliva* (see p118), *Mexicana* (see p119) and the rather grand-looking restaurant of the *Hotel Respublika Lyux* (see p111). For incredible value try the pizza-pasta-salad buffet at *Il Gusto* (see p119). Or, for more choice and great quality, have the ever-popular AZN15 buffet at *Old Mill* (∂L16, see p100), unmarked and deep within the Landmark Building. It's aimed at the executives working in the same building but is available to all if you can find a seat!

Caravanserai restaurants

For sheer ambience it is hard to beat one of the old caravanserai restaurants,where full 'cultural shows' or Muğam music are likely to accompany your banquet, in Baku's Old City. The wonderful multi-niched *Muğam Club* (ΣK11, ☎ 492 4085, garnished mains AZN10-20, Xirdalan AZN4) is a photogenic two-storey covered courtyard caravanserai that's colourfully lit at night. It's a good if pricey place to taste Azeri standards including ash/plov. Note that the whole restaurant is fairly frequently booked for private events but you might still be able to

peep inside for a few minutes to see the extensive programme of local music and Caucasian dances that are often organized for such evenings.

The splendidly atmospheric *Karavansara* (ΣO13; ☎ 492 6668) has two separate dining areas and often features muğam music in the evenings. The main site has small, individual stone-niche rooms around a shady courtyard; the rooms are smoke-blackened from centuries of candle flames. Across the street dining is in a vaulted dungeon. Menu prices are reasonable (saj AZN6, monastirsky AZN5, lävangi AZN16, garnishes AZN1, Xirdalan beer AZN2, wine from AZN5 a bottle) but watch for extras and check your bill before paying.

Mediterranea (ΣL12; ☎ 492 9866) is also within an old caravanserai but the attractively modern furnishings mean it lacks the same immediate feeling of antiquity. The central dining area is a covered winter courtyard with trees growing through while in summer there's also an outdoor terrace. The cuisine, ranging from Moroccan to Lebanese to Iranian (mains AZN12-17, Xirdalan AZN4), can be very good though my recent experiences were rather disappointing. Biz lunch 12:00-14:30 Mon-Sat.

Other Old City options

Airy but with enclosed sections for winter, the rooftop *Open Space* (above Sultan Inn, ΣN11, main courses AZN20-35) has for some years been one of the top Old City dining spots thanks to the phenomenal views down across to the Maiden's Tower. Their Caesar salads (AZN12) are reliable but coffee costs a whopping AZN10 and Xirdalan beers AZN7.

Museum Inn's newer summer-terrace *restaurant* (ΣO11) is noticeably cheaper and has similar views. *Meridian Hotel*'s *restaurant* (ΣI7) has served up some fine dishes over the years though the views are less spectacular. Designed as an ethnic-style cavern *Köhnä Shähär* (ΣG8) is a pleasant place to sample a good range of Azeri and Caucasian cuisine at prices that aren't exorbitant if you choose carefully (smallish dishes AZN6-40). However, the

BAKU

atmosphere feels a little more sanitized than at the Karavansara or Muğam Club opposite. For lounge-sushi there's *Kill Bill* (p119; ΣI9).

The one Georgian option, over-bright *Georgia Cafe* (ΣH7, mains AZN4-12, khajapuri AZN5) is rather lacking in atmosphere and its house red wine (AZN15 per litre) is slightly astringent.

Two appealing branches of *Chocolate* (ΣN10, ΣU11) serve good coffee while cosy *Kişmis* (ΣU9) is delightful (if pricey) for tea; see pp120-1.

Garden restaurants

These create a mock-rural ambience then frequently shatter it by pumping out deafening levels of live music. The music quality ranges from the inspirational to the crassly annoying depending on the artist and where you sit. Prices can vary enormously without necessarily reflecting the quality of the food. Check carefully whether there'll be a cover charge or minimum fee on the night you go.

If you're prepared to venture into the unglamorous '8th Km' suburb, *Xari Bül Bül* (see map below, Chobanzade St, ☎ 423 7545, kebabs AZN3, beers AZN3, no cover) is a reliable garden choice that's been popular for years with middle-class Bakuvian families. It's unusual for combining modest prices (with no surprise extras) and high musical standards but the mosquitoes can get annoying.

Tonqal (ϑC5, 82 Inqilab, ☎ 449 9198, 🖥 www.tonqal.com, no cover charge) has a lightly wooded garden that's less 'artificial' and manicured than most and the few old wooden horse carts add a heritage feel. Nice in summer, but on colder evenings dining is in contrastingly unrefined wooden cottages. There seems to be no written menu to hand. Most kebabs cost AZN3-4 but salads can be as much as AZN8 and various other 'extras' that appear can bump up the bill very significantly.

Niaqara (ΨK6) has a truly vast banqueting hall and a highly manicured restaurant-style garden that's handy for the Ambassador Hotel but not necessarily worth a special journey. Kebabs AZN3.50+, beers AZN2, lemon chicken AZN7.

Lido (ΨN8, ☎ 436 2021, 🖥 http://lido.az/main.swf) is a dauntingly nouveau-riche modern palace entered across two small pools from Atatürk Ave. It's a fascinating place that oozes more exclusivity than taste and showcases musical performers who are nationally known stars (so check the night's cover charge before booking!).

Appealing, cheaper local places

Art Restoran (∂K9, 51 Xaqani, ☎ 598 2224) has trendy red seats, golden wall panels and an indoor gazebo-like décor that looks dauntingly pricey. In fact most meals cost only AZN3-10 washed down with AZN1.50 beers and while the food quality isn't exactly gourmet (AZN5 'steaks' are as chewy as the price implies) there's a vast trilingual menu and the place stays open all night. Co-owned *L'Aparte* (φU7, Monolith Bldg) has the same menu and a remarkably suave interior. *Restoran Port* (∂G3) is bright, bustling and similarly inexpensive.

Next door *Bäh Bäh Club* (∂G3, ☎ 498 8734, 🖥 www.bah-bah club.com, meals AZN5-14) is airy, decorated with local handicrafts and serenaded with gently inviting live music. There's a wide range of very fairly priced Caucasian favourites: book a table. *Fayton Club* (ΣQ12, 17 Behbudov; ☎ 498 8101, meals AZN6-25, beers AZN2, evening cover charge AZN5) is pricier and the evening music more invasive but the antique Azerbaijani

EATING IN '8TH KM'

BAKU PHONE CODE: 012

rural-cellar décor is effective. *XVII Äsr* (∂Q10, 215 Säfäroğlu; meals AZN5-25) attempts a similar effect less successfully with old guns and carpets but their AZN5 lunch is a bargain. Popular for romantic local couples is the female-run *Nostalgie* (φU5) with divided booth seating. The slightly twee *Buena Vista* (Monolith building, ∂G1) claims a hard-to-see Latin twist.

Simple

Bland but inexpensive places for meals under AZN5 include *Estrella* (∂P6) and *Trulaila* (∂N5, not Georgian despite claims on its sign).

If price is all that matters the very cheapest eateries you're likely to find in central Baku are near the railway station or around Vurğun Gardens. Many are male-dominated, dingy and far from welcoming. Indeed *Kähräbä* (αO19) seemed intent in on driving me away rather than serving me. Other cheap dives include *Qoç* which is handily open 24 hours (but double check their prices!) and *Xayal* (∂U13) which hasn't really changed anything for a decade. It still serves simple meals for AZN2.80 and lets you have tea by the glass for 'dva mammad' (ie 40q) if you don't want a whole pot. Better than most are nearby *Pitixana* (∂U13) supplementing *piti* (p355) with popular pork chops, and especially *Yeni Bakı* (αR22, mains AZN2-6, beers AZN1.40). The latter serves Azeri favourites such as soyutma, düshbära (AZN1.20), buğlama and dolma (AZN2.40) supplemented by succulent chicken-in-orange (AZN3) and some curious 'enchiladas'. Unlike most cheaper places it's not overly male-dominated and one of the waiters can manage fairly passable English.

Turkish

For AZN4-8 including side-dish many Turkish restaurants offer satisfying pre-prepared meals, usually in well-appointed surroundings. You can choose by pointing at what you fancy should you lack linguistic dexterity to deal with menus. Long-term favourite *Anadolu* (🖥 www.anadolu.az) has branches at 5 Pushkin (∂E6) and 3/5

Räsul Rza (αK18) and like spacious *Iskändär* (αK16, opposite the Landmark) opens for early breakfasts around 7.30am. Both *Izmir* (∂L9, most meals AZN6) and *Zero* (∂I13) have a good buzz with contemporary design within older vaulted buildings. *Divan* (φV6) is a pleasant choice near the Old City.

Sultan's Restaurant (∂G7, ☎ 598 0555) gets mixed reviews. Its vast charcoal grills fire up kebabs (AZN6-7) and whole fish (from frozen, priced by weight) served at ranks of long tables with oddly cheap-looking plastic chairs. Xirdalan AZN3.

Star (∂F10) and *Inter-Grand* (∂E4 and ∂U6-7) are known for their döner kebabs though cheaper, lesser versions are widely available notably along Bül Bül St.

Lahmacun (Turkish 'roll-pizzas', see p24) are available on request at most Turkish restaurants but there are certain specialists such as *Büyük Firat* (∂S14 and πS2) and *Markaz Lahmacun* (φU5). Expect to pay around AZN1.20 plus extra for fillings.

Russian

TrinTrava (αK19, ☎ 437 9857, 🖥 www.trin -trava.com) is a wonderfully atmospheric basement with a Russian rural design theme and costumed waiters who somehow don't seem ridiculous. The prices are fair and most meals come with a garnish. Wines cost from AZN9, beers AZN3, stuffed mushrooms AZN2.80, pork chops with pears AZN5.80. Advance bookings are virtually essential.

Also emulating a Russian Izba (log cottage), smaller *Yolki Palki* (aka Ëlki Palki, meals AZN6.50-12) is often lively with gypsy music in the evenings. They have branches at 15 Qoqol (∂P6, ☎ 494 2492) and 88 M Hüseyn (πL7, ☎ 492 6427). With similarly costumed waitresses and a village-style atmosphere *Xutor* (φW4, Muxtarov 9/3, ☎ 437 2223) serves Ukrainian specialities including pig fat (sala) to accompany your vodka shots.

Georgian

Fine food and particularly imaginative terracotta décor makes *Georgian Home* (∂O3, Hotel Hale Kai, ☎ 494 4385) a tempting

BAKU

choice but the prices are discouragingly high, especially the wines (cheapest around AZN40) meaning that the place can feel eerily empty. 10% service charge.

Similarly named but much cheaper, **Georgian House** (∂O11, mains AZN4-6) does khajapuris for AZN5 and house wines from AZN20 per litre. It's tastefully decked out with copperware and the tables are inlaid with posies of dried grasses and are set around a piano.

Much more down market but similarly priced is *U Dali* (∂N2, Qorki ☎ 494 9356; mains AZN6-10, wine AZN10/l, Khajapuri AZN8) in a cosy cellar room with dining booths but oddly it's missigned as Café Napoli.

Several other Georgian restaurants serve great food but in offputtingly bland, bare-walled eateries as at *Imereti* (∂K8), **Kavkasioni** (∂R12) and *Georgia Cafe* (ΣH7).

International

Assados (∂C4, ☎ 598 1022, pastas AZN10-13, surf-n-turf AZN26, beer AZN3) has a great reputation for steaks (AZN16-23) served in a Klimtesque modern décor with starburst coloured-glass art-lamps, swirl of stairway and well-spaced tables. Long-lasting *Churasco* (∂G8) gets very mixed reviews.

No Name (∂L14) has stylish café-style seating with dark leather sofas and red cup seats ranged around a central bar island. It serves steaks (AZN11-15), beluga in pomegranate (AZN18), pastas (AZN9-10) and cocktails (AZN8.50+). *Fillet House* (αE22, ☎ 598 0573, 🖳 www.fillethouse.com) hides in the small basement of one of the few oil-boom mansions to have survived this area's total redevelopment (the fast-gathering builders' dust can make the place look closed from outside). Fully garnished AZN23-40 dishes justify their elevated prices by using fresh meat sourced carefully from their own farmers. Coat-hanger seats, Swedish flags and car-boot-sale bric-a-brac give a bit of atmosphere and there's a sweet little two-stool bar.

Azza has a rapidly expanding series of cafés, chocolate shops and restaurants all with fashionably appointed trendy-casual décor and coffee-coloured fittings. The original (∂I2) occupies a lovely century-old pavilion on Fountains Sq.

● **Upmarket** Behind discreet façades there are now a growing collection of little-advertised upmarket eateries. *Giakonda* (∂B3) is so incredibly discreet that you'll only ever get in by invitation from the nation's very top brass. Walk-in guests well-enough dressed to get past the officious bouncer, may eat at *Aristokrat* (∂Q8, ☎ 208 8811, 🖳 www.aristokrat.az, mains AZN14-55) whose décor oozes gold around a glass piano. The gold-on-black menus offer caviar blini starters (AZN190) washed down with champagnes (AZN320-3200) or Chateau Mouton Rothschild 1997 (AZN2000). However, the Italian chef also cooks pastas that mere mortals might be able to afford providing they don't take the caviar-topped vodka-sauce variant.

The double brick towers with water pouring over a golden nameplate make one doubt whether *Mesa* (∂I15, open 17.00-02.00) isn't really a private club. In fact it's a euro/sushi restaurant with main courses AZN22-39 and bottles of 1925 Laroque St Emilion Grand Cru for AZN1200. The broodingly indulgent interiors have black walls and gilded highlights, food comes on Villeroy & Boch china and the German chef turns out duck in an orange-pernod sauce on cauliflower mousse. The owner seems oddly proud of the bathroom designs which have mosaic floors depicting naked females.

● **Relaxed** A long-term expat favourite is the congenial diner-style *Sunset Café* (∂D3, 8 Äziz Äliyev) with appealing cinema décor, good coffee, unusually reliable salads and interesting twists on fast-food including vegetarian lavash wraps. Amusingly named *Pizza Hat* (∂K12) is a nice, arch-vaulted place aimed at younger locals and serving stuffed-steak, calamaris and various other alternatives in addition to their perfectly acceptable pizzas. Similarly *Pizza Inn* (∂I4, Fountains Sq) has a range of cuisines and while the décor is nothing remarkable it is the only place still to directly overlook the main strolling strip.

● **Italian** *Scalini* (τG3, ☎ 598 2850; 12-14.30 & 19-23.00), opposite the Hyatt, hits the perfect balance of casual cool with airy bistro-style sophistication. Great pastas come with crustini and ample Parmesan.

More central and pleasantly relaxed, the next-best Italian is *L'Oliva* (∂H4, ☎ 493 0954, 🖳 www.trattoria-oliva.com, pastas AZN10-19) offering good lunch specials and featuring a sushi lounge downstairs. The elegant *Ristorante Filharmonica* (φM3, ☎ 492 7788, pastas AZN11-18), within the philharmonia's south flank, gets the look right but struggles sometimes with the food.

Corleone (αK19, 40 Xaqani, ☎ 493 6473, mains AZN9-30, beers AZN5) has a hushed, overly intimate upmarket feel that can feel intimidating. There's a bar-menu for those eating in the more relaxed upstairs section but if menu prices seem too cheap they probably are. I was charged much more than the menu stated, though unusually they decently refunded the difference when I complained.

Il Gusto (∂M7, ☎ 494 8318, 🖳 www .ilgusto.az) has a particularly good value midweek lunch buffet (AZN7 including pizzas, salad bar, drink and dessert).

● **Middle Eastern** The city's two Lebanese restaurants are within a block on Tağiyev St,: the basement *Lebanese* (∂G4) does a 30-piece meze for AZN20; *Beyrut* (∂H4) has a more contemporary look; *Bibi* (τF1, ☎ 510 2632) is an inviting place to sample Iranian cuisine including fesinjan and käshki badimcan.

● **Spanish** With elegantly high-ceiling vaults *Tasca* (∂O7, 7 Qoqol, ☎ 596 2470, mains AZN12-18) is calm and suave but the leg of jamon is a plastic fake, the tapas isn't pre-prepared and the paellas (AZN27-37 for two) are serious investments.

● **Mexican** Several restaurants offer pseudo Mexican 'enchiladas' while Indian-owned *Mexicana* (∂H4, ☎ 498 9096) has a fuller range and various biz-lunches at AZN7-9. *Travellers' Coffee* (∂M9) serves quesaillas (AZN2.80-5.50) and *Sunset Café* (∂D3) generally has a Mexican Night once a week.

● **Indian** *Adams'* (∂D4) is primarily an unpretentious expat sports bar (Xirdalan AZN2) but Sarita's superb curries and espe-

cially the succulent Malai Chicken Tikka (AZN10) are unbeatable in Baku. For lavishly evocative Mugal-oriental décor along with good-value lunch deals try *Maharaja* (∂D4, ☎ 492 4334) or the marginally cheaper *Taj Mahal* (∂M13, 18 Xaqani, ☎ 493 0049). Tatty *Bombay Palace* (∂P9) is much less appealing.

● **Oriental** Expansive and mood-lit, *Hong Kong* (τE2, ☎ 436 9001) is about the most elegant Chinese place in town, main dishes AZN9-18, rice AZN2. Chic *Taboo* (αJ17, 33 Ü Hacibäyov, ☎ 598 1761, 🖳 www .taboo-baku.com) offers a range of fusion dishes along with showman-style teppanyaki. *Shanxay* (∂N5, 31 Räsul Rza, ☎ 495 4510) and cheaper *Great Wall* (∂H11, 26 Ü Hacibäyov, ☎ 493 7672, meals AZN7-15) offer little by way of décor but the Chinese food is well rated.

A recent fashion is for sushi served in lounge bar-style environments much as in Russia. However, as all fish must be flown in frozen, the maguro tends to be as flaccid and tasteless as it is expensive (typically nigiri-zushi costs AZN2-3 per piece) so Baku is unlikely to appeal to those who are genuine sushi fans. *Kill Bill* (ΣK11, Xirdalan beer AZN3, shisha AZN12) is typical, a black arched bar-café with leather settees, pink-purple walls and loud trance music. Mojitos by the jug cost from AZN14. Some readers enjoyed the sushi but mine was entirely lacklustre and not even served with wasabi or sushigari. Those are oversights you can forget at *Mado* (☎ 497 5544; τG1; nigiri-zushi AZN4-7 for two) which is much the grandest and most authentic-looking Japanese eatery, complete with stylish ceramics and kimono-clad waiting staff. However, even here the sashimi isn't always inspiring.

● **Fast food** Serving Biq Mak's (AZN3.20) and Dabl Çizburqers, *McDonald's* on Fountains Sq (∂L4) or at Gänclik Sq (θA6) is worth visiting if only to photograph the menu.

Apart from the name, the only thing French about *La Baguette* (∂I4) is the TV5 you watch while they pack your sandwiches (AZN2.80-6.30) or takeaway houmous.

BAKU PHONE CODE: 012

Rotisserie chicken is increasingly available from the spit but for freshness stick to high turnover places such as at αK16 opposite the Landmark.

Otherwise the local idea of fast food is the ubiquitous **döner kebab**, available from a myriad of booths and windows across central Baku. While AZN1 döners are available, paying AZN1.70 is generally worth the extra.

● **Bakeries and snacks** Baku is blooming with great bakeries, most of which have stand-and-snack tables and serve tea/soft drinks. Some have salad bars attached. The most visible is a chain called *Chudo Pechka* (*Çudo Peçka*, Magic Oven) with branches at ∂K1, ∂F10 and many other points including a large one, 300m east of Velotrek Hotel. Its signs are in pseudo-Russian script and the interiors are simultaneously modern yet evoke a Siberian cottage feel. There's a fabulous range of sweet and savoury delicacies including various styles of (pre-cooked) khajapuri and pizza. A good alternative is *Sari Sünbül* (∂P15) which does delicious *Kartoflu Chudu* (herby potato-stuffed pastries) and the city's best *Almalı Qatlama* (apple turnovers). *Häyät Bakery* (αQ15) opens 24 hours. In the arches of Nizami St you can still find a handy **khajapuri stand** at ∂M6.

CAFÉS, PUBS AND BARS
Terraces
Relatively inexpensive terrace bars are to be found at the north-west corner of Fountains Sq around the Araz Cinema. On Nizami St ever-popular *Shoarma #1* (∂L7) is the place to watch fellow strollers doing their passeggiata. For years there was a great bar-restaurant perched above a pond in Molokan Gardens, but the whole park was closed for a makeover at the time of research. The archetypal Soviet-era promenade café *Mirvari* (∂A7) is a curious open-sided structure with a clam-shell concrete roof. There are various summer tea terraces at ∂A6, ∂A11, ∂P11, ∂P9, or the City Park rotunda at φN2.

Cafés
Baku is now awash with coffee shops. Many are impressive fashion statements and most

now serve a reliable Italian-style brew, but so they should given that an espresso/cappuccino typically costs AZN3/4.50. Most also serve cocktails and light meals.

There are two Old City branches of *Chocolate*. The high-ceilinged original (ΣN10) near Sultan Inn has a gentle 1920s atmosphere with tasselled embroidery on wrought-iron tables. They serve Baku's best club sandwich (AZN7). A new *Chocolate II* (ΣU10) inhabits a large, appealing cellar room near the double gates.

Aroma Café (∂G9) has good cakes and great street-view sofas upstairs. Other chic sipping spots include *Fashion Café* (∂L7), *Vanilla* (∂K9) and *Hazz* (Landmark 1, αL16) which does sushi and cocktails as well as coffee.

Less indulgently opulent, *Café Caramel* (∂E4) has clean lines and good coffee comes with a biscuit and glass of drinking water. Split-level *Travellers' Coffee* (∂M9) is similarly styled but less intimate. *Dalida* (∂L4), atop the Nargiz Mall, has an appealing outdoor balcony with seating in summer but the interior is lacklustre. The best coffee in the ElmAk area is at *Baku Bean Roasters* (πN4).

Çayxanas and teahouses
Traditional downmarket çayxanas for a (male-only) 20q cuppa or AZN1 pot are becoming increasingly few and far between in central Baku though Çinar (πI9) and the summer-only garden places at βB7 and τG1 can still oblige.

Terraces on the Bulvar promenade and around Fountains Sq might charge anything from AZN2 to AZN8 for a pot and a cut-up Snickers-bar so double check. Meanwhile there's a whole new range of comfy teahouses specializing in qalyan/shisha ie hubble-bubble water pipe. Generally you'll pay around AZN15-30 for a tea-&-pipe set. Ironically it's often much cheaper to sip a beer (AZN2.50-3.50) in these places than to have tea and jam! If you're going to do the upmarket teahouse thing choose carefully as there are many that charge high prices without really giving you an atmosphere to match. A top choice is oriental extravaganza

Shadurvan (πT2). *Armudi* (αP23 Sarafieva) plays out an odd culture-clash with its comfy sofas and bow-tied waiters. The most upmarket teahouses aren't always 100% male but still it would be most unusual for unchaperoned women to venture in. One exception is *Kişmis* (ΣT9; 💻 www.kishmish.az, ☎ 492 9182), a cosy, quaintly inviting little Old City place that's more like an English tea shop albeit with sensibly relevant décor. Teas/coffees cost from AZN2.90/3.50 per cup, or AZN10.40 for a pot of tea with jams.

Somewhat cheaper if less salubrious places include *Çay Evi* (αE21), hidden inconspicuously beneath the wonderful oil-boom mansion at 145 Neftchilar, which serves a wide range of bag-tea by the cup (AZN2). Little *Sofrakhane* (τC4) is basic and the air's thick with fruity hookah smoke but the Iranian owner is delightfully hospitable.

Expat pubs

There are a dozen or so central pubs with Anglo-Irish pub décor and a significant proportion of expat clientele. Five years ago these places seemed disproportionately expensive and wafted a vague feeling of us-and-them economic apartheid. These days, however, locals often significantly outspend foreigners so many of the pubs have become comparatively fair-priced places to while away an evening. Pints of lager from AZN2 versus AZN20 for tea-&-jam... you choose!

Long-lasting favourites include the 'Cheers of Baku' *Adam's* (∂D4, happy hours, pool table), *Finnegans* (∂E4) and the *William Shakespeare* (∂K7). *Corner Bar* (∂N5) is a personal favourite with AZN2 '33' beers, good music and a pub feel that's not overly contrived. A series of other bars and pubs are gathered nearby including *Crossroads Sports Bar*, inexpensive *Stranger* (beers from AZN1.40), perennial down-market survivor *Madonna*, and *The Garage* (∂N5) pitting Teesiders against Geordies. Cosily appealing little *O'Malleys* (∂M4) shares a summer terrace area with *Tequila Junction* (pool table) and *Caledonian* (Scottish crowd). Up a notch, *The Lounge* (τG3) has the rather

exclusive feel of a gentleman's club.

Baku's one microbrew-pub, *The Brewery* (φP2) occupies a large Germanic cavern and its ales are very quaffable, the darkest being the most successful of three varieties.

Sunset Cafe (∂D3) has more of an American bar-café feel; *Azza* (∂I2) and *No Name* (∂L14) have upmarket cocktail lounges but a better choice given the fabulous views is the top-floor of the ISR Plaza (∂M4). *The Lab* (∂L3) is a calm, chocolate-toned midmarket lounge-style bar with fashionable furniture, prints of Old Baku and (small) beers at AZN3.

Pint for a pittance

A youthfully atmospheric (if smoky) place for AZN1 Xirdalans is *Elephant* (∂F3). *Çinar* (πI9) beside the Funicular base station has an OK terrace and tea or Xirdalan beer costs only AZN1. If you need to rendezvous near the station or wait for a train, *Elite* (∂U13) has cheap NZS and a calm, pine-and-bearskin interior.

Some smaller bars in the north-western corner of Fountains Sq are relatively inexpensive and have terraced seating. Cheap, unexotic places not far from Axundov Gardens include *Arbat* (φW4, NZS 60q) and next-door *Shark Pub* (Xirdalan AZN1). the summer-only tea terraces at τF1 and βB7 also sell cheap beers.

NIGHT CLUBS

The ever-changing club on the Bulvar was known as *X-ite* (φN10, Thur-Sun, 8pm-late, variable cover) at the time of writing. *Le Chevalier* (τL2, cover AZN5) beneath the Europe Hotel is popular with business types while unsophisticated *Black Jack* (∂O10) is better value (no cover, drinks AZN3-6, bar 22-24:00 then disco till 04.00). The latter is likely to close at least for a while once the Nizami Cinema building's renovation gets underway. *Infiniti (ex-Key) Club* (∂P7) is popular with Peace Corps volunteers on R&R. Several expat pubs have live music. *Chill Out* is a misleading name for a small, ever-thumping DJ bar at ∂F3.

BAKU

BAKU

Le Mirage (∂L3) has occasionally been amusing if a little raunchy. Dozens of other mini-clubs, mostly in small underground rooms, attract a male clientele plus girls with price tags. These places can be fun if you're with the right crowd or if you actually like to buy your dates. They're easy enough to spot on or near Bül Bül St, notably around ∂P9.

ENTERTAINMENT
Live music
● **Classical** One of the proudest achievements of the Soviet system was patronage of the fine arts. However, both the splendid Philharmonia (φM2 [2], p85) and ornate Opera-Ballet (∂M12, p95) considerably predate the revolution. The latter has a great proscenium arch, gigantic chandelier and cherubic pillar support figures. It's worth the extra for a seat in the stalls (*parter*) since chattering students in the gallery (*amfiteatr*) can be distracting.

Classical recitals are also held from time to time at the Conservatory (Academy of Music, ∂S11) and in the Mamedova Opera Salon beneath.
● **Organ and chamber music** Concerts are held occasionally in the old German Church (∂Q14, ☎ 493 7537). Take a hot water bottle in winter and pretend you don't notice the metro rattling beneath you every few minutes.
● **Jazz** The **Jazz Centre** (∂R12, ☎ 437 5533) hosts regular live performances with food and drinks available. The much-cosier and brilliantly quirky *Karavan Jazz Café* (∂B3), beside Giakonda, has sadly become largely dormant though it might be worth checking to see if it's been reincarnated.

In late May or early June **Baku Jazz Festival** has, for several years, been reason enough to come to Azerbaijan. Star guests have included Herbie Hancock (in 2006) (much quoted as saying that President Ilham Aliyev was a 'very nice guy') and the stupendous Aziza Mustafazadeh (in 2007). However, at present its funding is in doubt.
● **Muğam** Regular muğam ensembles wail mournful ditties about the beauties of Azerbaijan and the loss of Shusha as you dine at the Karavansara (p115), Elbara (p103) and as part of an extensive dinner show at the Muğam Club (pp114-15). The big new Muğam Evi (Muğam House) on the Bulvar will hopefully organize more Muğam events in future.
● **Pop music** Azer-pop musicians play at most upmarket local restaurants on busier evenings and are on call for parties and wedding feasts. Many offer cheesy Casio Organ oriental singalong favourites in darkened glitter-ball halls. However, for reliably high standards try Bäh Bäh or Xari Bül Bül (good, reasonable food too, p116). The best-known stars play at whichever restaurant is in vogue at the time.

Heydar Aliyev Saray (formerly Republican Palace, ∂U9, tickets ∂T10) is the main rock-concert venue hosting most Western stars that blunder into town (if you can classify Imagination or Matt Bianco as 'stars'); although fully renovated the sound system leaves a little to be desired. Elton John's much-discussed September 2007 gig was played at the **Tofiq Bahramov national stadium** (see p107). For interesting stories ask those who went to that show how the ticketing worked!

Cinemas
Near Fountains Sq, Azerbaijan Cinema (Aziz Aliyev St, ∂D3) is Baku's most comfortable air-conditioned multiplex, though when completed the new Bulvar Shopping Mall (∂C14) should have an eight-screen multiplex while the big Nizami Cinema (∂O10) is due for total reconstruction. Less salubrious cinemas include the Araz (∂K2), Vartan (∂M6), Dostluq (βH7) and Shusha (ϑD7).

Theatres and other venues
Baku has a vibrant scene though getting information as to what's on where can prove surprisingly difficult. Sudden postponements are not uncommon especially for one-off shows and recently a number of high profile events have been mainly restricted to VIPs. Don't be put off – the challenge adds to the excitement of getting in. The local press should have partial event details as does 🖳 www.bakuguide.az, and AzTV has a brief events slot at 8.59am (in Azeri) but the best source of info is word of mouth. Note that

most theatres only operate October to June.

If you don't understand the local language, the best bets are the musical-based spectacles at the **Opera-Ballet** ∂M12 (☎ 493 3449, p95), **Philharmonia** p85, **Musical Comedy Theatre** ∂B5 (p91), **Puppet Theatre** ∂A3 (p124) or **Behbutov Song Theatre** ∂M12 (p96). Lively pantomime-theatre is staged at **Şafaq** (βC7), a former chapel that's also used as a low-budget cinema. Bigger events are also held at **Heydar Aliyev Saray** (see opposite). If there's a concert in the **Green Theatre** (πH8, Yaşil Teatr) be aware that it's an open-air auditorium so bring warm clothes on a cold evening and don't waste your time showing up if it's raining! However, on a clear day there are great views over the bay, especially from row 34 at the very top.

If you're more linguistically adept, Baku's most creative new drama is showcased at the very intimate **Üns Theatre** (φF4, 69 Neftchilar, ☎ 437 2395) and at **Ibrus Theatre** (πL7, ☎ 497 1910) owned by (and named after) Oscar-winning film director Rustam Ibrahimbeyov (see pp365-6).

Milli Theatre (Füzüli Sq, ☎ 494 4840, ∂U1) is the top spot for bigger-scale Azeri and Turkish drama and also offers some lighter-hearted productions. The **Russian Drama Theatre** (∂L7, ☎ 493-0063, 🖳 www.rusdrama-az.com) is the equivalent for Russian-language productions. The **Bälädiyä** (Kamera/Chamber) **Theatre** (∂G12) and hideously ugly **Young Performers' Theatre** (∂L11) were under total reconstruction at the time of writing.

Sports and pastimes
(See p61 for a national overview.)
● **Bowling (ten-pin)** At Baku Entertainment Center (BƏM, ΨH11, ☎ 490 2222) lanes cost AZN18 *per hour*, double after 5pm and at weekends. Reservations cost AZN10 extra! A cheaper option, unless you're with a big group, is Olimpik Star (ΨK6, 5A Chamanzamanli, ☎ 449 4001) at the very top of Vurğun, close to the Ambassador Hotel. Bowling costs AZN6 per person per game, there's a toddler zone (AZN2) and various video games (80q).

● **Chess, dominoes and nard** The childhood chess club of famous Bakuvian world champion, Garry Kasparov, is still in regular use at 42 Hüsi Haciev/Azerbaijan St (∂R1, ☎ 437 1345, 🖳 www.chessclub.az) with the best chance of a game on Saturday mornings. Nard, dominoes and chess are played in çayxanas and city parks (eg ∂B7, βI7) often by old men.
● **Football** Roughly half of Azerbaijan's top league sides are from Baku, while Bailov Rovers, a team of expats, has proved good enough to play in the national third division! Big matches and internationals are played at Tofiq Bahramov national stadium near Gänclik metro (ϑA7). Advance ticket sales are available from the football association, AFFA (☎ 490 8721; 🖳 www .affa.az, 2208 Nobel Avenue) whose website lists fixtures. Several expat bars televise British and international matches.
● **Golf** At the time of writing there was a golf-driving range (ΨM1, AZN5 per bucket of 50 balls) at the Olympic Shooting Center but its continuation is in doubt.
● **Gyms** All the top hotels have sports clubs with a selection of facilities (swimming pool, training gym etc), with annual non-guest membership fees from $800-2500 or around AZN 30 per day as at Olympus in the Hotel Europe (p111). Crescent Beach Hotel (p113) has squash and tennis, jet skis, wind surfing and various water sports.
● **The Hash** The Hash House Harriers meet for non-competitive fun runs most Sundays. See 🖳 www.bahhh.com.
● **Horses** Azerbaijan Jockey Club (☎ 447 4505, 🖳 www.ajk.az) is just beyond Bina Airport off the Mardakan highway. It's an impressive complex with racetrack, VIP stand, private restaurant and a vast complex of stables where you can get horse-riding lessons at AZN10 – call Sveta ☎ mobile 050 314 5938 (English spoken). Horseraces are at 5pm on Saturdays (May to Sept). Four categories of horse are raced: thoroughbreds, Arabian, Turkmen (Akhalteke) and local Karabaghs (strong but slower).
● **Martial arts** There's a strong martial arts scene with major competitions held at the

BAKU

Idman Sarayi (φB4). Baku hosted the WTF Taekwondo Team Championships in 2009. Useful contacts: Taekwondo Federation (☎ 496 3987, ✉ taekwondo@azeurotel.com), Aik-ido Federation (☎ 467 5895), Contact Karate (☎ 476 9721), Karate Federation (☎ 498 1100). Aiki-Jiujitsu (✉ www.azcra.org).

● **Motor sports** While hardly Formula 1, you can drink, dine and drive go-karts at MET Karting (ΨM12, ☎ 490 8222, 1993 Aliyar Aliyev St near Keshla Station) several kilometres out of the centre.

● **Mountain-bike excursions** The well-organized BBC (Baku Bike Club, ✉ www .bakubicycleclub.com) arranges pedal-powered expat excursions and they have excellent route-maps based on Google Earth views of the Baku region.

● **Other sports** Spectator volleyball, boxing etc usually takes place at the Idman Sarayi, usually translated rather dubiously as the 'Palace of Handgames'. Basketball matches are held at the Olympic Center (ϑA9) in Gänclik. To play volleyball and mini-football, pitches can be rented at the nearby Gänclik Sports Center.

● **Paintball** Organized at the Delfin Hotel (p113, ✉ www.delfinhotel.az/paintball), AZN12 for 50-shots. Call ☎ 406 6400 or mob ☎ 050-250-1912.

● **Rugby** Baku Exiles are a mostly expat rugby team. See ✉ www.bakuexiles rc.com.

● **Shooting** Clay-pigeon shooting (AZN30 for ten rounds including rifle hire) is possible at the Olympic Shooting Center (ΨM1) on the north-west edge of the city. Contact Francis Matthew (mob ☎ 050-624 2002).

● **Squash** The Hyatt's Oasis fitness club (τH2, ☎ 490 7551) has two squash courts.

● **Swimming** Of hotel pools my favourite is the Ramada's (p113). For serious sportsfolk there's the covered Gänclik pool (ϑA9, ✉ www.ganjlik.net) where swimming lessons can be arranged, ladies only 2-4pm. For more casual splashabouts try Delfin Hotel's pool (with swim-up bar) or Baku Entertainment Center (ΨH11, AZN30, ✉ www.bem.az) whose eccentrically shaped indoor pool has its own waterfall. Head out to the Absheron for waterslides: there are two at Märdäkan Beach (p150) or the full-

blown waterpark at Novxani Beach (p159).

Note that the Aquapark Building on Behbudov St no longer actually hosts a pool or waterpark.

● **Tennis** There are functioning tennis courts at the Hyatt, Delfin and Crescent Beach hotels, on the Bulvar near the puppet theatre, at Gänclik sports centre (ϑA9, ☎ 465 8400, ✉ www.ganjlik.net) and at Old Gänclik. The cheap Leyla Tennis courts (βE3, ☎ 494 8836) closed during the reconstruction of Officer Park and their future is uncertain.

● **Windsurfing** Expats with their own boards favour the Bilgah beach 'around the corner' from the more popular bathing spot at Amburan (Absheron Peninsula, p146). Winds here are usually good, though the waves are choppy. You can rent boards and jet skis at Crescent Beach Hotel.

BAKU FOR CHILDREN

Zum Zum (αR22) and **Baby Bom** (∂R11, ☎ 437 5686) are toddler play zones cum creche. **Koala Park** (βH6, ✉ www.koala park.az, 10am-11pm, entry AZN3) has miniature fair rides (80q-AZN2.50 per go) and amusements aimed at 4 to 8 year olds. **Electric kiddy-cars** have once again started to harry pedestrians on Fountains Sq and the Bulvar as well as in the busy park near metro Narimanov. **Skateboards**, roller-blades and **mountain bikes** are sold at the sports shop at α18. There's a variety of **video games** and simulator rides at Aquapark (βD5). Many internet clubs offer **network games**, albeit usually with a violent terrorists-v-cop theme. There are some **pinball machines** in the bowling alley at Baku Entertainment Center (ΨH11).

The **Children's Railway** offers 10-minute rides at walking-speed pace (20q) that kids might find a little dull, though toddlers seem to love the train's bright colours. In summer it departs Dädä Qorqud station (βH9, near the **zoo**) at 11am, noon, 1, 4, 5, 6 and 7pm returning 20 mins later from Bahar station (ϑA6, behind the Ramstore at Gänclik). The **puppet theatre** (∂A3) has enthralling shows but they're not in English. A peep behind the scenes makes a visit even more interesting.

MAP SYMBOL KEY Ψ p77; Σ p83; φ p86; ∂ pp92-3; α p99; τ p105; π p101; β p106; ϑ p107

❏ Crossing the city centre: car and taxi logic

By car/taxi, crossing town **eastbound** you have two main choices: either go along the Bulvar/Neftchilar with no turns possible until Dom Soviet, or squeeze along Safiroğlu (Shors) or M Aliyev streets. Plans to demolish a whole city block south of Füzuli St to create a wide park-boulevard between Füzuli Sq and Heydar Aliyev Saray will likely add a new option. **Westbound** cars can take Zärifä Äliyeva (formerly Azerbaijan) pr, Füzuli St, or 28th May Ave (continuing onto Aslanov St to reach the Radisson/upper Fountains Sq area). However, there's no way across 'new' Azerbaijan pr (formerly Hüsu Haciyev St, one-way northbound). So to reach Içäri Şähär metro you'll have to go all the way up and around Füzuli Sq and back via the Wedding Palace on Muxtarov or alternatively loop right around the Old City via the Bulvar/Neftchilar and Azneft Sq. There's no easy way to drive from the south-east to the northern side of Fountains Sq so it's much quicker to walk. If you take a taxi, don't be surprised to see half the city en route!

There's a **Mothercare** shop at (πV3) and **All 4 Kids** (τG4) is well stocked.

GETTING AROUND
Walking

The Fountains Sq/Nizami St central area is reasonably compact and increasingly pedestrianized making walking the most sensible option, even though this can be a sweaty business in midsummer.

Taxis

Most taxi drivers do not use meters. Fares have rocketed over recent years and it's now tough to find a ride across town for less than AZN5 or AZN3 for a very short hop. To the airport you're looking at AZN15-20. However, for around AZN40 you could charter a taxi around the city for a whole afternoon.

During the day it's easy to flag down passing cabs on almost any city street. At night the easiest places to find one are at the bigger hotels (the prices not quite as inflated as one might expect), directly south of the main station, and on a small rank behind the south-west corner of Fountains Sq. Taxis also buzz around the most popular expat bars ready to scoop up the dizzy revellers from whichever bar is currently in fashion. Note that older drivers tend to be more competent and also generally speak better Russian than youngsters.

Locals tend to keep the mobile phone numbers of a few reliable drivers with whom rates tend to be comparatively favourable so ask friends for recommendations. Or you can call one of the central taxi agencies such as Grand (☎ 437 9999, ⌨ http://taxi.az).

Driving

Driving in Baku is quite stressful for the uninitiated. Although comprehensive resurfacing has removed the tram-tracks and once-ubiquitous pot holes, the one-way system is nightmarish, nobody sticks to their lanes, there are stupidly parked cars and any vehicle (especially minibuses) may decide to stop abruptly in front of you without warning. Cars start to accelerate away from traffic lights when they are still flashing red. However, don't try to go through such a light when it starts flashing green at the end of the cycle, let alone amber – you'll be pulled over immediately by lurking cops.

Street parking is generally free but old codgers with red armbands guard the busier roadsides. When you leave they'll wave you out into the oncoming traffic with reckless abandon, a dangerous pleasantry for which you're perversely expected to tip. Park for long and you may find that your car has been washed for you. Failing to pay the 'washing fee' for that unwanted service can result in mysterious punctures should you park in the vicinity again!

See p18 if you still dare to hire a car.

Metro

The metro can get crowded and sweaty at peak times but several of the stations have very stylishly designed platforms (eg Elm Ak, Neftchilar, Gänclik). The mosaics at the bottom of the escalators in Nizami station are especially splendid. But don't take photos; you'll risk having your camera confiscated. The staff retain a Soviet mentality towards transport infrastructure secrecy spiced by strong memories of the 1994 metro bombings in which a little-known Lezghian Independence group killed 20 commuters including jazz pianist-composer Rafiq Babayev. A year later, a mysterious fire between Ulduz and Narimanov stations killed 300 in what was the world's worst metro accident.

The metro is great value at only 10q per hop. But before you use it you'll need to pay AZN2 (refundable) for a plastic metro-card similar to a London Oyster-card. This card is then 'loaded' with credit (minimum ten-rides) and tapped against a reader on entering the station.

At the time of writing the metro line was being extended. By 2010 the line will continue three stops east from M Acami to Därnägül and a second spur line is planned from M Acami to the new bus station out at ΨΟ1.

Note that Cäfär Cabbarly and 28th May (Yirimi sekis mai) are different platforms of the same station. However, contrary to the implications of almost all published maps, all trains use the 28th May platform except for the one-stop Cäfär Cabbarly–Xatai spur). Metro maps still misleadingly imply that through trains run from Xatai to Memar Acami. In fact you'd need to transfer at 28th May/Cäfär Cabbarly.

Buses and minibuses (Marshrutki)

For 20q, bus and minibus services cover the city with remarkable frequency until around 10pm (some routes continue more sporadically till around midnight). However, the cumbersome one-way system makes many routes rather convoluted. Don't assume that a service that takes you in one direction will necessarily take you back the same way!

Buses have fixed stops but beyond the city centre minibuses will often screech to a halt wherever flagged or whenever an alighting passenger yells 'Sakhla!' (stop).

Route numbers are clearly displayed. Minibuses list primary stops on boards in

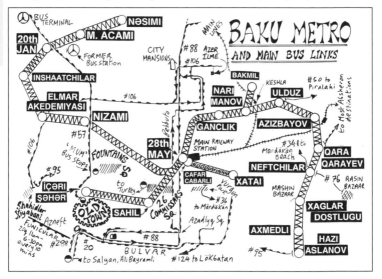

the window but there are many abbreviations (see box pp128-9) and stop-names to
learn and given the sheer number of possible route options, it's worth memorizing at
least a few key routes. Usefully many of the
most common routes tend to use standardized vehicle types and colours making iden-
tification easier.

● **#1 minibus** Vurğun Gardens to Araz
Hotel, Ramstore and straight along Heydar
Aliyev pr.

● **#1A minibus** From north side of the station east to Sharq Bazaar.

● **#5** Links Bayil and Shahidlär Xiyabani,
sometimes using a curious back route.

● **#3 minibus** From City Centre Mall
(φW8) via Axundov Gardens, Narimanov
Statue, Azizbäyov Heyk (πK4), botanical
Gardens, Patamdar.

● **#20 new full-sized buses, often green**
Heads west from Xatai metro, along 28 Mai
St, then Zärifä Äliyeva (ex Azerbaijan pr)
emerging onto Bulvar at the carpet museum
and continuing round the bay to Bayil.

● **#88 & 288 usually boxy 'Otoyol' vehicles often painted in national colours**
Southbound the routes follow Azadlyq
from way out in the suburbs all the way to
the Landmark then swing west on Zärifä
Aliyeva (ex Azerbaijan pr), pass Sahil
Metro and Cänub Hotel before emerging
onto the Bulvar at the Carpet Museum. The
#88 turns round at Azneft Sq while the 288
continues to Bayil passing the Sälyan and
Qobustan bus stands. Returning, both fol-
low the Bulvar to Dom Soviet, then climb
Behbutov past the Milli Bank and
Aquapark. At Bakixanov St, they shimmy
three blocks east then continue north beside
Irshad Hotel, sidestepping a block west on
Ingilab before continuing north up Azadlyq.

● **#52/57 various vehicles** From Içäri Şähär
(Bakı Soveti) Metro past Ismayıllı Palace,
Fountains Sq and MUM to Füzuli Sq (Besh
Märtäbä), up Akhmedbekov and beneath
Bakikhanov at KöhA/V (a short walk from
the Hyatt Regency), past Europe Hotel and
on to 20th Jan and the main bus station. The
return route is approximately the same but
passes Nizami Metro and from Füzuli Sq
diverts via either Muxtarov or Zargarpalan Sq
according to the driver's whim.

● **#59 minibuses or Otoyol** From Vurğun

Gardens (αP18, [V2]) cuts across town
along Füzuli St to 5Märtäbä then follows
the #52/57 routes. Returning it again follows Füzuli St thence cutting south to the
Landmark and back up to the AZAL
office/Vurğun Park.

● **#71** Is similar to #88 in the city centre
but continues northbound on Behbutov at
Zorge Park.

● **#75** Basically the 95 loop but in reverse.

● **#95 new full-sized buses, generally
orange** Starts at Shahidlär Xiyabani,
descends past the old city then crosses right
across town Hazi Aslanov Metro. Returning
it passes Vurğun Gardens and loops right up
past ElmAk.

● **#106 boxy 'Otoyol' vehicles, usually
orange** Starts at Shähidlär Xiyabani (πH7)
loops past Azizäyov Heyk, Avis, ElmAk,
Cavid Sq, Olimp Shop and the Hyatt
Regency then shoots east along Bakixanov
past the Russian embassy turning north past
Irshad Hotel.

● **#124** Starts from αM17 [V4] and runs
along the coast past Bibi Heybat and Shix(ov)
Beach all the way to Lökbätan (map p139).

● **#127** Starts from approximately outside
the Behbutov Song Theatre (∂M12) and
heads up Vurğun passing Taza Bazaar.

● **#145** Runs across town from the station,
turns right at Füzuli Sq, then right again on
Bakixanov.

● **#338** From Milli Bank via Täza Bazaar
and Gänclik to Narimanov Metro.

● **#345 minibus** Heads west from Milli
Bank (∂U13), turns north at Füzuli Sq, west
again up Nakhchivani St then loops labori-
ously round via Olimp, ElmAk and
Shähidlär Xiyabani finally returning via
MUM/Fountains Sq.

Tram

Baku's juddering old tramway system has
now been entirely dismantled and the tracks
removed. As their main function seemed to
be to cause traffic disruption, few have
mourned their passing.

GETTING TO/LEAVING BAKU
By air

Baku's Heydar Aliyev International Airport
is a kilometre off the main Baku–Märdäkän
road at Bina. The terminals are clean and

pleasantly efficient. Beware of pushy porters who have been known to demand nonsensical rates to carry your bags.

Airport transport A taxi should cost AZN15 from central Baku. From the airport drivers typically ask AZN20 or more but by day you'll get a better price simply by walking across to the domestic terminal and bargaining with drivers there. I once managed AZN10. You might save a manat or two by getting a taxi to Azizbayov then

taking the metro. The cheapest solution (albeit hard with any baggage) is to walk/hitch 1km down to the main Mardakan road and wave down a #36 minibus. Guests at the airport's Holiday Inn (see p113) are provided with a free shuttle service into town.

By train

Some of the station buildings are attractive and the Moorish-style waiting room is well worth a look. Several cheap restau-

---

❏ Useful bus stop names and abbreviations to recognize

● **5Märt** (Besh Mertebe) is bus terminology for Füzuli Sq (∂U1).

● **20Jan** (Yirimi Yanvar, ΨL3) is the self-explanatory square near 20th Jan metro, close to the former (now defunct) main bus station.

● **28May** (Yirimi Sekis Mai, αV15) Train station area, typically Azadlyq St (αV15) but can also mean that the bus passes within a few blocks, the term overlapping somewhat with **Vurğ Bağ** (see opposite).

● **AxBağ** (Axundov Bağı, ie Akhundov Garden, φU-V2), five minutes' walk from Içäri Şähär (Bakı Soveti) metro.

● **A/V**, **Avtovaqzal** means bus station so should mean the new main bus terminal (ΨO1). However, some buses haven't changed signboards since February 2009 before which A/V was synonymous with 20 Jan Sq, previous site of the main bus station. That might eventually come to be known as **KöhA/V** or **Köhnä Avtovaqzal** ('Old Bus Station')... but beware that that term at present still refers to the site of an even older bus station long ago removed from the junction of Bakixanov and Moskva/Tbilisi streets where the Natavan Residence (τH4) now stands.

● **Aviakassa** refers to any stop near the AZAL office (αO21). The term overlaps somewhat with Vurğun Bağı.

● **Äzizbäyov hej** is the site of a former waving Azizbäyov statue (πK4) not to be confused with **Azizbayov M**, the metro station.

● **Azneft** (φI5) is at the south-west corner of the Old City.

● **BakSov** means the north edge of the Old City (Istiglalyyat Ave) referring to Bakı Soveti, the old name for Içäri Şähär metro station.

● **Basin** old term for Füzuli St (∂U1-U14).

● **Besh Märtäbä (5Märt)** means Füzuli Sq (∂U1).

● **Bulvar** is the seaside Boulevard, ie Pr Neftchilär.

● **Dost K** refers to Dostluq Cinema at the corner of Azadlyq and Bakixanov streets (βG7).

● **Elm Ak** is metro Elmar Akademiyasi (πR3).

● **KöhA/V** used to imply the Natavan Residence junction (βH1), but see A/V above.

● **M** often written in red denotes a metro station.

● **M/R** refers to any of the sprawling, numbered MicroRayon suburbs at the northern edge of town.

● **M/R3 baz** is the bazaar (ΨL5) between 20th Jan and the Hippodrome.

● **Mehm Nax** is a now-rare abbreviation for the Hyatt Regency (former Naxçıvan Hotel).

MAP SYMBOL KEY Ψ p77; Σ p83; φ p86; ∂ pp92-3; α p99; τ p105; π p101; β p106; ϑ p107

rants nearby such as *Pitixana* and *Elite* (both ∂U13) are handy while you're waiting for a train. The nearest grocery stores for provisions are on Azadlyq St. The station has two left-luggage rooms (*saxlama kamerasi*, AZN2 per day). The one beneath the platforms off the passage between *kassa* (ticket desks) 18 and 19 seems the more reliable.

There are various trains to Russia (including 3/week to Moscow's Kursk station). However, foreigners aren't allowed to use these. Ticket clerks check your passport when selling tickets so you can't 'pretend' to be local.

The nightly sleeper to Tbilisi costs AZN26, kupe.

Daily domestic sleeper services leave for Ağstafa (21.10), Gänjä (23.10), Qazax and Böyük Käsik (21.20), Astara and Horodiz (23.55), and Bärdä and Balakän (via Shäki, 21.40). The first three (plus the Tbilisi service) all go via Gänjä. Dual destination trains divide part way. There are also

---

- **Milli Bank** (Behbutov St west of the copper tower, ∂U12) is a very busy collection of stops.
- **MUM** is technically the department store (∂L1) but in fact there are several widely spaced stops for Fountains Sq that can go by this name. Southbound it means anywhere along Muxtarov or Zargapalan streets. Depending on the mood of the police north- or eastbound buses might or might not be allowed to stop at ∂H1 south of Standard Bank (for Fountains Sq). If not, try flagging one down at MUM [A] (∂F1) or walk up to MUM [C] (∂N1) on Azärbaycan pr (Hüsi Haciyev) between Tagizade and Tolstoy streets. MUM [B] (∂H1) is the starting point for several services towards Shähidlär Xiyabani via AxBağ.
- **Narimanov Pr** refers to the street between **Narimanov hej** (the big statue, π N6) and New World Supermarket (τE1). Note that **Narimanov M** (the Metro station) is on the opposite side of town at ΨK11.
- **Näsimi Baz** (ΨJ8) is on Azadlyq north of Bakixanov St.
- **Olimp** refers to a long-established shop (πU5) halfway down Inshaatchilar between Cavid Sq and the Hyatt Hotel.
- **Ramstore** refers to the big Ramstore supermarket (ΨI11). In fact most buses so marked pass the Araz and Excelsior hotels but bypass Ramstore itself by around 300m.
- **Sahil M** Westbound buses marked Sahil M drive along Zärifä Äliyeva (ex Azerbaijan pr) stopping across Bül Bül from Cänub Hotel (∂F10). Eastbound they pass along the Bulvar a block further south.
- **Sahil Bağ** means Sahil Gardens, typically the north-west corner (∂K10) but possibly Behbudov St ∂H-L12.
- **Sabunçu Dairasi** A spaghetti junction of new flyovers at the intersection of the airport and Mashtaga highways makes this a very awkward place to attempt to change buses.
- **ŞX** or various other abbreviations = Shähidlar Xiyabani (πH7).
- **TiBB Uni** (ΨJ6) – top end of Vurğun St
- **VurgBağ (Vurğun Bağı)** implies one of almost a dozen stops dotted round Vurğun Park just south of the main train station (see list and map p99).
- **Yirmi Sekis Mai** (see 28th May).

NOTES:
- For **Fountains Sq** use MUM
- For the **Old City** use Azneft, BakSov, AxBağ or Bulvar
- For the **Station** use 28May or VurgBag
- For the **Hyatt area** jump off at KöhA/V or Nax Mehm.

❏ Airline offices

• **AZAL** (☎ 493 4004, 🖳 www.azal.az, 08-20.00) General ticketing for Azerbaijan's state airline is normally at αO21 though while that building remains under renovation visit SW Travel (∂M14)

• **Aeroflot** (∂I15, Hacibäyov 25, ☎ 488 1167, 🖳 www.aeroflot.ru/eng) to Moscow Sheremetyevo

• **AeroSvit Ukrainian Airlines** (τH2, Hyatt ☎ 436 8785, 🖳 www.aerosvit. com) To Kiev... or via Kiev to New York (JFK, Fridays, from US$950 return), Hamburg, Naples, Budapest, Prague, Sofia and Warsaw (from $560 return). Most Western nationals can now stopover in Ukraine without a visa.

• **Austrian** (τE4, Caspian Plaza, ☎ 497 1822, 🖳 www.aua.com) Wide international network via Vienna.

• **Belavia** (c/o Meridian Travel, Nizami 100/1, ☎ 493 0494, 🖳 www.belavia.by) to Minsk, Belarus

• **BMI** (τH3, Hyatt, ☎ 497 7701, www .flybmi.com) to London Heathrow

• **China Southern** (αP19, 54 28th May St, ☎ 598 1165, 🖳 www.csair.com/en) Connect via Ürümqi to a wide selection of Chinese destinations.

• **Imair** (∂K8 c/o Improtex, 16 Vurğun, ☎ 598 4587)

• **Iran Air** (∂K6, ☎ 498 5886) Mon & Thu to Tehran by Fokker 100. Just a few international connections are feasible without the need for an Iranian visa.

• **Kolavia** (∂K8, c/o Improtex, ☎ 493 0896, 🖳 www.kolavia.ru) to Surgut in northern Russia (flights from Ganja)

• **Perm** (🖳 www.aviaperm.ru) flies to Perm

• **S7 Airlines** (αN20; Zorge St, ☎ 498 3077, 🖳 www.s7.ru) Connects via Novosibirsk or Moscow to most cities in Russia

• **Scat Kazakhstan Airlines** (αN20, 🖳 www.scat.kz, ☎ 498 1918, Nizami 135) to Atirau (AZN220), Aktau (AZN200) and Astana (AZN355), Kazakhstan

• **Lufthansa** (τH3, Hyatt, ☎ 490 7050) to Ashgabat, Turkmenistan and world-wide via Frankfurt, Germany.

• **Rossiya** (αP22, 29/11 28th May St, ☎ 598 2931, 🖳 www.rossiya-airlines. ru/en/) to St Petersburg

• **THY Turkish** (∂N1, 11 Azerbaijan [Hüsi Haciyev], ☎ 494 1943)

• **Turan Air** (αO21, 68/64 28th May St, ☎ 498 9431, 🖳 www.turan-air.com)

• **Tatarstan Aero** (🖳 www.tatarstan .aero) to Kazan on Tuesdays

• **Ural** (αN20, 135 Nizami, ☎ 493 9139, 🖳 www.uralairlines.ru/en) to Yekaterinburg on Thursdays

• **UTAir** (c/o Aeroplan, Nizami 102, ☎ 493 9260) to Moscow Vnukovo (thrice weekly), and Ufa (Fridays). Summer services to Nizhnevartovsk via Khanty Mansysk (Saturday)

• **Uzbekistan Airways** (αM19, 98 Nizami, ☎ 598 3120, 🖳 www.uzair ways.com).

day trains to Gänjä (8am, 7hrs) and Astara. For the first 85 minutes all of the above wind round the back of Baku so should you just miss your train, you'll probably be able to catch it up at Qaradağ station (near Sahil, p139) though the taxi fare would be considerably more than your original ticket.

Suburban 'elektrichka' services to the Absheron peninsula towns also use the main railway station for now but might eventually be relocated. Buy tickets aboard.

Stopping day-trains/elektrichkas to Xachmaz and to Älät leave from Keshla station (reached by minibus #221) but buses are faster and much more frequent for those destinations.

By bus and minibus
Baku's vast new bus terminal (ΨO1]) finally opened in February 2009. However, the completion of a metro spur that should link it to Memar Acami station remains at least

a year or two away. Till then bus 284 (10q) shuttles every 3mins from 20th Jan metro to the terminal. These buses are currently very overloaded with the constant stream of Sumqayit-bound passengers whose marshrutki services have also been shifted to the new terminal.

The bus terminal handles almost all long-distance services plus numerous marshrutki including #14 via Corat. However, for the following destinations you'll need to start elsewhere:

● For **Sälyan**, **Şirvan** (formerly Äli Bayramlı) and **Neftchala** use **Salyan bus station** (ΨC6), accessed by city buses 5, 20 and 288.

● For **Qobustan** take Älät-bound minibus 105 starting outside 30 Qurban Abbasov, opposite the Moon Crown restaurant (πA9) in Bayil. Access by bus 20 and 288.

● For **Lökbätan** take minibus 124 from [V4] αM17 near the Landmark Building.

● For **Märdäkän** town and **Shüvelan** take minibus 36 from Vurğun Gardens ([V7] αR18) or bus 24 from Metro Qara Qarayev (map below).

Qara Qarayev Area

● For **Märdäkän Beach** take bus 341 from Metro Neftchilar (map p116)

● For **Novxanı** and **Yanar Dağ** start at Gänclik Metro (ϑA7).

● For **Pirallahı (Artyom Island)** take minibus 50 from Ulduz Metro (ΨM14).

● For most other **east Absheron towns** start at one of several stops around Metro Qara Qarayev (above) or Metro Neftchilar.

● Turkish buses to **Istanbul** (US$60) via **Trabzon** ($50), operated by various companies, all depart en masse around 3pm on Tue, Thu, Sat from near their respective ticket offices. Most are around Sahil Gardens including Gürsoy (☎ 498 3034,

ϑK10); Kavasoğlu (☎ 498 1445, ϑG10 downstairs); Öy Nuhöğlu (Vurğun 94, ☎ 444 7203/447 3434, ϑK11, Istanbul 212-632 9718). Öz Gülhan (☎ 418 8256, ϑU13) is near the main railway station.

By Caspian ferry
Expect frustration and endless delays. See p14 & p15.

LISTINGS
Below is a quick reference A-Z overview by category including a listing of museums, galleries, ministries etc with coded map references of where to find them. Page numbers when given refer to additional text.

● **Airline offices** see box opposite.

● **Antiques and souvenirs** There are many collectors' and artists' stalls in so-called 'Art Alley' (Passaj; ϑK5; see also p91) and in the Old City (eg ΣH7, O14, I9). Other interesting shops at ϑG7 (the colourful 'Silk Wind'), βC7 (Dar-Us Salam), ϑE3 (Qlobus, facing the Natavan Statue, sells Soviet-era postcards), ϑI5 (off Fountains Sq), ϑG3 (stocks old Lenins and Soviet memorabilia) and Amber (ϑM11).

● **Art galleries and studios** For those in the Old City see p82. UAA Gallery (ϑN1), National Art Gallery (φL2, see p85), Yusif Mirza's studio (ϑI7). The Artists' Union Gallery (ϑK10) hosts varying exhibitions. At the time of writing Bahlulzade Exhibition Hall (αJ16) was under reconstruction. The Landmark Building and Park Hyatt Hotel display fine 'incidental' Azeri art on their walls. See 🖳 www.Azgallery.org and pp58-9 for more on individual artists.

● **ATM cash machines** ATMs are increasingly common in the city centre, dispensing up to AZN200 on most major credit and debit cards.

● **Bakeries** See p120. Chudo Pechka (ϑF10, ϑK1 and many more), Sari Sünbül (ϑP15), Aslan (αT16), Häyät (24hrs, αQ15).

● **Bazaars** Most central are Taza Bazaar (βC4, text p105) opposite the circus and a small but historic covered vegetable market (ϑK1). Bus 33 from Sahil Gardens (ϑK10) is the 'Bazaar Express' running past the cele-

BAKU

brated 70s-futurist-oriental-style Sharq
(Vostok) Bazaar (ΨJ10, alternatively take
minibus #1A or 224 from αW15) and on to
the big *tolguchka* (push-&-shove) market,
aka Rasin Bazaar (or take bus #73 from
metro Neftchilar). Other popular local markets include Montin Bazaar (south of
Narimanov metro, ΨJ13) and Nasimi
Bazaar (ϑA2). The huge flea market out by
Baku Airport was a virtual town of its own
until recently, but the new Ziğ–Airport highway has cut right through the site which is
due to be moved altogether to Lökbätan.
Some of Baku's TV stations display each
bazaar's commodity prices for household
produce (mutton, butter, tomatoes etc) to
help shoppers decide where to head.
● **Books and maps** Chiraq Books (φV6)
has the best choice of English titles, sells

this book, stocks regional Lonely Planet
guides, and many other locally relevant
titles. Ali & Nino Bookshop Café (∂M10)
sells a very limited selection of books but
does often stock the excellent Heron *Baku
City* map. The shop at αJ16 stocks inexpensive local maps. Other options include
ΣN14, ∂E6, ∂G1, ∂K3, ∂P1. Second-hand
from occasional stalls on the small square
outside AIT (αK17). Al Hoda (αM19) sells
Iranian books.
● **Boutiques** You can now find virtually
any global-brand boutique in Baku, notably
within the grand old buildings on Rasul Rza
and Aziz Aliyev streets. Quite who buys
anything in these glamorous but ever-empty
shops is a topical question.
● **Bus stops** see pp128-9.
● **Bus stations** see pp130-1.

❑ **Consular representation in Baku**

● **Armenia** No representative, nearest
in Tbilisi (see p320).
● **Belgium** 19 Suleyman Dadashev St
(πN3, ☎ 437 3770).
● **Bulgaria** 13 Etibar Godjayev St (☎
441 4381).
● **China** 67 Xaqani, entry in Safaraliyev
St (αL22, ☎ 498 6257). Visa US$60. A
notice says that tour-bookings are
required but in reality several travellers
have received a visa within 24 hours
without any special paperwork.
● **France** 7 Rasul Rza (∂F6, ☎ 490
8100, 🖥 http://ambafrance-az.org).
● **Georgia** 15 Yashar Husseynov (☎
497 4557).
● **Germany** ISR Plaza (∂M4, ☎ 465
4100, 🖥 www.baku.diplo.de). German
cultural centre at ∂Q14.
● **Greece** 86/88, Kichik Qala (ΣR4, ☎
492 0119)
● **India** 31-34 Oktay Karimov St (ϑE4,
☎ 564 6354). Six-month tourist visas
AZN40 for locals, AZN50 for most resident foreigners, AZN70 for US citizens. Two photos. Apply 09.30-12.30
Mon-Fri, collect same afternoon.
● **Iran** 4b Saradov St, (φT3, ☎ 492
8006). The consulate is in a completely

different location opposite Nizami
Metro station (πU8, Cäfär Cabbarly 10,
☎ 495 9542); apply for visas Mon-Fri
09-12:00.
　　Women must cover their hair for
visa photos and before being allowed
in the consulate. Before applying see
Iran visas box, p15.
● **Iraq** 9 Xaqani St (∂K7, ☎ 498 1447)
in the pretty 19th-century Gayibov mansion near the Russian Drama Theatre.
● **Israel** 7th Floor, Hyatt Tower 3
(τH3, ☎ 490 7881).
● **Italy** 44 Kichik Qala (ΣO2; ☎ 497
5133).
● **Japan** 5th Floor, Hyatt Tower 3,
(τH3; ☎ 490 7818).
● **Jordan** Caspian Business Centre, 44,
(τE4, ☎ 437 3121)
● **Kazakhstan** 82 Ak Hasan Aliyev
(Inglab) (ϑC6; ☎ 465 6248). Consular
section Mon-Fri 09-12.00. Visas
require invitation through an Almaty
agency. With such a letter visas are
issued within a day or so but the visa
will only be valid for the exact stated
dates so plan carefully.
● **Kuwait** Caspian Business Centre
(τE4, ☎ 596 8172)

• **Carpets** There are nearly a dozen atmospheric carpet 'dens' around Maiden's Tower including one in the dome of a partially restored 15th-century hamam at ΣN12. Azerilme (ϑB4) is a fascinating carpet factory allowing visits to its workshops and dyeing rooms (see pp107-8). For carpet repairs try 'Oguz', ΣK6. For export certificates visit 19 Böyük Qala St, Thursdays 10am (ΣN9) or via the carpet museum (∂C7). See pp60-1 for more on carpets.

• **Car wash** Numerous back-street carwasher folk await your mud-caked Pajero on Kaverochkin St (βF9).

• **CDs and DVDs** For a varied selection of local, Russian, jazz and Western artists from Radiohead to Sweet try ABC (∂H4) on Fountains Sq, or Grand (∂L6) on Nizami St. DVD rental βE7.

BAKU PHONE CODE: 012

• **Chocolates** Several branches of Valonia look upmarket and charge hefty prices presumably expecting customers to associate Valonia with Wallonia and thus Belgium. Sadly the products don't taste anything like the 100% cocoa-butter marvels that one gets from real Belgian choccies. Azza also has a growing chain of upmarket sweet shops.

• **Churches** Like its holiest mosque, Baku's most splendid Christian cathedral (Alexander Nevski) was demolished in the 1930s. Attractive and active Russian Orthodox churches include the 1860, silver-onion-domed Church of Archangel Michael (πQ9/∂Q1), the silver-roofed Nativity Church (βC7, with turquoise bell tower) and the recently restored Cathedral of the

---

• **Latvia** Caspian Business Centre (τE4, ☎ 436 6778)

• **Libya** Suleyman Dadashev St (πN3, ☎ 493 8548)

• **Norway** ISR Plaza 11th floor (∂M4; ☎ 497 4325/6)

• **Pakistan** 30 Ataturk (ϑF7; ☎ 436 0839; Mon-Fri 09.00-12.00) Foreigners can only get visas if they are registered as Azerbaijan residents. For Azerbaijani nationals 15-day visas are free when showing return tickets and booked accommodation.

• **Poland** Kichik Qala 2, Old City (ΣF4; ☎ 492 0114)

• **Russia** 17 Bakixanov St (βH3; ☎ 498 6016, 🖳 www.embrus-az.com)

• **Saudi Arabia** 44/2, Suleiman Dadashev St (πM3, ☎ 497 2305)

• **Slovenia** 13/4 Qäsr (ΣQ4, ☎ 494 9305)

• **Switzerland** 9 Böyuk Qala, Old City (ΣL7, ☎ 437 3850)

• **Turkey** 94 Vurğun St (βG4; ☎ 444 7320)

• **Turkmenistan** 14 Shanti Rahimova (☎ 465 4876) After seven years of frosty relations over the disputed status of the

Kyapaz oil field, diplomatic relations restarted in April 2008. Still, Turkmen visas are never easy to organize. Contact Almaty-based Stan Tours (🖳 www.stan tours.com) for tour information.

• **UK** Landmark Building (αN15; ☎ 497 5188, 🖳 http://ukinazerbaijan.fco .gov.uk)

• **Ukraine** 49 Chemenzenli, Gänclik (ϑE4, ☎ 441 2706, 🖳 www.mfa.gov .ua/azerbaijan).

• **USA** 83 Azadliq (βF6; ☎ 498 0336, 🖳 www.usembassybaku.org)

• **Uzbekistan** Batamdar Şosesi, side street 9, #437 (☎ 497 2549). Visa applications Mon, Wed, Fri 09-18.00. Once you have a voucher/invitation letter (eg from 🖳 www.stantours.com or 🖳 http://asia-travel.uz/) the visa is issued the same day for US$75-100, but the fee must be paid into International Bank of Azerbaijan's central office (Nizami St, beside ISR Plaza), a long schlep away by minibus #3 to/from MUM [B].

• Offices of the EU, World Bank, OSCE and British Council are all in Landmark Tower 3 (αM16).

BAKU

MAP SYMBOL KEY Ψ p77; Σ p83; φ p86; ∂ pp92-3; α p99; τ p105; π p101; β p106; ϑ p107

Holy Myrrh-Bearers (τI1, pp104-5) which has fine new murals.

The spired 'Kirkha' (∂Q14) is an 1899 German-Lutheran church which reputedly survived the 1930s' anti-religious demolitions when its congregation promised Stalin that they'd pray for him in perpetuity. It's now used for organ recitals though a Sunday service has been revived.

Heydar Aliyev presented land for the new Catholic Church of the Immaculate Conception (ΨH13, ☎ 416 8782, 🖳 www .catholic.az) during Pope John Paul II's visit to Baku in May 2002. The church was officially inaugurated in 2008.

The chunky stone Church of Gregory the Illuminator (∂L3; Armenian), off Fountains Sq, is abandoned but reasonably well maintained.

● **Embassies** see box pp132-3.

● **Flowers** Particularly attractive places for fresh flowers are at ∂I8, φU4 and ∂L12; ∂M1 has a wide variety of plastic flowers. My Flowers (βE1, 36 Cäfär Cabbarly, ☎ 418 3840) deliver. An original if shockingly expensive alternative to flowers is to send an 'edible bouquet' from Fruit Couture (🖳 www.fruitcouture.net, ☎ 418 1100) which has branches at 8 Tagiyev (∂E4) and 100 Nizami (αM22).

● **Graveyards** Shähidlär Xiyabani (Martyr's Alley, πH7) is Baku's best-known graveyard (see p102). However, most national greats are buried in nearby Faxri Xiyabani (πI5, p103) including Heydar Aliyev and his wife amid a veritable sculpture-fest gallery of fine tombs. Faxri Xiyabani 2 (πI1) mourning Tofiq Bahra-mov (see box p107) among other celebrities, lies on the ridge above a vast cemetery which includes large Christian and Jewish sections. The decision to demolish the Montin Cemetery in Gänclik (former entrance ϑE10) caused a furore in summer 2007. Relatives, who wished at least to rebury their loved ones' remains, were given minimal notice.

● **Guides** Baku's never been the same since poet and encyclopaedic motor-mouth Fuad Axundov left. Should he return to Baku try and track him down and do one of his mindspinningly inspired themed tours. Asya Shiraliyeva (mob ☎ 50 328 0985), the feisty, multi-faceted Carpet Museum guide also offers Baku city walks albeit a considerably more staid experience.

● **Hairdressers** There are thousands: *Qadin Salonu* for women, *Berber* or *Kişi Salonu* for men.

● **Hamams** Most atmospheric are the very 'local' Aga Mikayil (Old City) baths (p84), the indulgent 1886 Tazäbäy Hamam (πM7, p102) and the classic Fantasia (∂R2, see p98). There are other functioning hamams at ∂P2, ∂R4, πP7, πT7 (vaulted 1889 structure, men/women alternate days).

● **Hats** ∂P13, ∂P1, ∂M1, ∂U14 and, more expensively, sold in 'antique' shops. See box below for hat types.

● **Hunting/fishing equipment** Ovçu-Baliq ΨP6, Bossa ∂N14, Winchester φV1.

● **Internet** Clusters of internet places are common but individual *klub*s rarely seem to

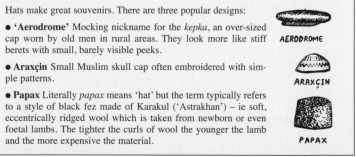

❏ **HATS**

Hats make great souvenirs. There are three popular designs:

● **'Aerodrome'** Mocking nickname for the *kepka*, an over-sized cap worn by old men in rural areas. They look more like stiff berets with small, barely visible peeks.   AERODROME

● **Araxçin** Small Muslim skull cap often embroidered with simple patterns.   ARAXÇIN

● **Papax** Literally *papax* means 'hat' but the term typically refers to a style of black fez made of Karakul ('Astrakhan') – ie soft, eccentrically ridged wool which is taken from newborn or even foetal lambs. The tighter the curls of wool the younger the lamb and the more expensive the material.   PAPAX

survive more than a year or two. They typically charge 60-80q/hr, or AZN2-3 for a midnight-8am session. Wolf (upstairs at ∂S15) is long-lasting and handy if you're waiting for a train. Others include αR15, αQ15, βF7, ∂I13 (24hrs), ∂G13, ∂I14, ∂H4, ∂K8, ∂K6 (several), ∂Q5 ∂M5, ∂P12, ∂Q15, ∂Q14 & S14, Kredit (βF7), Lamer ∂U3, πS2 (several).

● **Key cutting** ∂G4, ∂T1.

● **Language lessons** Several language teachers advertise in the local press. While I haven't used any of these personally, readers have recommended Dilbar Gasimova (✉ dilbargt@gmail.com, mob ☎ 050 731 1892) and more punctual if less experienced Afet Suleimanova (✉ afetstf@mail.ru; mob ☎ 055 685 2664). At the time of writing rates averaged AZN8-10 per hour.

● **Laundry/dry cleaning** Salavan Express (∂O8, ☎ 498 9339, shirt/trousers AZN3/4), Borçali (αI21, Xaqani 46, ☎ 498 9276, AZN2 shirts or trousers), Mr Pak (☎ 498 6365, βB6 and ∂S12), Milnaya Opera (πM4, ☎ 497 5767) charges from AZN1.50 per kg. Dry clean (βE7).

● **Left luggage** (*saxlama kamerasi*) AZN2 per bag per day both beneath and beside the train station.

● **Legal** Notary (∂E8), Ministry of Justice (πS4), Supreme Court (∂Q9).

● **Libraries** The Bookplace (βD6, ☎ 441 6744, Mon-Sat 10-18.00) is a free English-language library service at Information World in Baku Languages University (opposite Aqua Park). Axundov Library (☎ 493 1806) occupies the grand 1959 statue-in-arches building on Sahil Sq. As the national book repository it holds around 4.5 million books, maps and documents with sections in a variety of Western languages. There's quite a palaver to register before entering and books must be read in situ. Ramida Aliyeva is the very helpful librarian of the modest but interesting English-language section (Tue-Sun 10-20.00).

● **Manicures** While many a Qadin Salonu will work on your nails, many are off-puttingly smoky or smell overpoweringly of solvents. Nail Spa (∂L13, manicure AZN12, pedicure AZN18) has been recom-

mended and has two amiable, English-speaking Philipino staff.

● **Maps** Heron (140/10 Alovsat Guliyev, 498 3930, 498 0449) produces the best available Baku city-centre map (1:8000 scale) and their very useful *Baku Street Directory* covers the whole city in good detail, though obviously no such atlas can hope to keep up with the furious pace of recent road-building.

An easier-to-find 1:23,000 city map that sells in bookshops for around AZN3, is viewable online at ✉ www.dtxk.gov.az/maps/maps_r.html (click Карта столицы).

For the Old City, Ismayil Mammadov's splendid graphic map comes complete with pictures of every major building: if you can't find a copy to buy, there's a ceramic version adorning a public wall near the Maiden's Tower so you could snap a digital photo and use that for exploring.

● **Media** Azerbaijan International (see p32, ✉ www.azer.com). See p32 also for Baku's free English weeklies.

● **Medical** Hidden away amid Ganclik apartment blocks, MediLux (∂G6, Salamzade 66b, ☎ 413 5505; ✉ www.medilux.az) charges from only AZN12 but you'll need local languages. Medi Club (αJ20, ☎ 497 0911, ✉ www.mediclub.az) has English-speaking local doctors (consultations from AZN24) and an ambulance service. SOS (AEA) (∂S12, ☎ 493 7354, ✉ www.internationalsos.com) has Western physicians but the charges are much higher and membership is required for many services. Turk-American Medical (βC3, ☎ 497 3784, ✉ http://tamc.az) has consultations from AZN20. Some doctors speak English.

The Chinese Medical Center, 82/1 H Aliyev Av (INAM, ☎ 447 9877; ✉ www.inam.az) offers acupuncture, deep intestinal cleaning and many other hi-tech cures. Near the Funicular, SEBA (φD2, ☎ 437 1825) is a Korean Hospital for Oriental Medicine offering accupuncture, moxibustion, bioenergetic measurements and herbal treatments.

X-rays are cheap at ∂H7 if you dare: the device looks like a remnant from an early James Bond movie, complete with gold-toothed Blofeldt at the dials.

There are numerous aptek (pharmacies): Hayal Aptek (∂S10, 30 Bül Bül, ☎ 493 6161) is one of several to open 24hrs; Taza Bazaar peddlars and the Yasil Aptek (ΣF5) sell herbal remedies.

● **Ministries** Communications (ΣF11, 💻 www.mincom.gov.az), Anti-Corruption (βF7), Customs (💻 www.customs.gov.az), Economic Development (ϕK2, ☎ 492 4110, 💻 www.economy.gov.az), Ecology (πQ4, ☎ 439 0126, 💻 www.eco.gov.az), Finance (βG4, ☎ 493 0562, 💻 www.maliyye.gov.az), Foreign Affairs (πT9, 💻 www.mfa.gov.az), Health (∂Q11, 💻 www.mednet.az), Internal Affairs (∂I1/ϕY7), Justice (πS4, 💻 www.justice.gov.az), Parliament (Milli Mäjlis, πH6, 💻 www.meclis.gov.az), President's Office (Aparat; ϕM1, ☎ 492 3543, 💻 www.president.az), Sports (ϑA8, 💻 www.mys.gov.az), Tax (πQ4, 💻 www.taxes.gov.az), Tourism (ϕC3, 💻 www.mct.gov.az).

● **Mobile phone shops** If there isn't a mobile phone shop within about 3cm of wherever you're standing, you've probably been abducted and are no longer in Baku. Should you need a mobile made of solid gold, Ant Hill (∂D7) is your place. If you just want a local SIM card but don't have Azeri residence papers try the shops on Vurğun Gardens (or better find a local friend to sign the papers for you).

● **Money** The best rates are from booths around Vurğun Park (eg αP17) or on Hacibayov and Xaqani streets close to Sahil Metro (eg ∂K8, ∂H9). Rates near Fountains Sq are marginally poorer but unless you're changing hundreds of Manat the difference doesn't offer enough incentive to hike across town for. Standard Bank (∂I1) and IBA (∂L6) buy and sell travellers' cheques. ATM cash machines are ubiquitous.

● **Mosques** The impressive 1914 Täzä Pir Mosque (πP8, p100) is the seat of Sheikhul Islam Haji Pashazade, spiritual leader of Muslims in the Caucasus. Other fine oil-boom-era mosques include the solid Töybä/Imam Hussein Mosque on Shaig St (πO7, p102), the 1912 Blue Mosque (βF4, not blue at all) and the 1910 Haci Sultan Hasan Mosque (πU8) with its recently gilded minaret. Much older mosques are found in the Old City (see p82). The city's most important (if newly built) Muslim shrines are well out of the centre at Bibi Heybat (p104), Nardaran (p151) and more controversially at Shuvälän (p154).

● **Museums** Aliyev (ΣR13), Azimzade House ∂S5 (very rarely open, ☎ 494 0569*), Bül Bül Apartment ∂K10 (pp96-7), Carpets ∂C7 (p91), Cavid Apartment ϕT6 (p89), Füzuli Institute of Manuscripts* ϕT6 (p89), Hacibäyov House πT8 (p102), Historical Museum ∂D6 (p91), Maiden's Tower ΣM14 (p80), Miniature books ΣP3 (p84), Nariman Narimanov apartment ϕT3 (p87), Muzeyi Märkäzi ∂C7 (overall name for former Lenin museum, now the Carpet, Theatre and Independence museums, p91), Niyazi Apartment ∂O10 (p95), Nizami Literature Museum ∂G2 (p90 [21]), Ordubadi Apartment ∂K10, Rostropovich apartment πO7 (p102), Shaiq apartment πO7 (p102), Shirvanshah's Palace ΣP4 (p81), Vagif Mustafazade House [VM] ΣI7 (p84), Vurğun apartment ∂C4 (p91).
* = by appointment

● **Musical instruments** For both Azeri instruments (see box p56) and classical ones, Royal (πO9, Nizami 24, 💻 www.royal.az) is very upmarket. Or try Melodiya (βH6), αG15, αL18, ∂S1, or ΣK9. For keyboards go to ∂K14.

● **Office supplies, stationery** Best range at Nil (αL16). Smaller selection but more central at ∂L8 and ∂I1. Cheap at Kartriç Evi βJ6.

● **Optical** Anar Optik ΣG9.

● **Photocopying** Handwritten notes in shop and pharmacy windows saying *Kserokopiya* are ubiquitous but relatively few machines actually work. Typically you'll pay 5q per sheet but less from the stationery shops at αL16 and ∂J6.

● **Post and parcel services** GPO (∂F14/αG15) – for Poste Restante use the fifth bank of windows on the right marked 'Talab Olunanadak Korespondensiyasi'. Other city-centre post offices include ∂M2, ∂S1, αR19 and ϕT4. PX Post (☎ 494 5024, ∂Q7) offers a private international letter service. Philatelists can buy Azeri commemorative stamps at Azärmarka (∂I14), some at face value, others for much more. YAPS

MAP SYMBOL KEY Ψ p77; Σ p83; ϕ p86; ∂ pp92-3; α p99; τ p105; π p101; β p106; ϑ p107

courier service (βB2, 102 Ak Sh Azizbäyov ☎ 497 7700) offers express courier delivery within Baku. Other international shippers include DHL (∂Q12; ☎ 493 7414), OCS/ASE (αI15, ☎ 497 3775, 💻 www.ase.com.tr), TNT (∂K13; ☎ 498 6448), UPS (∂G5, 14 Mammedaliyev, ☎ 493 3991).

• **Printing, business cards** Printing House (∂G15, downstairs), Max (∂N8).

• **Restaurants and cafés** See pp114-21.

• **Repairs** Clothing (Atelye Mod, Zorge St, αL20), Shoe repair ('*Ayaqqabi Tämiri*', Minutka ∂L15 (beside Bossa), αR18, ∂Q2.

• **Shoe shine** A freelancer often works in the attractively rebuilt puppet theatre underpass (ΣA4).

• **Sports** (see pp123-4).

• **Statues** The intricately allegorical Vahid has moved to ΣN2 (see p82). Other greats include Zorge's expressive Eyes (βI4), throw-off-the-veil 'Free Woman' (βC1/πU8), swirling Cavid (πR4), enormous Nariman Narimanov (πN6).

• **Supermarkets and food stores** The Almali Supermarket chain has a wide and growing number of shops (eg πT2, αM19) and feels more inviting than competitor Kontinental (most central at ∂I10). Ramstore has small hypermarkets off the airport road (ΨI11) on Cavid St (πO4) and at Gänclik Square (θA6). Other expat favourites are Citymart (∂Q8) and New World (Yeni Dunya, τE1). Most demand that you check your bags before entry.

Ubiquitous minimarts often stay open late eg Romashka (∂E5) or even 24 hours cg ∂R15 and Qastronom (∂Q10). The timewarp Monolit (∂G1) grocery still operates Soviet-style like a DIY café. Buy bread, salami and salads then stand at a high table and make your own lunch. See also bakeries.

• **Synagogues** The most attractive old synagogue is now used as the Behbutov Song Theatre (p96). Of the active synagogues the most dramatic is the strikingly modern new Ashkanazi one, a white-stone fortress at 171 Mustafayev St (aka D Aliyev St, ∂S6). A shop next door sells kosher food.

• **Telephone offices** Long-distance calls are possible from φR2, φS3, ∂H11, ∂E4, αR19 and in the GPO (∂F14).

• **Theatres** – see pp122-3.

• **Toilets** Baku is not strong on public con-

veniences. Best to go to a café or top hotel.

• **Tourist information** The friendly Tourist Office (∂I15; Hacibäyov 6, ☎ 598 5519, 💻 www.tourism.az, 10-13.00, 14-18:00 Mon-Sat) has bundles of free brochures, maps and booklets but the staff aren't always good at answering detailed queries. The Ministry of Youth, Sports and Tourism (65 Neftchilar Pr, φC3) is not really set up to receive walk-in visitors but they have some friendly English-speaking staff should you have specialist questions that the Tourist Office staff can't deal with.

• **Tours** Several travel agencies run tours around Azerbaijan if you don't want to organize your own. Improtex's 'incoming' agency is hidden away in a courtyard at ∂O9.

• **Travel agents** The following have at least some English-speaking staff and can discount most Western airline tickets. SI Travel (τH3, Hyatt Tower 2, 💻 www.si-travel.com, ☎ 497 0800) is particularly helpful; AIT (αL17, ☎ 498 6500); STI (∂M11, 497 0880, 💻 www.sti.az) operates city and Absheron tours. IN-ternational (τL1, ☎ 510 1388) a reputable expat-friendly agent; Caspian Travel (∂N13, ☎ 498 2508, 💻 www.caspiantravel.com); CGTT/Elegant Travel (αM20, ☎ 598 1222, 💻 www.eleganttravel.az), Elite (βC6), Improtex (∂L8, ☎ 493 0896); Skylife (ΣK13, ☎ 492 5577, 💻 www.skylife-travel.com). SW Travel ∂M14 for Azal tickets and Derviş (∂Q10). There are many cheap agencies around Vuŕğun Park (αP18-20) dealing mostly with air tickcts to the former USSR.

BAKU

□ **Exhibition/conference halls**

Several big international exhibitions and trade fairs take place at the 'Sports Palace' (τK3), an enclosed stadium on Moskva (formerly Tbilisi) Ave, imaginatively named after Heydar Aliyev. Best known of these exhibitions is the Oil and Gas show (💻 www.caspianoilgas.co.uk) though there are many others (see 💻 www.ite-exhibitions.com and 💻 www.iteca.az). Some smaller conventions are held in Gülistan Palace, originally built for a visit by Soviet premier Leonid Brezhnev.

PART 3: AROUND BAKU

Baku to Älät

Just an hour south of Baku, the petro-glyphs and mud volcanoes near Qobustan make an easy half-day trip combined per-haps with a dip at the Shix(ov) beaches and lunch at Sahil. Sadly the potentially fascinating Soviet tank graveyards at Puta remain off-limits.

BAKU TO SAHIL
Shix(ov) beaches
Popular for its easy proximity to Baku (10km) the beaches here offer the surreal sight of bathers having fun with a backdrop of offshore oil rigs. Swimming isn't neces-sarily wise though the murky water does appear to clear when the wind direction blows its oily scum out to sea. There's sand underfoot despite the mainly rock and shell forebeach. Virtually the whole strip is now hidden behind a roadside strip of restaurants, summer night-clubs and the Ramada and Crescent Beach hotels (see p113) where you can rent jet skis and windsurfers. Most charge for access to their beaches in the summer.

Lökbatan
South of Shix(ov) is a construc-tion/reconditioning plant for semi-sub-mersible oil rigs which sit with their long retractable metal legs poking up at the sky-line. The landscape is desolate with large commercial salt-pan lakes either side of the turn-off to Lökbatan. The lake water comes from oil-well run-off and the salt derived from its evaporation is rich in minerals such as uranium: not the healthiest condiment to sprinkle on your chips.

The most impressive views are from the low, grey hill south-west of town that's

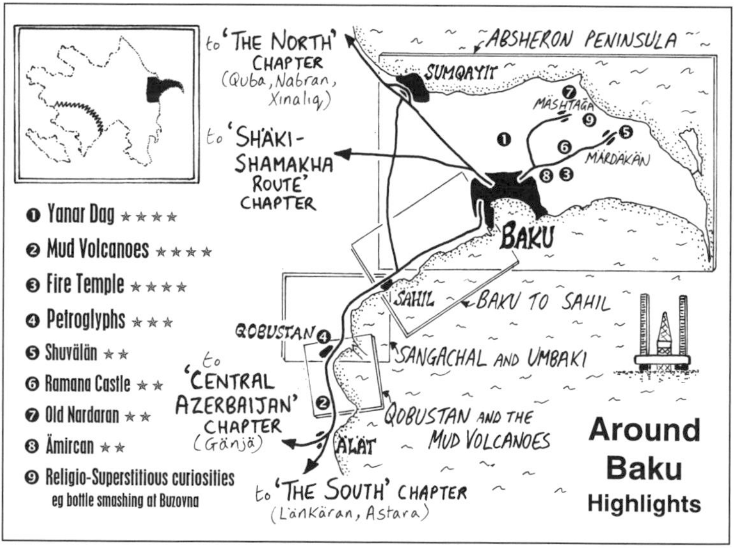

to 'THE NORTH' CHAPTER (Quba, Nabran, Xinalıq)

to 'SHÄKI-SHAMAKHA ROUTE' CHAPTER

❶ Yanar Dag ★ ★ ★ ★
❷ Mud Volcanoes ★ ★ ★ ★
❸ Fire Temple ★ ★ ★ ★
❹ Petroglyphs ★ ★ ★
❺ Shuvälän ★ ★
❻ Ramana Castle ★ ★
❼ Old Nardaran ★ ★
❽ Ämircan ★ ★
❾ Religio-Superstitious curiosities eg bottle smashing at Buzovna

ABSHERON PENINSULA
SUMQAYIT
MASHTAGA
MÄRDÄKÄN
BAKU

SAHIL — BAKU TO SAHIL
QOBUSTAN
SANGACHAL AND UMBAKI
to 'CENTRAL AZERBAIJAN' CHAPTER (Gänjä)
QOBUSTAN AND THE MUD VOLCANOES
ÄLÄT
to 'THE SOUTH' CHAPTER (Länkäran, Astara)

Around Baku Highlights

speckled with lazily turning nodding don-key pumps and plenty of curiously twisted metallic scrap. You can climb the mud flow to the summit of the mud volcano which exploded catastrophically in 1887, 1975 and 2001. The burning gas flares were visible for months in Baku. On its summit there's none of the Clangerland-style bubbling (see p142) but the small central crater remains 'burnt' into brightly oxidized colours. Driving onwards from here to Puta is com-plicated by run-off pools, pipes and rail lines so it's easier to backtrack via Lökbatan.

Puta
Beneath the imposing cliff-capped peak of Mt Kyarkas near nondescript little Puta, 'graveyards' of tanks and military vehicles have been simply left to rust. Once some-thing of a tourist attraction, the command-ers of these places have now erected 'Keep Out' notices and visitors are likely to be interrogated as potential spies. Avoid until further notice! A less controversial Soviet relic is the regularly repainted **silver Lenin** which stands somewhat obscured by trees in the forecourt of the 'industrial mud' fac-tory (a place producing the goo that's pumped into oil bores equalizing pressure once the oil itself is extracted). To reach it

leave the main M3 southbound after Km22 on a diagonal turning towards the big gas refinery (*Qaz e'mell Zavod*).

Sahil and Qaradağ
Approaching Qaradağ railway station the coast is dominated by the outline of mas-sive drilling platforms under stalled con-struction in the SPS/Kaspmorneft yards. The station serves **Sahil (Primorsk)** which simply means 'seaside'. This outwardly dismal tower-block town hides an old mosque and a most unexpectedly pleasant boulevard with decent beachside dining, notably at Xäzri. Buses 17 and 97 run regu-larly to Bayil (southern Baku).

The town's main industry is the gigan-tic Qaradağ cement factory whose belching chimneys are infamous for creating one of the country's worst respiratory disease blackspots. Though not open to visitors, the plant reputedly still conceals a faded Lenin mural along with the collected sayings of Calvin Coolidge. It has what was once boasted as the longest single kiln in the USSR at 180m (now dysfunctional). In January 2000 the plant was the scene of an exciting skirmish as the British sales direc-tor was holed up during an occupation in support of the former management.

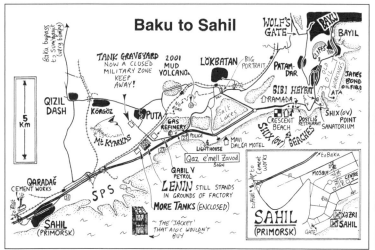

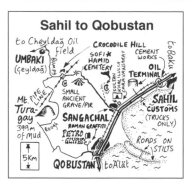

Sahil to Qobustan

SAHIL TO QOBUSTAN
Sangachal
Vivid blue sea contrasts with stark semi-desert as you reach Sangachal, the terminal for the offshore Chirag 1 oil field and for the new Baku–Ceyhan (BTC) pipeline. In the Caspian nearby, incredible stilted road-ways extend for miles on wooden piles to more offshore oil workings, best viewed with binoculars from the hills above Qobustan. Lying half-forgotten at the north-ern end of Sangachal Town (some way south of the terminal) the cream-stone 1439 **Sultan Khalilulla caravanserai** is very near the main M3 but to access it you'll need to walk across the railway tracks.

Sangachal to Umbakı
A bumpy side road into the dry hills behind Sangachal takes you deep into moonscape. Visible to the right after a few kilometres, is the intriguing **Sofi Hamid Cemetery**. Graves, new and old, some brightly coloured and oddly shaped include a large concrete camel which people slither beneath for good luck. The story goes that a local holy man's last request was that his dead body be placed on the back of a camel and buried wherever the animal stopped walking. That sup-posedly explains the isolated position of the graveyard, though the *mollah* assured me that the place had once

been the site of Old Sangachal (the ancient city). It's a considerable way off the road but the two possible mud tracks are smooth enough for the Ladas of the many pilgrims. See 🖳 http://azer.com for a detailed photo essay about the cemetery.

Even further inland you'll pass a cou-ple of mud volcanoes where you'll have to look very hard to find the small active nos-trils. Then the road dives through some rocky scenery passing a **crocodile-shaped hill** after which it divides. The dusty track ahead later swings south past the gigantic mud-volcano mountain of **Turagay** and back, eventually, to the main road at Qobustan. Or veer right to the strange vil-lage of **Umbakı**. Despite its ludicrously isolated position in mid-desert, almost all the homes are made of wood and locals claim the little bungalows were imported ready-built all the way from Finland to house post-war oil prospectors. This is probably a linguistic confusion as 'Finnski Dom' (Finnish House) is a Russian term for a type of wooden hut. Hidden away behind Umbakı, the still-functioning **Leprosy House** has become a cause célèbre of expat charity Community Shield (🖳 www .csabaku.org). Somewhere around 15km inland is the ancient caravanserai complex of Miadjik.

QOBUSTAN
Qobustan is a drab strip-town on the main highway but the hills above offer great Caspian views and hide a fascinating series of truly ancient petroglyphs that now form the core of a State Reserve (☎ 544 4208). Azerbaijan's best-known mud volcanoes are 10km further south.

Petroglyph site
(40°06'42"N, 49°22'43"E)
The climate here has not always been as harsh and parched as it is today. Indeed for thousands of years the now arid Caspian coast was alive with forests and wildlife. Neolithic man found it conducive to good hunting and depicted various

IS THIS REALLY AN
ANCIENT BOAT SAILING
TOWARDS THE SUN?

QOBUSTAN
PETROGLYPHS

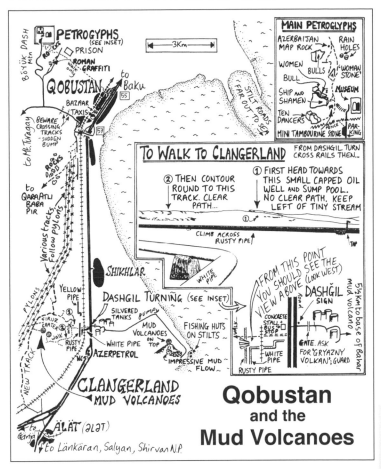

Map labels:

PETROGRAPHS (SEE INSET)
BÖYÜK DASH Mtn
ROCKS
PRISON
ROMAN GRAFFITI
QOBUSTAN
to Baku
55
BAZAAR
TAXIS
57
BEWARE CROSSING TRACKS - SUDDEN BUMP
to Mt. Turagay
STILT ROADS - FAR OUT TO SEA
←—3Km—→

MAIN PETROGRAPHS
AZERBAIJAN MAP ROCK
RAIN HOLES
WOMEN
BULLS
WOMAN STONE
BULL
MUSEUM
SHIP AND SHAMEN
TEN DANCERS
MINI TAMBOURINE STONE
FENCE
PARKING

to QARAATLI BABA PIR
Various tracks Follow Pylons
ROCKS

TO WALK TO CLANGERLAND
FROM DASHGIL TURN CROSS RAILS THEN...
② THEN CONTOUR ROUND TO THIS TRACK. CLEAR PATH...
① FIRST HEAD TOWARDS THIS SMALL CAPPED OIL WELL AND SUMP POOL. NO CLEAR PATH. KEEP LEFT OF TINY STREAM
CLIMB ACROSS RUSTY PIPE
TAP

SHIKHLAR
WHITE PIPE
FROM THIS POINT YOU SHOULD SEE THE VIEW ABOVE (LOOK WEST)
DASHGIL SIGN
5½ km to base of Bahar mud volcano
YELLOW PIPE
DASHGIL TURNING (SEE INSET)
SILVERED TANKS
bumpy
MUD VOLCANOES
FISHING HUTS ON STILTS
CONCRETE STALL SHOP
PYLONS
FIRUZ CRATER
JAIK
RUSTY PIPE
WHITE PIPE ON TOP
AZERPETROL
IMPRESSIVE MUD FLOW
WHITE PIPE
RUSTY PIPE
GATE. ASK FOR 'GRYAZNY VOLKAN'. GUARD
NEW TRACK

CLANGERLAND MUD VOLCANOES
to Ganja
ÄLÄT (ƏLƏT)
to Länkäran, Salyan, Shirvan N.P.

Qobustan and the Mud Volcanoes

animal forms in the dwelling caves above today's Qobustan. Erosion and the subsequent collapse of the outer caves has revealed thousands of carved figures: shamen, cattle, deer, and most famously, an ancient ship sailing towards a stylized sun. Famous adventurer Thor Heyerdahl believed that this suggested an ancestral link between Azerbaijan and the Vikings.

Older Stone Age petroglyphs are deeper and more rounded than the later Iron Age ones cut with metal blades. But none of them are immediately easy to spot: photos that you might see of the images standing out starkly in white were in fact taken after filling the crevices with toothpaste to improve the contrast. The toothpaste has long since been rinsed! Included in the site entry fee (entry/camera fee AZN 3/2, 10.30-16.30) is a small museum, long overdue for renovation. For AZN6 extra the helpful staff can guide you round the most important petroglyphs and show you a miniature 'tambourine stone' (Gabal Dash), which resounds like a drum when hit. In fact there's a vastly bigger Gabal Dash far into the hills but getting there requires a major hike.

Part of Qobustan's charm is the lonely, meditative mood as one gazes from the museum's terrace out across the Caspian and its long oil-working stilt roads. So try to avoid coming up here on summer weekends when the main site can be noisy and overcrowded.

Roman graffiti
(40°06'08.6"N, 49°23'15"E)
Roughly 2000 years ago a bored centurion called Julius Maximus scribbled some lines of graffiti with his spear on a rock near what is now Qobustan prison, around 2km from the petroglyph site. It's the furthest east such a Latin inscription has ever been discovered. The letters aren't very easy to make out even if you manage to get inside the site's small fenced enclosure (some guides and taxi drivers know where the key is hidden).

Getting to Qobustan
Baku taxi drivers want around AZN40 for a half-day trip to Qobustan and the mud volcanoes. Alternatively you an reach Qobustan town from Älät-bound minibus #105 from opposite the Moon Crown restaurant in Bayil (πA9); the last ride back leaves around 19.30/21.00 winter/summer. From Qobustan the petroglyph site is over 6km by asphalt road above the town, taxis charging AZN10 return including a quick detour to see the graffiti rock. Going one way saves a couple of manat if you're happy to walk back – about an hour descending a short cut through hefty rocks, passing the prison and following a rough track to cross the railway line at Qobustan station.

CLANGERLAND MUD VOLCANOES
Azerbaijan's most appealing collection of loveable little mud volcanoes lies atop apparently uninteresting dry hills inland from the Baku–Älät road, about 10km south of Qobustan. Anyone who remembers the Clangers from British Children's TV will expect to find the Soup Dragon lurking behind the hypnotically gurgling pools and

mini-cones. Apart from a small Chinese oil test-well at the base of the hill, the site is wonderfully lonely and atmospheric. There's no fence and no sign though this might change if the government decides to protect/commercialize the area as has been mooted. (See pp62-5 for more about mud volcanoes).

Access
By vehicle It's possible to reach the site from the petroglyphs road on a bumpy, slightly confusing track that approximately follows the pylons. See map p141 or for more accurate directions use the waymarked trail on 🖥 www.everytrail.com/view_trip .php?trip_id=70269. However, a new and much easier access track has been built starting from the big Älät junction. Head north 100m then exit 1km following signs to ŞPAL Zavodu. After crossing the rail tracks turn north (at 39°59'48"N 49°23' 53"E) and climb an unsurfaced but decent track for 3.2km more.

Whichever way you come, when you reach a slight saddle-shaped 'pass' (at 39°59'48"N 49°23'53"E), turn steeply uphill to the east for 350m (or walk if you don't have a 4WD) and park in front of the first cones. Please don't drive directly onto the mud flows as you may sink, get stuck or damage the very special environment.

Taxi drivers at Qobustan will do a combined petroglyphs/mud volcanoes trip for AZN20 return including waiting time.

On foot It's possible to reach Clangerland on foot from the M3 highway in about 35 mins (impossible this way by vehicle). Get off bus #105 at the Dashgil turn-off where you see silver storage tanks to the left. Walk away from these tanks on a track beside a bus stop/concrete shack. Cross the rail line and briefly follow the white pipeline. Where the white pipe turns left, continue, climb over a second rust-coloured pipe and use the diagram on p141. The trail that you want to hit is a pair of old tyre ruts just visible rising up the low hillside in the distance. To get there walk straight ahead for 10 minutes, climb up to an oily black pool (where there was a decapitated test well) and then curve round to the left. When you reach the clear trail, follow it up until it starts to double back on itself. Then, instead of descending, take the smaller trail straight on and after a few minutes scramble up the red-tinged hillocks for a view onto the first of the volcano pools, the biggest, watery *salse* (bubble pool). The classic *gryphon* cones are a five-minute walk further to the west.

Qara-Atli Baba Pir
Part way between Qobustan and Clangerland, if you follow the track that veers higher to the west away from the pylons, you'll end up weaving for some 5-6km between the curious boulder-strewn lower slopes of Mt Kichik Dash (more petroglyphs here) to an old cemetery.

Three hundred metres beyond, visible between the rocks where the track ends, is Qara-Atli Baba Pir, the miraculous 'cave of the black-horse granddad'. In a story that seems to be lifted straight from the Koran, an old holy man being chased by pagan enemies jumped off his horse and ran into the cave. A spider's web instantaneously formed across the cave's mouth, hiding it from view and saving the fugitive.

These days the superstitious make curious offerings: one man presented a wig made by shaving off his own hair. Someone else had made a baby's cradle out of matchboxes. To ensure general good luck, believers try to throw seven stones to lodge on top of 'happiness rock'.

ÄLÄT (ƏLƏT, ALYAT)
Where the main Baku–Gänjä road turns inland and forks to Länkäran, Älät is a small oil and stone-quarrying town that has been mooted to become Azerbaijan's new port city, to free up space in Baku. It was here that the White-Russian commander Bicharakov and a small British contingent landed in the doomed 1918 Dunsterforce campaign to thwart the Turkish army's advance on Baku. The best that Marvin could find to say about the place in the 1880s was that 'there is a small buffet at the station where an excellent tea may be made'. There's still no reason to hang around.

Absheron peninsula

If Azerbaijan is an eagle flying towards the Caspian sea, the Absheron (Apsheron) is its eczema-plagued beak. The landscape is faintly disturbing – an eerily fascinating wasteland of parched hillocks and plains which sprout pylons, nodding-donkey oil derricks and pools of oily effluent amongst ragged scrub. It is not the most immediately appealing area for tourism. Yet there are some almost passable beaches and several medieval castle towers in modestly interesting villages.

On the Absheron you'll find the country's most religious area (Nardaran), dozens of older mosques and several big new shrines (eg Shuvälän) yet close by in Buzovna, Märdäkan and Mashtaġa you can witness some of Azerbaijan's oddest superstitious folk-rituals. There's the Suraxanı Fire Temple, the Yanar Daġ burning hillside, and century-old remnants of the early oil industry including old wooden-lined pit-wells and archaic drilling rigs. Not a bad selection if you can cope with the often drearily disappointing settings.

Though not covered here, archaeologists have found well-preserved Stone Age 'cart tracks' (near Turkan), standing stones and unexplained stone cup-holes. Sites are hard to find/discern without a competent guide. For more information see the Spring 2003 edition of *Azerbaijan International* on 🖳 www.azer.com.

There's a range of beach accommodation at Novxanı (p159), Märdäkän Beach (p150), Zagulba (p148) and Pirshaġı (p152).

HISTORY
Though Baku has always held a great strategic importance, until the 19th-century oil boom the city's population was fairly small while various Absheron villages such as Qala, Nardaran and Saray were relatively bustling market centres.

The whole area was vulnerable to attack from the sea and consequently developed a formidable string of castles

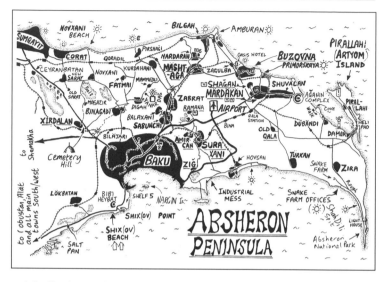

and fortifications, a few of which have been renovated. In the 19th century, while Baku became increasingly cosmopolitan, the Absheron remained the bastion of traditional Azeri culture and a centre of religiously conservative Islam. Nardaran and Mäshtaga retain this image today, but Qala, Saray and several other ancient settlements withered away or were refounded on new sites. There were two reasons for these changes. Firstly, improved communications made the Absheron's short-hop caravanserais obsolete and undermined the area's ragged agricultural economy by making better, cheaper food available from the more fertile regions (Quba, Länkäran). There was also a deliberate Communist-era attempt to break the religious spirit of the strongly Islamic towns; places which resisted the secularization were rendered virtual ghost towns.

'When its oil fountains are playing 200 or 300 feet high, the Absheron might not unfitly be compared to a huge spermaceti whale' a 17th-century traveller reported. By the 19th century as the Absheron's agricultural importance waned so its oil industry took off. Indeed what are usually called 'Baku's oilfields', actually had their epicentre in a small area around Balaxanı.

Today much of the peninsula bears the scars of actual, or aborted, oil and gas workings. International statistics rate the peninsula amongst the world's most polluted places, with an estimated 40,000 hectares rendered uncultivatable by pollution or excessive use of pesticides and fertilisers. But this does not deter local holidaymakers who still see the region as a recreation area with its shady sanatoria and accessible beaches. Like the khans of yore who had a summer palace at Nardaran, today's elite from the president down, retain holiday homes on the peninsula. Since the 1990s, an ongoing building boom is slowly turning much of the peninsula into a sprawling semi-suburbia. Officially the whole area is already classified as Baku City.

BEACHES

In 1883, British tourist, Charles Marvin noted that even at Baku the sea was 'so full of fish that [a swimmer] never loses the impression that he is in an aquarium'. That abundance is much diminished today. But the murky Caspian waters still attract

AROUND BAKU

swimmers despite all the sewerage, pesticide run-offs and the detritus produced by the oil industry.

Not all oil spilt in the Caspian is produced by messy, meddling man, as natural vents leak gas and petroleum from the sea beds and the many submarine mud-volcanoes. Even in Marvin's time 'when wind is ill set there forms a black scum of oil which can prevent swimming for two days at a time'. The observation is still partially true.

The widest sandy stretches are along the north coast. Marginally less commercialized than Shix(ov) (p138), and with somewhat cleaner water, the most developed are at Märdäkän/Primorskaya, Novxanı and Amburan. Some beaches are now cleared of litter occasionally but be prepared that fellow bathers often have a taste for noisy music and love to cruise their Ladas along the hard-packed sand. In contrast, the south-coast beaches tend to be narrow and awkward to reach behind marshy pools.

The west coast coves and Shah Dili spit (now a national park) can be plagued with sandflies and swimming snakes but at least you'll have them largely to yourself.

GETTING AROUND
Driving and suggested routes
Modest distances and relatively good roads mean you can reach even the most remote spots in two hours from central Baku. But don't drive too fast. Over-zealous police line the main routes and have a very unscientific sense of 'speeding'. An additional conundrum is that the thundering new highways to the airport built in 2008 have yet to be equipped with more than a couple of exits so even for locals it's a puzzle as to how to get on or off these roads.

A good half-day car-trip loops through Ämircan, Suraxhanı and Ramana though crossing the new airport highway adds a challenge in reaching the latter. With more time you could continue via Shaǧan and Märdäkän to Shuvälän then backtrack slightly and continue up the coast to Buzovna returning via Mäshtaǧa, Nardaran and Yanar Daǧ, preferably reaching the latter around dusk. A seven-hour taxi charter to do all the above is liable to cost at least AZN50. The north-west Absheron towns are less interesting and could be seen as part of a longer journey to the north (p161).

If you plan to do much exploring it's well worth buying the excellent 1:100,000 Absheron topographic map sold in Baku bookshops. It shows fairly accurately which routes are asphalted and helps you through the confusing maze of certain Absheron towns, though not the new motorway intersections. Versions of the map appear on the back of certain 1:23,000 Baku city maps.

By public transport
Getting around the Absheron by public transport is straightforward and mostly involves taking one of the minibuses that depart from certain suburban metro stations in Baku (pp130-1). Most then pick up passengers near the vast spaghetti junction of concrete flyovers at Metro Azizbayov, but by that stage you can expect standing room only. Along the most popular route, Märdäkän–Baku, share-taxis and minibuses run till around 23.00. Further from this main artery, services are less and less frequent. Transport to and from Baku is easier than between Absheron towns, though Hovsan, Märdäkän and Suraxanı are better than other towns as local hubs. Sumqayit is served by packed but ultra-frequent minibuses from Baku's new bus terminal with some services routed via Corat and Saray. Mid-sized bus 998 takes a slightly slower but much more comfy and scenic route to Sumqayit from Gänclik Metro (map p107) via Novxani beach and Corat beach.

Elektrichka **trains** are slow, uncomfortable and crowded at rush hours. Departures become less frequent every year and the service has been threatened with complete closure. However, at the time of writing they still operate, are very cheap (20q flat fare), are handy for reaching Suraxanı without changing buses, and could be considered a cultural experience. Most trains loop round Suraxanı, Märdäkän, Mäshtaǧa or the same in reverse, with one or two daily using the spur line from Qala to Pirallahı (Artyom) Island.

AROUND BAKU

PLACES TO VISIT

Sumqayit, Saray, Corat, Novxanı and Xırdalan are covered in the north-west Absheron section (pp156-9). Other towns are listed alphabetically below.

Absheron National Park

The Shah Dili peninsula, 'nose' of the Absheron, has been declared a national park. The site is a narrow strip of coastal sand dunes that might appeal to ornithologists but whose visual impact is very limited and not much different to the similar dunes you'll see en route to the entrance gate. That gate is manned but a guide won't necessarily be waiting so it's best to make prior arrangements through the Ecology Ministry (🖳 www.eco.gov.az). Entry AZN4 for foreigners. The nearest village, reached by bus 87 via Qala, is **Zira**, once site of a former *gurza* snake farm producing venom for antidote serum – until all the snakes escaped. Don't assume you'll be able to find a taxi here.

Amburan

Probably the Absheron's liveliest stretch of shore, Amburan (eastern Bilgah) has a good **pay-beach** and a lesser free beach accessed from beside the MiniMart (parking AZN1). The amusingly tongue-in-cheek restaurant-café *Retro* (☎ 453 6082, kebabs AZN3, Efes beer AZN3) has a courtyard displaying a selection of vintage cars while in the dining room a Lenin bust surveys a tight-packed display of classic B&W photos.

Bus #171 comes via the airport, #72 via Mäshtäğa and Bilgah.

Ämircan

One of the peninsula's most interesting towns, Ämircan was formerly known as Xille, under which name it was famed for its buta-motif carpets. Boom-era industrialist Muxtarov (see box p88) was born here and graced the town with his elegant **mosque**, arguably Azerbaijan's finest. A new, ornately carved gravestone including oil-rig motifs has recently appeared in the mosque's yard. Ämircan was also the birthplace of great modern artist Sattar Bahlulzade and a splendid **Sattar statue** by Omar Eldarov stands in the large lakeside graveyard.

Minibus #213 passes close to Ämircan

mosque and links on very usefully to Suraxanı.

Artyom Island (see Pirallahı, p152)

Balaxanı (Balakhany)

Three sq km around Balaxani were the most important in all Azerbaijan during the original Baku oil boom. Travellers and writers

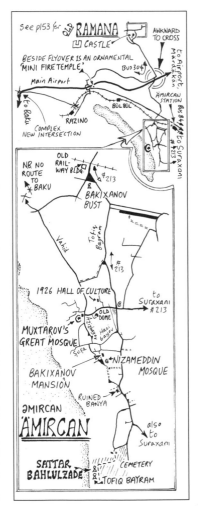

have noted in some detail the curious sight of its 'oil springs' which Von Thielmann described in 1875 as spurting to a height of 35ft 'like geysers in Iceland'. Valuable oil like this could run to waste for weeks for lack of storage capacity until the Nobel brothers installed a pumping station with two then-enormous 400,000 gallon reservoirs. Today the township is a depressingly non-descript mess but if you wander up onto the hill behind town there are still some of the hand-dug original well-pits of the 1880s complete with wooden interior-linings. See Yanar Dağ (p155) for directions and map.

Buzovna (see map p148)

If you have a taste for the Absheron's off-beat minor attractions, Buzovna is a rewarding hunting ground. There's a small **Nestorian (*Nasranilar*) monument** tucked behind #7 Eyvasov St, an old graveyard, a couple of turbes and several mosques to seek out.

For pious locals, the primary attraction is the **Äli Ayağı shrine** (aka *Qadamgah*), a new gold-domed, silver-windowed building beside a marshy armpit of Caspian shore. Pilgrims come here in considerable numbers to pay respects to a comically oversized 'footprint' of Imam Ali within the central octagonal glass display ('Yes, Ali was REALLY big' notes the attendant!). It was first discovered and encased 250 years ago by Sheikh Aliyar, but the footprint's original shrine virtually collapsed during the Soviet era. Outside on another holy rock, a blue mini-shrine covers the supposed hoof-print of Ali's faithful horse Dül Dül. Beside the shrine is the twin-towered **Fatimeyi Zährä mosque**

❏ Balaxani's revolutionaries

In 1904-5 when Baku was rife with political agitators (including Stalin) trying to pave the way for a Bolshevik revolution, it was the workers in Balaxanı that were the main targets of their propaganda. Many of the agitators were rich, educated Russians for whom communism had been a philosophical concept before arriving here. Seeing the appalling conditions in which men worked, digging with hand shovels while almost submerged in the toxic naphtha, had a great influence on their ideas.

The culture shock, difficult conditions and revealed prejudices of the revolutionaries make their recollections particularly interesting reading. The memoirs of Eva Broido have the added piquancy of a female perspective in a totally male world (men outnumbered women almost 3:1 in the oilfield areas):

'Life in Balakhany was fraught with particular dangers for women ... the local Tatars ... inspired me with real horror. No woman could go out on her own in Balakhany without being molested. Certainly not after dark.' Tatar (ie Azeri) and Armenian women's lives were entirely spent behind closed gates in the yards of their houses, notes Broido, which was 'all very awkward for a professional revolutionary'. She would walk about the muddy 'streets' 'with a revolver my constant companion, stuck into my belt; a man on either side and a third if possible behind.' The one time she relaxed this she was grabbed from behind and only escaped thanks to a passing Russian carriage driver. On another occasion when walking with 'only' one chaperone, a 'huge Tatar watchman at the Benckendorff Factory armed with a revolver demanded "Give me the woman".' The companion finally managed to dissuade him from kidnap or violence 'after a long parlay, compliments and one rouble for beer.' A few days later, however, another woman was found raped and decapitated in a forgotten cemetery nearby. 'It was only too easy to lose one's life in the oilfields; men were trigger happy and fired at the least provocation.'

Popular myth has it that the bell of Balaxanı's domed Greek-Russian-style church tolled mysteriously all of its own accord as the September 1905 massacres began. This was possibly a planned signal, rather than a ghostly campanologist's outing.

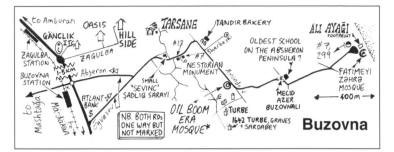

and a computer-equipped madrassa funded by pilgrims' donations.

The curious **Tarsane** appears to be the remnant arched dome of a medieval church or mausoleum. Local lore says this is the place to come for superstitious 'insurance' before undertaking a long trip. To make your wish tie a rag onto one of the nails in the wall or smash a bottle: judging from the vast pile of glass, Buzovna's citizens are very well travelled.

Buses #7 (via Zabrat and Mäshtağa) and #299 run from Baku passing all the way through Buzovna to terminate at the shrine. Driving from Baku it's faster to go via Märdäkan than through Mäshtağa.

Zagulba, 1.5km north of Buzovna, has a handful of accommodation options misleadingly portrayed in some literature as 'beach hotels' despite being well set back from (and without easy access to) what's anyway a pretty grotty area of Caspian shore. The best option here is the modern yet classically styled *Hillside* (☎ 453 1661, 🖥 www.hillside.az); AZN80-130 double rooms are bright and airy with gingham bedcovers and wicker chairs. AZN250 'cottages' are more like full-blown homes. There's a butterfly-shaped swimming-pool and wide views from a sensibly priced café-bar. Better known but somewhat bland and with peeling wallpaper, the *Oasis* (☎ 453 4456, AZN85 dbl) has a very small pool. There's an oddly located **tourist information booth** at the gates of the so-called 'Gänclik International Tourist Centre'. It seems to be permanently closed.

Dübändi

The trans-shipment port that receives Kazakhstan's oil for export to Europe and is the terminus of a pipeline from Oily Rocks (Neft Dashlari), built in 1983.

The port itself is hardly a place to visit but around two headlands to the north-west is an attractive sandy cove, sheltered by low cliffs. The cliffs and some patches of rocks on the grassy shelfland above are cut with caves. Like at Qobustan, some ancient petroglyphs have been found here showing bulls and open-armed stick figures (N40°27'32.3", E50°15'24.6"). Beware of snakes.

Fatmai

One of the older, slightly more appealing Absheron villages, little Fatmai has three old mosques and a low-rise, whitewashed homogeneity which gives it a slightly Greek-island flavour. Very slightly. Bus #108 runs from Gänclik metro.

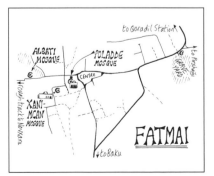

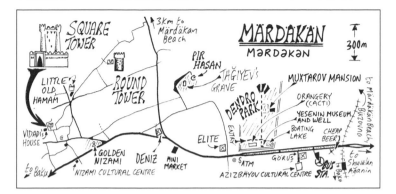

Märdäkän (see also Shuvälän and Shaǧan) Märdäkän has a wealthy air with numerous upmarket datchas and several oil-boom mansions, tucked away in large gardens. The town sprawls from Shaǧan across a considerable area, merging into Shuvälän at the railway line just beyond the theatre, bus station and central bazaar.

The main points of tourist interest are two **fortress towers**. Both are extensively restored stone structures of which the 22m **square tower** is much the more impressive. Built in 1187 and rebuilt in the 14th century, it's set back from the quaint little 1482 **Tubashakhi Mosque** which exhibits photos of other Absheron castles. Here you might encounter the tower's key-holder, Vidadi Yaftumov (if not try his home, nearby house #17). Vidadi can show you Stone Age tools found en site and 'refrigerator holes' beneath the castle tower's floor. He claims that a network of tunnels once led all the way to the Caspian and to Shaǧan from here. The highlight of a visit is the sweeping view from the tower's upper ramparts.

The smaller **round tower** (built in 1204, 15.5m high) is stuck incongruously amid dreary suburban homes in a scraggy handkerchief of park. It has been substantially restored but is not usually open.

For locals, Märdäkän's big draw is a stroll, pot of tea or paddle-boat ride in **Dendro Park** (9am-10pm), once oil baron Muxtarov's datcha and grounds. However, the AZN4 foreigner price entry-fee is highly discouraging (locals pay AZN1). The park contains a rather scraggy **botanical garden**, an '**orangery**' (ie greenhouse full of cacti) where you might be asked for a further 20q (officially there's no need to pay). A more intriguing feature is the great well with spiral stairs descending a wide, cool shaft beside a modest bungalow that's now a **Yesenin Museum**. Yesenin, the fast-living 1920s' poet, stayed here on the rebound from a tour of the USA and two short-lived, high-profile marriages (to Isadora Duncan and to Tolstoy's granddaughter!) He had set off to Persia for inspiration but was so drunk by the time he reached Baku that he was persuaded he'd already arrived. His 'Persian Poems' were thus written while comfortably installed in the fine pseudo-moorish house (still standing at the northern end of Dendro Park) that had recently been confiscated from oil baron Muxtarov. Guest rooms here are available to rent by arrangement (call ☎ 012-454 1050).

Another oil baron, Taǧiyev, while still an all-powerful millionaire was warned by a Koran-quoting holy man (Molla Abuturab) that all wealth was transitory – a gift from Allah who could take it back at any moment. It was a conversation Taǧiyev was to rue when dispossessed by the communists. In Taǧiyev's will he asked to be buried at the sage's feet as a token of religious penance, and today the two graves lie side by side in a garden under a fine stone cupola surrounded by architectural fragments of oil-boom

AROUND BAKU

Märdäkän Beach

buildings. Just beyond is the small but high-ly regarded **Pir Hasan shrine**. If Mashtağa's *childağ* folk-cure for jumpy nerves failed you, seek out a bottle-wielding old crone near this shrine. Stand beside the pile of smashed glass, bow your head and see what happens! Don't forget to tip her a manat.

The best restaurants in central Märdäkän are *Deniz* and *Görüş* though El and Oasis in Shuvälän are more upmarket.

Märdäkän Beach Around 3km north of Tağiyev's grave, Märdäkän's decent beach has two **waterslide parks** (neither as extensive as the Novxanı Aquapark) and many summer dining options. Of several hotels, by far the best is professionally managed *Khazar Golden Beach Hotel* (☎ 012-554 0710, 🖳 www.khazarbeachhotel.com). Its series of balcony-sporting two- and three-storey blocks range around a good central swimming pool but don't expect peace and quiet in summer when disco nights are almost inevitable. Rack rates are a thumping AZN250-400 though discounts are likely outside summer weekends.

The downmarket, summer-only *Dalğa* is reserved for workers' families arriving in pre-booked groups but if you can talk your way past the gruff guard-post it's worth dropping in to sample the sensory overload of its acid-trip lobby – a technicolour undersea fantasia of oversized starfish, sharks and sturgeons diving surreally from garish walls beneath discordant chandeliers and gaudy-classic stairway statuettes.

Transport From Baku, minibus #36 starts from handily central Vurğun Gardens sever-

al times hourly or take more frequent #24 from Qara Qarayev metro. Both pass Dendro Park en route to Shüvälan where they terminate at the shrine. Get off at the tiny Nizami Cultural Centre for the castle towers or at restaurant Deniz for Pir Hassan.

Bus #341 starting from Baku's metro Neftchilar goes to Märdäkän beach. For the Märdäkän–Suraxanı run take #77. From Märdäkän bus station, the #220 goes a few times daily to Qala and Pirallahı (Artyom) Island. Eight trains a day in each direction run from Baku looping through Märdäkän and Suraxani, though every year this service seems to dwindle. Take the anticlockwise route one stop to the derelict-looking Primorskaya station for Märdäkän beach.

Mäshtağa
Prosperous Mäshtağa is known for piety, business sense and limp wrists. Goltz, who stayed here in 1991, claims it was the centre of the USSR's 'florist-mafia'. The astonishing 'AzPark', a private mansion in a garden of grandiose rock-mountain follies (partially visible behind a wall from the Nardaran road) is itself partly used as a nursery for flowers and cacti. It's unmarked and not open to the public but the courteous owners are sometimes prepared to show polite visitors around, especially if you're interested in flowers.

Juma Mosque has a fine new minaret in the shadow of which is the pre-eminent venue for the rather more animist custom of *Childağ*. To conquer a nervous disposition, bring the panicky individual here on a Saturday or Wednesday, queue with the other faithful, and get burnt on special energy points with a blue fuse of smouldering cloth. A donation of around AZN2-5 is appropriate as you leave.

Minibus 72 from Metro Qara Qarayev serves Mäshtağa and continues via Bilgäh to Amburan beach.

Nardaran

Nardaran is one of the most interesting Absheron towns, though you'd never guess it if you just drove by. The old centre of town atop a steep, north-facing slope, was built around the summer palace of the 15th-century Shirvanshahs. At that time the level of the Caspian Sea was higher than today so the castle would have had an even better view of potential invaders arriving by sea. Local historians claim that the eastern approaches were simultaneously watched by a look-out post near Zagulba linked to Nardaran by an improbably long tunnel, now closed and mainly collapsed.

Nardaran and bigger Mäshtağa, to which it now clings as a virtual suburb, are Azerbaijan's most piously Muslim towns. Backstreet walls are occasionally daubed with Islamic slogans and cartoons designed to guide moral behaviour. Though hardly Iran-strength fanaticism, you'll see a fair few women in chador. Nardaran held Azerbaijan's most significant anti-Israel marches deploring Israel's January 2009 war against Gaza.

The gigantic **Rehime Khanım Mosque** was built between 1997 and 1999 on the site of the former khan's summer palace and is arguably the most impressive religious structure in Azerbaijan. But what draws visitors is the little subterranean tomb beneath which the faithful peep through a tiny window under an artificial rose to offer prayers to the grave of Rehime Khanım, another sister of the 7th Imam (like Okuma/Herkume at Bibi Heybat). A donation here is considered an effective approach to conquering infertility. Women visitors should wear a scarf: you can borrow one from the shoe deposit desk.

In the winding streets and alleys nearby

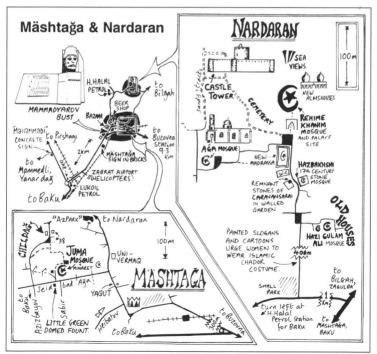

you'll find several other mosques, most notably the blue-domed **Ağa Mosque** with its fortified round tower minaret. There's also a **castle** whose simple crenellated tower (built in 1301) and inner curtain wall have been heavily restored, while most of the outer defences have long since vanished. The **Shah Abbas Caravanserai** has been reduced to one small, insignificant building in the corner of a private vegetable garden.

Minibus #89 from Baku's Qara Qarayev metro runs all the way to the gate of Rehime Khanım Mosque.

Neft Dashlari (Oily Rocks, Neftyanye Kamni) (map p63)

Local tradition holds that a range of underwater mountains (hills really) once divided the Caspian between the Absheron and Turkmenbashi (Turkmenistan). In a few places these rise high enough to create small islets, of which the most intriguing is surely the 'Oily Rocks', 45km offshore. In the 19th century people observed 'Naptha' (ie petroleum) bubbling to the surface here; since 1949 the site has been a commercial source of oil.

It is now the world's only town to be built entirely on stilts in the middle of a sea, with nearly a hundred kilometres of photogenically rickety plank-and-stilt roadways. A real town, it has its own power station, road signs and even a mini Heydar Aliyev Park so that the roughly 6000 workers can feel really at home. Men (families are not allowed) work two-week shifts and live in eight- and nine-storey apartment blocks which were featured proudly on a 1971, 4-kopek Soviet stamp.

Visitors are not allowed unless by invitation of the state oil company SOCAR, which remains apparently disinterested in the great tourist potential. Should you get an invitation, helicopters leave regularly from the south end of Pirallahı (Artyom) Island.

Pirallahı (Artyom) Island

Alternatively known as Svyatoi ('Holy Island'), this long, low, shrinking raft of land was a sacred spot for ancient Zoroastrian fire-worshippers. It was also the first place favoured by the Persians to extract oil. In the

Russian era the extraction continued sponsored by a brother-in-law of rebel leader Imam Shamil who went into partnership with Dutch-Baltic entrepreneurs. Still, when founded in 1823, Artyom village had just two buildings – one for the Europeans to live in, the other for refining paraffin.

Today, rising water levels have made 'old' Artyom village unstable. The place has been abandoned and the people moved to **Pirallahı** ('God's shrine') township where uninspiring 5-storey apartment towers straggle north from the railway station, itself built in 1948 by German prisoners of war. The northern end of the island, around 2km beyond the terminus point for Baku-minibuses, is fascinatingly ugly with assorted offshore debris, rickety moorings and oily mud pools. The southern spit has virtually disappeared into the rising Caspian along with a former causeway to some offshore oil platforms – a phenomenon more clearly visible from the hill opposite on which stands **Damba lighthouse**.

Minibus #50 runs several times per hour from Baku's Ulduz metro (AZN1) taking 1½ hours. There are two daily trains, one from Baku the other from Qala station (one hour).

Pirshağı

The two long, winding main streets of this sprawling village divide at a fork whose left branch leads past the little Talaz Pir (new), through some vaguely atmospheric areas and ends up close to a curious two-domed tumble-down ruin on a sandy pre-beach area. The right fork leads to better sand if you're swimming and to the *Sunset Beach* restaurant. Bus #73 stops a short, obvious walk from the beach.

Qala

Although there's a new 'Qala' around the railway station of the same name, Qala proper is an 800-year-old village 4km further south. Today it's a strange partial ghost town with five little mosques scattered about a gently undulating landscape of sand-mud homes, old petrol workings and oil-effluent pools. Yet in pre-Soviet days this was one of the most prosperous and

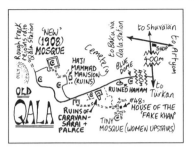

pious towns on the peninsula. According to local historian Haji Shabran it had a population of around 20,000 (there are now just over 900) and 316 shops. The population has been dropping since 1905 when the Tsar's police accused local Mollahs of stirring up anti-Armenian sentiment. In fact the town retained most of its Christian Armenian minority until 1918 when they fled to avoid the Turkish invasion.

Qala became a particular focus of the USSR's anti-religion drive with many mosques closed or destroyed. Today what's left is in a sorry state. The **caravanserai/palace complex** whose highest walls once soared 28m is now an easy to miss, one-room shell. Some 2006 restoration work prevented its collapse and you can now clamber inside but the floor passage optimistically said to lead to Bibi Heybat (!) is secret once more.

The home of former philanthropist landowner **Haji Mammad** also stands empty and derelict. Haji Shabran claims that there are the ruins of a substantial city beneath today's foundations and ruins, but as yet his hopes to publish a history of the village haven't come to fruition. Pirallahı minibuses pass near Qala.

Ramana

Ringed with sturdy crenellated outer walls, Ramana's **castle tower** is the most impressive on the Absheron. It sits on a rocky outcrop, panoramically surveying a vast expanse of photogenically ugly oil pools and old derricks. With the key, available for a donation, you can climb the crenellated outer walls for even better views. Sources vary as to the age of both the tower and the small box-mosque clinging to its side; perhaps 11-12th, perhaps 16-17th century. Outside is an intriguing rock with a bowl-shaped indentation. Such rocks occur quite frequently on the Absheron and archaeologists suggest that they may have some pre-Islamic ceremonial importance. In previous centuries, dust scraped from special stones was considered a talisman against various ills. The relatively interesting adjacent village of old Ramana is worth a wander. Take bus #304.

Note that New Ramana is an entirely different place, an uninteresting village close to the main airport road.

Shağan (Şağan, map p154)

Now almost a suburb of Märdäkän, quiet Shağan was reportedly once a minor centre for Nestorian Christianity. Like nearby Buzovna it has a small, rare 14th-century Nestorian grave/shrine on a little roadside rock. More visually memorable is the tumble-down **castle tower** (at 40°29'51.2"N, 50°07'45.7"E) now incorporated into the perimeter wall of a local home. Hurry to see it before it collapses. **Museji Kasim mosque** is unassuming but has an interesting sword-bearing lion motif above the

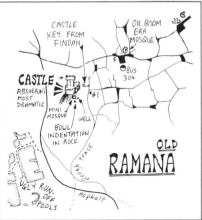

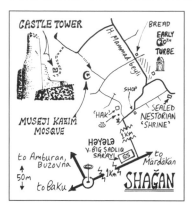

door. Yesenin's famous ditty *Shağan Maya Shağan* was in praise of a beautiful Shağan milkmaid who refused the 'shagoholic' poet's repeated advances and ended up needing her wares in Märdäkän.

Shuvälän (Şuvələn)

The 'place of snakes', Shuvälän merges into Märdäkän at the railway line near **Safar Aliyev's villa**, now a sanatorium, with turreted 1912 gates. Shuvälän's main claim to fame is the **Mir Mövsüm Ağanin** at the other end of the town's long main street (known variously as 26 Commissar St, Yesenin St, or Almas Ildirim St). An impressive Central Asian style blue-majolica dome and some dazzling (if new) mirrored stalactite vaulting give it the feel of an Iranian Imamzade.

The Ağanin is the last resting place of Mir Mövsum (Aga Seyid Ali Mirmövsumzadeh), nicknamed Ataĝa, ('the Boneless One' or literally 'Meat Lord') much to the annoyance of his respectable Seyid family. This odd figure apparently spent his decalcified life slumped in a chair, unable to manoeuvre himself or even stand as his body lacked a skeleton. With typical oriental optimism, his deformity was seen as a blessing. Those who encountered him reported miraculous turns of fortune. Soviet authorities finding his presence incompatible with communist rationality tried to banish him from his Baku home but the vehicles sent to remove him invariably developed mysterious technical faults rendering them immobile. Some claim he was even used as a secret weapon in WWII – wheeled towards the Dağestan frontier to ward off a possible German invasion. It worked. After his death, the Boneless One was interred in the graveyard in Shuvälän and pilgrims began to visit the site bringing gifts as well as prayers.

Inside, pilgrims circle the grave three times before retiring to the nearby madrassa building for free cups of tea sweetened with Nazir offerings (sugar, halva etc). Even the most level-headed Azeris seem to believe in the Meat Lord's power, and return to 'repay' granted wishes. I was handed a spiced pastry by one couple whose son had 'miraculously' got into university following a visit to the meat lord's grave. Of course, passing the exams helped too.

Minibuses #24 and 36 from Baku and #77 from Suraxanı terminate at the shrine.

Suraxanı

Suraxanı town is an unappealing sprawl but the unique **'Ateshgah' fire temple** makes it by far the most popular Absheron destination for foreign tourists. Surrounded by a cloister of pilgrim cells, the temple's central stone shrine stands like a castle tower across a flaming central hearth and shoots jets of burning gas from four roof-corner flues. At least when it's lit. These

days the gas fuelling the temple is piped from the mains as the natural gas pocket directly beneath the shrine has become exhausted. This is not some new 'deception'. The last Hindu 'priest' sold the site's gas extraction rights to the Baku Oil Company in 1879 who considered the Ateshgah an uneconomic waste of resources. To economize they switched off the gas supply and as early as 1881 travellers reported the temple 'closed and only re-lit for tourists'.

The exact history of the temple is uncertain. Some historical sources wager that the site was holy to the Zoroastrians from the 6th or 7th century BC, others that there was a temple here only after the 13th century AD. Whatever its precursors, the present Ateshgah is not Zoroastrian at all, contrary to assertions by many writers including Alexandre Dumas, and early editions of this very guide. Essad Bey reports that it was briefly the centre of a weird pantheist religion in which reverence to mother earth was symbolized by kissing the breasts of naked female devotees. However, the present structure was built by Indian merchants in the early 18th century and used by Punjabi mystics who were probably devotees of Jawala-ji, a flame-faced incarnation of Devi. Suraxanı was a sub-temple to Jawalamukhi, 56km south of Dharamsala (in Himachal Pradesh's Kangra Valley) where even now Hindu pilgrims go to see spontaneously burning gas emerging from a holy rock within a Mughal-domed temple.

Entry costs AZN2, add AZN2 for a camera and AZN6 for a guided tour of the pilgrim-cell rooms, some of which are dotted with amusingly wobbly mannequins of Hindu ascetics some undergoing daft self mutilations in the tacky fake lamplight.

Behind the temple site there's some classic old oil-field detritus though some visitors report being far from welcome to photograph the rotting old derricks.

Public transport A filthy, wooden-seated commuter train runs several times daily from Baku stopping just two minutes' walk from the temple entrance. By minibus take #84 from metro Narimanov, or #213 from metro Qara Qarayev via Ämircan. The #77 connects to Märdäkän.

Yanar Dağ (Burning Hillside) (map p156)

An extraordinary little hillside between Digah and Mammedli (Mähämmädi, Magomedli) burns day and night thanks to seeping subterranean gases which were accidentally ignited in 1958. The site is on the edge of a desolate windswept moorland, hidden behind the rather decrepit *Yanar Dağ teahouse* (40°30'06"N, 49°53'28"E) where a tea-and-jam set costs AZN8 and can take half an hour to prepare. On cold winter evenings, adjust the temperature to your comfort level by settling a terrace table at the appropriate distance from the flames. Arriving alone in the middle of the night, the atmosphere is at its most surreal with the teahouse closed and barely a car on the road – the only sound is the escaping gas licking at the slope with its multiple-flaming tongues. Although there *are* other such 'fire-places' in Azerbaijan, none is as impressive or as accessible.

A bizarre rumour claims the teahouse was once closed for possession of a rocket launcher, presumably for express delivery of tea to planes taking off from Bina Airport.

Taxi drivers want around AZN20-25 return (and you might need to help them with directions). Minibus 47 from Gänclik Metro (p107, ϑA7) usually terminates at the eastern end of Digah. From there walk 1.2km north-east and Yanar Dağ is 100m beyond the new barn-like disposal plant (blue and yellow flue-chimney).

Hand-dug wells

An odd moonscape, 2.5km south of Yanar Dağ, is the site of **Baku's oldest oilwells** especially in the area between 40°28'25-47"N and 49°53'19-58"E. The earliest ones were shallow, hand-dug affairs with timber cladding inserted to the pit-sides to prevent collapse. Life expectancy here was very short. Ironically the worst thing for the digger was to strike oil. The result could often be fatal, whether poisoned by gases, burnt by explosion or being gey-

AROUND BAKU

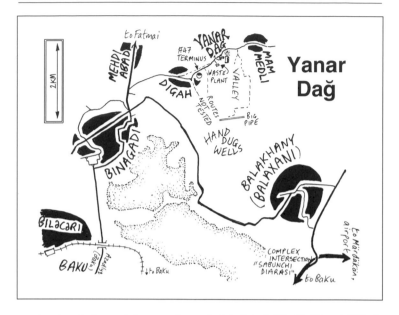

sered out and drowned by a gusher. Incredibly a fair number of these 1880s pits are still there, while the stumps of later Nobel-drilled versions are also visible. Coming directly from Yanar Dağ, a pipeline across the intervening valley means you can only drive part way (park around 40°29'10"N, 49°53'30"E then walk south up the hillside beyond). Access is easier if uglier and less peacefully thrilling from the west where a track leads off the asphalt road at 40°28'11.8"N, 49°53'07.2"E allowing 4WDs up onto the main well-hole hill.

NORTH-WEST ABSHERON

Should you wish to see the fairly minimal sights of Xırdalan (drinks factories), Sumqayit (industrial horror), Saray and Corat (smaller, more historic) and Novxanı (mosques, beach), a day should be more than ample by car. By bus take the #14 from Baku's main bus terminal (p77, ΨΟ1) to Saray and on to Corat and Novxanı beach. The #998 then takes you back to Baku's Gänclik Metro (p107) via Novxanı village. Continuing to the rest of the Absheron is slightly inconvenient as there's no easy road from Novxanı to Fatmai/Yanar Dağ without back tracking to Binagadi.

Xırdalan and Ceyranbatan

One of Baku's larger suburban townships, Xırdalan is most noted for its cola-bottlers and its eponymous brewery. Hidden behind a grave-covered hillock, the older part of town hides a 1884 **mosque** with a fine minaret added in 1996. Its prize possession is a splendid seven-stepped 1902 wooden *minbar* fashioned with shäbäkä-style panels. A visiting group of Uzbeks who vainly tried to purchase it in the 1990s apparently offered $300,000. The notches and scars are souvenirs from 1918 when the mosque was attacked by Armenians during the March Days.

Incredibly the water for the **Ceyranbatan reservoir** is brought all the way from the Russian border by the

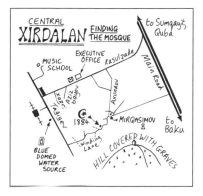

Samur–Absheron canal. Without it Baku would not be viable as a city. The banks of the reservoir are partially forested with mini-pines amid which are several outdoor restaurants popular with those weekend picnickers who lack the time or the wherewithal to go to Quba or Nabran. However, you can't actually reach the waterside as the reservoir is too strategically important.

Sumqayıt

Until 1940 Sumqayıt was a village of 4000 souls set on an idyllic curve of wide sandy beach. It might have been developed into the country's foremost resort. But Soviet planners had a better idea: a concrete-tower city of 250,000 people and as many rusty pipes. By the 1980s it was home to 80% of Azerbaijan's heavy industry, a brave new world of chemical factories that belched colourful fumes so acrid that locals passing through by train found their white clothes stained yellow!

Today, promotional brochures still poetically extol a city 'well known to users

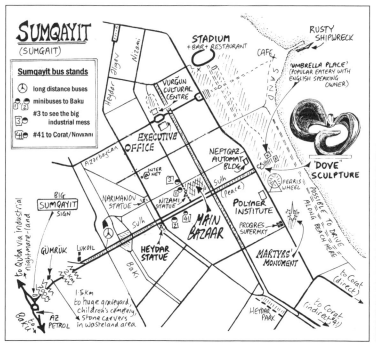

of sulphanol, superphosphates and synthetic cleaning substances'. In fact, a perversely positive side effect of the 1990s' economic dislocation was that many of the dirtiest factories ran out of money and the air quality has improved dramatically. Relatively few factories have been recommissioned. That still doesn't make the city's smoke stacks and regimented apartment blocks much of a tourist attraction. But the neat central area is pleasant enough with a beautifully creeper-draped **Executive Office** building facing the columned **Vurğun Culture Centre**. The waterfront retains its wide, hard-packed sandy beaches and is attractively backed by an expansive park, a dramatic **martyr's monument** and a stylish modernist **'dove' sculpture** at the culmination of Sulh (Peace) avenue. The tangled mass of **industrial debris** in the north-western zone is photogenically ghastly (see p161). Also moving is the children's section of the vast **city graveyard**: a poignant reminder that Sumqayıt once held the unenviable world record for infant mortality. Locals seem keen to show visitors the **German Graveyard** in the 'Koteji' district (entrance at 40°36'07.5"N, 49°39' 08"E) but there's virtually nothing to see there.

Modern historians' interest in Sumqayıt stems from 1988-9 when inter-ethnic conflict erupted here between Azeris and ethnic Armenian residents who had previously lived as perfectly amicable neighbours. While the recent arrival of ethnic Azeris displaced from Armenia added to local tensions, there is some evidence that the disturbances were deliberately stirred up by a gang of *agents provocateurs*, probably at the bequest of the Russian secret services.

Minibuses leave every few seconds from Baku's new main bus terminal taking various routes. To go the slow, 'scenic route' via Saray and Corat take #14. Or start from Metro Gänclik (θA7) and take bus 998 (80q) via Novxanı.

Saray
Old Saray is marked on some Absheron maps with the intriguing icon 'destroyed or half-destroyed'. This hilltop former caravanserai town was systematically depopulated in the Soviet era and, apart from a clutch of half-finished new farm buildings, only the old mosque remains. From outside that appears tattily rebuilt and rather ordinary but the interior reveals very elegant stone vaulting and loving restoration. The hill is not steep enough to make views really dramatic but they are fairly wide with a long, grassy foreground and a spooky feeling of desolation. Access is via new Saray, a small low-rise town with a modest, new mosque which bus #14 passes en route between Baku and Corat.

Corat (Jorat)
Although it's the north coast's most historic village, Corat is now little more than a suburban limpet at the eastern edge of Sumqayıt. Locals claim its squat little mosque was founded by Arabs in 1007AD

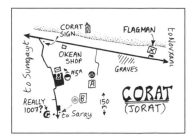

but if so only one stone appears to be original (inset above a new side door). I've labelled the two hamams 'A' and 'B' on the map: 'B' is a typical 19th-century brick-domed affair; 'A' is a curious subterranean chamber beneath a small glass dome. It is claimed to be 480 years old and still operates. It's free (women Mon and Fri, men other days) if you can find it – descend via the unmarked blue metal door.

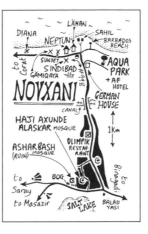

Novxanı

In summer salt diggers appear to walk on water as they work the fluorescent purple-pink surface of Masazyr Lake. Directly north in Novxanı's old village centre is the heavily restored **Haji Axund Alasker Mosque** with a fine interior. You'll see the mosque in passing from the 998 bus which also passes a Rasulzade statue beside the graves of the ADR hero's father and son. Upmarket datchas sprawl most of the 4km from here to **Novxanı Beach** which has been considerably improved in places by the addition of imported shell-sand.

Restaurants, club-cafés, pay-parking lots and mini-hotels now stretch from here almost all the way to Corat. From mid-June each year *Novxanı Aquapark* opens Azerbaijan's biggest complex of water-

slides (AZN15 per day, AZN5 after 8pm). They get very busy and the poolside is often a venue for summer concerts. So don't expect peace and quiet at the smart-looking *Af Hotel* (☎ 012-448 3043, 🖳 www.afhotel .info/en/) that wraps around them. Rooms were good motel-standard when the place opened in 2006 but some are already getting a little musty so look before you book. Doubles cost around AZN150 in summer (including three institutional meals) but drop to AZN60 in winter. The waterslides are free to residents.

For around AZN60 (AZN30 in winter) some of the beach restaurants offer air-conditioned rooms. The best bet is to choose whichever has been most recently constructed: at the time of writing that was the *Neptun* (☎ 012-447 3987) and especially the *Läman* (☎ 050-521-7188) approximately opposite *Sindibad*, a restaurant that's amusingly shaped like a pirate ship complete with concrete canons.

Comfortable and frequent in summer, bus #998 from Gänclik Metro goes through Novxanı village to the beach then runs along the coast to Sumqayit. Buses #5 and #41 come along the coast from Sumqayıt with a wiggle through Corat.

PART 4: THE NORTH

INTRODUCTION

North of Baku, the scrubby desert gradually transforms via orchard lands (around Quba) into oak forests nuzzled around Nabran's grey sand beaches. Short, easy diversions en route take you to the dramatically coloured 'Candy Cane' mountains, the castle ruin at Chirax, and the mysterious shamanesque pinnacle of Besh Barmaq.

Further inland lies Azerbaijan's loveliest scenery – breathtaking chasms, canyons and bald-peaked mountains with excellent hiking, climbing and camping opportunities. An asphalted lane built in 2006 makes it possible to reach the timeless villages of Cek and Xınalıq without a 4WD. At least for a few seasons until the road deteriorates. Lovely Laza remains hard to reach but might become more accessible as work procedes on the big new Shahdağ ski resort.

REGIONAL HISTORY

During the Albanian period the coastal plain represented a profitable trade route or a devastating invitation to invaders according to the era. Thus the main architectural efforts were put into a massive series of fortification projects: three great walls aimed at funnelling any movement of trade (or potential invaders) through controllable gateways. Most impressive was the 120km long, 10m-thick earthen ramparts whose famous Great Iron Gate was at Derbend; 42km of this was later reinforced by the 16th-century Azeri-Persian emperor Shah Ismail I (Xatai). That now lies within Russian Dağestan.

The two more southerly wall routes were (a) from Chirax Castle to Gilgilchay (near Dävächi); (b) spanning the shorter plain between Besh Barmaq and the coast.

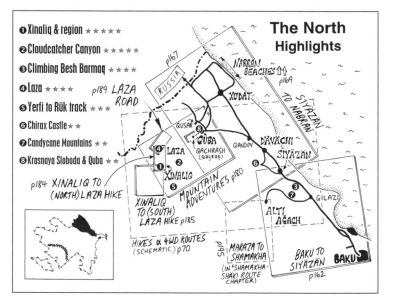

The North Highlights

❶ Xinaliq & region ★★★★★
❷ Cloudcatcher Canyon ★★★★
❸ Climbing Besh Barmaq ★★★★
❹ Laza ★★★★
❺ Yerfi to Rük track ★★★
❻ Chirax Castle ★★
❼ Candycane Mountains ★★
❽ Krasnaya Sloboda & Quba ★★

p167
RUSSIA
NABRAN BEACHES p169
XUDAT
TO NABRAN
p189 LAZA ROAD
QUSAR
QUBA
GACHRASH (QƏÇRƏŞ)
QANDOV
DÄVÄCHI
SIYÄZÄN
LAZA
XINALIQ
MOUNTAIN ADVENTURES p180
p184 XINALIQ TO (NORTH) LAZA HIKE
XINALIQ TO (SOUTH) LAZA HIKE p185
GILAZI
ALTI AĞACH
HIKES & 4WD ROUTES (SCHEMATIC) p70
MARAZA TO SHAMAKHA (IN 'SHAMAKHA-SHAKI' ROUTE CHAPTER)
BAKU TO SIYÄZÄN p162
BAKU

There would have been further defences along the Samur River which forms today's Russo–Azeri border. As in China, these 'Great Walls' were never demolished as such, just left to decay. The stretches which were built of stone have since been cannibalized for house building, so today it takes a lot of imagination to make out where they once stood.

Power over the area was wielded alternately from Derbend, Shamakha or Baku until the late 17th century with the rise of a minor local khanate based at Xudat.

In the 18th century the Xudat khan transferred his power base to Quba which rose rapidly to regional prominence. Quba briefly became one of the strongest power centres in Azerbaijan under Fatali Khan who tried, semi-successfully, to unite the squabbling Azeri potentates as a counterbalance to the growing threat from Persia. However, his 1784 defence treaty with Russia paved the way for eventual annexation and, in 1806, Russia abolished the khanate altogether.

BAKU TO GILĀZI (see map p162)

There are two routes around the rusting mess of **Sumqayıt**. The westerly bypass offers sneaky views over the bunkers of the Nasonaya military airstrip leaving you wondering how many of those fighter planes are actually wooden decoys. Alternatively, the straight-through route presents mile upon mile of awesomely dilapidated factories and overhead chemical pipes plus a bus graveyard on the left as you reach the far end of town. Grimly photogenic stuff.

The recombined road thereafter follows the railway line and later the Samur–Absheron canal which supplies most of Baku's water. For 70km the landscape is dry, empty steppeland dotted with a few villages, refugee settlements and ageing oil workings. Very minor sites viewed from the main road include a train graveyard (km46.8) and the lonely, vaguely handsome stone **Yaşma Station** building (km52.7).

Several kilometres east of the road are several potentially nice beaches (golden shells, not sand). However, military zones and waterlogged forelands obstruct most access routes. Perhaps the easiest 'beach' to reach is 4.5 pot-holed kilometres east of **Shurabad**. Beware of swimming here, however, as there are submerged rocks.

GILĀZI TO ALTI AĞACH (map p162)

Beside the main Quba road, **Gilāzi** is a windswept non-event marked out by its *kamikoma fabrik* (factory) beside which the A6 road turns inland. The A6 is asphalted as far as Xızı village (31km) climbing slowly between dry, eroded tiger-paw hills, through rolling sheep-nibbled hills. After Xızı the road gets bumpy en route to Altı Ağach beyond which you'd need dry weather and a 4WD to continue. A handful of Xizi-bound buses pick passengers up at the Gilāzi junction (40°52'10"N, 49°21'15") where alternatively the Bizim Market shop can help you organize a taxi.

'Candy Cane' mountains

Around 14km from Gilāzi, the dry mountains start to develop beautiful rose and white 'candy' stripes and swirls. For a stretch the other-worldly scenery is reminiscent of Death Valley, USA, except rather more vividly coloured and littered with little conical fossils.

These 'Candy Cane' mountains have no well-established local name so if taking a taxi from Gilazi (around 10AZN return) ask for 'Mushviq Ojach'. This will get you to an isolated bust of poet Mikayil Mushviq surveying the scene from across a small footbridge. A kilometre back towards Gilāzi is an isolated, recently restored stone house that was said to have been Mushviq's birthplace.

Xızı (☎ 0199)

The *rayon*'s comically petite administrative centre Xızı (population 1200) has a few shops, an internet centre and the world's most pointless set of traffic lights. The architecture has none of the attraction of much-older Altı Ağach but the viewpoints at the western edge of town look out across the Atachay valley. There are some pleasant walks in the hills above Xızı, including a hike to/from the Candy Canes using a parallel ridge and passing a curious ski-jump-

THE NORTH

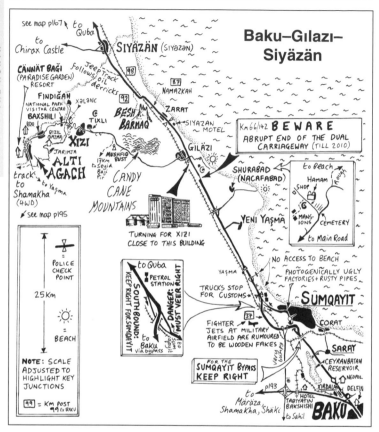

Baku–Gılazı–Siyäzän

like rock en route. See 🖥 www.everytrail
.com/view_trip.php?trip_id=36010 for photos and waymarked GPS points. There's a
cosy little **camping** spot at 40°52'30.7"N
49°04'53.9"E.

Transport Buses to Baku via Gilazi leave
at 09.30 and 18.00, to Sumqayıt at 13.30.
To Altı Ağach minibuses should run at
11.00 and possibly 14.30. Alternatively,
find an impromptu 'taxi' by asking at the
small central row of shops. Be aware that
some maps show a direct Baku–Xızı road
(the A7) but in reality that's just an indistinct 4WD track.

Altı Ağach National Park (☎ 0199)
Beyond Xızı the road descends a ladder of
hairpin bends. At **Xälänc** a single track lane
diverts south-west taking a pretty forest
route through dwarf oak and beech trees to
Qizil Qazma Hotel (☎ mob 50 224 0708,
new rooms AZN100, old bungalows
AZN20-40), under reconstruction at the time
of writing. It sits on a hilltop ridge that was
once the most beautiful place in this region.
Sadly the best viewpoints here are now used
for private datcha sites and a vast, secretive
official retreat complex. All very ironic as
the surrounding area has become a national
park. On the main Xälänc–Altı Ağach road

the National Park has an under-used **animal rehabilitation compound** and **visitor centre** (☎ mob 50-326 2205, Pasha, 09-18:00, Mon-Fri) with a small 'museum' – a single locked room with a few pressed leaves and some badly hung nature photos. You're supposed to stop here and pay a park fee (AZN4 foreigner, AZN2 local) but unless a barrier is erected, most cars will continue to ignore this and drive straight through.

Beyond **Baxshili** there are a few shashlyk places scattered amongst the trees including *Merjan* (☎ mob 50-494 4104) with AZN30 twin guest rooms that come with a shower and a seatless toilet, and *Cil* (☎ mob 50-426 2160) with AZN50 rooms and an AZN100 stone bungalow.

Altı Ağach village (☎ 0199)

From its now isolated position you'd never guess that venerable Altı Ağach once controlled a major trade route linking the entrepôt towns of Shabran and Derbend with then all-important Shamakha. Today this straggling village retains several older, Russian-style wooden cottages with a fair degree of charm. However, they're too few and far between to create a really memorable ensemble and every year new walls and swanky newer modern datchas further diminish the effect. Still, some of the pensioner inhabitants offer AZN10-15 **homestays** in traditional village houses. Utterly charming Rosa Samedova (☎ 44073, ☎ mob 050-478 7429) has one such, speaks Russian and will heat buckets of water for guests, at least when water is available. The toilet is at the end of the yard.

Most visitors, however, stay at the *Paradise Garden/Cennet Bağı* (☎ 44215, ☎ 012-454 0909, ⌨ www.cannatbagi.com, 40°51'13"N, 48°54'60"E), a popular getaway resort for Baku folk. The room quality is variable in both the hotel-style building and the surrounding bungalows set rather haphazardly across a large grassy area. Prices range from AZN60 to AZN240. The swimming pool is only filled in July and August and the fairly extensive zoo is likely to upset any animal lover. When there's sufficient snow, tobogganing is possible but the rather wobbly-

looking short-distance **cable car** doesn't inspire confidence.

The *BDU turbaza* is for university students but occasionally accepts tourists off-season.

ALTI AĞACH TO SHAMAKHA (map p195)

It was via Altı Ağach that the amputee Russian General 'Golden leg' Zubov clippety-clopped his regiment into Shamakha in 1795. He later fled along the same route when he got wind of the Persian army coming the other way.

Two hundred years before, the intrepid British wool traders Turnbull and Tolboys, had brought their wares this way, nearly getting themselves butchered as the 1579 Turkish take-over happened around them (see box, p40).

Today Baku–Xızı–Shamakha–Baku makes a challenging but satisfying daytrip but only if you have a very sturdy 4WD. In the wet the route would be miserably slippery.

GILÄZI TO QANDOV (see map opposite and p167)

Back on the coastal road, the landscape is punctuated by the abrupt rocky crag of Besh Barmaq (literally 'five fingers') on top of which weird animist rituals merit a detour. Into the hills west of Siyäzän is Chirax Qala, one of the most impressive castle ruins in Azerbaijan. At Qandov (aka Gandob) the road divides for Nabran (beaches) or Quba (orchards and mountains).

Besh Barmaq (Five-finger mountain)

Visible for miles, Besh Barmaq (Xizr Zindä Ziyaratgah) is a natural fortress. For centuries it guarded the narrowest strip of the coastal plain and a wall between the crag and the sea funnelled all commerce through a controllable gateway near which was a great caravanserai.

Its antiquity and cosmopolitan clientele are clear from 18th-century travellers' reports which noted that the caravanserai walls were covered in the graffiti of a dozen languages including French, Polish and Arabic. A painting in Baku's Historical

Museum shows it as being close to the water's edge but this is either artistic licence or represents the Caspian in an unusually high mood.

The caravanserai has now vanished entirely. In its place is a small roadside *Namazkah* (prayer room) and new mosque paid for by *nazir,* donations of passing motorists who almost unanimously stop to sip from the water source.

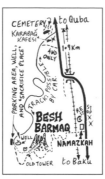

Climbing Besh Barmaq

The curious Azeri blend of Islam and Animism is nowhere more vividly portrayed than amid the dramatic rocky pinnacles on the abrupt summit of Mt Besh Barmaq. All prayers and genuflections, pilgrims struggle the mountain in their Sunday best. In places the rock has been kissed smooth by a procession of devout lips. And twigs are tied with very Tibetan-looking prayer knots. At the top, old women hold out knarled begging hands and several mendicant sages lead prayers on precarious ledges with spectacular views. Some of the faithful let forth a superhumanly rapid babble of prayers. Though supposedly Islamic and led by a Mollah, the ceremonies are to all intents and purposes ancient animist rites evoking the dark powers of the rock beneath. It's an odd and eerie atmosphere albeit often over-busy at weekends.

From the Namazkah stone mosque-shrine where Baku–Quba buses stop it's a steep, sweaty 1½-hour walk up to the base of Besh Barmaq's rocky knob. With a vehicle you can drive most of the way up in dry conditions even without a 4WD. The access track turns inland about 3km north of Namazkah, just beyond Qarabağ Kafesi. Beside the mountain-top parking area is a 'sacrifice' point where many a sheep baas its last. A well of holy water here is also in considerable demand. From here it's a 10-minute walk across a steep grassy bank to the base of the rock pinnacles. These are laced with metal stairways, steps and footholds which can seem daunting at times.

Nonetheless, even the most rotund pilgrims seem able to climb them... even in high heels.

Siyäzän

Originally Siyäzän was 80% ethnic Tat though why they chose the name meaning 'black women' (in Persian) is unclear. Today it's an oil-servicing town with a four-columned cultural centre behind which lie a collection of brightly white-washed war memorial sculptures.

A minibus leaves for Qala Altı at noon. If driving from Baku to Chirax Castle you can take a short-cut around Siyäzän by turning inland at 41°03'59"N, 49°07'17"E.

Chirax Castle and Qala Altı (☎ 0115)

The remnants of Chirax Castle sit very impressively at 1200m on a forested cliff top above the Qala Altı Sanatorium and associated Mäshrif village. It's one of the few fortress ruins in Azerbaijan to retain a real castle-shaped silhouette. You can loop past when driving between Baku and Quba but both approach roads (from Dävächi and Siyäzän) are desperately in need of resurfacing.

Part of a defensive chain for 1600 years, the name Chirax means 'lamp' for the beacon fires that were lit here to warn of approaching enemy armies. During the 18th century it was the southernmost outpost of Quba's Fatali Khan and was never stormed. It simply fell into disuse. Today a lofty knob of stone and brickwork teeters ever more perilously on a rock which is being eroded from beneath. Hidden in the forest beneath are many more wall sections.

The hike up to the castle is one of many healthy exercises prescribed by *Sanatorium Qala Altı* (☎ 32656) which specializes in 'Balneo mud treatments' using the local, sickeningly sulphurous mineral spring waters plus additives taken from the Kainarja mud field, 7km away. Both of the two main routes to the castle start from the gated sanatorium grounds. If you can persuade guards to open those

gates it's possible to drive up a rutted road to within 15 minutes' walk of the ruins (keep right at both road forks). Alternatively there's a steep footpath trail that heads up more directly in around ¾ hour from opposite the concrete shell of Hotel Qala Altı. That route is hidden within thick woodland but is fairly obvious until close to the top where a couple of slightly scary scrambles are necessary. With a 4WD there's a third alternative route from the Siyäzän road avoiding the Sanatorium altogether.

Accommodation Several restaurant-camps have bungalow accommodation along the sanatorium approach road. None is luxurious but better options are reputedly planned. The best option at the time of writing, if also the least conveniently situated, is *Göycha* (☎ mob 50-451 8841, AZN30-40) where two rows of fairly neat, relatively new cottages come with fold-out settee-bed, TV, towels, seatless toilet and tap-shower. *Zaur Huts* (☎ mob 50-719 7517, AZN 30), which should be finished, has rather hard new beds and partial views towards the coast. *Bal Bulaq* (☎ mob 50-356 8024) has very ropey container-box huts (AZN20) and newer roomlets with sickly wallpaper (AZN30). *Qala Altı Huts* (☎ mob 50-682 8801, Seymur) are mostly aged Soviet-era cabins in which two twin rooms (AZN15 per bed) share a sitting area with long-drop toilet away across the garden. One smaller, neater hut has a new private toilet along with squeaky bed and cacky vinyl floors.

At the *sanatorium* itself, two-week cure-stays cost from AZN375 and can be arranged through Baku tour agencies such as Shabran-D (☎ 012-496 9530, 🖳 www .shabrand.com). One-off overnight stays can sometimes be arranged informally and cheaply if you track down the doctor in charge. The facilities in the simple wooden cottages are basic with cold water and grubby toilet areas shared between pairs of rooms. The walls are thin and though most people go to bed early to prepare for a hard day's 'curing', some work off the strains of healthy living with noisy vodka binges. But the setting is pleasant amidst trees and gushing streams beneath the looming castle.

Much the cheapest option at just AZN5 per bed is *Hotel Qala Altı*. Once an exclusive apparatchik retreat, this sad concrete structure stands out all too obviously amid the otherwise thick forest cover in the shadow of the castle crag. A fine candidate for eventual renovation, for now the place looks derelict but four suites with lovely balcony views and just-functioning old bathrooms can still be rented informally by talking to the watchmen. It's a curiously eerie experience staying in the totally deserted building: the loose windows clatter all night in the eddying wind and you'll probably be locked in once the watchman goes to bed.

There are a few summer **teahouses** and shashlyk burners dotted about the area including a couple in seemingly quite uneconomic hidden spots along the pathways towards the castle.

Transport Taxis from Dävächi want at least AZN10, or AZN12 return. Clunky old minibuses trundle to Siyäzän (80q) at 06.45 and 17.00 starting from the sanatorium gates. Arrive a little early or talk to the driver (Oktay, ☎ mob 50-352 6997) the night before to be picked up outside your accommodation for the morning service which continues to Baku. En route it passes Gilazi around 08.30 giving you enough time to connect with the morning minibus to Xizi.

Dävächi (Dəvəçi, Devechi, Devichi)
Although only officially founded as a town in 1930, Dävächi's bus station occupies

THE NORTH

the site of a much-older, once-famous camel market (*deve* means camel). There are a few old wooden houses, a quirky crenellated '**chay castle**' (now closed) and a **historical museum** with interesting exhibits on historic Shabran. Discussions in parliament during 2009 suggested renaming Dävächi as Shabran which would cause confusion given that the real site of Shabran (see below) is 15km further north.

Hidden behind Ansanta kiosk-shop the town's *hotel* (AZN3 per person) has collapsing ceilings, beds held up on bricks and a nightmarish outside toilet.

QANDOV TO NABRAN
(see map opposite)
The road is quietly attractive with stands of mature woodland. Notice the occasional passing Zhiguli cars packed to the ceiling with fruit.

Shabran
The open-air excavations at Shabran (41°17'43"N, 48°52'53"E) are not visually exciting. The few half-collapsed domes and the subterranean remnants of a small 16th- to 17th-century castle give little impression of the town's great historical significance. Still, the site is easy to visit while 'driving by' and worth a two-minute detour if you're heading for Nabran or Quba. There's no entry fee.

History The ancient city of Shabran developed to exploit the then 'ideal climate' of the narrow, fertile Caspian shore plain. Officially founded during the reign of Sassanid Shah Khosrov Anushirvan (531–579) it rapidly became one of the five main towns of Caucasian Albania and an important Caspian spur to the great Silk Routes.

Excavations indicate that it had advanced sewerage systems in the 9th century and piped fresh water from springs some 14km away. It later developed its own silk industry and, from the 9th to 12th centuries, was famous for 'Amilin Shabran' glassware. It was here that the great 12th-century poet Xaqani was incarcerated and produced his famous 'prison poems', *Hebsiye*. Shabran was rebuilt after the Mongol destructions but when British wool merchants arrived in the 16th century they found its markets too small to bother with. Raids by Khazar/Ossete gangs, Dağestani Lezghians and even (according to one source) Crimean Tatars, continued to undermine the city's reputation and eventually it withered away to nothing.

Incredibly the site was forgotten altogether during the 18th century and was only rediscovered by archaeologists in 1980. Nobody has yet found the mythical *Mekhak* gold-divining stone.

Transport The site is in a field 300m off the main Baku–Nabran road, 4.4km from the Qandov junction. At the relevant point a small unmarked junction faces an information board and a brick-and-bottle freshwater spring.

The public transport to/from Nabran, Xudat and Xachmaz sometimes stops at the spring for a 5- to 10-minute bottle-filling break. That's just about long enough to run over and catch a glimpse of the excavations.

Xachmaz (☎ 0172, pop 66,000)
The north's biggest town, Xachmaz has a rather splendid Tağiyev-funded **railway station** (1898) and a couple of typical northern-style **mosques**. Through the **Qoşa Qapi** gateway, the **local studies museum** might not wow you with its displays of local tomato purée, but the super-keen

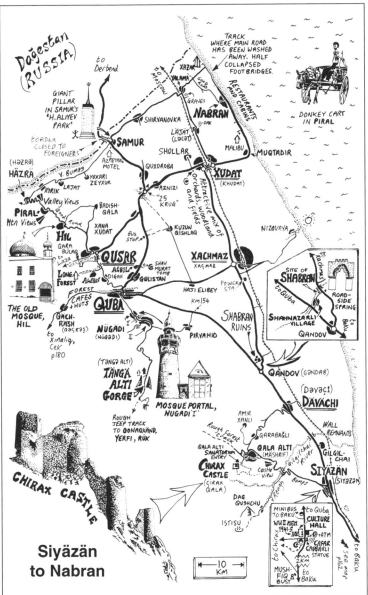

THE NORTH

Siyäzän to Nabran

THE NORTH

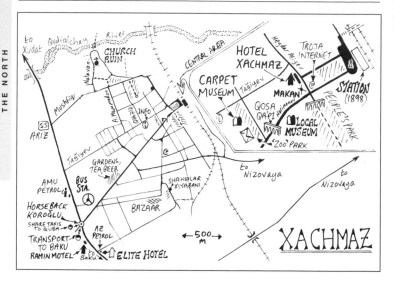

XACHMAZ

director could inspire you to seek out some of the region's practically invisible archaeological sites, gravestones at Gülalan (2km), *kurgan* burial mounds at Canaxır or the scant vestiges of a 3rd century AD city at Särkär-Täpe (12km). More accessible is an **'Albanian' church** ruin hidden away in the yard of #25 Natavan St.

At the free **Carpet Museum** you can admire a fine rug showing Heydar Aliyev in full Soviet military regalia. Nearby there's a helpful **tourist office** (Tağiyev St, ☎ 51651, 09.00-18.00 Mon-Fri, 09.00-14:00 Sat) and one of several internet clubs.

Providing much the best accommodation in town, *Elite Hotel* (☎ 50083) sits in a manicured garden 400m down the Baku highway from the big Koroğlu roundabout. Attractive Baku watercolours enliven the corridors. The air-con rooms (from AZN44) are new and pleasant enough with decent bathrooms (showers uncurtained). Bigger 'lux' rooms (AZN88) sleep four. Table tennis and a weights machine are available.

Also on the highway, *Ramin 'Motel'* (☎ 55149) opposite Xäzär Mebel has three basic if reasonably homely fan-cooled rooms (AZN12) sharing a bathroom, and two more with private shower (AZN20).

In the town centre, the Soviet-era *Hotel Xachmaz* (☎ 54040) charges just AZN3 per person. Its entrance has a certain (extremely) faded grandeur that gives way to predictably rough old rooms with cold tap.

Near the historical museum, *Makan* offers simple snacks in a décor incorporating dried fish, hazel fencing and a little 'stream'. Upstairs the pleasant beer terrace has views down Peoples' Park lined with busts of famous Azeris.

Share taxis to Baku depart regularly from the south side of the Koroğlu roundabout. Buses use a slightly hidden station directly north east. The very cheap *elektrichka* train departs at 05.43 and 17.38 for Baku's Keshla (not central) station.

Around Xachmaz There's a **beach** of sorts amid the rush-grasses 17km from Xachmaz (at least AZN10 by taxi plus waiting time). The last 2km beyond **Nizovaya** is a rough track alongside a gently picturesque creek dotted with naval-coloured fin-boats. This was supposedly the site of a port in the early middle ages but there's no visible remains nor any sign of archaeological workings.

THE NORTH

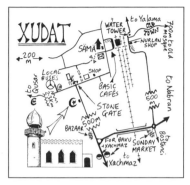

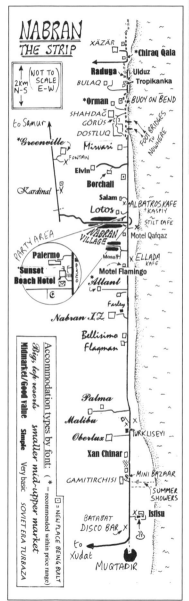

Xudat (☎ 0173)

Twenty-one kilometres north of the Xachmaz turning, Xudat was a royal town before the khanate moved its base to Quba. However, there's no apparent sign of any palace remnants and the older part of town, tucked away on the far side of the rail tracks, is frankly unexciting. The oldest (and visually least impressive) of Xudat's mosques is set on the edge of an ancient cemetery.

The ageing but friendly little *Hotel Säma* (☎ mob 55-686 9087, AZN5 per bed) has clean sheets but the taps don't work, doors don't lock and the dismal shared squat toilets are flushed by bucket with water from an outside well.

Transport to Baku and Xachmaz picks up from the southern edge of town. Buses to Qusar (08.30, 11.30 and 15.00) start from the small bus station. Taxis outside here or at the train station can whisk you off to Nabran for around AZN8. Alternatively Nabran through-buses (summer only) pick up near the big bridge across the railway.

NABRAN (☎ 0172)

Bakuvians sigh and look puppy-eyed at the mere mention of Nabran, a 30km strip of forest-backed beaches. Don't get overexcited. The beaches are unexotic, improving somewhat towards the south, but mostly with pebbles or dark-grey sand. For locals that's not so important as it's parties, romances and woodland picnics that are the main attraction.

THE NORTH

At the northern end of the 'strip', notice how the rising Caspian has washed away part of the road and left bizarre pedestrian 'bridges to nowhere'.

Nabran means 'fighting place' in Lezghi and tiny Nabran village in the middle of the strip was historically renowned for its fearsome mercenaries. These days the fight is over a hotel room in mid summer. There's a vast choice of accommodation but the resorts are very widely spread making it rather awkward to shop around if you don't have a vehicle.

Accommodation (see map p169)

With half of Baku holidaying here a **reservation** will be virtually essential in July and August. In spring or late September, however, there are often bargains to be had and you'll have the whole beach to yourself. Well, yourself, a few cows and the odd dead seal that is. Naturally **prices** fluctuate wildly according to season, demand and your bargaining ability. I've quoted June rates. In winter prices can drop to half but most cheaper places close (or are unheated). In summer prices rise and you can assume that there'll be a noisy disco either in situ or close by. People don't generally come here for peace and quiet.

In each category below hotels are described in the order they appear on the map (south to north).

Major resorts The swankier resorts with hot showers, A/C, satellite TV, swimming pool and winter heating are often guarded by forbiddingly grand gateways. Several have tried to recreate an Edward Scissorhands image of American suburbia with transplanted rose bushes lining little lanes of Lego-like apartment-houses. Some are over a kilometre from the beach.

Oberlux (☎ 012-418 3665, 💻 www .oberlux.az) hides behind a daunting granite-faced entrance that contains a four-lane **bowling alley**. Its houselets recreate an upmarket suburbanism around an impressive swimming pool. Prices from AZN60 per person including meals.

In a garden setting, *Malibu* (☎ 012-598 1816, 💻 www.malibu.in-baku.com)

has densely packed huts and a holiday-camp busy-feel, but its standard bungalows (AZN100-150) sleep four (double + twin) and there are a few AZN40 fan-cooled twins sharing good hot showers between pairs of rooms.

Nearby *Palma* (☎ 012-404 4434) is less homely and the central disco can be noisy. The two-storey cottages (AZN50++) are reasonably sized with somewhat saggy beds and worn carpets. The balconies have broken plastic furniture and varnish peeling off the balustrades. Willows attractively surround the rectangular pool overlooked by a sturdy open-sided restaurant building but contrary to the shamelessly fictitious brochures there are neither palm trees nor sea views!

Nabran I.Z. (aka Aquapark; ☎ mob 50 372 4372, AZN50-80) seems a little disorganized. Between willows and roses, their cottages form rigidly straight lines and have crumpled carpets and small bathrooms. The tennis court is falling apart but the swimming pool seemed clean and it has a waterslide.

The classic Nabran brochure image shows a fanciful pirate boat sailing across a bright turquoise swimming pool. That's *Atlant* (☎ 012-418 6647, 💻 www.atlant-az.net) and its big pool complex really does seem cleaner and more child-friendly than most. The biggest resort on the strip, Atlant heaves with up to 740 people at a time and non residents can pay AZN6 to use the facilities. The acceptable if heavily used rooms start at a fair AZN45 (AZN55 in summer).

Greenville (☎ 012-493 8950) is a big complex off a quiet back lane where the pleasant rooms (AZN50) have real art, good showers and wooden floors. There's tennis, volleyball and a forest restaurant as well as the good-sized pool. Good value.

Smaller mid-market choices Several smaller places now have full facility cottages and may be somewhat less impersonal but without bargaining prices can be unrealistically high.

Istisu (☎ mob 50-351 2853 Abbas) is the only place in Nabran that sits right on the beach. Typical rooms use naturally heated (if pretty grey and gritty) water in the en suite showers. The good-value café-restaurant serves 80q NZS beers but is at the road-side end. Small air-con rooms cost AZN30-50. Non residents can use the bathhouse showers for AZ1.

Open year-round, **Sunset Beach Hotel** (☎ 25375, dbl AZN50, AZN30 off-season) is a well-pitched real hotel, rather than a resort, with decent colour-tiled bathrooms. Seaview rooms cost double and the small L-shaped pool suffers inevitable music-overload in summer.

Lotos (☎ 25252, dbl/quad AZN50/80) has tight-packed if relatively comfy, fresh-smelling units but the cisterns run constantly and there's no toilet paper. Summer disco.

Borchali (☎ mob 50-660 9440) feels a little sad and its views are now obscured by new buildings. The unique centrepiece restaurant at **Kardinal** is a very eccentric if somewhat jerry-built 'castle'. It's in an isolated field 1.3km south of Greenville making for a calmer stay than the strip resorts. The rooms (from AZN60) aren't as crazy inside. Breakfast is included.

Sea-facing **Mirvari** (☎ mob 50-380 7651) is well positioned on a slightly elevated ridge from which its tea tables have good sea views. The bungalows have AC, OK bathrooms and a terrace with flowers though the carpets show wear. Rates for a double are AZN20-60.

Orman (☎ 25350, ☎ mob 50-627 3672) remains a well-ordered, simple but good-value place and they're planning additional rooms closer to the beach. The rooms are AZN20/30 sgl/dbl, add AZN20 per person for full board.

Raduga (☎ mob 50-455 9428, Tofiq) has a new, fairly attractive arc of upper floor rooms with sea views (AZN40) where pairs of twin rooms share a decent bathroom and balcony. The downstairs rooms are slightly cheaper but lack the views and hence the attraction.

With hot showers and a WC shared between pairs of rooms **Chiraq Qala** (☎ mob 50-382 4666, twin AZN20) is great value given its sea views.

Cheaper options *Motel Flamingo* (☎ mob 50-586 5330) AZN20 has a simple arched stone terrace, torn flooring and musty toilets but it's not too bad for the price and there are glimpses of sea through the willow trees.

Above Nabran's supermarket, **Motel Qafqaz** (☎ mob 50-311 0352, Lala) has a surprisingly pleasant garden and seven rooms (AZN30) have balconies. The showers are a little rusty, there's no AC and it can get noisy in the disco season.

Elvin (☎ mob 55-297 2520, AZN20-40) is pretty basic but set in an attractive woodland-clearing behind an arc of canal with sweet little mini-bridges.

Bulaq (☎ mob 50-760 1301, Eldar) is a budget possibility for individual travellers as they charge per bed (AZN14) in units set back in the woods with three rooms per tiled, shared bathroom.

Tropikanka (☎ mob 50-334 6696) feels tired and squashed but the sound of waves is pleasant off season. **Ulduz** (☎ mob 50-376 4545) sleeps up to three in two-storey units that are plain and slightly musty (AZN30-40) but its nice little restaurant terrace overlooks the sea.

Soviet-era resorts The big old Soviet-era holiday complexes such as **Gamitirchisi**, **Görüs**, **Shahdağ**, **Xäzär** and the massive **Dostluq** rarely take drop-in tourists. Most sell all-in two-week packages and are noisy with families. However, in late September you might get a basic cheap bed if they're empty. Dostluq has several *cafés* and a popular woodland *disco*.

Food
Most places will provide full board for between AZN10 and AZN25 extra. There's a growing sprinkling of summer restaurants, **grocery shops** (opposite Istisu and at Motel Qafqaz) plus a small **bazaar** near Gamitirchisi.

Transport
In mid summer, buses and minibuses operate fairly frequently from Baku and they'll generally drop off at any cabin site along the strip. Out of season you may need to go first to Xudat or Samur then take a taxi.

THE NORTH

QANDOV TO QUBA (see map p167)

Shabran (p166) is an easy, detour through Shahnazarli. Otherwise the road is fast all the way to Quba through flat, progressively greening landscapes. Children flag down motorists to sell little buckets of walnuts, apples or pears depending on the season.

QUBA (KUBA) (☎ 0169, pop 55,000)

Originally built around the ancient village of Kudial, Quba really only came of age when the regional khan moved his entourage here from Xudat in the early 18th century. The town rose rapidly to prominence under Fatali Khan who used a combination of diplomacy and coercion to form a temporary alliance between the usually squabbling local lords and khans. Once the Russians had muscled in and abolished the khanate they needed to keep a close eye on the area so Quba was developed as an imperial administrative centre. Numerous quaint 19th-century town-houses survive from that time along with a curious selection of brick mosques that give the town's central grid a certain low-rise charm.

The central *Meydan* is a grassy square around which lie a few archetypal old houses though to the south the effect is diminished by the dumpy concrete ordinariness of the **House of Culture**. Hidden within that lies the **tourist information office** (☎ 53618, 🖳 http://guba.azeriblog.com, 🖳 tic _guba@box.az, 10.00-18.00 Mon-Fri). Facing to the north is Quba's very distinctive 19th-century **Juma Mosque**, an octagonal brick structure with an over-sized lemon-squeezer dome that creates an impressive interior space whose floors are colourfully carpeted. Its latterday minaret is visible from afar.

Other passingly curious structures include a bizarre old **beehive hamam**, the **Saxina Xanum Mosque** (built for Fatali Khan's wife) and two colourfully painted square-form mosques, **Ardebil** and **Haci Cafar**. Both were originally churches and the latter has a vine-draped sitting area and heavily colourful inner doors.

The huge main **cemetery** is worth exploring with some interesting royal brick tombs as well as newer, kitschier memorials.

The **Historical Museum** (AZN1) is housed in the home of famous 19th-century historian Bakikhanov (1794-1847). **Qadim Quba Carpet Workshop** (132 Heydar Aliyev pr, ☎ 53270) is unusually welcoming with an appealing carpet and souvenir shop where you can request to be shown around the working looms directly behind.

Food

Quba is known for its nuts and fruit, especially apples, which are sold cheaply on the town's main approach roads in season – bring a bag!

Most visitors head towards Qächräsh to dine in the attractive woodland or streamside shashlyk places. In Quba itself **Kafe Sərin** makes great use of a bird-serenaded lawn/field summer terrace while unusual heavy stone effects add some life to the interior. They can whip up a wide range of reasonably priced dishes from düshbärä to chicken'n'chips. Unlovely but more central **Chinar Café** serves simple AZN2 qrechki (qreçka) meals and has a piano. Ask at the very basic **Mahir Kafé** for a 'Sachin Special', a truly delicious AZN1.20 lavash döner sentimentally named after the Peace Corps volunteer who told the world about them. Tea costs just 10q a cup, pirozhkis are 10q too but only two of the tables have seats.

The Meydan becomes one big çayxana in summer and there's cheap draft beer from beer-&-tea places around Nizami Park where triumphant Soviet-era sportsman statues line the stairway to the Krasnaya Sloboda bridge.

Accommodation

There's a wide range in the surrounding area (within 10km) but the only central options are modest. The best of these, near the bus station, is friendly **Oscar Hotel** (☎ 51516, ☎ mob 50-489-4715, Imran) with simple but cosy en suite rooms from AZN20 above a little courtyard eatery. You even get soap and towels.

Tucked away in the bazaar the **Xınalıq Hotel** (☎ 54445, AZN7-10) is a crash pad aimed at market traders. While not horrendous, the shared squat loos downstairs are not appealing and it's not really a place for

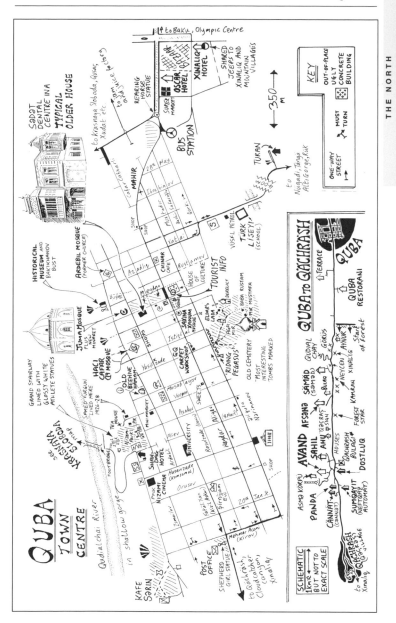

single women. Two AZN10 singles have private bathrooms.

Helpfully central, **Shahdağ Hotel** (☎ 52927, beds AZN3-5) is a modest Soviet-era pad which could look rather fine once it gets renovated. For now, though, it has no showers and only shared WCs that have a very unsavoury smell.

Overlooking a pear orchard at Quba's southernmost edge, **Turan** (☎ 52066, ☎ mob 50-612 8669) is rough and ready with a cracked toilet, very narrow 'double' beds and clunky metallic doors but you do get soap, towels, a top-sheet and hot water – not bad for AZN15.

Accommodation east of town Hotel-style accommodation at the **Olympic Complex** (☎ 51517, 🖳 www.gubaolympic .az) is spacious and neatly appointed; the bathrooms come with toilet paper and curtained showers. A job-lot of art prints and Greek Tourist-Office posters add colour to the walls. All for only AZN60 (suite AZN90) including use of the complex's full-sized indoor swimming pool. Xach-maz-bound minibuses from the bus station will get you within 1km for 60q.

Set in fields behind the complex, **Bärpa Spa Märkäzi** (🖳 http://ucs.az/ru/ clients/berpa/, ☎ Baku 418 8835, ☎ mob 50-313 4530) is a 21st-century upmarket sanatorium-resort complex where the AZN150 rate includes full board.

Accommodation beyond Asmar In a clearing 2km behind Asmar village, **Cännät Bağı Hotel** (☎ 51415, ☎ mob 50-200 1986, 🖳 www.cannatbagi.com, 41°18'32"N, 48°32'22"E) is a real hotel with a real reception featuring giant copies of historic Azeri coins. Some staff even speak English!! The lobby is hidden in the three-storey 'new' block where the odd-numbered rooms overlook streamside tables below. The pleasant AZN70 doubles have monogrammed towels, marble sinks, curtained towels and toilet paper. AZN160 luxe rooms sleep up to four and have patterened parquet floors. The older block has rooms facing the swimming pool across partly tended lawns. They have larger bath-

rooms and are slightly cheaper but might be mothballed out of peak season.

Bal Bulaq, around 2km further on, is extremely basic and aimed at school groups who will put up with the musty container-box rooms. Another 500m further on **Qırmızı Qäränfil** (☎ mob 50-403 2180) seemed more suspicious than helpful when I asked about their rooms.

Quba to Qächräsh

The road between Quba and Qächräsh is famed for the forests that are so thick they blot out the sun. Very popular with Baku weekenders the woodlands are full of hut-camps and shashlyk restaurants.

Accommodation and food In Quba's western outskirts, well before the forest area starts, is outwardly upmarket, **Terrace** (☎ 53015, ☎ mob 50-490 3015). It has been nicely designed, like a Mediterranean villa-hotel with vines, flowers and a central swimming pool. The pleasant AZN75 rooms come with satellite TV and curtained showers but the ornaments are tacky and the cleaning standards need attention.

Reliable if somewhat pricey food makes **Quba Restorani** a popular lunch spot but its proximity to Quba means that the surroundings are starting to feel semi-urban despite the trees that back the site. The rooms are unspectacular though the cheapest ones (AZN30) are only slightly musty and come with bathroom and towels.

One of the better woodland options so far, **Afsänä** (☎ mob 50-517 1274) has pleasant timber bungalows and dining booths amid mossy beech trees, some over-looking the river. The wrought-iron balcony tables are almost stylish if already starting to age. Towels are provided though the showers feed off the flimsy sink taps. Rom speaks some English. With slightly less style, **Sämäd** (☎ mob 50-310 5523, AZN50-100) has a similarly appealing location stretching into a local orchard. The tiled bathrooms are a decent size and have hot water; several huts have terraces.

Aynur (☎ mob 50-310 7973) offers well-built pine huts fairly deeply set back into the woodland from their discordantly big yellow banquet-hall. The staff are obliging, food good value and beers are cheap. However, despite the decent bathrooms the timber-walled rooms (AZN60-70) have little charm and are decked with some abysmal 'art'.

Avand (mob ☎ 50-335 6091) is a simple little 'hotel' with a garden, bar, restaurant, and billiard room. There's a stark lack of atmosphere and the small twins (AZN50) come with a fairly basic tap-shower. For AZN80 you'll get a second double bedroom and a dining room.

The dimly lit AZN50 'luxe' huts at *Äsmä Korpu* (☎ mob 50-562 8989) don't seem built to last but they do have bathrooms, seatless loos, and are soothed by river sounds. The cheaper AZN20 box-huts share WCs and have little concrete terraces. The simple teahouse serves cheap beers and big juicy kebabs (AZN3).

AHU Club (☎ mob 50-585 5151) has newly built sturdy bungalows (AZN80-120) but the wooden floors offer splinter dangers and as ever there's been little attempt at creating any atmosphere inside. There's a somewhat silly artificial 'waterfall' and the hay-field location is slightly spoilt by the surrounding area of new houses.

The pleasantly sited *Sahil* (☎ mob 50 674 4264) has a drinking-water spring and a grassy central area but most of the variable-quality rooms have concrete floors, camp beds and squat toilets. Effectively sharing the same site, *Soyuq Bulaq* (☎ mob 50-640 2851) has better if still overpriced pine-floored bungalows with hot water but no attempt at décor. *Görus* (huts AZN50), right at the roadside, serves 60q NZS beers.

Overpriced *Panda* (☎ mob 50-515 5100) is friendly but has aged, very basic cabins (AZN30), each with four camp beds, sharing two whiffy toilets. In a pleasant orchard setting, *Cännät* is also rather rundown while the very basic *Dostluq* is almost exclusively for children's groups: both are due to be redeveloped.

All the places above offer food but a good non-resort choice for outdoor dining remains *Qächräsh Bulaği*. Don't be put off by the unappealing roadside building you'll see first. Set back, tables are arranged around a charming amphitheatre in the beech forest, the staff are obliging, prices fair and flagons of free spring water are available.

EXCURSIONS FROM QUBA

It's a short stroll across the bridge to the unique Jewish village of Krasnaya Sloboda (see below), an easy drive to the Afurca waterfall via Tängä Altı Canyon (p177) or to the lovely forests and riverside restaurants of Qächräsh (opposite). But the most popular excursion takes you through fabulous mountain and canyonland scenery towards the fabled village of Xınalıq (p181), starting point for some of Azerbaijan's best mountain hikes and climbs. Since 2006 an asphalt road has made access comparatively easy but sections already show signs of falling apart.

A 4WD is needed to reach Söhub, Buduq or most places beyond Tängä Altı. A reliable driver with an indestructible UAZ-jeep is irrepressibly humorous Heybat Yagubov (☎ mob 50-391 4480). A former circus tight-rope walker, he speaks no English but fills his Azeri and Russian with endless diminutives and joke-ikos. He charges very fair rates for mountain explorations. Readers have also recommended Intigam Sultanov at Quba bus station whose ex-army 4WD minibus can carry up to ten people.

Krasnaya Sloboda (see map p176) (Qırmızı Qəsəbə, Gyrmyzy Gasaba)

The village's name 'big red village' sounds distinctly Soviet. But in fact Quba's twin-across-the river is the prosperous capital of Azerbaijan's 'mountain Jews'. Perhaps the only all-Jewish town outside Israel, the 3600 inhabitants are considered by some to be direct descendants of one of the 'lost tribes' scattered after the destruction of the Jerusalem temple in 722BC. Other theories suggest that they're descended from Jews fleeing Iran in the 17th century or that they were simply Khazars who converted as a way to stay neutral in feuds between Christian and Muslim communities. Krasnaya Sloboda itself was founded in 1735 with permission supposedly granted after a Jewish doctor had saved the life of

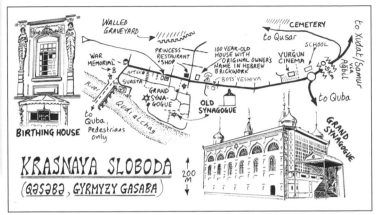

the khan of Quba. Jews from various mountain villages thereafter congregated here to be near the khan's court. According to one of his living relatives, the great Fatali Khan of Quba had apparently advised his citizens: 'Protect these people, and later you'll reap the fruit'. In the long term this paid off. The historical lack of discrimination against Jews is held to be one of the reasons why Israel and the US Jewish lobby were relatively supportive of Azerbaijan during the 1990s' crisis years. However, the intervening communist era had been predictably unkind to Krasnaya Sloboda. Stalin banned the use of Hebrew, forced the farming population to rear pigs and destroyed all but one of the 11 synagogues. Emigration to Israel halved Azerbaijan's Jewish population between 1979 and 1993.

Today, however, funds sent from these emigrants have made Krasnaya Sloboda look noticeably wealthier than Quba. Today there are two active synagogues. The newer **Grand Synagogue** is more architecturally eyecatching. However, the **Old Synagogue** is more regularly used (notably Mon & Thur mornings and Saturdays) and retains a collection of scrolls including a 200-year-old torah encased in silver. Phone ☎ 54519 or ☎ 050 321 8139 to organize a visit.

The town's school is named after Isaak Xanukov who compiled Tat language scripts as well as writing many an opus about Soviet Kolkhozes. The boys' **yeshiva** (religious top-up school) is well stocked with computers, carpets and chandeliers.

Nügädi (see map p167 and p180)

The prosperous agricultural town of Nügädi is divided by the Qarachay river. Nügädi I (Nügädi Birinci), nearer to Quba, has a curious lemon-squeezer **mosque** and a distinctive 'pepperpot portal' **gateway**. In Nügädi II, 1 May St is a rough side lane leading past a pond and the rather ragged Chanlibel Café after 1.5km (not 500m as the sign claims). Beyond is the decrepit Geofizik Turbaza whose lovely meadow setting offers considerable redevelopment possibilities. Further still the lonely little *Ceyran Bulaq* (☎ mob 050 330 2210) sits in rolling fields that are unexceptionally pleasant offering three AZN50 huts with toilet and hot water and sorry old blankets.

Rustov (see map p180)

After Nügädi the road rises through walnut orchards for some 6km before a panoramic pass with fine views across the rolling green landscape. The road descends to the valley bottom at Rustov before winding up across a second pass with great views if you look back. Rustov has an unusually complete old-village core 1.3km off the Tängä Alti road. It's centred on a sizeable brick **mosque** that locals date to 1899, though an

Arabic inscription says 1321 (ie 1903) beneath the unusual pentagonal upper window. Major ongoing restoration work plans to leave intact the mosque's nine original internal post-columns.

Qızılaçaç IZ (☎ 050 669 2722) is a widely advertised restaurant-resort 2km from Rustov. It's ludicrously awkward to reach. This adds to the comical anticlimax of finding that there's only one (dreadful) AZN10 single-bed 'guest' room. And that ordering the AZN2 kebabs requires an indefinite wait while the caretaker goes off in search of a dead sheep.

Tängä Altı gorge and Äfurca (☎ 0169, see map below, p167 & p180)

Straggling **Tängä Altı village** ends in a short rocky **canyon** that would be very photogenic but for the electricity wires dangling overhead. A 3.5km detour off the main road leads up through **Äfurca** village on a very rough, steep lane to one of Azerbaijan's most impressive **waterfalls**. The waters tumble from a slightly concave arc of cliff that various sources claim to be 60 or 75m high (I'd estimate that 40m was more accurate). To find the falls fork left after 2km, pass the Qizil Qaya tea house then descend to the parking area (AZN1 per car) from which it's five minutes' walk to the main falls viewpoint. You can continue walking on a narrow ledge-path beneath the falls' main cascade. A taxi from Quba to Äfurca charged me AZN12 return plus AZN4 per hour's journey time.

Accommodation

At the northern end of the gorge *Buz Bulaq* and a *castle-style hotel* both nearing completion look as though they'll be the area's most comfortable accommodation options.

Above a nearby shop, *Tängä Motel* (☎ 43649) has basic AZN20 beds sharing outside loo or

AZN50 rooms with bathroom. Willows block potential balcony views.

Marxal (☎ mob 55-333 6244) has a great gorge-end location beside the river accessed by a footbridge but three of its four huts (AZN30) are poorly maintained and don't have bathrooms. The restaurant (kebabs AZN3) is good for tea but serves no alcohol. Across the river *Koroğlu* has AZN20 bare-box rooms with unshaded light-bulb-lamps and ceaseless pounding music.

Between Tängi Altı and Äfurca, *Baki IZ* (☎ 43606) has a pleasant river-serenaded dining terrace (but check the prices carefully). The rooms have neat carpets and en suite shower, but the water's not always warm, the toilets are seatless and the curtains rather sad.

Higher up the slope beside an unkempt spring, *MMM* (☎ 43623) has very attractive views from the balcony of its one thick-walled bungalow where the AZN30 twins have very rough floors. It's a long walk to the outside WC.

Near the Äfurca turn-off there are several hut-camps. None is specially impressive though several newer 'rest zones' are under construction. With city folks prepared to invest US$500,000 for one of the smaller land plots here one can anticipate rapidly rising prices in all ranges.

Äfurca IZ (☎ 43593) looks slightly more upmarket than the competition but the riverside location isn't especially picturesque, the windows and fittings are poorly crafted and most of the AZN40-60 terraced bungalow rooms share bathrooms.

Guneşli (☎ 43482), the biggest complex to date, surveys a sweep of attractively varied landscapes but has rather the feel of a Soviet-era turbaza. The rooms, most with shared bathrooms, cost AZN30-60 and the atmosphere can feel a little over busy.

Map: Tangi Alti & Afurca — to Quba, BUZ BULAQ, TƏNGƏ MOTEL, CASTLE-STYLE HOTEL, TANGI BULAQ, KOROĞLU, MMM, MARXAL, GÖZEL MAKAN, BAKI I.Z., to Qonaqänd / Sohub, GÜNEŞLI, ƏFURCA, 3.5km to Waterfall

THE NORTH

□ **Side roads (see map p180)**
A bumpy road linking Nügädi II and the main Quba–Baku route passes through **Pirvahid**, a village that looks great in late spring as it's filled with blooming roses and blossoming cherry trees. Nearby the locally renowned holy place, **Jikhilan Baba Pir**, is merely a small glade of sacred trees in a cornfield.

Some maps show a road branching off at Rustov to **Zukhur** village. In fact, that track is in appalling condition after Xanagar. Locals loop round via Tängä Altı and Söhüb.

Around a kilometre north of Tängä Altı you can cut east to **Chichi** village (map p70), historically famous for its *akgul* (white flower) carpets.

Beyond Äfurca (map p180)

In perfect conditions experienced 4WD drivers may be able to link up with the main Xınalıq–Qächräsh–Quba track near Alik or to continue south towards Shamakha. Picturesque villages lie en route but the tracks are very rough even for the strongest off-road vehicles: you'll need winches and a sense of adventure.

There's a dramatic 270° view of grassy mountains above the bifurcation of the wide flood plain. The road then descends to this river junction. Fork right for Söhüb (see opposite). For Qonaqkänd fork left on the smaller track across multiple fords and continue 4km past a curious monument of stone balls.

Qonaqkänd, the unlikely provincial capital, is supposedly linked to Quba by a very bumpy daily bus. From Qonaqkänd it is possible to trek across to the Pirguli–Shamakha road, via Qaravatüstü, Nutah, Xaltan (hot springs in the forest), Pirbayili, Astrakhanka and Chukhuryurd. Though really a footpath, this has been achieved by at least one intrepid team of off-roaders in 4WDs. There is a passable area for camping, with a freshwater spring near a small graveyard where two rivers meet northwest of Nutah.

Söhüb and Rük Had you forked right before the Qonaqkänd ford you would have found yourself gently rising for 5km while following the river westward and passing through a tiny half-derelict stone hamlet. Above this point is a widening swathe of grassy downland. With no constraints, the track diverges at several points. The first divergence reconverges. However, 2.8km later at 41°05'37"N, 48°29'56"E avoid the left-hand branch that descends 1.5km to **Yerfi** (don't believe the maps that suggest there is a track between Yerfi and Qarxun near Rük). Instead climb to the right passing close to a perfect **picnic site** (41°06'00"N, 48°29'40"E) with superb views of little Yerfi, a dramatic ridge of knife-edge strata, and, on a clear day, snow-capped Shahdağ looming on the far horizon.

After the vaguely photogenic hamlet of **Qayadli** (41°07'25"N, 48°27'15"E) the track tumbles over an 1800m pass with trees on the upper north-facing slopes but rather barren grassy slopes facing south. Very unpleasant muddy ruts here can prevent further progress when the ground is damp.

Sturdy stone-walled homes give **Söhüb** (41°09'02"N, 48°23'44"E) a sense of basic rural prosperity. Dried disks of cow-pats (for fuel) are stacked on roofs, adding to the timeless, picturesque image. The rocky crag above the village, now crowned by a communications mast, was once a *dakhma*, a Zoroastrian 'tower of silence': where corpses were given a 'sky-burial'. There are fords before, in and after the village but within a kilometre of leaving Söhüb you should be descending on the southern bank of the main stream. A sudden turn provides great views across the valley to Zäyid and Buduq. Both villages are perched on their respective mountains, separated by deep canyons.

At times the ledge along which the descending road approaches Rük becomes a nightmarish sea of mud, impassably dangerous for

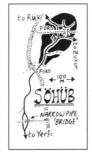

THE NORTH

all but the most foolhardy 4WD vehicles, though still possible for the 6x6 Ural truck-bus that does the Quba–Söhüb–Rük run. There is no alternative route so be prepared for possible disappointment here! When the descent is dry enough you'll need to ford the river to Rük as the flimsy bridge isn't really strong enough for vehicles. **Rük** has a small shop and an old cemetery. It's somewhat less attractive than Söhüb or Qayadli, but a kilometre above the village on a steep rocky track is a brilliant viewpoint which more than compensates.

Zäyid and on to Alik The track beyond the Rük viewpoint once led to Zäyid but mud slides have rendered it impassable to vehicles. So, near the landslide, descend the perilously steep grassy hillside to a tough, rocky track that follows a rough gully back up to Zäyid (some interesting views to the left across grassy hills towards diamond-faceted, stratified white canyon cliffs). This gully can also be reached from a track leading north across the river near Anvil Rock in Rük. However, the ledge to reach it from Rük is too narrow for vehicles and the ford from the Söhüb road is now virtually impossible. Continuing west from Zäyid an initially rocky track crosses a pass into a high, flower-filled plateau, then descends through a deep, muddy ford before slithering past a lonely farmstead down to meet the Quba–Xınalıq road.

Buduq
Rarely visited Buduq is 'another Xınalıq' with flat-roofed homes (here oddly whitewashed) on a mountaintop perch and a language all of its own (Budad Mitz). The river valley to the east of Buduq has impressive, hard-to-reach canyons. Getting to Buduq from Zäyid (6km) is extremely tough even with a 4WD. There's also reputedly a hiking route from Qriz Dahma though crossing

the river is a challenge. Boji Cabbarova and Shohba Azizova reportedly accept **homestay** guests (AZN10) in the unlikely event that anyone makes it this far.

QÄCHRÄSH TO XINALIQ
(see map p180)
After the picnic woods (p174), gently attractive little **Qächräsh village** has an old cubic mosque with a wooden terrace and a new, corrugated iron roof/tower. Beyond, the route to Cek and Xınalıq is one of the most beautiful rides in Azerbaijan. A major rebuild in 2006 surfaced the whole route and bridged the notoriously difficult fords. However, landslides and heavy snows can still block the road so check conditions before you go.

The most atmospheric and attractively sited accommodation en route, *Minarä* (☎ Quba 53015), was closed on my last visit. Hopefully it will reopen. Meanwhile, it's worth a brief stop to admire the chasm it surveys. In season itinerant tea makers fire up a samovar here. Complete with artificial waterfall, 48-room *Nazli Bulaq* (☎ mob 50-203 8321, dbl AZN50-80) is a jarringly insensitive pink eyesore either side of the road towards Qriz Dahma. The rooms seem well built if lacking style and with scrappy carpets.

After Qriz Dahma one of Azerbaijan's scenic highlights is '**Cloudcatcher' Canyon**, my name for an impressive gash through craggy grey rocks and thick forest

---

❑ **Cold alert**
Remember to bring warm clothes if sleeping in the higher mountain villages. On a sweaty Baku summer day it's all too easy to forget that in Xınalıq night-time temperatures can still be seriously frosty even in August. In winter, brass monkeys panic with -25° not uncommon.

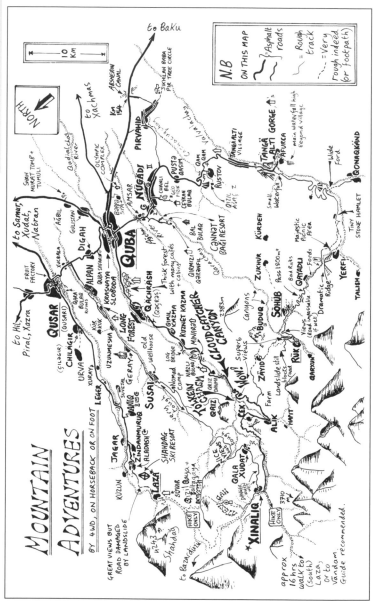

above which a dense mist floats mysteriously on many an otherwise sunny day. After two tight hairpins you emerge at **Chaigoshan**, the meeting of the Alik and Xınalıq rivers. It's a delightful viewpoint (marked 'Wow' on map opposite) where you can simultaneously glimpse the narrow yet unfathomably deep **Tolkein chasm**, imagine Angkoresque eroded faces in a Grand Canyon-style cliff wall, and watch the low sun burnish the voluptuously grassy mountains behind. Sadly careless jeep-driving visitors and army trucks have ripped up much of the once pretty grass here but it's still possible to camp. A nice, reader-recommended, alternative spot is 40°09'26.3"N, 48°21'43.2"E.

Cek (Jek) is a picturesque hamlet perched on a rocky knoll halfway up a steep grassy hillside. It's possible to offroad up the grass to a radio mast on the top of that hill for brilliant 360° views. Some Cek villagers speak a variant of the strange Qriz dialect.

XINALIQ (KHINALIK, GINALIG)
(☎ 0169, pop 800-1700, seasonal)

On a typical overcast day, viewed from the Qala Xudat trail, Xınalıq rises like a prehistoric stone boat floating on a heavy sea of clouds. When the clouds clear the vista of surrounding peaks is truly breathtaking. The village itself is a steeply stacked pile of 300 higgledy piggledy, rocky-grey homes. The flat roof of one house often forms the front yard of another on which men stand for hours staring, apparently transfixed by the dancing skyscapes. Colourfully dressed women collect water and beat clean fresh raw wool at communal water sources. Local girls weave beautiful carpets which adorn the massively thick walls of the houses.

There's no specific 'sight' though a new **museum** (50q) in a curious castle-shaped building displays some old stones and a collection of traditional copperwork. Craggy-faced old gentlemen wearing giant papax hats sit for hours outside the **Mädäniyyät Evi**. While strolling through the alleyways you can amuse your hosts by trying to spot the difference between Xınalıq's three variants on the formula dung+straw=winter fuel. If you don't want

the answer look away now! Brick-shaped *kukwa* and round wall-pressed *!kd* both use cow poo, while *gomra* is from sheep and is reckoned to burn best.

Sheep, the village's raison d'être, appear to know their way as they trot home at dusk to their respective pens. The grassy terraces on steep slopes across the river were cultivated up until the 1970s but these days even the hardy locals realize it's not worth the bother.

The new road has been a boon for locals offering vastly improved access to hospitals and facilities. With building materials suddenly much easier to ship in, many locals have been taking the opportunity to improve their homes. While one can hardly begrudge them added comfort, the downside for tourism is that several of Xınalıq's once picture-perfect older homes are sprouting discordant corrugated metal roofs while others have been abandoned altogether as people move to lower ground and build afresh. Still, the overall effect remains upliftingly beautiful as you'll see on 🖳 http ://christopherjanderson.googlepages.com/ xinaliqphoto.

Xınalıq

An unusual attraction is **Ateshgah** (see map p184), a three- to four-hour return hike from Xınalıq. Contrary to the very misleading claims of certain tour agencies this is NOT a temple but a mystical eternal flame burning naturally in the middle of the mountains, heating shepherds' tea pots and confounding vulcanologists. Though very small it offers a great excuse to walk into the fabulous mountain scenery and its setting is superb. Essentially you simply stride up the valley towards Shahdağ, criss-crossing the shallow river several times at first and continue as far as the third side valley on the right. (This far is possible if very uncomfortable by 4WD). Climb towards a rock that, from a distance, looks a little like a small hut. Continue up the steep grassy slope then skirt back to the right towards the stream within the side valley – the exact location is pretty hard to find without a local guide as it's hidden in an unassuming natural amphitheatre, but shepherds should be able to help.

Accommodation and food

Several homes offer bed and board for AZN15-20 and staying in one of these almost medieval homesteads is a great part of Xınalıq's attraction. I've previously stayed with **Badal Lalayev** (☎ 49076) who has an archetypal old town house and two horses that you can possibly hire. Other travellers have recommended **Zaur** (☎ 49003) whose family cooks great qutabs. The delightful Quba-based Xınalıqi **Xeyraddin Jabbarov** (🖳 www.xinaliq.com) rents rooms semi-formally in his family's home (AZN20 per person, B&B) and can organize a variety of excursions. He has also started a three-room **guesthouse** (AZN25, B&B) which, remarkably for Xınalıq, has an indoor bathroom with hot water.

Baku's 1000 Camels hostel run a two-room, ten-bed **hostel** (US$20, 🖳 www .thousandcamels-az.com) in the valley at the base of town. Arrange in advance through English-speaking Farid (☎ mob 50-422 5512, 🖳 xguidex@yahoo.com) or Turan Halil (☎ mob 50-569 1099, 🖳 halili turan@yahoo.com). All the above can help you engage walking guides.

Xınalıq now has a tea house and two tiny shops but for any kind of trekking bring your supplies with you.

Transport Shared, packed-full UAZ jeeps depart most mornings from outside Xınalıq Hotel in Quba bazaar taking around 1½ hours in ideal summer conditions. However, finding out when or if a jeep is leaving is pretty hit and miss. Try turning up around 8am and just keep asking. Chartering, the going rate is AZN50-60 day return – one-ways won't be much less unless you can track down a Xınalıqi driver. Quba

---

❏ Chetidi Mitz (Xınalıqi language)

Xınalıq and neighbouring Bostangesh hamlet have a language all their own. It is commonly known as Xınalıqi, though is referred to by locals as Chetidi Mitz. *Salam* (hello) and *Sa-ol* (thank you) are the same as in Azeri but numbers are more similar to Lezghi and are counted Georgian-style in base 20. The clucking plosive !k and !ch are also reminiscent of Georgian. Despite these similarities, some linguists contend that Xınalıqi is fundamentally unique. Note that different words are used according to the sex of the person to whom a phrase applies: eg sit down is *chii* to a man but *jeh-zi* to a woman.

Most locals speak a reasonable level of Azeri, Russian and/or Lezghi but using a few words of Xınalıqi can be fun and win friends.

ksan kwoma – it's good	*dadliqomä* – it's delicious
!knir – beautiful (woman)	*hayarde* – beautiful (view)
deylat – where?	*mkkel* – near
ché suleto – let's drink tea	*!ke* – salt
pshii – horse	*pshe* – bread

taxis often try their luck asking tourists AZN100 or more and in my experience often won't be easily bargained down. In such cases you'd do better to contact one of the Quba drivers (p175) or organize things through Xeyraddin Jabbarov (☎ mob 50-225 9250, 🖳 www.xinaliq.com) who speaks good English and charges sensible prices.

HIKING EXCURSIONS FROM XINALIQ
The following treks are only practicable during the short summer period. Ateshgah and north Laza can be reached from June but for Vändam and south Laza the snow doesn't clear sufficiently from the high passes till July. By mid-September it's probably too late.

Preparation
For any hike carry rain gear (the weather changes very fast), water bottles, food (bring supplies), your passport and a spare pair of shoes for wading through the freezing cold rivers. Bring a gas stove if you want hot food/drinks as there is generally no wood for camp fires. Consider downloading (eg from 🖳 http://maps.poehali.org/en/) and printing the 1:100,000 scale map, K-39-97 (last updated 1983) which covers Xınalıq, Cek, Laza and Shahdağ.

Guides and horses Finding someone to show you the way is advisable on more tricky hikes as clouds can appear amazingly suddenly reducing visibility to a few metres and rendering already indistinct paths almost impossible to find. Local guides can also supply packhorses for your baggage (highly recommended). Riding a horse yourself saves you a lot of trouble fording streams and makes the journey much more comfortable even though you don't travel significantly faster than walking pace given the difficult terrain. Note that if some of the group ride and others walk, it may be better to have two guides because the pedestrian and equestrian routes follow different courses along the river beds.

Amazingly it is often possible to rustle up a prospective guide and a couple of horses for a next-day departure. However, if you're time-dependent or want more than two horses you'd probably be wise to pre-arrange things through Xeyraddin (🖳 www .xinaliq.com) or the 1000 Camel Hostel folks (opposite). Costs vary fairly arbitrarily but typically start at around AZN30 per day for guides and a similar rate per horse. Although Xınalıq is getting increasingly accustomed to tourism, don't assume that all 'guides' are professional or that they'll speak any English. My old friend Badal Lalayev is charming, calmly meditative and looks brilliant in his black Papax but remains far from effusively communicative. Neither does he seem to have camping gear so had we not had a space in our tents he would have been stuck out on the freezing mountainside in just his shepherd coat.

Annoyances
Beware that since the installation of a new army camp across the valley from Xınalıq, soldiers have started checking trekkers' passports and sometimes prevent hiking groups from setting off at all. It's worth having a local guide if only to smooth out such annoyances. And don't forget to carry your ID documents. As with any hiking in Azerbaijan, ferocious sheep dogs can be a danger. Stay well away from flocks of sheep and if cornered by dogs, hold a stone as though planning to throw it then hope that the shepherd comes fast enough to 'save' you!

Xınalıq to (north) Laza There are two routes. With perfect weather it's possible to trek straight on up from Ateshgah making for the ridge just to the left of Mt Baltaqaya's rocky crown via a summer shepherd camp. From the top you get the most stunning views of Shahdağ. Descending is fine if you have visibility – just aim ahead/right towards Shahdağ then follow the main valley high above the river. Even on the clearest mornings, however, clouds can come in very fast and make the descent potentially lethal so it's worth having a guide. Allow a very full day and be prepared for steep gradients.

An easier if longer route is possible without a guide. It takes around 10 hours and initially follows the same river from

Xınalıq to (north) Laza hikes

to Qusar
GATES OF LAZA
LAZA
WATER FALLS
SUVAR
Shahdağ
to Base Camp
New Datcha
BETWEEN ROCKS IMPOSSIBLE FOR VEHICLES
HIGH ABOVE RIVER
Baltagaya Qızıl Qaya
No single path
NO MARKED PATH ACROSS GRASS BUT EASY
to Bazardüzü, Tufandağ
PASS
GOOD WATER
Very steep
Sharp Ridge
YAXIYER SHEPHERD CAMP
CONFUSING
Approx 2km
MUGAN PIR SHRINE
ATESHGAH   NATURAL FLAMES
'HOUSE ROCK'
POSSIBLE BUT UNCOMFORTABLE IN A HIGH-CLEARANCE 4WD
ARMY
to Qala Xudat
XINALIQ
to Quba
to Qabala

- = footpath
- = stream
- = 4WD track

vehicle. The route is extremely attractive (at least what I saw when the rain abated) but arguably not quite as stunning as the Xınalıq–north Laza route. The walk takes about 16 hours so non-masochists will need to camp en route. Qäbälä Laza's officious customs post can add complications to your arrival/departure (don't forget your passport, see the notes on p183) so these days it's wiser to head for Vändam, a similar distance and slightly easier to boot.

For either destination follow the course of the Qudialchay river leaving Xınalıq. The route basically hugs the right bank but there are several places where the safest route is to ford back and forth across the river. Unless on horseback you are very likely to get wet feet so it's worth carrying spare shoes. After some two hours a small side valley approaches from the right and there's a flimsy makeshift bridge across the main river. Some 50m beyond take the insignificant-looking path that zigzags back up to the left and on up very steeply, avoiding a dangerously narrow canyon.

After a high grassy area with nice views and picnic potential the path descends back into the river valley again at a small green area known as **Mecid Duzu**. From here the river valley forks twice – take first the left, then the right. Even in September there were remnant chunks of unmelted snow in these valleys – in June the route was impassable. Where the river

Xınalıq towards Shahdağ, crossing a pass where the valley ends (fill your water bottles before crossing over) and descends into a wide, delightful area of meadows; a great camp-site. Tough 4WD vehicles and trucks can make it all the way from Xınalıq and on towards Bazardüzü but not to Laza: there are too many great boulders.

Xınalıq to Vändam and (south) Laza

A hike to the other Laza (Qäbälä Laza or Kutkashen Laza) is a more serious proposition. The trip is satisfying in that it takes you right across into another part of Azerbaijan in a way that's impossible by

THE NORTH

forks once more is a **shepherds' camp** with stone enclosures. If it's getting late camp here: the next suitable spot is several hours' hike beyond.

To continue to Vändam take the left valley cross the Salavat Pass then essentially follow the Vändamchay River all the way to Duyma Hotel (p212). For South Laza take the left bank of the right valley fork, but very soon double back on the path that climbs to a grassy outlook knoll way above the camp you have just left. The map gives hints on how to proceed thereafter to descend via **Mucuk Dolma** but you'd be unwise to attempt this without a guide and having at least one horse is virtually essential to get you across the Damiraparanchay River just before Laza.

Mountaineering Even if you're not a real mountaineer the region offers some fabulous climbs. You'll need an experi-enced guide (reckon on around AZN50/ day), one or two porters/camp guards (AZN25/day) and good weather as there is no shelter on the flinty upper slopes. Climbing Shahdağ ('king's mountain', 4243m) takes you along a relatively narrow ledge and up a glacier for which crampons and an ice axe are normally necessary. The final stretch is somewhat anticlimactic except for the little Lenin statues at the summit, but the views from base camp are stunning. Coming via Laza you'll typically need four days from Baku. Driving via Xınalıq it is just about possible in 48 hours given perfect weather, but 3-4 days is normal. The same goes for Tufan Dağ ('hurricane mountain', 4191m), climbed from the north. Tufan Dağ's elegant triangular peak has a small lake way up above the tree line at 3800m. Three sub-peaks to the west, at about the same altitude, there is a grave and some animal bones, which

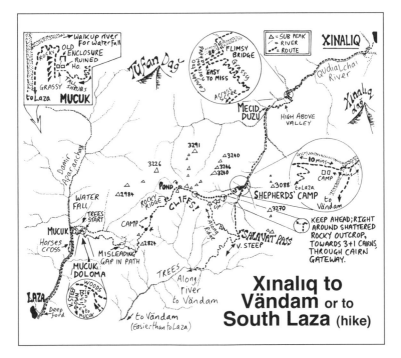

Xınalıq to **Vändam** or to **South Laza** (hike)

may mark the site of the now vanished Hun village of Askikand.

Bazarduzu ('marketplace', 4466m) is the highest Caucasian peak east of Kazbek but it's right on the border with Russian Dağestan so make sure you get clearance if you want to avoid unpleasant brushes with the army or customs services. The climb involves scaling a scree-sprinkled glacier. Visible in the valley below are some aged graves of bygone traders whose summer markets gave the mountain its name. Roughly halfway to 3527m Rüstamboz, is a curious point from which two streams flow in different directions, one south to Qamarvan near Qäbälä, the other north, eventually to form the Qusarchay river.

QRIZ (map p180)

With a timeless air and, like Xınalıq, a language of its own, mysterious Qriz is perched above the Cek canyons and just about accessible on a 4WD track from Xınalıq via Qala Xudat. Beware that this winds around very steep drop-offs on smooth, angled tracks that become perilous when wet, vehicles (and even pedestrians) tending to slip inexorably towards the daunting precipice.

Alternatively, Qriz is accessible on foot from Cek and from the western end of 'Cloudcatcher' Canyon (descend to the river where the road makes its abrupt hairpin – there's a foot bridge). The former 4WD track to Alpan via Susaı has fallen out of general use and can prove impassable by vehicle.

QUBA TO SAMUR (see map p167)

The main highway passes within 200m of the 1537 Shah Murat tomb (aka Ağbil Pir), to the right as you traverse **Ağbil** village. It's a dumpy cuboid structure set between two tumuli adorned with hundreds of colourful votive rags left by pilgrims. A friendly mollah welcomes visitors.

Turn north at '**25 Krug**' and cross some wide moorland hills to reach **Samur**. Set back 300m from the Russian border post (closed to foreigners), the AzPetrol station's neat new six-room motel (☎ 138-54545, sgl/dbl/air-con AZN7/10/26) is

cheaper than anything equivalent at Nabran but you might find a lot of questions being asked as to why you'd want to stay in this dreary place so near the border when the beach is just a AZN12 taxi ride away through pretty areas of fields and forests.

QUBA TO QUSAR (GUSARI) (see map p167 and p180)

Frequent minibuses shuttle between Quba and Qusar (20 mins) for 50q. As the road rises above Krasnaya Sloboda beside a Jewish graveyard there are some magnificent views of Quba, and (when clear) of Shahdağ. In season, apple and nut vendors laze around the villages of Xuchbala and Digah. Just south of the latter, **Quba Safari** (☎ 044-269 0747, ☎ mob 70-727 9608) is a sports and paintball recreation centre.

Alpan and Long Forest

Halfway between Quba and Qusar an apparently surfaced road heads towards the beautiful if distant mountains. Within 2km it degenerates into a gravel track which meets the river at **Alpan**. This is the site of a very ancient city whose history appears to have been totally forgotten after its destruction by the Arabs a millennium ago, though six Albanian coins and a golden coronet (since stolen) were found when digging a waterpipe. Otherwise, only the barest traces remain: illegibly inscribed stone fragments, pottery shards etc in a semi-sacred wood, 20 minutes' stroll above the upper town. Today's Alpan has a 150-year-old **mosque** with a simple square plan and central corrugated iron-nose cone. The 16th-century **Su Baba Turbe** is a six-sided tomb set in an old cemetery.

❏ **Man of the mountains**
The craze for renaming everything after Heydar Aliyev reached its grandest summit when Mt Qizilqaya was officially renamed Heydar Zirvasi Peak. To balance things out a little, Mt Tufan Dağ is now officially named after Karabagh journalist-hero Chingis Mustafayev.

Across the river and a further 4km beyond on woodland tracks at 41°21' 45"N, 48°23'03"E is *Long Forest 'Chalet Resort'* (☎ 012-496 9518, ☎ mob 50-526 4631, Ibrahim, 🖳 office@longforest.baku.az). One of Azerbaijan's very first rural retreats, the wooden bungalows with real fires cost from AZN75, horses (AZN10 per hour), skis and mountain bikes can all be hired and activities include table tennis, billiards and volleyball. The resort was originally conceived by Scottish dandy Alex Burnett as a means of testing the qualities of local timber. Alex subsequently went on to inspire considerable local agricultural development while Long Forest became a de rigeur expat weekend escape. However, since Burnett's departure, growing competition, a fire on site and the increasing impassability of the former Alpan–Xınalıq road have all led to a loss of popularity and some guests have complained that the generator doesn't get turned on midweek.

Alpan to Susaı

In the 1990s, a popular alternative 4WD route to Xınalıq connected via Uzunmesha, Geray and Susaı, crossing a bridge at 41°18'27"N, 48°17'05"E. However, since the paving of the Qächräsh–Xınalıq route the already-difficult track between Susaı and fascinating **Qrız** (another hamlet with its own unique language, see opposite) has

not been maintained and is now virtually impassable. Going by horse would be more pleasant. Ask at Long Forest.

QUSAR (Gusari, Ktsar; ☎ 0138)

Qusar is home to the 'Lezghian National Theatre' and a capital of sorts for the northern Lezghian minority. Although it's architecturally no different from other provincial centres, the town's cliff-edge location above the Qusarçay River allows views of the distant mountain backdrop towards Mt Shahdağ, sacred in local tradition. Qusar's finest building is the big, Turkish-style **Mustafa Kazdal mosque**. Built in 1998 it has a beautiful blue-tiled Mehrab and grand, spired minbar. Across the road, the **historical museum** displays a piece of a German WWII plane that fell nearby in 1942.

At the west end of town a little row of clifftop restaurant-cafés each has its own river view. *Kafe Xıdır* (☎ mob 50-551 8327) offers outdoor tables amid the willow trees and two more on a platform that hangs over the cliff edge with views of Shahdağ and Qizilqaya. Kebabs are only AZN2, beer 60q and tea comes with fudge and lemon. Music-prone *Edelveys* (☎ mob 50-775 6969) is less charming but the views are great. *Restoran Qusar* (☎ mob 50-719 8724) is grander and set around a fountain pool. Access is relatively easy as city marshrutkas (marked 'Şähär') loop anticlockwise around town from the bus

THE NORTH

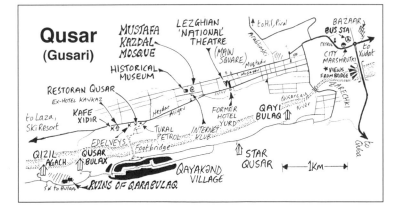

THE NORTH

station, passing a block north of the mosque then swinging back east between Xıdır and Edelveys.

Accommodation   Qusar's Yurd and Kavkaz hotels were both closed at the time of writing but there are a string of modest hut-camps and mini-resorts either side of Qayakänd village on the south bank of the Qusarchay.

On foot the swiftest way to reach the **west side** of Qayakänd is by using the long footbridge accessed from behind Tural Petrol (just east of Restoran Qusar). But distances are considerable. A spooky attraction here is the increasingly overgrown wreck of Qarabulaq Resort. The turreted forest-folly restaurant, formerly filled with clocks, still stands guarded by a concrete warrior-knight figure whose weapon once spurted fire. But the complex hasn't been used since the 2005 arrest of an infamous gang who reputedly used the resort as a holding place for its kidnap victims!

Qusar Bulax (☎ mob 50-525 1222) has white and gilt animal statues, a new lake and is walking distance from a curious stone pyramid. The clean if somewhat gerry-built two-storey cottages (AZN80) sleep at least four. Six AZN50 twins are set further back from the river and have hard camp beds. Tucked amidst the outer remnants of Qarabulaq, *Qizil Agach* (☎ mob 50-613 9507, Shakir) has promise and the simple three-bed domiks that had been constructed at the time of research cost only AZN40 including water heater. In thick woodland *Bulaq* (☎ mob 50-323 6721, Tahir) is a tatty Soviet-era place charging AZN30 for a musty but sizeable hut sleeping four. The rooms have an en suite toilet and water heater.

On the **east side**, for comfort *Star Qusar* is one of the best options with full bathrooms in pine cottages (AZN70-100) with carpet-on-wood floors, but it's away from the river and lacks any views. Kamil speaks English (☎ mob 50-390 7007).

Closer to Qusar, popular *Qayi Bulax* (☎ 53995, ☎ mob 50-332 7068) has something of a holiday camp feel with over 20 bungalows of varying styles and sizes. AZN50-100.

❏ **Lezghian issues and Lezghi language**

One of Azerbaijan's biggest minority groups (178,000), Lezghians are typically Sunni rather than Shi'ite Muslims though, like other Azeris, their faith includes some notable animist superstitions and reverence for natural *pirs* (holy trees, mountains etc). Historically Lezghians have been renowned for their fighting prowess – initially as raiders against settled towns and farmsteads, later as mercenaries notably in the pay of Tsar Nikolai. Nonetheless, the culture is not nomadic as some sources suggest: indeed they have a saying that one 'must return home when it's time to die'.

In the chaotic early 1990s, a small Lezghian minority group called Sadval campaigned briefly for an independent Lezghistan straddling the Russo-Azeri border. Sadval perpetrated a 1994 bomb blast on the Baku Metro. However, there was little or no popular support for their demands and the apparent funding/training of the terrorists by Armenians largely discredited any perceived legitimacy they might have enjoyed. The group gave up its independence manifesto in 1996.

Lezghians call their language Lezghi Chal. Useful words are:

Hello	*Salam*	How are you?	*won hikiya?*
Good (reply)	*ksanya*	...and you?	*bes won hikiya?*
Thanks/cheers	*saghurai*	Bon appetit	*nush khurai*
It's good	*im ksanya*	Delicious	*aiarti*
Water	*yad*	Beautiful	*para ksahn*

THE NORTH

Transport The bus station is beside the large bazaar area where money changers offer very good US$ rates. Buses leave for Baku (hourly till 17.30), Piral (09.30 & 13.30, 70q), Hil (07.00, 09.00, 11.00, 13.20 & 15.30, 50q), Yalama via Samur (13.00, AZN1.80), Aniq (11.20 & 16.20, 80q), Zindanmuruq (16.30) and Kuzun (16.40, AZN1). The latter was already packed full of waiting passengers at 2pm and impossibly crushed full when I squeezed aboard just before departure. Shared taxis and minivans shuttle fairly frequently to Quba.

QUSAR TO (NORTH) LAZA
(see map p180 & below)

At **Äniq** there are sizeable wall remnants of a medieval citadel, some curious ancient graves and an unusually ornate mosque. Buses return to Qusar at 07.00 and 13.00.

The road is now paved as far as **Aladash** but the surface will probably degrade quickly given all the heavy trucks using it as part of the construction programme for the big new **Shahdağ Ski Resort**. The first stage of the ski resort is due to start operating by January 2010, though given the limited natural snowfall, pistes will probably have to be artificially whitened for much of the season. The site will also pose a problem for local shepherds whose flocks have customarily watered at the meadowland pond that will now be at the heart of the resort.

Beyond this point, the final approach

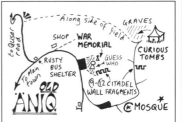

to Laza climbs through attractive grasslands rutted by struggling 4WD vehicles (beware of the sheep-dogs if walking) and reaches a bolderstrewn precipice known as the 'Gates of Laza'. The views here and for the rest of the descent are particularly impressive but the 'road' is in very bad shape if you're driving.

LAZA (Lazar, Qusari Laza)
☎ 0138, population 137

NB Don't confuse with the 'other' Laza near Qäbälä, p214.

Nowhere in Azerbaijan has a more majestic setting than little Laza. It's surrounded by curious erosion features and several high waterfalls. Emerald-green sheep meadows soar up to craggy mountain peaks of astonishing grandeur. Cue *The Sound of Music* soundtrack. Actually seeing any of this symphonic beauty is a question of luck given the frequent foggy whiteouts. And with Baku folks showing interest in buying

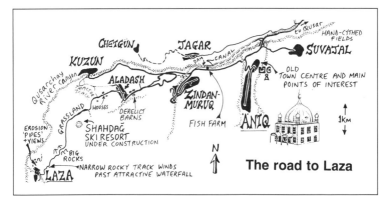

The road to Laza

THE NORTH

land here for datchas, it's worth hurrying to visit while the scene remains pristine. Laza village isn't architecturally notable in the way of Xınalıq. Nonetheless, in its tiny centre, a distinctive rocky knob and a rusty-roofed 1899 mosque add interesting foreground for the symphonic landscapes behind. In a cliff face behind lies the **Haji Zangi Baba pir**.

Laza is popular as a camping and climbing base for Shahdağ and Baltagaya and in January Laza's frozen waterfalls are the location for an ice-climbing competition (💻 www.fairex.az/buzad-e.php). Alternatively there's a gorgeous and relatively straightforward one-day hike between Laza and Xınalıq (impossible by vehicle). If you have the time it's worth camping en route in the lovely meadows beneath Shahdağ. Make sure you bring all your own food, water and cooking materials as there's no firewood en route and the river-water at the campsite is full of silt. Also be aware that in some recent instances hikers report a frosty reception from the army in Xınalıq so get local advice before setting off; see pp183-4.

Accommodation

Occupying a majestic viewpoint location 2km beyond central Laza, comfortable bungalows at *Suvar* (☎ 53671, 💻 www .suvar.az, 41°17'02"N, 48°06'42") with hot showers and satellite TV are widely spread around an appealing stone restaurant-bar. Prices start at AZN60/100 sgl/dbl but increase at weekends and peak holidays. Sadly, the inspiringly energetic long-term manager has left and road-access problems during 2008 might have a negative longer-term effect.

Homestays in the village (AZN10-20) are an appealing alternative. Last time I was ushered without ado to the home of the friendly *Azizov Family* (☎ 57035) who have a special guest-annex in their home-compound and can fire up a hot shower. For AZN20 you get a bed and two meals. The house is opposite Laza's main shop, Latsar, where teacher/store-owner Khalid looks like a gold-toothed Jeremy Paxman. Mevlud Azizov (☎ mob 050-684 4374) even speaks some English and can act as a hiking or mountaineering guide.

Transport

The last 5km into Laza from the ski-resort site is hard going for cars and even 4WD vehicles struggled for much of 2008 after a landslide temporarily reduced one ledge-section of the track to a scarily narrow ribbon. Direct buses no longer run to Laza. However, once the ski resort starts operating it's likely that transport will get you that far fairly painlessly leaving a very agreeable walk for the last section (beware of the sheepdogs though). Alternatively AZN1 public buses run daily from Qusar to Aniq, Zindanmuruq and Kuzun (at 16:40, returning 07.00 next day). I have walked to/from Laza from all three places: Kuzun is quickest (around two hours) but outside the long days of early summer that'll be too long to reach Laza before nightfall so you'd be wise to camp in or near Kuzun and continue next morning. Following a short-cut trail and tractor-path from Kuzun to the main Alasht–Laza 'road' only takes around 20 minutes.

Returning from Laza is generally easy as villagers can help you arrange a shared ride to Qusar for around AZN4 assuming the road is passable. Otherwise you might have to walk 15km to Aniq for the 13.00 Qusar bus. From Qusar the best taxi fares are obviously from Laza-bound drivers (AZN20). Try Elchin (mob ☎ 50-712 2818).

QUSAR TO HIL, PIRAL AND HÄZRÄ

A quietly bucolic and mostly well-surfaced road winds between Qusar and the Russian border at Häzrä where there is no legal crossing point. Sadly the Samur–Häzrä road is rather too bumpy to make the attractive loop really enjoyable.

Hil is a coil of very rough mud and rock tracks climbing a knoll beside the Qusar–Häzrä road. Hil's historic silver onion-topped mosque is curiously hidden despite being in the village centre. The mosque's walls are appropriately coated in *hil*, a form of mud and straw daub-plaster from which the village takes its name. Embedded in the front wall are several decree stones written in Arabic script. Until

1997 this building was the unlikely setting for the National Lezghian Museum.

Pleasant **Piral** has an attractive if somewhat distant backdrop of mountain ridges. There seem to be as many donkey carts as cars on the road here, though a daily bus does run to Baku (13:50). Approaching **Häzrä** the road switchbacks down a series of forest hairpins into the Samur River valley – a fairly wide floodplain across which the spiky peaks you see are in Russian Dağestan. Häzrä was the site of a 1456 battle between the Shirvanshahs and the Sheikhs of Ardebil led by Khaluli I. Sheikh Juneid, grandfather of the future great Shah Ismail Xatai, was amongst the invaders who died. His death was later viciously avenged by his Safavid descendants who sacked Baku in 1501 and finished off the Shirvanshahs altogether at Qalabugurt in 1538. Six years later Xatai's daughter sponsored a mausoleum-tomb at Häzrä for Sheikh Juneid which still stands.

A tough 4WD track leads west from Häzrä to the pretty wooded Lezghian mountain villages of **Quturgen** and **Sudur**.

❏ Thinking like a red-head

The Safavids are best known as a dynasty of Persian emperors (1502-1736). However, they started as followers of the 13th-century Sufi mystic Safi-Uddin from which the name derives. Safi lived in Ardebil (Southern Azerbaijan, ie Iran) where his splendid blue-tiled mausoleum complex still stands. Although Muslim, the early Safavids believed in the cyclical nature of time, in reincarnation and the attainability of paradise on earth. This *quluw* ('exaggeration') had them labelled as heretics, but proved the philosophically potent driving force behind Shah Ismail Xatai's fanatical Qizilbash (red-head) troops, so named because of their scarlet caps. Xatai himself saw the qualities of great kingship as a yin-yang balance of modesty and pride, of ruthlessness and mercy. Although quluw philosophy evolved closer to mainstream Islam over time, it was influential in shaping Shi'ite Islam which is still most prevalent in the areas which formed part of Xatai's great Azeri-Persian empire.

PART 5: SHAMAKHA–SHAKI ROUTE

INTRODUCTION

Rolling lifeless deserts turn to grasslands. Meadows become tree lined. Forests grow thicker. And within a few hours' drive there are white-topped peaks poking above the lushly rich green foothills. Add coppersmiths in Lahıc, royal palaces in Shäki and many curious Albanian church ruins for a remarkable palate of options: and all within a remarkable day's journey from Baku.

Planning a trip

This is much the most enjoyable route between Baku and Tbilisi. For a weekend away from Baku you could start by flying to Zaqatala on Friday. Or sleep on the overnight train to Shäki or Zaqatala saving a day's travel one way. Then return in taxi hops: chartering a shared taxi will be relatively cheap as the driver would be doing the trip anyway – just be sure to pre-arrange what stops you'll want.

By bus you'd have to do the route in stages changing in Qäbälä if you didn't want to miss the lovely Oğuz region. That's because direct Baku–Shäki/Zaqatala services divert via Aqsu and Göychay. If time is short don't waste much of it with the half-hearted 'sights' east of Shamakha.

For accommodation there's plenty of choice. Much is banally lacklustre but the Babayurd yurt camp (towards Pirguli) is very original, Duyma (Vändam) is pleasantly quiet and comfortable, and Shäki has both the professional Saray Hotel and the unbeatably atmospheric Caravanserai to choose from. Homestays, available in chaming Lahıc, Shäki and Kish, are a great way to see local life from the inside.

Eateries are common all along the route

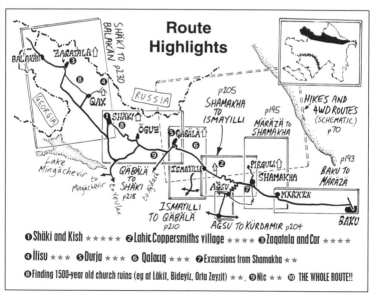

Route Highlights

❶ Shäki and Kish ★★★★★ ❷ Lahic Coppersmiths village ★★★★ ❸ Zaqatala and Car ★★★★

❹ Ilisu ★★★ ❺ Durja ★★★ ❻ Qalacıq ★★★ ❼ Excursions from Shamakha ★★

❽ Finding 1500-year old church ruins (eg at Läkit, Bideyiz, Orta Zeyzit) ★★ ❾ Nic ★★ ❿ THE WHOLE ROUTE!!

with particularly picturesque shashlyk spots in the forests and ridges east of Basqal, west of Ismayıllı and along the Ağsu pass.

BAKU TO MÄRÄZÄ (see map below)

Soon after you leave Baku heading west, the stark environment loses all vegetation except the roughest of scrub and one solitary tree after km43. The landscape appears to have been painted in by a divine hand suffering from too severe a hangover to bother with much detail. Arid hills undulate in stark shades of lifeless dun mellowing only slightly as you approach Märäzä. The main attraction is the post-holocaust bleakness of the scenery (see photo C9 btm L), but there are a couple of points of passing interest en route.

Note that the Baku–Shemakha road is undergoing a major rebuild so it's possible that the kilometre markings will be somewhat different by 2010.

Mud volcanoes

There are two very accessible groups of mildly active bubblers five minutes' walk (or a one-minute 4WD ride) off the main road. **Buraniz Jylgya** (aka 'Napier's Nipples', 40°28'50"N, 49°26'52"E) is directly north of the road at km41. Be careful driving off the road as the track crosses a deceptive gulley. Somewhat better, though still less impressive than Clangerland (p142), is the **Perekishqul** group some 500m south of the road at a turning that's 400m east of km38.

Further from the road there's a pair of sizeable, mineral-rich cones on the approach to Shikhzahirli, 2km of gravity-defying mud tracks above **Ceyrankachmas**; not an ideal trip in the rain! There are several big mud volcanoes deep into the desert, eg about 7km following the 4WD track that leads south at km74 (just west of the first bridge

where the main road crosses the Ceyrankachmas river). The latter track is reported to link all the way to the caravanserai at Pir Hussein (p241) and thence to Navahi on the Baku–Kürdamir road.

Babajanli Caravanserai

Ancient caravans from Baku to Shamakha used the so-called Shah's Road. This avoided the route of the modern main road, following closer to the course of the powerlines in a parallel valley. Built in the reign of early 16th-century Shirvan ruler Khalilulla II, Babajanli (aka Garachi/Gypsy) Caravanserai was once an important halt on that route. These days the remnants are exceedingly limited. There is an antique one-roomed stone building with an arch-domed interior now used as a casual sheep shed, but even that is quite unimpressive and looks likely to collapse. It is surrounded by more recent if semi-derelict buildings of a Soviet sheep station and is awesomely overpowered by the battalion of giant pylons (look west).

Pastel graveyard

At km71 a track curves off towards a sizeable graveyard containing a curious mixture of old, new and pastel-coloured tomb stones, reminiscent of Sofi Hamid cemetery, Sangachal (p140).

Narimankand

Just before Märäzä, the main road swerves to avoid Narimankand's hilly eastern flank. If you take the increasingly rough track directly opposite the turning to Diri Baba Mausoleum and follow it around the base of the town past a small reservoir you come to a cliff in which are several caves, once prehistoric habitations.

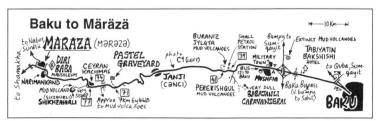

Märäzä (Mərəzə, ☎ 0150)

Diri Baba ('living granddad') was a Sufi mystic whose body, entombed here in 1402, mysteriously refused to decompose, leading to a posthumous declaration of his sanctity. Recently smartened up, the domed, stone **Diri Baba Mausoleum** is built into a cliff 1.1km off the main road, and accessed from above by a precipitous stone staircase. Across a rocky gully to the south, gnarled old Arabic-inscribed graves are photogenic at sunset against a desert horizon pimpled with mud volcanoes. The atmosphere is at its best when the muezzin calls forlornly from the mausoleum roof, though unruly mobs of pesky kids can spoil the charm. At the western edge of Märäzä, Heydar Park has sprouted an improbable glass pyramid.

MÄRÄZÄ TO SHAMAKHA

East of the Pirsaat bridge the road divides briefly, the northern carriageway passing **Pirsaat Pir**. Most motorists stop at this rather ugly green-domed shrine to leave a donation and sip the holy water. One driver described it as the 'insurance mosque': 'who knows what would happen if I didn't leave a donation?!'. According to a somewhat far-fetched local tradition, a medieval holy man, lost in meditation, disappeared here, carried away in the fast-flowing waters of the eponymous Pirsaatchay.

If you aren't in a hurry there are several mildly interesting diversions. Roads and bumpier tracks allow a loop from Märäzä to Shamakha via antique Sündü or cottagey Xilmilli without too much backtracking.

Sinners' Rock

An off-road diversion from the Märäzä–Xilmilli road leads to the very lonely **Abdul Karim Pir** where locals make superstitious sacrifices. Blood-stained boots are removed to place smooth pebbles on the black-draped altar within a squat, domed tomb-mosque

dated AH1247 (1899). Set back on a gentle muddy hill-shoulder that you'll pass before reaching the pir is the hollow **Kitchit Dashi** (Sinners' Rock). By popular belief, only the pure hearted can squeeze themselves through the hole in this man-sized boulder.

Xilmilli

Originally founded by Molokans, **Xilmilli** retains some old Russian houses and there's a timelessness to views of riverside life on the Qozluchay river. Although 4WD vehicles can ford the river when water is low, don't assume that you'll be able to reach Altı Ağach this way. A daily minibus links Baku and Xilmilli via Bäklä Junction.

Sündü

No-one seems to know the history of Sündü, an ancient stone-cutters' town which was largely destroyed in medieval earthquakes. The ruins of once-grand buildings have been cannibalized as an easy source of building stone as you can see in certain newer walls. Nonetheless, several extensive graveyards and the medieval mosque remain. And in the heart of the village, women still fill their jujums at a long, timeless stone-faced water collection point. The latter is vaguely reminiscent of ancient washing areas in India/Nepal and photogenic when colourfully saddled donkeys come to drink.

Half an hour's stroll below the village is a series of crumbly-edged canyons. All that remains of what locals call the **Onbesh Kul Palace** (literally 15 rooms) is a string

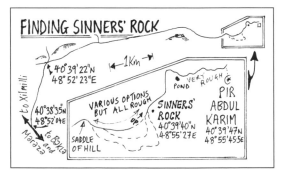

FINDING SINNERS' ROCK

To Xilmilli
40°39'22"N
48°52'23"E

40°38'35N
48°52'04E

Maraza and ...
to Baku

◄─ 1Km ─►

VARIOUS OPTIONS BUT ALL ROUGH

SADDLE OF HILL

VERY ROUGH
POND

SINNERS' ROCK
40°39'40"N
48°55'27E

PIR ABDUL KARIM
40°39'47N
48°55'45.5E

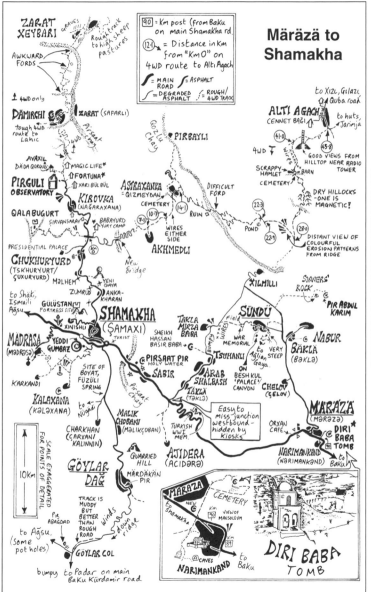

Märäzä to Shamakha

SHAMAKHA–SHAKI ROUTE

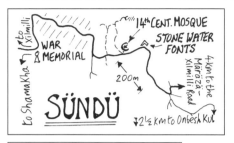

SHAMAKHA–SHAKI ROUTE

of smoke-blackened bandit caves cut into one of the cliffs. In another canyon the **Ağlian Gaya spring** flows out of the living rock and is said to be the collective tears of mothers mourning their lost warrior sons.

Sündü to Shamakha
Leaving Sündü westbound the road is rough and slightly confusing: coming up from the old mosque turn right and curl through the far side of town (more graves) to a lonely war memorial. Branch right, then left and cut across a field diagonally towards a row of telegraph poles beneath which you'll meet a degraded but formerly asphalted road. To the right the route leads to Xilmilli (see p194). To the left it returns towards Shamakha via **Arabshalbash** which has a new mosque and a couple of military statues. **Tsuhanli** also has a mosque and, out in a field sits the squat little Sheikh Hassan Basir Baba Pir.

Approaching **Täklä** there are some wide grassy views towards Shamakha. Where the route rejoins the main Baku–Qäbälä road, a track to the south leads to **Ajidera** (Acidərə) where the tomb of Sheikh Eyub commemorates an early 19th-century ethnic Arab philanthropist famed for his height (over 2m high), massive stature and his equally massive golden rings; the rings were made specially to fit his fingers which had a diameter of over an inch.

SHAMAKHA (ŞAMAXI) (☎ 0176)
For centuries Shamakha was the capital of Shirvan and a major trade centre for northwestern Azerbaijan. Yet today it's a surprisingly small town with little to show for all its historical prowess. The distinctive double hill around which the town originally formed now lies half-forgotten at Shamakha's western edge. Defeated by time, the once-impenetrable Güllüstan Castle on its grassy peak is quietly crumbling into memories along with the scars of endless invaders and earthquakes. Shamakha's low-rise homes are pleasant enough when viewed from Yeddi Gumbaz

❏ A victory of diplomacy
In the 8th century Shamakha survived the Arab caliphate's invasion led by Ibn Mervan. The cunning Shirvanshahs, far from adopting the customary chivalric practice of fighting unwinnable odds and having your cities burnt in retribution, tried a novel approach. They simply let the invaders march in. Over a few drinks, the Shirvanshah seems to have alerted Ibn Mervan to the dangers of the Dağestan horde on Shirvan's northern border which might at any time invade this new colony. Why not make a deal, suggested the wily Shirvanshah: if you don't demand the 400,000 Dihram financial tribute to the Caliph, I'll keep my armies to defend your northern borders for you. It seems Mervan agreed and went off, satisfied, to conquer elsewhere. The Arabs renamed Shamakha as Maziabiya but otherwise things stayed much the same. The Shirvanshah's army stayed where it had been all along and everyone was happy.

mausoleum across the valley, but the Grand Mosque is the only architectural attraction in the town itself. Outside that there's a **tourist information booth** (☎ 51022, 🖳 tic _shamakhi@tourism.az).

History

When Baku was still in nappies, Shamakha was already an incontinent grandparent. Possibly the Kmakhia described in Ptolemy's *Geography*, it spent most of its history as the capital and major commercial centre of Shirvan/western Azerbaijan.

The Shirvanshahs ruled from the 7th to the 16th century over varying-sized portions of the Shamakha–Derbent–Baku region and are said to have controlled a network of 360 fortresses. Their long survival was down to a relative lack of expansionist ambition and a preparedness, when necessary, to accept reduced status as mere governors in the empires of others (see box opposite). The Shirvanshahs were finally toppled during the Safavid Azeri-Persian era when even 'invincible' Qalabugurt (p201) eventually fell. Shamakha town was wiped off the map altogether in 1734 by Persia's Nadir Shah (see 'New Shamakha', p204). It was only just re-emerging when the Russians arrived first in 1795, then again in 1806 leading Shama-

kha's last independent ruler, Khan Mustafa to flee to his mountain retreat at Fit Dağ and thence obscurity. The Russians initially used Shamakha as their regional administration centre but after a massive 1859 earthquake, Baku seemed a safer option.

Shamakha was known for its Quba-style carpets throughout much of the millennium, though today there's little being made. Shamakha was also famed for wine: there are dramatic claims that France received its first vines from Shamakha cuttings. In the 1980s the region's annual harvest averaged 160,000 tons of grapes. In the 1990s this dwindled to barely a tenth and the curious balloon-shaped 'cloud-zapper' buildings sat idle on local hill-tops: they'd been designed to protect the vines from hail by pre-emptive cloud attacks. Today the region's wine industry is starting to make a very modest comeback.

Grand Mosque

A kilometre east of central Shamakha the active Grand Mosque is a very large, attractive if simple cuboidal stone construction. Built on the site of an ancient pagan sun-worshippers' temple, a mosque was reputedly founded here in 743AD leading tour-guides to proclaim it the Caucasus's second

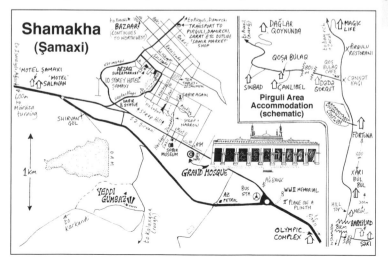

oldest mosque (after Derbend). That's a little misleading since the present design only dates from 1902 and even that only belatedly rebuilt long after the disastrous April 1918 fire. No accident, that inferno was part of the era's horrendous inter-ethnic conflict. Many of the Muslim faithful who were burnt in the conflagration had fled to the mosque seeking sanctuary from fighting in the town. A local man who lost two grandparents in the blaze, told me that a group of Armenians fired on the mosque with cannons, but that the 2m-thick stone walls held out. The mosque remained a ruined shell until the late 1970s. Today the building is complete again with its vast, dark prayer-hall powerfully impressive if rather bare.

In the courtyard garden some excavations show foundation stubs of older structures. The pumping mechanism here is not a bizarre oil strike: it simply produces the water for worshippers to perform their pre-prayer ablutions. Two blocks from the mosque is a **museum** dedicated to Shamakha's favourite son, the poet **Sabir**.

Gülüstan fortress

Shirvanshah Gubad first erected iron gates on his hilltop fortress between 1043 and 1049 and for the following centuries the site's walls enclosed the residences of the Shirvanshahs and later the Shamakha khans. Most of the walls have long ago collapsed and many stones have been removed for house building, but the views are lovely from the top where one can still sense the site's natural impregnability. Beneath the tallest remnant chunk of tower at the fortress's western end is a small hole, the now blocked entrance to a tunnel which led to a subterranean labyrinth. Locals remember playing in these tunnels as children: one of the tunnels was said to lead almost a kilometre down to the small ravine where a stream cuts the castle hill from the neighbouring Pir Derekos mount. The tunnel entrance at that end is still open though it takes a short but steep scramble (and possibly a guide) to find it. With a torch you can crawl some 40m inside before claustrophobia and cave-ins block further progress.

The easiest way to the top of the castle is by the fairly smooth track from near Xınıshlı village. It was in **Xınıshlı** that

archaeologists found several important relics including the approximately life-size stone idol which stands cross-armed in Baku's Historical Museum like a giant headless Oscar. Other interesting finds include grave jewellery that dates back to the 4th century BC and a more recent Kupe amphora containing the skeleton of an apparently murdered man whose skull had been punctured by a nail.

The deep well-like hole on top of the castle hilltop was also the result of recent, albeit freelance, excavations. As usual, locals believe that the diggers waltzed off with great caches of gold, though there's absolutely no proof.

The 'other' hill, directly across from Gülüstan on the Shamakha side is considered holy in a way that is typical of the Azeri brand of animist-Islam. The hill was topped by a Zoroastrian fire temple and ceremonial area 2000 years ago. Today there's the small Pir Derekos hilltop mausoleum.

Yeddi Gumbaz Across the valley from Shamakha, the famous Yeddi Gumbaz (seven tombs) are the 18th-/early 19th-century mausolea of the khans of Shamakha. Usseinov et al suggest that *yeddi* actually meant 'many' in this context, but today only three of these desecrated octagonal royal tombs are reasonably complete. Some of the surrounding gravestones are centuries older and the site is well worth the 2km detour if only for the excellent views back onto the city. A track continues from here to further grave-sites at Kalaxana (p202).

Accommodation and food

If you don't want to drive on up towards Pirguli (opposite), Shamakha's best accommodation is at the *Olympic Complex* (☎ 51130) where nearly new AZN50 air-con bungalows and AZN100 suites have full facilities, toiletries and use of the great indoor swimming pool (May-Sep). Despite being well set back there's still some road noise.

Dominating the town centre, the ugly *Hotel Şamaxı* is an utterly decrepit 10-storey Soviet tower. If you don't mind washing using buckets in a separate room, beds cost only AZN4 to AZN10. The lifts don't work discouraging anyone from reaching the view-rooms of the upper storeys. However, a full-scale reconstruction is supposed to start during 2009 which should transform all that.

Restaurants *Savalan* and *Şamaxı*, side-by-side at the western end of town both offer 'motel' rooms as well as garden dining with decent, sensibly priced food (though the road noise can be tiresome). Room standards at the Şamaxı vary enormously from stuffed-full waterless quads to nouveau-riche doubles with bathroom and chandeliered dining hall. Rates seem to be random and calculated according to demand and how much the chief waiter estimates you'll pay. I obviously looked poor and was offered the best room for just AZN20. The Salavan sensibly puts its guest accommodation around the back (less road noise). Upstairs rooms (AZN10) are fairly rough but downstairs (AZN20) versions are simple mini-suites with tiled bathrooms. Good value.

Other food options include some very simple *yemekxanas* in the town centre around the well-stocked **Arzaq supermarket**. Somewhat tatty *Shirvangöl* has a view across the reservoir towards Yeddi Gumbaz. Several **shashlyk eateries** are dotted along the road towards Pirguli.

Public transport
The main bus station was being totally rebuilt at the time of research. Minibuses (AZN3) and shared taxis (AZN4-5) to Baku depart regularly from outside until early evening taking around two hours. Heading west can be somewhat awkward with Qäbälä-bound minibuses often already full on arrival ex-Baku.

Six blocks north of central Shamakha is the pick-up spot for shared taxis to Chukhuryurd and Pirguli (rare off season but regular in summer supplemented by an 08.00 minibus). Jeeps to Zarat Xeybari and the 13.00 Damırchı bus via Pirguli (returns next morning at 08.30) also use this stop. Buses from most other regional villages including Mädräsä arrive early morning in the bazaar returning around noon.

There are no city buses. Taxis charge AZN1 per hop, more to Yeddi Gumbaz.

AROUND SHAMAKHA (NORTH)
On the hills above Shamakha, Pirguli/ Pirqulu offers a fresh-air escape from the summer heat or for undramatic but accessible informal skiing in winter. There's a fair selection of rural accommodation and several fairly good day trips should you decide to stick around.

Pirguli (Pirqulu) and around
North of Shamakha a 35-minute drive winds through farms and downland to high flower-filled meadows and the popular datcha townships of Chukhuryurd (Tskhuryurt) and Kirovka (Nağarxana) before reaching the forest reserve and observatory domes of Pirguli (Pirqulu). The best views are well before Pirguli itself. The area attracts picnickers and weekenders escaping Baku's summer sweat and the open grassy hillsides would make for pleasant hiking. In winter some people ski or toboggan but there's no lift infrastructure and aprés ski is limited to sympathizing with sad caged wolves, cooped up as 'attractions' at *Pirqulu Restorani*. Pirguli isn't a town, just a diffuse scattering of rural tourist hut-camps around the 1960 **astronomical observatory** whose alien silvered domes are a major local landmark. The biggest houses a 90-ton telescope that gained international attention for its high-quality spectra of Mars observed in 1971. A 1990s' funding crisis all but closed the place down but the equipment remains in working order. Getting in is hit and miss. Sometimes I've been shooed away gruffly from the site, other times invited in for interesting informal tours of the (smaller) telescope and some visitors report 9pm star shows in midsummer. Try calling ahead (Mushviq, ☎ mob 50-485 5363) or visiting with a tour agency.

Accommodation
There's lots to choose from. Hidden away off the Astrakhanka/Qizmeydan road, brilliant yurt-camp called *Babayurd* (☎ mob 50 390 0728, Said) is the most original accommodation in rural Azerbaijan. You sleep in one of its furnished Central Asian-style felt 'tents' that look as if they've materialized straight off the Mongolian steppe. Yet they're relatively comfy with hot water,

chemical toilet, natural (ie hole-in-the-floor) fridge, and each is decorated with skins, carpets, kilims and Azeri metalwork (AZN30 dbl). There's a large, characterful restaurant (kebabs AZN3, mains AZN6) with central fire-hearth, piano, stone walls and antique furniture. Or in summer dine at thatched dining booths in the pear orchard ranged around a pond full of bullrushes. Delightful and fairly priced.

Xari Bül Bül, 800m south of the observatory, is a frog-croaky pond with rickety tea tables and ten uninviting Soviet-era huts each with two or three saggy beds and a dining terrace (price negotiable). Outside shared squat toilet.

Fortuna (☎ mob 50 371 5390) offers a rather regimented row of small AZN50 huts whose selling point is their handy proximity to the observatory.

At *Magic Life* (☎ mob 50 520 0156, Ramiz) unpretentious timber huts with private bathrooms have tile effects and stone bases are spread about an orchard. The rooms start at AZN35-50 according to season.

The following fall along or near the first 2km of lane towards Avaxil. *Dädä Qorqut* has puke-green concrete bungalows

that are too close together. *Çanlibel* sits on a nice little knoll but trees hide the potentially lovely views. *Qoşa Bulaq* (☎ 50-423 3007, Asad) is worth considering with good views from the terrace of some of their two-in-one bungalows (AZN50). Room quality is fine but sizes vary, the bathrooms are very small and oddly a single water heater is shared between the two room-units within each bungalow. *Sinbad* looked good but appeared closed when I visited last. *Dağlar Qoynunda* (☎ mob 50-374 5176) is high on a hill-ridge with potentially great panoramas but the 35-bed accommodation consists of dreary pine boxes.

In **Kirovka** (see map p195) *Şirvansaray* (☎ mob 50 342 7842) has turquoise huts with very pink interiors (AZN30-50) and pleasant dining platforms beside a small pond. There's billiards and table tennis but the decor and settings could be better. **Chkhuryurd** has a roadside *motel* and a lakeside *restaurant* complex.

Beyond Pirguli

Beyond the observatory a bumpy track continues 8km to the attractive stone village of **Dämırchı** – allow half an hour. This is 4WD

❏ **Azerbaijan's astronomical pedigree**

Extraordinary new ideas have been known as 'revolutionary' ever since the Polish astronomer Copernicus published his theory of 'planetary revolution' in 1543. Copernicus's idea of a spherical, spinning world was revolutionary in political as well as physical terms. But new it was not: some 300 years earlier, astronomer Nasruddin Tusi and his Azeri students had taken for granted that the world was round and had accurately calculated its diameter (see box p314 for more of Tusi's exploits).

Tusi's great 1261 observatory and his 400,000-volume library at Marağa (now Maraqeh, Iran) were sadly destroyed by Timur a century later. Nonetheless, Tusi remains a posthumous regional hero. This is quite in line with historical precedence. Court astronomers were the most respected scientists in a khan's mediaeval palace. If you visit Baku's Shirvanshah Palace, note that the most visible turbe marks not a prince's tomb but the grave of the royal astronomer. Azerbaijani Islam's animist undercurrents add to the obvious universal appeal of space and the stars as a subject for local writers, eg:

> Full of enigmas the sky opens like a book
> Infinite and boundless invites us to look
> Deep and still deeper into wide unfathomable depths
> Of mysteries profound

(Roughly translated from *Astronomer and Poet* by Bakhtiyar Vagabzade who also wrote a ditty called *The Observatory*.)

territory and one of the perennial off-roader challenges is to reach Lahıc from Dämırchı. Some years it's possible, others the route becomes totally impassable. With patience and a good 4WD it is slightly easier to continue north from Dämırchı past **Zarat** (across the river, marked Safali on some maps) to Zarat Xeybari (around 70 minutes from Pirguli). Note that neither of these Zarats is the Zarat marked on most published maps (near Varna), which is known locally as Baba Zarat and is better reached from Lahıc (tough river drive) passing Gurbanca, the access point for climbing Mt Babadağ.

Zarat means 'shiny horse' and refers to the apocryphal visit of a local khan who exclaimed with pride at the jewels with which the local valley folk had adorned their steeds. The tribe then applied the honorific term to each of their villages.

Attractive **Zarat Xeybari**, known 'pre-khan' as Tchukhar, is a lush oasis between otherwise stark-grey mountain ridges. A pleasant day hike takes you up through thistles, barberry and juniper bushes onto the highest ridge for views of Shanazardağ and the forest way below.

It's possible to hike (a day each way) across a dramatic pass between Shanazardağ and the Jarlija mountains, then down a dangerously steep scree into **Mayil's Forest**. It's named after a pro-independence outcast who hid here following his unilateral refusal to recognize the Soviet takeover in 1920. A party of 1000 Red Army guards failed to flush him out and he remained undiscovered for 15 years till betrayed, ironically by his own feuding son. Take a guide if you go or you too may get lost amid the 60ft oaks in this beautiful but disorientating and extremely isolated place. Take a tent also.

Qalabugurt Castle

(40°45'13"N, 48°34'26"E)
Amid sharp rocky pinnacles on a very steep wooded knife-edge ridge, this dramatically situated ruin was once the Shirvanshahs' fortified treasury. It was enlarged in the 12th century by Memuchekhr I and was the scene of an intense siege during 1538. This was the last stand of Shirvanshah Shah Rukh who holed up in his most impenetrable cas-

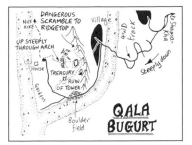

tle for months before being starved, bombarded and finally tricked into submission by Safavid Emperor Tahmasp (son of Shah Ismail Xatai) who promised mercy but promptly had him and his entire entourage put to the sword. Bye bye Shirvanshahs. The castle was fairly systematically destroyed thereafter. Nonetheless, today, if you peer carefully you can still make out ruined wall segments and the one minor round tower on a lower rock ledge. Scrambling up through the trees, there is a lot more to discover – lengths of wall up to 6m high with the odd arch. Half-collapsed vaults of the treasury chamber remain and there are fantastic views from the very top ridge if you dare to scurry up the perilous scree-covered path that leads to it. Villagers were keen to guide us to many of the harder to find relics. Even if you don't venture beyond the base of the complex there are some interesting walks and plenty of old discarded pottery shards to search out amongst the stones.

Just reaching the base of the castle is difficult enough. The access track leads 11km west starting 1km north of Chukhuryurd (at 40°43'25.4"N, 48°38'23"E). Initially deceptively smooth, the track rapidly deteriorates and the latter sections require a sturdy 4WD. At Qalabugurt village, ford the wide bolder-strewn river, then skirt along the river bank and loop around to Qaladerasi hamlet at the foot of the castle crag. Allow nearly an hour each way for the very rough drive from Chukhuryurd.

The tracks to Xızı

There is a Friday livestock market at the crossroads where the Qalabugurt road heads west. If you take the road to the east at the same point passing Babayurt yurt-tent accommodation (p199), it is possible to reach Altı Ağach, Xızı and the 'Candy Cane' mountains as long as you don't get lost en route. Beyond Astraxanka/Qizmey-dan, fords and rough sections make the route exclusively 4WD or horse territory. The route passes some intriguing rock forms including a magnetic mountainette. And in summer some shepherd tents look like upturned coracles. However, the dangerous wolf-dogs seem to have something to prove and the pleasant scenery is much less spectacular than 4WD adventures further north. See maps on p195 and p70.

AROUND SHAMAKHA (SOUTH)

A network of relatively smooth downland tracks link Yeddi Gumbaz, Kalaxana and Mädräsä. Many are driveable without 4WD as long as there's no rain. A quick circuit is possible in two hours.

Kalaxana

Set amid fig trees, Kalaxana is a friendly village hidden in a fold of rolling grassland, 8km south-west of Yeddi Gumbaz. When Cornelius DeBruin visited in the 18th century there were nine sharply pointed **turbe** tomb-towers, five with porticoes. One was identified as the tomb of Sheikh Ibrahim, son of Mir Mohamed, buried in 1663/4. Today, seven tombs remain. One resident told me how gangs of evil Armenians had destroyed the others but later confessed that he had in fact taken some of the stones to rebuild his own house.

Mädräsä

Mädräsä shares a name with the grape most commonly used in Azeri wines and was itself Azerbaijan's most famous wine-producing area until the 1980s. It was populated by ethnic Armenians until 1990 when almost the entire population fled during the ethnic conflicts. The large church still stands albeit earthquake-cracked and used as a hay barn. Today Mädräsä's population is a disparate mixture of refugee groups, notably Mesketian Turks – Georgian Muslims who Stalin deported to Kazakhstan but who

returned to the Caucausus especially after the USSR split. Unlike Kalaxana, the people here seem uncomfortable with tourists.

Göylar and the long loop to Ağsu

A little-used alternative link to Ağsu runs through two villages both called Göylar. In winter much of the population moves with their flocks of sheep from upland Göylar Dağ to the much less attractive settlement of Göylar Cöl on the plains. The road between the two is becoming increasingly degraded but offers sweeping views across central Azerbaijan as it wiggles and bumps down the balding ridges where the 1985 Robin Hood-style movie *Gachagnabi* was filmed.

Known as Engels Kolkhoz during the Soviet era, Göylar Dağ (40°29'07"N, 48°41'03"E) grew around a 13th-century caravanserai. This was established by an Arab commander who, like most rulers of the day, claimed direct descent from the Prophet Mohammed. The most visible remnant of that era is **Märdäkän Pir**, the stone turbe-tomb of Tair Taj Al Huda Mardakani. It's guarded by a cross-eyed crone who can barely squeeze through the narrow entrance hole. Nonetheless she's all too eager to bless visitors by spooning dubious holy water into their mouths. A cache of gold

was found nearby along with a stone inscription demanding that the finder use the treasure to renovate the tomb. The actual finder decided to ignore this request and keep the loot. Few locals doubt that this behaviour brought upon him a curse as shortly afterwards he was left deformed and dumb by a mysterious stroke. Göylar means 'blues'. According to the friendly amateur historian who now cranks the low-tech petrol pumps at the northern edge of town, the people here were famed for their blue eyes and Shamakha men would raid the village to carry off beautiful brides across the Galni (blood) river in the valley below.

The surrounding hills hide many more pirs, each renowned more for its purported curative properties than its hazily remembered history. With the necessary time and enthusiasm you might seek out:

• **Shkhröb Baba** (madness), visually similar to Märdäkän pir, it's in an old Arab graveyard, about 30 minutes by 4WD along the Pir Saat river. It's so awkward to reach that a sub-shrine and collection box have been set up beside the main Märäzä–Shamakha road.

• **Pir Gasanov** (arthritis, leg problems).

• **Pir Abagdad** (general ailments), accessible but insignificant tomb in the cemetery just west of Göylar Çöl.

• **Zigir Pir** (skin problems) via Bagirli.

• **Keshtimas Baba** (skin problems) on Langabiz hill.

From Göylar Çöl a very degraded road continues south to eventually join the Kürdämir–Baku main road. Alternatively, a bearable but pot-holed asphalt road loops round to Ağsu passing south of **Orculu** (more blue-eyed people), **Bagirli** (hike to some of the pirs), Geshed,

Kechdimaz/**Büjo** (an oasis of green once famed for carpets) and **Kalkani**.

Shamakha to Ağsu

A much easier drive to Ağsu swings south 10km west of Shamakha (for Ismayıllı, Qäbälä, Shäki etc keep straight, see p204 onwards). The road winds down numerous hairpins through attractive woodlands and is lined with dozens of small restaurants and shashlyk barbecues in cosy little roadside glades.

Ağsu (☎ 0198)

Neat and well cared-for, Ağsu is an undistinguished provincial town with a fairly typical **historical museum**. Facing the derelict hulk of a never-finished government building is a gigantic flag-waving Rasulzade which appears to have been remodelled using parts of a former Lenin statue (a theory denied by locals). Basic but much better kept than other Soviet-era mini-hotels the little *Hotel Ağsu* (☎ 54247, AZN4 per person) has been repainted and provides new sheets on the contrastingly worn beds.

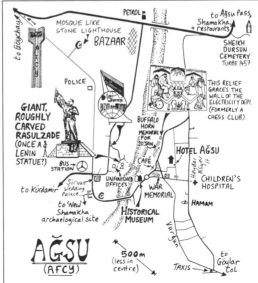

New Shamakha When Nadir Shah, the Persian 'Cromwell', destroyed Shamakha in 1734 he refused to allow the survivors to rebuild their city and forced them to resettle at a more controllable site on the plains. The move was unpopular and after Nadir's power waned, people started to drift back to Shamakha proper leaving 'New Shamakha' to fade away. All that's left are some antique graves and a dry moat enclosing some vague muddy undulations. The site is 2.8km from Ağsu: half a kilometre south of Uluclu village: turn left where an unpaved track crosses the drainage gully and proceed for 400m.

Ağsu to Kürdamir

As you head to Kürdamir, the dreary straight, flat road diverges slowly from a low dry ridge in the lee of which lie a number of small, unspectacular wine- and fruit-producing ex-*kolkhoz* farms. Die-hard enthusiasts might find some interest in tracking down forgotten tombs and turbes. The most attractive and accessible is the roofless 19th-century **Ağ Gümbäz tomb** where Khydayat Baba and Haji Niftali Shah are buried beside some willow trees at the far end of Qaraqoyunlu village.

Ağsu to Mingächevir

Most minibuses bound for north-western

Azerbaijan use the route via Shamakha, Ağsu, Yekäxana (see p210), Göychay (p244), Ağdash (p245) and Xaldan (p246). However, you can expect this to change once the upgrade of the less attractive main Baku–Älät–Kürdamir highway is complete.

SHAMAKHA TO ISMAYILLI
(see map opposite)

Within a kilometre of the Ağsu turn-off, the Shamakha–Shäki road tumbles down a series of hairpins into the Ağsu River valley giving marvellous views of a diverse patchwork of fields, mountain peaks and woodlands. The hairpins come straight back up the other side and the road then follows an increasingly forested ridge reminiscent of the Blue Ridge Parkway. There are several more clearings for panoramic views across towards Fit Dağ and the higher Caucasus mountains with a choice of attractively situated open-air places to stop for tea or shashlyk. Although the dining here is more modest than at equivalent places on the Shamakha–Ağsu road, the views are better. Of the possible side trips, Lahıc is the most popular, though Basqal is easier to reach.

Basqal (☎ 0178)

Famed for its silk weaving (now much reduced), Basqal village claims to have been one-time temporary home to two former presidents, Rasulzade and Elchibey! Today the narrow cobbled streets are pleasant, but beyond the eerily quiet central core the town's semi-agricultural suburbs are a little over punctuated with new homes to create a really atmospheric ensemble while full-on renovations have left the antique mosque looking effectively new. A pair of *hajis* were happy to show me the (normally locked) former hamam which functioned until the 1990s, with its blackened furnace-room walls in the cellar behind. Nearby is a massive *chinar* (plane tree) whose hollow trunk once made a handy tea house and later a barber's booth. At present it's 'preserved' ie not in use, though a smaller version still occasionally shades a tea table at which the white-beards sit meditatively clicking their prayer beads.

Ämräki Turbaza (map opposite) rents out so-so huts in a charming beech-wood

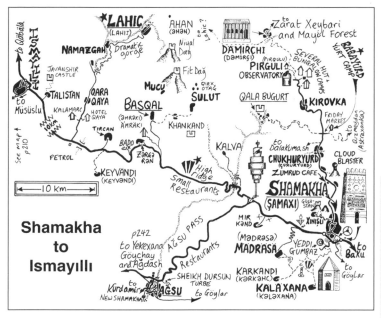

Shamakha to Ismayıllı

See map p210

clearing that's nice for a cup of tea even if you don't stay. It's 2km along a steep, narrow, once-asphalted track, reached via the first left turn when approaching Basqal from the Shamakha road.

Around Basqal
The spiky ridge of green-speckled mountains between here and Lahıc is reminiscent of France's Vercours region. **Mucu** was a Jewish village until the population was shifted by the Soviets to a kolkhoz near Shamakha. And **Sulut**, around 10km north-east of Basqal (by rocky 4WD track, river-bed drive and

BASQAL

FURNACE ROOM
EX HAMAM
HOLLOW ÇINAR

Narrow Cobbled Lane

to Sulut

SILK CO-OP
KIOSKS

4km to main road

hike), are the ruins of Haram Fortress also known as the '40 Rooms' (**Qirx Otağ**). At the first river fork bear left through meadows keeping to the right bank (the opposite side from Fit Dağ). The ruins are above the next fork, most easily accessed by heading to the right then scrambling back up to your left.

It was at a fortress atop **Fit Dağ** that the last Shamakha Khan staved off a Persian attack in 1806 and to which he again retired in the face of the approaching Russians. Guides in Lahıc can take you to the site on an interesting multi-day trek ending up in Basqal.

Towards Lahıc (☎ 0178)
Loveable Lahıc is 19km off the Shamakha–Ismayıllı route, signposted opposite a lonely petrol station. The landslide-prone route is currently useable by normal cars and scheduled to be fully asphalted soon. Near Qaraqaya there are a pair of rural resort-complexes more luxurious than anything in Lahıc itself. The sizeable new *Qaya Hotel*

SHAMAKHA–SHAKI ROUTE

(☎ mob 50-215 8090, from AZN80) is well equipped by rural hotel standards with good linen, clean if stark white décor and '70s retro-style furniture in the better AZN100 'luxe' rooms. However, there are no balconies and the rooms don't face the best direction for views. No air-con either. *Kalamarc* (☎ mob 050-730 2408, chalet AZN80-90) has vaguely upmarket cottages around a roadside clearing with a tendency to overheat. There's walking potential from Qaya.

Further north a long pedestrian suspension bridge quivers perilously across the river. It accesses a path towards Zärnava village, see 🖳 www.everytrail.com/view _trip.php?trip_id=56326 for an attractive hike description.

Some 11km from the main Baku–Qäbälä road, the Lahıc lane turns right, slithers along a ledge and passes attractive **Namazgah** where there's a mineral spring. Continue through a gorge of striking rocky pinnacles and vertical shale strata and notice the old shepherd's track clinging terrifyingly to the far side of the valley: until the 1980s that was the only access route to Lahıc!

Lahıc (Lahij/Lagich ☎ 0178)

Ancient Lahıc (commonly mispronounced 'La Heej') is one of Azerbaijan's most picturesque villages. It has a distant high-mountain backdrop and a photogenic cobbled main-street dotted with copper beaters' and blacksmiths' workshops. As one of a few places in Azerbaijan to draw a steady stream of summer tourists, the locals here are unusually foreigner-savvy making this a charmingly rural getaway where there's a decent chance of finding English-speaking assistance.

History Lahıc was founded well over a millennium ago by Persian-speaking settlers from Lahijan (hence the name) and even today the local dialect retains many elements of Farsi. Some claim that the site was chosen for the valley's medicinal cold springs but it was copper craft that became the population's trademark. Despite its inaccessibility, by the 18th century Lahıc was one of rural Azerbaijan's bigger settlements. As easily

processable local copper ore became exhausted, most of the copper used was 'recycled' from older unwanted or broken objects laboriously lugged across shepherd paths. By the late Soviet era copper was shipped in from Kelbajar (now under Armenian occupation) but locals claim that in the 1980s Soviet engineers had located a potential site for a new copper mine across the Girdmanchay river. They started building Lahıc's big, very visible 'bridge to nowhere' to connect with those potential mining sites but left it unfinished when the USSR collapsed. It was only belatedly completed in 2007. The new mines were never developed.

Things to see It's fun to seek out half a dozen **old mosques** and find the partly ruined **Haji Qurban mansion** whose interior courtyard was once a traders' market. However, the main attractions are the village **workshops**, **smithies** and **craft shops** along the **cobbled main street**. Every year these become more like tourist boutiques but for now several shops still combine their souvenir selling with genuine craftsmanship. You can still see old-fashioned pump bellows feeding the crucible fires and hear the tap tap tapping of finishing hammers shaping a range of traditional copperwork items (see box p208 for typical designs). Similar items show up in the little **museum** housed in the former Ağoğlu Mosque on Nizami St (a muddy track). A second mini-museum lurks in a walk-in cupboard behind one of the classrooms in the school. The proud principal is all too keen to disturb a strictly regimented lesson to show visitors in!

Note: when the copper workshops are closed (as many are most Sunday mornings) the premises are shuttered so effectively that it's impossible to distinguish them from other traditional houses.

Hikes A short, if bracing 1¼-hour hike takes you to **Niyal Castle ruins**. In the 10th century Niyal was described by Masudi as being the 'most firm of all the world's fortresses'. These days it's just a heap of stones but a good excuse to clean out the lungs and once you've found the main sheep-track pathway the route is

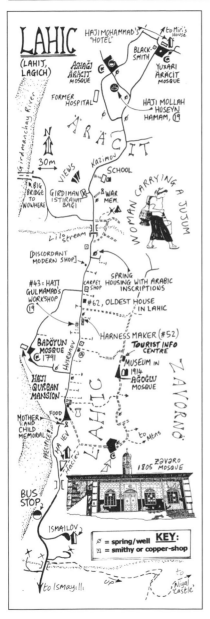

pretty obvious even without a guide. If you have a tent, many longer-distance treks (Babadağ, Fitdağ etc) are possible; guides and pack horses are usually fairly easy to engage through both the **tourist office** (☎ 77 571, 10-14.00 & 15-19.00 summer only) and Ismailov Homestay (see below).

Accommodation If you arrive in summer you're likely to find a selection of **homestay** options touting for your business. This is a great opportunity to experience Azeri village life and bed & breakfast rarely costs more than AZN15. Do double check whether or not the breakfast is included and remember that many homes don't (yet) have running water let alone indoor bathrooms. Out of season you'll need to knock on relevant doors or contact Dadash Aliyev (☎ 77303, ☎ mob 50-677 7517, ✉ dadashaliyev@yahoo.co.uk) who runs the tourist office and can make arrangements for you. Long-standing favourites (and friendly rivals) are the homes of the **Ismailov** (☎ 77 200) and **Hajiyev** (☎ 77357) families. Both families have English-speaking sons, though off season they're likely to be away working in Baku. The Ismailovs have a hamam and more English speakers. Both families and several others offer camping spaces. The nearest thing to a hotel in town is **Haji Mohammad's** (☎ 77494, ☎ mob 50-554 6174) with very simple twin rooms that share bathrooms which are, at least, indoors. Haji's daughters Zöhrä and Ruxsärä Ahädov speak some English. Off season the place is dormant but you can seek out the caretaker, Miri, and have the place spookily all to yourself for AZN20 per person. Six hotel-style rooms were under construction at the time of research above *Girdiman Istrahat Baği*, a garden restaurant from the edge of which are some fine tree-framed views towards the distant mountain horizon.

Transport Buses to Lahıc depart Ismayıllı at 07.00, 11.00 and 14:00

❏ Azerbaijani metalwork

Along with carpet-making, bronze and copper work are Azerbaijan's most developed handcrafts. For centuries, the forms of bowls, jugs and lamps have been formalized into the accepted styles depicted below, the best examples are ornamented with ornate etched or hammered design details – usually floral motifs or stylized 'Paisley' arabesques developed from ancient Zoroastrian symbolism.

During the 20th century copperware mostly drifted out of daily use, supplanted by cheaper ceramic and plastic alternatives albeit often using the same designs. Original metal items now fill local and national historical museums, but in traditional villages such as Kish and Lahıc women still used heavy copper jujums slung over their shoulders to collect water from the communal water sources. In Lahıc that era is likely to end within a year or two as long-delayed piped water supplies finally start reaching the houses.

Common designs (§ = depicted)

aftafa	Water jug for use where there's no toilet paper
aladdin §	Term used by Lahıc salesmen attempting to explain in English the function of a *chirax*.
ash-gazan	Rice tray for serving *plov*, covered with a *särpush*.
badya §	Bowl
chirax §	Long-armed paraffin lamp
dolcha §	Water jug
gaby §	Heavy-stemmed tankard/goblet used for serving sherbet
gazan	
hammamtasi	A type of cooking pot/urn for use in washing
jujum §	Heavy-duty water-carrying vessel. Also spelt *güyüm*.
kasa	Soup bowl (often ceramic)
kilab§	Long-stemmed water jug for ceremonial ablutions, notably wakes.
käfkir	Ladle
parch	Handled cup
piala	Small tea bowl
sähäng §	A more bulbous *jujum*
satyl §	Handled pot
särpush	Pointy-topped cover used to keep meals warm without dripping them with condensed steam.
tavar	Cast-iron cooking skillet.

CHIRAX

KILAB

SÄHÄNG

JUJUM (GÜYÜM)

SATYL

DOLCHA

GABY

BADYA

returning at 09.00, 13.00 and 16.00, shared taxis (rare) cost AZN2, or pay AZN15 for the whole car. A minibus to Baku leaves around 08.00 (four hours, AZN6) but reserving a seat the night before is wise.

ISMAYILLI (☎ 0178)

The thickly wooded mountains are majestic behind Ismayıllı and conceal at least two royal fortress ruins. However, the town itself has no special charm and is rather spread out.

Niyal Hotel (AZN4 per person) is central but appallingly decrepit. *Talistan Motel* (☎ 536 32) is not enormously better. The ground-floor rooms (AZN6/pp) share unlovely squat toilets, upstairs (AZN20 dbl) you get your own bathroom which is a mixed blessing. I've heard reports of a newer restaurant called *Mähsul* (☎ 51520) which apparently has acceptable cabins (around AZN40) at the south edge of town. However, sleeping in Lahıc is more interesting. The public transport options depart from a variety of pick-up points (see map) rendering the bus station virtually redundant except for services to Göychay.

AROUND ISMAYILLI
Talistan

Cavanshir Castle was an early Shirvan fortress first constructed in the 7th century. Two sections of very degraded ruins survive amid pretty forests in a bowl of valley around 3km beyond Talistan village (itself 2km off the Baku–Ismayıllı road). The track is so horribly

rutted and stream-cut that it's better to walk at least the last 2km. If you take a taxi from Ismayıllı to Talistan at dawn, there should be ample time to visit the ruins and get back for the last bus to Lahıc.

Ismayıllı to Qara Märyäm
(see map p210)

About 5km south-west of Ismayıllı, a side lane winds up 8km to the sprawling hilltop village of **Ivanovka**, now synonymous with Azerbaijan's cheapest vaguely drinkable wine. Ivanovka was founded by and is still populated by blue-eyed Russian Molokans. They continue a Soviet-style cooperative ownership of land and machinery and are reputed to produce the nation's best vegetables, dairy products and grapes. The village maintains its own little shop on Baku's Nizami St (p94, ∂L6) and its farmers are suspected to be the richest in Azerbaijan. For tourists the neat village offers no specific attractions (Molokans don't believe in churches) but the views are lovely driving back towards Ismayıllı.

Just before a village called 'Fish' (**Balıq**) side roads peel off to Ivanovka (above) and to the part-Jewish village of **Mücünäftärän** (Mijaftaran). Directly south there's a small restaurant at the southern end of Balıq-Göl lake ('Fish Lake'). Close beside the road as it curves around the attractive village of **Talish** is an old tile-roofed mill with a wooden waterwheel, somewhat obscured from view by trees.

SHAMAKHA–SHAKI ROUTE

**Talistan &
Cavanshir Castle**

Ashığ Bayramlı is named after a famous Armenia-born Sass player who resettled here while 10km beyond **Qara Märyäm** was the site of a major WWI skirmish on 17 June 1918.

A 2.3km detour east (on the Ağsu road) then 1.1km north, **Yekäxana** is a vaguely attractive village whose 'Tepe' (kurgan tumulus) has been the source of local superstitions following the alleged discovery of human bones and gold on the site. Visually it's just a muddy mound surrounded by houses.

South of Qara Märyäm, the road wiggles through some dry hills before dropping onto the featureless plain rejoining the main Baku–Gänjä road at Müsüslü. The bridge across the railway line here remains unfinished resulting in some bumpy improvised diversions.

ISMAYILLI TO QÄBÄLÄ

Scenic variety continues all the way to Qäbälä with many patches of thick, beautiful forest. Most 'historical sites' consist of very meagre stone-piles, though Häzrä does have four complete tomb towers. Delightful Qalaciq is better for mountain scenery.

Xänäyä Forest and Qız Qalası

The attractive village of Xänäyä (marked Xanagah on some maps) perches on the left

İsmayıllı to Qäbälä (42km)

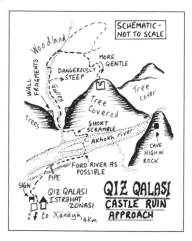

SCHEMATIC - NOT TO SCALE

QIZ QALASI CASTLE RUIN APPROACH

bank of the wide Akhokh river. The river's name is derived from the 'Ah's' and 'Oh's' of a tired khan who struggled trying to cross it. Or in different versions, the more desperate sighs of a distraught mother who had dropped her baby in its swift-flowing flood waters. A newly asphalted lane follows the river bank 4km to *Qız Qalası Isträhat Zonası* (☎ mob 50 613 6490, Anvar). A new hotel section is being built but for now all the bungalows are well spread out through lovely forests. The AZN100 versions are fairly impressive, carpeted with good bathrooms and a nard set provided. However, the AZN50 ones are cramped, over priced and too near the generator. Bring a torch to find your room at night.

A forest reserve officially begins on the riverbank directly north of the resort and some visitors report that they have been prevented from proceeding beyond. However, assuming you can go on, a pleasant half-hour ramble takes you up to the 11th-century **Qız Qalası** (Maiden's Tower) 'fortress'. It's nothing more than a heavily ruined pile of white stones almost entirely hidden within the ash and beech woods on a knoll on the far side of the river. But the hike to reach it involves the fun of fording the river (not feasible after rain) and scrambling up leaf-covered slopes having walked up a very charming stream gully.

Qalacıq

A side lane through **Sumaqallı** was recently asphalted for 4km as far as the ***Green House Resort*** (☎ mob 50-342 1443, photos on 🖳 www.nyusfera.com/tourism.php), three comfy but oversized new hotel blocks which go for the straight, suburban look and lack any local flavour or sensitivity to the otherwise charmingly rustic environment. Rooms cost AZN100-130, bungalows AZN60-70, there's a clover-leaf-shaped summer swimming pool and a restaurant that hides its lack of décor beneath a barrage of over-loud music.

Beyond, the road is unsurfaced and pretty rough in places. Despite the name, **Istisu** ('hot water') has no known thermal springs. Its name apparently derives from a large wooden public bath that once graced the centre of the village.

Qalacıq village is a particularly delightful pastiche of tree-shaded lanes where white-beards in their 'aerodrome' caps sit with their backs to dramatic views over the wide, deep-cut river valley. Distant mountains rise in tempting arrays beyond. If you have a day or two to spare there's great hiking up to the bald-headed peak of Qaraburga and a waterfall en route. A possible trail north-east from Istisu leads to the top of Babadağ.

Back on the main road near Sumaqallı, ***Vändam ZI*** (mob ☎ 50-421 2444) offers reasonable AZN50-100 new huts in the mossy roadside forest but suffers from car noise. (NB Despite the name it isn't in Vändam but 7km east opposite the fortress-

style construction that marks the Qäbälä Rayon boundary).

Häzrä (Həzrə, map p212)

Don't confuse this village with Häzrä in Qusar district (p191) nor with Häzrät Baba (a pir on top of Mt Babadağ).

Meaning 'holy presence', Häzrä village is interesting for the overgrown cemetery whose mossy trees conceal four classical pointy-topped stone turbes. At least one of these was constructed by master builder Shamsaddin of Shamakha in 1572. Another has been dated 1446. However, some claim that the occupants had lived centuries earlier, possibly four brothers who arrived during the Arab invasions. Locals claim that the Soviet regime had once discussed selling the Häzrä tombs to an undisclosed Arab state. The sale finally fell through, perhaps because the underground 'treasure vault' (which was supposed to provide funds for the maintenance of such turbe) was found to have been looted long before – by Armenians if you believe very partisan villagers. The tombs were heavy-handedly renovated in 2007.

The site is 2km off the main road on an unsigned dirt track through a cornfield gap in the woodland. Turn south 4km east of Vändam at 40°55'47.5"N, 47°58'50.5"E. Alternatively, coming from the east, turn where 'Həzrə 4km' is signed off the main road at 40°55'20"N, 47°59'43"E. You'll wiggle through **Bunut** village and will have two alternatives for crossing Häzrä village. The more northerly one crosses a very precarious bridge that's unsuitable for anything heavier than a Lada Zhiguli.

The turbes are in woodland accessed by a foot path that starts at a little wooden stile at 40°54'44"N, 47°57'51"E.

SHAMAKHA-SHAKI ROUTE

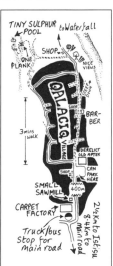

TINY SULPHUR POOL / to Waterfall / SHOP / ONE PLANK / NICE VIEWS / QALACIQ VILLAGE / SHOP / BAR-BER / 3 mins walk / DERELICT OLD APTEK / CAN PARK HERE / SHOP / SMALL SAWMILL / CARPET FACTORY / 400m / Truck/bus stop for main road / 2½km to İsfisu / 8·4km to main road

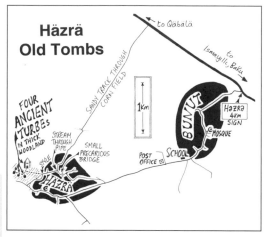

Häzrä
Old Tombs

to Qäbälä

Ismayıllı to Baku

SANDY TRACK THROUGH CORN FIELD

1Km

FOUR ANCIENT TURBES in THICK WOODLAND

STREAM THROUGH PIPE

SMALL PRECARIOUS BRIDGE

STILE

HÄZRÄ

BUNUT

Häzrä 4km SIGN

MOSQUE

POST OFFICE

SCHOOL

Vändam (☎ 0160) (see map p215)

The hill which rises to the west of the Häzrä turn-off is crowned by *Girvä Restaurant* (☎ mob 50-503 1261, Xalid) where you can enjoy AZN2 kebabs and 60q beers on a long terrace with fabulous sweeping views. At the rear are three interlinked windowless **guest rooms** (AZN30 dbl) should you drink too much to drive on.

Just beyond is a bustling little roadside market selling fruit, nuts and conserves including pickled walnuts and the tart plum sauce *alcha turshusu*. This is Vändam village whose name derives from 'Min dam' (1000 houses) rather than homage to Jean-Claude 'muscles from Brussels'. Vändam offers several decent accommodation options and makes a preferable alternative to Qäbälä Laza as an end point for the two-day hike from Xınalıq. Heading *to* Xınalıq from here is tougher as it's not so easy to rent pack horses, though you could try by asking at the recommended *Duyma Hotel* (☎ 91600, ☎ mob 050-346 0888, 🖳 www.duyma-hotel .com, dbl/tr from AZN70/90). That's hidden at 40°59'12"N, 47°57'15"E, ie at the very back of Vändam right at the trailhead but 5km down rough tracks from Ibrahim Petrol on the main road (taxis want AZN5!). The well-equipped rooms (AZN70-140) are bright with art to give you nightmares and

jugs of fresh spring water to wake you from them. Some staff even speak English and claim to take credit cards (I didn't test that). There's a big if unflashy summer swimming pool and an eccentric kids' play area.

Vändam has three other hotels near the river-bridge. Follow the concrete camels 400m up the riverbank from there to *Semerana IM* (☎ 91117). It has a good open-air swimming pool and a little artificial stream flowing between comfortable two-storey houselets. The rooms (AZN100-120) open with car-style keys, feel comparatively luxurious but have relatively small bathrooms. Neman speaks some English.

Nearer the bridge *Yeddi Gözel* (☎ mob 50-674 8426, AZN60-120) has some odd triangular-shaped rooms near its swimming pool but the generator and disco noise can be disturbing and the paint is already bubbling on the walls. *Selbasar* seems shamelessly overpriced with bare floorboards, share-pair bathrooms and bad construction.

Seven Beauties

Almost opposite the latter two hotels, a small, progressively degenerating lane leads north, dead-ending after a somewhat confusing 3.5km. Continue 200m on foot to reach the quaint open-air *Seven Beauties Waterfall Restaurant* (map p215) with open-air tables ranged idyllically on the ledges of a multi-level cascade. Some summers the place stays closed if the road gets too bad but even then it's an attractive scramble up to the waterfall's higher levels.

QÄBÄLÄ (QƏBƏLƏ, QEBELE, KUTKASHEN, GABALA; ☎ 0160)

Like Shamakha, Qäbälä is one of the most ancient towns in Azerbaijan. But misleadingly the present site is over 20km from the original Qäbälä citadel which now stands as a lonely, lumpy ruin south of Mirzäbäylı (see Old Qäbälä p217).

The present town, called Kutkashen till 1991, was the home town of Ismailbey Kutkashenli, the first Azeri commander in the Tsarist Russian army. Qäbälä's centre is Times Sq (Saat Yani) but don't dream of Manhattan. The town's a modest, mainly low-rise place with some older stone-built courtyard homes in the northern quarter of town and a Soviet-era **mosaic** mural that gives the cultural centre a colourful dazzle. The 19th-century **mosque** was reconstructed in 1983 but has only welcomed the faithful since 2006 having been used as a museum in the interim. It has a typical collonaded side and a tall minaret that twinkles with golden fairy lights at night.

The new **History Museum** (40q, closed Mon) is accessed through a merrily kitschy Stone-Age-effect gateway. Its exhibits include coins from ancient Antioch and other curiosities found at old Qäbälä whose original appearance is shown in an

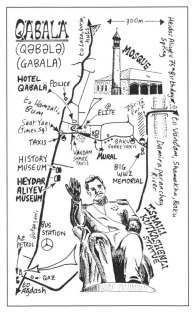

artist's impression model. There's a curious photo of an apple from which an image of Imam Ali supposedly sprang in a Lourdes-like miracle.

Next door the **Heydar Aliyev Museum** (free) has a grand modernist chandelier. Whatever one's cynical view of such typically hagiographic places, somehow the video of costumed children kissing the old president manages to embody the spirit of the times when the nation's future really did seem to depend entirely on this one man.

Entering Qäbälä from the east there are some really lovely mountain views (north-west) while to the south, the strange great concrete lump on a distant hill is not a huge Soviet monument but Qäbälä Radio Location Station (see RLS, p216).

Hotel Qäbälä (☎ 52408, 🖳 http://qeb elewelcomesyou.wordpress.com, sgl/dbl AZN40/60) has been extensively remodelled and at first glance appears fairly plush. However, corridors stay unlit, the showers barely run warm and the miniscule sachets of shampoo provided could claim a world record for worst product-to-packaging ratio. Nonetheless, the rooms have been comfortably refurbished and the staff are remarkably obliging.

There are several central places selling 10q piraşqi and a little *garden restaurant* opposite Hotel Qäbälä has beers from 60q. *Elite Club* has willow-shaded tea tables and an Internet room.

Frequent **shared taxis** shuttle up and down Qutqashenli St from Saat Yani past the museums and bus station to the bazaar. Some continue past Gilan Hotel to Zarağan circle whence shared taxis depart when full to Nic (80q). Services from the bus station include Baku (up to thrice hourly via Shamakha), Gänjä (08.00, 08.30), and Shäki (09.00, 12.00, three hours) via Oğuz. There are special share taxi stands for Vändam (60q) and Baku.

Accommodation around Qäbälä (see map p215)
Towards Shäki Slightly better kept than the outwardly similar Hotel Qäbälä is *Hotel Gilan* (☎ 52408), 5km south.

The corridors feel a bit like you're in an office block, but the rooms (dbl AZN50, suite AZN70) have minibars, toiletries, excellent enclosed shower booths and 500-channel TV. A few AZN20 singles lack air-con. Xaqani at reception speaks English.

Towards Laza The big, new *Qafqaz Resort* (☎ 54200, 💻 http://caucasresortho tel.net) is Qäbälä's swankiest hotel with rooms from AZN79 (AZN79 at weekends), bungalows AZN149 (AZN169) and a presidential suite for AZN1000 including butler service and 'surprise gifts'.

Spread across a considerable area of pretty woodland and around a central grassy clearing *Pavilyon Xanlar* (☎ 51799) has a range of styles and prices, mostly good value. The AZN100 three-room cottages have their own fireplaces. The best deal is in the divided AZN40 bungalow-rooms where balconies survey the river. They're far from the noisy generator but you may need to bring a torch to find your way through the mossy forest. The ever-popular restaurant has a little water-chime and consistently good food.

Ay Ishağı (☎ 50901) has a pleasant if not pristine setting between two rivers with strolling deer and ponds providing fresh fish for the fairly priced restaurant. Average bungalows (AZN80) sleep five. Simple AZN30-40 triple rooms in the main building have bathroom and toiletries but the carpets are very wrinkled.

The vaguely dysfunctional *Çanlibel* (☎ 51934, from AZN30) is set back on the wrong side of the river. *Soyuq Bulaq* (☎ 51025) has three creaky AZN40-50 bungalows with an outdoor sitting area but the grounds are ragged and the staff proved less than friendly.

Towards Vändam Popular restaurant *Sahil* (mob ☎ 50 668 1568) is set above a reservoir lake where families rent AZN5 boats for a weekend paddle. The food is good but the AZN50-90 cottages are fly-blown and lacklustre and the AZN20 rooms very basic. Duyma and Semerana in Vändam (p212) are better.

NORTH OF QÄBÄLÄ (map opposite)
Durja
Founded in the 19th century as a summer pasture village for shepherds from Dağestan, Durja is now only seasonally inhabited. Between October and May it is totally deserted as resident shepherds move with their flocks to lowland winter pastures.

In a bracken-speckled amphitheatre, Durja's pastoral setting doesn't have Laza's panoramic approach. However, its antique houses climb steeply between walnut trees looking more attractive than those of Laza's mud-cobbled maze. Most are red tiled, stone-walled and built in short, raked rows with wooden balconies and ogee-arched fireplaces on the lower storeys. At least one now ruinous home had an 'escape window' which would formerly have been hidden by carpets and through which fugitives could have 'disappeared' at times of trouble.

Durja is a delightful place to relax, stroll and watch the charcoal burners. Or you could get the shepherd folk to show you the steep paths through the woods up to the high grasslands where there are sweeping views of the high Caucasus (allow approx 7-8hrs up and back).

Durja is 3km from the Qafqaz Resort (see column opposite), a pleasant walk or a pretty bumpy car ride taking nearly 20 minutes on a stony track that peters out by an ancient cemetery in which a few graves have gnarled wooden 'headstones'.

Laza (Qäbälä Laza)
From Qafqaz Resort a very poor mud-track leads 4km to Laza – along the banks of the infamously powerful Damiraparanchay ('iron gets washed away') River. Sheep-mown meadows rise on the opposite bank and soaring distant peaks to the north remain snow dusted even in mid-summer. Picturesque little Laza (different from the Laza on p189) is potentially very cute. Sadly the access road is often impassable by vehicle and the officious *Gümrük/Tamozhna* (Customs Department) treats visitors with unguarded suspicion making passport checks likely and a full interrogation possible. In addition, the village's location on the 'wrong' side of the deep, ice-

cold Damiraparanchay River means that tough hikes to the 54m Mucuk Falls and Xınalıq must start and finish by an awkward ford (you'll probably need a horse). All in all you'd be better to start cross-Caucasus hikes from Vändam instead.

NORTH-WEST OF QÄBÄLÄ
(see map p218)
Hämzäli

A quaint village with a pir/cemetery set in dark woods, Hämzäli is known locally for its excellent *halva*. Unlike Shäki halva, this is not a glorified paxlava, but more like nougat made with either roasted nuts (*göz*) or sesame seeds (*kunjut*). Its production is very much a cottage industry. Rövshan sells his informally from his house: the first rusty gate on the muddy lane that curves away to the south from the gates at the back of the school.

Bum

Most visitors only venture to Bum to take snigger-worthy photographs of the town sign. Sadly the joke isn't quite as funny when you realise the name should be pronounced 'Boom'. According to questionable interpretations of Movses Kaghankatvatsi's *History of Albania*, a few (generally Armenian) historians believe that Bum rather than Kish (p227) was the site of St Elisey (Elishe)'s first-century church. There's little proof to back this up however, and certainly no visible sign of great antiquity.

The village is famed for its traditional dance troop 'Zopu Zopu' which originally formed here in 1981. The group has reportedly split but might re-form and a children's troop still practises. Try calling mob ☎ 050 541 5718 or asking at the Department of Culture in Qäbälä for more information.

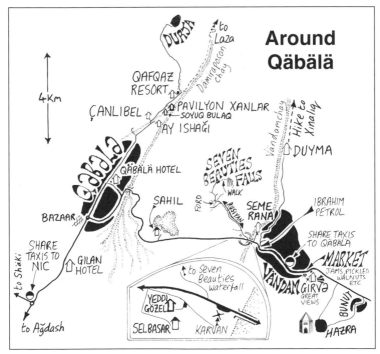

Continuing west from Bum is tough as there's a wide river to ford and water becomes dangerously deep after rain. Alternatively, there's a track to Xirxatala (without doubling back to Hämzäli) where a rough once-asphalted lane leads to the Shäki road. Allow plenty of time.

❏ Cads in Qamarvan

Yeld and Baker's 1890 experience:
There was one gentleman about the premises who ... had been sent to Kamaroffka into banishment for having killed two men. We thought it possible that this caitiff might visit our room and accordingly we prepared a trap at either door – an effective precaution, as it turned out, for in the dim light of early morning we were all aroused by the noise of overturned tins and platters, and distinguished the homicidal varlet, who made some excuses and hastily withdrew.

Qamarvan (Kamaroffka)

Bum's mountain backdrop is dramatic and the view should be even better from Qamarvan (Kamaroffka). According to Yeld and Baker's Alpine Club report of their 1890 climbing expedition, the 'view of Mt Bazardüzü from here resembles that of the Jüngfrau from Interlaken'. Sadly any such views have been obscured by clouds each time I've visited. The setting is certainly lovely though the village itself is an unfocused sprawl of metal-roofed homes. The road peters out in an impressively wooded gorge leading north which reputedly leads to a hot spring (Istisu) and a magnificent overlook if the soldiers allow you to go that far. Returning to Bum there are some very sweeping views over the plains below.

SOUTH OF QÄBÄLÄ
Qäbälä Radio Location Station (RLS)

This curious concrete carbuncle was built in 1985 as part of the USSR's missile defence radar-tracking system. Leased to Russia post independence, the RLS was in particu-

larly heavy use during the US invasion of Iraq in 2003 despite yelps of protests from environmentalists and opposition politicians who claim that it's a major cause of unexplained illnesses in local villages. One report quoted by *AzerNews* claimed babies were being born with strange deformities and that up to 90% of the 18- to 35-year-old population of nearby Amirvan/Amili village have malignant tumours that might be linked to radiation emitted by the facility. In 2007 the site made international news when Russian premier Vladimir Putin offered the US partial use of the station as an alternative to what Russia saw as a politically provocative US move to build missile-watching stations in Eastern Europe.

The RLS is a prominent landmark but is certainly not open to visitors. Snooping around or asking too many questions may raise suspicions as it's not the sort of thing tourists are 'meant to' be interested in. Saying that you're looking for the old Armenian cemetery on the hillside below is not likely to help! Somewhere nearby are the circular foundations of Böyük Amili ancient Albanian church.

Kyomarat Baba

This pointy-topped mausoleum perched on a dominating hilltop commemorates a local Muslim holy man, Seyid Ko Murad Ibn Ali Talib, whose black marble tombstone lies within. The monument looks intriguing spied from a distance but close to it's a rather ham-fisted new construction worth visiting only for the wonderful views. Some claim that the site was originally occupied by an Albanian church, but if so there are no visible remnants. In dry weather a Lada Zhigouli can miraculously get up the earthen tracks to within about five minutes' walk of the summit (20AZN return from Qäbälä). However, after a little rain the surface turns to squirming mud and then even a 4WD is unlikely to make it.

Access is from the Qäbälä–Ağdash road. Turn west 200m south of **Hacialılı**, beside the black, long-closed 'Chaichi Buffet' café. The road becomes a concrete-slab tank track and heads through Charxand village. It narrowly bypasses **Dızaxlı**

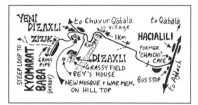

(Düzağli) where an old, three-storey *bey*'s house is claimed by wildly exaggerating locals to be 1000 years old. Note that looping from Yeni Dızaxlı to Old Qäbälä is no longer possible as the bridge between Chuxur Qäbälä and the archaeological site has collapsed: you'll have to return via the A15.

QÄBÄLÄ TO SHÄKI (see map p218)
The remarkably quiet A10 to Shäki passes close to the ruins of Old Qäbälä, to the former Albanian Catholicos of Nic and the curious town of Oğuz with its lovely mountain backdrop. Mountain views get even better after Oğuz, especially near Muxas, and there are plenty more minor attractions if you have time to seek them out.

The site of Old Qäbälä
Pliny describes 'Kabalaka' (Old Qäbälä) as 'a prominent town in Albania' and it remained a major fortress city for more than a millennium. In the 10th and early 11th centuries the town was ruled by the ethnic Arab descendants of Anbasa al-Avar who called it Khazar City. They were engaged in a series of wars with the neighbouring Shirvan who later absorbed the mini state as a vassal.

In 1386 Timur used Qäbälä as a military camp and it was briefly the refuge of Shirvan Shah Farrukh Yasar who regrouped his forces here after Shamakha had fallen to Safavid Shah Ismail Xatai in 1500. The Safavids soon grabbed Qäbälä too, and further fortified the town which became something of a pawn in the constant Turko-Iranian wars.

By the 18th century Qäbälä had regained autonomy but Khan Surkhay made the mistake of quarrelling with Persian expansionist Nadir Shah. Nadir

first attacked the town in 1732 and returned in 1742 to finish the job. Old Qäbälä was completely destroyed. It never recovered and a series of floods in the 1830s drove away the few remaining villagers. Remarkably the site was lost altogether until rediscovered by Azeri archaeologists in 1959, just across the river from Chuxur Qäbälä.

For all its historical significance, most of the site is about as interesting as an overgrown football pitch. The nearest thing to a 'star attraction' is a pair of powerful round brick-tower stubs. Suitably massive these once formed the gateway to the 'Qala' section of the city. But the rest of Qala is just a bare field, albeit with some nice mountain panoramas. Selbir is visually similar to Qala but with even less masonry: you'd never guess that it once had no fewer than 17 towers. A short drive or 12-minute walk across the Qala site, Kyamal Tepe is so overgrown that a machete might help you reach the excavation sites. A *kupe* amphora full of human bones found here is now displayed in Qäbälä Museum.

The pointy-tipped monument that you might spot on the distant peak is Kyomarat Baba (see opposite).

Lonely little **Qala Sälbir Kafesi** is a pretty little pondside café amid trees where Arif (mob ☎ 50-396 5246) is happy to show off the remarkable collection of coins, some very ancient, that he's fished out of the Old Qäbälä mud over the years.

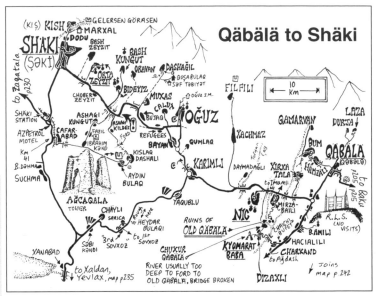

Nic (Needj, Nidshe)

Very ancient Nic was mentioned by Ptolomy and was the Catholicos (spiritual centre) of the Albanian Christian church from the 11th century. It is the only village in Azerbaijan which retains a substantial population of Udi people (65%) – an ethnic group who still consider themselves Christian, though other Christians might not easily recognize the fact. Historians trace the Udi to a warrior tribe who attacked southern Mesopotamia (today's Iraq). They were later driven back into Azerbaijan where they became a major force within the multi-ethnic make up of Christian Albania. The churches here maintained their Albanian-Christian masses right up until 1836 when the synod of St Petersburg coerced them into accepting Armenian priests.

In the Soviet era Nic's last Christian pastor was banished to Siberia but was allowed a brief trip home for good behaviour. While back in Nic the mayor forged his death certificate so the pastor could avoid returning to icy exile and instead go back to preaching, albeit underground. Or so the story goes.

Anthropologists are interested in the Udis' semi-animist reverence for fire *(arukh)* and the sun *(b'gh)*: an Udi swears an oath by invoking b'gh rather than by touching a Bible or Koran.

Nic sprawls along a considerable network of winding, mostly muddy lanes with almost every house hidden at the back of a tree-filled garden. Tucked away within this maze are three old churches. The **Göykilsa** and **Bulun** churches are described locally as 'Echmiadzin' (ie they followed the move to an Armenian-style faith in 1836) and both remain in atmospheric states of ruin. However, **Chotari Church**, considered pure Albanian due to the floral cross motif above its door, has been fully renovated. Still considered holy, though more as a *pir* than a place of worship, the 'bird stone' outside remains waxy with votive candles and you might find the doors hung with strips of coloured prayer-cloth.

Nic has two 'centres' where men while away the mornings: one is opposite school #5 but the bigger one is at the war memorial junction where there are a few shop-

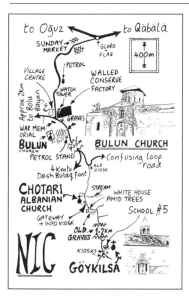

The week's focus is the big **Sunday market**, held near the Qäbälä–Oğuz road junction (turning at 40°56'33"N, 47°51'04"E). There is no sign of the 'massive portals' of a caravanserai noted by English visitors a century ago.

Elsewhere near Nic is a small 19th-century arched **stone spring-font** (Dash Bulaq) and hidden in a garden is the attractive arched façade of **Bolu Bayin Evi**, the house of a former Bey.

Kärimli

This small junction town, formerly known as Chelibi, was once a major stopping point on the northern caravan route. British mountaineers Yeld and Baker stayed in a very substantial caravanserai here in 1890 but this has completely vanished like its equivalent in Nic. Apart from two 2-3km rough sections, the road south to Xanabad (and thus to Mingächevir) is in passable condition. Northbound FROM Xanabad there are some superb mountain views across sweeping expanses of flower-filled fields (best in early May, see Heydar Bulaqi photo: C12 top R).

Filfili

A couple of kilometres beyond Filfili some degraded wall remnants of 18th-century stone Churxay Qalasi watchtower. The

kiosks, a mini-restaurant serving pork chops and a çayxana. If you speak Azeri or Russian, the latter is a good place to seek out Zhora Kechari, head of the Udi Cultural centre and a great authority on local history and monuments.

❑ Udi

There remains a mild tension between Nic's Muslim Azeri population and their pig-producing Udi co-citizens. In Soviet days, claim Nic Azeris, Udis were allocated land on the basis of 50 nut trees per son. Azeris got only 20 nut-trees worth! Udis were apparently excused military service (their loyalty being in doubt) so they didn't have the expense of maintaining them in the service (or bribing them out of it!). And it surely didn't help in the 1990s that Udi names look confusingly similar to Armenian ones, often ending ...*ian*. Some Udis are still suspected of being Armenians in disguise! The communities are not exactly antagonistic. But neither are they intermarrying any more.

The Udi language, considered to be related to Caucasian Albanian, is not only different from Azeri but it also has its own 53-letter alphabet. An Udi Bible reportedly exists in a collection in Cambridge, UK. Some words in Udi are:

Hello	*Khé gambai*	How are you?	*Hetarnu*
Fine	*Shad*	Not so well (bad)	*Pees*
Thank you	*Dris baka*		

(See pp373-4 for Udi numbers)
An interesting source site is 🖥 www.lrz-muenchen.de/~wschulze/udinhalt.htm.

16.00 bus from Oğuz runs via sizeable Xachmaz village and terminates where the Filfili bridge has been washed away.

Oğuz (Vartashen; ☎ 0111)

The Oğuz were the first major Turkic tribe to settle in Azerbaijan. However, Oğuz the village is misleadingly a recent rename for Vartashen – a village that was, until the 1980s, a curious ethnic mix of Udi (see Nic p218), Armenians and mountain Jews.

During a three-year experiment in the 1930s, Vartashen school kids were given the option of studying in the Udi language (see box p219). However, during the inter-ethnic conflicts of the early 1990s most Udi residents fled, fearing they might be 'mistaken for Armenians'. Roughly 500 of the Jewish community decided to stay and two **synagogues** are now operative (on Dalan 1, and at A. Aliyev 27), though architecturally they're hardly distinguishable from other town houses.

The town is basically a pair of converging roads with the bazaar two-thirds of the way up. At the upper end of town, an attractive old stone church is used as the local studies **museum**. Just to the north, at the back of the Abdullayev Hospital compound, is a second three-domed **chapel** whose ruins you can enter by crawling in under the overhanging foliage.

Above town, 2.5km beyond the hospital, *Oğuz Istirahät Märkäzi* (☎ 53545, ☎ mob 50-599 2665) has five new pine cottages (AZN80-100) in a delightful mossy forest setting. The cottages have two or three rooms apiece, big double beds, small tiled bathrooms and nice balconies but minimal décor. Prices are very fair at the on-site restaurant. Whether you stay or not, this is an ideal trailhead for strenuous forest treks up to the mountains behind – some of Azerbaijan's

most glorious. It takes around seven hours to the nearest peak-top following a thickly forest ridge spine whose fine mature trees make this *Lord of the Rings* territory. A shorter 2-hour hike brings you to a quartet of mini waterfalls (reputedly accessible by tough 4WD). For either a guide would be useful. Campers report seeing 'scarily large droppings but no bears as yet'.

The bus station has a handy **left-luggage service** (20q). **Buses** run to Baku (10/day, AZN6), Gänjä (08.00, 9.20), Qäbälä (08.00, 15.00), Shäki (09.00, 10, 12, 15 and 17.00, 80q), Dashagıl (16.00, 17.00) and Filfili (16.00). Village bus services generally drop passengers near the bazaar and might collect there too and thus be almost full on arrival at the bus station.

Muxas and Dashağil (map p218)

In the wooded hills that back on to **Muxas** are the ruins of a 14th-century stone tower (*bashnia*). In the village itself a stone pillar-plinth sits awaiting the return of its long-lost Lenin bust. Maybe Heydar could help? Twelve rough but Lada-passable kilometres beyond the village marked on maps as Daşağıl is locally pronounced **Dashağlı**. Several of its old stone houses have two-in-one gate-doors like in Kish (p227). Its mosque is reputedly one of the region's oldest but a missile minaret and shiny corrugated roofing date from a 2005 rebuild that has left only the qibla niche showing any real sign of antiquity. The views up the wide river bed north of the village tempt one to trek into the high mountains but there are usually soldiers posted here to stop you going any further towards Russia.

Around 800m south of Dashağil bridge notice the Uğan tunnel cave cut into uplifted strata across the river. Another 1km south is a grassy side valley with two attractive-

OĞUZ ISTIRAHÖT MƏRKƏZI

ABDULLAYEV HOSPITAL 1·5KM

CHAPEL RUIN

MUSEUM CHURCH

BAZAR

Heydar Aliyev

A. Əliev

Dalan 1

SYNAGOGUE

WWII MEM.

MOSQUE

BUS STA

to Main Road

Oğuz

ly located but significantly overpriced rest zones. *Säf Täbiyät* (☎ mob 50 575 6349) has horizon views of layered rock and forest ridges but the pink-purple-turquoise huts (AZN70) have wonky toilets and mattresses that feel a little damp. Still it's much better than the pitiful converted container-boxes for which *Qoşa Bulaq* asked me AZN50. AZN5 maybe!

Aydinbulaq

Far from the main road, the lonely, shattered 12-13th century **Ağcaqala** watch-tower stands 8m tall in a bramble patch between Aydinbulaq and Kishlaq Dashalı. Variously (and inaccurately) known as Qız Qalası or Torpaq Qala by locals, it was thought to have had a role in managing the caravan traffic passing through this section of the silk route. Today the peaceful spot is an obvious ten-minute trudge across ploughed fields from the upper road. The area would be a pleasant driving loop if the

road were better but all those puddles and potholes are off-putting.

Fazil

Shäki tourist brochures advertise a prehistoric '**Labarynth**' in Fazil village. Great marketing but forget the Minotaur. In fact the site is a small Bronze-Age tumulus that has been partly excavated and covered for protection by brick vaulting. While the site is pretty small the presentation is impressive with some pottery discoveries left 'half discovered' in the earth. Labels are in English and Azeri and when there's no electricity the visit by candle-light adds atmosphere. The twice-daily **Ashagi Kungut/Ibrahimkand** bus from Shäki passes within 300m of the site (the driver can show you where). If you're very quick there's just about time to see the site before the same bus passes by again on the way back to Shäki around 20 minutes later. But you'll need to be sure that the caretaker (Farman Mammedov ☎ 91144)

❏ Foothill churches

In the Albanian era the mountain foothills were dotted with monastic settlements and churches. Several very ancient ruins still exist. Although less impressive than at upper Läkit (p233) and less complete than at Qum (p232) or Kish (p227), it's fun just tracking down these long forgotten 6th-century stone structures. There are two in **Bideyiz** and one in **Bash Kungut** (where you could also seek out the 'lost' ruins of 5th-century Hazret Ali tower). The lower Bideyiz church has some finely finished masonry. It sits on a lovely grassy hillside a kilometre from the village. There's no road but you can drive across the grass and the site should be very conspicuous if the fog lifts! There are two more church

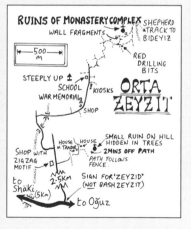

RUINS OF MONASTERY COMPLEX SHEPHERD

WALL FRAGMENTS — TRACK TO BIDEYIZ

⊢500m⊣

RED DRILLING BITS

STEEPLY UP ↑

SCHOOL KIOSKS **ORTA ZEYZIT**

WAR MEMORIAL

SHOP

HOUSE w. TANDIR HOUSE SMALL RUIN ON HILL HIDDEN IN TREES

SHOP WITH ZIG ZAG MOTIF 2 MINS OFF PATH

PATH FOLLOWS FENCE.

to Shäki (5km)

2.5KM

SIGN FOR 'ZEYZID' (NOT BASH ZEYZIT)

to Oğuz

ruins in **Orta Zeyzit**. The lower chapel is roughly formed and very decayed, although you can still make out the walls and doorway. Somewhat more complete and retaining its creamy stone facing, the upper monastery church is now used as a hay-barn by the encroaching village. In their childhood, local whitebeards remember a whole complex of 1300-year-old buildings here but these have been progressively cannibalized for their building stone and the ground re-used for farm housing.

actually has the key and is waiting for you! You'd be wiser to pre-arrange a visit with archaeologist Näsif Muxtarov in Shäki.

SHÄKI (Şəki, Sheki, Nukha; ☎ 0177)

Voluptuously rounded mountains generously slavered with thickly layered forest rise behind Azerbaijan's most inviting historic town. With attractive royal palace(s!), a sea of old tiled roofs, speciality silks and confectionery and the chance to stay in a real caravanserai, it's hardly surprising that Shäki is provincial Azerbaijan's main tourist draw. Yet it's a remarkably quiet, relaxed place whose citizens are renowned for their laconic sense of humour: ask anyone to tell you a few Haji Dayi jokes. There's a gaggle of internet clubs, a theatre, an Olympic centre with big pool and plenty of tempting excursions. The food is good, accommodation fairly priced and temperatures are especially pleasant in spring and early summer (though winters are cold and foggy). All in all Shäki makes a great long weekend getaway, or an ideal break in a Tbilisi–Baku journey.

History

Shäki has had a swashbuckling history. It grew rich as a market centre linking Dağestan mountain traders with the main east–west Caucasian commercial route. Then, in the 1740s under upstart leader Haji Cheläbi, Shäki thumbed its nose up at the ruling Persians and braced itself for retribution. Legend says that the Shah sent a battalion demanding to know who was foolhardy enough to deny Persian sovereignty and Cheläbi's answer was 'gelersen göräsen' (come and see for yourself), a name thereafter given to his mountain fortress (see p228) which miraculously survived the Persian onslaught. The town itself was not so lucky – 30 years later most of the homes were washed away by a disastrous flood of the River Kish and the town centre moved to its present position around Cheläbi's second fortress, Nukha. As a khanate, Shäki retained its independent status into the 1820s although the town was known as Nukha up until 1968.

Information

The **tourist office** (☎ 46094, 🖥 tic_ sheki@ box.az, 09-13.00, 14-18:00 Mon-Fri) was

dormant for some time. However, it has been relaunched under former Caravanserai manager Näsib Imamaliyev who speaks English and German and is likely to inspire a bit more dynamism. They currently sell bearable AZN1 town maps and flimsy AZN5 pamphlet-brochures. A somewhat better *Girdman Guide to Shäki* costs AZN10 from Saray Hotel whose friendly English-speaking receptionists are also a great potential source of help.

What to see and do

Palace/'old' city area Shäki's star attraction is the pattern-fronted 1762 **Xan Saray** (**Khan's Palace**; ☎ 43666, 10-18.00, entry 80q) set in an ornamental garden with towering Chinar trees. It's relatively small and unfurnished but unusually complete and full of colourful murals that guides will happily interpret in interminable detail. Legend has it that the right-hand balcony (as viewed from below) was the khan's 'amnesty' window. Supposedly he'd stand here to announce the sentences passed upon assorted foes and criminals... or on a whim, he might decide to let them off altogether. The other balcony was for his wives. If you arrive after hours tipping the guards might still allow you a quick whisk around or at least the chance to peep within the outer garden wall to see the palace's colourfully ornate external facade.

The palace sits quaintly amid sheep-nibbled lawns surrounded by sturdy citadel **walls** which are historic, albeit reconstructed in 1938. The palace area boasts several small if rather dull museums. The very scanty **Crafts Museum** (AZN1) occupies an unusual dome-roofed old church. The fairly standard **History Museum** (AZN1) in a 19th-century brick barrack-room is somewhat more extensive and has photos of local attractions in its Video Room. More interesting is the **Shäbäkä Workshop** (☎ 40932, 9-15.00, free) where craftsmen create the *Şäbäkä* windows, intricate jigsaws of coloured glass and hand-shaped wooden crosspieces that you'll see in the palace itself.

Below the walls are three **caravansarais**, the most atmospheric of which is now used as a hotel with little shops and very cheap bars set into its lower street-side arches. Nearby back streets wind appealingly between traditional houses and a scattering of little old brick minarets, finally petering out in forests or valleys beyond. There are half a dozen old mosques, some rather hidden away such as the 18th-century **Chelåbi Mechid** in the yard of which a severely damaged white stone is said to be the tomb marker of Chelåbi Khan. A more complete tomb is that of his son Salim Khan.

One of the more intriguing discoveries in the convoluted backstreets is that the khan actually had a second palace. The 'other' one known simply as the **Xan Evi** is hidden and not officially open to the public but you might be able to gain entrance by climbing the low wall from the garden of house #12 whose charming owner **Hasan** (☎ mob 55-619 7588) is generally prepared to show visitors around. The building is rather decrepit but that makes the murals seem that much more authentic than the bright but heavily renovated ones in Xan Saray.

On Axundov St but entered from behind, the new **Çingis Klub** (☎ 47700) is an appealing little cultural centre celebrating Çingis Mustafaev, a celebrated Azeri journalist who died covering the Karabagh conflict. The basement museum section (40q) is more imaginatively presented than the equivalents within the fortress, the 'cinema' has comparatively off-beat screenings and there's a gallery of paintings and photographs.

Juma Mechid, Shäki's most immediately noticeable mosque, has a tall archetypal brick minaret. However, seeking out a selection of other, smaller mosques and minarets is a great excuse to get yourself lost in the veritable maze of footpaths, alleys and lanes that give Shäki much of its charm. It's generally possible to climb the 1880 **octagonal minaret** simply named 'minarä' (minaret) if you ask at the shop in whose garden it lies (tip appreciated). On a corner of the lane that leads to Mustafabey, the stubby **Gilåhi Minaret**

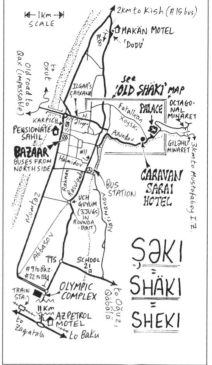

looks less stable and the wooden access steps have rotted away but the structure makes a great foreground to photos of the wooded mountains.

After Chelåbi Khan, Shäki's most famous son is the 'Muslim Molière', Misr-Fatih **Axundov** (aka Sabukhi) whose **house museum** is surprisingly small but furnished, carpeted and gently interesting. If Axundov's writing seems too mainstream there's always the house museum of **Rashidbey Äfändiyev** who mostly stuck to school text books.

The 'New' Town Even the 'new town' is mostly charmingly low rise and relatively old, the main square is a great place to sip tea. Bustling if less picturesque is the

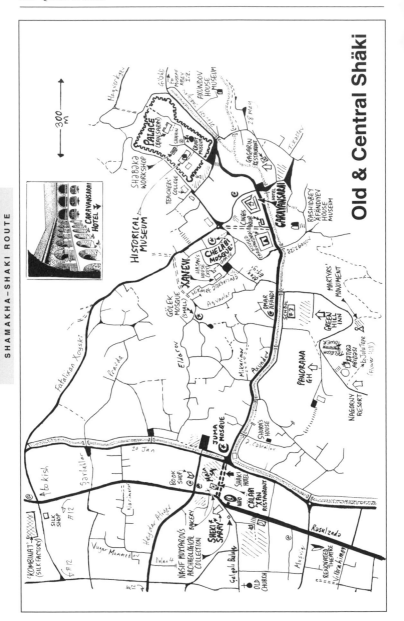

Old & Central Shäki

colourful main **bazaar** which comes to life between 8am and 2pm. From this part of town the white peak of Baziki Dağ is visible beyond the Kishchay valley. The once-important silk industry has recently restarted though the former 'Lenin') **silk factory** ('Kombinat') runs well below capacity and doesn't allow visits. They have a small store outside and another on Axundov St.

Näsif Muxtarov has a collection of intriguing historical finds in an unmarked room near Shäki Saray Hotel (upstairs through the doorway beyond the photo shop and barbers'). Ask the tourist office to arrange a meeting, especially if you plan to head to Fazil's Labarynth (p221); Näsif is the main key-holder and archaeologist.

Accommodation
Old and central Shäki (map opposite)
A stay in the atmospheric **Caravansarai** (☎ 44814) is one of the off-beat highlights of a visit to Shäki. Accommodation is far from luxurious but the rooms are unique vaulted nooks ranged around an arched inner courtyard that's entered through a timelessly sturdy gateway. The rooms (dbl/tr AZN30/40) have simple bathrooms and loveably dowdy sitting areas. A couple of AZN20 singles are unheated in winter.

For considerably more comfort, the splendid **Sheki Saray Hotel** (☎ 48181, 🖥 www.shekisaray.az) is the ideal choice. Central, understatedly hip and well managed the only minor gripe in this wonderful place is that the noise in the impressive atrium can disturb light sleepers. English is spoken, the décor is tasteful and rates (AZN90 dbl) are very fair.

New upper market options include **Green Hill Inn**, nearing completion in front of the stadium, an unmarked **new hotel** beside **Gagarin Restaurant** and a curious festival of mock medieval castellated brickwork beyond the **Panorama**, colloquially referred to as the '**Nagorny Resort**' (☎ mob 50 551 4939).

Family-run **Panorama Guest House** (mob ☎ 50-622 9027) has seven tastefully decorated rooms (dbl AZN35-50) with elements of local flavour and a great view across the valley from beneath the mulberry tree in its little garden. Rooms 1-3 share a little lounge area and their shared WC is indoors. However, the shower, along with the toilet for rooms 7 and 8, is across the yard.

The tragi-comic **Hotel Shäki** (☎ 42488) is a central but crumbling Soviet-era concrete tower known to locals simply as the 'Dokuz Märtäbä' (nine-storey building). A few AZN30 suites have renovated bathrooms but this is not the place for a holiday. The corridors feel more like the set for a C-rate disaster movie.

Greater Shäki (map p223)
Some expats have managed to stay in very nice bungalows with en suite hot shower and WC at the **Olympic Complex** (bus #9). However, the complex is far from central, is currently being reconstructed and tourists won't necessarily get a room if sportsmen are in town.

Looking outwardly closed behind tall wrought-iron gates at the back of the Bazaar, the simple **Pensionat Sahil** (☎ 45 491) has flimsy but clean en suite rooms from AZN20 dbl and an inexpensive courtyard restaurant pleasantly set with roses.

Other fall-back options include little **Motel Makän** (☎ 60372, ☎ mob 50-356 7454; off map) with pleasant unfussy AZN40 rooms above a courtyard restaurant at the Dodu terminus of minibus 8, and a good-value **AzPetrol Motel** (☎ 40270) that's 16km from central Shäki at the A16 junction (from AZN12 per person). Some 3km beyond the fortress, lonely **Mustafabey IZ** (☎ mob 50-341 3241, Farukh) is an aged Soviet rest-house with twelve big, entirely lacklustre rooms each with five survivable beds (AZN10 per person) and an approximately useable bathroom. The attached restaurant looks vaguely as though it survived a bomb attack. However, if the spartan conditions don't put you off the forested rural location is pretty and an ideal base for hikes. It's often full with groups mid-summer.

Homestays The tourist office can arrange homestays (AZN10-12). So can obliging English-speaking guide **Ilgar Ağayev** (☎ mob 55-623-8295, 🖥 ilqaragayev77@ yahoo.com, AZN12-14) who runs a tiny local *çayxana*. A third system, the B&B Network, seems to offer somewhat more comfortable homestays for a similar price, but you'll need some Russian or Azeri to telephone the organizer Farhad Azizov (☎ mob 50 612 6564) who will arrange for a car (AZN1 extra) to pick you up and take you to a host family. When I tried this I arrived at a truly charming family courtyard house where my hostess, Shura (☎ 43101) spoke two or three words of English. There was air-conditioning and even an indoor toilet plus tea and breakfast included for just AZN10. Fantastic.

There's also a lovely homestay at Kish (p228).

Food
Shäki is much esteemed for its *halva*. Cut from big circles dribbled with lurid red syrup, the taste is more like a kind of paxlava. It's sold from dozens of specialist shops which will usually let you taste before you buy and which also stock other local confectioneries such as *mindal*, *bamiya* and (in winter) *tel*.

Shäbäkä restaurant, at Shäki Saray Hotel, is suavely upmarket and serves some Western dishes yet charges under AZN6 for most choices. Middle-Eastern colours and modern yet traditional flourishes make the hotel's *Buta Bar* the most appealing watering hole in provincial Azerbaijan.

Çäläbi Xan has funky wooden décor inside and a congenial park-terrace for dining al fresco. Meals cost only AZN2-4 though don't expect a massive choice.

The *Caravanserai* has a pleasant garden restaurant and atmospheric vaulted eatery for winter dining but check prices carefully. Their teahouse is appealing but never seems to function and when it does wants AZN6 for a tea-&-jam set. Very basic *Shahin Cafe* facing the museums in the walled palace area does great baby-dolma and the outdoor terrace is pleasant if the wasps abate.

City transport
Shäki sprawls over a considerable area. Taxis (1AZN per ride) are easy to find around the bus station, the central square, the

bazaar and outside the Caravanserai but are otherwise a relatively rare sight. Within town there's a fairly reliable and frequent network of minibus routes (20q per ride) though by 19.00 most have stopped for the day and some routes only run until 16.00 as with cross-town #3 between the Kombinat and Caravanserai via Fatalixan Xoyski St. The most useful is #11 which shuttles between the bazaar, the bus station, the central square (Kohna Bazaar), the Caravanserai and the Khan's Palace (Xan Saray). The #9 Olympic Complex– Kombinat and less frequent #22 Olympic Complex–Xan Saray pass outside the bus station. From the Bazaar #8 runs to Dodu via the theatre and #15 continues all the way to Kish for the same 20q fare.

Getting to and from Shäki
The nightly **train** from Baku should arrive at 06.55 returning at 22.10. Be aware that the railway station is 17km from the centre. Trains are met by taxis and a ragged minibus (#21; 50q) which returns to the station from outside the post office at 20.00. Alternatively take any vehicle heading south from Shäki to the AzPetrol Motel and walk 700m east.

Long-distance buses depart from behind the big, virtually disused shell of the Soviet bus station (☎ 44617, 6.30am-5pm & 8pm-midnight). Big, slow but relatively comfortable coaches for Baku (via Kürdamir) run several times daily (7hrs with a meal stop). These include some overnight services but the train offers a much better chance to sleep. Additionally, there are 1-2 **minibuses** per hour from 06.30. These travel via Ağdash and Shamakha (6 hrs) for now but will probably re-route via Kürdamir once the main Baku–Ganjä road has been fully rebuilt.

Other destinations include Bärdä (09.00, 11.30, 16.30), Gänjä (08.00, 08.30, 13.30; 1.8AZN), Mingächevir (6.50, 9.40, 13 and 16.00; 1AZN), Naftalan (15.10), Oğuz (7.20, 10.30, 11.40, 13.20, 15.00, 16.00), Qäbälä (6.50, 14.00), Qax (7.40, 10.30, 13.40, 16.10) and Yevlax (10.30). There are direct buses to Balakän (10.10, 14.00) or hop via Zaqatala (dep 7, 9, 11, 11.40, 15, 16.30).

You could also try heading for the

main A16 road and flagging down rides from near the AzPetrol station, though traffic is pretty sparse and almost non-existent in the evenings.

Shared taxis to Baku (mornings, 5hrs) generally cost 10AZN per person. Once you've checked the price, consider offering the full 40AZN to get the whole car for yourself with stops and perhaps a few small pre-agreed side trips.

AROUND SHÄKI

A series of ever-plusher rest-zone resorts are springing up between Shäki and Gelersen Görasen, bypassing little Kish which remains one of Azerbaijan's more charmingly authentic old villages.

Marxal (Markhal) (see map p218)

The area's oldest 'resort' *Marxal* (☎ 51265) fills a thickly wooded cwm across the river from Kish with accommodation that varies from dreadfully old-fashioned crash-pad rooms with institutional beds (rates negotiable) above the ropey central restaurant to decent four-room timber cottages (AZN150) at a considerable distance up the enfolding mountain slopes. A funky if dated ski-chalet-style mansion still stands on pillars overlooking an artificial lake and includes the large-scale chess set on which Garry Kasparov reputedly used to play during his stays here.

A 12km coil of forest track zigzags up from Marxal to the fabulous mountaintop summit-meadow of **Xan Yaylaği** (king's pasture). For now at least it remains negotiable by 4WD (in about 30 mins, toll AZN2). Horsemen can do the trip almost as fast and on foot there are short cuts. At the top, look north for truly stunning alpine views towards the Dağestan mountains. Look south to distantly spy the beak of Mt Kyapaz way across Lake Mingächevir. But only on the rare days with good visibility, obviously.

It would be possible to hike back down into Shäki using shepherds' trails on the eastern side of the mountain. Hidden on the

forested sides of the mountain locals claim there are many stones with ancient inscriptions, including stone lions.

Kish (Kiş, ☎ 0177)

The original site of Shäki was somewhere near Kish, the road to which is heavily buttressed against the river's destructive moods. Kish village sprawls attractively up the Kishchay valley and its central knoll is graced by a simple but uniquely intact **Albanian church** (☎ 98833, entry fee 80q, 41°14'56"N, 47°11'35"E) that's been heavily restored and now houses a very well-presented museum about Caucasian Albania. An unproven theory suggests that a church here was first founded in AD78 by Yelisey (Eliseus), a disciple of Thaddeus of Edessa (one of the '70 apostles' appointed by Jesus in Luke 10: 1-20). Extensive excavations between 2000 and 2002 failed to provide

SHAMAKHA–SHAKI ROUTE

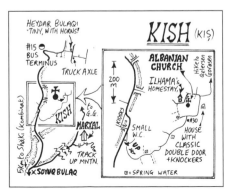

any evidence of this, though the discovery of 1st century BC human remains (now visible under glass outside) suggest that there was probably a pre-Christian place of worship at the site. The present structure is probably 12th century. The church-museum complex operates a sweet little *café*.

Living very close by, charming Ilhama Abdulhämidova (☎ 98416/7) speaks some English and offers a very personal, welcoming **homestay** in her typical traditional orchard-set house (AZN10 with dinner and breakfast). The outside bath-hut is clean. If Ilhama's is full, she can generally organize beds in neighbouring homes.

Kish is a delightful place to experience village life with local women filling traditional copper jujums at the spring-heads and old men bantering away all day.

Gelersen Göräsen

What little remains of the **Gelersen Göräsen castle** (Cheläbi's 'come and see') castle is hidden in woodland on a small knoll about 3km beyond Kish. The very basic, somewhat tacky *Pensionate* (mob ☎ 50 335 7933) at the base of the castle hill has simple single rooms (AZN15 including food). It's generally full of kids throughout summer but could make a decent base for hikes if you find a space. Minimum stay three days.

To reach the castle site from behind the Pensionat, follow the boggy, progressively steepening footpath up and after five minutes or so look for a junction in the water pipe on your right and a small stone cairn. At this point a barely discernible path swings right beneath the trees and up, eventually very steeply, to an old stone arch that is the start of the ruins. Climbing on top is slightly nerve-racking as some of the stones are loose but once on top there are attractive 360° views.

In a plantation of aligned

pines, *Narin Qala* (☎ 45300) is the furthest the resorts have yet spread. There's a pseudo antique watch tower and model falcon guarding a mineral spring and the AZN100 family-sized cottages smell fresh and woody. However, the timber is already warping and implements aren't provided in the attached kitchen. Some of the smaller AZN60 cottages are better value but still have flaws and it's hard to imagine preferring this to the Caravansarai or Shäki Saray Hotel.

SHÄKI TO QAX
(see map p230)

Travelling the direct road between Qax and Shäki in 1889, 19th-century tourist John Abercromby halted at Geinuk [**Ashağı Köynük**] where it was 'absolutely necessary to load the guns and prepare for action' against 'bad characters' (ie robbers) along the 'horrible road'. Today the road is still virtually unusable east of Ashaği Köynük but for a different reason – because its bridges have been long-ago washed away by floods. You'll probably need a 4WD to attempt it. Drivers who value their vertebrae still detour via the main A16. This

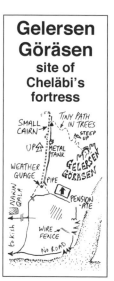

Gelersen Göräsen
site of Cheläbi's fortress

'long route' is particularly attractive on clear days. To the north the added distance from the mountains gives a good perspective of the wooded foothills and some glimpses of the higher ridges which are snow-capped much of the year. To the south of the road the landscape of arid hillsides comes briefly to grassy life in spring.

Just beyond Shäki station is **Kürdülü**, an old village with historic graves and burial mounds. In dry weather you can try the earth track side trip to **Dashbulaq**, attractively set in rolling grasslands and backed by a rocky cliff. Very far beyond, **Ajinohu** lake is infamous for its bitterly salty water.

The main road continues past tobacco-drying shelters and a small reservoir which sometimes attracts flocks of wading birds. **Baba-atma**, nearby, is famed for a fountain of water (well, OK a dribble) which appeared where a holy man struck the ground with his staff.

West of km post 76, a poorly signed road to the north offers a 1.5km excursion to the supposed **grave of Haji Murad**. The hero's grey gravestone has an Arabic inscription and slightly singed photo-oval, clearly anachronistic! It's with a few other memorials in a small glade of old trees at the point where the asphalt ends. The deputy of Imam Shamil (box p237), Haji Murad was immortalized as the rough-cut hero of an eponymous Tolstoy novel. Having finally and brutally escaped his Russian captors, he got bogged down in his desperate dash out of Shäki, though Tolstoy places his demise a little further north, 'near Belarjik minaret' (possibly **Ikinci Biläcix** on the upper Qax road).

QAX (Gakh; ☎ 0144) (see map p231)

A channelled stream gurgles beside winding Azärbaycan St, Qax's cute commercial lane. Charming Ichäri Bazar St has a couple of wooden-pillared Russian-era houses and almost hidden at its upper end are two stone stumps which probably once formed the gatehouse in a now defunct town wall. The main Ilisu road (20th Jan St) rises gently passing gardens full of fruit trees and the recently renovated **Georgitsminda Georgian church** with its stand-alone bell tower and impressive 2001 murals. A large proportion of the population here is Georgian and the somewhat dilapidated school behind the church teaches in the Georgian language. There was said to be a Stalin statue here though I could only find Nizami.

At the far northern edge of town the former Qala Restaurant is being converted into a large new hotel resort. The site has been surrounded by a crenelated wall joined to the sturdy round-tower of a real **castle ruin**, Hasan Qala (at the southern end).

Qax is known for its **mineral water**, bottled beside the road to Zaqatala, 6km west of town, just beyond Shafa Pensionate. There's a free spring there too.

Accommodation and food

Qax Hotel (☎ 54868, AZN3 per person) has presentable if basic rooms sharing decent new shower rooms. A few en suite rooms are under construction. When rebuilt *Qala Restaurant* should have rooms.

It's also possible to sleep at *Shafa Pensionate* (see map p230); ☎ 53514) west of Qum though as that's a Soviet mini-sanatorium aimed at recuperating octogenarians you're unlikely to find a party atmosphere! It's much nicer to stay in Ilisu.

Central Qax's best dining is at *Märkäz* (☎ 54144). It might look derelict but behind the empty façade the restaurant actually hides in a rear courtyard. Excellent kebabs cost AZN1.40 and beer is 50q a pint.

On the Ilisu road, *Migidana* (☎ 54333) has a vine-covered streamside terrace and is the nearest thing to a Georgian restaurant but other than khajapuri (AZN2) the menu is mostly kebabs.

Transport

If arriving by train be sure to alight at NEW Qax station. The old one is extremely isolated down a dead-end lane near Kötüklü.

Buses to Tbilisi are timetabled 8.15, 9.00, 14.00 and 16.00 though you may need to contact the driver to reserve a place. Antiquated old buses rumble to Zaqatala ten times daily, but only half use the 'köhnä yolu' route passing near to Läkit, others looping around on the main A16 road. For more afternoon options take a shared taxi to the A16 junction (AZN1). Buses to Shäki (7.40, 10.30, 14.00 and 16.10) also loop round on the A16 due to broken bridges on the direct road. Minibuses run up to Ilisu at 7.00, 9.00, 12.00, 14.00 and 17.00 but for AZN5 (return with stops) you could hop in a taxi. Buses to Läkit run at 7.30, 13 and 17.00, Gänjä at 08.00.

AROUND QAX
Kötüklü (map p230)

The 'old' Qax–Shäki road (köhnä Şäki Yolu), now virtually impassable beyond Ashaği Köynük, starts off by crossing a long

SHAMAKHA–SHAKI ROUTE

CINGIS QALA, CAR

Shäki to Balakän

FACADE OF THE KHAN'S PALACE, SHAKI

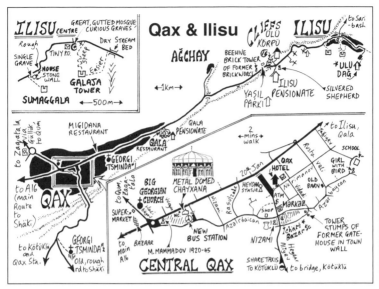

bridge, then wiggles down the riverbank for 2.5km to a fork-junction. Keeping right here takes you through thick, almost jungle-like, forest to the Georgian ('Yengilo') village of **Kötüklü**/Qotoklo which has a little watermill and a small, rebuilt church. Forking left, you'll drive by a much more impressive Georgian church, lonely **Georgitsminda #2** perched on a rocky bluff at (41°23'21"N, 46°55'17E). It's only 800m east of the Kötüklü turn-off and visible from the road but to get up to it take the footpath starting at the Kötüklü fork-junction by crossing a small stream on a concrete slab.

ILISU

A splendid, high-sided valley leads up to quaint Ilisu, a delightful single-street village of old-fashioned stone homes built on the foundations of even older structures, many with sturdy stone-arched entry portals. The unusual village mosque is intriguing, too. Long a regional power centre, Ilisu was the capital of an autonomous sultanate from the mid-18th century. Guarding the village's southern flank, the 19th-century **Sumaggala**, is a square, plastered brick

watch tower which is not especially photogenic but recalls the era of Daniyal-beg (see box p232). Crumbling remnants of an older, probably 16th-century, **Galaja** stone tower are a short, steep scramble above the centre of the village.

The village's alley-ways make for appealing strolls toward the river drop-off or into the chestnut groves. Seven kilometres walk beyond the usually relaxed (or unmanned) army checkpoint at the end of the village there's a hot-and-cold waterfall just beyond a disused building daubed 'hamam'. You'll need a good sense of balance for the multiple stream crossings! There are plenty of other hikes possible and with a 4WD you can drive on to the lovely village of **Saribash**. Easier to reach and also quaint is **Ağchay** village just off the Qax–Ilisu road.

Accommodation and food

The most appealing and best-value accommodation choice is *Ulu Dağ* (☎ 93425) at the far end of the village. The series of small blocks climb the hillside (be prepared for a fair walk) with certain rooms (eg 35, 36) offering wonderful views from shared balconies. Beds are a little soft but the rooms have fridges, water heaters and fragrant pine panelling. In summer they fill their huge 25x50m outdoor swimming pool. Waiter Elvin speaks a little English.

Three alternatives lie in a dramatic grassy valley hemmed in by magnificent, soaring cliffs and overlooking a 16th-century bridge between Ilisu and Ağchay. *Yaşil Park* (☎ 54575) sells itself on its indoor swimming pool but the five-bed houselets (AZN200!!) are a little musty with the wooden floors already losing their varnish while rooms in the smaller six-room terrace (AZN80-130) are presentable but lacking style. *Ilisu Pensionat* (☎ mob 50 763 0288, Gullya) is the area's original hut-resort though its once breathtaking views are no longer pristine thanks to Yaşil Park. Manageress Gullya is friendly and speaks a little English but getting past the officious guard at the gate to talk to anyone can be awkward. The simple hotel-style rooms start at AZN40 but the cottages with three narrow beds, bathroom and fake-parquet floors are better value (AZN52). The food is good with fresh fish from their own pond, but alcohol is not served.

Nestled directly above the river *Ulu Kö-rpü* (☎ 54140) has modest huts that are somewhat wonky and have pretty basic squat toilets but at AZN20-30 one can't complain.

Another resort is taking shape closer to Ilisu and there are several attractively situated *summer restaurants* along the road.

QAX TO ZAQATALA (see map p230)

Shäki/Baku to Zaqatala buses bypass Qax altogether taking the A16 via Shäki Station and Äliabad (an Inghiloi-Georgian village with a 17th-century minaret). However, most Zaqatala–Qax services use the partially unsurfaced direct road offering several interesting side trips:

Qum

One of Azerbaijan's most accessible **Albanian church ruins** ('məbəd') is in central Qum village 3.2km off the Qax–Zaqatala road. If it really is 5th century as claimed it must have been remarkably large for its day. The apse has collapsed but twin side aisles and three 6m-high arches remain in the nave. Across the road is an 18th century mosque, now roofed with corrugate.

If you continue another 3km through the Tssakhur-speaking village of **Çinarli** (on an unpaved road that becomes astonishingly rutted) you emerge at **Bali Bulaq**, an idyllic clearing between two forest streams where simple tea-tables are perched precariously over small waterfalls. When the simple 'hotel' building is complete, this could make an excellent base for hiking.

From Qax bazaar buses run to Çinarli via Qum at 7, 9, 12, 14 and 17.00. Don't assume it's easy to find a taxi back.

❏ Niedhardt versus Shamil

General Niedhardt's previous job had been governor of Moscow. It was not the ideal preparation for commanding the Russian Caucasus forces against Shamil's Chechen raids (see box p237). He soon became infamous for his military and diplomatic blunders. Perhaps the worst of these was the needless loss of Ilisu. The sultanate had till 1844 been a willing Russian vassal and Ilisu's sultan, the happily Russified Daniyal-beg, was a serving major general in the Tsar's army. Until, that is, Niedhardt decided to abolish his ancestral leadership rights in Ilisu. Outraged by this tactless gesture, Daniyal-beg switched allegiance to Shamil who, thanks to another piece of Niedhardt incompetence, had recently escaped certain death in a mis-managed Russian ambush.

Daniyal-beg's daughter Kherimat, pining for the salons of St Petersburg, instead found herself sent to an *aoul* in windswept Dağestan as she was married off to Shamil's son Qazi Mammed – then the 'finest horseman in the mountains' not a dull central Azerbaijan railway town. Niedhardt was rapidly sent back to Moscow in disgrace. But his mistakes allowed the Murid wars to drag on for more than another decade.

Läkit (Lǝkit, Lekit)

Läkit has two **Albanian ruins**. The more visually impressive is **Yeddi Kilisä** (seven churches), a once-walled Albanian monastic complex on the track up to **Läkit Kötüklü**. The beautiful spot is idyllically peaceful and only 15 minutes walk uphill beyond the northern end of Läkit village. It's possible by 4WD, though during rain the rough track becomes a torrent. Several tufa buildings and a gate-house remnant are clearly visible. A hole behind the empty apse of the former main church supposedly leads to a warren of tunnels extending, some claim, as far as Qum.

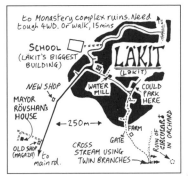

The other 7th-century ruin is more central but harder to find being only a few stones high and hidden at the back of an unmarked nut orchard. It's nonetheless the most accessible example of an ancient Albanian round-plan church design; only two others are known [one at Böyük Amili (out of bounds near the RLS, p216) and the other above Gözparaq (see below)]. From the village centre you'll walk 10 mins down a very rough track, scramble across a small stream then cross a fence but you'll probably need to ask directions to find the correct orchard-garden.

Güllük, Gözparaq and Mamrux

Eight kilometres west of the Läkit turning is the attractive village of **Güllük**. A tree is growing through the roofless shell of what appears to be an old chapel behind the newer of its central graveyards at the eastern edge of town.

Beyond Güllük and 500m west of the Zaqatala provincial border marker, a road to the north leads directly into **Gözparaq** (**Gözbarax**). This is backed by a flat-topped, tree-covered hill called Armatai Meshasi atop which there's a circular, supposedly 5th century, Albanian church ruin. Amid the ivy a few arches and wall fragments do at least give a vague sense of its former form but you'll need a guide to find it. Mohammad Gassanov, a teacher who lives in the Tssakhur-speaking village of **Mamrux** north of the hill might be able to help. Mamrux itself has a tiny Albanian chapel (or is it a store hut?) with its ancient stone roof still intact (in front of the new mosque). An older mosque, dating from 1129AH (1717) is directly behind the new one but is now used as a barn.

Muxax and Perigala

The locally renowned 'old' mosque in **Muxax** is similar to that of **Tala** (map p235) with multiple brick arches, a corrugated iron roof and no minaret. It's set

❏ The mysterious Tssakhur people

One of Azerbaijan's least-known linguistic groups, the Tssakhur, live in Mamrux, Çinarli (above Qum) and Läkit Kötöklü though you'll also find Tssakhur-speaking villagers living in Zaqatala. Some apparently straight-faced locals claim that Tssakhurs are descendants from Roman legionnaires and that Mamrux was founded by the Roman leader Pompey in 66BC. Linguists consider the language a Lezghi dialect and it's named after Tssakhur village in Dağestan. In Tssakhur *mijag-da/mijag-na* means beautful for things/people, *yug-da/yug-na* means good. Greetings are as in Azeri. Website ⌨ http://www.sil.org/silesr/2005/silesr2005-016.pdf offers an interesting analysis of the language's viability.

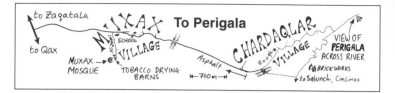

behind heavy wooden gates and tobacco-drying barns. The classic **Perigala** (fairy castle) is a remarkable structure sealing the entrance to a cave dwelling, high on an inaccessible cliff overlooking the upper end of Chardaqlar village. A viewpoint is reachable by normal taxi (AZN8 return from Zaqatala) but to get up into the cave-fortress itself is extremely perilous. If you attempt it (not advised) you'll need a very full-day's hike and a guide to show you how to shimmy along the minimal cliff ledges to the entrance.

Even with a sturdy 4WD, getting to **Cimcimax** in the high reaches of the Karachay is extremely challenging. Locals do make it in Ural 6-wheel truck-buses but your presence close to the Russian border might cause suspicion especially if you attempt to camp or walk the shepherds' trails to seasonal **Ağdam Qalay**.

ZAQATALA (☎ 0174)
The Qara, Car and Jinjarchay rivers cleave a gap into the wooded foothills behind Zaqatala that give the town a beautiful backdrop. Its partially 19th-century heart has several quiet avenues of cottage-style homes. The main street, **Heydar Aliyev pr**, sweeps up from the bus station roundabout passing the Islamic university and an imposing new Turkish-style stone **mosque** with tall twin minarets. After 1.5km it reaches a central square and (nominally) turns left in front of the post office. It then becomes a much more pleasant, low-rise street with sweetly ragged old shopfronts, an **internet room**, and a modest **historical museum** (AZN1, 09-18:00 Wed-Sun) which had neither light nor heat when I last visited. The street culminates beyond the *tourist office* in a hushed old-town square graced with **700-year-old plane trees**. Just behind (though hidden) is the shell of a once-fine **Georgian Church** beneath the powerful battlements of the Russian-built **fortress**. Still in military use and thus closed to visitors, this castle was built in 1830 to protect settlers and occupying Russian troops from raids by the Lezghian mountain tribes. In 1853 and 1854 there were fierce battles here as Imam Shamil (see box p237) made several attempts to seize the town before retreating back into the mountains. The fortress is also famed as the prison for the perpetrators of the *Battleship Potemkin* mutiny (1905) who became immortalized in the Soviet era for their perceived role as early revolutionaries. A vaguely simian **bust of Stepan Demeshko** (one of the mutineers) is tucked away in the attractively wooded Heydar Aliyev Park along with an obligatory Heydar statue, Aliyev museum, funfair rides and some attractive spots for tea overlooking a fine sweep of forested mountains.

Accommodation
Zaqatala *Görush Motel* (mob ☎ 050 322 5289) isn't a motel at all but a simple (if unexpectedly good) **restaurant** with three handy if somewhat ageing rooms (AZN12 twin or double) sharing a clean but broken-tiled bathroom. There's no reception: ask a waiter. *Hotel Qafqaz* (100 Heydar Aliyev pr, ☎ 53353, ✉ qafqaz-hotel@mail.ru; sgl/dbl AZN50/60-75) is Zaqatala's newest offering. The façade looks grand and the rooms are clean and sizeable with good showers but there's no air-con and neither the wall-art nor the leopard-patterned bedspreads offer much inspiration. The top-floor dining room is soul-less and road noise is possible.

Hotel Zaqatala (☎ 55709, Heydar Aliyev pr 92; dm/tw/ste AZN5/15/30) is the old Soviet-era hotel but its ground-floor rooms have been decently renovated and standards are acceptable given the price.

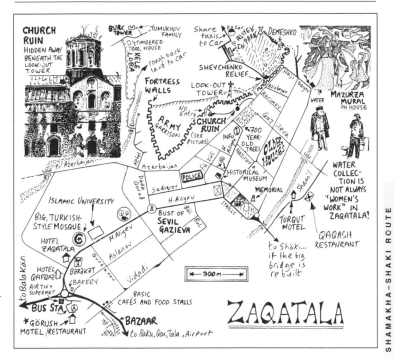

Even the six-bed dorm (men only) has a private bathroom. The much tattier upper floor should be stylishly redecorated eventually.

Turqut Motel (Shamil St, ☎ 56229) charges AZN30 for newish double rooms with tiny bathrooms and air-con, AZN15 for the ones without.

Greater Zaqatala *Iş Hotel* (☎ 56959, rooms AZN35-120) is a well-equipped, all-AC 3* motel tucked behind the IşOil petrol station at the western edge of town, accessible by Balakän minibuses (AZN1). Rates depend on size not quality so the smallest room (#4) is a bargain. AZN100 room #8 has a private balcony and the option of in-room Internet. Across the parking lot are AZN50-60 'cottages' above closeable garages. The big sauna with dining area and 2 by 3m pool costs AZN14 for the first hour, AZN10 for subsequent hours.

SMU-2 motel (aka Goycha, ☎ 52142) is beneath the Tala roundabout, across the bridge 1.5km east from the bus station. Twin rooms with shared OK bathroom

start at just AZN10. Much better-value rooms at AZN14 have air conditioning and private bathrooms.

Also in Tala, the **Karvan** (formerly Pensionat Tala, ☎ 56860) is due to re-open in 2009. The original place had a swimming pool and small football pitch but the rooms had gone to seed so they'll need to do a lot of restoration. To find it go 700m south from the SMU-2, turn right at the Ashaği Tala sign then first left.

An appealing alternative option is Läzzät (see p238) in the idyllic nearby village of Car.

Food
Handy for the bus station area hotels, **Bäräkät** serves Turkish food and pizza in a comparatively modern restaurant where women venture to dine unchaperoned upstairs. Tucked away near Turqut Motel, the characterful **Qaqash Restaurant** makes innovative decorative use of old bottles and has a series of wooden dining areas behind. Kebabs (AZN2) and beer (60q) are great value. There are picturesque outdoor spots for summer tea amid the çinar trees of the old town square and on the valley-lip eastern edge of Heydar Aliyev Park.

Public transport
Flights to Baku (AZN52) depart Mondays, Wednesdays and Fridays. Tickets are sold from a small office (☎ 55466, ☎ mob 055-380 0880) beside Ağsaray Supermarket near the bus station. Air services are planned to Moscow and Makhachkala (Dağestan).

Useful **long-distance buses** from the main bus station run to Baku (several mornings and nights), Gänjä (five daily via Mingächevir, last 15.00), Shäki (nine daily, last 17.00) and Qax (six daily, last 16.15).

Minibuses for Balakän (60q) leave from the front of the bus station when full. Services to local villages pick up further east towards the bazaar.

Shared/private taxi hops around town cost 20q/AZN1. Shared/private taxis to Car cost 50q/AZN2 from the north-west corner of Heydar Park. Waiting for a ride back requires some patience.

The **train** from Baku arrives around 09.30 and despite the protestations of taxi drivers to the contrary, it is met by a small bus which trundles the 8km to the bus station passing the Karvan Pensionate turning and SMU-2 Motel. Returning it leaves town at 19.30.

NORTH OF ZAQATALA
Keleloba fort (see map p235)
Hidden away in Muhuma Yumukhov's private orchard-garden in rural Keleloba village lies the three-storey 14th century **Burc Tower**. These days the top section retains some stone castellations though one wall is dangerously cracked, causing a degree of nervousness for the family who uses the inside shell as a dump for old tin cans. There are two possible routes back to Zaqatala, the shorter, rougher one passing a timeless half-timbered house and a viewpoint surveying the town. Turn left here for a short-cut up to Car.

Car
Some 6km above Zaqatala (shared taxi, no bus) is the charming Avar village of Car (pronounced Jar, ✤ Djari). Chocolate-box houses in part-stone, part brick are semi-hidden in orchards of apple, chestnut and walnut trees behind mossy dry-stone walls. Like Ilisu, this was once the centre of its own mini nation spending much of the 14th to 18th centuries as a free (*jama-atlik* ie kingless) state. Car was frequently allied to the Georgian kingdom of Kaheti which may explain why Car's most photogenic building, **Cingis Qala tower**, is vaguely reminiscent of Georgian mountain tower houses. Certainly any spurious link to Genghis Khan is purely mythical as the tower was only built in the 16th century (according to experts in Baku), or as late as 1816 according to the owners, the convincingly named Cingisov family who now live next door. The tower was damaged when the roof collapsed under heavy snows in 2003, but it has been partly patched up and the orchard setting is lovely. There are antique wall remnants including two Arabic inscription stones on the streamward side of the tower's compound.

Chamois and a few remaining specimens of near-extinct Dağestan goats roam on highland pastures way above the tree line. The most accessible path zigzags up

❏ Shamil, Haji Murad and the 'Murid' mountain guerillas

By the early 19th century Russia had captured the lowlands of Georgia and Azerbaijan but was left with a problem – the fearsome Caucasian mountain tribes had yet to be pacified and the situation became one of constant guerrilla attacks that lasted from 1832 till 1860. As with the Soviet invasion of Afghanistan (1979-89), 'freedom fighters' were funded by Western powers (notably Britain) to give the Russians as tough a time as was possible, keeping them too busy to consider pushing on towards Iran and India. Just as in Afghanistan, the West turned a blind eye to the fiery brand of Islam being preached by the guerillas preferring to class the fight as territorial rather than religiously inspired.

The Murid movement's most famous, charismatic leader was Imam Shamil, an ethnic Avar who operated mainly in Dağestan and Chechnya, but also launched violent but short-lived attacks on Zaqatala and north-west Azerbaijan. Born in 1797 Shamil was a sickly child who, by self discipline and strenuous exercise, developed into a powerful athlete. His great height, fair hair and striking red beard made him an eye-catching figure, especially when dressed in his white turban, yellow boots and bright green cape. The wild glamour of the 'freedom fighters' appealed greatly to journalists and writers of the day. Alexander Dumas wrote in some detail about Shamil and his supposedly cruel treatment of prisoners. However, not all his hostages were abused – one Armenian lady who Shamil had originally kidnapped became Shamil's devoted concubine and, to the horror of her nephew who spent eight years tracking her down, refused to leave even when her family sent a large ransom.

Shamil practised meditation, fasting and a mystical form of abstinent Islam which inspired respect and awe amongst the men he came to lead. By persuading the infamously fractious mountain tribes to drop their age-old blood feuds and focus their attention instead on a 'holy war' against the invading Russians, he fashioned an extremely tough and disciplined fighting force. His most famous commander was Haji Murad whose story was glamorized later in the eponymous Tolstoy novel.

Murad's lightning attacks were even more effective than those of Shamil such that the sound of his chanted name could send groups of Russian troops fleeing in panic. In the end, Haji Murad's prestige grew too much for Shamil who felt his command slipping away. The very feuding he'd stamped out amongst others thus divided Shamil's forces from Murad's and the Russians took advantage. Haji Murad was caught and imprisoned in Nukha (Shäki). After a blood-thirsty escape plan was botched, he was executed in 1852 and his severed head was toured around the Caucasus to prove his demise.

The collapse of the Murid movement was prevented, however, by Ottoman Turkey which funded Shamil's 1853-4 attacks on Zaqatala as a diversion to the brewing Crimean War. However, once that war was over in 1856, the Russians had 200,000 battle-hardened troops to re-assign to the Caucasus. Shamil finally surrendered in 1859 and such was his mystique that in Russia he was treated more as a retired film star than a prisoner. Remarkably he spent his final years in relatively comfortable exile in the provincial town of Kaluga, though his son Qazi Mammad went on to launch a further rebellion in the 1870s.

Shamil was a controversial figure during the Soviet era – a useful symbol as an anti-colonial revolutionary but sensitive due to his potential adoption as a Muslim icon. Since independence many streets are now named 'Şeyx/Sheikh/Imam Şamil' after him in Azerbaijan despite his relatively tenuous link with the country. For the full story read Lesley Blanch's fabulously florid *Sabres of Paradise*.

the western side of the valley from the southern end of Car. After around three hours steep uphill walking you should emerge on Mt Shamil. It's supposedly riven with hidden tunnels as the one-time hideaway of 19th-century anti-Russian resistance fighter Sheikh Shamil (see box, p237). Here there's a *pir* surrounded by a series of small grave mounds thought to date from a Shamil-era battle in which the whole former mountain village of Qoloda was destroyed, never to be rebuilt. Others date the graves to the 1730s when Car was attacked by Nadir Shah before he stormed Shäki and Bash Kungut.

Accommodation/food
Läzzät (☎ 52266; mobile ☎ 50 383 4573) rest zone has a wide-ranging restaurant, a fun tree-top tea-table and a selection of modest hut bungalows with en suite WC and a shower which should run hot once the electricity comes on after 7pm. The owner, the self-styled 'King of Zaqatala', is quite a character.

ZAQATALA TO BALAKÄN (see map p230)
Several villages in the area have painted their stone-inlaid walls in eye-catching zebra-leopard polka-dot designs. This is especially noticeable in the ancient little town of **Katex** which was once home to a

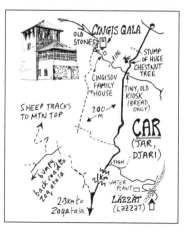

SHEEP TRACKS TO MTN TOP
OLD STONES
CINGIS QALA
PIPE
STUMP OF HUGE CHESTNUT TREE
CINGISOV FAMILY HOUSE
TINY, OLD KIOSK (BREAD ONLY)
200→M
CAR (JAR, DJARI)
SIGN
bumpy back road to Zaqatala
1 Km
WATER PLANT
2·3 Km to Zaqatala
LÄZZÄT (LƏZZƏT)

> ### ❏ Some Avar words and phrases
> *Kansu-ugo*   How are you?
> *Khiksa-ugo*   I'm OK
>   (an appropriate reply)
> *Khiksa*   good
> *(Amir) bertsena* (very) beautiful
> *(Kuda) barkala* thank you (very much)

notable Polish community. Right beside the Balakän road there's a long stretch of medieval wall ('Qala Divandari'). Katex also has a small, box-shaped, five-arched mosque (14th century), a large WWII monument at its western end and the *Sähil garden-restaurant* at the east.

Well beyond the Katex sawmill ('kombinat') is a waterfall that makes a popular summer picnic spot, but in places the riverbank road has been washed out and now you can only get there by driving (or walking) some sections along the river bed – not feasible if the water level is high.

Optimistic taxi drivers may assure you that a viable alternative route goes via **Mazix** (an attractive village of sturdy stone homes, sometimes written Matex or Matsex) and **Qäbiz Därä** (an Avar village). This road passes the attractively positioned, summer-only *Shälälä* riverside restaurant and ends up in some lovely beech woods which are abuzz with dragonflies in autumn. However, the bridge that crosses a narrow canyon of the Katexchay river to reach the waterfall has become impassably buckled. It is quite a sight but utterly unsafe to cross.

BALAKÄN (✛ Balakani; ☎ 0119)
The nearest town to the Kaheti-Georgia/Azerbaijan border, Balakän has a thriving, colourful **bazaar** and some attractive if unremarkable back streets overhung by kaki (persimmon) trees whose orange fruit make for colourful scenes in early winter. The lovingly restored, cuboidal 19th-century **mosque** has a splendid 17th-century brick minaret that's arguably the finest in Azerbaijan (for photos see ❏ www.belokan turizm.narod.ru/mon.html). On clear days

there are wonderful mountain panoramas from the top. Another good viewpoint is from the waving hilltop Aliyev statue at the back of Heydar Park. In the summer heat (May-Aug) you can save the sweaty 15-minute walk by taking the new **ropeway** (cable car; AZN1 return).

AzBank (9-13.00 & 14-17.00 Mon-Fri) changes US$ and euros and also has a handy **ATM**.

Accommodation/food

Balakän's plush new *Hotel Qubek* should be open by the time you read this. Otherwise the best accommodation is the *AzPetrol Motel* (☎ 52401) where neat air-con double rooms cost AZN20-25 and equally good triples can be used dorm-style at just AZN7 per bed. A last resort are the utterly decrepit rooms of old *Hotel Balakän* (☎ 53589, AZN8 per person) which trics to fool potential guests with a misleadingly smart, redecorated foyer.

Türk Restorani and *Kafe Avropa* are marginally better than most eateries on the central street. Pleasant *Güney Doğu* overlooks parkland and is close to Balakän's best Internet place.

Transport

There are direct buses to/from Baku (08.00, 09.00, 18.30, 19.30, 21.00, 21.30, 23.30). Or it's easy to nip aboard a raff (Soviet-made minibus) to Zaqatala (40 mins, 60q) which depart as full roughly every 20 mins until around 19.00.

The Balakän–Baku night train leaves at 19.50. Note that the railway station is

4km down a dead-end road at the far eastern edge of town (AZN2 taxi).

For Georgia take a shared taxi (AZN1) from the MMOil petrol station to the Postbina border where a shiny new customs complex is being built. Formalities are ponderous but no longer shady and the Georgian immigration check is just a short walk beyond from which a taxi to Lagodekhi should cost only 5Lari. Alternatively direct buses run between Qax and Kabali (an ethnic Azeri village just west of Lagodekhi) around three times daily and there are Qax–Tbilisi minibuses most days but these are generally full by the time they reach Balakän.

Note that there are no exchange facilities at the border. Taxi drivers will informally change Lari but at atrocious rates.

Around Balakän

Despite a luxuriantly forested mountain backdrop Balakän is not the best base for excursions: the tracks are too rough even for a 4WD and a modest castlc ruin on the Mazimchay river is out of bounds thanks to its border-zone location. If you can get permission to enter the forest reserve you could wadi-bash up the Balakän river in search of the rare Caucasian black grouse.

Overloaded horse-drawn hay-carts are the main attractions of the wide fertile plain south of town. When I stumbled into the large, undistinguished agricultural village of **Qabaq Chöl** seeking attractions nonplussed tea-drinkers at the *çayxana* were merrily amused to meet their first-ever tourist... but why had I come? Why indeed?

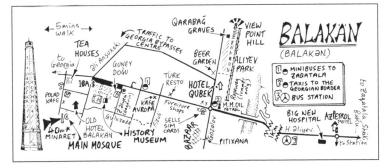

PART 6: CENTRAL AZERBAIJAN

INTRODUCTION
On a typical, hazy day, the main M4 manages to cross the nation without even hinting at Azerbaijan's scenic wonders. Most of the central region is flat and undramatically agricultural and would not be high on any tourist's itinerary. Nonetheless, on exceptional spring days when the air clears, distant glimpses of snow-topped Murovdağ (to the south) and the high Caucasus (north) transform the experience especially around Goranboy. There are battered historical sites, some ancient (if utterly rebuilt) cities such as Bärdä and Gänjä and the foothills of the lovely Lesser Caucasus mountains are worth exploring.

The pageant of autumnal colours on dramatic Mt Käpäz (Kyapaz) reflected in Lake Göy Göl is perhaps the single most beautiful view in Azerbaijan. It would be all the more delightful if you could get there!

Sadly the Armenian occupation of nearby Nagorno Karabagh renders much of the surrounding area inaccessible.

PRACTICAL INFORMATION
Comparing east–west routes
From Älät the main M4 highway runs relatively straight all the way to Qazax and the Georgian border at Qırmızı Korpü (Red Bridge, Krasny Most). Until major upgrading works is complete (probably 2011), several sections remain dusty and slow with potholes, diversions and construction traffic. A somewhat more scenic and (for now) better-surfaced route to Gänjä starts out through Shamakha then cuts down across the Ağsu pass (p203) to Göychay (p244) and Ağdash (p245) rejoining the main road south of Mingächevir.

Note that if you're heading for Tbilisi, the route (pp213-39) via Qäbälä and

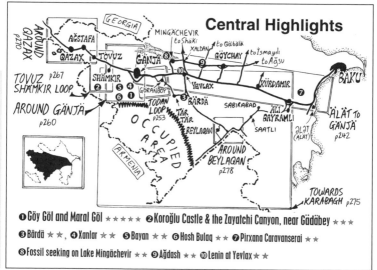

Central Highlights

❶ Göy Göl and Maral Göl ★★★★★   ❷ Koroğlu Castle & the Zayatchi Canyon, near Gädäbey ★★★

❸ Bärdä ★★,   ❹ Xanlar ★★   ❺ Bayan ★★   ❻ Hosh Bulaq ★★   ❼ Pirxana Caravanserai ★★

❽ Fossil seeking on Lake Mingächevir ★★   ❾ Ağdash ★★   ❿ Lenin at Yevlax ★★

Zaqatala is far more attractive than either of the above, if somewhat slower.

ÄLÄT TO KÜRDAMIR

Dull, scrubby agricultural plains made almost fertile with laborious irrigation have backdrops of low, arid hills and mud-volcano out-flows. Villagers en route forlornly wave fish, rabbits, fruit or clothing for sale to passing cars. I've marked police checkpoints, unexpected diversions and speed traps on the map on p242 but most of these should disappear once the roadworks are complete.

Pirxana/Pir Hussein Caravanserai

This modestly interesting caravanserai (variously known as Hanega, Xanaga, Pir Hussein and Pirsaat) was once a major stop on the busy Shamakha–Tabriz trade route, the region's most prosperous according to a traveller's report of 1318. The complex incorporates the minaret and mausoleum of Sheikh Hussein, built in 1256 by Mahmud Masudi even though the Sheikh himself had died nearly 200 years before (1074). Glazed brick-tiles once adorned the interior but were carted off to museums in Tbilisi and St Petersburg. A whole frieze decorated with a Ferdowsi poem was reputedly purloined by 19th-century British collectors. Pictures from 1963 show the complex on the verge of collapse but two tasteful restorations, most recently in 2007 have renewed the place.

Today the complex's appealing isolation is diminished somewhat by a long, low dam directly behind it that creates a seasonal reservoir. Locals still come to make superstitious offerings at the mausoleum and picnic in the wooded area next door. Beside the complex is an ancient graveyard.

Transport From the main M4 west of Navahi take the road to Qubalı Balaoğan (Qubalı) that leads north under a railway bridge. Coming from Baku there's a new white-on-brown sign board but the turn is still easy to miss (east of Pirsaat village where a tall TV transmission tower comes into view). From Qubalı the caravanserai is 5km further by manageable dirt track. From the last bridge in Qubalı maintain a basic west-north-west line aiming towards the

left side of the gap in the distant ridge where you can just make out a long concrete building in the single clump of trees. The caravanserai complex is behind that.

Buses from Qazi Mammad market leave for Qubalı at 8.30, 10.30 and 13.30 returning an hour or so later but beyond that there's no public transport and in Qubalı it's hard to find a taxi. You might be able to hitchhike with a road-stone lorry then walk the last 1500m. I flagged down a Qubalı-bound driver at the M4 turn off and paid him 8AZN return to take me to Pirxana and back with an hour's sightseeing time. Tea at his modest Qubalı home was an added bonus.

Qazi Mammad
(Gazi Magomed, Haji Qabul; ☎ 0140)

The town's official name honours the favourite son of Imam Shamil (p237), with Qazi meaning 'saintly warrior'. However, most locals still call it by the original name 'Haji Qabul' which roughly translates as 'stopping place for pilgrims'. That name seemed appropriate in the 1880s as the site evolved from isolated army barracks into the terminus of the planned railway to Mecca via Tehran. Visiting in 1883, Marvin describes Haji Qabul as 'a place with a future'. That future never really came to much – today it's a modest, unprepossessing junction town where the once-grand Moorish station remains the only feature of note along with its graveyard siding of old trains. With a guide, however, there are some potentially interesting hikes to be had on the dusty hills to the north where, at one point there's an abrupt 'secret canyon'.

Transport Through buses to Baku and most points west depart from the roundabout on the southern edge of town. Buses to Qubalı Balaoğan (for Pirxana/Pir Hussein) leave from the bazaar area two blocks south of the railway station in the town centre. Frequent minibuses shuttle between Qazi Mammad bazaar and Äli Bairamli/Şirvan.

Şirvan (formerly Äli Bayramlı, ☎ 0197)

Officially renamed Şirvan in 2008, the large town of Äli Bayramlı hosts oil extraction companies, a pipeline junction and large

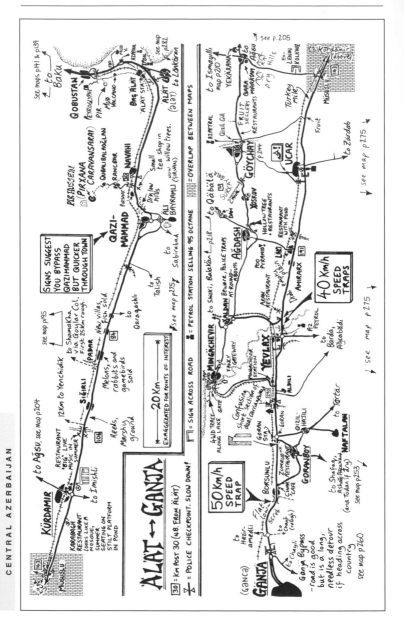

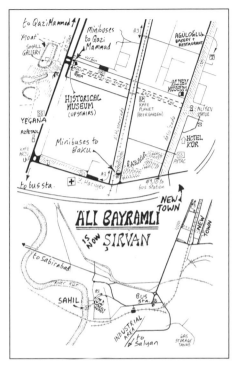

strategic gas reserve. It's hardly an attraction, but should you find yourself living here (it happens!) there's a friendly little expat community, acceptable pizza/Turkish restaurant (*Agüloğlu*) and an upstairs **historical museum** whose hospitable guides are keen to illustrate centuries of human habitation in the area. Signs of such antiquity aren't obvious from the New Town's leafy but archetypical Soviet streets. The 'Old Town' is only slightly more atmospheric with a century-old warehouse and, on the nearby riverbank, the simple *Sahil Restaurant* where you can savour kebabs on a stilt platform above the waters.

Renovated first-floor rooms at the outwardly decrepit *Hotel Kür* (☎ 51456) are better than expected, most with tiled bathrooms, Western toilet and new air-conditioners (AZN14). However, the beds have

thin mattresses and the mosquitoes like to meet and greet.

SABIRABAD (☎ 0143)
Agricultural centre Sabirabad (see map p275) sits at the junction of the great Araz and Kura rivers. Apart from predictable statues of Sabir, the town has nothing to show for millennia of history. Previously known variously as Galagayin, Petropavlovka and Javad (Djevat) the site has always proved strategic enough to warrant a thorough destruction by passing invaders. Changes in the course of the rivers have left so little for archaeologists that the Khanate of Javad is now one of the least-documented entities of medieval Azerbaijan. Yet it was here in 1736 that Nadir Shah was grandly crowned ruler of Persia at a *kurultai*-style tent-city erected to emulate those of Genghis Khan. And 60 years later Aga Mohammad chose the site as his winter camp.

Today's villages of Cavad (5km north) and Qalaqayin (2km west, whose castle was sacked by Nadir Shah) are sentimental recent namings and don't appear to represent the site of their historical forbears. The only attraction of visiting today's Cavad is crossing the low-slung pontoon bridges across quietly scenic riverbanks to reach it.

If you're continuing via **Saatli** to fly-blown **Imishli** or vaguely interesting **Beylaqan** (p277) there are three pleasant roadside restaurants at **Bulaqlı**, 5km east of Sabirabad.

KÜRDAMIR (☎ 0145)
Historically Kürdamir is a place that has demoralized even the toughest of visitors. In 1795 it was at Kürdamir that Russian General Zubov learnt of the impending Persian invasion and sensibly decided to run away. Two thousand years before, the local 'Albanian' warriors had proved no match for

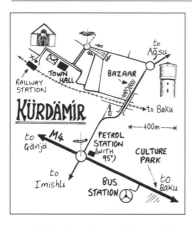

be up to 400 years old, though the town itself was only officially founded in 1858. One of the trees was sliced in half 'by Armenian bombardment' during 1918. Its trunk has since grown 'miraculously' into a curious quintuple-stemmed 'hand' that some consider to have magical powers. Göychay translates as 'blue river', perhaps misleading for a rather big, sprawling market town on a wide silt-filled stream.

The region is famed for pomegranates. You'll see them on sale everywhere from late September and on October 19th there's a Pomegranate Festival (Nar Bayrami). The town's most distinctive building is the **Äbulfäz Äbbas mosque**, a colourfully painted 1902 brick building with round, Moorish-style windows.

You must wear slippers to enter the well-kept **museum** (9-13 & 14-18:00, free) which displays medieval pottery from the inaccessible Surxay Qala castle ruins (see opposite) and a twist of metal that was the handiwork of 1960s muscleman Chingiz Göychaylı, whose portrait features in a wonderful old poster.

Behind summer tables of pensive tea-drinking veterans, the central **Chinar Hotel**

the disciplined, well-armed Romans. However, the legions were tricked into following a local 'guide' who led them not to Shamakha as they'd hoped but into the Kürdamir marshes where they quickly became lost and disoriented amid the bogs, mosquitoes and *gurza* snakes. Kürdamir is still infamous for its night-time plagues of mosquitoes and its summer heat, though it's drier and less marshy than in previous centuries.

The town centre, across the railway tracks from the main highway, has a neatly whitewashed, ghostly atmosphere. For a planned Soviet town ensemble the design is not unpleasant but like all Kürdamir's historical visitors, you'll probably be keen to hurry on. For the Kürdamir to Aqsu road see p204.

UCAR (Ujar, ☎ 0270)
Track three on Sparks' 1976 '*Big Beat*' album sums up this dreary steppe town: go on, look it up! Actually Ucar does have one surprise up its dusty sleeve, a supermarket that Peace Corps volunteers have dubbed the 'Awesome Store' for its remarkable selection of Western groceries.

GÖYCHAY
(Göyçay, ✪ Geokchai; ☎ 0267)
Backed by curiously eroded mud-walled canyons, Göychay has a pleasant central area full of plane trees that are claimed to

has been redecorated but the new paint is already peeling off. The AZN4-5 per person charge is reasonable given the newish toilet/shower booths in most rooms though the beds themselves are prehistoric and rather offputting.

The best central restaurant is the *Karavansaray* (off Rasulzade St) with tables set beneath peach-trees in a paved if unexotic courtyard. The *buğlama* is better at *Qizil Gül* (formerly Zehrab) restaurant set in an overgrown rose-garden terrace by an artificial streamside. It's unsigned and well away from the town so access is awkward without a vehicle although rare #5 buses pass within 300 metres.

City bus routes 2 and 3 link the town centre to the bus station roundabout where through transport is common especially for Ağdash. Shared taxis to Baku cost AZN8 per person.

XOSROV

Between Göychay and Ağdash, Xosrov village has a new mosque, the view of which is masked westbound by an ugly four-storey apartment block. Across the road,

Xosrov grave posts

behind a wall is a cemetery containing the Haji Bulat Baba Pir, the last resting place of a 19th-century Lezghian holy man who lived to 112 years old. More interesting are the nearby simple wooden graveposts of more ordinary folk: the **posts** with sharpened rhomboid tops denote women's graves.

Xosrov is one possible starting point for attempts to reach **Surxay Qala**, a castle site probably named after Khan Surkhay of Shirvan (ruled 1721-34). Its minimal ruins sit on an inaccessible, perilously crumbly clifftop to the north via Arabjabali/Kukar villages. Explorers venturing into a tunnel at the site claim that spookily their lamps would consistently fail at the same point, nine metres in. The castle is the mythical setting for an Azeri variant on *Taming of the Shrew*: a local ruler kidnaps the beautiful Lady Gülgaz and whisks her off to Surxay where she perversely falls in love with him despite her enforced captivity.

AĞDASH (☎ 0193)

Known as Arash Mahal until 1919, Ağdash ('white stone') was ravaged by a June 1999 earthquake but has since been extensively restored. Today it's a relatively appealing small town with several late 19th-century brick buildings including two surviving sides of a former brick **caravanserai** now inset with a pair of exceedingly slow-connection internet rooms.

The **museum** (10-13 & 15-17:00, closed Sunday) is housed in the Jashaji Bey mansion. Model soldiers breaking through the blackened wall-cracks create an unusually imaginative dramatization of WWII

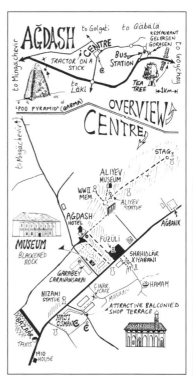

action. There's also a recreated village home scene illustrating local spinning crafts. One of the guides speaks a few words of English and is happy to sell you the hand-painted ceramic works of local artist Taleh Salehov.

The town's social whirl revolves around tea and strolls in attractive **Heydar Aliyev Park**. Here Heydar Baba's statue and museum compliment a dolphin gateway, a notable WWII memorial and a concrete stag. Amid the pretty cypress trees, four çayxana-eateries are full of noisy slappers – ie çay-sipping nard-playing men who whack down their pieces with maximum possible force.

On Ağdash's eastern outskirts 1.5km east towards Göychay, Çinar restaurant's giant, 560-year-old **hollow tea-tree** was used for years as a çayxana.

The best accommodation is an unmarked *Qonaq Evi* above Ağ Bank where five rooms with air-con and toilet cost AZN10 per bed. Phone Sabukhi (☎ mob 050 347 6803) to reserve.

Otherwise you'll be stuck with the Soviet-era *Ağdash Hotel* where just two dorm-style rooms are operable. The power-points dangle loose, doors don't close let alone lock and partly smashed, taped-closed windows are held together with plastic sheeting. If the scratching, snorting and chain-smoking of your roommates doesn't keep you awake, the evening's voracious mosquitoes and unexplained gunshots just might.

For more choice continue 40km to Mingächevir.

Ağdash to Qäbälä

The mostly paved Ağdash–Qäbälä road follows the Turyanchay river, crossing a dam and heading into a gorge of lion-paw cliffs. The views are best driving north-bound: heading south is less interesting as the erosion effects are hidden by the trees on the north-facing slopes. Around 2km north of **Savalan** the route rises along a narrow plateau between two gorges and later forms a tree-lined avenue. Approaching Qäbälä (see p212) there's a possible excursion to **Kyomarat Baba**

(p216) before passing the access road to the **RLS** tracking station (p216).

Xaldan

Xaldan is not a place anyone plans to visit but you may need to change buses here (eg Zaqatala–Mingächevir) and drivers passing through should watch very carefully. No fewer than three poorly signed road inter-changes count as roundabouts to lurking traffic police who delight in catching you as you unwittingly drive the 'wrong way round'. There are similar 'money round-abouts' on the eastern side of Ağdash and just north of Ucar.

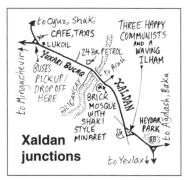

Xaldan junctions

MINGÄCHEVIR (☎ 0147)

Azerbaijan's fourth-biggest city, Mingä-chevir (Mingachaur in Russian) is one of those towns that, with residual Soviet zeal, many locals describe as 'beautiful'. While there are some well-designed government buildings and plenty of parks to break up the regimented grid of concrete homes, 'live-able' would be a better description. Or 'relaxed'. Even Lenin (while his statue lasted) used to sit cross legged on a park bench rather than standing and pointing.

Today Lenin's gone to bed but some other fairly imaginative sculptures remain and there's a hypnotic charm to staring at the surreal opal-blue waters of the River Kura from one of the terrace restaurants and tea houses scattered along either bank.

Smaller than it looks, the **History Museum** (9-13 & 14-18.00, Mon-Fri)

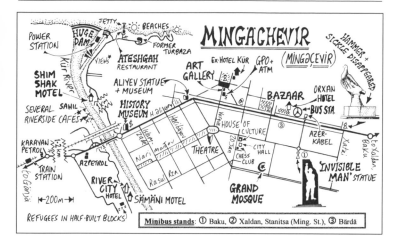

Minibus stands: ① Baku, ② Xaldan, Stanitsa (Ming. St.), ③ Bärdä

shows some interesting cut-aways of pre-historic grave-sites, has decent models of ancient homesteads and recreates the interior of a Lahic-style smithy. The guides speak limited Russian.

Mingächevir's modest **Art Gallery** (same times) has some excellent modern and Soviet realist works, eg by Fikret Hasimov.

The large **Grand Mosque** is a new, sandstone edifice in lovingly tended grounds. Its grey marble interior has an impressive giant chandelier. The twin, silvered minarets look like intercontinental ballistic milk-churns.

West bank cafés offer pretty river views backed by arid hills behind a ribbon of trees. *Sahil Café* puts summer tables at one of the nicest viewpoints. However, the café itself is a scaly metallic hemisphere that looks like an alien space pod designed by a Soviet *Blue Peter*.

Mingächevir's raison d'être is its large **hydro-electric dam**, built between 1948 and 1954 with the help of German PoWs who had still not been allowed home years after WWII ended. The dam provides citizens with a supply of water/electricity which is unusually reliable for provincial Azerbaijan. The population is vocally happy about this and seems immune to killjoy experts who have been warning for years that the dam

faces a catastrophic collapse if it's not strengthened. The **reservoir** that the dam created is Azerbaijan's biggest lake and has submerged many rich archaeological sites, the best finds from which are displayed in Baku's Historical Museum. During the ultra-dry summer of 2000 the water retreated exposing many new finds – one group of expats stumbled upon a fossilized mammoth. With a 4WD it was possible to drive for miles along the shore. In contrastingly wet years, however, the water can rise so high that even the beaches disappear.

The most accessible such 'beach' is just beyond the dam. On the gentle rise above the rotting jetty nearby is the summer-only *Ateshgah Restaurant* (☎ 43399). Its terrace is pleasant for tea (60q) or beer (AZN1) with fish sudak and lake views. However, hidden beneath the once-attractive main building, an off-beat attraction is its surreal acid-trip cavern bar guarded by a giant spider and facing a dance-floor where glass-fibre stalactites have a stream cascading through the middle. It's worth a look even when the bar is not officially operating.

Accommodation

The four-star *River City Hotel* (☎ 49373) should be the best in town when/if it's finished. Till then the nearby *Sämäni Hotel* (☎

42998) is a reasonable choice with acceptably furnished box suites, air con and a quiet riverside location.

Just off the road to the dam, *Motel Shimshak* (☎ 43730) has just two suites (AZN20 & 30) where the dining areas are much bigger than the beds. Handy for the bus station, *Orxan Hotel* (☎ 56920) is a functional, traders' hotel with curious views down onto the covered hardware/cloth market from its upstairs corridor. Friendly manageress Mila seems to share Sybil Fawlty's coiffeur, though fortunately not her management style. Beds cost AZN6 in neat, unsophisticated rooms that share a frequently polished squat loo and hot shower. That's much better value than at the mostly refugee-filled *Ex-Hotel Kür* (also AZN6 per bed) whose former reception office is now used as a school room. To organize a bed head up to the third floor and seek out the harridan *dezhurnaya* (floor lady) if you dare. She rapidly started screaming at me for asking to see a room: 'Not until you pay'. In fact the rooms are predictably bare. They've been repainted within living memory and share a seatless WC and cold water.

Transport
Services from Mingächevir's main bus station include 11 daily to Ağdash, five to Gänjä and Tärtär, four to Oğuz and Shäki plus daily to Länkaran (8:30), Balakän (8:30), Qäbälä (11:00) and Ashaği Ağcakand (9:30). Qazax buses (7:10, 9.30 and 13.50 run via Gänjä. Most Baku-bound transport leaves from the 'Invisible Man' roundabout. Minibuses to Bärdä depart when full from opposite the bazaar.

Mingächevir is sweatily spread out but taxis cost only AZN1-2 per hop and various city buses run regularly down Heydar Aliyev pr. Useful #7 passes the Grand Mosque, takes in 20th Jan St and Heydar Aliyev pr, crosses the river bridge then turns immediately north under the railway. Rare Bus #2 goes from the bazaar to the former turbaza passing the dam (but only eight times daily).

There's a train to Baku at 07.45 each morning except Wednesdays (AZN3.10 seat-only).

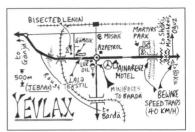

YEVLAX (EVLAX, YEVLAKH, JEVLAX; ☎ 0166)
The one potential tourist attraction in dull Yevlax is a fine, pink-granite **Lenin statue**. Sawn in half and pocked with bullet-holes in his back, he's been dumped at 40°36'19.6"N, 47°07'50.5"E where he surveys a maudlin domain of collapsing factories. 'I always kiss his head when I pass' said an old shepherd man. Less-respectful kids scramble across the decapitated torso, squealing 'Good morning children, a table, a table' and other random English phrases that they've learnt at school. To find him follow the main road 1.2km west from the AzPetrol roundabout. After the big new Lalä Tekstil factory (and before the bridge) turn right. After 450m, having bumped across an old freight railtrack, the statue is in the muddy walled yard to your left.

BÄRDÄ (Bərdə; ☎ 0110)
For most of the 'Albanian' period ancient Bärdä (known then as Partav) was politically subservient to Qäbälä though it grew

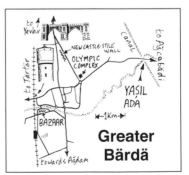

Greater Bärdä

in stature after Qäbälä effectively collapsed during the 6th century Mekhrane dynasty. Wall fragments of the Torpaq Qala (Earthen Castle) are held to date from this era. In the summer of 943 Bärdä was capital of Aran, an emirate loyal to the Arab Caliph when one of the bizarrest incidents in Azeri history occurred. Asmut and Sveneld, a pair of Viking warriors had negotiated free passage right down the Volga for them, their classic longboats and their small, private army. In a veritable Odyssey, they then traced the western shore of the Caspian and sailed up the great

Kura river, finally mooring at the junction of the Tärtär river.

From there they launched an audacious raid on Bärdä. Understandably, the locals were not exactly expecting a gang of drunk Varengians to roll into town and much of the town's superstitious population simply fled from what were assumed to be devils. For two months Azerbaijan was thus a nominal Viking colony! However, an unfamiliar surfeit of fruit soon had the invaders clinging to their medieval toilets. The Emir regrouped his forces and marched into town. Lacking Imodium, the Vikings fled

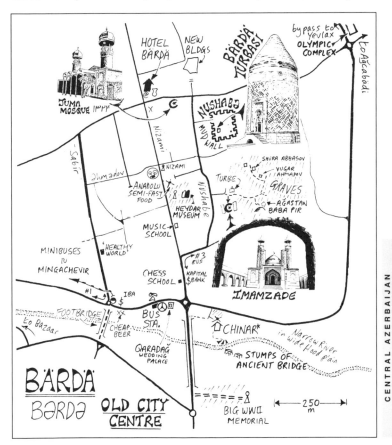

CENTRAL AZERBAIJAN

under cover of night carting off a fair cache of treasure with them. Incredibly around 300 of them eventually made it all the way home again. That home would have been somewhere in today's Ukraine where the Varengian Vikings were progressively Slavicized becoming the Kievan Rus, ie proto-Russians. Varang meant 'keeper of oaths' in old Norse.

What to see

The familiar teamwork of earthquakes, redevelopment and Genghis Khan have been cruel, but Bärdä retains some intriguing hints of the town's former glory. Three **brick arches** (out of an original sixteen) show where a classic 120m ancient bridge once spanned the Tärtär river diagonally.

Built in 1322 by Ahmed Ibn Ayyub al Hafiz, the brick and blue-tiled tomb-tower called **Bärdä Turbasi** (Akhmed Zocheibana Mausoleum) is second only to Nakhchivan's Momine Khatun tower for works of this genre. But don't get overexcited: 'restoration' in the Soviet era added an unsightly concrete conical top and some of the kufic inscriptions are crumbling. Nonetheless the tower is attractively set in a pretty rose garden in the centre of the modest mud walls of **Nushabä/Torpaq Qala** (supposedly 6th century). Local whitebeards claim that it once served as a keep/watch tower controlled by Dağestani princes and that a warren of unexplored tunnels lead out from beneath it.

The sizeable **Imamzade** is an important Muslim shrine at the supposed grave of Prince Ismail, grandson of Imam Jaffar Sadiq. It had already been a place of pilgrimage for generations when 12th-century merchant, Tajir Ibrahim, decided to sponsor the brick-domed mausoleum. The four minarets were added in 1868 by Kerbelaji Safi Khan who also built mosques in Ağdam and Shusha and lived to the ripe old age of 122. Within the shrine is a stone draped with a green flag and topped with an Arab sabre. The complex is bracketed by barn-like metal-roofed prayer areas, and set within a very extensive mixed (Christian and Muslim) **cemetery** with several other notable tombs. Unobtrusive with a small

brick dome, the **Bakhman Mirza tomb** was for a nephew of the Qajar Shah of Persia who was a minor poet. A curious ring of stones is all that remains of the **Ağastan Baba Pir**, destroyed decades ago in an earthquake. The muddy mound beside it is not a *kurgan* tumulus but the debris from the excavations, with plentiful fragments of blue-glazed ceramics. Contemporary 'portrait' memorials include those of Shura Abbasov (shown in a traditional hat but holding his electric guitar and mobile phone). A little beyond is the full colour depiction of 16-year-old Vugar Ahmadov who was killed by an electric shock in a faulty sauna.

Accommodation and food

There are four decent air-con rooms with bathrooms (AZN20-50) at the back of the very popular *Chinar Restaurant* (mob ☎ 050-456 9995, Jamal). The unreconstructed Soviet-era *Hotel Bärdä* (AZN5 per person) is as bad as it looks. Enquire for keys at the shop units in its ground-floor area.

Pleasantly perched at the crossing of a river and canal 3km towards Ağcabädi, *Yaşil Ada* (see map p248) aka Green Island, is one of Bärdä's best dining options.

BÄRDÄ TO TÄRTÄR AND NAFTALAN (see map p275)

Near **Buruch** a series of muddy mounds is visible north of the main road. They look like *kurgan* burial mounds though a local archaeologist insists (rather unconvincingly) that they're actually ancient look-out posts for surveying the flat expanses of farmland.

Tärtär has a fine twin-minaretted mosque and an atmosphere that's surprisingly upbeat considering its proximity to the occupied zone. During the Soviet era Tärtär was renamed Mirbashir after a revolutionary 'hero'. It reverted after independence in 1991. 'That's democracy', explained one resident inscrutably. The town's simple but bearable *hotel* costs AZN3-5 per night, showers are AZN1 extra. Minibuses start near the bridge for Bärdä market, Naftalan and Mingächevir.

From the Tärtär–Goranboy road the mountains of Karabagh rise hazily on the

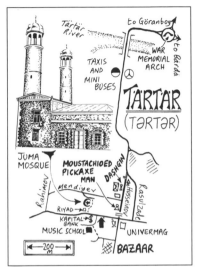

name means 'to take the oils'. Apocryphally the source was discovered when a medieval herder decided to leave behind a particularly sick, mangy camel. The beast rolled over into an oily pool and was left for dead. But when the herder returned some weeks later, he found the camel miraculously cured. Remarkably he chose to credit the oil rather than divine intervention. With the liberalizing of the imperial Russian economy in 1874, a German chemist by the name of Jäger developed Naftalan oil into a major export product. By the turn of the 20th century, jars of Naftalan ointment were so common that even the Japanese soldiers attacking Russia in the 1904-5 war were found to be carrying jars of the stuff. Enemy soldiers being protected by a 'Russian' product was yet another embarrassing irony for the Tsar facing military defeat, revolution and the chagrin of his wife's improprieties with Rasputin.

Attractively nestled amid hundreds of pine trees, Naftalan village became one of the USSR's more vaunted sanatorium towns, cadres flying into its exclusive airport from all across the Soviet Union. Naftalan's fame was such that a 'sister' clinic was founded in Ivanić Grad (then Yugoslavia, now Croatia, 🖥 www.naftalan.hr).

During the 1990s, however, Naftalan was flooded with refugees/IDPs fleeing the nearby Karabagh conflict. The airport and all but one sanatorium closed down and the whole town went to seed. Around 2005 the situation started to improve. Although many rotting buildings remain over stuffed with long-suffering refugees, these days Azerbaijan tourism authorities see Naftalan as having major potential for attracting local and East European hypochondriacs. After all who wouldn't want to soak in a bath full of gooey chocolate-marmite petroleum?

The first of a new series of sanatoria is already attracting visitors from as far afield as Moscow. Imaginatively named **Naftalan Sanatorium** (31 Shirvan pr, ☎ 23038, 🖥 www.naftalan-tour.com) the three-storey building is comfortably institutional with attractive tiling, 11pm cur-

western horizon. The best views are some 2km south of Qizilhacili (the Naftalan turn-off), eternally snow-topped Mt Murovdağ looking majestic above a wide field-filled foreground.

NAFTALAN (☎ 0255)

Marco Polo wrote of a magical oil which made an excellent 'unguent for the cure of cutaneous distempers' – ie it helped skin diseases. Though he never visited Azerbaijan the oil he was referring to was most probably from today's Naftalan, whose

fews and an aroma of school dinners. It's fun to be shown around the complex and its bizarre series of treatments, mud tubes and four oil types (of which one is drunk!). They'll take walk-in guests hotel-style (sgl/dbl/suite AZN40/70/90) should beds be available, but normally it's AZN550-700 for two weeks including meals and one change of bed-sheets.

The multi-storey eyesore that was once *Hotel Naftalan* is full of refugees, but a few of these friendly long-suffering folk supplement their minimal incomes by renting out AZN3 beds in dilapidated but movingly personal former guest rooms that otherwise double as part of their adopted 'homes'. Staying here is cheap and gives an insight to the plight of the forgotten refugees' existence. Ask at the second minimarket down towards the bus station.

Kafe Samovar serves good fish/sudak for only AZN1.60 at tables set in the trees around an eccentric samovar-shaped building.

Transport

Minibuses and shared taxis shuttle regularly to and from Goran on the main Gänjä highway (25 mins, AZN4 taxi). From the wrecked shell of Naftalan's bus station, departures include Gänjä via Goranboy (7:05, 9, 11:50 & 13:00), Shäki via Mingachevir (7:50), Baku (8:30 and 16:00) and Tärtär (8:50, 9:30, noon and 12:30).

GORANBOY

Compact Goranboy (aka Jeranboy, formerly Kasim-Ismailov) has an attractively tree-shaded central area around the new **Heydar Aliyev statue** and sweet little **history museum** (closed on Sundays) whose director

might entertain you by playing the *tar*. The **English Center** in School No 2 delights in receiving foreigners to 'practice on' but there's neither a restaurant nor a hotel here.

Buses run half-hourly to Gänja or it's a 5-minute taxi hop to Goran where longer distance services stop. **Goran** is a 1km roadside strip of wholesale shops selling electronics and 'white goods'. If you're on a less-than-full bus, don't be surprised if your driver nonchalantly stops here for as much as an hour filling every available square inch with TVs and washing machines.

At **Rähimli** (see map opposite), west of Goranboy, there are dome-topped brick tombs in an old graveyard. And the views south-west towards snow-capped Mt Murovdağ can be superb when the haze clears. However, the most likely touristic reason to come to Goranboy is to attempt the scenic but heart-rending and problem-filled Todan Loop.

THE TODAN LOOP

The potentially fascinating loop from Goranboy to Gänjä via Shafaq, Ağcakänd and Todan is made difficult by the appalling roads around Todan (impossibly muddy after rain) and especially by official sensitivities as Ağcakänd is still classified locally as a 'war zone'. Getting beyond the Shafaq police checkpoint was always hit and miss but on my last attempt the police told me they'd become much more vigilant in stopping foreigners since some annoying reporter 'got through and wrote about this place in a book!' I wonder who that could have been? You might get through if you're with locals whose car is known to the barrier cops or using the Gänjä–Ağcakänd bus which sails straight through. If you do, beware that there are still some mine-fields (mostly marked) so don't stray from the well-used tracks.

Shafaq

The oldest village in the valley, archaeologists have been investigating a suspected Timur-era settlement on the spooky hills to the south-east of Shafaq town amid extensive shattered **graveyards** and the ruins of former Armenian homes.

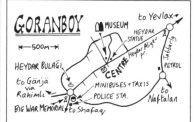

GORANBOY

← 500M →

to Yevlax →

MUSEUM

HEYDAR STATUE

Heydar Aliyev pr.

HEYDAR BULAĞI

to Gänjä via Rähimli

CENTRE

MINIBUSES + TAXIS

POLICE STA.

BIG WAR MEMORIAL

to Shafaq

PETROL

to Naftalan

CENTRAL AZERBAIJAN

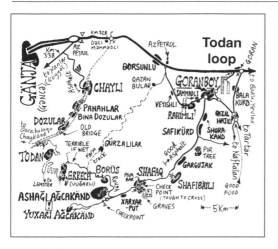

The asphalt turns abruptly to squelching mud 3km before ruined but picturesque **Erkech** (now officially named Vugarli). Steep muddy hairpins undermine the beauty of the road's tortuous continuation into **Todan** whose new metal roofs glitter on the next ridge. The whole town has been rebuilt since the early 1990s when Muslim Todan and largely Armenian Erkech blew each other to bits in a senseless artillery exchange across the deep valley that separates them. Halfway between Erkech and Todan a hiking track reputedly leads to the site of the German mountain village of **Lemster** while near Todan, **Monashid** was once a cheese-making village founded by Swiss exiles!

A rough track supposedly links Todan to Chaykand near Hajikand. A better (if still unsurfaced) lane descends steeply into the Kurakchay valley rewarded by some attractive panoramas. There's an old bridge in **Dozular** where the houses are made of distinctive purple, grey and cream stone. Asphalt finally returns at **Chayli** where the road descends with sweeping views over Gänjä.

Ashaği Ağcakand (formerly Shaumian or Shaumianovsk), a large formerly ethnic-Armenian village, was utterly devastated in the fighting and looting of the early 1990s. Part of the village has now been resettled with rows of pastel pink and blue box-style refugee houses but the effect remains movingly depressing. More such homes are planned 5km beyond in much lovelier **Yuxari Ağcakänd** (formerly Bashkand), an idyllically set ghost town where fruit trees line a gurgling stream and grassy meadows are layered all the way up to the triangular summit of 3340m Mt Murovdağ. This could be one of the most beautiful places in Azerbaijan were its shattered stone homes rebuilt to tasteful original designs. But getting anywhere near is likely to send you to the KGB without passing Go let alone collecting £200.

On via Todan

If you've made it past Ashaği Ağcakänd the problem becomes one of road quality rather than the police. In perfect dry weather Zhigulis can make it to Todan. If it's wet even a UAZ will weep. After the attractive but partly devastated village of **Börüs** one gains false hope from the little single track asphalt lane that winds merrily up unsigned hairpins and over a small grassland pass.

GÄNJÄ (Gəncə, Kirovabad, ☎ 022)

Gänjä is Azerbaijan's second city with a population of nearly 300,000. Very few local people have heard enough Jamaican English to realize the funny side of the town's name nor the irony that Hash (Xaş) is a local delicacy. A 'Gänjä kiss', like the Glasgow equivalent, is in fact a head-butt. But the caricature of short-tempered citizens is exaggerated.

Gänjä makes a logical starting point for touring the lovely mountains and forests of the Lesser Caucasus (see Around Gänjä p259). Its pleasantly calm city centre has several mosques and churches (most now disused or converted into theatres), an

CENTRAL AZERBAIJAN

GREATER GÄNJÄ

the city fell to the Seljuk Turks under Togrul 1. Seljuk rule did not interfere with the city's growth and in 1063 the khan's builder Ibragim Gänjävi constructed the celebrated Gänjä gate. This was partially ruined in a massive 1139 earthquake. The remnants were seized by a Georgian raiding party and taken to Gelati monastery near Kutaisi where its stones remain to this day, forming the King David gate.

With Seljuk power weakening, the regional governor Shamsaddin Eldegyz ran the Gänjä-based region ('Atabeys') as an autonomous state. Although the power centre shifted for a while to Nakhchivan, Gänjä flowered as the cultural capital during an unprecedented golden age. Famed for its liberal multiculturalism the city fostered Azerbaijan's greatest classical poet, Nizami Gänjävi, as well as the gifted poetess Mähsäti Gänjävi. The golden age collapsed along with the state of Atabeys with the Mongol invasions. Though the first raid in 1220 failed, the city fell in 1225 to Jalaladdin, the Turkoman-Mongol ruler of the expanding Khorazem sultanate (centred on what is today's western Uzbekistan). Plucky Gänjä did not give up without a fight. In 1231, a peasant-and-craftsman's revolt led by the unfortunately named 'Bender', destroyed Jalaladdin's governor's palace and killed his servants. The rebels redistributed money and jewels to the poor. Inevitably Jalaladdin was not a happy Sultan. His troops returned and gruesomely beheaded poor Bender. But no sooner had they restored 'order' than the 'real' Mongols arrived. The city was pillaged and left in lifeless ashes for four years before limping back into existence.

Hulugu Khan, the Mongol-Persian 'Il Khan' emperor (reigned 1256-65), incorporated the region into his slice of empire ruled from Soltaniyeh in today's Iran. Gänjä became a major link in the Il-khannid defensive ring but couldn't stand up to Timur, who stormed through a century later. Timur not only sacked the city but expelled

imposing Stalinist city-hall, the former National parliament building and the quaintly kitsch 'bottle house'. Photos, a schematic map and extensive city history notes appear on 🖥 www.ganca.net.

History

Gänjä derives its name from Dzhanzar (Arabic for 'Treasury/Harvest store'). Or, according to some sources, from a long-forgotten Gandjak tribe that once built primitive huts in the area. Like all cities of the region it has been repeatedly flattened, initially by the Persians in the 7th century and by Arabs soon after.

Although the city celebrated its 2500th anniversary in 2006, its first period of preeminence came with the weakening of the Arab caliphate in the mid-10th century. Gänjä's semi-independent Salarid dynasty was succeeded by the Shadadids who built fortresses, bridges and caravansarais to underline the town's importance on intercontinental trade routes.

Though partially Islamicized, Gänjä remained a centre of Christianity – the seat of the Albanian Catholicos until 1054 when

CENTRAL AZERBAIJAN

❏ 1918 – Gänjä leads the Islamic world to democracy

In the confused months concluding WWI, Tsarist Russia collapsed and the three Caucasus nations, Azerbaijan, Georgia and Armenia formed an unstable Trans Caucasian Federation. As the Ottoman Turkish army marched east, the federation fell apart, Georgia declared its independence on 26 May. Two days later the Tatar National Council in Gänjä followed suit and the Azerbaijan Democratic Republic (ADR) was born. Significantly, Baku was not initially included as that city had been temporarily seized by communists, supported by a bizarre triad of mutually loathing Cossack, British and Armenian forces if only to prevent the impending Turkish invasion. In contrast the ADR welcomed the Turks as 'ethnic brothers' and following their arrival in Gänjä on 20 June, they were joined by around 12,000 Azeri volunteers forming the 'Army of Islam' to march on Baku under Ottoman commander Nuri Pasha.

Meanwhile, Gänjä had become the capital of the world's first democratic Islamic nation. De facto ministries were set up in the homes of activists while the city council office (later used as a WWII hospital and now the agricultural academy) became the ADR's parliament. It held its first session at 2pm on 17 June. As yet 'democracy' was an abstract principle as no national vote had been able to confirm the leadership. Nonetheless, the leaders were later to impress US President Woodrow Wilson with their advanced, principled philosophy.

most of the native population to central Asia, replacing them with thousands of captured Syrian families.

For several subsequent centuries, the region returned to a mostly Persian orbit. Eclipsed culturally by Tabriz, Gänjä nonetheless rebounded yet again as a trade and Islamic centre with an important mosque built in 1620 by Shah Abbas (still standing). 'Verily tis one of the fairest cities in all Persia' gushed Polish traveller Cornelius DeBruin in 1718 admiring the 'wide streets, large caravansarais, a river through the town and all surrounded by gardens and orchards'. The positive impression reinforces Philippe Avrille's 1681 nickname 'paradise garden' for a Gänjä which he found to be surprisingly bustling with foreigners.

By the 18th century, Gänjä was 'the principal centre of Islam in the Caucasus'. Although briefly absorbed into King Irakli's Christian Georgia, it remained an independent khanate till 1795 when the city fell to Aga Muhammad, founder of the ruthless Persian Qajar dynasty. British diplomacy briefly restored the local Khan Javad to the throne but after a fierce struggle the city was grabbed for Russia by Viceroy Tsitsianov in 1804. The battle is depicted in a huge painting in Baku's Historical Museum. Russian rule was by no means popular and in 1826 Gänjä opened its gates to the Persian forces of Abbas Mirza. But the Tsar's forces under Matadov counterattacked and drove the Persians back across the Araz river. The permanent division of Azerbaijan into Russian north and Persian south was settled two years later by the Treaty of Turkmenchai.

Incoming Russians settled several kilometres west of the original city centre, around a then-massive pentagonal star shaped fortress. This colonial 'new town' was re-christened Elisavetpol for Tsar Alexander I's wife. Population shifts had already made this the city centre by 1918 when (known as Gänjä again) it was briefly capital of the Azerbaijan Democratic Republic (see box above). In Soviet days the town became a sprawling semi-industrial city and was renamed Kirovabad after Sergei Kirov whose murder Stalin covered up by launching a vast personality cult. It regained the name Gänjä yet again in 1991 though most Azeri inhabitants had never called it anything else.

CENTRAL AZERBAIJAN

What to see

The **central square** has been transformed into a very attractive stroll-park with musical fountains performing around 9pm surveyed by an obligatory Heydar Aliyev statue. But the area is still dominated by the fine Stalinist arches of the grand city administrative buildings built in 1948-9 by architects Ismailov and Leontieva. The Soviet insignia over the doors at each end have been painstakingly replaced with gilded Azeri national symbols. The rest of the façade, however, retains good old communist-era motifs – tractors, helicopters, bridges and industrial scenes topped off with flag designs. It is photogenically illuminated at night.

The 17th-century **Abbas (Juma) Mosque** in the central square is a relatively modest brick affair with two minarets but has an attractive domed interior. Built about the same time, the Çokäk hamam (former bath-house) is now labelled **Decorative Arts Centre** (☎ 565547, 5-9pm, 20q). In reality this means it displays a lot of 20th century teapots and some unremarkable ceramic miniature-work.

The **Bottle House** (15 Guseinli/36

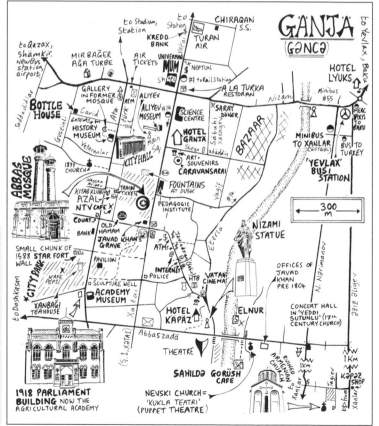

Cavid) is one of Gänjä's more off-beat attractions. More impressive than its better-known relative in Rhyanon, Nevada, it's the work of Ibragim Jaffarov who used 48,000 glass bottles to decorate an existing two-storey home. Though the use of bottles was purely aesthetic, the pictures peeling off the gables commemorate Ibragim's brother Yusif (depicted in the portrait that looks like Mao). Yusif never returned from WWII. He didn't die as the family received a mysterious letter from him in 1957 but have received no word since. The prominently painted word 'Ждем' (Zhdem) means 'we wait for you'. Visitors are encouraged to buy something from the motley selection of overpriced gum, beer and Snickers bars sold from the creeper-enveloped porch to finance the house's much-needed renovation.

Museums The **History Museum** (☎ 563 594, Tue-Sun 10-13, 14-18.00, AZN2) is housed in the former mansion of the Zhiadkhanov brothers, who were among the founders of the 1918 Democratic Republic. Exhibits include a model of how the ancient city may once have looked plus all the usual photos, mammoth bones and *kupe* amphorae. In the garden is the remnant brick archway of the Hüsniyyä mosque with token towerlets and a small gallery.

The 1918 Parliament convened initially in the building that's now the **Agricultural Academy** (closed to the public). Across the road is the **Academy Museum** (Akademiyanin Muzeyi) which formed the parliamentary annex at the same time. On my last two visits it's been closed but previously this museum was a brighter, more interesting version of the History Museum with the added bonus of being free. The interior itself is attractive thanks to the old bronze-and-white-tiled fireplaces. The overpoweringly gaudy Nizami room painted by Rustam Guseinguliev with scenes from Khamza and multilingual translations of Nizami's aphorisms.

Other curiosities Though quite large, the supposedly 17th-century brick **cara-vanserai** is relatively unspectacular. The inner courtyard is graced by a massive plane tree, but the structure is part of the Gänjä State Humanitarian college and not officially open to the public.

It is pleasant to stroll or sip tea in the city park where a small remnant section from the **old fortress** has been built up into a commemorative brick arc. The fort had originally been built in 1588, was reinforced by the Turks in 1712 and 1724 and later became the heart of Russian Elizavespol.

Of Gänjä's several **churches**, two are used as theatres. The biggest but hardest to find is a gutted Armenian 1869 drum-towered edifice set almost invisibly behind locked gates at the rear of a small tea garden. The tea-drinkers there are likely to look somewhat askance at your interest in the building. Try calling it 'Albanian' if asking directions! Minibus 14 gets you close.

The tiny brick cube known as the **Khan's Office** was supposedly where Javad Khan did his paperwork before 1804. The building is touted as a museum but is actually used as an office by city bureaucrats.

En route to Xosh Bulaq (or accessible by bus 7A), the green domed 1677 **Qizil Hacili Mosque** is worth a very brief stop.

Accommodation
A new 'five-star' hotel is nearly finished out near the Olympic Complex in New Ganja. Meanwhile the best choice by far is the grand *Hotel Gänjä* (☎ 565106) occupying a fine Stalinist stone edifice facing the city hall. The best rooms have a great view over the central square. Totally renovated twin rooms from AZN50 have A/C, fridge and good clean Western bathrooms. The lobby would be even more impressive if they'd turn on its pseudo art-nouveau lamps. The AZN200 suite has a sauna.

If Ganja Hotel is full try *Hotel Lyuks* (☎ 574652), a relatively new place near Yevlax bus station. Twin rooms with full facilities start at AZN40. Slightly bigger but not better versions cost AZN60. They're presentable enough though the curtains look cheap and colour schemes aren't exactly artistic. Oddly you have to enter from the pine-shaded courtyard at the rear.

The new motel-style *Mehmanxana Karavanşaray* (☎ mob 050-245 3000) is on

CENTRAL AZERBAIJAN

the thundering Baku highway 1km east of the big castle-style gateway. When I visited it was operational yet totally deserted, *Marie Celeste* style. The big plus here seems to be its little outdoor swimming pool with unparalleled views of the aluminium factory!

A last resort for backpackers, **Hotel Kapaz** (☎ 565106, Käpäz Mehmanxanasi) is every bit as dismal as it looks. The 1970s' concrete block lacks the slightest architectural charm, the receptionists seem half asleep and dezhurnayas (floor ladies) proved unconcealedly contemptuous that I was sad enough to require their services. Prices start from AZN15 for dowdy old single rooms with collapsing plumbing and seatless stained toilets. The creaky lift works but only up because there's no way to call it from the 6th to 8th floors where guests stay!

On the southern platform of the train station, the toilet caretaker claims he arranges **homestay** crash-pads from AZN5 for the needy, but I didn't test this.

Food and drink

Upwardly mobile city folks tend to dine in the woodland cafés towards Hajikänd (pp261-3). In town *Hotel Gänjä* offers a very grand dining room and with some insistence the staff can sometimes rustle up a menu. With a new stone-façade, *Eleqans* (☎ 568224, 9am-10.30pm) offers sensibly priced doner kebabs, pizzas and kebabs (meals AZN3-6) on sturdy wooden furniture and plonks its welcoming beer terrace in the 'mouth' of pedestrianized Cavadkhan St. For cheaper beer (60q) try *Elnur* or *Sahilda Gorüsh*, both of which overlook the river near Kapaz Hotel. *A la Turka* serves freshly baked lahmacun and a range of point-and-pick Turkish pre-cooked meals from AZN2.40 including rice. Shiny metal furniture.

Around an ugly new green building, *Xanbaği teahouse* has attractively set outdoor tables amid plane trees and palmyra palms. Tea costs 20q, open till 11pm. A little deeper within the same park, *Kafe Pepsi* serves AZN1.20 beer and ice cream till midnight in a similarly attractive environ-

ment beside an ornamental pond though here the trees are draped with fairy lights.

Services

Pedestrianized Cavadxan (Sabir) St has three **Internet Klubs** and several banks with **ATM cash machines**. There are many money-change booths notably around Univermaq (MUM/TsUM); some, including Kredo Bank, operate till late at night.

The **bazaar**, just east of the city centre, is an interesting if chaotic bustle. According to one journalist you should be very careful talking to jewellers here – apparently 'buying gold' is a coded way to arrange a narcotics deal.

Close to the caravanserai entrance, **Antikvar** is an antique/souvenir shop and a small art gallery. You might need to call ahead (☎ 50-313 0217) to have it opened.

Transport

Taxis charge a flat AZN2 rate almost anywhere in town, AZN3 to the airport. There are two bus stations linked by minibus 20 via the northern side of the main square (MUM). The **Yeni Avtovaqzal** (opened 2008, 3km west of centre) has very regular minibuses to Qazax and Aqstafa plus less frequent runs to Dashkäsän. Most other services use the **Yevlax bus station** including half hourly Yevlax (07.30-20.30), Goranboy and Baku (07.30-01.00) buses. Other useful routes include Balakan (09.30, AZN4), Bärdä (10.10, 12.50, 13.30, 15.00), Ismayıllı (08.00, 15.00), Länkäran (08.00, 09.00, 20.00) via Beylaqan, Naftalan (09.00, 12, 13, 14.20, 17.00), Qax (14.30, 15.15), Qäbälä (13.30, 14.15), Oguz (13, 16.00), Shäki (08.20, 13.45 & 16.30, AZN3) and Zaqatala (08, 11, 15.30, 16, 17.00).

For Xanlar (now officially renamed Göygöl) very regular minibuses depart from nearby when full for 20q.

The railway station is 4km north of MUM up Shah Ismail Xatai St by minibus 1. Minibus 2 loops clockwise round to Yevlax Bus Station. There's no left-luggage office. Four overnight trains run to Baku plus a not-so-fast 'express' day train oddly timed to leave at 16.00. Daily elektrichkas run to Böyük Kasik (4hrs via Ağstafa) and Ucar (2hrs).

The **airport** (international code KVD) has flights to Istanbul (Turan Air, 3T, ☎ 562 800) and Moscow (Turan and Moskovia, 🖥 www.ak3r.ru). AZAL's Gänjä–Nakhchivan flight has been suspended but might restart.

AROUND GÄNJÄ (see map p260)
Ancient Gänjä and the Nizami Mausoleum

Modern Gänjä has moved with the shifting course of the Gänjä River. The original site is some 5km east of the present centre. Archaeologists have found a few scrappy flint and mortar walls but most of the site is now on military land with little to see even if you are allowed in.

The main visitable attraction is the space-shuttle-shaped Nizami Mausoleum which has a certain brooding elegance but dates only from 1991 (replacing various older versions). Inside the sombre 22m-high structure the interior is veneered in white marble. Behind the mausoleum, some scenes from Nizami dramas are depicted in metal statuary with the jarring backdrop of the huge aluminium smelter. Driving along the main road through the underpass beneath the mausoleum don't be alarmed if the car behind starts sounding his horn – some locals 'hoot for Nizami'!

Imamzade

Within a beehive-gated old cemetery, the Imamzadeh is the revered mausoleum of Imam Mohammad Bagira ibn Ibrahim. He was a distant 8th-century relative of the great Imam Ali though a plate suggesting that the mausoleum is a millennium old is doubted by scholars. The complex was nonetheless a major religious centre and at its peak had its own fortress walls, gates, tombs, mosques and assorted religious buildings.

The present, much-reduced form of the mausoleum with its Central Asian-style blue majolica-tiled dome dates from an 1879 restoration during which the shape of the dome was changed. The reason was not artistic but part of the devout benefactor Jadigarzade's desire to remove an ancient kufic inscription he regarded as blasphe-mous. Perhaps similar motives were behind the recent removal of portraits of Babek and Imam Ali that were previously displayed inside.

Non-Muslims are welcome to enter though women should cover their hair. It's appropriate to drop a small donation in the alcove where the candles are burning. The tomb itself is ringed in black curtains and, to show respect, pilgrims shuffle out backwards so as not to turn an impolite back on the saint.

The site is beyond Bagbanlar on a road leading north from near Gänjä railway station. Taxis cost AZN5 return or take hourly bus (not minibus) 18 from opposite Gänjä railway station for 20q.

Xanlar (Göygöl town, Khanlar, Helenendorf, ☎ 0230)

Ninety years ago Franco-Armenian entrepreneur Calouste Gulbenkian advised travellers to get out of 'insupportable' Elisavetspol (Gänjä) and 'seek the shade of Hajikand or Hellenfeld'. By Hellenfeld he meant Helenendorf, later Xanlar and now Göygöl: during 2008, Azerbaijan's ever-fiddling State Toponymic Committee decided to confuse everyone by renaming Xanlar as Göygöl even though it's far from the closest village to Göy Göl Lake.

Despite all the name changes, Gulbenkian's advice remains highly appropriate. Göygöl/Xanlar has a distinctive village atmosphere with tempting

CENTRAL AZERBAIJAN

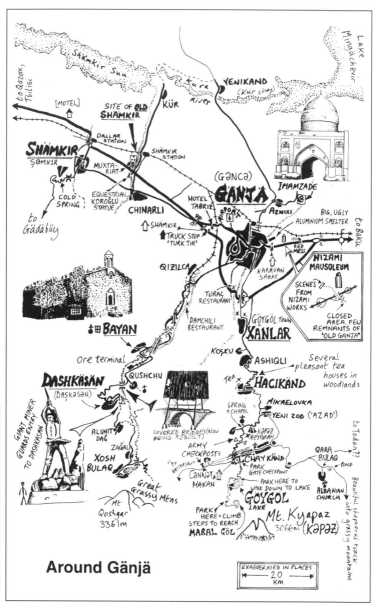

Around Gänjä

EXAGGERATED IN PLACES
20 Km

glimpses of the snow-capped lesser Caucasus peak and its six central tree-lined streets retain most of the original chocolate-box wooden homes. Several of these have now (re)inserted 'olde' style inscription key-stones into their entrance archways. Altogether the quiet town makes a delightful contrast to the dull lowlands. The area has been cultivated for centuries and a picturesque 12th-century bridge still crosses the river at the precipitous south-western edge of the village. But the village itself was only founded in 1819, the most important of many German homesteads (see box p262).

Sights In the heart of the peaceful old town, across a narrow little central park from the obligatory **Heydar Aliyev museum**, is a simple, red-stone **1854 German church**. It's been painstakingly restored within and now hosts a very sparse little **history museum** (1AZN). Most of the museum's original exhibits are reportedly now in Ganja.

Much more intriguing is the **House of Viktor Klein** (50 Aydin Haciyev St). Viktor was considered Xanlar's 'last German man' until his death in 2007 and his former home is a truly fascinating time capsule. The typical if somewhat rundown building has all the classic village elements – a big wine cellar, a loft winch and fruit-drying eaves – but also numerous faded Germanic wall decorations, a dust-coated plastic Christmas tree, German books and a kitchen full of implements that usually show up in museums. The very personal and unrenovated nature of the place makes a visit a particularly intriguing experience, but the authorities plan eventually to clean it all up and museum-ize the place which could radically alter the experience. For now, getting in is one of those delightfully hit and miss palavers so typical of rural Azerbaijan. The key-holder Fikret Ismailov (☎ 54142, mob ☎ 055-748 1718, pr Heydar Aliyeva 33) works at the town hall. He speaks some Russian but no English and you'll need to persuade him that you're deserving enough to be shown inside.

Accommodation and food Diplomats and official guests might be hosted at the unmarked *Qonaq Evi*, a clean if unpretentious guesthouse set in an overgrown walled garden on Tusi St. There's hot water and a kitchen.

For mere mortals, the only choice is *Hotel Koroğlu* (☎ 52274, mob ☎ 055-306 7855, beds from AZN5), housed in a typical balconied wooden house where Herr Forer reputedly once installed Azerbaijan's first telephone. There's no record of what he did with it until there was someone else to call. The hotel looks attractive from the outside and the interior exudes a certain atmosphere of times gone by, but conditions are basic, bedrooms somewhat dowdy and there's no heating or hot water. Toilets are communal. The hotel isn't always manned so consider phoning ahead to ensure it's open.

The appealing little *777 Restaurant* is the most central eatery. In a pretty garden, *Cännät* was run for several years by one of Xanlar's very few surviving Assyrian-Christian (Ashur) families and sporadically served great pork ribs. On my last two visits the place seemed semi-permanently closed but it's worth checking.

Alternatively there are many attractively rustic **woodland cafés** along the road to Hacıkänd after Ashiqli. For most locals a picnic at one of these places is the highlight of any trip to Gänjä.

Access From Gänja drive straight up Narimanov pr passing vineyards and a vast newly walled palace site. Or take one of the frequent Göygöl minibuses (20q). Coming from Baku use the easy-to-miss Gänja bypass swinging north at a barely-signed turn at the police check-point several kilometres east of Gänjä.

Hacıkänd (Hajikand) and around
While the teahouses in surrounding woodlands continue to multiply, **Hacıkänd** village remains strangely run-down. Several splendid old mansions appear to be falling apart as you watch. The old pink-stone **chapel** to the left of the road isn't looking too healthy either.

Above Hacıkänd the road rises through

CENTRAL AZERBAIJAN

❏ Germany's wild east

The year 1816 was a bad one in the German duchy of Würtemburg. Famine and instability had followed in the wake of the Napoleonic wars. Meanwhile, Russia hoped to spread the legendary German work ethic amongst the peasants in its newly conquered colonies, notably in the Caucasus which was considered Tsar Alexander's 'hot Siberia' for political exiles. The Russian government positively encouraged emigration with a gift of 148.85 roubles and one horse to each arriving German family. The Caucasus were made to sound like a 'promised land' to pious immigrants by stressing the proximity of Biblical Mt Ararat. However, for poor peasant families, the journey was painfully difficult. Their stories are the Caucasian equivalents of US wild-west pioneer epics.

Out of the first 'column' of 1400 families that left Würtemburg almost half died en route. Many others got only as far as Ukraine or Bessarabia (today's Moldova). The 488 families that did finally make it were settled initially in Elisavetspol (Gänjä). Two later columns of settlers were given an idyllically set but untended pasture area which they named Helenendorf (now Xanlar/Göygöl). They planted crops and vineyards but, in 1826, before development had got far, the town was burnt down by the Persians. Nonetheless, the resilient population rebuilt what rapidly grew to be the nucleus of Azerbaijan's 'Concordia' wine business. Many of Xanlar's attractive timber-eaved homes still retain the cool original wine cellars. Helenendorf also developed a reputation for producing the finest horse carts in the Caucasus and by the 1880s it had become one of the most prosperous villages in the land.

The town's fortunes collapsed in 1941 when the still predominantly German population was deported en masse to Central Asia. This bore similarities to the wartime internment of ethnic Germans and Japanese in the UK and USA, except that after the war they were not allowed to return.

an orchard onto a tree-speckled grassy ridge with ever better views across the Kurakchay Valley to the distinctively cracked-peak of Mt Kyapaz. The road passes the twin ridge-villages of **Mikaelovka** (aka Molokanka) and **Yeni Zod** (formerly Kamo/Azad). The former was founded in 1867 by Ukrainian Molokans, a few of whose descendants still remain. The main asphalt road on towards Lake Goy Göl offers wonderful views over the mountains and valleys: a particularly superb vantage point is the terrace of the *Käpäz Restoran* on the sharp bend where the road starts to descend into the valley. A checkpoint beyond prevents you descending to scraggy but vaguely historic **Chaykänd**. However, you can usually get there instead by backtracking to Yeni Zod then descending the passable unpaved road to the south from the east end of the village.

Until they were expelled during WWII, Chaykänd's population was mainly ethnic German. Their sturdy stone homes were filled by Armenians in the post-war years when the village was renamed Getashen. An Armenian inscription and an almost-collapsed church ruin remain from this period. The Armenians left during the Karabagh war and were themselves replaced by Azeri refugees.

Roads beyond Chaykänd lead up onto wide, sweeping pastures and wheat-fields with a distant mountain backdrop. The main track just bypasses the small village of **Qarabulaq** where locals have very carefully protected the turf-roofed ruin of an ancient **Albanian church** with beautiful interior stone columns and an altar area whose ogive-shaped mouldings recalls a Persian qibla niche. Across a deep-cut gully from the village is a tiny chapel and locals claim there are two other churches in the surrounding forests.

Reputedly horse and 4WD tracks lead up to Lake Göy Göl from here.

Accommodation and food Shashlyk sizzles merrily at many a woodland café on the multiple hairpins approaching Hacikand from Gänjä. *Käpaz Restoran* (see opposite) is somewhat more upmarket and has a fabulous view from its terrace. A few woodland eateries have ludicrously overpriced accommodation, eg *Laçin Qaya* who want AZN80 for fanless rooms in old container boxes.

Lake Göy Göl and the 'Tears of Kyapaz'

The distinctive rocky beak of Mt Kyapaz (Käpäz) cracked open in the September 1139 earthquake and disgorged such a mass of rock that it dammed the mountain streams in several places. The result was a string of seven idyllic mountain lakes known as the 'tears of Kyapaz'.

Most famous are Göy Göl (Blue Lake), formerly a popular sanatorium and camping retreat and the more secluded Maral Göl (Deer Lake). Lesser known Zali Göl (Leech Lake) and Sara Göl (Yellow Lake) never sounded as appealing. The area is especially magnificent in autumn when green forests are burnished yellow, auburn and red like a pointillist painting rising from Göy Göl's still blue waters to Kyapaz's dramatic crown. The best views are part way to Maral Göl.

Sadly it's far from assured that you'll be allowed to see these delights. Checkpoints prevent foreigners getting anywhere near, citing the dangers of Armenian snipers. Yet residents and VIPs with military clearance (and/or an official escort from the Xanlar or Gänjä mayors' offices) are allowed. Perhaps they're bulletproof?

Even if you get through the first checkpoint (sometimes avoidable by sneaking round via Yeni Zod and Chaykänd), there's a second even tougher one right beside Cänät Makan hotel. Even if you can't get as far as the lakes, the drive as far as the first checkpost above Chaykänd still offers delightful views of weird Mt Kyapaz and its very attractive

forest scenery. If, as reports claim, a big tourist complex is really planned up at the lake, it's surely just a matter of time before access is formally reopened.

Accommodation *Cänät Makan hotel* (mob ☎ 050-316 1150 or 649 6660) is tucked amid small trees into a gushing stream gully beyond the first Göy Göl checkpoint. However, you'll need a reservation so that the guards at the first check point are alerted to your names/numberplates. Otherwise you simply can't get there! The pine bungalows (AZN90) are comfortable though no more than you'd expect at this price. There are also some acceptably clean, new AZN40 rooms in a more basic accommodation block but these share common toilets. The hotel's quaint streamside dining booths offer meals at around AZN9 per person (no menu). Several more basic kebab-shacks line the river valley for a few kilometres on a road which spookily is still signposted to Kelbajar. There is no accommodation YET at the lakes themselves but this may change.

Transport Göygöl Town to Lake Göy Göl would take about 45 minutes driving were you able to whizz straight through the checkpoints. In October 2000 I managed to get through by chartering a local Xanlar taxi with darkened windows and a driver who knew the soldiers and thus got waved through the barriers. But security has increased since. Turning up with yellow (expat) or red (diplomatic) number plates on your vehicle will severely diminish your already small chances of getting through.

Gänjä to Xosh Bulaq

After 10km of arid plains the road from Gänjä reaches more intriguing landscapes of rocky hills and pinnacles dusted lightly with greenery. **Qizilca** has some older houses and *Damchili restaurant* sits in an appealing crouch above the river. The trees get gradually thicker as the road switchbacks across the railway 2km before the striking village of Bayan.

Slithering up a green-speckled rocky hillside, **Bayan** is a snaggle of balconied, camouflage-grey stone houses with angled

tiled and corrugated roofs. Unblemished by concrete the whole ensemble looks unlike any other village in Azerbaijan. At its heart is a spireless, very ancient Albanian stone church, partly rebuilt in 1863 by its then-Armenian population. They left en masse in the early 1990s replaced by a mixed population of Muslim refugees who now use the church as a grain store. Notice the long 'sword stone' set in the base of the tiny, heavily concrete-restored side chapel.

The mineral railway ends 4km beyond Bayan where **Qushchu (Quşçu)** iron-ore terminal is fed by rusty buckets dangling precariously on a steep cableway that swings down from the Dashkäsän quarries. The road is protected from stray falling rocks by triangular hat-like structures of corrugated metal. In complete contrast to the ugly terminal, Qushchu village is a pleasant green hamlet tucked in a side spur of valley with sparse remnants of a 5th century monastery.

After a long series of hairpins, a massive silvered statue of a pick-axe wielding

worker indicates the short diversion into **Dashkäsän**. The town takes its name ('cut rock') from the marble quarries which form an impressive amphitheatre along the Xosh Bulaq road. Its mines yielded cobalt for Siemens and copper and iron ores for the USSR with up to 500,000 tonnes produced annually after WWII. However, the main customer was the massive Rustavi steelworks (in Georgia), and when that came close to bankruptcy in the mid-1990s the obvious knock-on effect hit Dashkäsän. The town has a Soviet feel softened slightly by its mountain-top location and by some older three-storey European-style 'Nemski-Dom' buildings. The central square has a certain austere grandeur and a blue-glass Heydar Aliyev museum. There are sweeping views from the fenced sports pitch above town.

Xosh Bulaq and beyond Xosh Bulaq is a mountain reservoir-lake mostly surrounded by a grassy sprawl of datchas. Many belong to rich Gänjä folk though some of the structures look like squatters' lean-tos. City dwellers come for the fresh air, clear spring water and to get hammered on *tutovka* while barbecuing shashlyk. Behind the lake hilly fields and rolling grasslands rise towards **Mt Qoshgar**'s summer shepherd camps. Although some areas are boggy with hidden streams, the hand-scythed flower-filled meadows and upper pastures make for great rambles, wide open panoramas and offer good camping possibilities. The long, narrow pipe which follows the valley up towards Mt Qoshgar provides Dashkäsän with most of its water supply.

Transport From Gänjä's Yeni Avtovaqzal, several minibuses run daily to Dashkäsän (one hour) but only one continues to Xosh Bulaq. Hitching back to Gänjä is usually quite possible in the summer as many people spend the day at their datchas and return in the evening.

Beyond Xosh Bulaq is 4WD territory: there are several off-road possibilities but beware of boggy patches.

GÄNJÄ TO SHÄMKIR
There are two almost parallel routes. The fast, if longer, main road passes near the ruins of Old Shämkir. A quieter route transits the prosperous village of **Chinarli**, known as Lenin during the Soviet era. Chinarli residents seem to be engaged in an eccentric competition to see who can top off their house with the most ornate aluminium roof.

SHÄMKIR (✪ Şəmkir, ☎ 0241)
The low-key town today called Shämkir actually started life as Annanfeld. Settled like Göygöl (Xanlar) by German refugee-colonists (see p262), it suffered a similar partial depopulation when the ethnic Germans were banished by Stalin in 1941. In January 1918 nearly 1000 people died near the train station in an infamous confrontation between red-Russian troops and Azeri nationalists who were trying to requisition their guns. This further aggravated relations with the Bolsheviks contributing

perhaps to the *March Days* massacres later that year.

Today Shämkir's neat, tree-lined avenues hide a 1909 square-towered **church** and a few older **German-era houses** like that at 129 Vurğun. Nearby is the attractive central **stroll-park** named after Zärifä Äliyeva, the president's mother. This is home to the unusually tempting *Annanfeld Café*, a new but timelessly designed wooden building with a wraparound veranda. At the park's east end, facing an attractive contemporary mosque, the town's unmarked *hotel* is currently undergoing renovation. *Efes Café* has a curious beer garden set amongst a maze of fake rocks.

Public transport From Shämkir's bazaar minibuses leave every 15 minutes or so to Kür (till around 17:00) and occasionally to Gänjä via Chinarli. For Gädäbäy shared taxis depart from Vurgun St supplemented by a handful of daily buses and minibuses. For Baku, Gänjä, Tovuz or Qazax you're usually better off heading to the main roundabout 2km north (by Dallar minibus or taxi) and waving down one of the regular main-road minibus shuttles.

NB If you plan to use the train, note that Shämkir town is served by Dallar station. The so-called Shämkir station is in the middle of nowhere near Old Shämkir.

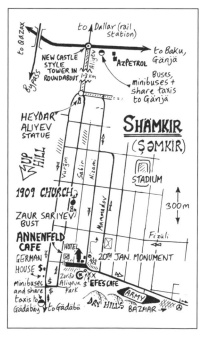

Old Shamkir
Modern Shämkir takes its name from an historical city whose scanty ruins actually lie nearly 10km further east on the northern outskirts of Muxtariat village. For centuries a fortress here guarded a key crossing point on the seasonal Shämkirchay River. In 1195 this was the scene of a decisive battle where Arran's Atabey ruler, Abu Bakr, was defeated by Queen Tamara's Georgian army. The Georgians reinstated the recently deposed Shirvanshah ruler, Agsartatan, but no sooner had Shamkir recovered than it was flattened again by the Mongols in 1235. Shämkkir's fort saw battle once again in 1826 during Persia's last ultimately unsuccessful attempt at

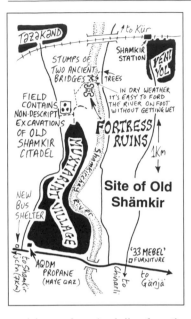

regaining northern Azerbaijan from the Russians. Thereafter the site seems to have simply withered away in favour of Annanfeld ('new' Shämkir).

Today archaeologists, led by jovial Rashid Bashirov, continue to excavate the silent, forgotten site. As they work so stubby chunks of fortress bastion are appearing from a muddy riverside hillock, their wall-remnants fashioned from brick interlaced with rock strata, several metres high in places. On the river's stony flood-plain the decapitated stumps of two former bridges remain visible. The newer 18th-century bridge was never finished while the earlier (possibly 6th century) stumps are so wobbly that discordant brick-tiled concrete supports have recently been added to preserve their last vestiges.

When the water is low, access to the fortress is an easy 15-minute walk from the Kür road (40q by minibus from Shämkir) crossing the wide shingle flood-path of the Shämkirchay river beside the old bridge stumps. That crossing is often possible by

4WD though by car it's easier to wind through Muxtariat village starting near the AQDM Qaz propane kiosk.

SHÄMKIR–GÄDÄBÄY–TOVUZ LOOP (see map opposite)

With at least one spare day, an interesting alternative to the dull Shämkir–Tovuz main road is the scenic loop via Gädäbäy. This drive is more attractive heading clockwise because the Qızıl Torpaq–Qovlar section faces into the craggier views. However, that road section is becoming increasingly rough and sometimes gets washed out altogether.

The loop doesn't really work by public transport. Getting to Gädäbäy is easy enough but the next leg (to hotel-less Saratovka) would need to be done on one of the pre-dawn village buses that arrive overnight from Baku in order to connect to the (somewhat uncertain) Saratovka–Tovuz morning bus. Renting a taxi allows for photo stops but will probably cost around AZN50 Gädäbäy–Tovuz.

Note that while this trip doesn't take you into the high mountains, you gain nearly 1000m altitude and the air in Gädäbäy is significantly cooler and fresher than on the plains.

Shämkir to Gädäbäy (45km)

South of Shämkir the Gädäbäy road starts curling up some 6km of hairpins providing wide views, though the distant High Caucasus horizon is rarely visible through the haze. After some woodland, the scenery is mostly rolling upland cornfields and hummocky meadows. A small but dramatic roadside crag after Slavyanka offers more views.

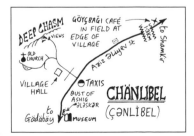

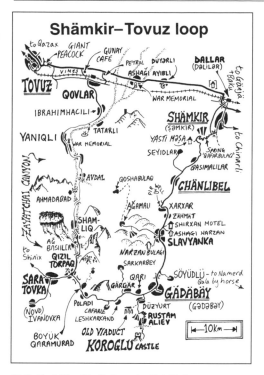

Shämkir–Tovuz loop

cian. Grass is now growing on the well-preserved stone roof of the **old church**, whose multicoloured walls form a mesmerizing pointillist study when seen close to. Just beyond is the lip of a deep, grassy **chasm**.

Slavyanka The sizeable village of Slavyanka was founded in 1844 by Russian Dukhobors ('spirit wrestlers'), members of a non-conformist Christian sect whose belief in pacifism and the irrelevance of priests led to their banishment from mainstream Russia following an imperial decree of 1830. The village retains a scattering of attractive Izba-style wooden houses, notably up the road that leads to Ağmali. The nearby countryside is locally noted for several fizzy, metallic-tasting **cold-springs**, two of which are nicknamed Narzan after the famous Russian spa-water. Above one of these, *Narzan Bulaği* (mob ☎ 50-550 55 55) is the nicest of the three accommodation options. Comfy, well-equipped cottages of various sizes (AZN70-180) have multi-coloured stone-cladding, thick rugs on wooden floors and double beds with frilly golden covers. The cottages are ranged around a copse of mature trees behind a rather grand wooden restaurant sweeping up from a pond and crenellated outer wall. In a garden of wild rhubarb at the rear are a few contrastingly plain, pre-fabricated 'wagon' huts (AZN20) with a single bed and scrappy shower. The location, 2.5km south of Slavyanka down a rough streamside track, has hiking potential.

Easier to find is *Shirxan Restaurant/ Motel* (☎ mob 50-547 4757), close to the main Shamkir road, 2.7km north of Slavyanka. Above what was once an old mill

Chänlibel (Çənlibel) In myths Chänlibel was home to the great Turkic warrior Koroğlu. However, attractive as *this* Chänlibel may be, the name is recent. Formerly it was the Armenian village of Chardakhlı, birthplace of Ivan Bagramian who was declared a hero of the USSR for his leadership of the Red Army in the battle of Kursk and the 1945 drive on Berlin. In September 1987 a local demonstration here was brutally repressed by the Soviet authorities, an action which Armenian nationalists now portray as ethnically motivated. During the Karabagh conflict the population was 'switched' with ethnic Azeri refugees from Göycha and Basar Kechar (Vardeniz) in Armenia.

Outside the village **museum** is the sass-playing bust of **Ashıg Äläskär** (born 1821), Basar Kechar's most celebrated folk musi-

CENTRAL AZERBAIJAN

(rebuilt beyond recognition), five relatively new if somewhat musty en suite rooms have balconies overlooking the lightly wooded valley. Stream-side meals are available.

Accessed off the main road just 200m further south (then 800m down a track crossing the river on a small bridge), *Ashaği Narzan* has solid double cottages (AZN80-100), delightful little 'Finnski dom' wooden hut-bungalows (AZN30-50) and a small motel-building under construction (rooms AZN20-40). All are pretty good value but the location is slightly lacklustre on a rather bare hillside with no focus to the views.

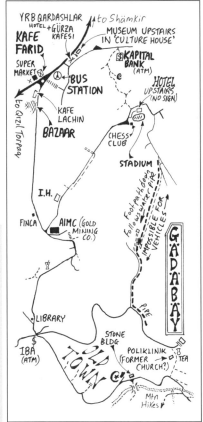

Gädäbäy (Gədəbəy; ☎ 0232) From 1865 to 1920 Gädäbäy was a small-scale mining town producing copper for the German company 'Siemens'. At least, they were supposed to be mining copper. Recent evidence suggests that in fact they found gold which was smuggled out secretly in wine barrels. Gold-mining operations restarted in 2007 but today Gädäbäy is better known for its small, lozenge-shaped potatoes reputed to be the best in Azerbaijan.

The new town is a dusty curve of road that's the nearest this region comes to 'busy'. The once-industrial older section of town below is softened by a gurgling stream, appealing tumbledown buildings and attractive woodland ridges which fold into its south-eastern edge. There's a small unmarked **museum** room upstairs in the **culture house**.

Near the bus station *Hotel YRB Qardashlar* (☎ 53133) is a series of crash-pad rooms above the Gürzä Kafesi with carpeted walls (!) and saggy beds (AZN6 per person).

A better option is an AZN10 bed in the unmarked '*Hotel*' upstairs in the new Sports Complex building beside the stadium. Bathrooms are shared but well maintained. You'll probably have to phone the caretaker Sabir (mob ☎ 050 632 3568) to make arrangements. A pleasant hike leads down from here to the 'old' town – follow the water pipe (see map).

Kafe Farid is the most inviting of several central eateries though atmospherically downmarket *Kafe Lachin* does a great bread-and-honey breakfast.

To Koroğ lu Castle An audacious **narrow-gauge railway** originally transported Gädäbäy's copper ore across the mountains to Shämkir. The rails have long since vanished but you can follow their former course to a graceful **old stone viaduct** now standing all alone at 40°31'50"N 45°55'07.5"E. The surrounding alpine pastures could make for great camping. The bridge is 8.2km from Gädäbäy: head west, turn south on the Rustam Aliev road for 3km (passing

through **Düzyurt** village) then turn right
onto an insignificant earth track which follows a water pipe for one kilometre.

South of Düzyurt there is a spectacular
view from a rocky knoll. Immediately
beyond, the very rough road tumbles down
a series of treacherous muddy hairpins into
Rustam Aliev village. Taxi drivers want
AZN20 return from Gädäbäy to attempt it
in dry weather. It's quite impassable after
rain. The evocative ruin of 16th century
Koroğlu Castle is a kilometre beyond the
stream at the base of the village: you might
have to ford this if your vehicle is too wide
for the tiny metal bridge. From the base of
the castle hill it's a stiff 10-minute hike up
to see some chunky wall remnants, a cave-
room and fabulous views to the south. A
legendary spring that emerges from beneath
the castle was once said to flow with gold.

Gädäbäy to Qovlar
Beyond Düzyurt the road from Gädäbäy to
Qızıl Torpaq rollercoasters gently through
attractive countryside dotted with small settlements. Near **Gärgär** an eagle-headed
mountain peak rears up to the north. Just
before **Poladi** a rocky valley appears to lead
the road away from fertility and habitation
but soon the alpine foothill views are back.
Behind **Böyük Qaramurad** a sweet little
stone bell tower still survives as a last vestige
of **Väng**, one of Caucasian Albania's foremost monasteries back in the 13th century.

Qızıl Torpaq has a basic *café* and
petrol station (95 octane not available).
Here the A64 continues west to dead-end at
Ivanovka or Shinix dividing at **Saratovka**,
a quaint village of picturesque Russian cottages built by protestant-Dukhabor sect settlers. Note that this area is close to the
Armenian-occupied zone and was once
closed to outsiders. Roadblocks have been
removed for years and travel seems to be
unrestricted now, but be sensitive when
exploring and expect questions. There's no
hotel but there are night buses to Baku at
19:50 and 21:10.

Heading north from Qızıl Torpaq the
road is steadily deteriorating but when not
blocked by landslides it's possible to loop
back this way to Qovlar on the A62. A sce-

nic highlight, **Zayatchai Canyon** (aka
'Diktash') is a soaring series of eroded strata bluffs liberally doused in trees. Several
isolated homes at the upper end of the
canyon are built in an unusual tricolour
combination of grey rocks, white stones
and brick. And en route are several quaint
hamlets and more rumours of Albanian
churches in the rugged hinterland.

Landscapes become much drier after
Yanıqlı, where there's a shop, mosque and
war memorial facing an old cemetery. The
views remain pleasant across the widening
river to a ridge that is crowned by the rocky
knob of Tauz Koroğlu fortress (11th-12th
century), another Qız Qalası. **Qovlar** is a
faceless junction town with a useful railway
station (overnight expresses stop here). It's
on a parallel route the 'wrong side' of the
tracks from the M4 reached by somewhat of
a detour.

TOVUZ–QAZAX (see map p270)
Tovuz (Tauz, Traubenfeld; ☎ 0231)
German settlers overspilling Helenendorf
(aka Xanlar, now Göygöl) founded
Traubenfeld in 1912. The town's new name,
Tovuz, is a shortened form of the Azeri
word for peacocks (*Tovuz Qushu*) which
were once common in the region. Now the
only peacock you're likely to see is the
giant, garishly painted concrete one standing in a traffic circle at the eastern edge of

town. The last-known living specimen was kept as a mascot in the grounds of the Shafaq (now I Äliyev) cinema. It disappeared in the early 1990s, feared eaten.

A small free **museum** (Axundov St, 09-12.00, 14-18:00, Mon-Fri) is dedicated to the nationally famous Ashıǧ musician Hussein Bozalganli. Bozalganli is said to have known the whole epic poem *Koroǧlu* off by heart and was champion in many 'muǧam battles', a traditional local version of the 'poetry slam'.

Tovuz town centre is tucked away on the south side of the railway tracks where a new Heydar Aliyev statue stands in a manicured square in front of the station. For some reason local police decided I deserved

an inquisition just for coming to look!

Should you get stranded in Tovuz there are a few **basic rooms** (dbl/tr AZN4/6) above the bus station but the only toilets are public squats across the yard, used and abused by passing passengers. Halfway to Aǧstafa on the main Baku–Qazax highway (km443) the better *Hasansu Motel* looks like a latterday castle on its lonely perch.

There are several **minibuses** per hour to Qovlar, Gänjä (AZN1.20) and Aqstafa/ Qazax from outside the bus station. To reach the southern centre of town take **buses** marked 'Shahar Arasi'. These take a long loop as they can't get through the narrow tunnel under the railway on Vurǧun St. A Tovuz–Saratovka bus runs at 07.00 (AZN1).

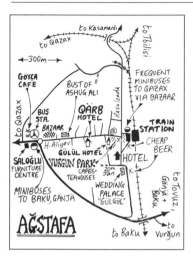

Ağstafa (✪ Akstafa; ☎ 0244)

Founded as Elisavetinka in 1914, Ağstafa grew as the railway junction/departure point for trains to Yerevan. That line is now closed due to the Karabagh war but the strategic importance of the junction remains. In September 1989, and again in 1991, opposition activists made ground-breaking anti-Russian demonstrations by sitting on the rails in protest. Simultaneous demos also occurred at Yevlax, Baku and Bilajari paralysing the whole national railway system for a week until being broken up by Soviet troops.

There's little to see but the town has a friendly, laid-back quality and **Vurğun Park** is a pleasant place for tea. The best of the three hotels is *Hotel Qärb* (H Aliyev 35, ☎ 53091) with comfy little AZN25 en suite rooms above the town's best **restaurant**. A cheaper unnamed *hotel* (*mehmanxana*, Rasulzade St) near the station has saggy AZN5 institutional beds and non-descript bare walls, but there's a scrap of garden behind and the very friendly owners put fresh-cut roses in my room.

Three night trains run to Baku. Coming from Baku note that the Qazax-bound train stops for almost an hour here so you'd be wise to jump out like everyone else and take one of the Qazax-bound

minibuses that depart every 10-20 mins (till around 22.30) from outside the station. Twice hourly minibuses to Gänjä leave from the roundabout at Saloğlu Furniture Centre. Baku buses also pick up here (mornings) with more starting from the bus station (mostly evenings).

Qirakh Qäsämänli (Qirax Qəsəmənli)

On the banks of the Kura, this once important settlement was ploughed into the soil in advance of flooding by a Soviet dam project. Ironically the dam was never built! All that remains is a crumbling mud castle tower and mosque, overlooked from the deserted ridge-top by a manor house once owned by **Israfil Ağa** (see p272). But the views from here across the Kura river to the stark arid hills beyond are quietly memorable. And the ancient graveyard on the approach road from Ağstafa is especially eerie considering that it was part of a huge triple-domed tumulus constructed by Timur as a place to bury mountains of corpses after a bloody battle on this site. The graves feature in a classic Nizami movie. There's no public transport; expect to pay around AZN15 for a two-hour return excursion by taxi from Ağstafa.

Some 4.5km beyond the Qäsämänli turning, a pair of bridges cross the whirlpools of the Kura River (nicknamed Däli Kur – 'crazy Kura'). Immediately after the road bridge is a checkpoint. A bumpy 2.5km beyond (assuming the customs offi-

cers let you through), look left when you see the decaying cadaver of a former container box. The rusty stand pipe gushing water into a puddle is a **Yanar Bulaq** ('fire spring') and the water will burn impressively if you're prepared to wallow through the mud to set light to it.

The road beyond continues to **Böyuk Kasik** (the border station for Baku–Tbilisi trains) but it's rough, is used mainly by smugglers and the military, and isn't ideal for casual tourists. Foreigners can cross the border here by train but NOT on foot/ by road.

QAZAX (Gazakh, Kazakh; ☎ 0279)

Qazax has a modest charm, two old churches, a 19th-century mosque, functioning domed hamam, and a quietly attractive tree-shaded central area but see box opposite. There are moneychangers at Nargiz Café in the bazaar and IBA (75 Sabir St) exchanges US$.

History

A town by the name of Gazaka was capital of the ancient state of Atropatena in the 2nd century BC and later formed the seat of the Sassanian-Persian governor. That city was close to modern Didivan and only moved to the present site of Qazax after being destroyed by Timur in the 14th century.

From 1767 Qazax became an autonomous sultanate. It was nominally subservient first to the Ottoman-Turkish empire and latterly to the Georgian kingdom of Kartli-Kaheti. When Kaheti was annexed by Russia in 1801, Qazax fell into the Tsar's *gubernia* of Georgia. Unlike Gänjä, the Qazax Azeri population proved enthusiastic to Russian overlordship and contributed a 'Tatar' cavalry to fight against the Qajar-Persian army in the 1826-8 war.

The town owes much of its century-old architecture to **Israfil Ağa** (born 1862),

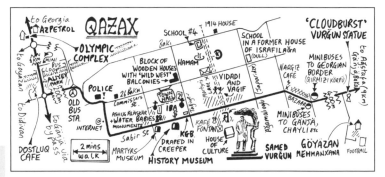

❏ Bertubani Monastery

On the 6th century meditation spot of 'Syrian Father' David, this lonely cave hermitage developed in the 12th century at the same time as the David Gareja complex (p331) just across the Georgian border. Its frescoes included one of only four known originals showing Georgia's classic Queen Tamara. However, Bertubani suffered severely from being used for target practice by the Red Army during the Soviet period and now only a muralled apse remains amid the rubble. By an administrative quirk the site falls within Azerbaijani territory but it's virtually impossible for casual visitors to reach from Ağstafa. It would be easier from Georgia (though still 25km on dirt tracks from Udabno) given a good guide and border-crossing permission. Informal discussions with Georgia have considered a 'swap' giving Azerbaijan a vaguely equivalent piece of land in return for Bertubani but as yet there's no progress.

❏ **Hassles**
Given the province's recent history and proximity to a still hostile Armenia, it is not surprising that the Qazax police are excessively suspicious. On my first visit I was questioned for four hours for snapping an uncontroversial photo of the hamam, albeit politely and over ample pots of tea. Nearly a decade later little seemed to have changed. Once again simply walking in the streets proved provocative enough for the KGB to be called. Police advise tourists to stay in a car or taxi (or just change buses at the bus station) rather than wandering into town where the authorities are apparently **required** to laboriously establish the identity of any foreigner. Curiously the paranoia seems limited to Qazax centre – I was not stopped at Göyasan, Didivan or Demceli (luck?) and many foreigners report staying at the Olympic Centre or AzPetrol motel without incident. Of course if you've always wanted a chat with the mayor's henchmen and a few free cuppas…

nephew of a celebrated Crimean war hero. As a leading local landlord he invested large sums in town improvements, built the mosque, bath-house and several homes while also gaining limited fame as a writer.

Meanwhile Israfil Ağa's contemporary and former school friend, **Gachakh Käräm** ('escaping' Karam, so named due to his nifty disappearing act with enemies), had become a leading anti-Russian agitator. He engineered a short-lived uprising but was quickly forced into exile in Tehran where he ended up as bodyguard to the Shah. Israfil Ağa stayed put, becoming one of many pro-Tsar figures to die during the anti-Russian upheavals in the wake of the 1917 St Petersburg revolution.

Qazax *yezd* (ie province) became part of the Azerbaijan Democratic Republic during 1918. At the time it retained most of the carpet-making lands that had been associated with the old sultanate and which stretched to the north-eastern shores of Lake Sevan. However, Stalin later redrew these borders, giving the southern two-thirds of the province to Armenia and creating anomalous 'islands' of Azeri territory completely surrounded by Armenia. The 'ethnic cleansing' of these enclaves – Yukhari Askipara and Barkhurdarli – between 1988 and 1990 has rarely, if ever, made the Western press, but thousands of refugees still languish in Qazax.

What to see
The attractive **History Museum** suffers from frequent power cuts making the exhibits hard to make out. There are several **literary monuments** in the town's neat parks including two to local hero Samed Vurğun. Young Vurğun had studied at the Seminariya Pedagogical Institute (1918-59) founded as the 'Tatar' branch of the then-famous Trans-Caucasus Educational seminary of Gori, Georgia. The institute's main building is now **school #4**: behind a plain façade it retains its attractive enclosed courtyard. 'Wild west' balconied **wooden houses** across from the town hall were originally built as accommodation for the institute's students.

On attractive stroll-street Sh Xiyabani (Martyrs' Lane) lie the active twin minaretted brick **mosque** and still-functioning 19th century **hamam** (shower and bath booth AZN1). The supposedly **'Albanian' church** [1] has been restored and painted in cream-and-white but remains disused. The red-brick **former Russian church** [2], now hosts the Mähämmädäli Qazaxlı wrestling club. Neat Heydar Aliyev park is expansive and there are very distant views of Goyazan from the bridge but nosy, underemployed police are ubiquitous here.

Accommodation and food
On the road to Georgia, just beyond the last roundabout at the western edge of town, the sleek *Olympic Complex* (☎ 55400) is a titanium-grey curl of contemporary modernism. Rooms (AZN60 double, AZN70-150 cottages) are stylish and well equipped with a/c, fridge, fluffy towels and bathrobes.

CENTRAL AZERBAIJAN

There's a bright restaurant with hip, high-backed chairs in magenta-leather. Almost directly across the road *AzPetrol motel* (☎ 55206) has standard unfussy doubles with small en suite bathrooms for AZN24-30 or you can pay AZN10 per bed in twin rooms 8 and 9 if you don't mind potentially sharing with a stranger. If these are full, the cheapest alternative is the *Göyäzän Mehmanxana* (☎ mob 070-326 2325) whose neat new rooms (from AZN20) are a pleasant surprise given the building's dowdy appearance and lack of signs; it's tucked behind the local football club.

A pleasant if unpretentious garden place for breakfast, cheap beer or kebab dinners is little *Dostluq*, around a rectangular fountain-pool hidden behind a shop marked 'Topdan'. Drinking at the various more central tea-houses is likely to attract police attention.

Transport

Minibuses run from various spots around the bazaar, notably to Gänjä and to Qırmızi Körpü (the Georgian border aka Krasni Most). **Buses** to Baku are more sporadic, some originating at Qırmızi Körpü, others at the decrepit old bus station. For both Baku and Gänjä, should no transport appear, it's very easy to continue 9km to Ağstafa and connect there. An almost continuous stream of Ağstafa–Qazax minibuses (30q, 15 minutes) run along Sabir St passing the bazaar. Most continue to the roundabout near the Olympic Complex following a westbound diversion through a residential area across the river.

For **trains** to Baku, there's more choice (and more comfortable options) from Ağstafa. The single Baku–Qazax train is in fact just a couple of carriages pulled by the nightly Baku–Böyük Kasik train. As these spend 40 minutes being shunted at Ağstafa station, virtually all passengers prefer to take trains to/from there.

Around Qazax (if the Mayor and KGB allow)

West of Dash Salahlı (10km) there are around 100 caves in the cliff-sides of chapel-topped Mt Avey-Dağ, where traces of Palaeolithic man have been found. At the celebrated **Demceli** picnic-spot is a rocky recess from above which spring water drips constantly into a drinking font. It's most interesting to visit on summer weekends when daytrippers celebrate this freak of nature with shashlyk, music and dancing.

Goyazan is a photogenic, abrupt rocky pinnacle visible for miles around but best viewed from a point just beyond Abbas-beyli village (formerly Alpout).

On a hill above Xanliğlar village, overlooking Ağstafa reservoir, is the relatively well-preserved 16th century defence tower of **Didivan**. It's nicknamed Koroğlu Bochäni (Koroğlu's cask) due to its barrel-shaped tower. There's a basic *restaurant* with nice views where the narrow access-road dead-ends near the hill top. However, the tower, just 30 metres above, is within a military compound so you'll need to ask for permission if you want to crawl through a small hole into the empty remnants.

QAZAX TO THE GEORGIAN BORDER (see map p270)

As you head towards the border the villages become further apart. The road passes at first through avenues of drunkenly leaning trees. The landscape becomes increasingly barren except for the ribbon of forest occasionally visible along the banks of the Kura beyond.

Yuxkhari Salahlı is a long thin strip village whose main claim to fame is as birthplace of the much-loved writer, Samed Vurğun. His home is preserved and a 15-minute walk away is a separate Vurğun Museum in well-watered gardens.

Famed for its carpets, **Shıkhlı** also has literary connections as the birthplace of the poet Vidadi. There's an old graveyard on the northern side of the road.

The border (**Qırmızı Körpü aka Krasni Most, Tsitelis Khidi, Red Bridge**) is named after a brick-arched bridge spanning the Khram River and reputed to be 12th century albeit rebuilt 500 years later. It carried cross-border traffic until bypassed by an EU-funded replacement in 1998. A once-bustling no-man's land bazaar here was recently closed as part of Georgia's anti-smuggling campaign, but minibuses do still run to the border post from Qazax bazaar along with 13 daily MTrans buses from Baku (all leaving westbound before noon or after 8pm).

The Georgian border post is walkably close and from there minibuses depart when full to Tbilisi station and to Marneuli (an ethnic-Azeri village in Georgia). If there's no sign of a Tbilisi-bound minibus you could save a little taxi money by going only as far as Rustavi whence very frequent city buses to Tbilisi cost a few cents.

Towards Karabagh

Contemporary travel articles by Azerbaijani authors tend to brush over the fact that Nagorno (Mountain) Karabagh is under Armenian occupation – at least until they've finished whetting your appetite for the richly forested mountains, ancient monuments and artistic magnificence of fortress city Shusha.

Sadly, the occupation is more than a detail. Many of the most beautiful villages

have been torched and looted to total destruction and anyway, there's no way you can visit from the rest of Azerbaijan. Given the impracticality of a visit, this chapter is consequently restricted to a brief overview. Be aware that the subject of Karabagh remains intensely sensitive. Attempts at giving what may to you seem a 'balanced' view of the historical perspective, even if apparently harmless and reasonable, may be taken as a pro-Armenian bias given the painful sense of loss that almost every Azerbaijani feels. After all, the country is dealing with the occupation of over 15% of its land area and hundreds of thousands of refugees/IDPs remain stranded.

BACKGROUND

Karabagh (Qarabağ) is an historical entity considerably bigger than Nagorno Karabagh, the disputed region. Indeed according to the *History of Karabagh*, 'The first city in the velayat of Karabagh was the fortress city of Bärdä.' The text continues, innocuously enough, to explain that until the Arab invasions, the area was populated by non-Muslim Albanians. Or does it? Another translator castigates the use of the term

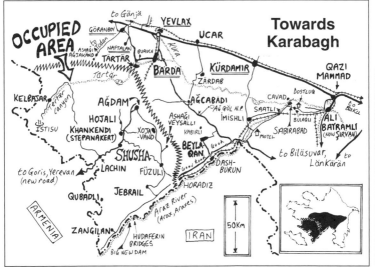

Albanians saying it should read Armenians. A nonsensical but fiercely political debate has raged over such fine points, as politicians try to claim that they can prove that Karabagh is rightfully Armenian or Azerbaijani. From an outsider's perspective, the argument fails at a fundamental level ie the term 'Armenian' was used carelessly by historians and travellers to describe the region's Christian population, just as the term 'Tartar' was used as a highly inaccurate description of Muslim Azeris. Accurate translation cannot improve historical sloppiness. For much more insight read Thomas de Waal's *Black Garden*.

SHUSHA

Shusha is considered Azerbaijan's main cultural heart which adds to the general bitterness felt over the town's continued occupation. Shusha sprang to prominence when Panakh Khan of Karabagh built his capital here and immodestly named it Panakhabad. He erected a palace reminiscent of a Kew Garden greenhouse where he and his successor son, Ibrahim, encouraged artists, writers and thinkers to congregate in what later became known as the 'Conservatory of the Caucasus'.

The name Shusha ('glass') comes not from the brittle structure of the palace but from a challenge by Persia's eunuch-Shah Mohammad Ağa. As the ruthless Persian army approached, their leader supposedly warned Ibrahim Khan: 'God is pouring stones upon your head. Sit ye not then in thy fortress of glass'. However, thanks to Mohammad Ağa's sudden death, the city held out and the ironic title 'Shusha' stuck. Nonetheless by this time Ibrahim Khan had already fled and in his absence the whole Karabagh government was overthrown and executed by Ibrahim's nephew. Amongst those to die was the great writer and philosopher Mollah-Panakh Vagif who had been Ibrahim's foreign minister.

Shusha's reputation for invincibility may have been one of the many factors which led Azeri leaders in 1992 to provide woefully inadequate protection for the city against Armenian attack. Shusha's carpet collection was rescued and taken to Baku.

Other cultural monuments (busts of Hacibeyov, Natavan et al) were lost only to be miraculously salvaged from a Georgian metal dealer who'd bought them for scrap. The bullet-ridden busts are now displayed behind the National Gallery in Baku.

Today Shusha is in a sad state: in contrast to the city of Khankändi (known to Armenians as Stepanakert) which has been totally rebuilt.

LESSER-KNOWN SITES IN THE OCCUPIED AREA

● **Ashağı Veysälli** Mir Ali Mausoleum has a smooth, sharp-pointed, conical-domed turbe estimated to be 13th-14th century. It would have been on the old Bärdä to Pälätakan (Beylaqan) caravan road.

● **Azikh cave** A 350,000-year-old Neanderthal woman's jaw bone was dug up here, the oldest human remains to have been found in the ex-USSR.

● **Ağdam** Once one of Azerbaijan's bigger towns, Ağdam is now a completely devastated ghost town, plundered by the Karabagh Armenians as a free source of building materials. The attractive twin-minareted mosque still stands though its interior has been defaced, see 🖳 www.armeniapedia.org/index.php?title= Aghdam.

● **Füzuli** Divided. According to Baku's Historical Museum the caravanserai was still standing in 1990.

● **Hojali/Khojaly** Hojali field has over 100 historical tumuli (2000-500BC), some of which have been excavated. However, in Azeri minds the now-destroyed town has become synonymous with the events of 25/26 February 1992 when over 600 Hojali residents were infamously massacred. The tragedy remains arguably the single most painful post-Independence event for Azerbaijan where that night is remembered as the 'Khojaly Genocide' (🖳 http://khojaly.org).

● **Hudaferin bridges** The impressive remnants of two Araz River bridges, one 11th century, are visible from the Iran-side border road just east of the big new Araz dam.

● **Jebrail** The small, ruinous 'Maiden's Tower' at Xalflı Village had fine views.

● **Kelbajar** This partly Kurdish region

was full of attractive villages before 1993 but many were burnt by the invading Armenian forces.

• **Dozens of churches** See website 💻 www.cilicia.com.

GETTING TO KARABAGH

The only practical way into Nagorno Karabagh at present is via Armenia. But be aware that the Azeri government considers such visits to represent illegal entry to Azerbaijani territory. Thus having a Karabagh entry stamp proves criminal activity and could render you liable for arrest should you get into the rest of Azerbaijan. However, having such a stamp will most likely mean that you won't be issued with an Azeri visa in the first place.

Visas are required for Nagorno Karabagh but can be procured on arrival at the MFA (💻 www.nkr.am) in Khankendi/Stepanakert where you'll need to register anyway. Five-day visas cost AMD11,000 (around US$36) though you could save AMD4000 by applying a week before travel at the Nagorno Karabagh office in Yerevan. For more info see Lonely Planet's *Georgia, Armenia & Azerbaijan* guide or 💻 www.armeniapedia.org.

TOWARDS THE OCCUPIED AREA

The frontline meets the Araz River at Horadiz, a town which had fallen to the Armenians but was retaken at the end of hostilities on 3 January 1994. Sixty-five per cent of its 2000 homes were destroyed or left roofless after the Armenian withdrawal and more damage was done by looters in the aftermath, but reconstruction is progressing. There's an overnight train from Baku but apart from

mine clearing, voyeurism or the desire to be suspected of espionage, there's little reason to visit. Most buses stop short of Horadiz at Dashburun or Beylaqan.

Beylaqan (☎ 0152)

Palakatan/Paitakaran (Old Beylaqan) was the capital of Albania in 451 and it remained a major fortress city until Chamaghan marched the Mongol armies through in 1235 and totally devastated it. Timur's plans to rebuild the city never materialized and today the site (near Kabirli) is no more than a flat, slightly raised field locally known as **Oränqala**. Visually it's entirely neutral but the loose 'soil' is a potential treasure trove for archaeologists, consisting as much of crumbled mud-brick and pottery shards as of real 'earth'? For now the site is considered out of bounds and is too close to the sniper-prone ceasefire line for any excavations to proceed.

Today's Beylaqan is 22km away, the renamed one-horse town formerly known as Zhdanovsk. There's a fine **Beylaqani statue**, a distinctive square and a small bazaar but the main attraction for local pilgrims is the **Jerjis (Cärciz) Shrine** complex (aka Peygamberä, 08-21:00) 4km north-east. According to some, holy-man Jerjis was a

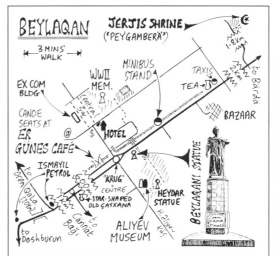

BEYLAQAN   JERJIS SHRINE ('PEYGAMBERÄ')

3 MINS' WALK

EX COM BLDG

WWII MEM.

MINIBUS STAND

TAXIS

TEA

to Bärda

CANOE SEATS AT ER GÜNES CAFÉ

@ $ HOTEL

BAZAAR

ISMAYIL PETROL

"KRUG" CENTRE

STAR-SHAPED OLD ÇAYXANA

HEYDAR STATUE

BEYLAQANI STATUE

to Oran Qala (Kabirli)

Jannat Bağı

to Dashburun

ALIYEV MUSEUM

Haliqi Köç

disciple of Jesus. They're probably confusing him with Yelisey (see Kish, p227) and most sources date him a millennium later (AH315-392, ie AD927-1001). Whoever he was, his importance was such that Jafargullu Khan, ruler of Shäki-Shirvan, felt the need to be buried beside him. Once he was dead, of course. In the green-domed shrine building (rebuilt 1902) after tomb kissing and three circumambulations, pilgrims score a blessing by hanging a scarf from the central whiplash chain-hook that was originally designed to holds a 'magic' chandelier.

The town's six-room *hotel* (☎ 52347, AZN4-10) has old floors, seatless toilets and no showers at all, but some rooms are air-conditioned and the 'Super-Lux' one has been redecorated.

The simple but very original *Er Günes Café* serves 50q beers at seats fashioned like a canoe over a small canal. Around 600m south-west of the central junction ('Krug'), there's a distinctive if run-down *çayxana* with the cross section of an Azeri star. Turn south here for the out-of-town *Cännät Bagi*, Beylaqan's foremost garden-restaurant.

Reaching Beylaqan from Baku is most comfortable using the Horadiz-bound overnight train (AZN3.40). Get off at Dashburun from where a 60q minibus shuttles to Beylaqan. Note that it starts from a hidden point around the north-west side of the station to give taxi drivers a fair chance of getting business from the unwary.

Minibuses/buses from Beylaqan run to Baku via Şirvan (Äli Bayramli) at 8, 8:30 and 11:30, and to Gänjä via Tärtär at 07:30 and 10:00. A taxi to Oränqala costs around AZN15 return but bear in mind that visiting Old Beylaqan isn't technically permitted so don't linger (nor remove any 'souvenirs') if you do go.

Ağ Göl National Park

This recently declared National Park comprises a patchwork of shallow lakes fed by 'collector' canals which wash leeched salts off the region's fields. The resultant briny waters and marshlands attract migratory birds in winter with spoonbills and nearly 20,000 Little Bustards reputedly resident between November and March. Access is by a gravel road cutting inland from the road between Dashburun and **Ağcabädi**, the latter famed as the birthplace of classic Azeri composer Üzeyir Hacibäyov.

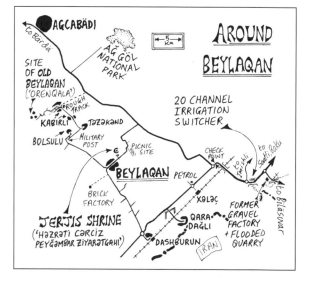

PART 7: THE SOUTH

INTRODUCTION

The main M3 slips imperceptibly from scrubby steppe through wide waterlogged marshlands and corn fields to woodland and rainforest. And with the border to Iran painlessly open to foreigners (assuming you have an Iranian visa) it is no longer a dead end. The unexpectedly green Talysh (aka Hirkan, Qirkan) region west of Länkäran is the real highlight. It has its own language and super-hospitable culture and progresses geographically from rolling forests into sheep-mown hills and gently impressive mountain canyons. *Shafag* (🖳 www.southtourism.az) offers some low-key rural tourism ideas.

In the Talysh language thanks and greetings are as in Azeri but good=*chuk-eh*, delicious=*lazatineh* and beautiful=*gashang-eh*. See pp373-4 for numbers.

Regional history

The Talysh region spent centuries oscillating between independence, Persian control and local confederations. Russians first took an interest in the area between 1728 and 1735 but withdrew on signing the Ganja Treaty in the face of a resurgent Persia under Nadir Shah. Once Nadir Shah had died in 1747, the Talysh Khanate was one of many Persian provinces to declare itself as an independent local fiefdom. Talysh's 'Black Khan' reforged links with Russia and pro-Russian Quba much to the annoyance of Gilan (the khanate further south). A series of skirmishes followed and for decades the area was a pawn in the geopolitical game between Russia and Persia being repeatedly conquered then reconquered by either side. In 1809 the Persians took control yet again

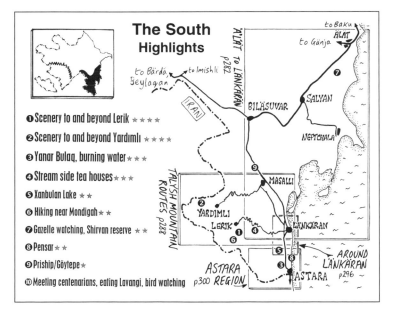

The South Highlights

❶ Scenery to and beyond Lerik ★ ★ ★ ★
❷ Scenery to and beyond Yardımlı ★ ★ ★ ★
❸ Yanar Bulaq, burning water ★ ★
❹ Stream side tea houses ★ ★
❺ Xanbulan Lake ★ ★
❻ Hiking near Mondigah ★ ★
❼ Gazelle watching, Shirvan reserve ★ ★
❽ Pensar ★ ★
❾ Priship/Göytepe ★
❿ Meeting centenarians, eating Lavangi, bird watching

and invited in British troops and engineers to help fortify Länkäran as part of a mutual defence agreement. However, events in Europe put the Brits in an awkward position. The Napoleonic wars meant that Britain needed Russian support against France. Thus in Talysh where they were supposedly helping in the Persian defence of Länkäran, the Brits quietly slipped out of town as the Russians advanced in 1813. The Shah's troops were left understrength and rapidly capitulated. The fall of Länkäran pushed the humiliated Persians into signing the Gülistan treaty which signed away most of today's Azerbaijan.

But Russian rule proved unpopular. In 1826 rumours of Tsar Alexander's death set off a rebellion in Länkäran as well as in Karabagh and Gänjä. The Persians returned in support but a Russian counter attack drove them out within a year. By 1828 there were Cossacks in Orumiyeh and Ardebil threatening to advance on Tehran. The Persians sued for peace and signed the Treaty of Turkmenchai on 22 February 1828 which confirmed Russian control over the Talysh khanate.

During the confusion that followed WWI, the Talysh region initially followed Azerbaijan to independence. During April 1919 the region fell under the control of the Bolsheviks and set itself up as the Talysh Mugam Soviet Republic, only to be forced back into the Azeri Democratic Republic three months later.

History repeated itself in August 1993 when the Talysh Mugam republic was declared by Alikram Hümbätov, supported by the crack local tank regiment. His 'international declaration of independence' was actually made very informally to a collection of four journalists and seems to have had very little popular support. Again, within three months, the independent republic crumbled. Former mayoress Jamalova arrived at the city hall, carried in on the shoulders of her massed supporters, while abandoned Hümbätov escaped out of the back door. He is thought to have hidden in the forests around Ballabur Castle (p297) in a feeble attempt to draw Babek comparisons, but was later arrested and imprisoned.

PRACTICAL INFORMATION
Permits and hassles
Until 1993 even Azeris needed a permit to visit the Talysh/south-east region. Passport checks and an internal borderpost were removed following the Alikram Hümbätov incident (see column opposite) and the only restricted areas are now within beer-throwing distance of Iran. Don't be intimidated if you're interviewed once in a blue moon by over-zealous policemen who have yet to hear of Brezhnev's death.

Transport
Like most of Azerbaijan's main roads, the M3 is being upgraded. However, heading inland the only mountain roads readily passable by car are those to Yardımlı and Lerik. Other routes, including all possible interconnections between the Yardımlı and Lerik roads will need a strong 4WD. Even indestructible UAZ jeeps can struggle reaching Allar or Sım.

Länkäran-bound buses and minibuses depart surprisingly frequently from Baku's main bus terminal (p130; p77 ΨO1) stopping at intermediate points along the M3 from which Masallı, Celilabad etc are short taxi-hops away. Sälyan and Neftchala transport uses a separate Baku bus station (p77 ΨD9) towards Bayil.

There's a useful overnight sleeper train (AZN4-6) to Astara via Länkäran and a 6-hour daytime 'express' (AZN3). Länkäran's railway station is helpfully central but be aware that the stations of several other southern towns are nonsensically far from the cities they purport to serve. Länkäran 'International' Airport reopened in late 2008. As yet the 'International' bit is wishful thinking.

Accommodation
There is now acceptable mid-range accommodation in all of the southern towns and a remarkable plethora of AZN30-50 bungalows along the Lerik and Yardımlı roads.

The people in this region are particularly hospitable. It can be difficult to refuse offers of food or accommodation. Even though a guest may be 'sent by Allah', the Almighty doesn't always send the cash to

THE SOUTH

mop up the expenses incurred, so please try not to take undue advantage.

There are many possibilities in the mountains for camping 'rough' though it's hard to get away from civilization altogether – don't be surprised to see a bemused shepherd standing staring at your tent in the morning.

Climate
Quite the opposite of conventional wisdom, as you head south towards Iran, the landscape becomes progressively greener. Indeed the Talysh region (Länkäran/Lerik/ Astara rayons) is the wettest part of Azerbaijan and, especially in the autumn, it is likely to rain almost every day. This is not just depressing but also turns normally rutted mountain tracks into impossibly muddy quagmires. Summer temperatures are not necessarily as high as in Baku but with high humidity it can feel very muggy. May is the ideal time to visit with temperatures cool and less chance of rain. Winter is short and mild on the coast, but Lerik and Yardımlı can get snowed in.

ÄLÄT TO SÄLYAN
Near Xırdılı school kids shun their studies to sell live rabbits to passing motorists. On one occasion I saw a group of camels saunter along the roadside here. But basically the scenery is uninspiring. A dual carriageway is under construction and km posts are being renumbered causing some minor confusions.

Shirvan National Park
At first glance the pan-flat, 70,000-hectare Shirvan National Park looks very dull. But amid grasses of beguilingly subtle hues live 220 species of birds (the majority winter migrants) and the last surviving herds of *ceyran* (wild Caucasian Gazelles). Pushed to the edge of extinction before a hunting ban was imposed in 1949, the ceyran has recovered significantly from 200 in 1960 to over 5000 today. There's a good chance of seeing these cute mini-antelopes on a jeep safari in the park, but you'll probably have to provide your own vehicle (the site is vast and there are no set tours). Note that if their tails go up hurry your ceyran photo as they're about to run away. The entrance to the park is clearly marked through a new gazelle-topped gate.

Park entry costs AZN4 but it's worth calling the amiable German park director (Hartmut Müller ☎ 050-796 6882) ahead to check opening details. If you don't have access to a 4WD it might occasionally be possible to charter a park vehicle by advance arrangement.

At the eastern edge of the park there are reportedly fine beaches (albeit some 30km of rough tracks away). Off a cape called **Bändovan** (see box below) archaeologists believe there's a submerged Caspian *atlantis*, a once-important town whose remnants are reputedly visible to scuba divers and were surveyed by a Russian expedition in 1975.

Sälyan (☎ 0163)
Central Sälyan is a quietly attractive grid of low-rise, tree-shaded streets enclosed on three sides within a dyke-sided loop of the flood-prone Kura (Kür) River. There has been an agricultural presence around here for nearly a millennium though it only real-

---

❏ **Stepan Razin, more than a Russian beer**
Even if there's no lost city at Bändovan, there might be considerable offshore treasure. After all it was on Sängi Muğana (Svinoy) Island that Cossack rebel Stepan ('Stenka') Razin hid out in 1669. Razin, better known now as a Russian beer than a historical figure, had rampaged down the Volga on a revolutionary looting spree. He then crossed the Caspian, raided Rasht (Iran) and retreated with his booty to Svinoy off Bändovan. In 1670 the Persians sent a fleet to punish him here but Razin turned the tables and sank virtually the entire Persian navy. Thereafter he returned to Russia where he set up a Cossack republic that came close to toppling the whole Russian state.

THE SOUTH

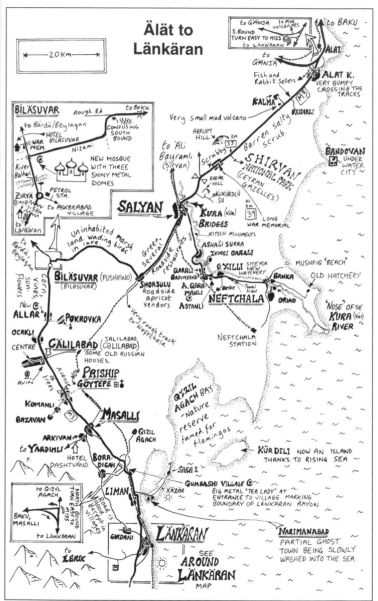

Älät to Länkäran

◄— 20 Km —►

to GANJA · to Mud volcanoes · to BAKU
S.BOUND TURN EASY TO MISS
to LÄNKÄRAN
to GANJA
ÄLÄT

Fish and Rabbit Sellers
ALAT K. VERY BUMPY CROSSING THE TRACKS
KALMA M3 OXIDIRLI

BILÄSUVAR
Rough Rd to Baku
to Bärdä/Beylaqan
HOTEL BILÄSUVAR
WAR MEM
Nizami
River Balhar
NEW MOSQUE WITH THREE SHINY METAL DOMES
ZIRYÄ (Ziryk)
PETROL STA.
to Askerabad VILLAGE
to Länkäran

Very small mud volcano
ABRUPT HILL Km 33
to Äli Bayramlı (Sirvan)
Scrubby
Barren salty scrub.
BANDOVAN UNDER WATER CITY

SHIRVAN NATIONAL PARK (CEYRAN GAZELLES)
RADAR HILL
KÜKÜRDLÜ SU
at km 39

SALYAN
KURA (Kür) BRIDGES
LONG WAR MEMORIAL

Uninhabited land. Wading birds in lake.
Green: several roadside restaurants
KITSCH MONUMENTS
ASHAĞI SURRA
İKİNCİ QARALI
MUSHFIQ 'BEACH'
OLD HATCHERY

BILÄSUVAR (PUSHKINO) (Biläsuvar)
to Bärdä/Beylaqan Sun-flowers
Corn, vines
QARALI
QADIMKAND
SITE FOR NEW HATCHERY
BANKA

New ALLAR
POKROVKA
SHORSULU Roadside apricot vendors
A. QARAMANLI
ASTANLI
BOYAT TOWN SIGN
XİLLİ
NEFTCHALA
ORIAD
'NOSE' OF THE KURA (Kür) RIVER

OCAKLI
CENTRE
GÄLILABAD (JALILABAD) (CÄLILABAD)
SOME OLD RUSSIAN HOUSES.
Very rough track to Neftchala
NEFTCHALA STATION
RUIN
Avenue of trees

PRISHIB GÖYTEPE

QIZIL AGACH BAY
- Nature reserve famed for flamingos

KOMANLI
BAZAVAN
M3
MASALLI
QIZIL AGACH
KÜRDILI NOW AN ISLAND THANKS TO RISING SEA

ARKIVAN
to YARDIMLI
P.
HOTEL DASHTVÄND
BORA-DIGAH
SARA II

to QIZIL AGACH NORTH BOUND TURN EASY MISS
BAKU, MASALLI
to LÄNKÄRAN
LIMAN
Road is good to villages
GIRDANI

QUMBASHI VILLAGE
XÄZÄR
BIG METAL 'TEA LADY' AT ENTRANCE TO VILLAGE MARKING BOUNDARY OF LÄNKÄRAN RAYON

to LERIK
LÄNKÄRAN
SEE AROUND LÄNKÄRAN MAP

NARIMANABAD
PARTIAL GHOST TOWN BEING SLOWLY WASHED INTO THE SEA.

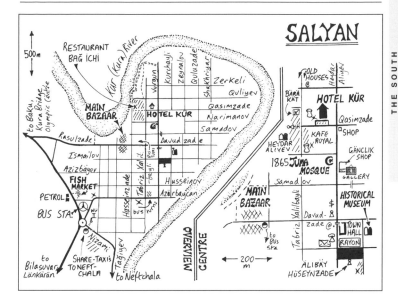

ly became at all urban in the 1920s. Centuries before that, at least in peaceful years, Sälyan was the site of a bi-annual market catering mainly to Caspian fish traders sailing down from the Russian port of Astrakhan. Misjudging reports of such a market, Peter the Great sent an army to occupy Sälyan without realising that there was barely even a port. He built a garrison here nonetheless only to find that most of the 400 Russian troops dropped dead of tropical diseases within a year.

Old pictures show Sälyan's 1865 **Juma mosque** with *shebeke* windows and a central golden dome. The structure was much diminished during the Soviet era, and in 2007 was virtually demolished for a renovation so extensive that it's effectively a total rebuild. Opposite, the small, basic **Baqqaliyyä art gallery** is upstairs above the Gänclik shop among vaguely photogenic old brick shop-fronts.

Amid the usual pots, banknotes and mangy stuffed goats, the five-roomed **historical museum** (10.00-13.00 & 15.00-18:00, Mon-Fri) has interesting photos charting Sälyan's 20th-century history. The curious bags of earth are WWII mementos, each coming from a different Russian 'hero-city'. Exhibits on more local heroes feature artist and 1918 independence figure Älibäy Hüseynzadä (1864-1941) whose generously bearded **statue** adorns the main square. The very tatty late-Soviet *Hotel Kür* has beds from AZN3. Room 11 (AZN12-18) is marginally more comfy despite scattered piles of bricks and a seat-less en suite WC. Water comes in buckets provided by a flirty, bouff-haired Russian matriarch. Hopefully by the time you read this, the whole place will have been rebuilt.

Bäräkät restaurant serves fish and good kebabs while local bureaucrats pour the lunch-time vodkas.

Minibuses shuttle between the bazaar and bus station via Tabriz Xalilbeyli northbound, returning via Hüseynzadä. Leaving town if you're heading towards Länkäran keep right at an unmarked fork near a level crossing. The left branch (signed '*Plastik Zavodu*') passes the train station then dead ends near a gigantic old flour mill.

THE SOUTH

Around Sälyan

Most visitors miss central Sälyan altogether, simply driving through the Soviet-era western outskirts using the main Länkäran road. The most notable feature en route is the pair of bridges across the Kura (Kür) River at Sälyan's northern edge. The older **rail bridge** was built by WWII German prisoners in a real-life River Kwai-style drama. Suspecting that the PoWs might have deliberately weakened the iron girders, the Soviet commandant ordered the whole construction gang to stand underneath while overloaded trains rolled across the new bridge. The structure held. Indeed, it still stands and was only bypassed by a new road bridge in the early 1990s. That bridge is adorned with appropriate big-cat statues (*Kür* = lion) honouring the river's wild reputation for evil currents, whirlpools and spring floods. At the southern end of the bridge Sälyan's new Olympic Centre is under construction.

Almost 3km north of the bridge, a rough road turns east off the main Baku highway and curls around through a mini smoky-mountain rubbish dump then skirts an arid hill topped with a military listening post. About 2.3km from the main road a track leads 300m to a desolate scrubby amphitheatre at the back of which is **Kükürdlü Su** – an evil-looking murky, bubbling pool which locals believe to have a variety of curative properties – notice all the discarded bathing towels!

SÄLYAN TO NEFTCHALA

A few years ago a trip down the 'nose' of the Kura was worthwhile to seek out some of Azerbaijan's best (if illegally poached) caviar. However, the little markets at Banka and Oriad, at which one could formerly make the necessary contacts, have been closed down. The caviar business is now centred on Neftchala market which is easier to monitor.

The road to Neftchala/Banka is paved and generally fast but with a few sudden holes to catch you out. Beware that standard maps of Azerbaijan show the A28 linking Neftchala to Shorsulu; that road is in fact very rough and struggles across

many canals, so attempting a loop can not be recommended.

The terrain is entirely flat but the monotony is alleviated by occasional views of the meandering Kura river, most peacefully from the high bridge at **Ikinci Qarali**. Numerous motorcycles with side-cars add a photogenic touch especially when overloaded with hay. In **Ashaği Surra** notice the clay-walled tandir stoves right on the roadside. There are attractively minareted mosques in **Ashaği Qaramanli** (new) and **Xilli** which also has an eccentric, gone-to-seed former tea-house and an ugly but much-needed new sturgeon hatchery.

Banka, Oriad and Neftchala (☎ 0153) (see map opposite)

Both **Banka** and **Oriad** have some older houses and pleasant river views but neither is idyllic and Banka's 1928 caviar-processing factory is now derelict. **Neftchala** is larger and much more 'Soviet' with an eerily quiet, disproportionately wide central boulevard. The **museum** (9.00-18:00, Tue-Sun) is spacious and well presented if slightly aging and welcomes you with a huge if not especially informative relief map. A mock underwater scene dangles with Caspian fishes. A prominent scale model triumphantly touts the town's Iodine-Bromine plant baldly ignoring the fact that it closed years ago.

Plans are mooted to make Neftchala a centre for eco-tourism and bird-watching boat tours. I saw no sign of this on my last visit. Instead the main entertainment was courtesy of the local police who, after walking me all round town to various abrupt interrogations, turned friendly and started buying me tea, coaching me at nard and effectively preventing me from leaving town till the next day.

The once-comfortable three-storey *hotel* (☎ 21824) has some partly restored ceiling mouldings and the survivable rooms cost from AZN4 per person without water, AZN5 with. Room 14 has a water heater.

Sporadic **minibuses** cost AZN1 to Sälyan (70 mins). **Shared taxis** (AZN2 per person, AZN8 per car) taking half the time depart from an oddly inconvenient

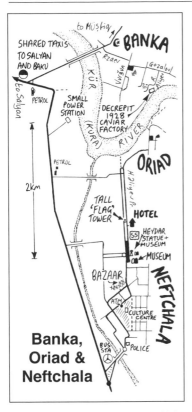

Banka, Oriad & Neftchala

spot at the Banka junction. Many vehicles continue to Baku.

SÄLYAN TO MASALLI

The lakes and marshes between Shorsulu and Biläsuvar take on a variety of colours according to the season and look best when flocks of wading birds arrive. Wheatfields and scraggy vineyards stretch south of Biläsuvar. The road becomes more attractively treelined after Cälilabad, which, like Priship/Göytepe, has some mildly quaint older Russian-style wooden homes.

Biläsuvar (Biləsuvar; map p282; ☎ 0159)

Known officially (but not popularly) in the Soviet era as Pushkino, the name Biläsuvar has two popular derivations. 'Place of skilful irrigation' makes sense given the contrast between the steppeland wastes further north and Biläsuvar's rich wheat fields. A more imaginative interpretation is 'station for military elephants'. Don't expect to see any! To really appreciate the 'skilful irrigation', drive 60 monotonously flat kilometres through cotton-wheat-alfalfa-cotton rotated fields towards Beylaqan. After several refugee villages you'll reach the point where a bridge-dam crosses the Araz River, a stone's throw from the Iranian border. Here a complex switching system diverts the river water into some 20 canals, guarded by a gaggle of mildly suspicious soldiers (see map p278).

In Biläsuvar itself the **history museum** has artifacts from an ancient city site nearby and a Talysh kitchen diorama where museum staff have been known to dress up in traditional costumes for your photos. Biläsuvar's **central mosque** is rather eye-catching with triple silver domes.

Zirvä Restaurant (☎ 32515, mob ☎ 55 785 7761) at the southern edge of town serves delicious food (try the fish with narsharab) but beware of the extras. Its decently equipped *rooms* (air-con, hot water, AZN40-50 twin) are fair value but can get noisy in the 'wedding season'. *Biläsuvar Hotel* (dbl AZN18) is an older structure with clean but shared bathrooms. It's unsigned next to Mäisät Evi; call ☎ 055-716-5942 if it's locked. The management can supply plates and utensils for cooking and maybe even a camp stove.

Allar and Pokrovka

The Allar tribe was a sub-group of the Shahsevans. These renowned Turkic warriors initially fought against 17th-century Persian ruler Shah Abbas. However, they later changed sides and for serving him faithfully, Abbas rewarded the tribe with various gifts of land. Thus Allar is a fairly common village name in these parts (see also p291). This **Allar**'s original incarnation was destroyed during the 1918 intercommunal turmoil by a raiding party from Puchkov, 4km away. Today renamed

THE SOUTH

Pokrovka, Puchkov was founded by Ukrainians and grew rapidly following Stolypin's agricultural reform programme (1906), when an audacious irrigation project piped fresh water all the way from a mountain spring above Cälilabad. However, the pipes broke in the late 1980s and many Christian families left during the political turmoil of the early 1990s playing havoc with Pokrovka's agricultural economy. The one sight here is a church ruin beside the war memorial. Disused since a 1963 crackdown on religion, the church was already derelict when its onion-domed cupola was removed as part of planned repairs in 1990. The USSR dissolved before the process was finished. In 2000 the hospitable mayor told me of his valiant plans to prevent the building's total collapse by turning it into a mosque but so far this has come to nothing and the original 416kg bell which he rescued remains in his yard. The road from Allar is very degraded and patches can be impossibly muddy after rain.

Cälilabad (Cəlilabad, Jalilabad, Astrakhan Bazaar, ☎ 0114)

Astrakhan Bazaar, once a predominantly Russian town, was renamed Cälilabad in 1967 to honour Azeri writer Cälil Mämmädguluzadeh, one-time editor of the classic satirical magazine *Molla Nasruddin*. Few tourists bother visiting Cälilabad but it's a pleasant town stretching several kilometres west from the main Länkäran road. In the central area, Heydar Aliyev pr loops around an attractive park full of teahouses. The nearby **central mosque** has a curious new minaret and the paved back streets have plenty of older homes with wooden-framed windows and weather-worn roof tiles. A

great deal of care and money has been lavished on **Heydar Aliyev Seyrangahi**, a layered park of fountains and shrubberies leading down to an ornamental lake with paddleboats. There's also a **Heydar Park**.

At the eastern side of town are three abrupt little hills. The first is topped with a rusting fairground and the second covered in old graves. The third hosts the town's foremost restaurant *Kral* (☎ 35449). It has a lovely outdoor setting in a lush garden, with tables sheltered from rain by sideless but sturdily roofed pavilions. Prices are reasonable (small shashlyk portion AZN1.80, chicken AZN7) though the walk back into town at night is very dark and the short-cut involves crossing a small stream by a plank bridge (bring a torch). You can avoid this by staying at the attached *Kral Hotel* (mobile ☎ 50-664 7793). It's new and very friendly and the air conditioned AZN40 double rooms are good value if you can face the clashing colours, blue furniture and tasselled orange-gold beds. Bathtubs are clean and the AZN50 suite has a big dining area.

For those on a tight budget the unsigned Soviet-era *hotel* (☎ 33130) still operates ten crumbling rooms at AZN6 per person. While far from lovely, most rooms have seatless toilets and perhaps a rusty cold tap that once sported a shower attachment. If nothing else you could see this as an educational experience: just five years ago hotels all over Azerbaijan were mostly like this! The building is marked 'Nuranä Tibb Märkäzi' for a medical centre that occupies the building's ground floor but a reception desk within can provide the hotel keys.

The impressive-looking *Göl Hotel* was complete but yet to open on my last visit.

Passing Länkaran–Baku minibuses

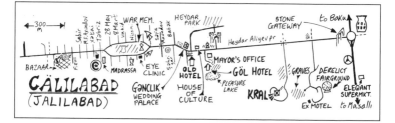

collect passengers at the M3 roundabout rather than the nearby, little-used bus station. The nearest train station is 12km further at Novo Golovka.

Göytepe (Priship)

'Blue Hill' (Göytepe) seems an odd name for a flat town surrounded by potato fields. Many inhabitants stick to the older name, Priship, under which the place was a Russian garrison town. Its modest 'sight' is an appealing 1878 **Russian church** in the grounds of School number 2. Otherwise Priship's charm lies in the wide sprinkling of Siberian-style **wooden homes**. The

town's central stream looks almost attractive from the popular bridge-side *teahouse* (tea 40q), at least when twilight renders the rubbish on the banks less conspicuous.

During the first years of the 20th century, Stalin spent much of his life escaping from a selection of Tsarist prisons across the Russian empire. According to locals, after one such occasion he spent some time lying low in **Bazavan**, beyond Komanlı west of Göytepe.

MASALLI (☎ 0151)

During the chaotic years of the early 1990s with the army fighting Armenians and the government fighting itself, opportunistic farmers around Masallı quietly started cultivating a lucrative crop of smokable weeds that would have seemed more appropriately grown in Gänjä. Renewed police vigilance means you'll no longer see waving fields of marijuana. But for a different type of greenery, consider staying the weekend at one of the various woodland getaways towards Yardımlı. Masallı itself is a busy market town whose typically southern-styled **mosque** and **madrassa** can be seen in 15 minutes as you drive through.

The nearly central *Masallı Hotel* (☎ 53 231, sgl/dbl AZN22-32/42-50) has made a

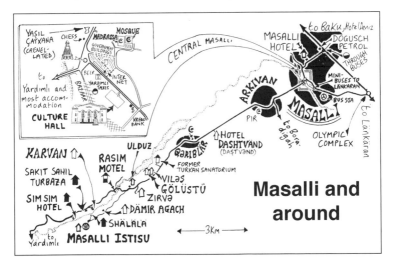

Masalli and around

THE SOUTH

fair stab at turning a concrete Soviet block into a semi-presentable hotel, but it's far nicer to sleep in the woodlands a few kilometres west. Between the bazaar and bus station there's a *tandir-bakery* that also sells AZN5 fish lavangi to take away.

Masallı's **bus station** is south of the market but only handles a few longer distance services (mostly mornings) and Baku minibuses. Occasional **minibuses** shuttle to Länkäran from the southern end of the bazaar but it's often quicker to go to the main Baku–Länkäran road junction and flag down passing vehicles from there (especially in the afternoon). Baku–Yardımlı minibuses (AZN2) pick up near the bridge in the town centre mostly mid-morning. **Shared taxis** to Yardımlı (AZN3) depart from outside Aptek Nur in the bazaar but it's generally worth paying for the whole car (AZN12) at least one way to allow for photo stops. Yardımlı–Masallı regular Safar (mob ☎ 50-375 5344) speaks Russian.

MASALLI TO YARDIMLI

The main Yardımlı road is a country lane which wriggles inexorably higher above the river, mostly in fairly thick forest. The occasional viewpoints are attractive rather than spectacular. The interest starts 7km beyond Arkivan ('Azerbaijan's biggest village') with charming woodlands that hug the southern, raised bank of **Vilash Lake**. Here an understandably popular picnic area is rapidly becoming more like a holiday camp with all the new bungalow hotels and restaurants. Beyond this the trees get thicker and the valley narrower but accommodation is dotted along the entire stretch. A short diversion brings you to **Masallı Istisu** (38°58'05"N, 48°32'41"E), a flower- and tree-filled natural amphitheatre from which mineral water springs emerge at a scalding 68.7°C. Once the water's cooled a little you can bathe in it. The once-ragged Soviet-era spa-sanatorium here has now been upgraded though there's still something vaguely 'Carry On' about those lugubrious doctors prescribing you your ten-minute medicinal bath. Each dip is said to give the bather one year of pain-free life so people are happy enough to cough up the AZN4 fee.

For something less commercial and altogether more magical head for the bungalow camp *Yanardag* 500m off the Yardımlı road at km15. Cross the green footbridge below its restaurant tables and head to your left to find hot water emerging from

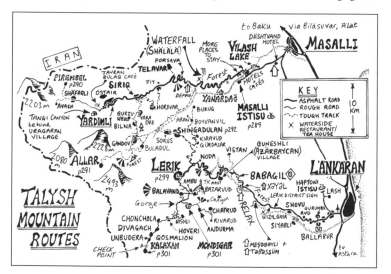

between the river stones. The fizzing bubblings here are flammable and when ignited at dusk the whole surface of the river appears to burn. It's a memorable sight. A guide can show you more burning springs in a forest clearing in the hills above; hence the name Yanardag (fire mountain).

Twenty-five kilometres out of Masallı as the trees start to thin, the road reaches **Shälälä** waterfall (see photo C12 top L). Approximately 20m high, the upper of its two drops is impressive in the spring but a disappointing trickle after a dry summer. At a popular teahouse near the base itinerant peddlers may proffer hand-carved souvenir spoons. One kilometre beyond the waterfall a rough side track descends sharply to the river; this is one of several possible equestrian/4WD routes to Lerik.

The forest fades away as the main road winds on through increasingly steep, barren grasslands towards **Sırıq** where a tough 4WD side-trip leads to Allar (see p291).

Accommodation (see map p287)

The area's only real hotel, *Hotel Dashtvänd* (☎ 21230, mob ☎ 50-371 0345; 💻 www .dashtvend.com/index.htm, 39°00'22"N, 48°37'13"E) is continually enlarging, transforming and renovating itself such that standards tend to stay higher than at typical build-and-forget places elsewhere. Set in an oddly unglamorous flat-field location at the km5 post (ie 3km west of the Arkivan road fork), the hotel has put considerable effort into creating willow-edged artificial pools that now echo with peacock cries and clinking tea-glasses. There's also a new-ish indoor swimming pool. The rooms in the main block have good bathrooms and are excellent value (from AZN40). The bungalows around the pond cost a whopping AZN200 but are virtually full houses sleeping up to eight.

Vilash Lake area The former sanatorium *Türkan* was once the region's best-value option in a rose-garden overlooking Vilash Lake (km9) but was closed (for reconstruction?) on my last visit.

A kilometre beyond are several closely grouped eateries and rest zones in an undulating grassy wood perched above the same lake. Of these my favourite remains the growing *Gölüstü* (mob ☎ 50 220 6377). Its café and balconies enjoy the best lake views; rooms in its three-storey building start from only AZN30 dbl. The wooden huts at nearby *Viläş* (mob ☎ 50-678 1477; AZN60) have carpets, sitting room, TV and air-con but are set further back from the views in the pleasant grassy woodland. Dominated by a tall concrete goat and 'waterfall mound', *Zirvä* (AZN40-60) is on a low grassy hilltop above the road so it's quieter with no passing traffic. *Ulduz* (AZN30) is basic and annoyingly near the road.

Istisu and around The ongoing gentrification of *Masallı Istisu* (☎ 41262) means doubtless many new rooms will become available while the cheap, cheerless old Soviet hut-wrecks will soon be history. Rates are AZN30-80, the mid-range options having sitting rooms with a see-and-be-seen balcony plus a dark double bedroom at the rear. The mustier upper rooms come in varying sizes.

If you still want something super-cheap you could try descending to *Shälälä* (open May-Sept only), 200m below the Istisu car park where the ultra-spartan concrete cubes shouldn't cost more than AZN10 given that you wash in the river. Entered via a somewhat tacky gateway of fake rocks, *Damir Agach* (mob ☎ 50-689 9798) is set in a thick stand of ironwood trees high above the river; the AZN50 huts have fold-out couch beds, a fireplace for winter and a tiny WC/shower booth with water heater. Non-residents can dine at the pleasant outdoor tables high above the river.

Back on the Yardımlı road, just after the bridge beyond the Istisu turning, the circular, eight-room *Motel Rasim* has stuffy, claustrophobic rooms with saggy beds and separate WC (AZN12). *SimSim Hotel* (mob ☎ 50 357 6529), 1.7km further then steeply down to the riverside, has strange, stilted concrete box rooms, reached by spiral metal stairs, for AZN30 (sleeps up to five).

Beyond Istisu (map opposite) Well off the road near km15, huts at *Yanardağ* (mob ☎ 50-325 5826, Vugar) are less polished than many but they're well spaced amid the trees and are the ideal place to stay if you want to burn that river at night (p288). Dining tables are positioned streamside.

At km28.9, 2km beyond Shälälä *Demen* (☎ 51038) has AZN50 red and yellow huts that look rather 'plastic' in their thin woodland but they have sizeable bathrooms and carpets on the wooden floors. Pre-erected tents can be rented at AZN12 or pay AZN2 to put up your own. The grassy areas above could make for good hiking and the higher elevations here keep temperatures refreshingly cool.

YARDIMLI (☎ 0175)

Strung along several kilometres of narrow-cut river valley, Yardımlı's eastern end starts with some small, olde worlde cottages – some tiled, others re-roofed in corrugated iron. At the bazaar the road chicanes across a small bridge near which the new **history museum** is being built. A rough cobbled section of main street leads up to the **WWII memorial** then the road curves towards the **Heydar Aliyev Museum** and neat new *A&E Hotel* (☎ 51246). It has just four pleasantly appointed en suite rooms (AZN30-40). The helpful owners can help you find UAZ drivers for trips to Pirembel or even Lerik, reputedly now possible in under three hours on a track via Horovar (which I've never personally taken). In dry conditions the route is reportedly fairly straightforward.

Where the village peters out there's a modest **carpet-weaving factory** where visitors are at liberty to watch women creating

portrait carpets (9-19:00, Mon-Sat). Strangely there's no shop.

Around 2km further on, just beyond a small shopping centre where the asphalt ends, there's a good view over the brooding Tangi Canyon. A tractor track cutting up the hill behind this point leads 700m, most improbably, to *Javran Bulaq* a tiny café/restaurant with outdoor tables ranged in a little copse surrounded by pretty meadows and a small artificial pond. Despite its unbelievably uncommercial position it's a popular place for succulent shashlyk, home-made cheese and fragrant tea.

Shared taxis depart when full (how long you wait depends on whether people turn up or not) from Masallı's bazaar charging AZN3. Renting the whole vehicle for a return day trip with many stops cost me only AZN25, though I suspect I was lucky. There are a couple of **minibuses** to/from Baku daily.

AROUND YARDIMLI (see map p288)

West beyond Yardımlı the road is bumpy until Shäfäqli where it degenerates into a muddy mess. Although I miraculously made it by Lada Zhiguli, you really need a 4WD to reach **Pirembel**, an attractive village filled with quince and walnut trees, cupped in a steep-sided, wooded valley with some exposed sections of reddish cliff. At the village's centre, two ancient stone rams form a gateway just past the white-washed war memorial where the road ends. A track contours around to the sizeable new mosque. Or hike uphill for some fine views back across the valley. There are some tempting trekking possibilities on the ridges high above but given the proximity of Iran you may get yourself into trouble for attempting them.

Even harder to reach is **Abu Darda** cave-memorial, a pilgrimage site near Lazran, 1km from Arsila. The area was the scene of Khuramid battles in Babek's day (9th century). Accessible only by horse, **Avarak** is a 1000-year-old cemetery on the Iranian border (called the 'Ardebil border' by the old man who told me about it). The skeletons found here measured up to 2.5m long. As these super tall people were not

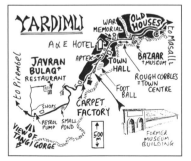

THE SOUTH

buried facing Mecca it is assumed they were pre-Islamic pagans. Rumours abound of a *kupe* urn full of gold that was supposedly found here. Some stones from the site and another kupe (without gold) should be displayed in the Yardımlı Historical Museum once it reopens.

Peshtasar and Allar (see below) have celebrated mineral water springs but neither village has anything resembling a road.

Sırıq to Allar

Allar remains very isolated. Well into the 1990s the only way to get there was by horse or on foot. There is now a jeep track from Gandov/Buladul villages. The very steep, muddy sections are feasible in a high-clearance UAZ but very tough in a Niva and utterly impossible if it's been raining.

Start in Sırıq (38°55'08"N, 48°19' 07"E) where there's a pair of small car-repair workshops. At one of these Azad (mob ☎ 50-532 8007) can sometimes arrange a UAZ and driver for the return trip (a bargain at AZN40), but one can't count on a vehicle being easily available. Take the track descending between the workshops, ford the river and rise steeply up the other side. Follow the grassy ridge beside **Värqädüz**, veer left at a track junction and skirt around **Bilna** village. This is another grassy ridge with great views of the forested mountains ahead. You then descend very steeply on horribly rutted mud tracks to a ford just before **Gandov** where there's a choice of routes (see map p288). Heading left for Shingadulan should bring you out eventually at Lerik. This, or the steeper diagonal left, could loop you through to Allar via Buladul (where the road through the village is extremely muddy and difficult). But it's best to bear diagonal-

ly right, rising very steeply through Gandov and on up through the forest beyond where the muddy track has been heavily mashed by trucks.

At around 1300m elevation the track levels out and bears right along the top of a wooded cliff high above the Allarchay river. There are more great views and from here the track improves, though it's narrow and strewn with rocks in some places. From Sırıq the spine-crunching trip took me roughly two hours out, 70 minutes back.

Allar

Not to be confused with the dull town of the same name near Cälilabad (p285), this Allar is a mysterious mountain village hemmed in by a maze of forest-covered cliffs and crags. It's entirely dominated by the soaring perch of **Qız Qalası** on which the Khan of Yardımlı's mythical castle once stood (see box p292). Visible on the skyline from as far afield as Yardımlı, the 2266m rocky peak is a classic volcanic plug, rising from a pyramidal sheep-mown grassy mountain. Viewed from the village there appear to be substantial wall remnants ringing the top of the crag, but those who have climbed it (taking just over an hour) claim that there are no clear remains beyond a few pottery shards and a tandir hole. Locals claim there is a tower called Olan Qalası a little further east.

Bemused villagers are friendly if suspicious towards visitors. A lady who presented me with some bread, butter and home-made cheese for the journey back was light-heartedly aghast at my culturally insensitive attempt to shake her hand. 'You're not my husband so if you touched my arm I'd have to cut it off!' she said. She was only half joking.

At the approach to the

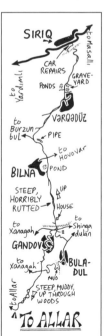

village a tiny spring hidden within a small waterfall five minutes' walk from the 'road' produces a fizzy, heavily mineralized water. Locals consider it therapeutic, despite the frighteningly vivid scarlet stains it produces on surrounding rocks. The village sprawls appealingly up the rocky valley and a handful of homes retain classic wooden-tiled roofs. Tucked away to the west of the village are some more impressive crags and canyons.

Yardımlı to Lerik

Trips into the mountains would be much more satisfying if you could link Lerik and Yardımlı to make a loop. Sadly this is only possible with a very sturdy 4WD or a horse. After rain, the tracks become effectively impassable except for 6WD Ural trucks which carve ever deeper ruts into the route.

The toughest section is within Shingadulan village itself, so at least there's some chance of getting pushed out of trouble. Every day or two in the summer a truck-bus rolls in to either town from intermediate villages along the 'road'. But for Lerik–Yardımlı even locals find it more comfortable and possibly quicker to go via Masallı and Länkäran!

MASALLI TO LÄNKÄRAN
(see map p288)

There are two manageable roads. Marginally shorter but much slower, the A31 cuts slightly inland to **Arkivan** then

winds through a series of quietly prosperous villages with neat, semi-traditional houses, Pensar-style mosques (like the graphic on p66) and the odd donkey-cart.

If you stick to the faster main road, look out for the big, metal '*tea lady*' in **Qumbashi** welcoming you to Länkäran region. That village also has a typical southern mosque. An excursion to Narimanabad is uncomfortably close to car-crash voyeurism but the empty beaches beyond are pleasant enough.

Liman (Port Ilich) and Narimanabad

With Lenin's first names long out of fashion, **Port Ilich** has been renamed **Liman**. That means 'port' in Azeri/Turkish for its harbour that was once a tsarist naval base and was further dredged out in 1922 by the Soviets.

Across the bay, **Narimanabad** was known as Sara until the 1980s. It was so named by a Russian general in honour of his sick daughter and was renamed less for political reasons than because of the big Narimanov fishing cooperative which came to be synonymous with the town. Sara was an island until the unusually low Caspian Sea level of the 1950s allowed the building of a causeway to Port Ilich. People also built fine, sea-view houses despite the warnings of the old men that the sea might return. Now it has. Although the causeway has held, on the town's southern shore whole homes have succumbed to the lapping waves. It's a maudlin site echoed by

---

❏ Escape from the skylark fortress

Once upon a time the big brave Khan of Yardımlı was beset by an invading Arab army. Like all folk-tale kings the Khan had the world's most beautiful daughter. To protect her from the marauding Arabs he hid her in the impenetrable castle at Allar, which 'soared like an armoured skylark' above a dark, forgotten valley.

Predictably she was eventually tracked down and the Arab commander promptly fell in love with her. At this stage her father turned sleazy politician and offered the invader his daughter's hand in return for his reinstatement as ruler. But the spunky princess was having none of it. She slipped out of the castle by moonlight, reversed her steed's horseshoes to leave false tracks, then rode like the wind to find her secret love in the safe haven we today call Ardabil (now in Iran). From there she sent a curt note to her father: 'Ar da var' ('already found a husband'), from which the name Ardabil is said to be derived.

the town's gigantic concrete war memorial – an 'unknown soldier' statue with an eerie resemblance to the grim reaper.

The road north continues another 14km before dead ending at the edge of the Qızıl Ağach wetlands reserve. As far as the fishing village of Sara II (Narimanabad Ikinci) it passes right alongside some appealingly deserted golden shell-beaches. Shore access is impeded by marshes or sea channels but a few connecting paths exist.

Qızıl Ağach is famous for its spectacular flocks of **flamingos** but even if you're granted a permit to enter the (normally closed) reserve beware that to see them you'll have to push and punt a small boat significant distances through the marshy shallows. Enquire at Baku's Ecology Ministry (☎ 012-438 7085).

LÄNKÄRAN (Lənkəran, Lenkoran; ☎ 0171)

A symbolic figure is picked out in embossed metal on the wall of the **ARZU wedding palace**: a powerful female form holding a tea cup in one hand and a heavy battle-sword in the other. This image of friendship balancing strength appears elsewhere (eg inside Baku Old City's double-gates) but is especially appropriate in Länkäran. To most Azeris, Länkäran is synonymous with tea; and tea is synonymous with hospitality. Tea production has fallen off of late but the hospitality remains as intense and generous as ever. Nonetheless Länkäran does occasionally brandish a sword: it was also the capital of the very short-lived breakaway Talysh-Mugam republic in 1993.

Even though its languorous tree-lined streets seem ill-fitted to any military excitement, the town centre remains home to a big tank regiment. And the city's favourite son is not a writer or artist but a battle commander, Hazi Aslanov, who is immortalized

NARIMANABAD

WAR MEMORIAL
4km Causeway to Liman
to Beaches
BOATS
OLD SARA CAFE
FISH CO-OP
BUST OF NARIMANOV
SHOP
HOUSES AT THE END OF THIS STREET HAVE BEEN PARTLY WASHED AWAY
50 m
Niriman Narimanov

in the central square standing atop a symbolic stone tank. Still, the overall atmosphere is tranquil and best summed up by Samed Vurğun:

Länkäran smiles with dazzling flowers
Refreshed by tea and welcomed showers.

What to see

The town's most visible landmark is the whitewashed **Mayak** – a round-towered, operational lighthouse-cum-former prison. A similar but unpainted brick building near the river bridge is said to have once incarcerated Stalin. It's now being slowly renovated. Ideas as to its future purpose are still hazy but a Stalin-themed café has been suggested which could be a hoot. The Talysh khan's palace no longer stands. However, the **History Museum** (free, closed Mondays) is housed in the elegant former home of Mir Ahmad, one of the khan's dapper descendants. His moustachioed portrait in full bow tie and tails hints at a turn of the 20th-century playboy. He died in France in 1916, just three years after the house was completed. The museum contains a typical series of archaeological, photographic and Karabagh memorial items, plus a room decorated to show the interior of a traditional Talysh home.

The lack of thrilling landmarks is underlined by the fact that Länkäran's official website (🖳 www.lankaran.az) lavishes many of its precious photos on the railway station façade. In the square outside is the **Hazi Aslanov statue** standing on a white-brick raft supposed to represent a tank. Until recently a real **tank** sat on a plinth just across the railway line, lapped by the waves of the rising Caspian. Although within a closed army area, spotting it from a distance was one of Länkäran's off-beat attractions. Sadly it was removed in 2006 and although Länkäran's tourist officer told me that he

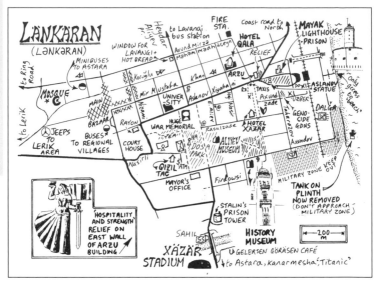

planned to have it restored to its now-empty plinth, I wouldn't hold your breath waiting.

Länkäranis are proud of their gardens, most notably the neatly groomed **Dosa Park** where a bolt-upright Heydar statue watches locals making their evening passeggiata to the strains of amplified piped music. The free **Heydar Aliyev Museum** is worth visiting if only for the great air conditioning. A large, dramatic **war memorial** depicts a soldier bursting out of a bronze-coloured boulder.

Now almost hidden by foliage is the metallic relief of the 'heroic tea lady' (see introductory paragraph, p293) on the wall of the ARZU wedding palace (formerly MUM). Originally a caption beneath her read 'Long Live Azerbaijan, the great Soviet state'. It's been removed, obviously.

Accommodation and food

The highly presentable **Hotel Qala** (☎ 50 284, 🖳 www.abqala.az) has excellent, modern rooms from AZN51/72 sgl/dbl with upper floor rooms costing more (same facilities, better view). The *restaurant* is stylish but keeps relatively little in stock.

The lobby of **Hotel Xäzär** (☎ 51663) retains a certain sense of olde worlde charm but the rooms (AZN32/55) are fairly functional and poorer value than the Qala's.

Behind the railway station **Dalğa** (☎ 51 769) serves reliably good food in a pleasant garden restaurant, though the mosquitoes are smarter than the narsharab and you'll need to check the bill. Several good-value hotel rooms (sgl/dbl AZN21/25) are attached and come with bathrooms and towels.

Hotel Qizil Tac (☎ 51664, rooms from AZN30/50 with shared/private bathroom) is new and well kept but oddly managed, there's no real reception and your experience is likely to be hit-or-miss according to which caretaker is on duty.

Widely nicknamed **Titanic** (see map p296) due to its boat-shaped main restaurant building (kebabs AZN2.40, plov AZN1.20) the Palidli Sahil (mob ☎ 55-750 8618) has a selection of nine AZN50-100 en suite bungalows in a woodland area two minutes' walk from the Caspian shore. It's near the Olympic Centre, 3km by road from the Stalin Tower, considerably less if you walk along the rail tracks.

A series of rustic alternatives are available along the Lerik road (p299). For those on a tight budget, AZN10 **homestays** are available at Haftoni Istisu (below) and at Hirkan village. *Shafag* (💻 www.south tourism.az) c/o Vamig Babayev (47 Mirsalayev St, mob ☎ 055-719 2068 or ☎ 50-368 3078) has started advertising interesting eco-tours to many of the region's more offbeat attractions and claims to organize homestays in several rural villages.

There are several modest eateries and teahouses in the area around the train station.

Transport

When British dering-doer Fitzroy Maclean showed up back in 1937, passenger boats from Baku provided a great alternative to the two-day cart-track from Astrakhan Bazaar (Cälilabad). However, with decent roads and a railway these days, attempts to introduce a hydrofoil service from Baku have so far failed to prove profitable and rough seas tend to make timetables unpredictable. Nonetheless, now that Länkäran's port facilities have been rebuilt waterborne services just might resume.

Länkäran 'International' Airport was officially reopened in October 2008. Now all it needs is a few flights. Till then the most comfortable way to Baku remains the 21.17 night **train** (arriving Baku 06.00). However, as it's cheaper than the bus, train berths are often sold out several days ahead especially on Friday and Sunday nights. On such days the ticket office (supposedly open 08.00-13.00 & 14.00-21.30) typically stays closed behind a 'bilet yoxdur' sign. The seat-only 'express' train is inconveniently timed leaving Länkäran at 16.59 arriving in Baku around 23.00.

An overloaded overnight **bus** to Baku leaves around 21.00 from outside the train station. Other Baku-bound buses and minibuses depart approximately hourly (07.00-18:00 from **Lävängi bus station** (☎ 45928). That's 3km north-west of the centre on the ring road. Get there by marshrutki 1 or 2 or using the Liman-bound local bus from the main bazaar. With wood and thatch interiors, 50q beer and AZN6 chicken lävängi, *Xan Länkäran Restaurant*,

right at the bus station, is a great place to wait. Also from here there are buses to Gänjä (07.15), Qazax (06.30), Mingächevir (08.30) and Lerik (07.30). Further Lerik minibuses (ex Baku) pick up around noon and 13.00. However, the joy of heading to Lerik is the journey itself so you'll generally do better to charter a vehicle. That's cheapest from the Talysh share-taxi stand on Koroğlu St in the town centre.

Local bus services to regional villages depart sporadically from various points around the main bazaar. To reach the airport or to get close to Haftoni Istisu, take a 'Laş/Läj/Lash' minibus.

AROUND LÄNKÄRAN
Beaches

North of Länkäran there are some tatty shore-side cafés close to the Baku road with relatively easy access points to the sea. South of town the beaches are somewhat nicer and more secluded, thanks to the lack of a coastal road and the resultant difficulty of approach.

At **Känarmeshä** the beaches are black-sand strips dotted with rocks but a couple of restaurants have sea views and/or beach access. *Dalğa* (☎ 96600) serves decent fish kebabs on a pleasant balustraded lawn overlooking the sea. Around 600m away **Yeddi Bulaq** (mob ☎ 50-379 8791) is named after a fresh-water spring that gushes out right beside the beach where you'll find more people washing their cars than swimming.

If you just want to gaze at the Caspian, one possibility is to take the Astara-bound train (60q) at 07.23 or 14.20 which trundles along the seashore at little more than walking pace.

Haftoni Istisu and Kirov Istisu

Around 700m north of the Lash turning, a hot-springs sanatorium is under reconstruction in a grove of oak and iron-wood trees. For now, renting out ad-hoc bathing booths (AZN1 for 10 mins) provides a little income for refugees. The site is through Soviet-era gates and across a little gully from where the road ends beside Shaiq's shop. Attached to the rear of that shop are some very inexpensive but dismal *rooms*

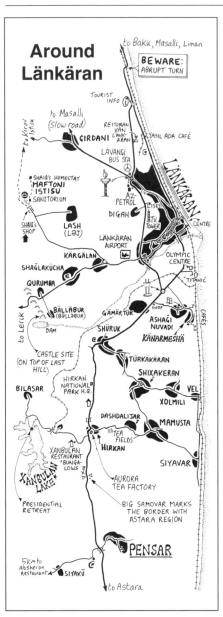

of close-packed, saggy beds (4M per person). Owner Shaiq (mob ☎ 050-564 9170, no English) also offers much more appealing homestay accommodation (AZN 10-15 per person) in his clean, well-kept house, a ten-minute walk away behind the sanatorium.

This could make a pleasant base for gentle hikes into the forested hills above or, much more straightforwardly, following the canalside path through gentle birdsong to another Istisu (aka Kirov). After about 40 minutes' stroll, just after the aqueduct, turn right to a rubbish-pile junction from which it's five minutes more to central Kirov whence occasional shared taxis run back to Länkäran via Girdani. Alternatively double back more sharply to the right and descend into the little grassy hollow where you'll find the very basic warm-springs baths (20q, 15-mins dip) for which the village is known. A friendly çayxana sets tables in the surrounding overgrown flower garden and serves tea with fudge-flavoured home-made sugar lumps.

Hirkan National Park

The vast Hirkan National Park covers much of the beautiful (if inaccessible) forest lands that stretch south-west from Länkäran to the Iranian border. Entry costs AZN4 (AZN2 for locals) but oddly to pay it you must go out of your way to find the visitor centre (☎ 171-76266) on the Astara road, and odder still that's closed on Sundays when most visitors want to go. The park's most visited attraction, **Lake Xanbulan**, is a pretty, forest-ringed, reservoir whose banks are picturesque picnic spots. It's a pleasant place for woodland strolls despite the fair amount of rubbish left along the short trails. However, ten minutes is enough to get the idea so AZN4 seems an entirely disproportionate sum to charge. Local families appear to ignore (or be unaware of) the park's entrance fee altogether. After all there's no barrier or ticket booth anywhere near. Also note that the finest lake views have always been from a waterfront official guesthouse ('gastavaya'), originally built in 1978 for the visit of Urho Kekkonen (then Finnish president). This is now totally out of bounds having been turned into a complex for the president's entourage. Keep well away from the electric fences.

A much more enticing side to the national park is a series of guided routes around which you can be shown local flora and animal tracks. However, you'll need your own vehicle to access the trailheads (and to pick up the guide from the park office). Deputy Park Director, Haji (mob ☎ 50-687 1009) speaks English and can help organize AZN10 **homestays** in local villages including Hirkan itself. Around 3km short of the lake, *Xanbulan Restaurant* (☎ 171-57190) does an excellent chicken lavangi with garlic susma and has several decent **bungalows** (AZN40). There are no views but it's a peaceful spot (closed mid-winter).

Aurora tea factory

Länkäran's heavily tanic tea has an almost meaty flavour that is in great local demand. However, production remains limited: the Soviet-era collective farms were broken up into private smallholdings that are often too small to render tea-growing economic. Nonetheless some tea-fields can still be seen around **Mamusta**. And in the season (late May to early June and late August to mid September), Aurora tea factory allows visits by appointment (call Mirzaga Gasimov, mob ☎ 050-576 5217). If admitted you can to watch the fermentation, roasting, dying and stem-filtering processes, the latter using a curious disco-wiggler of a machine. The factory sits in a pretty rose garden behind high, unmarked blue-metal gates off the main Astara road in Hirkan village.

Bälläbur Castle site

The 9th-century Khuramid leader **Babek** is a major, semi-religious hero in Azerbaijan. Part Robin Hood part King Arthur he had his dramatic mountaintop 'Camelot' at Bazz Castle near Kaleybar (now in Iranian Azerbaijan) from which he launched raids on the Arab Caliphate. However, in August 837, after a tremendous battle with general Afshin, Bazz finally fell. The scene is depicted in a celebrated painting now in Länkäran's Historical Museum. Although much of his rebel army was killed and Afshin took Babek's son hostage, Babek himself escaped. According to locals he headed for Bälläbur near Qurumba where he holed up in a small hilltop fortress. This might be where messengers tracked him down only for Babek to refuse Afshin's deceptively magnanimous ransom note. Babek fled once more (locals insist that there was another fight here in which he

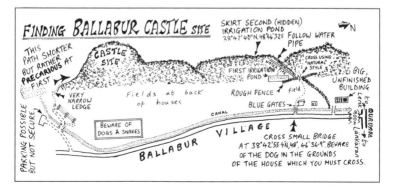

THE SOUTH

was injured) before being caught and executed in January 838.

Today the only remains of Bälläbur castle site are a few almost invisible brick sections on the contours of a powerful defensive position. Hidden within the iron-wood trees, several lip-and-mound terraces culminate in the small, flat central area where the commander's residence would have been. One legend says that Babek thrust his sword into the ground here and it mysteriously transformed into a massive double-headed snake that is still said to haunt the place. Beware while exploring as small prosaic snakes, if not the legendary giant one, are common here. Another legend says that there's a trove of treasure which was dropped into the well, a site now marked by a metal pole held in wobbly concrete at the summit. A local man who tried to dig for that treasure escaped the great snake but apparently went insane having seen a ghost, adding further to the mystical power that this unassuming hill casts.

LÄNKÄRAN TO LERIK (map p288)
Beyond the recently re-inaugurated Länkäran Airport and Qurumba (the Bälläbur turning, see p297), the Lerik road winds up through the first of several layers of wooded hills interspersed with smaller villages. Three kilometres beyond Shovu a section of

thick forest hides several roadside cafés with more around km34 (see accommodation opposite). Woodland walks can take you to small waterfalls.

Just before the km40 post passing motorists usually stop on a bend of the road to leave a donation at the **Babagil** holy site (the very short access path starts at 38°48'11"N, 48°30'57.2"E). Baba Gil, a Muslim mystic from Gilan (northern Iran) who lived here as a hermit, apparently sanctified the surrounding forest. He is now commemorated by a slap-dash new mosque-shrine which rather spoils the peaceful glade with its two ancient stone rams. One of these is now tucked away in a nearby area of graves and locals claim without apparent justification that it dates from the Babek era (9th century).

After the Vistan turn-off, the road crosses and recrosses the attractive, ever diminishing river – in summer you may find the odd steaming samovar and tea table temptingly ranged at strategic waterside points. Beyond is **Guneşli**, a large village that was patriotically named Azärbaycan until 2005 when, the story goes, the President drove through and demanded a change considering that an address of Azerbaijan, Azerbaijan simply was not suitable. After several hairpins you get the first good views of Lerik.

Four kilometres before Lerik the side

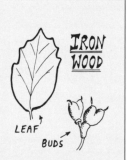

❏ Iron-wood tree
The wood of the *Dämir Ağach* (Iron-wood Tree) is so dense that it sinks in water. It is almost indestructible by pests and has thus been valued for centuries as a building material especially for rot-proof foundations. The nearest equivalent is English 'bog oak'. Unlike the latter, iron wood doesn't have to spend decades maturing in wet peat to become flameproof. However, iron-wood trees grow extremely slowly and often into contorted shapes. This renders much of the wood unusable, so what little is workable is particularly expensive. The species is only native to a narrowly restricted area in the Talysh hills around Länkäran. Yet ancient iron-wood tomb supports have been found way across the country near Mingächevir. This is seen as evidence of a long-distance trade in the timber dating back over a thousand years.

road marked to Shingadulan degenerates rapidly becoming the very, very tough route to Zuvuc and eventually to Yardımlı. Keep left for Lerik.

Accommodation en route

Relax (☎ 56068, mob ☎ 250 8464, 🖥 www .relax.az) at km34 is a full-blown resort with hotel block, two-floored villas with plush carpets (dbl AZN95 B&B) and stone cottages (AZN140) with traditionally styled walls but modern interiors. There are various entertainments, mini-golf, billiards, a blaring summer disco but contrastingly peaceful hiking possibilities running 5km into the mossy, muddy woods behind. Off-season discounts are possible. Aijan speaks English.

Xayal (mob ☎ 50-362 4362, Azad) has relatively well-built huts facing the river (but without balcony) for AZN50 fully equipped, AZN30 with shared bathrooms. Disco alert.

Mesäbäyi (☎ 56112) has a remarkably smart rose garden and tea-terrace above the river. Some distance away their three divided cottages come with golden bedspreads and ogive windows over the doors. Riverside rooms (AZN120) sleep four, set-back doubles cost AZN100. A hotel section has four twin rooms (AZN50) sharing a lovely communal balcony and graced with rare architectural flair. There's a vast AZN100 room in the mansard roof which has eight beds but could sleep dozens.

The all-enveloping pine fragrance makes *Täbässum* (☎ 56150) inviting for dining at woodland platform tables. Relatively simple AZN40-50 wooden huts have neat little bathrooms, double beds and sitting areas in and outside. A few very dark AZN20 rooms are also available above the main building but sharing an outside toilet.

LERIK (☎ 0157)

Lerik has a beautiful setting. Behind are grassy mountains, sharp peaks and a series of deep craggy ravines. In front are wooded valleys with agricultural hills rolling away towards Yardımlı. Lerik itself, however, is not a lovely town. It sprawls fairly formlessly and few buildings give any impression of history. Soviet planners are not

entirely to blame – earthquakes have taken their toll. One on 9 July 1998 scored 6.5 on the Richter scale and damaged 4200 homes in the region. Better viewpoints and more appealing villages start a few kilometres further into the mountains along passably drivable tracks. Excursions are very rewarding and there are great opportunities for wilderness hikes if you can handle steep gradients.

Lerik's five minutes of global fame came in 1973 when Shiralev Muslimov died aged 168 at nearby Bazarvud. There is some doubt that he was really born in 1805, but even if he sneaked an extra decade onto his tally he remains one of the longest lived humans since the old testament. His great-great-great-grandchildren would fill a small stadium. Centenarians are still far from rare with over 50 in the Lerik region. American dairy advertisements once tried to claim this longevity was caused by yoghurt. However, white-beards interviewed by *New York Times* journalist Stephen Kinzer claimed they never touch the stuff. Scientists suspect that a good Lerik innings is probably down to strong genes combined with pure water and hard work. Yet nutritionists would shudder at the lack of vegetables in a shepherd's diet. And one 123-year-old claimed it was the daily 100g of vodka that stoked his fire.

The only accommodation in Lerik itself is *Hussein's Canteen* (☎ 54276), a handful of acceptable if simple new-ish rooms (AZN10/dbl) around a very simple eatery. Toilets are shared squats but reason-

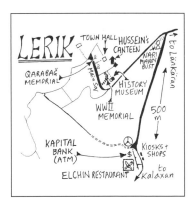

THE SOUTH

ably clean. Hussein ('Gussein') himself is quite a character and speaks conversational Russian (but no English).

Locals tell of a Lerik shepherd who donated a small flock to feed refugees from Karabagh. Apparently then-President Heydar Aliyev wanted to visit the donor of such a symbolic gift but discovered that the road was too bad for the presidential limousine. So he had it paved. That was somewhat astonishing for a mountain village back in the early 1990s. While the main Länkäran–Lerik road is asphalted, a 4WD will prove virtually essential to continue beyond or divert from it.

Morning **minibuses** run to Baku via Länkäran's Lävängi Bus Station but other public transport is rare.

TOWARDS KALAXAN (see map p288)

The scenic Kalaxan road passes through memorable scenery with deep-cut chasms hemmed in alternately with grassy-topped ridges, and towering rocky bluffs. Though increasingly degraded, the main road is still possible (if uncomfortable) without 4WD, and several villages close to the route offer fabulous vantage points and hiking potential.

At a small crossroads marked by an isolated hillside tea house, turn right for the quaint hamlet of **Balavand**, or left, and through Ambu to reach **Bazarvud**. This splendidly situated mountain-top village was the birth place of record-breaking 168-year-old Shiralev Muslimov (see p299). Ironically unidentified radiation emanating from the prominent TV transmitter tower

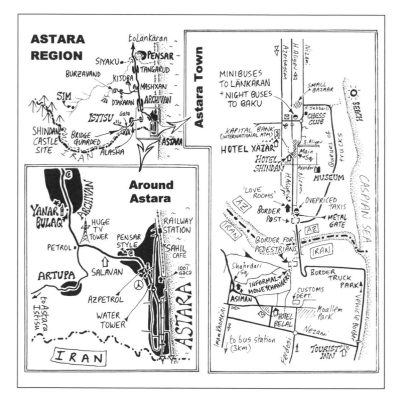

immediately above is commonly suspected of causing the spate of 'early deaths' of the region's centenarians who rarely make 115 these days!

Across a mostly forested 'grand canyon' you can see the villages of **Mondigar**, Andurma and Chayrud, though reaching them requires a circuitous route branching off the Kalaxan road beneath Balavand and using very steep down-then-up tracks that get dangerously slippery after rain. If dry, continue just over a kilometre beyond Mondigar, then walk around 15 minutes across flower-dappled meadows in the direction of the distant TV tower to find a great viewpoint atop a rocky precipice. The chasm falls away before you and on a clear spring day the mountains on the western horizon look very dramatic.

Beyond the Mondigar turning, the Kalaxan road enters a deep rocky gorge but thereafter the scenery becomes tamer. A military checkpoint blocks the final drive into **Kalaxan** village whose position on the Iranian border makes it sensitive. At least one Western visitor, however, has managed to convince the astonished guards that a tourist should be allowed to climb the 'castle rock' on the left of the road as you drive in. This is not actually a castle at all, but an outcrop of hexagonal columnar basalt – geologically reminiscent of the Giant's Causeway in Northern Ireland. Think twice before sneaking through if the checkpost doesn't appear to be manned. By the time you return it probably will be and by then you may be accused of coming illegally from Iran, preposterous as it may seem! Don't forget your passport.

ASTARA REGION

The coastal region is 86% ethnic Talysh, lushly forested and is known particularly for its citrus fruits. Rising rapidly behind this narrow fringe, the first phalanx of wooded hills is vaguely evocative of South-East Asia with big, slightly sparse tree cover on thin, red soil. Behind are folds of forested mountains hiding numerous villages. These offer intriguing opportunities

for horseback exploration but by vehicle the roads are impossibly muddy even in dry weather. It's enough to make a Pajero weep. Pensar and several other coastal villages have distinctively rectalinear mosques with arched, stained-glass windows and a small central turret (depicted in the box on p66). En route to the Iranian border at Astara Town, make a quick stop at Archivan's Yanar Bulaq (see p302) to see water 'burn'.

Pensar and around

Pensar's present site was settled after the older village of Alakaran ('away from the sea') was washed away by severe floods in the 1650s. Initially the new town was known as Butäsär, named after the Talysh troops of Shah Ismail Xatai who had retired here having worn the imperial *buta* emblem (depicted on p60).

Today the centre is graced with a pair of attractive 18th- to 19th century mosques, each in local style. **Haji Teymur Mosque** was originally for Sunni Muslims and is now for men, while the Shiite **Haji Jahan Bakhshihi Mosque** is for women. You may visit either outside prayer times and enjoy the multi-coloured light strained through the simple stained-glass windows. The **Said Jamal Pir** at the entry to the village is the tomb tower of a Skif tribal elder and supposedly dates from the 12th century.

According to superstitious locals the rough road opposite goes through **Siyaku** to **Toradi** (10km, where there's a lake in which everything sinks), **Galindashi** (the legendary home of a dragon statue with medusa-style powers) and **Kluputi** (where the *plashatka* is an underground cellar that emits an unexplained glow). A little easier to find is the charming, nonsensically hidden

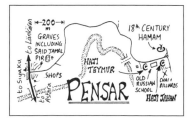

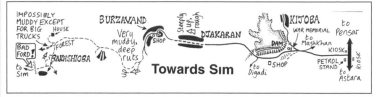

Absheron Restaurant, a simple but friendly streamside hut-camp 5km beyond Siyaku.

Towards Sım

Unlikely as it seems, Sım was apparently a cultural centre in the Middle Ages. Sheikh Nasrullah was buried here, Sultan Sanjar had properties in the region and Shah Anushervan had a summer palace at nearby Askhakaran. In a fairy-tale version of the latter's history, two rich nobles had fallen in love with the daughter of an impecunious local lord. For the damsel the choice was easy – one was honest, strong, young and handsome. The other ugly, old and peg-legged. But the girl's father set a contest: the first man to construct him a fine palace would take her hand. The young noble built much quicker, but the wily older man had his spies undermine his opponent's work so it kept falling down. The contest was won by the ogre and the girl was swept away to an unknown fate. Her father, lonely and ashamed about his silly idea, gave the palace to the shah in return for help to retrieve her. To no avail.

Utter nonsense of course, but supposedly the ruins of the palace really exist. What it looks like I can't say: I have consistently failed to reach Sım, once almost losing a rented Niva in a gigantic mud-filled pothole en route. However, **Shafag** (🖥 www.south tourism.az) has recently started advertising three-day homestay-based trips that include Palikash and Sım, meeting honey farmers and visiting an 'ancient watermill'. If you do one of these trips please drop me a line and tell me what you think!

Archivan

Along the Astara–Länkäran road in sprawling Archivan you can see a Pensar-style old **mosque**, an antique bath-house, a small shaduf well and the intriguing **Yanar Bulaq** spring. The water here is so full of bubbling methane that it catches fire. An enterprising local peddler will sell you matches to test the theory. Locals swiftly blow out the flames again: they're more interested in collecting gallons of the water for its supposed curative properties.

Astara Istisu

At this popular picnic site in a bend of the river, locals bathe in naturally heated water using a makeshift bath surrounded by flapping screens. Others collect the waters from a rusty standpipe to wash their cars. Beyond is some attractive woodland with hiking potential. To reach Istisu head south at the big TV aerial near Archivan and simply follow the rubble-asphalt till it runs out. En route there's a charming little mosque in **Artupa**. After Alasha/Sanjadi (once a royal village), arguably the greatest thrill of the visit is the glimpse of Iran across paddy fields as the road passes right alongside the decaying barbed wire of the border fence. Technically Astara Istisu now falls within the Hirkan National Park so you'll probably be expected to pay an entry fee.

ASTARA TOWN (☎ 0195)

Low-rise Astara town is a not unpleasant staging post en route to Iran. Its accommodation is reasonably priced, the free historical **museum** is welcoming and there's a grey sand **beach** that's pretty good by undemanding Caspian standards. And there are plenty of relaxing if all-male summer tea and beer gardens at which to nard the day away. The Kapital Bank ATM dispenses money on international cards, something that seems miraculous if you're arriving from Iran.

Accommodation and food

Much the best accommodation is the smart new *Hotel Shindan* (☎ 34177), superb value (sgl/dbl AZN30/50) with marble fittings and even minibars in the modern rooms.

Also central and bargain-value, the family-run *Hotel Xäzär* (☎ 53530) has simple but well kept rooms (AZN10) sharing very clean bathrooms and shower.

If you're driving you might prefer the setting of *Savalan* (☎ 33116, mob ☎ 50 322 8325), primarily a restaurant set in a rose garden well beyond the north-west edge of town. It's named after a snow-capped mountain across the Iran border which can supposedly be glimpsed from the balcony across lush green paddies if the haze clears. There are seven rooms: AZN10/20 sgl/dbl with private bathroom and shared kitchen, AZN12 dbl with shared toilets. For just AZN3 per person you can use the sauna.

The cheap *1001 Gäcä Motel* (mob ☎ 50 576 5262) has moved from its formerly ideal beachfront location and is now inconveniently located 1.7km further north. Clean but extremely simple rooms (AZN twin) attract lorry drivers whose trucks rumble past regularly. A five-minute walk away between algae-clogged ponds there's a black-sand beach dotted with fishing boats and tackle.

On the Iran side there are several lower mid-range choices near the pedestrian border, the somewhat-worn *Tourist Inn* (Mehmansara Jahangardi, ☎ 22134) is nearer the beach while the swanky *Espinas Hotel* (🖳 www.espinashotel.ir, US$100+) is beside an ornamental lake 8km south.

Transport

The most useful transport is the AZN1 minibus that shuttles to and from Länkäran when full (last around 5pm). Night buses to Baku depart from the main square at 22.00, 22.30, 23.00 and midnight but it's more comfy to shuttle into Länkäran and take the train from there: cheaper than paying a taxi to reach Astara's awkwardly located railway station. Day buses to Baku (hourly in the morning) use a bus station 2km north of centre.

Beware that cheeky taxi drivers still sometimes quote prices in Shirvans (ie AZN2 units) giving recently arrived travellers from Iran an expensive shock.

Crossing the border to Iran

The river which divides Astara into two, also forms the Azeri-Iranian border. Vehicles queue for hours via Cafar Cabbarli St. However, on foot there's a special crossing point hidden away behind an unmarked grey metal door at the point where Azadlyq St appears to end. It's an easy walk from the town centre so don't believe taxi drivers who claim otherwise when 'greeting' arrivees from Iran! On the Iran side pedestrians should use the 'Moasaferi Gümrük' outside which moneychangers offer better rates than you'll get on the Azerbaijan side. South-bound buy enough rials here to reach Rasht, Ardabil or Tabriz where you'll find the nearest banks with official exchange counters. Don't forget that nowhere in Iran accepts Western ATM-cards nor travellers' cheques.

The exact border opening times seem to vary but are approximately 9-12.30 & 14-17.00 Azeri time (ie 8.30-12.00 & 13.30-16.30 Iran time). Customs and immigration procedures are straightforward, though there are sometimes longish breaks while officers stop for tea, lunch or whatever. Still, I have twice crossed in under 20 minutes.

From Hakim Nezami St in Iranian Astara it's easy to find a taxi for the 3km ride to the bus station whence buses leave roughly hourly for Tehran via Rasht.

See box p15 for tips on getting the Iranian visa.

PART 8: NAKHCHIVAN (Naxçivan)

INTRODUCTION

Nakhchivan (Naxçivan) is the magnificently stark, disconnected chunk of Azerbaijan stretching from the awesome shadow of Mt Ağrı (Ararat) to the historic town of Ordubad. For most of the Soviet era this was a secretive military zone. Its only moment of international press coverage occurred in 1988 when jubilant crowds, sensing an end to the USSR's iron grip, tore down the frontier posts with Iran and reunited themselves with long-lost relations. In 1991 Nakhchivan upstaged even Lithuania to be the first Soviet republic to declare independence, only to rejoin Azerbaijan two weeks later. The place remains a little-known entity for most Westerners even though it consistently produces Azerbaijan's leaders and is the only part of the country with a direct land border to Turkey. With dramatic semi-desert mountain landscapes and two magnificent tomb towers, the region certainly has attractions, though finding English speakers can be tough and a sense of police paranoia can detract from the overall experience.

The most obvious disincentive of a visit is that to get there from Baku you'll have to fly. That is unless you're happy to loop round via Iran or Georgia/Turkey. Nakhchivan's isolation from the rest of Azerbaijan remains a critical economic issue. In his 'Globe Plan', US scholar Paul Globe has suggested that a mechanism for a lasting peace with Armenia might be to give Azerbaijan Armenia's southern province of Meghri (thus reconnecting Nakhchivan) in return for Baku's agreement to cede Nagorno Karabagh and Lachin to the Armenians. That might look good on paper. But it seems hardly credible in reality.

HISTORY

The name Nakhchivan comes from Noah Jahan, 'colony of Noah'. The biblical ark is supposed to have grounded itself upon the slopes of Mt Ağri/Ararat (or on Nakhchivan's Mt Gamigaya according to some Azeri sources). However, local legends claim that its hull had earlier crunched into the submerged summit of Nakhchivan's **Ilan-dağ** ('snake mountain') causing the great cleft in that very dramatic peak.

Known to ancient historians as Naxuana, Nakhchivan City as well as Ordubad, Culfa and Qarabağlar were powerful trading cities on the international caravan routes. In the second century BC, Ptolemy describes Nakhchivan as an already well-developed city. Sixth-century coins have been discovered embossed 'Nakhtch', suggesting that the region retained a high degree of autonomy during the Sassanid era. In 654 Nakhchivan was

---

❏ **Nakhchivan highlights**

✫✫✫✫✫	The abrupt rocky knob of Ilan Dağ mountain, especially as viewed from Alinca Castle.
✫✫✫✫	The stark, sharply eroded geology of the Nakhchivan–Ordubad road is contrasted, in places, with the green oasis villages.
✫✫✫	Ordubad old town.
✫✫✫	Qarabağlar – visiting the mausoleum complex gives you a good reason to poke around this quiet, friendly village.
✫✫✫	Momine Xatun Mausoleum, Nakhchivan City.

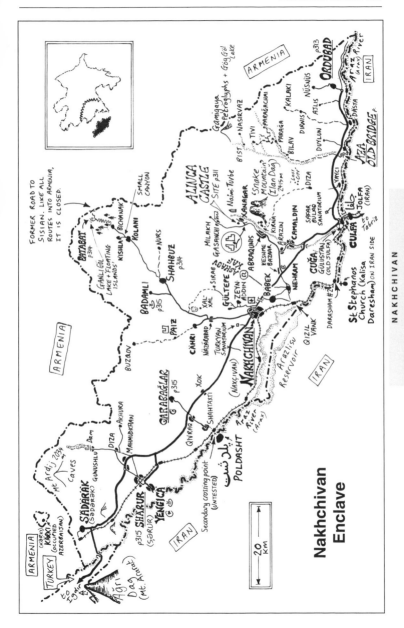

Nakhchivan Enclave

ORDUBAD p313

NAKHCHIVAN

invaded by the Arab forces of Emir Habib. Locals put up a considerable fight and thereafter the region became a major centre for the Khuramid resistance (see Babek, p297).

In a movie version of the Babek story, the Nakhchivan village of Camaldin was used as the setting thanks to its spectacular backdrop though Babek's real Bazz castle is some 50km south-east within Iran.

In the 9th and 10th centuries Nakhchivan was an independent kingdom, surviving until 1064 when conquered by Alp Arslan and incorporated into the Seljuk Turkish empire. The Seljuk empire fractured in 1121 following a military defeat to Georgia. This left central and north-western Azerbaijan virtually independent under the 'Atabeys' dynasty of former Seljuk governor Eldegyz (Ildeniz) who moved the regional capital from Gänjä to Nakhchivan in 1138 following Gänjä's sacking by Georgia. He built the impenetrable fortress of Alinca (p311) and, during 40 years of strong-armed rule, enriched Nakhchivan with great madrassas, public buildings and tombs.

The Mongol invasions, so destructive elsewhere, had a relatively minor impact on Nakhchivan. Despite some damage in 1221 and 1235, the region retained some of its monuments, libraries and reputed craftsmen allowing a relatively quick rebound. Timur was rather harsher when he stormed through in 1386.

For much of the 15th to 18th centuries Nakhchivan was at the heart of greater Azerbaijan united within Persia. An autonomous khanate emerged from 1747 under Heydargulu and lasting until 1827 when Ehshan Khan, whose palace is now the carpet museum, accepted Russian rule and became governor instead. Russia also took the Ordubad sultanate and the Turkmenchay treaty of 1828 formalized a split with southern (Persian) Azerbaijan which has remained ever since.

On today's map, Nakhchivan is a disconnected raft floating away towards Turkey. However, this politically contrived isolation has come from a series of relatively recent historical quirks. It remained firmly joined to the rest of northern Azerbaijan throughout both the Tsarist era and the brief 1918-20 independent republic. Following the Bolshevik takeover, the Soviet government considered giving Nakhchivan to Armenia as a 'fraternal symbol'. That plan displeased 90% of local residents in a 1921 referendum and was prevented by the insistence of Kemal Atatürk's nationalist Turkey. However, as part of the December 1920 treaty sealing the Russian reconquest of Armenia, the Soviets presented Armenia with the previously Azerbaijani province of Zangezur, the sleeve of land that had attached Nakhchivan to the rest of Azerbaijan. As a result many ethnic Azeris fled from Zangezur to Nakhchivan. Nakhchivan's isolation was sealed when Stalin gave up on the Trans-Caucasian SSR. The reinvented Armenian and Azeri SSRs were defined within the 1924 borders while Nakhchivan ASSR was left in limbo, administered directly from Moscow for two decades.

Throughout the period, Turkey maintained at least a nominal concern for their increasingly isolated brother Turks in Nakhchivan. A footnote to the post WWI Treaty of Kars allowed Turkey the right of intervention if Nakhchivan were threatened by a third force (ie Armenia). In 1932, Turkey also arranged a land swap with Iran to provide it with the long thin nose of territory which today forms the main trade route to Nakhchivan. This was remarkable foresight considering that for 60 years there was no bridge across the border river there. The eventual construction of this bridge in May 1992 provided Nakhchivan with a crucial lifeline once the Armenian blockade cut off all road and rail connections from Baku. That Armenia didn't invade the enclave could be credited to several factors: the Kars Treaty, the relative impenetrability of the border except along two roads, or the strong and decisive leadership of the then Nakhchivan parliamentary speaker – none other than Heydar Aliyev. Thomas Goltz recounts a story of Aliyev rallying morale in Shärur when an Armenian bombardment had caused inhabitants to flee there from nearby Sädäräk. His mere presence, it seems, smoothed a virtual riot into a pro-Heydar rally.

With heavy pressure from Turkey, Armenia backed down from further attacks (except for the seizure of the small, disconnected village of Kärki). Aliyev's popularity in Nakhchivan remains deep: while Aliyev statues are now ten-a-penny across Azerbaijan, the Heydar bust in Nakhchivan's central park long pre-dates his 12-year spell as national president.

POSSIBLE HASSLES
No special permit is required to visit the enclave. However, while local people are very friendly and hospitable, the same can't be said for the police and officials in smaller Nakhchivani towns where your presence is liable to cause confusion, suspicion and thinly veiled accusations of spying. Visiting Cuğa or Gamigaya requires ministry clearance which is unlikely to be granted to casual tourists.

NAKHCHIVAN CITY (☎ 0136)
Although its long history is mostly hidden beneath a neat 20th-century exterior, Nakhchivan City does sport Azerbaijan's finest medieval tomb-tower and makes a logical base for touring the whole enclave. It has virtually all of Nakhchivan's accommodation and most attractions lie within two hours' drive. Its hazy, swelteringly hot summers are made more bearable thanks to the dry climate, reasonably reliable breezes and torpid pace of life. Winters get briefly very cold and the abrupt mountains that ring the city look especially attractive when still snow-sprinkled That can last till May which is a good time to visit given the mild temperatures and relatively clear skies: on super-clear days you might even see Mt Ararat from near the carpet museum.

Useful addresses
Natig Travel (🖳 www.natigllc.eu.tp, mob ☎ 050-567 2506) Tour and translation services from very obliging English-speaking agent-fixer Aliheydar Pashayev. He even managed to get me an air ticket to Baku minutes before departure when to all

appearances the ticket office was closed.
Turkish Consulate (H Aliyev 17, ☎ 457330).
Iranian Consulate (Atatürk 13, ☎ 450343, 10:30-12:00 Mon-Thu) see box p15 for notes re Iranian visas.

What to see
The splendid 1186 **Momine Xatun mausoleum** is the city's icon and focus. Despite a slight Pisa-style lean, it remains the finest single antique monument in Azerbaijan. Experts differ over exactly which royal lady it was intended to honour but the real star is the architect, Acami Nakhchivani whose **statue** sits on a traffic island nearby. The tower was self-consciously designed to awe the observer with its soaring 26m height and its splendid exterior band of majolica-tiled Kufic script. This reads 'we are temporal, the world is eternal, we shall die but the memory remains'. And so it does. The tower's contrastingly unremarkable interior displays some interesting pictures of old Nakhchivan but the original graves were moved to St Petersburg in the 1950s.

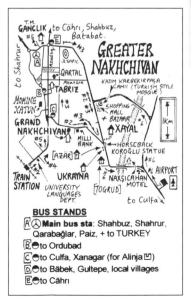

BUS STANDS
Ⓐ Ⓝ **Main bus sta**: Shahbuz, Shahrur, Qarabağlar, Paiz, + to TURKEY
Ⓑ ● to Ordubad
Ⓒ ● to Culfa, Xanagar (for Alinja 🏛)
Ⓓ ● to Bäbek, Gultepe, local villages
Ⓔ ● to Cähri

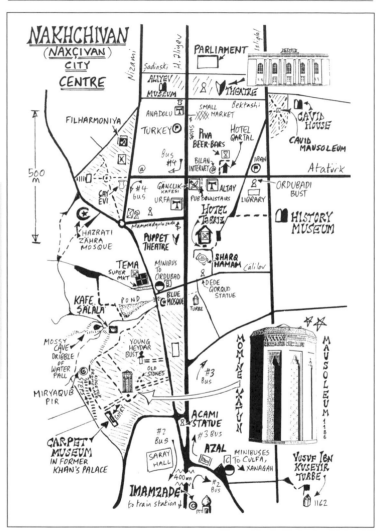

NAKHCHIVAN

Ranged around the tower are well-watered gardens containing a collection of ancient stone rams, the squat little blue-domed **Miryaqub Pir** and a medal-spangled **Soviet-era bust** of the young Heydar Aliyev. Overlooking the Araz reservoir and

Iranian mountains from the park's cliff-like southern edge there's a well-presented **carpet museum** (09.00-13.00 & 14-17:00, closed Monday, entry 50q) housed within the former Khan's Palace. The building is an impressive brick structure somewhat reminiscent of Shäki's Xan Sarayi albeit without the murals. Don't miss the museum's intriguing historical section.

Other historic sights include the pointy **Yusuf Ibn Kuseyir turbe** hidden amid unexotic backstreets, and the 18th-century **Sharq Hamam** in front of Tabriz Hotel. The latter is an historic bath-house that's received a truly bizarre restoration: the yellow-metallic cladding covering its multiple brick domes means it now resembles an alien landing craft.

The over-restored, blue-domed **Imamzade** is the modest Central Asian-style tomb of Abu Mustafa Bahdur Khan who reigned over independent Nakhchivan 1722-32. A large graveyard slopes up behind to the minimal muddy lumps that constitute the last remnants of Nakhchivan's former citadel ramparts.

Near the bazaar the 1997 **Kazim Karabekirpaşa Camii** is Nakhchivan's finest mosque, the name of Allah picked out in repeating gold script around the gorgeous white-marble doorway. From one angle a view of Ilan Dağ is framed by its portal.

The **Blue Mosque**'s only blue bits are tiles set into the boxy 19th-century brickwork, though recent renovations have added attractive Shäbäkä windows.

Iran funded the large but stylistically schizophrenic yellow-brick Häzräti Zähra Mosque.

Museums The cute wooden courtyard **House of Hussein Cavid** (9-18.00 daily, free) is set behind his attractive 1990s white marble **mausoleum**, built very symbolically during the Armenian blockade. It celebrates the writer whose bones Heydar Aliyev had famously repatriated from Siberia at the end of the Soviet era. Predictably Heydar Baba gets his own **Aliyev Museum** too (9-13.00, 14-17.00 Mon-Sat, free) in a palatial new building full of polished stone.

The bright, spacious **Historical Museum** (Dövlät Tarix Muzeyi, 9-13.00, 14-18:00 daily, AZN1) has new chandeliers and nicely presented displays of the usual handicrafts, farm-tools and banknotes along with petroglyph fragments from Gamigaya.

Most interesting is the Davud Kazimov painting showing how the city might have looked back in the 12th century. No English and little Russian is spoken.

Accommodation

The 13-storey **Hotel Täbriz** (☎ 447701, sgl/dbl/tr US$50/75/100) has been totally refurbished and now has an upscale modern look with rainbow-coloured floodlighting at night. Its compact rooms have all amenities and the obliging receptionists speak decent English which is startlingly unique in Nakhchivan. The fair-value top-floor restaurant has some pseudo-European options and is one of very few Nakhchivan eateries to serve alcohol.

Although the rooms at **Hotel Grand Nakhchivan** (☎ 445930, dbl/suite AZN50/100) are bigger than the Tabriz's, the upkeep is poor and the facilities are temperamental.

Motel Näxşicahan (☎ 441441) is primarily a plush wedding hall set in a willow garden out near the airport but they also have AZN70 rooms with air-con and decent bathrooms. Don't expect spoken English.

Hotel Xayal (☎ 445915, sgl/dbl/suite AZN12/25/35) is hidden away in a very unlikely back lane and isn't plush but you do get air-con, a big double bed and a private bathroom. The paint is peeling but service here seems far friendlier than at the more central **Gänclik** (☎ 446215) where the relatively new but already deteriorating AZN20 twins share bathrooms on the top floor of block 1 above Ticaret Märkezi Gänclik shopping mall.

The faded, 34-room **Hotel Ukrayna** (☎ 455383) has rust-speckled columns and the downstairs rooms are miserably gloomy but the bare upstairs double rooms (AZN30) are acceptable with new air-con and old-fashioned but functioning bathrooms.

Qartal (☎ 452125, AZN10) is a lacklustre budget fallback. Ultra cheap Hotel Tehran has reputedly closed.

At the northern city limit, **Düzdag Sanatorium** treats respiratory ailments by confining patients in a former salt mine March to October. Natig Travel (see p307) can help you make arrangements.

Where to eat
Hotel Tabriz's restaurant is Nakhchivan's top choice. Of several reliable if unsophisticated Turkish-style restaurants, *Gänclik Kafesi* is a good choice and it hides a bar-cavern beneath (enter from the side). Almost as good for food are *Tema* (above the eponymous supermarket), *Altay* and *Anadolu*, all offering dishes from under AZN2.

In a narrow alley marked *Fiçi Bira* behind Hotel Qartal are two little **piva bar** beer gardens serving cheap NZS and strips of dried Sazan fish from the Araz: expect plenty of friendly but intrusive attention.

Teahouses (pot from 60q) are often attractively shaded by willows or tucked away in parks. Only *Kafe Şälälä* is at all accustomed to female customers and, while its amphitheatre-style terrace is attractive, the jams that come automatically with your AZN1 pot of tea can quadruple the cost. There's also an unthreatening *çayxana* in the shiny-glass shopping mall beside the bazaar.

Transport
City transport City buses operate 07.30 to 21.00 (20q). The most frequent is bus #3 looping anti-clockwise from the Olympic Complex round to the big Koroğlu Statue near Hotel Xayal via the bazaar then returning past hotels Ukrayna and Grand Nakhchivan and the Culfa bus stand, swerving diagonally right at the Acami statue and returning north up Inqilab. Almost as common is bus #2 making a clockwise loop crossing town southbound on Nizami, diverting to the train station then doing the rest of route 3 in reverse.

To/from Baku and beyond Despite some very misleading online info, trains haven't connected to Baku or Russia since 1991: that would require transiting hostile Armenia where the tracks have been ripped up anyway. The only direct way is by air. AZAL flies in from Baku around six times daily (locals/foreigners AZN16/US$100). Despite apocryphal horror stories the planes are neither overcrowded nor filled with sheep. Indeed the flights are often worth the money for the great views of Mt Ağrı (Ararat) and Armenia's Lake Sevan.

The airport is a mere 3km from Nakhchivan City, 20q by bus No 6, or AZN2-3 by taxi. Buy air tickets from AZAL's Aviakassa (9-17:00 Mon-Fri, and 9.30-13:00 weekends) or the ticket counter at the airport (opening hours seem random). Getting a seat on an apparently full plane is not necessarily impossible given the help of a well-connected friend or a reliable agency.

UTAir (c/o Aeroplan, 7 H Aliyev pr, ☎ 457 327, 🖳 www.utair.ru) flies Nakhchivan–Moscow Vnukovo on Sundays. AZAL flies to Istanbul on Tuesdays and Fridays (AZN180-210).

To/from Turkey Incredibly there are eight buses a day running between Nakhchivan and Istanbul (AZN40, 26 hours) via Iğdır (AZN5). Most start from Nakhchivan Airport before 10.00, briefly picking up extra passengers at the main bus station.

To/from Iran The border at Culfa is open to foreigners (with visas, obviously) but cross-border trains no longer operate.

Getting around the enclave Inter-town buses run fairly intermittently in the morning and very rarely in the afternoon. Renting a taxi need not be fearsomely expensive (around AZN35 return with stops, to Batabat or to Ordubad) and paid hitch-hiking is fairly common. There are two trains daily: both depart at 08.00, one from Ordubad the other from Shahrur. Both take almost four hours and return from Nakhchivan City at 15.00. However, the rail line hugs the Iranian border. Foreigners are liable to be under intense scrutiny from both staff and police who can only conceive of one reason that you'd take the ultra-slow train instead of a vastly faster taxi or minibus: you're a spy. Try if you dare. The experience should add handsomely to your KGB-encounter tales. Don't take photos without a get-out-of-jail-free card.

SOUTHERN NAKHCHIVAN

Leaving Nakhchivan City, the watermelon fields rapidly give way to abrupt crags and wild mountain deserts with scenery that's inspiringly memorable all the way to Ordubad. By train you'll travel even nearer to the Araz river, emerging through a dramatic red valley just before Culfa with a tiny shepherd's church and ruined caravanserai visible across the river on the Iranian side... lovely if you're not so busy being interrogated that you miss all the views.

Ashabu Kaf

Surah 18 of the Koran relates a tale in which seven holy men manage to fall asleep in a cave for 309 years. Some scholars believe this was a reworking of the Christian tale of the 'Seven Sleepers of Ephesus'. Others say the tale was a parable told as part of a rabbinical test when arguing law with Jewish scholars, so doesn't refer to a real place at all. That doesn't stop local pilgrims coming in considerable numbers to this intriguing network of 'holy' caves and crevices tucked into a cliffside 6km off the Nakhchivan–Culfa road. A good road dead-ends at a series of cafés and souvenir shops from which you'll need around an hour to climb all the various stairways and visit the two minishrines. At the back of the site a ladderstairway leads into a larger cave area but there's nothing to see there apart from the cairns left by other confused visitors.

Alinca Castle site

Eldegyz's once-great fortress is today just a scattering of 7th- to 11th-century wall fragments but excellent views and a bracing climb to reach them makes this a rewarding side-trip between Nakhchivan and Culfa. Scrambling up to the crag-top summit ponds and ruins takes nearly two hours but all you need is 15 minutes to reach the first two outer wall sections and even here the views are tremendous towards dramatic **Ilan Dağ**, a wild ridge of jagged rock teeth to the north and the **Naimi Turbe** across the valley on the other side of a village called **Xanagar** (literally 'House of Dervishes'). Start the climb from near Xanagar's 'Alinca Goyuiçulag Sovxoz'. That's around 20 minutes' drive beyond Abraqunis which has marginally more public transport. If driving, turn off the main road at **Keshme Bazaar**'s attractive little Heydar Aliyev Mosque.

Culfa (Julfa) (☎ 0136)

In the Tsarist era Culfa was the Russo-Persian border crossing, and in Soviet times a railway built across the Araz allowed Tehran–Moscow rail travel. The border remains active and crossing it is the most likely reason foreigners would risk a KGB inquisition for stopping here.

History Mongols stormed through from Tabriz in 1235 destroying all before them, but by the 16th century Culfa was thriving again, a predominantly Christian craft town whose globetrotting merchants were known in Rome as *Chiolfalino*.

In 1603 Culfa's mayor, one Xawjay Xalchil, must have made some pretty bad after-dinner conversation while hosting Persian Emperor Shah Abbas – the next year Abbas was back and not as a guest. He had the whole town demolished and deported its skilled craftsmen to beautify his new capital, Isfahan. That Iranian city still has a suburb called 'New Julfa' where, even today, the community maintains their distinctive lifestyle, churches and the Vank Cathedral whose gruesome murals depict the tortures suffered in maintaining their Christian faith.

Culfa today All that's left of the original Culfa is a large, decapitated turbe and the controversially cleared site of the former Gülistan graveyard (aka Cuğa), once one

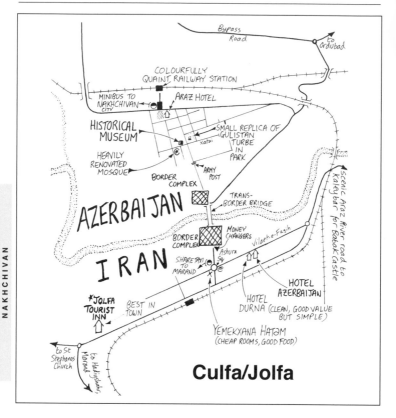

Culfa/Jolfa

of the largest medieval Christian cemeteries in the Middle East. Strangely, although pictures of the turbe are featured prominently by the tourist ministry, the site (at 38°58'16.4"N, 45°35'13.3"E) is entirely out of bounds to casual visitors unless specially invited. Visa permitting, it's much easier and less stressful to observe it from across the river on the Iranian side.

Modern Culfa, 3km further east, has a hotel (*Araz*, 30 Hağiyev, ☎ 461807) but there are no real attractions and entertainment is limited to multiple police interrogations. If you're crossing the border, Iranian Jolfa suffers none of the police paranoia and there's a range of accommodation, an (unmarked) internet club, a market and many freelance moneychangers. Day-time share taxis run to Hadiyshahr and Marand whence minibuses continue to Tabriz.

Culfa to Ordubad

The desert road to Ordubad is dramatically craggy but the only specific 'sight' is the attractive medieval bridge at Aza. It's visible as you drive by.

Ordubad (☎ 0136)

At certain periods of history Ordubad has been a semi-independent sultanate and for much of the Middle Ages it was a centre of learning which attracted the great scholars of the day including the family of Nasruddin Tusi (see box p314) whose daughter was buried here. It was also one of the early centres for printing and an ancient Alem Khomig *Koran* is displayed in the excellent local museum. Perhaps Ordubad's most famous recent son was Mammed Ordubadi, nationally renowned author of historical novels (eg *Patpol Baku*) and the librettist of the classic opera *Koroğlu*. Former Azerbaijani president Abulfaz Elchibey (died 2000) came from Käläki village in Ordubad region whence he returned to 'lie low' for several years after fleeing from power.

Historical quirks which nudged Nakhchivan out of the geo-political mainstream left Ordubad in a particular cul-de-sac. A positive result is that the town retains a lot of its original charm, but with minimal experience of tourism and the Armenian border very close, wandering around town without local contacts might cause considerable suspicion. To avoid trouble start your visit at the **Historical Museum** (09-13.00, 14-17:00 Mon-Fri) where the loquacious director speaks good Russian and will help you register your presence with local police. The museum is housed very atmospherically in a domed, building, formerly used as both a silk bazaar and a *zorkhane* (venue for a typical sufi-Iranian strength-sport). If you're a fan of petroglyphs there's plenty to whet your appetite about Gamigaya but the site itself is completely out of bounds near the Armenian border.

Of Ordubad's 18 mosques, some are virtually indistinguishable from houses, others are disused. However, the **Juma mosque** has a palatial appearance and was once the office of the Persian vizier. A nearby **madrassa**, reconstructed in 1714, was the only Muslim seminary in Azerbaijan to remain operative throughout the Soviet era.

Ordubad's mud-path backstreets wind between traditional courtyard houses, many incorporating parts of original 19th-century and older wooden structures. Most are hidden behind tall mud-block walls

NAKHCHIVAN

which also enclose lush gardens and orchards fed by channelled underground streams which provide the rich oasis fertility. These channels can be accessed through several simple **ovdans**: if you see a simple arch over a few steps try going down and see if you strike water.

A satisfying short stroll leads to the well-used **Saatabad** mosque, historic if heavily renovated with shäbäkä windows and framed by chinar trees.

East of Ordubad the road towards Armenia heads into a picturesque canyon but unless you're an official guest here, you'd do much better to experience it from the Iranian side of the border (no crossing point in Ordubad).

Ordubad has a few simple **eateries** and an attractively tree-shaded çayxana near the bus stand but there's no hotel.

Several morning **minibuses** run to/from Nakhchivan (AZN2, 1½ hours) but by afternoon transport virtually stops except for a single 5pm service in each direction. Returning by **taxi** makes sense and allows photo-stops and side trips to Alinca and/or Ashabu Kaf en route but agree the details before getting aboard. That's not just for the cost: the taxi driver will report your movements to the authori-ties before departing so won't want to deviate from the plan.

NORTH-CENTRAL NAKHCHIVAN

The mountains north of Nakhchivan City are higher but less dramatically craggy than Ilan Dağ or the ridges behind Alinca. The main attraction here is **Batabat**, an unpopulated alpine valley high above the quaint, partly wooded village of **Bichanak**. Batabat's main feature is **Ganli Göl** ('blood lake', photo C12), on which float a couple of large, flat turf islands moving at the whim of winds and currents. Though curious this is less dramatic than it sounds as it can take days for them to move a few metres. For Nakhchivanis, Batabat's meadows are synonymous with refreshing summer barbecue-picnics, but personally I prefer visiting in late spring when the mountains remain prettily snow-frosted and there are no music-blaring crowds. However, the access road can be snow-blocked till early April. Beware not to take the right fork at the top of the first ladder of hairpins approaching Batabat. That would take you towards the Armenian border and inevitable trouble. As it is you might find some annoyance en route at **Shahbuz** (the regional capital) where foreigners are sup-

---

❏ **Tusi**

Nasruddin Tusi (1201-74) was one of those remarkable all-round medieval Muslim scholars who took education to remarkable heights while feudal Europe was still in dark-age elementary school. He found 38 ways to prove Pythagoras's Theory, developed trigonometry as a separate discipline and found methods for solving cubic equations. Many of his treatises on mathematics and morals were written at the 'Assassins Castle' at Alamut (Persia), though opinion is sharply divided as to why he was there: as an Ismaili convert availing himself of the famous library, or as a prisoner of the infamous 'Old Man of the Mountains', Hasan Sabbah.

Following his release/departure from Alamut in 1256, Tusi found time to create the greatest astronomical telescope of the day (at Marageh in south Azerbaijan – now Iran), make fundamental advances in the mathematics of spherical geometry and write such boffin-baffling books as *Counting Totality*, *The Measure of Poems* and *Perpetuity and infinity in the Cosmos*. The branch of Tusi's family which settled in Ordubad occupied a succession of senior positions in the 16th-century court of Shah Ismail Xatai and of later Persian rulers including Shah Abbas who reportedly exempted the family from all taxes. A carved stone originally incorporated into the façade of Ordubad's main mosque, confirmed the fact.

posed to sign in at the police station. On one occasion that process took me over an hour of farcical if not unamusing banter. It's tempting (though potentially unwise) to simply drive straight through and avoid the hassle.

Between Nakhchivan and Shahbuz there are views of Alinca and Ilan Dağ. Just beyond at **Näzärabad** the road forks to **Cähri** and **Paiz** above which a wall remnant of the 3000-year-old Jalkhan Fortress snakes along a ridge.

After winding attractively around a reservoir, another fork leads to **Badamlı** source of Azerbaijan's most celebrated mineral water.

NORTH-WESTERN NAKHCHIVAN

The scenery north-west of Nakhchivan City is less dramatic than the road to Ordubad, but on a clear day the ghostly apparition of distant Ararat (Mt Ağri) is haunting. A minor attraction is Qarabağlar beyond which the painted deserts widen into increasingly fertile plains dotted with relatively prosperous agricultural villages.

Qarabağlar and Shahtaxtı

Little **Qarabağlar**'s peaceful green groves and fruit gardens soften otherwise barren red-brown crags rising toward the arid Qarakush foothills. It's hard to believe that this was once the bustling caravan town that 17th-century travellers reported having 70 mosques, 40 minarets and 10,000 buildings. Today just two minarets and the fluted tomb tower of the **Jehan Kudi Xatun mausoleum complex** recall Qarabağlar's past glories. This impressive complex is thought to date from the reign of Abu Said Bahadur Khan (1319-35) and its intricate blue majolica tile-work finally received a much-needed restoration in 2008.

Archaeological digs around **Shahtaxtı** unearthed the beautiful 2000-year-old animal urn now displayed in Baku's Historical Museum. Shahtaxtı also houses a Huseyn Cavid House Museum.

The only Nakhchivan–Qarabağlar **bus** leaves at 13:00 (AZN1.20). Otherwise take Shärur-bound transport and walk/hitch the last 6km. There's a **train** to Shärur from Shahtaxtı railway station at around 16.00 but suspicious locals wouldn't let me reach the station let alone buy a ticket.

Yengicä (Yengicə) & Shärur (Şərur)

The oldest town in northern Nakhchivan, **Yengicä** has several aged mosques, an old bazaar and the maudlin shell of what my hosts tried to convince me had once been the third greatest bath-house in Azerbaijan. The streets have something of the 'hidden courtyard' feel of Ordubad but with little of the latter's charm thanks to the busy central road and the flat terrain.

Shärur (see map p316), originally named Ilich (Lenin's middle name), developed in the 1920s around the then-new railway station some 2km from Yengicä. Today it's the district headquarters and hosts a castle-style museum. On a clear day Mt Ararat appears to float above the town, remaining snow capped even in summer.

Sädäräk (Sədərək)

Back in 1992, Sädäräk became the unwitting fuse that might have started World War Three. Shelling from Armenian forces across the border resulted in the town's brief evacuation but reminded Turkey of a clause in the 60-year-old Kars agreement.

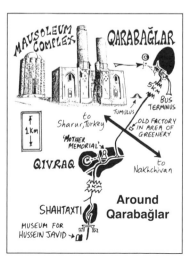

NAKHCHIVAN

This allowed Turkish intervention in the event of any threat to Nakhchivan. The then Turkish president, Turgut Ozal, was quoted as being keen to 'lob a few shells' across the border to frighten the Armenians off. But then wouldn't the Russians lob a few straight back to help their Armenian friends? Whoops, suddenly that's NATO versus Russia. Hey presto, global war. Fortunately this didn't quite happen and the Armenians looked east instead for territorial expansion.

Other than this thankful historical anticlimax, Sädäräk's last main claim to fame was as a primitive fortress/citadel in the territory of Uratu. It may date back as far as 2000BC and was known for much of ancient times as Bash Norasen. A few blackened stones are all that remain.

The main reason to pass nearby is to reach Dilucu, the Turkish frontier post.

Officials here were once notoriously corrupt and on my first visit one particularly blatant guard simply took my passport then demanded $100 for its return. Things have much improved since and now crossing procedures are much more transparent. Foreigners even seem to be exempt the AZN1 per bag fee that locals pay.

Heading westbound Turkish visas are available on arrival for most Westerners. However, on my last crossing, contrary to all official information, I was refused such a visa and was told that British citizens were NOT eligible. They sent me back to Nakhchivan – thank goodness I had a double entry Azerbaijani visa.

Note that heading to the border by taxi rather than by bus will leave you the minor logistical problem of arranging a subsequent ride across the 500m of no man's land: pedestrians are not allowed to walk that.

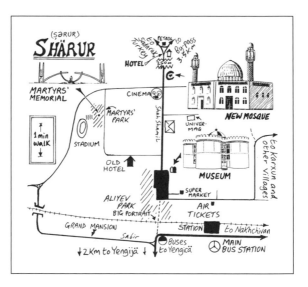

PART 9: EXCURSIONS TO GEORGIA
(Sakartvelo)

Facts about the country

INTRODUCTION

Georgia is an ancient Christian land dotted with elegant churches, fortified mountain villages and impressive medieval castles all set amid fabulously varied landscapes. Home of the Golden Fleece, birthplace of Stalin, land of music, wine and blood feuds, Georgia overflows with history, myth and character. It is populated by some of the planet's most passionate, most hospitable and at times its craziest people. They have a unique language, alphabet and distinctly European features with the black-eyed, timeless faces of incense-darkened icons.

This chapter gives you a concise guide to cosmopolitan Tbilisi, its surroundings and the gloriously wine-soaked region of Kaheti, the areas you'd be most likely to visit as a weekend trip from Azerbaijan. *Sakarvelos gaumarjos! (Cheers to Georgia)*

HISTORY

While God was busy dividing the world amongst primordial tribes, the Georgians were out drinking. They flattered the not yet omniscient deity that they'd been toasting His honour and God decided to give them the most beautiful land of all, the land that he had been saving for himself: today's Georgia. But for most of Georgia's history, God's favourite mountains have formed a shifting jigsaw of smaller kingdoms, principalities and feudal estates that swooped in and out of neighbouring empires. They only formed a united Georgian kingdom for two significant historical periods prior to the 20th century. The most important of these, Georgia's Golden Age (11th-12th centuries), ended abruptly with the Mongol invasions.

After further depredations by Timur and a couple of centuries fighting with the Turks (during which most of the country was sacked at one point or another) two of Georgia's sub-kingdoms (Kartli and Kaheti) reunited under King Irakli II but became increasingly overshadowed by Russia. Briefly deserted by their supposed new 'protector' (Russia's mad Tsar Paul I), Georgia faced a massive onslaught in 1795 from Qajar Persia (Iran). Despite the heroically embellished exploits of King Irakli and his '300 Aragvi' warriors, the Persians took Tbilisi and utterly destroyed it.

Russia was quickly back to scoop up the mess, annexing Georgia bit by bit between 1800 and 1804. They rebuilt Tbilisi, recaptured long-lost Batumi and Akhaltsikhe and

---

❑ **Geo-political facts**
- **GNP per capita**: $4400 (2007), $968 (1997), $5135 (1989)
- **Major exports/economy**: Wine, fruit, mineral water, manganese, oil-transit revenues
- **Leaders**: National President US-educated Mikhail Sakashvili; de facto President of Abkhazia, Sergei Bagapsh; de facto President of South Ossetia, Eduard Kokoity
- **National flag**: The red cross of St George, like England's flag but with further red crosses in each white quadrant
- **Population**: 4,631,000 (2008 est), 4,400,000 (2002), 5,400,000 in 1989! The 'missing million' are assumed to be working in Turkey, Russia and Europe
- **Capital**: Tbilisi
- **Area**: 69,700 sq km (just over half the size of England)

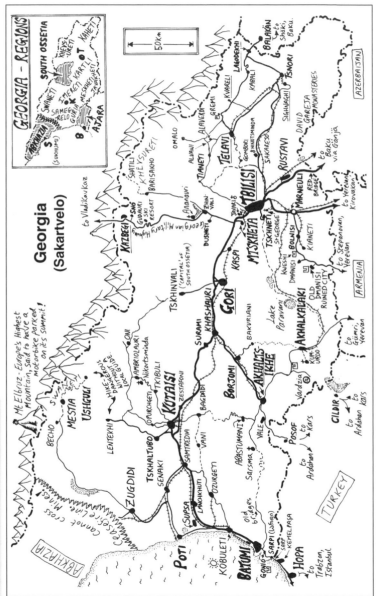

used the region as a place of internal exile. This unintentionally turned Georgia into an alternative axis for the Russian liberal intelligentsia. Tbilisi became the capital of Russian Trascaucasia and in 1876, though then 'only the size of Brighton', Lord Bryce described it as 'a little Paris'.

Independent Georgia was declared on 26 May 1918 following the confusion of WWI but was snuffed out again by a Red Army invasion in February 1921. Though Georgian born, Stalin didn't spare his own people from the horrific purges of the 1930s. Nonetheless, when Krushchev later denounced his excesses, a pro-Stalin demo erupted on Rustaveli Ave in Tbilisi. Initially peaceful, dozens died when the Red Army heavy handedly rushed in. History repeated itself with 20 dead on the same spot during a 9 April 1989 rally that shook any faith people had had in the Soviet state. Thus, as the USSR collapsed in 1991, Georgia gleefully elected as president a popular dissident, Zviad Gamsakhurdia (son of a great writer). Paranoid and authoritarian Gamsakhurdia swiftly proved to be a tragically poor leader. Popularly but unwisely he refused to let Georgia join the CIS and generally thumbed his nose at Moscow. Russia responded by stirring up a civil war and arming independence movements of Ossetians in South Ossetia and ethnic Abhaz in Abkhazia. Gamsakhurdia was swiftly ousted in a 1992 coup but already the country had been torn apart. South Ossetia and Abkhazia declared de facto independence and Abkhazia ejected around 80% of its population (the ethnic Georgian majority) who still languish as IDPs. After Gamsakhurdia was replaced by Gorbachev's former sidekick, Eduard Shevardnadze, Georgia grudgingly joined the CIS and Russia responded by stopping overt attempts to undermine the country. Nonetheless, serious jousting continued over Chechens holed up in the Pankisi Gorge who Russia claimed to be terrorists. Meanwhile, Georgia's shattered economy got mired in corruption and patently failed to recover as a large proportion of the able-bodied population simply left to seek work abroad. Many war-scarred buildings remained unrepaired for over a decade.

Never popular, Shevardnadze was finally ejected in November 2003's peaceful 'Rose Revolution' to general jubilation. The new government of pro-Western Mikail Sakashvili led an impressive anti-corruption crackdown (firing all the infamously bribe-seeking traffic police!) and reduced taxes (albeit actively collecting them in a more comprehensive manner). The result was a comparative boom in the economy. Sakasvili's brinkmanship politics brought Adjaria back into the fold, but created greater tensions with South Ossetia and serious strains with Russia who imposed a boycott on imports of Georgian goods, seriously undermining wine exports. Tensions came to a head in summer 2008 when Russia invaded South Ossetia and subsequently formally recognized South Ossetian (and also Abkhazian) independence in a very obvious quid-pro-quo for the West's recognition of Kosovo. Georgians remain incensed that Russia needed to 'grab' parts of little Georgia when Russia's 'already so big', and somehow imagine that the world will one day find a way to get their lost territories back again.

RELIGION

Georgia's link with Christianity dates back at least to AD55 when St Simon and St Andrew preached their way through, en route to Scythia. One legend says Georgian merchants witnessed the crucifixion and brought back Christ's holy cloak to Mtskheta (p344, then the capital). Most outlandish is the myth that somewhere on Mt Kazbek is the original Bethlehem manger. However, the nation's conversion came in the 4th century when teenage St Nino arrived in Mtskheta from Cappadocia. Nino bound two vine fronds with her hair to show King Miriam the sign of the cross. Bob's your uncle, Miriam saw the light and demanded that his people converted with him. For over a millennium, despite long periods of Persian and Turkish Muslim rule, the Georgian church was independent under its own Catholicos/ Patriarch until, under Russian rule, the church was forced into the Russian orthodox hierarchy. Under the Bolsheviks most

EXCURSIONS TO GEORGIA

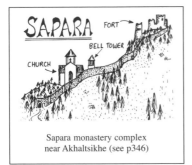

Sapara monastery complex
near Akhaltsikhe (see p346)

churches were closed altogether. Since 1991 rejuvenation has been in full swing, the church is once more independent and across the country you'll see young priests with bushy black beards looking like characters from *Alice's Restaurant*.

Practical information

GETTING THERE
Airport transfer Taxis from Tbilisi to the airport cost about 25L. Between 07.00 and 21.45 bus #37 runs every 15 minutes from the main train station (40q) via Rustaveli St. There are also seven direct daily trains (2L, 25 minutes) departing 00.30, 04.30, 08, 10, 17, 20 & 22.00 from the main station, returning around an hour later from the snail-shaped glass building opposite the airport terminal.

Overland
To Baku Every night the Tbilisi–Baku train (kupe 34.84L*) departs at 18:15 taking around 12 hours. Buy tickets at counter 9. By road making the trip in stages via Lagodekhi and Balakän is much more attractive than going via Gänjä. Either route is possible in 24 hours but ideally take at least three days stopping en route at Sighnaghi, Telavi, Zaqatala and Shäki. See p324 for more details.

To Turkey For details of the two main routes to Istanbul see p346. Either is possible in around 48 hours if you don't hang around.

To 'Kansas' Should you want to head to Armenia from Azerbaijan you'll have to transit Georgia (or Iran). Some foreign residents living in Azerbaijan tactfully avoid even mentioning such trips to Azeri colleagues and refer to Armenia as 'the other place' or, more wittily, as 'Kansas'. Armenian tourist visas are available in three working days in Tbilisi (Armenian Embassy, ☎ 22-959443, Tetelashvili 4, near Marjanishvili metro) but the costs are the same as if you got one (almost instantly) on the border so it's much easier to get one on arrival – possible at all major land borders (including the one from Iran).

Morning-only Tbilisi–Yerevan minibuses via Sevan depart hourly from Otrajala bus station (30L), and there's also a 16.00 Yerevan minibus from outside Tbilisi's main train station. The overnight Tbilisi–Yerevan train (platskart 13.64L, kupe 20.65L, SV 39.58*) departs at 16:40 on odd-numbered dates looping via Gyumri.

*Note that international train fares vary depending on the exchange rate of the Swiss Franc in which they are officially calculated.

GETTING AROUND
Trains are slow enough that you can get a night's sleep between Tbilisi and Zugdidi, Akhaltsikhe, Poti, Batumi, or even Kutaisi.

Big, decrepit **buses** and some of the **minibuses** (marshrutki) work approximately to a timetable while others don't leave till they're 95% full. Destinations are usually written only in Kartuli – daunting at first but learning the alphabet is easier than you might think (see box p323).

Taxis are worth chartering for longer trips given the many curiosities, churches and castles that dot several routes. One-way taxi trips generally work out cheaper starting from the relevant bus station/share-taxi stands as the driver will easily find passengers for the return leg.

MONEY
ATMs are available in all major towns. Changing euros or US$ is often easiest in booths at supermarkets. However, hardly anybody seems to want Azeri manats so convert them to dollars in Baku before leav-

❏ Essential information for visitors

● **Visa** No longer required for most Westerners. Incredibly you can stay up to 360 days; further details on 🖳 www.mfa.gov.ge (click top right for English). Special rules apply for Abkhazia and South Ossetia.

    If visiting from Azerbaijan don't forget that you'll need a double- or multiple-entry Azeri visa to return unless you fly back to Baku.

● **Currency (Exchange rate)** 1Lari=100 Tetri (Oct 2009 $1=1.68L, €1=2.46L, £1=2.66L). Re-exchange is no problem. Rates are OK for euros but poor for pounds sterling.

● **Accommodation costs** Homestay beds from around 20L, en suite mini-hotel rooms from 50L.

● **Food** A khajapuri snack costs from 0.50L at bakeries, 5L in restaurants.

● **Safety** Before the 2003 revolution muggings were common on Tbilisi's dark streets and organized pickpockets worked with apparent collusion from corrupt cops. All this has changed radically and today one feels pretty safe anywhere. Even the wild mountain districts of Swaneti are fairly lawful these days. However, the 2008 summer war with Russia has left the situation tense around the South Ossetian border and has made crossing into Abkhazia harder than ever.

● **Driving** International licence required.

● **Time zone** 4hrs ahead of GMT year-round. That means the same as Azerbaijan and Armenia in winter but 1hr behind in summer (2hrs ahead of Turkey in winter, 1hr ahead in summer).

● **Religion** Christian since 4th century but famously tolerant. Muslim minority (around Batumi).

● **Language** Georgian (Kartuli); see box p323.

● **Best seasons** Spring and autumn for central Georgia, mid-summer for the mountains.

● **Telephone codes** Country code ☎ 995. When calling within the country use the codes given in the chapter but when calling from abroad, remove the first 2 from the city code and replace with a 3. To dial out use code ☎ 8-10 (not 00).

● **Problems** Abkhazia and South Ossetia have claimed independence since 1991 but this was forcefully recognized by Russia during the brief summer war of 2008. Approaching either breakaway zone from Georgia at present is very unwise: you'll probably be suspected of being a journalist. Power cuts are less frequent than in the past but still not uncommon.

● **Things to buy** Wine, drinking horns, icons, herbal remedies, handicrafts.

● **Key tip** Tap water is generally OK to drink but prepare your liver for plenty of alcohol if planning to visit locals.

ing. Changing leftover manat at the road borders is possible with taxi drivers but rates are very poor. Prices are generally markedly cheaper in Georgia than in Azerbaijan especially for restaurants and mid-range accommodation.

ACCOMMODATION

Many of the big Soviet hotels were looted, burnt out or filled with refugees following the civil strife of the early 1990s and only started being properly refurbished after

Sakashvili came to power. Meanwhile the accommodation gap was filled by a range of small B&Bs, mini-hotels and ad hoc homestays.

FOOD

See pp23-4 for an overview of Georgian cuisine. Tbilisi has some excellent, small, cosy restaurants with buckets of style. Elsewhere, however, dining options are limited. In rural villages people tend to be largely self sufficient so there may not be

EXCURSIONS TO GEORGIA

more than a simple grocery shop or kiosks proffering vodka, cigarettes and chocolate.

HEALTH
IMSS (☎ 22-938911, emergency ☎ 22-920928, 💻 www.imss.ge) at 31 Makashvili, Tbilisi, near Betsy's Hotel is a Western-standard medical support service.

CLIMATE
Summers are best in the mountains but can get pretty hot in Tbilisi which is nicer in autumn and spring. Expect rain any time especially in Batumi which is one of Europe's wettest cities. Winter can get pretty cold even in the lowlands, especially so in Gori and Akhaltsikhe, while in the mountains of Khevsureti, Swaneti etc, villages can be cut off by snow for weeks or months. Snowploughs attempt to keep the Georgian Military Highway open year-round to ensure access to the Gudauri ski area (peak ski season December to April), but the direct Batumi–Akhaltsikhe road closes.

SOURCES OF INFORMATION
Books
The most practical guidebooks are Bradt's *Georgia with Armenia* (Tim Burford) and Lonely Planet's *Georgia, Armenia & Azerbaijan*. The latter is necessarily fairly thin on any one of the countries and might be confiscated on entry to Azerbaijan as the Azeri authorities are annoyed that LP treats Nagorno Karabagh as a separate country.

For photos and architectural interest supplement these with Roger Rosen's Odyssey Guide, *Georgia: A Sovereign Country of the Caucasus*.

For trekking there's both Peter Nasmyth's *Walking in the Caucasus* and Katharina Haeberli's *Under Eagles' Wings* aimed also for ski and horseback excursions.

For background Nasmyth's *Georgia – in the Mountains of Poetry* is a classic and Tony Anderson's 2003 *Bread and Ashes* is a well-written travelogue.

Georgia's greatest literary classic is Rustaveli's *The Knight in the Panther Skin*, and although 800 years old it still offers great insights into the chivalric national psyche.

Many of the above are available at Prospero's (see p335) an excellent English-language bookshop off Rustaveli St, Tbilisi.

English-language newspapers
The Messenger (💻 www.messenger.com.ge) was severely affected by the Russo-Georgian war of 2008 with two brave photographers killed and other staff injured covering the conflict (💻 http://georgianmessenger.blogspot.com). The *Georgian Times* (💻 www.geotimes.ge) is easier to find.

Useful websites
💻 **http://places.ge.iatp.net/index.php**
Great resource for digging up accommodation options in places in Georgia that are beyond the scope of this book
💻 **http://tourism.gov.ge/start.php**
Georgian tourist department's extensive but slow-loading site
💻 **www.info-tbilisi.com** & 💻 **http://etbilisi.com**
Extensive listings for Tbilisi and beyond.

Movies
The brilliant documentary, *Power Trip*, gives a superb glimpse of Georgia before the Rose Revolution through the intriguing prism of a company trying to renovate Tbilisi's electrical generation system.

For a glimpse of Soviet-era Georgia seek out the early movies of Otar Iosseliani.

Maps
Roland Hardt's 1:625,000-scale *Travel Reference* map (💻 http://shop.itmb.com) gives tourist attractions and some Kartuli.

The *Tbilisi Guide & Map* pamphlet (7L from Java Internet, 10.50L from Prospero's, see p335) includes a usefully indexed 16-page mini atlas taken from Tbilisi's *Yellow Pages*.

TRAVEL SERVICES AND TOURS
Fluent English-speaking staff at **Caucasus Travel** (☎ 22-987400; 💻 www.caucasustravel.com), 44 Leslidze St, Tbilisi, can get you discounts on hotels and can help with visa applications as well as providing personalized city and country tours. Similarly helpful, if aimed primarily at German visi-

tors, **TTC** (☎ 22-985075; 💻 www.ttc.ge), 5 Perovskaya, Tbilisi, is owned by the indefatigable Rainer Kaufman and offers a network of village homestays.

The Georgian Tourism Association (GTA; 💻 www.tourism-association.ge) lists many more agencies.

VISAS FOR AZERBAIJAN

The Azerbaijan Embassy (☎ 22-252639), Kipshidze Diplomatic Enclave, takes visa applications from 10am on Monday, Wednesday and Friday. You'll need to pay the fee into the Transcaucasus Development Bank (at Marjanishvili 4) then return by noon with the pay-in slip (bus 59 links the two points).

❏ Language

In Tbilisi a surprising scattering of people can manage a little English, German or French, but in the countryside it's pretty difficult to get around without at least a grasp of basic Georgian (Kartuli), Russian or one of the regional languages (Swan, Ossete, Laz). Learning to speak even a few words of Georgian will delight and amaze your hosts. At first, correctly pronouncing those extraordinary consonant-clusters feels like a mild choking fit. However, getting a feel for the different 'p's, 't's and especially the curious 'k's is ultimately most rewarding and exercises muscles in the lips and throat you never knew existed. Georgian has its very own alphabet. There are no capital or lower case differences to worry about and unlike English each letter has one specific sound. Thus learning the spaghetti-like letters is a lot easier than you may at first expect. And letter recognition is very useful for getting you on the right bus.

Key phrases in Georgian

Hello	*gamar jobat*	How much is it?	*Ra ghirsa?* (for numbers see p373).
Thank you	*didi madloba*	reply: *ara-prees*	
It's beautiful	*lamazia*	How are you?	*rogor rakhat?*
It's delicious	*gemrielia*	reply: *gargi/gargat* (good)	
Bon appétit	*a-amot*		
Cheers	This crucial word varies according to whom you are toasting. *Gaumarjos* is a safe start. S*akartvelos gaumarjos*: ('Cheers to Georgia') or *gagvimarjos* ('cheers to us') will impress.		

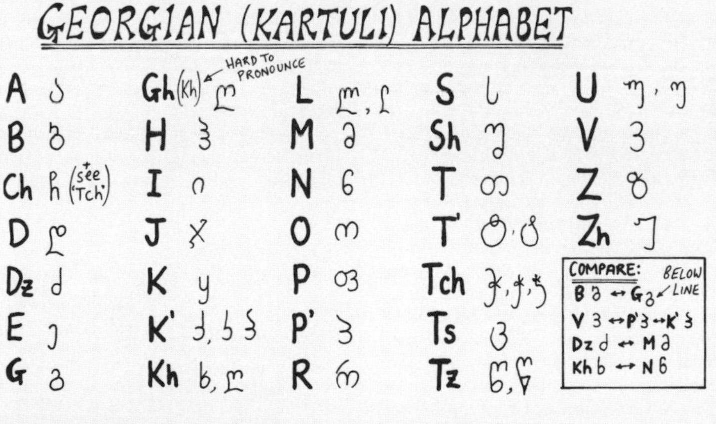

GEORGIAN (KARTULI) ALPHABET

A ა Gh (kh) ღ — HARD TO PRONOUNCE L ლ, ʃ S ს U უ, უ
B ბ H ჰ M მ Sh შ V ვ
Ch ჩ (see Tch) I ი N ნ T თ Z ზ
D დ J ჯ O ო T' ტ, ტ Zh ჟ
Dz ძ K ყ P ფ Tch ჭ, ჭ, ჭ
E ე K' ქ, კ, ქ P' პ Ts ც
G გ Kh ხ, ხ R რ Tz წ, წ

COMPARE: BELOW LINE
B ბ ↔ G გ
V ვ ↔ P' პ ↔ K' კ
Dz ძ ↔ M მ
Kh ხ ↔ N ნ

Processing takes five days. To find the embassy get off bus #17, 39, 59 (which picks up near Marjanishvili metro) etc at the stop beyond the Turkish Embassy, facing a small new stone church in a little garden. Take the footpath between that church and the stylishly modernist Czech Embassy into the diplomatic village behind. Alternatively Caucasus Travel (p322) can sort out invitations and make the embassy visits for you.

Kaheti and routes from Azerbaijan

Kaheti, the area closest to Azerbaijan, is the heartland of Georgian wine and offers plenty of scope for exploration en route between Baku and Tbilisi. Historically it was quasi independent on and off before the 11th century and from 1465 till the Russian annexation in 1820. From capitals at Ujarma, Gremi (see p326; destroyed in 1614) and Telavi, Kahetian kings played off Russian, Turkish and Persian colonial ambitions, most famously under Irakli II who built the Telavi fortified palace in the 1750s and went on to reunify Georgia between 1762 and 1795.

There are two main routes between Azerbaijan and Tbilisi. The route via Gänjä is relatively uninteresting, crossing the Red Bridge border (Tsitelis Khidi, Krasni Most, see p274) then crossing empty moorland and flat agricultural land and narrowly bypassing Rustavi, Georgia's ugly steel town. Direct share-taxis and minibuses (7L) run between Red Bridge and a stand outside Tbilisi train station (lower level).

It's much more interesting to travel via Shäki crossing the border at Lagodekhi (map p230 and opposite). Every hour or two, minibuses shuttle between Lagodekhi and Tbilisi's Isani metro station (map p337) via Tsnori (where shuttles connect twice hourly to Sighnaghi) and Bakhurtsikhe (stopping briefly to let you drink from a fresh water spring). Share taxis cost little more and by chartering the whole car you could stop en route at the 6th-century **Ninotsminda church** (heavily fortified since the 17th century, an easy 1km detour) and snap photos of **Old Manavi**, high on a hilltop above the main road.

Consider detours to Sighnaghi and/or Telavi en route, and possibly a longer detour to the David Gareja monasteries by taxi from **Sakarejo** (frequent minibuses from Samgori metro, Tbilisi, 3L). Alternatively some Sighnaghi and Tbilisi homestays can organize Sighnaghi–David Gareja–Tbilisi excursions (around 100-120L per car).

Another option is to take one of the minibuses between Telavi and Tbilisi's Ortajala bus station (see map p337). Note that the Tbilisi–Telavi route goes via Bakhurtsikhe at least until the now-dreadful Gombori road is rebuilt (supposedly work is due to start in 2009).

Lagodekhi–Kvareli–Tbilisi minibuses run twice daily but a taxi (50L) is worth the expense to see Kvareli, Gremi and Alaverdi (see p329) en route.

LAGODEKHI (☎ 254)

This architecturally neutral strip town is set at the base of thickly wooded hills leading up to a nature reserve renowned for its waterfalls. Lagodekhi's church is a large but atypical, red-brick affair of little interest. However, if you're stuck here the friendly *Lago Guesthouse* (mob ☎ 899-349932, sgl/dbl 40/70L) is a new homestay-B&B with very clean, uncluttered wooden-floored guest rooms sharing good new hot-water bathrooms and a balcony with mountain views. There's also a summer dip-pool and a billiard table.

Minibuses run roughly hourly to Tbilisi (Isani metro, 7L) via Tsnori (for Sighnaghi) and to Telavi via Kvareli at

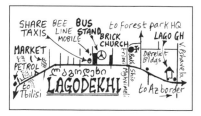

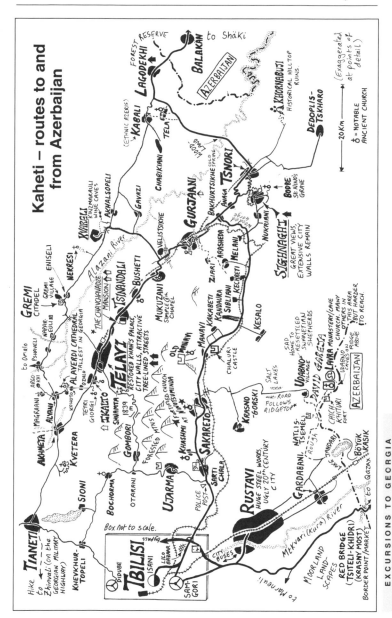

Kaheti – routes to and from Azerbaijan

(Exaggerated at points of detail)

20 km

ð = NOTABLE ANCIENT CHURCH

Box not to scale.

09.00 and 13.30 (4L). The Azerbaijani border is a 5L taxi ride away.

LAGODEKHI TO TELAVI
Kvareli (☎ 252)
A 2km detour off the main road is gently attractive Kvareli whose sturdy if oddly placed fortress encloses a sports pitch. There are two interesting house museums. Referred to as 'our director' by the obliging English-speaking guide, **Marjanishvili** (1872-1933) is considered the founder of modern Georgian theatre. He is celebrated in the delightfully rickety house of his grandfather Solomon Chavchavade (not Alexander whose house is at Tsinandali). Impoverished by robberies, the museum's most impressive feature is the 52-jar marani wine store, original despite the concrete floor.

Ilia Chavchavadze (yes, yet another Chavchavadze but no close relation) was the writer and intellectual behind the modernization of the Georgian language. A leading nationalist, he was assassinated by Russian agents in 1907 but was made a saint in 1987 on what would have been his 150th birthday. His house and the defence tower where he was born in the midst of a Chechen-Lezghian raid are hidden in the garden of the dramatic whitewashed modern museum building (10-17.00 Mon to Fri, 2L).

Kvareli's other claim to fame is its **Kindzmarauli wine** which matures in a series of industrial-scale wine-caves that have been carved into the cliffs east of town. The winery is not officially open to the public so visiting is hit and miss. Read 🖥 www.hansrossel.com/travel-information/georgia-tbilisi/kvareli-kakheti.htm for a traveller's personal report. A short-cut access track to the winery starts from beside the motel-style Hotel Kavkasioni.

Nekresi
Halfway up a wooded mountain foothill ridge and visible in the mid-distance from the main road is the active **Nekresi monastery**, founded in the 4th century. Access is via a 4km detour plus a 20-minute hike.

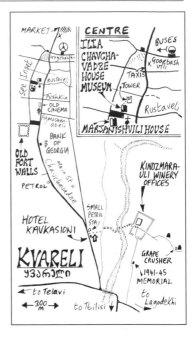

Gremi
Ancient Gremi became the capital when Kaheti separated from the rest of Georgia in 1465. The original town was razed and depopulated almost entirely by Shah Abbas in 1614, but a fairy-tale mini-citadel remains on a small crag, directly above the main road (a three-minute stroll up). On top the church has damaged frescoes and an appealing belfry (entry 2L) with a pitiful 'museum' room and views from the roof. Various remnant chapels, watch-tower stumps and monastic cells are littered around the sides of the citadel.

TELAVI (☎ 250, see map p328)
Sprawling down a long slope that surveys the Alazani valley, Telavi was an ancient capital of Kaheti and the summer capital of Georgia from 1762 under King Irakli II. In front of Telavi's heavily restored 19th-century fortress walls Irakli sits as a **horseback statue** proudly displaying a

mighty sword. Within the walls are Irakli's simple mansion-**palace**, an art **gallery** and historical museum, a sculpture garden, school and a couple of 18th-century churches. On a clear day you can see the spire of Alaverdi from the walls. Outside the fortress gates a curvaceous feminine **wine statue** suggests that Kaheti was the original home of breast implants.

Accommodation

The highly recommended *Rcheuli Marani* (154 Chavchavadze, ☎ 483030, 🖳 www .rcheuli.ge) is Telavi's best hotel with tradi-

tionally styled balconies, valley views and a good restaurant (see p328). It's 1km north-west of the centre.

Hotel Lia (Chavchavadze St, ☎ 71631, 🖳 http://lia.ge.iatp.net/welcome-eng.html) is a small, friendly if slightly lacklustre fall-back above a small grocery shop.

In a traditional old house on the central square, the **tourist office** (closed off season) can help you locate some of Telavi's numerous **homestays**. Three good options at 20L per bed: *Tsitso Galandadze's* (26 Giorgiashvili, ☎ 731255), with a swing-chair on the balcony overlooking

---

❏ **Kaheti – land of wine**

Wine, a word locals claim derived from the Georgian term *kvino*, is fundamental to the local psyche. It is consumed in vast quantities, traditionally from animal horns. To ensure that a plentiful supply is always at hand, many Kahetian homes have a *merani* – a cellar room into whose floor have been set a collection of large wine-filled earthenware amphoras (*qvevri*). Drinking the stuff at a local *supra* (feast) is a roller-coaster of passions led by a *Tamada* (toastmaster) whose unenviable task is to move, amuse and lead the assembly in endless down-in-one glassfuls without getting himself paralytic. The Tamada's word is law and drinking out of turn can earn penalties, much like a fraternity booze up. Generally at some point the table dissolves into music and somehow everyone seems genetically able to harmonize. The locals will be especially delighted if you can join in a song or two. Try this for size:

Kvino Kahuro-o	Kaheti Wine
Var sheni msmeli	We drink you
Ginda tetri iikho	Doesn't matter if you're white
Ginda tsitel-i	Or if you're red
Shena khar chweni-i	You are our beloved
Sweba da lkhena	Our contentment and our joy
Shengan ar gwakhsows	Never do I recall the time
Namtsetsi skkhena	You ever caused offence
Adan dali dan dali	La la la la
Chemi okros shandali	HEY! (by this time you should be too drunk to care!)

Wine tourism The best time to visit is *Kvinobistve* (the 'month of wine' ie Sept-Oct), with marvellously chaotic harvest festivals all across the region, most notably at Alaverdi (p329). In late October winemakers take the remnant solids from already fermented grapes to rural stills to extract the last alcohol as *chacha* (a sort of Georgian grappa). Trying to visit a winery can prove a little frustrating as the bigger producers are mostly industrial enterprises without much understanding of tourism. However, this is changing and some wineries do now accept visitors, eg: **Twins Cellar** (🖳 http: //twinsoldcellar.ge), small and personal in Napareuli; **Teliani Valley** (🖳 www.teliani valley.com) major producer on the Tsinandali–Telavi road; **Tsinandali** (🖳 www .shumi.ge/eng/index.html) see p329.

a vine-draped garden; **Georgi Narik-liashvili's** (10 Amir Rajibi, ☎ 71829), with a big, ultra-comfy double bed and hot water in a perfect shared bathroom that even has a bidet; **Svetlana Tushishvili's** (15 Nadikvari, ☎ 71909), peaceful, nicely furnished house with an obliging English-speaking hostess and a whole upper floor dedicated to homestay guests.

A cheaper alternative, **Manana Zamukashvili** (9 Nadikvari, ground floor apt 1, ☎ 73431) charges only 15L but the beds lie awkwardly in a thoroughfare within her cramped flat. Although officially at the same address, the **Shaverdashvilis'** (9 Nadikvari, ☎ 72185, 25L per person) more spacious homestay is actually in the courtyard behind.

Food and drink

The best choice is at **Rcheuli Marani Hotel** whose restaurant has both semi-formal and tavern sections and a preserved old marani (albeit wildly over-renovated). Their menu is translated and excellent khajapuris cost only 5L.

Pikris Khidi is a surprisingly large

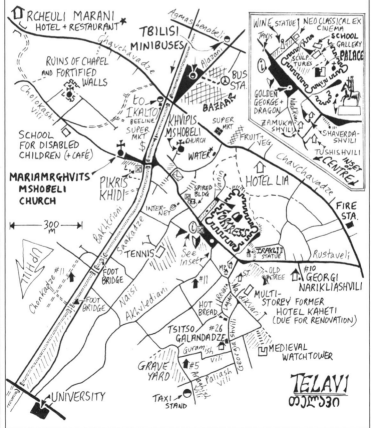

stone-and-brick arched basement restaurant with beers at 1.50L. However, the menu's all in Kartuli and my eggplant meal was unusually disappointing here. Between here and the main square there are three other options including an OK **pizzeria** and a small **cocktail bar**.

There's a very sweet little *café* albeit with entirely unpredictable opening times at the **School for Disabled Children** (Cholokashvili 37, ☎ 76103) and English-speaking Nata Rostomashvili, who works there, can organize a large but sparse and rather oddly located guest room upstairs (25L per person).

Transport
From two possible points near the bazaar minibuses depart fairly regularly to Tbilisi (Ortajala, 6L) via Tsnori. Most other services start from the little bus station hidden right within the bazaar including the 08:40 and 15:00 services to Lagodekhi via Kvareli, the 15:00 bus to Signaghi (returning at 09:00) and around four minibuses an hour that pass through Tsinandali. Minibuses to Ikalto pick up from outside the Beeline mobile phone office.

David Luashvili (mob ☎ 893-761216) is an English-speaking taxi driver.

AROUND TELAVI (see map p325)
In tiny **Alaverdi**, an 11th-century Giorgitsminda church has Georgia's tallest tower/spire (76m) and is the venue for a chaotic vindage festival (last week of Sept and first weeks of Oct, especially on Saturday evenings) when wine horns are everywhere as gaggles of merry locals dance informally on the lawns in front of the cathedral's impressive 18th-century fortifications. En route, **Tetris Giorgi** hilltop church, a 1.5km detour just before the Alaverdi road turns north, offers great valley views.

There is a watch tower and hilltop chapel outside **Pshaveli** and some crenel-lated castle walls remain in **Napareuli** village which has a renowned winery.

Also famed for its wines, **Shuamta** has two attractive monastic complexes. New (Akhali) Shuamta was founded in 1519 by Queen Tinatin to get out of the way of her moody husband, King Levan II of Kaheti. Old Shuamta is 2km further up the same spur. The great 12th-century Georgian poet Rustaveli studied at the **Ikalto Academy** (5L entry fee), the attractively set modest ruins of which are 2km above Ikalto village.

From Telavi all the above can be seen on a short-day 50-60L taxi tour.

Tsinandali
At km35.5 of the Akhmeta–Tsnori road, Tsinandali is considered the Nuits-St-Georges of this wine-growing region. Its famous vintages are created in an historic winery (⌨ www.shumi.ge/eng/index.html, visits/tastings 3/8L) set behind a manicured park (entry 2L, 10-18:00) of cypress avenues in which is set the 22-room summer **mansion of Alexander Chavchava-dze** (1786-1846). To see the mansion's slightly dowdy interior with some fine, sup-posedly original furniture costs 5L, or 15L if you take the tour (in German) by Nunu Patiashvili (Tue-Sun, 10-14.00 & 15-18.00). She explains the Chavchavadze family's love-hate historical links to Napoleon, the poetic salons and Decembrist mutterings held here and tells some of the fruity tales related to the distinguished family. Look out for the 'foldaway' piano and the side by side tactical 'love seat'. A hollow tree in the grounds once hid the only family member to survive a raid by Imam Shamil's guerrillas (see p237), a story brilliantly retold by Lesley Blanch in *Sabres of Paradise*.

If heading to Telavi from Tbilisi (but not necessarily vice versa) it's easy to stop, visit Tsinandali, then flag down any onward minibus to reach Telavi, 10km beyond.

SIGHNAGHI (☎ 255)
Recently undergoing a major makeover to be reborn as Kaheti's tourism hub, the little walled town of Sighnaghi (map p330) is perched attractively on wooded hills above Tsnori. It's a great place to do very little. Many streets (eg Dadiani St) look beautiful in their colourful evening floodlights hav-ing had their balconied houses painstaking-ly restored (or entirely rebuilt). An attrac-tive stretch of Rustaveli St has also been restored and the whole area around the eye-

EXCURSIONS TO GEORGIA

catching round-towered **Tsminda Georgi** church is worth exploring.

Sighnaghi's long city walls seem illogically placed but are pimpled photogenically with dozens of small, heavily reconstructed turrets, notably along Chavchavadze St. A small shrine built into one tower here offers great views across the whole Mediterranean townscape. A section of walkable wall is accessed from Gorgasali St. Behind the modern yet architecturally sensitive town hall, the recently rebuilt **history museum** (11am-5pm Tue-Sun) includes a gallery of Pirosmani works while the cute little house museum of **Sandro Marianashvili** is a contrastingly old-fashioned traditional home.

Old Town Studios (18 Baratashvili, mob ☎ 899-534 484) is a US-run private gallery (10-17:00 Tue to Sun) where you can also do wine tastings. The **carpet-weaving factory** next door to Hotel Kape (see below) can also be visited.

Around 2km from town, **Bodbe church** (see map p325) has been so thoroughly restored that from outside it looks virtually new. However, the vastly more atmospheric interior is full of old murals including a fine Adam-and-Eve over the central nave. In an alcove to the right of the altar area lies the grave of much-revered St Nino, the saint who Christianized Georgia. The marble tablet over her tomb was the gift of patriotic Georgian professional soccer stars playing in Turkey. The **bell tower** can be climbed.

From behind the church (beside the souvenir shop selling 30L icons and 12L litre-flagons of wine!) steep stairs descend around 600m to Nino's 'holy spring'.

Accommodation

For a town of 2000 people, Sighnaghi has an astonishingly wide selection of accommodation with even more under construction.

The best deal in town is the spacious, well-appointed *Hotel Kape* (19 Dadiani, ☎ 31951, dbl/suite 60/120L) above a pleasant cellar **restaurant**. Good bathrooms, wrought-iron furniture, kilim-covered wooden floors and lots of exposed brickwork.

Hotel Crown – almost complete when I visited – occupies a four-storey theatre-style building with wreath mouldings outside and an attractive brick-arched bar-restaurant. The cheaper rooms have oddly

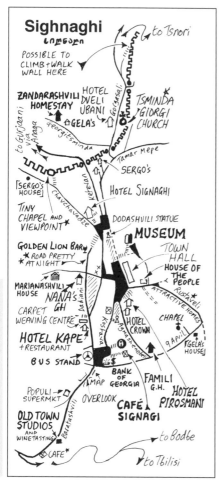

Sighnaghi სიღნაღი

POSSIBLE TO CLIMB + WALK WALL HERE

to Tsnori

ZANDARASHVILI HOMESTAY

HOTEL DVELI UBANI

GELA'S

TSMINDA GIORGI CHURCH

to Gurjaani via Anaga

Georgismindа

Gorgasali

Tamar Mepe

SERGO's

SERGO'S HOUSE

HOTEL SIGNAGHI

Chavchavadze

Ketevan

TINY CHAPEL AND VIEWPOINT

DODASHVILI STATUE

GOLDEN LION BAR
★ ROAD PRETTY ★ AT NIGHT

MUSEUM

TOWN HALL HOUSE OF THE PEOPLE

ATTRACTIVE HOMES

Rustaveli

MARIANASHVILI HOUSE

NANA'S GH

Dadiani

CARPET WEAVING CENTRE

HOTEL CROWN

CHAPEL

HOTEL KAPE + RESTAURANT

Kistava

9 April

GELA'S HOUSE

BUS STAND

POPULI SUPERMKT

BANK OF GEORGIA

MAP OVERLOOK

FAMILI G.H.

CAFÉ SIGNAGI

HOTEL PIROSMANI

OLD TOWN STUDIOS AND WINETASTING

Baratashvili

CAFÉ

to Bodbe

to Tbilisi

cramped bathrooms where sitting on the throne requires squeezing your legs under the sink, but the upper-floor rooms (200L) are much better with fine balcony views. The communal second-floor shared terrace has café potential.

Hotel Pirosmani (6 Agmashenabeli, ☎ 43030, 🖳 info@rcheuli.ge) has a luxurious white-on-white **restaurant** and the better rooms (from 165L) elegantly use pieces of fine, typically 1940s, furniture. Off the art-decked top corridor are some much cheaper 88L double rooms; very simple and tucked into the roof eaves with limited natural light.

Just completed, boutiquey, four-room *Hotel Dzveli Ubani* has pleasant views from the back. Rooms cost about €50.

Although totally renovated and with decent views, the Soviet-era *Hotel Signaghi* (dbl 150-200L) feels a little bland for the price.

Homestays Above Sighnaghi's most conspicuous souvenir shop, **Nana's Guesthouse** (☎ 795093, 🖳 nanahouse.ge.iatp.net) has ten beds in four rooms. Wine-tastings are planned in her old merani and Nana's daughter, Nino (mob ☎ 855-292 333), speaks English.

Famili Guesthouse (☎ 31855, mob ☎ 895-575 146; 30L per person) is the three-bed, high-ceilinged homestay of sweet-bearded babooshka Rusana Gogosashvili. There's a kitchen, dining room, renovated shared bathroom and functional but good-sized balcony. Rusana works as a nurse (10.00-15.00) so you'll need to arrive early or late to get in.

David Zandarashvili's (11 Georgitsminda, ☎ 31029, mob ☎ 899-750 510) is a five-minute walk out of the centre but has a great family atmosphere. David speaks excellent English and his father offers bargain trips to David Gareja (from 80L return). The rooms aren't sophisticated but this is a great place to meet fellow backpackers in season. Bed/half-board from 15/30L.

Rather than family homestays, *Gela's* (mob ☎ 899 554 371) and *Sergo's* (mob ☎ 899-393 808, 🖳 sergocowboy55@yahoo

.com) both offer 30L beds in rented houses. As there's nobody in residence you'll have to seek out the owners whose homes are also marked on the map. Gela (home 2, 9th April St) works by day at the tourist office so is easy to find. Sergo's house is at 16 Chavchavadze but you'd be better off phoning him.

Food
In addition to the hotels' restaurants the town has a selection of eateries and is small enough to make choosing one easy. Stylishly upmarket *Café Signagi* near the tourist office offers 4-course French meals from 30L and espressos for 4L, yet charges only 4L for a khajapuri.

Transport
Minibuses run to Tbilisi (Samgori) at 07, 09, 11, 13, 16 and 18:00 returning 09, 11, 13, 17 and 18:00 though the timings are somewhat approximate. Roughly two minibuses an hour shuttle to Tsnori where you can pick up a Lagodekhi connection. The Telavi service leaves at 09.15 Monday to Saturday only.

DAVID GAREJA CAVE MONASTERIES
Sharply undulating grasslands interspersed with long salt lakes become semi-desert moonscape before tumbling over a cliff-edge above the Azeri border. Lurking here within clefts and cliff-lip caves are the remnants of numerous ancient meditation retreats, some retaining remarkable frescoes. Their collective name, David Gareja, comes from one of the originally 6th century 'Syrian Fathers' who started the tradition of isolated hermitages here. Sadly the Soviet army used the hills as practice artillery targets, leaving most sites utterly ruined. Nonetheless, several widely spread groups remain.

Lavra and Udabno
By far the most impressive and most accessible cave group is **Udabno**, a twenty-minute climb above the very isolated but active, multi-level **Lavra Monastery**. Follow a conspicuous metal wire up to the hilltop and descend just over the lip of the

EXCURSIONS TO GEORGIA

cliff where a well-trodden path leads past the mouths of over fifty long-disused caves. Several have rather impressive old murals partially preserved, albeit open to the elements. Reaching the higher ones is a bit of a scramble and the whole visit requires at least a degree of fitness. At the far end of the cave-cliff path there's a pair of tiny hilltop chapels from which a direct path returns to Lavra with no need to double back.

Don't confuse the Udabno caves with Udabno village, a maudlin, half-abandoned sheep-farming village of drab concrete structures to which Swanetians were transplanted in the late Communist era. It's the area's only permanent village.

The road between Udabno village and Sakarejo is now pretty well asphalted and even the last 12km unpaved section to Lavra Monastery is quite possible by ordinary car, passing close to the sturdy fortress tower of **Chichkhituri**, 2km before Lavra. A return taxi ride from Sakarejo should cost around 60L, from Sighnaghi reckon on paying 80-120L. Taking the one daily bus between Tbilisi and Udabno village isn't recommended as the village has neither shops nor accommodation nor are you likely to find a vehicle for hire (Udabno residents themselves call Sakarejo for a taxi!).

Other cave monasteries
There's a rougher alternative access track to Lavra from Rustavi. A 3km 4WD detour from that road takes you to **Natlistsemeli**, a monastery that functioned until 1924. I haven't been there personally but reputedly some small, brilliant frescoes survive in the big cave church and there's a tower reached by a small tunnel.

Bertubani (see box p272) is across the Azeri border but there's no legal crossing point so you'd be unwise to try and get there from Lavra unless you have high-powered contacts. The site suffered particularly badly from shelling practice in the Soviet era leaving the cave entrances as needles in the proverbial haystack.

Tbilisi

INTRODUCTION (☎ 22)
Tbilisi ('Hot Water') was named by founder King Vahtang Gorgasali in AD452 after the sulphurous hot springs in which you can still bathe today. Atmospheric old Tbilisi is an extensive tangle of wooden-balconied 19th-century houses, tree-lined lanes, mosques, synagogues and more churches than anyone can remember counting. All these are squeezed into the narrow spaces left between the cliff-tops of the Mktvari river and the steep slopes leading to the chunky ruins of Narikala Castle and tree-topped Mt Mtatsminda. Tbilisi has a different character at every turn that is best sniffed out on foot with generous café stops for khajapuri, Kazbegi beer or a flagon of Saperavi wine.

EXPLORING THE CENTRE
A good way to visit Old Tbilisi is to start from Avlabari (accessible by metro) from which there are some fine views across the old city notably from restaurants at hotels Kopala (see p338) and Dzveli Metekhi (see p338). Descend to Gorgasali Sq where the city's founder holds forth his sword in front of **Metekhi church** ([B], see box p336). Until 1795 the churchyard housed a fortress-palace and later an infamous prison (demolished in 1939). Crossing the bridge look back towards the twee cliff-top houses, then fork left for the ancient sulphur baths. Some hamams are underground domed affairs. In contrast the majolica-tiled portal of the **Orbeliani Hamam** looks more like it belongs on an Uzbek mosque.

Uphill past a real **mosque** with its unique if forgettable brick minaret, pay 1L to enter the **botanical gardens** for an oasis of cool. Or, just before the gates, follow a narrow path up to the impressive ruins of **Narikala Fortress** on the viewpoint crag above. From here it's a lengthy walk along the ridge to the gigantic metal mother statue, **Kartlis Deda**, whose sword and raised tea-

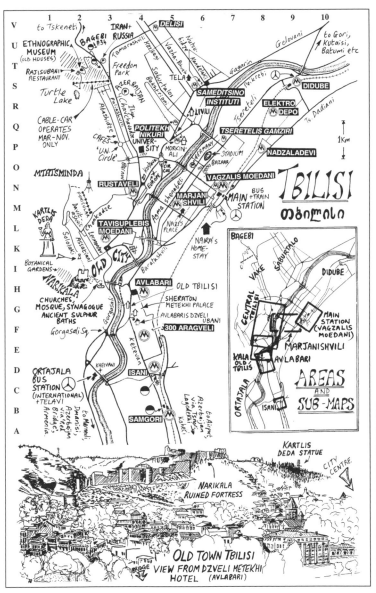

OLD TOWN TBILISI VIEW FROM DZVELI METEKHI HOTEL (AVLABARI)

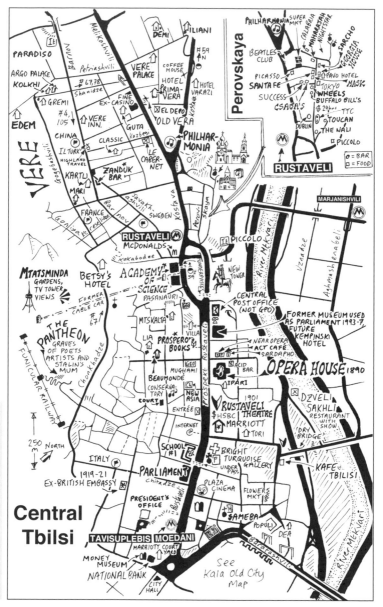

Central Tbilsi

cup are visible for miles. It's better to descend past the synagogue and **Armenian Cathedral** [E] into the **Kala/Old Town** area where a warren of alleys conceals many more fine churches.

In **Sioni Cathedral** [A] notice the heavy chair where the living Christ is believed to be enthroned (as in many Georgian churches). Sitting on his invisible lap is very bad form. Pedestrianized streets to the south-east now form one of Tbilisi's top café-districts while to the north beyond **Anchiskhati Basilica** [K], old, balconied, wooden houses nestle atop the remnants of the old city wall, colourfully illuminated at night.

Tavisuplebis Moedani

Tavisuplebis Moedani (Freedom Square) is the city centre's most attractive hub. A carved Lenin once directed traffic from the middle of the square until it was gleefully pulled down in 1991. Viewed from the square's north side, Kartlis Deda is visible rising above the clock tower of the appealing 1880 **City Hall building**. Coins, some dating back to Alexander the Great's Asian excursions, are displayed in the small but delightful **Money Museum** beside the rebuilt art-nouveau **National Bank** building. The **Fine Art Museum** (11-16.00, closed Mon, entry 1.50L) has a 'Treasury' full of icons, crosses and royal jewellery (guide compulsory) and a particularly good collection of modern Georgian paintings on Floor 3: notably stick figures by Pirosmani, impressionistic Kakabadzes, and Gudiashvili portraits easily identifiable for their subjects' lack of ears.

The **State Museum** has its own 'treasury' displaying small but curious preChristian items: hairpins thought to be 4500 years old plus relatively new (6th century BC) ring seals, horseman ear-rings and the tiny golden lion whose image appears on 5 tetri coins.

The slopes rising to the west are worth a stroll with several semi-grand government buildings. From Chonkhadze a funicular takes you up to Mtatsminda for great views. The hill is topped with a park, funfair, cafés and a 210m TV tower that competes with Kartlis Deda at dominating the city skyline. Halfway up is the Pantheon, a cemetery for Georgia's great and good (along with Stalin's mum). A steep path winds back down.

Pr Rustaveli

Bustling but attractive, **Rustaveli Avenue** is Tbilisi's main thoroughfare and cultural artery. Beyond Tavisuplebis Moedani metro station, the **Children's Palace** was once the Russian viceroy's residence and later that of Stalin's mum. The steps of the imposing **parliament building** (façade similar to that in Gänjä) was the site where the Soviet army perpetrated the infamous 9 April 1989 massacre. Opposite, behind a façade of muscular worker-caryatids, is the modern multiplex **Plaza Cinema**. Next door the prime empty space is one remaining reminder of the pitched battles of Christmas 1991. One faction occupying **School #1** (now fully rebuilt) would swap pot shots and lob shells at the other, holed up in the grand **Hotel Tbilisi** (now the Marriott). Luckily no serious bombs struck the garishly painted **Blue Gallery**, the misleadingly antique-looking **Kashveti church** [F] or the eye-catching neo-Moorish **opera house**. Across the road the Ministry of Justice building is carved with **griffin motifs** and hidden within the same block, **Prospero** (09.30-21.00) is a well-stocked *bookshop café* serving good coffee (espresso 3L).

At Rustaveli's northern end, the architectural grandeur fades somewhat. In the 1980s a vast square was gouged out here and tastelessly adorned with a set of concrete hoops commonly nicknamed 'Andropov's ears'. The ears have now been demolished, the square is renamed **Vardebis Revolutsis Moedani** (Rose Revolution Sq) and the once-vile Iveria Hotel tower is being reborn as a gleaming new glass skyscraper. The lumpy concrete **post office** is hardly attractive but the spired, Stalinist **Academy of Science** is striking and tastefully lit at night. Reaching it across the endlessly busy road requires finding the two unmarked underpasses. Or just continue north to the main entertainment district around Perovskaya St.

GREATER TBILISI

The so-called **Ethnographic Museum** (map p333, T2; entry 1.50L) is a hillside dotted with re-erected traditional houses, huts, a mosque and even a Swanetian hilltop tower. One of the ancient wooden houses hosts *Rajisubani* (☎ 235321), a full-on Georgian 'traditional' restaurant with Kaheti wine slopping from mini-barrels while customers sing in full voice. Take the (summer-only) cable car from the base of Victory Park to Turtle Lake and wander downhill for 10 minutes, or get a taxi from Bagebi.

Much further out (2.5km up a track from km16 of the road to Marneuli) the panoramic little **St George Monastery** is tranquil and looks down condescendingly at the sprawl of greater Tbilisi.

ACCOMMODATION, FOOD & DRINK

Tbilisi has dozens of house-, boutique- and mini-**hotels**. Unless otherwise noted all are clean, well maintained and have bathroom/ WC en suite. Some Avlabari hotels have fabulous views, while places in the Old City and around Rustaveli have the advantage of a perfect location. There are plenty more mid-range options in Vere, slightly less convenient but walkably close to the centre. Several business chain-hotels are under construction.

❑ **TOP CHURCHES**

Symbols: ❍ Barrel tower; ✚ Armenian; ✪ Russian; ✝ Other style; ✦ In use; ⊠ Disused or derelict; ☺ Atmospheric interior.

[A, map p339] Sioni Cathedral ❍✦☺+✝ Tbilisi's best. A powerful exterior and magnificent interior with dark murals detailed in gold. Across the road, the tower serves as a church bookshop. Note the Nino's cross in the window above the door.

[B, map p339 & p340] Metekhi Church ❍✦ Built in 1289 as Demetre II's palace church. Since then it has been knocked about and repaired with a mishmash of bricks and old gravestones. The interior was stripped for use as a theatre in Soviet days but it's since been reconsecrated.

[C, map p340] ⊠✝ A precarious ruin with a collapsed roof.

[D, map p340] St Echmiadzin ✚❍✦☺ An 1804 brick exterior with a soaring tower supported by pillars painted with a fake marble effect. Metro Avlabari.

[E, map p339] St Georg ✚❍✦☺ Tbilisi's main Armenian cathedral. Built in 1251, the exterior is plain and grey plastered; the interior is very dark and has an impressive multi-panelled altar screen; in the Old Town.

[F, map p334] Kashveti Church ❍✦ Built in 1910 but in ancient Georgian style with a carved stone exterior. George kills the dragon over the south door and there are window arches that look like toothpaste squeezings. The whitewashed interior is hung with naive-style paintings. Many worshippers drop by in their Nikes and shorts for a quick prayer; it's also popular for weddings. The bullet holes (from the 1990s) in the façade have been repaired and there's a tasteful new bell tower.

[G, map p334] Blue Monastery ❍✦ The 1873 brick renovations sit oddly on the remains of the 12th-century lower wall. The church is topped with a disappointing blue-metal spire and it has a modest, carpeted interior. The church was used as a medical museum in Soviet days. Beside it is the whitewashed 1901 Ivan **Bogosov Orthodox church** (☺✦) replete with spires and mini onion domes. Inside there are dozens of icons and an impressive altar screen.

[H, map p334 & p339] Sameba ❍✦☺ Small, brick exterior and dodecagonal tower. Gorgeous painted interior.

[K, map p339] Anchiskhati Basilica ❍✦ Founded in the 6th century, often rebuilt. Some 17th-century murals remain and it has a bell tower and cloister.

[L, map p340] New Sameba ❍ This gigantic new cathedral dominates Avlabari and illuminated at night appears to shine like gold.

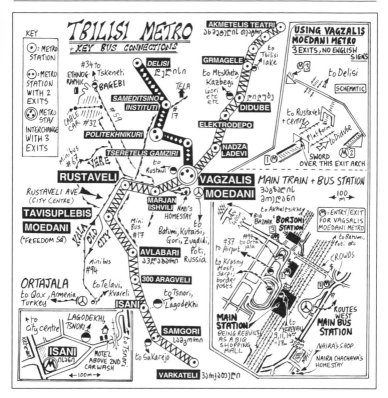

For cheap, rough-and-ready **home stays** look around Marjanishvili metro.

Tbilisi has a vibrant **café, bar and restaurant** scene. Good espressos cost only half the price you'd pay in Baku, while Turkish coffee can be had for a Lari in a less suave place. For **pubs, upmarket bars** and a whole range of food types look around lively Perovskaya (p341, many with live music) or more suavely in Kala Old Town. For cheaper drinks and excellent Georgian food be prepared to dive into local places that don't always have menus in Latin script.

Kala – Old City

Hotel Ambasadori (☎ 920403, 🖳 www .ambasadori.ge, sgl/dbl/suite from 250/325/ 530L) is the Old City's one full-scale hotel. It's new but oozes a splendid olde-worlde pseudo-Parisian charm. Breakfast is served on a fourth-floor terrace. It's a great upper-market choice but some front-facing rooms suffer a little from road noise.

Hotel Sharden (Chardin) (32 Khanzteli, ☎ 922027, 🖳 www.hotelsharden .ge, sgl/dbl US$110/130) is a stylishly appointed, very obliging mini-hotel with a glass-box elevator. Its big drawcard is the rooftop restaurant-terrace from where there's a superb view of New Sameba perfectly framed by the medieval spires from four churches (see photo C16, bottom).

Hotel Charm (11 Chakrukhadze, ☎ 985333, 🖳 www.hotelcharm.ge, sgl/dbl US$60/90) is charming indeed, a guest-

EXCURSIONS TO GEORGIA

house-style place decked with paintings and old furniture. The breakfast room has a fabulous fireplace and there are views of New Sameba from the ramshackle terrace. Great value.

Hotel Ata (☎/🖨 987715, 🖳 www .hotelata.com) isn't really a hotel at all, more a collection of reasonably priced (100-160L), well-appointed apartments. However, the building that contains them is rather offputting and someone had puked all over the dark stairwell last time I visited.

Dzveli Ubani Hotel (5 Duma St, ☎ 922404) is a friendly family hotel with 13 unsophisticated but recently redecorated double rooms at 90-100L and two bigger 160L suites. No air-con.

VIP Hotel (☎ 920040, 🖳 hotel@vip mail.ge, sgl/dbl US$60/80) is a decent eight-room house-hotel across the yard behind 31 Leslidze. From Room 7 there are great views of Mtatsminda and New Sameba. Sizeable sitting rooms, wooden floors, WiFi and air-con.

Dea/Deya (3 Mtkvari, ☎ 997045, dbl 120L) is a last resort option whose somewhat gloomy rooms are sometimes offered at hourly rates... It's close to **Populi XL**, the centre's biggest supermarket.

Old Town food and drink (map p239)
Most old town eateries are on Leslidze St (cheaper and fast-food options) or in the enchanting pedestrianized lanes nearby (more expensive) with an atmosphere somewhere between Paris and regenerated old Beirut. Contemporary and upmarket, *Meydani* (☎ 303030, khajapuri 13L, beer 4L) is a big, brick-arched cellar serving pricey Georgian fare at white table-clothed tables set with giant wine glasses or alternative seating on luxuriously comfortable divan cushions. Live music and dancing 9-11pm. Much cheaper cellar-restaurants include *Sarajishvili* (lobia 2.5L) and *Barakagogi* (khajapuri 5L, wine from 5L per litre) is recognizable from the chubby chef figurine outside.

With jade-effect fondue tables, *China Town* is a full-on upmarket oriental restaurant with an appealing sofa-lounge downstairs for pots of tea (6-30L) or 3L beers.

Cosy, classically French-European style cafés include *Taverna 33*, *Chardonnay* (Herzog beer 3L, steaks 20L), charming bric-a-brac-decked *12 Rue Chardin* and quirky *Premier* with upsidedown chairs placed on the ceiling. *Kon Café* serves coffee (espresso 4.40L) in an old tram carriage near Tbilisi History Museum, *Cafe Caché* is 1930s retro styled, *Café 19*'s all-weather terrace is THE place to see-and-be-seen. *Kala Café* has good live jazz, and next door *KGB* is 'still watching you'. *Bar No 1* (🖳 www.coffeeinn.ge) is hip-minimalist, *Chardin Bar* goes overboard with zebra-stripes, massive chandeliers and pumping house music.

Around Anchiskhati, several places are undergoing reconstruction, but the Irish-American pub-restaurant *The Hangar* (🖳 www.thehangar.biz) remains very popular.

Bread House (Puris Sakhli, ☎ 999537) somewhat isolated out beyond the **sulphur baths** is a popular local eatery with a few guest bedrooms available upstairs around the back (ask the waiters).

Avlabari (map p340)
Climbing steeply up the cliffside facing the old city just across the river, Avlabari now has several decent hotels, some with fabulous full or partial views across the old city.

In the original *Hotel Kopala* (☎ 775 520, 🖳 www.kopala.ge, twin/double rooms from €90) 13 of the 21 rooms have exceptional old-town views (€120-260), tasteful pseudo-rustic furniture and stylish new bathrooms. The rooftop terrace bar-restaurant is brilliantly located for the best panorama of all. However, beware that nearby there's also a 30-room *'new' Hotel Kopala* (☎ 775590, sgl/tw €80/100) which, while pleasant and comfy, has no views at all.

Dzveli (Old) Metekhi Hotel (☎ 747404, 🖳 www.oldmetekhi.com.ge), in a traditional stilted building, charges from US$80 for rooms in the roof eaves to US$200 for room 4, a superb apartment with three view balconies. There are also views from rooms 7, 8 and 11 (all $180).

Once the residence of the British Ambassador, *Boutique Hotel* (9 Metekhi, ☎ 266999, 🖳 www.boutique-hotel.dsl.ge)

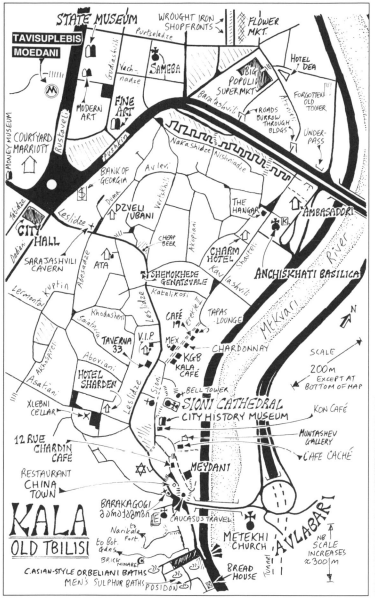

has utterly fabulous views from the balconies of its three suites and the little basement billiard room is built right into the rock of the Avlabari cliff.

Views from the *Old Tbilisi* (☎ 773840, 🖳 www.hoteloldtbilisi.com, $95-170) are nowhere near as nice. Despite liveried doormen and an airily oversized lobby, many rooms face away from the river, are surprisingly pokey, and have small shower-booths.

Hotel GTM (4 Metekhi, ☎ 273348, 🖳 www.gtm.ge) has mostly small but new rooms from US$70, while the pricier ones ($110-190) have balconies and partial views.

Hotel KMM (☎ 747185, 🖳 www.kmm .ge) has three different staircases leading to a warren of 19 air-con, not-quite-stylish rooms (sgl/dbl/tw from €40/50/70) many with Jacuzzis or multi-head showers. The €120 apartment is vast. The best feature is the shared open roof terrace.

Hotel Lile (☎ 773856, 🖳 www.hotel lile.ge, rooms 70-120L) is simple but friendly with air-con and hot water. It's right on Avlabari Sq so the front rooms can get noisy.

The best Avlabari **dining options** are the view restaurants of *Dzveli Metekhi* (☎ 774407) and (old) *Kopala* hotels but both get very busy so consider booking ahead.

Rustaveli and around (see map p334)

Perfectly positioned on Rustaveli, the top choice is *Tbilisi Marriott* (☎ 779200, 🖳 www.marriott.com, 13 Rustaveli Ave) combining grand colonial charm with 21st-century facilities (rack rates from 648L, breakfast 55L). When it's eventually finished the new *Kempinski* (🖳 http://development .kempinski.com/en/), expected to open in 2010, will prove strong competition. The *Courtyard Marriott* (🖳 www.courtyard .com) has an indoor swimming pool and is

right on Tavisuplebis Moedani.

Quiet yet fabulously central *Ipari Hotel* (☎ 996799, 🖳 ipari99@yahoo .com; $120-180) has a striking, bright black-and-white décor with vaguely art-nouveau touches in the seven rather small rooms. Similarly central *Hotel Villa* (☎ 920308, 🖳 www.investingeor gia.co.il; $100-150) has just four new, oddly shaped rooms that aren't especially charming but do have flat screen TVs. *Tori* (Chanturia St 10, ☎ 923765, 🖳 tori@access.sanet.ge) is a neat if rather bland tick-the-boxes business hotel with glass elevator and doubles from 260L. The gym and Turkish bath cost extra.

House-hotels On the slopes above Rustaveli about the nicest choice is *Beaumonde* (Chavchavadze 11, ☎ 996246, 🖳 bali103@hotmail.com), a splendidly airy, oversized modern home with balconies and 19 perfectly appointed rooms; $95/110 half-board including rich Mukuzani wine. The owners speak French and Russian. Five-room *Lia GH* (Arsena 35, ☎ 920858, 🖳 Arsena35@yahoo.com, $50-90 B&B) is an unsigned house-hotel richly furnished with antiques and stuffed with toys. There's a real family atmosphere and a pleasant communal balcony area. Also unsigned, five-room *Mtiskalta* (51 Zubiashvili St, ☎ 936397, 🖳 www.anano.ge; sgl/dbl $125/150 including breakfast) is Tbilisi's longest-running B&B, run by the irrepressible Manana Skhirtladze who is never short of an interesting tale or three. Her husband Alex is a prize-winning winemaker whose fine vintages are included in the price at an unusual basement billiard bar (guests only). Book ahead as drop-in guests are rarely accepted.

The only hotel on the Perovskaya strip is four-room *Pavo* (21 Akhvlediani, ☎ 98 6951, 🖳 www.hotelpavo.ge, sgl/dbl 165/ 200L). Its location makes it ideal for stumbling home post-party, but its attempts at art-nouveau class fall rather flat. Alternatively Vere (see opposite) is just a short walk further north-west.

Food and drink A meal at *Dzveli Sakhli* (☎ 982781/923497, most mains 8-15L) is one of those tourist 'must-dos' like dining at Baku's Muğam Club. The setting is a rustic-effect stone house and on weekend evenings there are several brief but thrilling dance-fight displays. Reservations essential.

A gaggle of appealing café-bars behind the opera house include the effortlessly stylish *Acid Bar* (beer from 3.20L), *Act Kafe* (coffee from 2L) with walls decked in B&W photos and the delightfully atmospheric *Near Opera* (espresso 3.30L, beer from 3.30L) with live piano-&-bass jazz, chequerboard floors and a crazy chandelier-fest. Good-value *Sardaphi* (beer 1.50L, wines 4-7L per litre) is a nearby basement eatery with four linked chambers.

New Asia (vegetarian/non-veg meals 7-11/13-50L, beer 3.60L) is one of Tbilisi's most appealing Chinese restaurants with oriental décor less intimidatingly OTT than at China Town.

For Georgian food at very sensible prices, try the 24-hour khingkali-and-shash-lyk restaurant *Mughami* (beer 1.50L) or the almost-atmospheric *Kafe Tbilisi* (29 Antoneli, ☎ 931773, beer 1.20L) with its high ceilings, drinking horns, canned local music and fine khajapuri/badrizhan (4/3L) washed down with Kahetian straw-wine (4L per litre) or very drinkable Evropuli (European-style) white wine at 2L per glass.

Still widely known by its former name, 'Perovskaya', Akhvlediani St is the spine of Tbilisi's longest-lived entertainment district where dozens of bars and pubs swing with a wide variety of canned and live music. Some pour local ales at 3L but most serve only imports (from around 5L, or 12L for draught Guinness). *Wheels*, *The Toucan*, *Dublin* and *The Nali* are long-term Anglo-Irish favourites. *Buffalo Bill's Saloon* hops with particularly infectious rock-country beats.

Several more intimate bars offer live Jazz-Blues sets, eg cosy *Csabas* and black-n-white *Nightstar*. Intriguingly wall papered with florid stars' faces, *Success* reputedly attracts a gay crowd. There are dozens more bars plus a good-rate 24-hour moneychanger within a stone's throw.

Virtually any world cuisine is available in upper-market restaurants here including including *Maharajah* (atmospheric Indian), *Tokyo* (chic if very expensive Japanese), *Sarcho* (Spanish), *Picasso* (Chinese),

Piccolo (very unpretentious pizzeria), *Calabria* (slightly lacklustre Italian but with good lunch deals), *Santa Fe* (Mexican-and-more in a charming café-ambience; fajitas 13L, beer 2.90L).

One of Tbilisi's most stylish places for local cuisine is the *Georgian House* (☎ 935057). Don't be put off by the immobile *maspinzelo* (the slightly aggressive-looking sheep-skin clad 'host') who blocks the door. Inside the style melds fashionably bright spaces with a traditional below-ground bare-brickwork. The food is somewhat pricey (eggplant starters 7L, khajapuri 9-11L) but the superb house Tswane ('green') wine costs only 7L per litre.

More colourful if slightly kitschy, the similarly priced *Mask* is presented dinner club style with carnival décor and live Georgian music after 11pm.

Vere (map p334)

Vere is the area directly north of Metro Rustaveli. While there's not much to see here, Vere's numerous accommodation options are handily close to the Perovskaya nightlife area.

Accommodation Classical music and indulgent Napoleon III furniture welcomes you into the impressive *Vere Palace Hotel* (☎ 253340, 🖳 www.verepalace.com.ge) There's a summer-only eighth-floor rooftop swimming pool and a swish sauna. The building has two halves. The older sgl/dbl €82/106 rooms are very slightly musty while the newer €130/147 de luxe rooms have nicer pale colour schemes, flat-screen TVs and mirror-fronted wardrobes giving a sense of space. Nearby *Hotel Primavera* (8 Kuchishvili, ☎ 251146, 🖳 www.primavera .ge) is a new, pleasant alternative.

High on the hill, the rooms at *Betsy's Hotel* (32 Makashvili, ☎ 931404, 🖳 www .betsyshotel.com) are not overly large and the bathrooms are petite but the fabrics are attractive and many windows have stupendous views. The stylish lobby coffee bar (espresso 3L) is a favourite expat meeting place. There's a small outdoor swimming-pool.

Draped in ivy and creepers, seven-room *Demi* (☎/🖷 252321, 🖳 www.demi-hotel.com, sgl/dbl US$106/130) has a

EXCURSIONS TO GEORGIA

342 Georgia – Tbilisi

handkerchief garden and a pleasant sitting area. The largish rooms have decent beds. Nearby *Iliani* (☎ 335710, 🖳 www.iliani .com, €100/120 sgl/dbl) seems comparatively overpriced.

Edem (formerly Victoria) (42 Petriashvili, ☎ 220160, 🖳 www.hotel edemi.ge, sgl/dbl €70/80) is a newish building but with very high ceilings, a shady garden (sadly getting increasingly shaded by the new building growing beside it) and nine sizeable, air-con rooms in very varying styles. Friendly, English-speaking management.

Guesthouse Mari (🖳 www.g-house mari.ge, sgl/dbl US$100/120) also has wildly varying styles in its eight rooms: some very ordinary, others impressively large with ornate fireplace (and a terrace in rooms 7 and 8). Some noise from the road.

Vaguely acceptable if lacking panache are nearby mini-hotels *Gremi* (☎ 252712), *Argopalace* (☎ 250461, 🖳 www.hotel argopalace.ge, sgl/dbl 100/120L), and *Kolkhi* (Shanidze 31, ☎ 234093, sgl/dbl 100/130L), the latter unusual in having a lift. *Hotel Guta* (☎ 250301, sgl/dbl US$70/100) refused to show me a room. Minimal spoken English these four.

Much better value is the friendly, English- (and German)-speaking *Kartli Hotel* (32 Barnov, ☎ 982982, 🖳 hot_kar tli@gol.ge) with six rooms above their decent *pizzeria* (three lack major windows) and six more across the street.

In older buildings the pleasant three-room *Vere Inn* (Barnov 53, ☎ 291252, 🖳 www.2.tbilisi.com, US$80-120) and quiet, three-storey *Classic* (18 Gurgulia, ☎ 227415, ☎ www.classic.ge, €50-70) both have antique furniture but the latter is let down by the bare bits in its cheap carpeting.

Food and drink Upmarket options include *Cabarnet* (French, modern) and *Paradiso* (pricey Italian, bland inside but nice summer garden). *Kartli Hotel's Pizzeria* (Italian/Greek/central European) produces intriguing twists on the khajapuri theme (7.50L) and has a narrow, vine-draped beer-garden (beer from 2.20L). *Zanduk Bar* (Russian/Caucasian) is an appealing wooden-floored pub-restaurant

decorated with typewriters and old radios and playing 1950s music (beers from 6L). Cheaper options include appealing *El Depo* (beer 1.70L, open 24-hours, a classic for 0.55-0.80L Khinkali), the slightly kitschy six-table Georgian cellar *Old Vera* (khajapuri 5L, wine from 4L per litre) and an unpretentious cheap *café* on Barnov St where 1L slices of large pre-prepared khajapuri and delicious lobiani can be washed down with a 1L Turkish coffee – it's beside **Highlands Travel** (🖳 www.highlands.ge). *Kafe Literaturi* is a small bookshop café with a good range of cakes.

Marjanishvili area (map opposite)

Around fifteen minutes' walk from both Rustaveli and the train station, the lively area around Marjanishvili metro has a decent range of for-locals dining places and virtually all of Tbilisi's backpacker homestay-based accommodation (15-30L per person). Most such places have beds haphazardly dotted about century-old homes and all have shared bathrooms. From outside none has any sign whatever but don't be put off! Ring the bell or ask.

The classic is *Nazi Gvetadze's Home-stay* (30/92 Marjanishvili; ☎ 950894) where the 25L beds are reasonably well spaced albeit oddly placed between Nazi's book shelves, desks and dining room furniture. Nazi speaks German and Russian and charges 1L extra for hot showers in the very small WC-bathroom. It's towards the rear of the 30 Marjanishvili courtyard on the right and is accessed through a low, ivy-draped fence.

Irina Japaridze's Homestay (🖳 www .iverieli.narod.ru, 🖳 irina5062@mail.ru, top floor, 19B Ninoshvili; ☎ 940611) is the nearest Tbilisi comes to a youth hostel. A central party/lounge room bristles with international flags and bunks are stuffed into every other space that the beautiful antique furniture allows. Irina's occupies the top floor of unmarked 19 Ninoshvili whose entrance (side) is guarded by two decapitated stone lions. The once-grand house was 'all ours till the family was sent to the gulag' remembers English-speaking matriarch Irina.

Dodo's Homestay (🖳 dodogeorgia@ gmail.com or 🖳 neliko@iliauni.edu.ge, 18

Marjanishvili; ☎ 954213) has beds from 27L to 35L in a series of comparatively spacious, high-ceilinged rooms (the front ones are noisy) sharing a good, hot shower and a rather grotty kitchen. Dodo is a delight and her niece Nelly speaks excellent English. Their house is on the left within the courtyard.

Green Stairs (53 Tsinamdzghvrishvili, 🖳 vazha@lycos.com, ☎ 941552, mob ☎ 893-331236) refers to four little, bright, if rather rough, twin rooms purpose built above English-speaking Vazha's courtyard home with its trademark green stairway. Quiet, with a place for bicycle parking, and bookable through HostelWorld (🖳 www.hostelworld.com).

Tsiala Siradze's Homestay (12 Chitaia, ☎ 566281) is the cheapest option at 15L per bed but the one twin bedroom or sofa spaces around the cramped dining room of this very modest home offer minimal privacy. Tsiala speaks Russian in a curious falsetto but her daughter Khatuna can manage some English. It's up the second of three short stairways on the right side of the 12 Chitaia courtyard.

Naira Cachava (9 Mamradze, map p333; ☎ 940611) speaks some German and her husband is a talented artist. Up beside his private top-floor studio (itself worth a look) there's a single-bedded room that polite foreigners might be allowed to rent

for 30L. Local travellers get palmed off with a grotty room in the courtyard. If you don't get a reply at the main door, try asking around the corner at Naira's small grocery shop. Handy for the main train station.

Prestige Hotel (51 Marjanishvili, ☎ 94 0505; 🖳 www.hotelprestige.ge; rooms from 120L) is this area's one little boutique hotel in an old house with surprisingly generous sitting areas.

Food and drink South of McDonald's is the indulgent *English Tea House*, Georgian restaurant *Marani* and an evocatively art-nouveau Parisian-style *café* attached to Marjanishvili Drama Theatre. But for great-value dining it's hard to beat *Shemoikhede Genadtsvale*, an appealing series of cavernous brick-walled dining rooms serving a wide range of local classics including superb mashed Badrizhan Nigvzit (large portion 4.30L), wines from 4.50L per litre and Kaz-begi beer at 1.80L. The menu is all in kartuli, but you can get a version in English (with just a few minor differences) from their branch on Leslidze (Old Town); comparing the two is a great tool for learning the alphabet!

Several **bakeries** have hot tandoor bread, freshly pre-cooked khajapuri and lobiani and there are **Turkish eateries** on Chavchavadze.

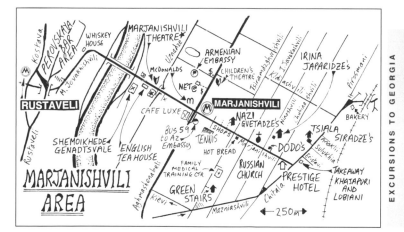

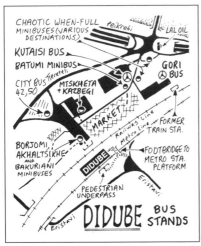

Beyond Tbilisi

MTSKHETA AND JVARI

About 40 minutes by minibus from Didube (see map above), **Mtskheta** remains the country's spiritual heart though it is now just a sleepy village backwater at the confluence of the Mktvari (Kura) and Aragvi rivers. Its architectural focus is the impressively fortified 11th-century cathedral, **Svetitskhoveli**. Considered 'the most beautiful church in creation', the master builder who'd created it

had his forearm lopped off to prevent him bettering his work elsewhere. The amputated right hand lives on, carved in stone high on the exterior north wall. Inside, the Madonna to the left of the present altar barrier was said to cry tears for a couple of weeks leading up to the 9 April 1989 massacre. 'Unbelievable isn't it' said my guide. 'But I saw it myself' (see box below).

Samtavro Monastery, five minutes' walk to the north, has another beautiful stone church where King Miriam is buried and a quaint, tiny chapel said to mark St Nino's favourite meditation spot. In the hills around town are several more churches and the remains of a Roman mausoleum have been uncovered near the station.

Little **Jvari** ('cross'), perched on a cliff facing Mtskheta across the Mktvari, is one of the oldest churches in Georgia. Built in 604 on the site where St Nino had originally erected a cross, it is plain inside but offers great views and an atmosphere of serene sanctity despite being defaced in the Soviet era. There's a steep short-cut footpath from Mtskheta but to reach it by road requires backtracking several kilometres towards Tbilisi. Then it's a fiddle to get off the motorway but when you've done so the road curls round pleasantly.

GORI (☎ 270)

Around an hour's drive by bus or car west of Tbilisi, Gori seems just too appropriate a name for Stalin's birthplace. But bad old

---

❏ **Miraculous Mtskheta**

Pre-Christian Mtskheta had already been capital of Iveria (Georgia) for 500 years when citizen Elias witnessed Jesus's crucifixion. By way of a memento for his sister Sidonia he bought Christ's cloak from a sentry before rushing home. In a vast over reaction, Sidonia was so overcome by emotion on receiving the holy garment that she died on the spot. Buried in the royal palace grounds, a gigantic cedar tree had grown from her heart by the time King Miriam was finally converted to Christianity 300 years later (courtesy of his wife and St Nino). This great tree's felled trunk seemed to be the ideal central support for Miriam's new church but engineers proved unable to erect it. Fortunately the teenage St Nino was at hand to levitate it into position through her prayers. Hence the name Svetitskhoveli ('Living Pillar') for the cathedral which was rebuilt in the 6th and 11th centuries and fortified in the 18th.

'man of steel' Dzhugashvili is still revered here as a local boy made 'good'. A massive **Stalin statue** stares out across Stalin Sq which leads up to Stalin Park. The highlight of the attractive 1957 palazzo-style **Stalin Museum** (💻 www.stalinmuseum.ge, Tue-Sun 10-18:00, entry 15L) is the spooky death-mask chamber. A modest hut-house outside is supposedly Stalin's original childhood home.

Gori's geographical focus is a central crag crowned with the chunky ruins of a **16th-century fortress**. A castle of one sort or another has stood here for over 2000 years – the Romans dropped by to besiege it in 65BC but the main town and trading centre of the region at that time was 8km away at **Uplitsikhe** (site open 9-18:00, entry 10L). That was an ancient city carved out of bare rock which later evolved into a monastic retreat. Although the scenery is less dramatic than at David Gareja or Vardzia, there's still plenty to explore. Taxis want around 30L return from Gori.

Gori's best **accommodation** is the com-

paratively modern **Hotel Victoria** (76 Tamara St, ☎ 75586) charging from 70L for sizeable en suite twins with air-con, shower, towels etc. The once-grand **Intourist** (☎ 72676, 50L/twin) lurks behind huge carved wooden doors but the crumbling corridors are nowhere near as grand and water rarely runs hot (if at all).

Buses run hourly from Didube, Tbilisi.

Mountain areas

The Caucasus's top ski resort is at **Gudauri** (💻 www.gudauri.info, ski-pass 25L, ski-rental 40L) around two hours' drive from Tbilisi up the Georgian Military highway passing the picturesque **Ananuri** fortress churches en route. Gudauri hotel prices almost halve in summer but at that time it's worth continuing to little **Kazbegi** from where it's a 1½-hour hike to the iconic peak-top Sameba church backed spectacularly by the towering peak of Mt Kazbeg (5043m). Kazbegi has several homestays and the more comfy **Hotel Step-antsminda**. Around 10km further north the almost-mythical **Dariel Gorge** leads into Russia (border closed to foreigners). Seven minibuses run daily from Tbilisi (Didube, see map p344) to Kazbegi via Gudauri.

Attractive if less awe-inspiring, Georgia's second ski-station is at **Bakuriani** (💻 www.bakuriani.ge). Accommodation here is generally cheaper than in Gudauri or you could even 'commute' up from Borjomi (one hour by bus, two hours by narrow-gauge train). **Borjomi** (map p346) is the spa-town producing Georgia's most famous mineral water, and is an easy stop between Tbilisi (two hours) and **Akhaltsikhe** (map p346).

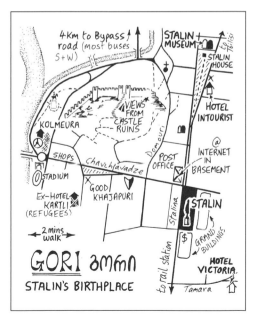

4Km to Bypass
road (most buses
S+W)

STALIN
MUSEUM

to Tbilisi

STALIN
HOUSE

VIEWS
FROM
CASTLE
RUINS

KOLMEURA

HOTEL
INTOURIST

@
INTERNET
IN
BASEMENT

SHOPS

Chavchlavadze

POST
OFFICE

STADIUM

GOOD
KHAJAPURI

Ex-HOTEL
KARTLI
(REFUGEES)

STALIN

GRAND
BUILDINGS

2 mins
walk

to rail station

$

HOTEL
VICTORIA

Tamara

GORI გორი

STALIN'S BIRTHPLACE

EXCURSIONS TO GEORGIA

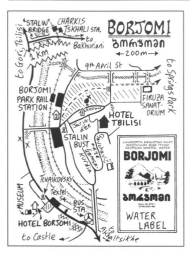

hotelinshatili.iatp.ge/en/index.htm) remains one of the most impressively medieval-looking fortified villages anywhere outside Ladakh.

Routes to Turkey

With partial funding from Azerbaijan, the long-mooted new railway link from Tbilisi to Kars (Turkey) finally started construction in 2008 but remains politically controversial by further isolating Armenia so some still question if it will ever be completed. Until then there are two main options: Batumi–Sarpi–Hopa–Trabzon or Akhaltsikhe–Vale–Posof–Ardahan. Starting from Tbilisi the journey to either Batumi or Akhaltsikhe is comfortable by direct overnight train but also interesting to do in hops.

SWANETI AND KHEVSURETI
Hard to reach **Swaneti** is a fabled Alpine land famed for the brilliant tower houses of **Ushguli** (🖳 http://lileo-ushguli.blogspot.com), 'Europe's highest village'. The Soviets never quite managed to tame Swaneti's fiercely independent people and until 2004 the area was still infamous for banditry. Things have improved greatly since then. A minibus runs most mornings to Swaneti's capital village **Mestia** (with numerous homestays) from the Swan tower in Zugdidi if there are enough customers. You should have no trouble connecting the same day having arrived off the overnight Tbilisi–Zugdidi train.

   Khevsureti is also a dramatic, inaccessible region where **Shatili** (see 🖳 http://

ROUTE 1: TBILISI–AKHALTSIKHE–POSOF–ARDAHAN
Apart from **Mtskheta** (p344), the main attractions en route are **Gori** (Stalin's home town, p344), **Borjomi** (see p345) and, after an attractive wooded valley guarded by the ruins of **Atskuri castle**, the town of **Akhaltsikhe** (☎ 265) where the somewhat institutional *White House* (Tetri Sakhli, 40/50L sgl/dbl) is better than the Soviet-era *Meskheti Hotel* (☎ 20420, from 25L). It's worth stopping in Akhaltsikhe for a few hours to see its old town and castle-museum then charter a taxi (around 70L return) to visit **Vardzia** (an extensive cave city and cliff church complex 15km away), splendid **Khertvisi castle** and **Sapara** (see graphic p320), possibly the most charming of all Georgia's monastic complexes.

   There are occasional buses between Akhaltsikhe and Turkey or take a taxi to the border (beyond the hopelessly dep-

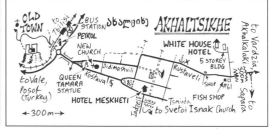

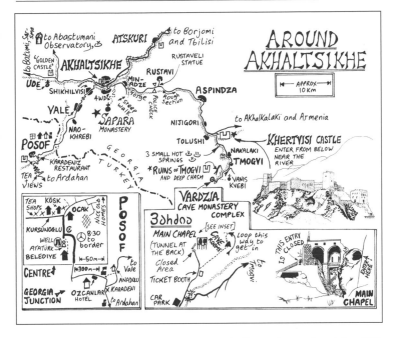

ressed mining village of **Vale**, pronounced *Var-leh*) and another to the quaint Turkish chalet-town of **Posof**. Here there are several inexpensive hotels and the onward drive to Ardahan (and thence Artvin/Trabzon or Kars) is very scenic.

ROUTE 2: TBILISI TO TRABZON VIA BATUMI

Beyond Gori (p344) Georgia's main cross-country road winds over an attractive pass to the manganese mining town of Zestafoni and on to historic **Kutaisi** which warrants an exploratory break and where *Lia's* (💻 http://hotellia.iatp.ge) is a reliable family hotel.

The route eventually transits **Kobuleti**, Georgia's 10km-long Black Sea beach resort before reaching **Batumi**. Batumi, Georgia's second city, has a steamy je-ne-sais-quoi and a wide range of accommodation. Buses are reasonably frequent on this route. If taking the overnight train to/from Tbilisi be aware that Batumi's station is

actually 5km to the east (by minibus #101 or 122) at Makhinjauri (which translates eerily as the 'place of death').

The Turkish border between Sarpi (Georgia) and Sarp (Turkey) is easy to reach by frequent minibus #142 (from Tbilisi Sq in Batumi) and passes **Gonio** en route where the substantial, square-plan fortress was originally Roman (albeit rebuilt by both Byzantine and Ottoman rulers).

On the Turkish side a taxi mafia pushes up prices to the first Turkish town Hopa, but coming FROM Hopa there are minibuses **to Sarp** (15 mins) from the Petrol Ofisi courtyard on the coast about 10 minutes' walk north then east from Hopa bus station. **Hopa** has many hotels and ATM cash machines, and frequent mini-buses to Trabzon (3hrs) from where buses run to Istanbul (18 hours) with considerable frequency. The Hopa–Trabzon mini-bus can also drop you outside Trabzon airport which has budget flights to Istanbul and Ankara.

APPENDIX A: BIBLIOGRAPHY

The following list includes both key reads and many off-beat sources that may be of inter-est to the more devoted aficionado of the region. If you just want one book to explain con-temporary history and the Karabagh problems start with de Waal (p351) adding Goltz once you have an idea of the characters involved. For the WWI period don't miss Kurban Said/Essad Bey or Peter Hopkirk while Altstadt and Swietochowski can add detail if you want further 20th-century insight. For the Shamil era there's no beating Lesley Blanch. Sources for more ancient history are sparse but if you don't want to rummage too deeply into the 7-volume Cambridge *History of Iran*, one possibility is van der Leeuw (p351). Note that I have omitted most of the sources which are available only in Russian or Azeri. Scanned versions of the books marked (Archive) are available for free download through 🖳 www .archive.com. A few others can be partly sampled through Google Books.
* denotes books often stocked at Chiraq Bookshop in Baku (see p132 and map p86, V6)
    Various colourful coffee-table books are sold in Baku but rarely prove very informative.

Abercromby, Hon John *A trip through the Eastern Caucasus* (London 1889) A six-week 'tourist' spree largely visiting Dağestan and the high Caucasus but with a visit to Zaqatala, Shäki and Kish.
Aliyev, Heydar Should you be aching to read something by the 'National Leader' you'll find plenty available in Azerbaijan or you can savour some of his speeches and addresses on 🖳 http://library.aliyev-heritage.org.
Altstadt, Audrey *The Azerbaijan Turks: Power and Identity under Russian Rule* (Stanford, 1992). Offers very useful insights into the Stalin/Bagirov purges and especial-ly the extraordinary Soviet decisions of the 1920s which still shape the nation and its rela-tionship with Armenia.
Atkin, Muriel *Russia and Iran 1780-1828* Includes some useful overviews of society in the various Azerbaijani Khanates during the era of the Russian takeover. Read sections on Google Books.
Baron, Charles *Au Pays de l'Or Noir* (Paris 1934) A rather dry analysis of the 1930s' Soviet oil industry enlivened by some fascinating photos of the Absheron and the Bibi Heybat oil-fields. The elektrichka train photographed at Sabunchi has hardly changed in 70 years.
Bechhofer-Roberts, Carl Eric *In Denikin's Russia and the Caucasus 1891-1920* (London 1921) Bechhofer-Roberts interviews the then Azeri president in this book's single chapter dealing with Azerbaijan (Baku: the Bolsheviks arrive).
Blanch, Lesley *Sabres of Paradise** Gushing with excitement in the wake of 19th century hero-warlord Shamil (see p237 and p232) whose story is told with unique, novelist's panache. Every detail comes to life and although little of the action actually takes place on Azeri soil, the book paints an unbeatably vivid portrait of Caucasus life in the mid-19th century Russian period. Highly recommended. The same subject is retold much less excitedly by Griffin (p349)
Broido, Eva *Memoirs of a Revolutionary* This autobiography of a prominent Menshevik involved in the February 1917 revolution also gives her fascinating account of Baku in 1905.
Brook, Stephen *Claws of the Crab* (1992) A very useful snapshot of Georgia during the madness of the Gamsakhurdia regime, with a less-interesting sojourn in Armenia. Reported through pro-Armenian eyes, the final section on Nagorno Karabagh offers a startling coun-terpoint to the Azerbaijani version of the events between 1988 and 1992.
Bryce, Lord James *TransCaucasia and Ararat* (London 1877) Travelogue from a 1876 'vacation tour' (Archive).
Buchan, John *The Baltic and Caucasian States* (1923) Historical overview of the then 'newly' Sovietized countries (Archive).
DeBruin, Cornelius *Voyages de Corneille de Bruyn par la Muscovie en Perse* (Amsterdam 1718) This Polish traveller was impressed by Gänjä and stopped to sketch such places as Kalaxana.

Dumas, Alexandre *Adventures in the Caucasus* Dumas visited Baku (Bakou), Shamakha (Schoumakha) and Shäki (Noukha) and tells tales of Imam Shamil. Locals love to tell you how much Dumas liked Azerbaijan, though few have probably read his book. The French original is readable online at 💻 http://gallica.bnf.fr/ark:/12148/bpt6k9935c.

Dunsterville, Lionel *Adventures of Dunsterforce* (1920) First-hand memoirs from the man who'd launched Britain's doomed 'defence' of Baku two years earlier (Archive).

Essad Bey *Blood and Oil in The Orient** (1930) Written under a pseudonym by the same author as Ali and Nino, this superb if embellished semi-autobiographical tale features the son of a Baku oil baron who flees to Central Asia following the Bolshevik takeover in Baku. It's fabulously evocative, offhandedly humorous yet historically vivid for the WWI period.

Freshfield, Douglas William *The exploration of the Caucasus* (1902, reprinted in 2000 by Elibron Classics) Various travels in the 1880s. Volume 1 covering Swaneti (Georgia) and much of Ossetia is partly readable online through Google Books.

Gallenga, Antonio Carlo *A Summer tour in Russia* (1882) A reporter for *The Times* passes through Baku in 1881.

Gmelin, Samuel Gottlieb *Travels through Northern Persia 1770-1774* Classic travelogue -cum-spy-report recently translated and republished in English in 2007 with useful footnotes. Although concentrating on Iran, Gmelin visits Sälyan and discusses Shamakha wines.

Goltz, Thomas *Azerbaijan Diary** (1998), An unmissable introduction to the turbulent Azeri politics of the 1990s written in a romping first-person style. But read de Waal (p351) first if you're not familiar with the events already.

Griffin, Nicholas *Caucasus: In the Wake of Warriors* (2002) A pale revisitation of Blanch's *Sabres of Paradise* (see opposite) spiced with bad-tempered and largely irrelevant travel tales. Griffin dubs the first edition of this guidebook the 'evil red book'.

Gulbenkian, Calouste Sarkis *Transcaucasie et la peninsule d'Apsheron, Souvenirs de Voyage* (1891) As with most travellers of the age, Gulbenkian was particularly concerned with technical observation of the oil springs but gives some descriptions of his trip through Georgia and western Azerbaijan on the way there.

Hanway, Jonas *Historical account of British Trade over the Caspian Sea* (1753) Travels from London to Russia into Persia and notes on 'recent' Persian revolutions.

Henry, JD *Baku: An Eventful History* (London, 1905) The author visited just after the September 1905 massacres.

Heradstveit, Daniel *Democracy and Oil, the case of Azerbaijan* (2001) Political analysis peppered with survey/interview findings from influential political figures.

Heyat, Farideh *Azeri Women in Transition* Based on a 1996 PhD with some interesting cultural details from marriage rites to words for 'hen pecked'.

Hopkirk, Peter *On Secret Service East of Constantinople** A rompingly readable view of the secret complexities of WWI: the last chapters home in on Baku.

Karny, Yo'av *Highlanders: A journey to the Caucasus in search of memory* (2000) Deals mostly with the North Caucasus but concludes with a chapter on the political motivations of 'historical' research into Caucasian Albania.

Maclean, Sir Fitzroy *Eastern Approaches* (1938) The gung-ho British diplomat-adventurer potters off towards Central Asia but, on his first 1937 attempt, gets stranded in Lenkoran (Länkäran), noticing en route the first signs of Stalin's snowballing mass deportations. He makes it in 1938 returning via Iran, Jolfa (Culfa) and Nakhchivan. *To Caucasus, End of all the Earth* (1976) has many further interesting observations on Georgia (plus five pages on Azerbaijan).

Marvin, Charles *The Region of the Eternal Fire* (1884) Marvin jumps on the train from London to Baku, gives practical details of his journey and quotes dozens of corroborating sources to encourage suspicious British entrepreneurs of the unbelievable oil wealth which, in 1883 was just waiting to be exploited. Reprinted by Elibron (💻 www.elibron.com) (Archive).

Minorsky, Vladimir *History of Sharvan and Darband* This hard-to-find 1958 publication comprises a translation of and commentary on an old Arabic text charting the history of north-

350 Appendix A – Bibliography

ern Azerbaijan in the 10th to 11th centuries. Minorsky's *Studies in Caucasian History* includes a section on the Shaddadid dynasty of Gänjä. Minorsky (1877-1966) was a leading Russian orientalist and was a diplomat in Tehran for the Tsarist regime before fleeing to Europe post-1917. His works are the subject of some debate between Armenian and Azerbaijani historians.

Morgan, Edward Delmar (ed) *Early Voyages to Russia and Persia* An 1886 compilation of travel accounts of daring Elizabethan English wool traders. Includes original source letters and an excellent contextual overview; two volumes.

Mounsey, Augustus *A Journey through the Caucasus and Persia* (1872) Calls Baku 'the Mecca of the Guebers' (ie fireworshippers).

Nersesov, Mirza Yusuf *A Truthful History (1850s)* Rather turgid material on the battles for Karabagh, available online at ⌨ http://digilib.am/texts/yusuf_nersesov/tshmartatsi_patmutiun_en/.

Osmaston, John *Old Ali* (1881) Reminiscences of a tourist's journey to Persia in 1861. Chapter 11 is the only section on Azerbaijan but it includes an intriguing 'burning sea tour' and a visit to the 'oil isle of Sviatoi' (Artyom).

Perkins, Justin *A Residence of Eight Years in Persia among the Nestorian Christians* (1843, reprinted 2006 by ⌨ www.elibron.com) The travelogue and memoirs of a US missionary to Persian Azerbaijan. Significantly he notes (on p130) that in the Nakhchivan area, poor Armenians who had been 'enticed into these provinces by the Russians from their more healthy homes in Turkey and Persia' would rather return but that the Russians wouldn't let them.

Reiss, Tom *The Orientalist* (2006) This fascinating, somewhat controversial, portrait of the life and times of *Ali & Nino* author Lev Nussimbaum aka Essad Bey aka Kurban Said actually spends most of its time focusing on Judaism in early 20th-century Europe.

Rohl, David *Legend – the Genesis of Civilisation* (1998) The TV archaeologist locates the Garden of Eden and the land of Nod in southern Azerbaijan (Iran).

Said, Kurban *Ali and Nino** This must-read classic is a sort of Caucasian Romeo and Juliet, set for part of the story in Baku in the pre-WWI period.

Salkeld, Audrey and Bermudez, JL *On the Edge of Europe: Mountaineering in the Caucasus* (1993) – an anthology of mountaineering tales from 1869 to 1986. Extensive bibliography and climbers' chronology.

Shaffer, Brenda *Borders and Brethren: Iran and the Challenge of Azerbaijani Identity* (2002) Argues that even in Iran Azerbaijanis are Azerbaijanis. Did that really need so much minutely detailed academic referencing? If you have the patience, there are some occasionally interesting insights into 20th-century Azeri history on both sides of the border.

Steavenson, Wendell *Stories I Stole* (2002) A Tbilisi-based Western journalist tells vodka-lubricated stories-behind-stories from Georgia and Abkhazia. Includes a brief trip to Baku in search of Ali and Nino. Her character 'Kurtz' sounds remarkably like Thomas Goltz.

Suny, Ronald Grigor Suny is a US (third-generation Armenian) political science professor and prolific author on the former USSR. Relevant books include *Transcaucasia: Nationalism and Social Change* (Ann Arbor, 1983) and *The Baku Commune 1917-18*.

Swietochowski, Tadeusz *Historical Dictionary of Azerbaijan* Useful but extremely concise at 144 pages. *Russia and Azerbaijan* (Columbia, 1995) is a useful resource on 20th-century history if you can find a copy.

Teague-Jones, R *The Spy who disappeared* Autobiography of the British agent who the Russians claimed to be the killer of the 26 Baku Commissars in 1918. The best part of the 1990 reprint is Peter Hopkirk's introduction.

Telfer, John Buchan *Crimea and TransCaucasia* A two-volume travelogue from the 1870s covering Georgia and Swanetia but not Azerbaijan. Telfer's 1879 book *The bondage and travels of Johannes Schiltberger* is fascinating but the slavery and adventures referred to actually happened between 1396 and 1427.

Thomson, Jason *In the Shadow of Aliyev* A Canadian NGO worker (resident 1998-2000) regurgitates the fundamentals of Azerbaijan's history in what's half travelogue, half lumpy thesis. The book is possibly worth buying for the 34-page postscript on Azerbaijan's 21st-century politics where the author finally gives up on all those tedious quotations and footnotes and tells us what HE thinks.

van der Leeuw, Charles *Azerbaijan: A Quest for Identity** (Palgrave Macmillan, 2000) Wide-ranging if somewhat turgid coverage of the whole range of Azerbaijan's history.

de Waal, Thomas *Black Garden** A brilliant attempt to explain the complex Karabagh situation debunking many wilder conspiracy theories with soundly argued in-depth research. Although its neutrality displeases both sides, the book offers a slight glimmer of optimism in highlighting the human closeness of apparently intractable enemies.

Wegge, Bjorn A *Azerbaijan – Where East meets West* (Oslo 1996) A brief, readable overview of Azeri history, ethnic groups and Christian links hinting at the opportunities for future missionary work.

Yergin, Daniel *The Prize* (1993) This wonderful romping read is the most thorough history of the oil industry available.

Zinger, L & Najafov, M *The art of Soviet Azerbaijan* Some great photos but dull text.

APPENDIX B: MENU DECODER

Key: ▲ = Azeri, ✤ = Georgian, ✦ = widespread throughout the Caucasus and beyond, ◯ = Russian, ♠ = Turkish, Ⅱ = Persian origin; # Other origin.

Note: The suffix *-si* is necessary in Azeri when qualifying a type of something. Eg Murabba is jam but apple jam is Alma Murabba<u>si</u>.

abgusht Ⅱ Piti (see p355) but served with a pestle: rather more appropriate for mashing than the aluminium fork you are likely to get in the Azerbaijan republic.

açma ✤ Layered like a lasagne but with only cheese (*Açma Pendirilä*) or meat (*Açma Ätlä*) between the pasta-like folds.

Adana kebab ♠ A spicy Turkish version of *Lule Kebab* (see p354)

adjika/ajika/adzhika ✤ Firey garlic dipping sauce

albuxara ▲ Dried plum

alcha turçusu ▲ Concentrated plum sauce used as an alternative to *narşarab*.

alfar # The Xınalıqı version of *qutab*

alma ▲ Apple

antreqot ▲ Mutton ribs served as *shashlyk*

arabuli ✤ Cheese/tomato-topped meat dish

araq/arak ▲/♠ Local name for any strong alcohol but usually vodka

ärishtä ▲ Soup with pasta strips

Arzuman küftä ▲ Imagine stuffing a chicken but in reverse – the bird is inside and the minced-meat/chestnut mix forms a ball around the outside. One is big enough to feed a whole family.

aseterina ▲/◯ The cheapest sub-variety of sturgeon; serve with *narşarab* (see p354).

ash/aş ▲ Special rice dishes, see p22 (◯ *plov*)

ätkyartof ▲ Meat and potatoes

ätli nohut ▲ Chick-pea and meat stew

axta ▲ Dried, stoned cherries

ayran ♠/▲ Refreshing watered-down yogurt drink. Often cheaper than water!

äzgil ▲ Pine nuts

azma ▲ Minced lamb's liver

Badamli ▲ Nakhchivan-sourced mineral water

badamli borucuq ▲ Sweet, almond-filled bready rolls

badımcan ▲ Aubergine/eggplant. ✤ badrizhani. *Badımcan dolmasi* are delicious mince-stuffed aubergines.

badrizhani nigvzit ✤ Strips of roasted eggplant with walnut paste (often served cold).

badrizhani nivrit ✤ Garlic eggplant strips but not necessarily using walnuts
bakhlava ♠ (▲ paxlava) Layered sweet confection of '*rishta*' pastry and crushed almonds or other nut-paste soaked in honey or syrup. There are regional variations.
balık ▲ Smoked sturgeon
balıq ▲ (♠ balik) Fish
balva ▲ A glutinous soupy-mush of greens and over-boiled rice thickened with egg.
bamiya ▲ Sweet, extruded fingers of dough with a star-shaped cross-section which are deep fried and sprinkled with icing sugar.
basturma ✤ Strips of dried meat from which the term pastrami is probably derived.
bekmes ▲ A thick, sweet syrup of mulberries used as a medication to cleanse the liver. Hard to find in the cities but is sold at the roadside stalls on the Ismayıllı–Qäbälä road.
beyin ♠ Boiled cow's brain, best with a splash of olive oil or lemon.
blini ◎ Versatile pancake-style snack. Add jam, sour cream, caviar or fill with minced meat and herbs. *Blinchiki* are smaller versions.
borş ▲ *borshch* ◎ Cabbage and beetroot soup. Typically served mornings only.
bozartma ▲ Meat dish that is started by boiling the meat then frying it with onions then returning it to the broth.
bozbaş ▲ In *köfte bozbaş*, a ball of *köfte* mince is wrapped around a plum or sour cherry (beware of the pip) and served in a tomato-based lamb stew.
bucanina ▲ Pork cooked in foil.
buğlama ▲ Boiled meat with vegetables but can be more exotic eg with eggplant and cherries. Served with *qatıq*.
burachniy salatı ▲/◎ Beetroot salad
...çaxırdä ▲ ...cooked in wine
burak ▲ Beetroot
çay ▲ Tea (a *çaynik* is a teapot, a *çayxana* is a teahouse)
chadi ✤ Georgian corn bread
chakapuli ✤ Herby lamb stew
chakhobkhbili ✤ Spicy chicken in onion and tomato sauce
chashushuli ✤ Tomato-stewed veal
chebureki ✤ Meat-filled pancakes or tarts
churchkhela ✤ Vaguely obscene brown, rubbery truncheons which are in fact strings of walnuts dipped in *tatara* (qv) and hung

to dry. Remove the string before eating.
chvishtari ✤ A cheese *chadi* typical of Zugdidi.
çiça ▲ Small dried fish like oversized whitebait, eaten with beer.
çiger ♠ Liver
çiğ köfte ✤ Balls of lean minced meat, onions, herbs and wheat-rice kneaded by hand for up to an hour but otherwise uncooked.
çığırtma ▲ Glorified omelette, typically heavy with garlic. Can be expensive especially if it is to include chicken (ie *toyuq çığıtması*)
cız-bız ▲ Mutton tripe and well-boiled potatoes fried to a mushy consistency. The name is onomatopoeic for the fizzing sound of the cooking process.
çoban ▲ The green salad of coriander leaves, tomato, cucumber, raw onion and various other herbs served before most meals.
cocuk (jojuk) ▲ garlic and herb mash
çolpa ▲ Chicken fried with onions, potato and berries (eg Zogol).
çorba ♠ Soup
çörek ▲ Bread. *Isti çörek* means it's hot from the baker.
cücä ▲ Chicken, younger more tender than *toyuq**
çudu ▲ Breadier version of a *pirozhki*
cuxa ▲ *Lavash* bread is called cuxa ('jukha') in Gänjä and west Azerbaijan.
dana bastırma ▲ Beef strips as kebab
dil ▲ Tongue
doğrama ▲ (◎ *okroshka*) Delicately flavoured cold yogurt soup with diced cucumber.
dolma ♠/▲ Vegetables or edible leaves stuffed with a minced lamb/rice mixture flavoured with herbs such as coriander, dill, mint, spring onion. Steamed or roasted.
dondurma ♠/▲ Ice cream
döner ♠ Similar to the infamous after-pub snacks in Britain but without the chilli sauce. Either *tavuk/toyuq* (chicken) or (*ät*) lamb meat is cut from a vertical rotating grill spike and served in bread with salad and maybe a few fried potatoes and/or sauce. Common in Baku but relatively rare elsewhere.
donuz ▲ Pork
döşünün ▲ Breast (of chicken etc)
dovğa ▲ Finely chopped green vegetables and herbs in a yogurt/water mixture which is

simmered laboriously with constant stirring.

düşbärä ▲ Azeri-style ravioli/*manti*. Teaspoon-sized balls of minced mutton with onion and coriander wrapped in a chewy local pasta and boiled in stock. Typically served with mint and yogurt/sour cream or with a garlic and vinegar dip.

düyü ▲ Rice

entrekot ✪ Mutton ribs served as shashlyk

ezme salad ♠ A sort of Turkish salsa. If you don't want it spicy ask for it *biber siz*.

fesenjan Ⅱ Classy Iranian dish using a rich, dark, walnut and pomegranate sauce.

fırında ♠ Roast

fisincan ▲ The Azeri equivalent of Fesenjan is typically meatballs with crushed nuts and garlic.

fisincan salati ▲ Chicken strips with a heavily garlicky nutty sauce.

'G' NB *Be aware that Azeri words spelt with a Q or H are often transliterated with a G.*

gaiganag ▲ Halfway between an omelette and scrambled eggs.

göbäläk ▲ Mushroom

goğal ▲ Lightly spiced pastry made for No-vruz, funerals or to give as Nazir offerings.

göy/göyarti ▲ Literally means 'blue'. In a restaurant this refers to the ubiquitous plate of salad herbs (most commonly *kinza* and spring onions). *Zelenye* in Russian.

gozinkali ✧ A honey and walnut confection common in the Turkic world as far away as Kashgar (west China) but relatively hard to find in the Caucasus.

gözleme ♠ Turkish name for *qutab*.

gubdari ✤ A meat-filled variety of *khajapuri*.

Gürcü mätbexi ▲ Azerbaijani term for Georgian cuisine.

Gürcü xingäl ▲ Azerbaijani term for Georgian *khinkali*.

gurza ▲ Semi-circular meaty parcels in a light pasta. They look similar to their Japanese namesake, *gyoza*, but are usually served in a herby broth rather than being fried.

hafta-bedjar ▲ Mixed pickled vegetables (aubergine, sweet-peppers, tomatoes). The name means 'ready in a week'.

halva ▲ Halva – ie honey/flour/butter made into a sweet confection, usually flavoured with a little cinnamon, fennel or saffron.

hash ✧ see Xash.

haydari ♠ Yogurt with garlic and herbs

(and aubergine) sometimes offered with starters/salads.

heyva ▲ Quince. In autumn, home-made heyva juice is ubiquitous though rarely sold.

Hindushka ▲ turkey (the bird)

ikra ✪ Russian name for caviar, see p21.

ikra ▲ salsa-style, if unspicy, mixture of tomato, peppers and carrot.

... izgara ♠ Grilled... .

ıskender ♠ Bread cubes fried and draped in döner meat, tomato sauce and yogurt

julyen (✪ *zhuliyen*) Partly mashed potato dish smothered with melted cheese.

kaban ✪ Wild boar

käklik ▲ Quail

kalapacha ▲ 'Head and toes': Lamb *xash* with extra brains! Eaten only by men, with vodka – or tutovka if you want to show off!

käläm ▲ Cabbage

käläm dolması ▲ Cabbage-leaf dolma, see *Dolma*.

karalok ▲ A type of persimmon that's harder and less digestible than *xurma*.

karişik izgara ♠ Mixed grill.

karni yarik ♠ Literally 'split belly'. Aubergines stuffed with herbs and minced meat – effectively the same as *badimcan dolması*.

kartof ▲ (*kartozhki* ✪) Potato

kartut ▲ Black mulberries

käshki badimcan Ⅱ Eggplant in Iranian whey

Kazbeguri ✤ Sizzling meatball and egg dish.

kbdari (see Gubdari)

kebab ▲/✧ Basically anything which is barbecued qualifies as a kebab! This could be meat, fish or vegetable: 'kartof kebab' are effectively jacket potatoes. However, if someone offers you 'kebab' without giving further details, you are probably going to get a crispy plateful of fatty mutton. See also Adana, Döner, Iskender, Köfte, Lule, Shashlyk, Şiş, Tikä, Urfa.

kharcho ✤ Rich, often spicy Georgian soup with ground walnuts, chicken and tomato. The Azeri *xarço* is usually blander.

khinkali/khingal ✤ Unpronounceable Georgian ravioli-like balls. To eat, hold the twisted doughy knob and try to bite into one without spraying yourself with boiling-hot meaty juices. See also Xinqal.

Kievski kotleta ✪ Chicken Kiev. The most commonly available alternative to shashlyk.

kilki ✪ Russian for Çiça (qv)

kişniş ▲ (also *kinza*) Sprigs of coriander leaves, as ubiquitous as tomatoes on an Azeri dinner table.

kızılgül sok ▲ Rose-water (literally 'golden flower juice').

kızıl ahmät ▲ A type of apple whose flesh goes red on being bitten.

köfte kebab ♠ Lightly spiced minced lamb/mutton and onion fried in balls or barbecued in strips.

kompot ✪ Mixed fruit in light syrup.

kotleta ✪ Minced-meat croquette.

kourma ▲ see Qovurma.

kuchmachi ✛ Boiled assorted tripe and lung, flavoured with walnut.

külcha ▲ Sour-dough rolls topped with a smear of semi-sweet flour/yogurt/herb paste.

kupati ✛ Georgian country sausage.

kuptari ✛ see gubdari.

kuri zharennie ✪ Roast chicken often served with mashed potato and gravy.

kutab ▲ see Qutab

kütüm/kuku ▲ Halfway between scrambled egg and an omelette, most commonly eaten with onion and tomato.

lahmacun ♠ Very thin bready circles dotted with minced meat: not pizza despite the appearance. Wrap around parsley and sliced tomato then add a squeeze of lemon.

langet ✪/✛ (▲ lanqet) Minute steak

lapsha ✪ Noodle soup

lavangi ▲ Talysh dish of chicken (or fish) with walnut/onion/plum stuffing.

lavash ▲/✛ Wafer-thin bread strips – should be eaten fresh from the bakery.

lavashana ▲ Wafer-thin strips of very sour dried plum purée used as a flavouring in cooking. A hard to find sweetened version makes a tangy snack.

lobya ▲/✛ Beans. Various bean-based dishes and salads are lumped together under this title. In Georgian cuisine expect a spicy bean hot-pot.

lülä/lulya/lule kebab ▲ Köfte-style spiced meat pressed around wide, flat skewers and barbecued (same as *kubideh* in Iran). Often served wrapped in *lavash* bread.

manti ♠✪ Like ravioli, served in a thin consommé-style soup or with garlic yogurt.

märci supu ▲ Lentil soup

matsonye ✛ A sometimes lumpy soured

milk or cream often used as a garnish/dip.

mecimek ♠ Lentils. Turkish lentil soup is excellent with fresh lemon.

mehr ▲ Tart, tasty citrus fruit which is half orange, half lemon.

mimosa salat ✛ Potato, carrots, mayonnaise and grated cheese.

mindal ▲ Hazelnuts with a sweet, crispy coating. Typical of Shäki.

monastirski ✪ Style of preparing meat fillets smothered with mayonnaise and melted cheese.

morok ▲ Blackberries or raspberries.

mtsvadi ✛ Georgian name for shashlyk.

murabba ▲ Jam/conserve usually served with tea rather than spread on bread. Eat with a spoon or stir into the tea as you prefer.

müsämma ▲ Stewed chicken in a tomato-based sauce.

myasa ✪ Meat

narşarab ▲ Concentrated pomegranate sauce, accompaniment to shashlyk/sturgeon.

nasuk ▲ Saffron-flavoured stuffed pastry.

nohut ▲ Chick peas. Boiled, lightly salted chick peas are de rigueur with beer.

ojakhuri ✛ Popular fried pork and potato meal.

okroshka ✪ Russian name for *doğrama*.

ovdux ▲ Alternative name for *doğrama*.

ovma ▲ A heavy pastry using cardamon, cinnamon and other spices.

ovrishta ▲ Chicken dish with a butter, cherry and onion sauce.

parpatöyun ▲ Pursane – a wild green vegetable. Pickled with garlic or as seasoning.

pashtet ✪ Liver and onions fried and ground into paté-like paste. Often served as a roulade.

patinlecan ♠ Aubergine/eggplant (*badimcan* in Azeri). Great as a purée with *lahmacun*.

patisson ▲/✪ Round, UFO-shaped green squash (vegetable).

paxlava ▲ see Bakhlava

paytaxt salat ✪ (stolichny salad) typical Russian-style potato salad in mayonnaise

pazı ▲ Beetroot (but *burak* more common)

pechen ✪ Liver

pelmeni ✪ Meat ravioli-dumplings similar to *manti*.

pertama ▲ Boiled on the bone hunks of mutton served in the broth, typically flavoured with onion and coriander and drizzled with sour cream.

phalki ❖ Various salads incorporating ground walnuts. Typically spinach based.

pide ♠ Thicker base, longer version of *lahmacun*. Various styles including *peynirli* (with cheese), *sucuklu* (with salami), *karishik* (mixed), *kiymali* (normal ie with minced meat), *etli/kush bashili* (with diced meat – not chick peas).

pilav ❖ Rice dishes cooked in a vast variety of styles, eg ▲ *govurma*/❖ *plov* (with lamb) ▲ *shirin* (dried fruit), ▲ *sudli* (milk), ▲ *toyug* (chicken).

pirojki ▲/*pirozhki* ◯ Greasy doughnut-style snack, normally with a potato (*kartoflu/kartozhki*) filling; ▲ *atli*/◯ *myasom* versions are loosely stuffed with mince and onion, ▲ *jiyar*/◯ *pechonkoi* with liver. Commonly sold in a scrap of newspaper on street corners.

pirzola ♠ T-bone steak

pistolet ◯ Ribs. More commonly called *entrekot/antreqot*.

piti ▲ Potato, chick pea, vegetable and fatty mutton stewed with fresh tomatoes or saffron, served in individual earthenware pots. Soak the juice in bread, then mash the solids together into a paste before eating.

piva ❖ Beer – also written as pivo, pivasi etc depending on the grammatical case.

plov see Pilav, Ash.

pomidor ▲/◯ Tomato

püre ▲ Mashed potato

puri ❖ Bread served with any Georgian meal. *Dedapuri* is a stretched version.

…qaburğası ▲ …chops (ie lamb or pork)

qamburger ▲ Hamburger but not necessarily McDonald's style – could be hot or cold and the 'burger' might be a simple slice of spam.

…qarnirlä ▲ … with garnish

qatiq ▲ Sour milk

qayğana ▲ Scrambled egg

qiymä ▲ Minced lamb

qızardılmış ▲ fried (as a way of cooking)

qlazok ▲ Fried egg

qoç yumurta ♠ Rams' testicles

qovurma Various fruity variations of *Bozartma*. Although often translated as 'kourma' on menus it is not related to an Indian korma curry.

qoyun ▲ Lamb

qoz ❖/▲ Walnut. If you're offered *qoz murabbasi* – literally 'walnut jam' – don't be put off by the appearance. The irregular black balls are sweet, conserved, immature walnuts with a unique and appealing flavour that defies description.

qreçka ▲ Boiled, split Bulgar wheat. Considered a somewhat low-class staple but is edible – often served in cheaper restaurants with a hint of eggy or tomato sauce.

qril ▲ Spit-roast chicken, usually sold whole.

quläş ▲ Goulash

qutab ▲ A thin pancake filled with spinach/greens (*göyarti kutabi*), meat (*at kutabi*) or occasionally pumpkin (*qabaq kutabi*). Served with sour cream in restaurants but cheap (around 40q) and good as a street snack if bought fresh from the grill plate.

quyruq kebab Much appreciated cut from the plump rear of a sheep, almost entirely fat.

quzu ▲ Lamb as opposed to mutton.

ragu ◯ Stew

rakı ♠ Colourless aniseed liqueur similar in flavour to Pastis/Pernod. Add water. Turks, especially from the Adana region, follow a raki with a *shalgam,* a carrot-extract chaser.

ramşteks ▲ Steak or meat cutlet

rheyma ▲ Talysh variety of vegetable dolma.

rhingkale ❖ See *Khingkali*.

riba ◯ Fish. See *Baliq*.

rulet ▲/◯ Roulet – ie a pastry roll with various, usually sweet, fillings.

sabsi Ⅱ Greens. See *Göy*.

sac ▲ Various pan-fried meat-and-potato dishes. Often very oily. Pronounced Saj.

sähär yemëkläri ▲ Breakfast menu

şalgam ♠ Carrot extract chaser drunk after raki; best with a squeeze of lemon.

şamama ▲ Variety of small, sweet melon used as a lewd metaphor in Vagif's poetry.

şampan ▲ Sparkling wine

şärab ▲ Wine

şatobrian ▲ Chateaubriand steak

satsivi ❖ Walnut, garlic and herbs combined to form a unique paste. Served with poultry.

…sayaği ▲ … style

sebzeli kebab ♠ Vegetable kebab.

semichki ◯ Sunflower seeds (▲ Tum).

shashlyk The ubiquitous skewered lumps of mutton that rule right across central Asia; see pp22-3.

shchi ✪ Cabbage soup

shkemeruli ✧ Chicken in garlic

shuba ✪ Literally 'fur hat' – a salad with potato, fish, carrots and beets layered in mayonnaise.

shurpa ✪ Vegetable soup

şilä ▲ A type of plov/ash in which the rice is boiled in mutton broth.

şirä ▲ Juice/soft drink (plural *şirälär*)

şirin ▲ Means sweet: in cookery it usually implies the use of dried fruit in the recipe.

sirka ▲ Vinegar. Add in moderation to your *Duşbärä*.

sir(om) ✪ (with) cheese

şiş/shish kebab ♠ see Shashlyk

şorba ▲ Soup (♠ *Chorba*, ✪ *Sup*)

şor gogal ▲ A puff-pastry snack

sosiska ▲✪ Sausage/frankfurter

soyutma ▲ The same ingredients as *Pertama* but the meat is served dry, perhaps with the broth in a separate bowl.

sucuk ♠ Spicy salami

sudak ▲ Pike-perch (fish)

suluguni ✧ White, home-made smoked cheese. Sometimes served fried.

sumak ▲ A common red seasoning which is said to bring out the flavour of mutton. Looks like paprika but is in fact made from the crushed petals of the *rhus* bush.

sup (suplar) ▲ Soup (soups).

şuyud ▲ Fine green herbs/dill.

suzmä ▲ White curd cheese (✪ tvorog).

tabaka ✧ Style of grilling poultry. Typically a whole bird beaten flat!

tandir ✧ A traditional clay oven, or the bread baked therein.

tarhun/tarkhuni ▲/✧ Tarragon, a spindly leaved herb which makes a minty-flavoured syrup, popular as a drink when mixed with soda water.

tatara ✧ Rubbery brown confection made from boiled, triple-pressed grape extract.

tava-äti ▲ A hot-pot of mutton and roughly cut vegetables/potatoes.

tavuk ♠ Chicken

tel A chewy sweet/candy

tikä ▲ Hunks of barbecued meat on a skewer, ie the most common form of shashlyk.

tkemali ✧ Georgian *naşarab*

toyuq ▲ Chicken

tum ▲ Sunflower seeds.

turac ▲ Small game birds the size of quail.

tut arağı ▲ A dangerously potent firewater distilled from mulberries. Was most famously produced in Zangilan province, now occupied by Armenia.

tutovka ✪ Widely used but technically Russian term for Tut Arağı.

tvorog ✪ White curd cheese

ukha ✪ Fish soup

Urfa kebab ♠ Two forms: one is virtually the same as lüle kebab, the other is like meat-balls skewered in between tomatoes then grilled.

vermişel ▲ Macaroni

vineqret ▲ Bean and red-cabbage salad

xama ▲ Smetana, sour cream

xarici ▲ Means 'Imported'.

xaş ▲✧ Khash, khashi, or hash. The ingredients vary but it's likely to be the least appealing bits of sheep (eg tripe and trotters) or cow, served up as a garlic-supercharged breakfast stew. A noted hangover cure, it is served with vodka: usually only to men!

…xämirdä ▲ battered (ie cooking style as per fish and chips)

xinqal ▲ Pasta squares served with minced lamb and broth. NB *Gürcü Xinqäl* is the Azeri term for Georgian *Khingkali*.

xiyar ▲ Cucumber; *xiyar pamidor salati* is simply slices of cucumber and tomato.

xot doq ✧/✪ Hot dog. The 20q 'hot dogs' from Baku bakeries are frankfurters baked into a bread roll. They're not necessarily hot.

xurma ▲ Persimmon/kaki/sharon fruit; in early December these trees are leafless but are covered with their brilliant orange fruit especially around Balakän. Xurma also means dates.

yarpag dolmasi ♠/▲ vine-leaf *dolma*.

yumurta ♠/▲ Egg

zharkoe ✪ Literally means 'hot' so you might get anything. In reality you'll probably end up with a plate of steak, fried potatoes, and the odd vegetable.

zirinj ▲ Tiny tart red berries.

zoğol Red berries the size of rosehips but with a more citric flavour (*kizil* ✪ from the Turkish word 'red'). Cornelian cherries.

zoğol arağı ▲ A zoğol version of *tutovka* but said to be a little less fearful for hangovers.

Key: ▲ Azeri; ✣ Georgian; ✦ Greater Caucasus area; ✪ Russian/ex Soviet; ♠ Turkish; Ⅱ Persian; # Other origin

Abkhazia ✣ The north-western geographical 'claw' of Georgia with lovely crag-backed beaches. Its de facto independence since 1992 was recognized by Russia in 2008 following the summer war with Georgia. Border with Georgia currently closed.

ADR Azerbaijan Democratic Republic (1918-20)

Aghovanq ▲ Ancient Georgian and Armenian name for Azerbaijan/Albania.

AH Abbreviation for Al Hijrah – Muslim years are dated from AH1 ie AD622.

Alans The ethnic predecessors of today's Ossetians, this historic people ruled much of the north Caucasus from the 10th century until their state was smashed by the Mongols.

Albania ▲ Confusing name for the region which was later to develop into Azerbaijan.

Albanian Church ▲ Formerly independent church with its own liturgy and a philosophy between Georgian Orthodoxy and Nestorian-influenced Assyrian Catholicism.

Ali Bayramli ▲ The name of Şirvan city between 1938 and 2008, in honour of a 1920s political activist.

aoul A fortified Dağestani mountain village/homestead.

Aragvi 300 ✣ The group of Georgian warriors who fought to the death with King Irakli II in 1795.

Aran/Arran # Former geographical name for lowland Azerbaijan used originally by Arab sources referring to the area between the Kura and Araz rivers. Along with Shirvan refers to the area once known as (Caucasian) Albania.

Aras/Araz The 1060km river which forms Azerbaijan's southern border, possibly the Biblical Gihon river.

Araxes # Alternative name for the Araz river as used by Herodotus.

Ardebil Former khanate and historically important city in southern Azerbaijan, now a regional capital in northern Iran.

armudi ▲ Literally 'pear' but also the name for the pinch-waist tea glasses.

Ashug/Aşiq ▲ Performer of *muğam* or praise singer.

Azadistan ('Land of Freedom') Name for Southern (Iranian) Azerbaijan while briefly autonomous under Khiyabani April-September 1920.

Azərbaycan Azerbaijan spelt the Azeri way.

bağ ▲ garden

banya ✣✪ Bathhouse/sauna. ▲ Hamam.

bayaty ▲ Four-line Persian/Azeri poem – a rough equivalent of haiku eg by Fuzuli.

Black Hundreds The Russian-led shadowy *agents provocateurs* who set about stirring up inter-communal discord and massacres in the Caucasus to divert attention from anti-Russian sentiment – most notably during 1905.

Black January ▲ On 20-21 January 1990 over a hundred Baku civilians were massacred by Soviet troops following earlier severe inter-ethnic fighting (12-14 Jan).

Brest-Litovsk ✪ After the 1917 revolutions, Russia was initially very vulnerable. But Germany was not in a strong position to attack as it was facing a strong push on the Western front so she decided to sue for a quick peace. At the resultant Treaty of Brest Litovsk, Lenin played political poker by signing away Ukraine, Finland, the Baltics and Georgia as independent states, and ceding Batumi, Kars and Ardahan to Turkey. Brest Litovsk also promised 25% of Baku's oil would be supplied to Germany. The Bolshevik commune, however, was in no position to fulfil this so the Germans continued their progress across the Caucasus to grab it for themselves, squabbling on the way with their supposed allies, the Turks, who eventually reached Baku first. Lenin's gamble eventually paid off – by 1922 the Red Army had reclaimed much of the 'lost lands', though Ardahan and Kars remain Turkish.

Caliphate The Arab empire of the 7th-10th centuries whose rulers claimed direct descendancy from the prophet Mohammad's brother-in-law Ali.

catholicos Pope equivalent in independent church hierarchies (including Albanian, Georgian etc).

çay ❖ means 'Tea'. As a suffix to a name however, it means 'River'

çayxana ❖ Teahouse. Assume a 100%-male clientele.

çimarlik ▲ Beach

CIS Commonwealth of Independent States. Loose successor to the USSR. Nominal capital, Minsk. All former Soviet states are members, except Estonia, Latvia and Lithuania. Georgia and Azerbaijan were effectively forced to join after extreme initial reticence.

Colchis ❖ A semi-mythical kingdom in Western Georgia based around Kutaisi.

Dashnaks Armenian nationalists.

Derbend Caspian city across in Dağestan (Russia) with strong traditional links to Azerbaijan. Famed for its 'iron gates'. Some consider it an historically 'Azeri' city.

Dighur Alternative name for Posof, the Turkish–Georgian border

Dukhabori ❍❖ Literally 'Spirit Wrestler' – a protestant religious sect similar to Molokans. Dukhabori villages in Azerbaijan included Saratovka. Read *The Spirit Wrestler*s by Philip Marsden.

Dunsterforce ▲ The rag-tag British forces operating during WWI in Persia, a detachment of which arrived too late to 'defend' Baku from Turkish invasion in August 1918. Commanded by General Dunsterville.

D/Y ▲ Damir Yol ie Railway

Ehsan ▲ On the 3rd, 7th and 40th day after somebody dies and at each anniversary, relatives give gifts (usually meat) to friends and neighbours on behalf of the deceased.

Ev/Evi ▲ House

Farsi Ⅱ The language of Iran

Favvaralar Meydan ▲ Fountains Square

gavür ▲ Non Muslim

Gazaka ▲ Former capital (or major settlement) of Atropatena. The site was probably near Didivan (on the Armenian border) rather than exactly where today's Qazax lies.

Gihon Biblical name for the Araz river.

Gonbad Ⅱ Persian equivalent of a Tomb Tower, see Turbe.

Guebers A name often used by Western visitors to describe Baku's fire worshippers (17th-19th centuries); alternately Magi.

Gülistan/Gülüstan ▲ Paradise

Gülistan Treaty The first of two Russo-Persian treaties dividing Azerbaijan signed in 1813 while Russia was weakened by the Napoleonic campaign. Later supplanted by the more definitive Turkmenchay Treaty.

Gyz Galasi ▲ see Qız Qalası.

hamam ▲▲ Turkic term for hot baths (❍ Banya).

Hurufism ▲ A 'blasphemous' belief that God exists in the heart rather than as a physical entity in His own right. It also held that special words and letters have a power of their own, ie somewhat like Transcendental Meditation. Initially propounded by Naimi and later adopted by the great poet Nasimi (NB not Nizami).

IDP Internally displaced person (ie a refugee within one's own country).

Il-Khan Dynasty Ⅱ Gradually Islamicized Mongol dynasty ruling Persia. Especially in southern Azerbaijan, they encouraged major regeneration projects and built the great (now ruined) city of Soltaniye. The empire slipped following Timur's invasion in 1380, allowing Turkey and Azerbaijan greater independence.

Isfahan Ⅱ Iran's most beautiful city, glorified by Shah Abbas I with the help of Christian craftsmen deported from Julfa/Culfa) – in Nakhchivan, Azerbaijan.

istirahät ▲ Rest. Hence Istirahät Zonasi (rest zone with accommodation), Istirahät Guçäsi (rest zone with food), Istirahät Märkäzi (with either).

Kachalka ▲ 'Nodding donkey' pump, invented by Azeri engineer Karim Aliverdizade.

Kartli ❖ Central region of Georgia including Tbilisi and Mtskheta, the ancient capital.

Kartuli ❖ 'Of Kartli' ie the Georgian word for Georgian.

Kaspiskoe More ❍ Caspian Sea, box p72.

Khan Ruler of a khanate, equivalent to a king.

Khanende ▲ The honorific name given to a master of Muğam music – theoretically only awarded to one who has mastered all seven forms.

Khazar/Xazar ❖ Invading tribes who attacked Azerbaijan from the north during much of its history.

Khazar Denizi ♣/▲ Caspian Sea (box p72).

Khazri ▲ Blustering wind blowing off the Caspian.

Khurufism ✧ see Hurufism.

kishlaq ▲ Winter pastures to which flocks are moved from summer mountain 'qaylaq' meadows.

Kür ▲ Kura River (Mktvari in Georgian)

kurort ✪ Sanatorium resort.

Kutkashen ▲ The former (and still commonly used) name for Qäbälä town.

LAOs (Large Abandoned Objects) A handy term coined by Wendell Steavenson (see p350), referring to the ubiquitous lumps of concrete, twisted metal and abandoned wrecks of unidentifiable buildings that are a major Soviet landscape legacy.

Mädäniyyat Evi ▲ Culture house

madrassa ✧ Islamic seminary. The Seljuks used these educational institutions to instil a conformity to Islamic ideology over their empire.

magara ▲ Cave.

magi The pre-Zoroastrian priestly class who probably wangled the reinstatement of fire reverence in later Persian state Zoroastrianism.

Mammed/Mammad ▲ Common first name. In the 1990s it was the nickname for the 1000 old-Manat banknote which featured Mammad Rasulzade.

March Days ▲ Baku street riots of 30 March to 1 April 1918 during which ethnic Azeris were attacked and their property looted and burned. Some suspect that the short-lived Communist leadership under ethnic Armenian Stepen Shaumian turned at best a blind eye.

maşrut ▲ Minibus/private shared taxi; ✪ Marshrutnoe taksı, marshrutka.

mehrab # The niche in a mosque which points the direction of Mecca (and thus of prayer).

MFA Ministry of Foreign Affairs

Miabanol Christian community of Nakhchivan which kept itself distinct from Catholic and Armenian Uniate churches and was subsumed into the Dominican order in 1583.

minbar # Stepped furniture within a mosque equivalent to a pulpit in a church.

Mktvari ✣ Kura River, Kür in Azeri

Mollah Muslim cleric.

Molokans ✪✧ Russian Christians of a sect which rejects the ornate churches of Orthodoxy in favour of simple piety. Prayers are said in local homes, not churches, without the aid of icons or crosses. Philosophically similar to Quakers in the West. Considered heretical, most Molokans were forced to leave Russia-proper during the reign of Catherine II (the Great) 1761-96. Many settled first in Ukraine before moving on to the Caucasus in 1867 and after the 1905 revolution. Unique in Azerbaijan, Ivanovka (p209) remains a largely Russian-Molokan village. There were once many more but during the early 1990s many Molokans left for Russia.

muğam ▲ The popular hypnotic if droning, improvised vocal style accompanying traditional Azeri music. The style was popularized in Shusha nearly two centuries ago as a way to jazz up teachings of the Koran. Aficionados divide the classical form into seven sub-types: Bayati-Shiraz, Chargah, Hamayun, Rast, Seygah, Shur and Shushter.

Mugan ▲ The steppe region on the Caspian coast area, south of Ğobustan.

MUM ▲ Central department store.

Murids ▲ Literally 'disciples' – fanatical, mystically puritanical Muslims for whom battling infidels was considered a form of religious purification. They conducted a holy war against the Russian invaders in the Caucasus from 1770 but especially after 1830 from a base at Gimri (Dağestan). See box on p237 for more on their leader, Shamil.

Musavat ▲ Rasulzade's Azeri nationalist party who fought with the Bolshevik Baku Soviet during 1918 eventually coming to power during the brief spell of independence. Today's opposition Musavat party has only the name in common with the original movement.

namaz ▲ Prayer

Natasha Common Russian female first name. Colloquially, however, it can be used as a slang term for a woman engaged in the 'oldest profession'.

nazir ▲ Religious or superstitious offering, typically money or sugar.

Neft Dashlari 'Oil Rocks', ✪ Neftyanye Kamni: the world's only mid-sea stilt town. See p152.

Niva Ubiquitous 4WD vehicle, cheaper but less sturdy than a UAZ

Nukha ▲ The original name for Shäki's 'new' (ie 1772) site, ie the present centre.

Oğuz ✧ A federation of nomadic Turkic tribes which expanded progressively westward, settling in western Kazakhstan around the 8th century and Azerbaijan from the 10th century.

Ossetia The divided 'homeland' of the Ossete/Ossetian people, a north Caucasus ethnic group with its own language, descendants of the historical Alans. North Ossetia is now part of the Russian Federation. South Ossetia is legally part of Georgia despite having declared 'independence' in the early 1990s. Russia recognized that independence as of 2008 following the short summer war during which Russian forces invaded.

ovdan ▲ Access point to reach an underground spring or stream. Before the building of the great canal from Samur to Xırdalan reservoir, Baku had a very limited water supply and in nearby desert villages such as Zığ, ancient ovdans can still be seen. A once-common alternative type of ovdan stored snow and ice.

Pajero Popular brand of 4WD vehicle, made by Mitsubishi.

Parsee The Zoroastrians driven out of Iran who settled in India.

Partakaran ▲ Ancient name for Beylaqan. Means 'capital'.

Partav ▲ Old name for Bärdä.

pir ▲ A holy place, not necessarily Islamic. Indeed many supposedly Muslim pirs seem to be distinctly animist.

Pontus ✧ Former kingdom in western Georgia/Eastern Anatolia.

Popular Front ▲ The umbrella opposition movement that brought Elchibey to power in 1992. Now a much less important political party.

Potëmkin Pronounced 'Potyom-kin'. Grigori Potëmkin had been Catherine the Great's foreign minister and lover (died 1791). A 1905 mutiny on a battleship of the same name became one of the catalysts for the first Russian revolution.

provodnik ❂ Railway-carriage attendant, *provodnitsa* if female (see p16).

putiovka ❂ The form – either a doctor's prescription or a permissory note from a local business or trade union – which allows you to stay in a sanatorium.

Qajar dynasty Ⅱ Ruthless 19th-century Persian dynasty whose attractive mosque designs are deemed 'insignificant' by architectural scholars. Overthrown in 1926 and replaced by the Pahlivis, Iran's last imperial dynasty.

qaylaq ▲ Summer pastures. The occupation of Nagorno Karabagh has not only displaced populations, it has also prevented the traditional annual movement of sheep between their winter *kishlaq*s of central Azerbaijan to their summer *qaylaq*s (qv) in the Karabagh mountains.

Qibla The direction of Mecca and thus of Muslim prayer. Mosques have a niche to point this out.

Qirkan ▲ Old name for the Talysh (Southern) region of Azerbaijan.

Qız Qalası ▲ Maiden's Tower. Name for a castle that suggests unviolated invincibility. Often applied to any tower for which the original history has been forgotten. *Orlan Qalası* (Boy's tower) and *Namerd Qala* (Traitor's castle) are less common but related terms.

raff ▲ A Soviet-made, sharp-nosed minibus.

şadlıq sarayı ▲ Wedding Palace, ie glitzy oversized restaurant that usually opens only for banquets. These places are generally the grandest modern buildings in most rural Azerbaijani towns.

Sadval ▲ Shadowy Lezghian separatist movement held responsible for the March 1994 Baku metro bombs.

Safavid dynasty ✧Ⅱ Dynasty who ruled the Persian empire 1501-1722. As the founder, Ismail I, was an Azeri poet, some claim that it was a 'Greater Azerbaijan' empire not Iran at all – at least until the accession of Shah Abbas in 1587.

Sahil ▲ 'Seaside' (❂ Primorsk).

Sakartvelo ✧ Georgia in Georgian.

Samtskhe ✧ Georgian for Meskhia.

scat A style of jazz singing where words are replaced by meaningless syllables giving an instrumental effect.

Section 907 1990s' US legislation passed preventing inter-governmental aid to Azerbaijan in punishment for blockading the Qazax–Yerevan railway. This very biased law was influenced by a strong pro-Armenian lobby in the US and overlooked the fact that Armenian forces had earlier cut the Baku–Nakhchivan railway for which they received no similar reprimand.

Seljuk (Selcuk) Turks ♠◇Ⅱ Originally a nomadic warrior tribe who gained control over Khorasan (Turkmenistan), the Seljuks consolidated an 11th-century empire covering most of Persia, Azerbaijan and the Middle East. Embracing Islam en route they defeated the Byzantine army and captured its emperor at the battle of Manzikert (northwest of Lake Van) in 1071 beginning the Turkish settlement of what is now Turkey.

Seyid A blood descendant of the Prophet Mohammad.

Sharia Law # A legal system based upon the word of the holy scriptures of Islam.

Shäki Khanate ▲ Lasted 1742 to 1820 though in the last 15 years merely as a Russian pawn.

Shi'ite From the Arabic shi'at Ali (followers of Ali). Originally referring to those who backed Ali's son following Ali's assassination, 24 January 661.

Shirvan/Şirvan ▲ (1) The historic kingdom of eastern Azerbaijan based at Shamakha and Baku; (2) The 10,000 Old-Manat banknote (3) the post-2008 name for Äli Bayramlı city

Shirvanshah ▲ Ruler of Shirvan.

SOCAR ▲ State Oil Company of the Azerbaijan Republic. SOCAR Circle is a nickname for AzNeft Square in Baku.

Sunni The majority form of world Islam in which faith is vested in the accuracy of the *sunnah*, the holy scriptures, without the need for a temporal religious leader.

Syrian Fathers ✣ Not Syrian at all but a group of 13 Georgian monks who studied in various Middle Eastern centres of Christianity and returned to found an ascetic monastic order in their homeland including Ikalto, Nekresi and David Gareja. David chose the uninviting caves of southern Kaheti.

Tamada ✣ The title for the toastmaster at any Georgian feast or celebration. He should be sensitive yet funny and able to down his drink at each round miraculously without getting drunk!

tarix ◇ History. Tarixi Muzeyi = historical museum.

Tatar ♠▲ A confusing term due to a multiplicity of inexact usages. Often applied to ethnic Azeris during the 19th century.

Tats ▲ A somewhat fuzzily defined term for the population/language of Persian-Aryans who were settled in the Caucasus centuries before the arrival of the Turkic peoples. By some definitions the term includes Azerbaijan's 'mountain Jews'.

tolkuchka ▲ Big, crowded 'push and shove' flea markets – Tolkat means push.

TRACECA ✣ The EU-sponsored 'new Silk Route' that aims to improve the transport corridor linking Europe and Central Asia, across the Caucasus nations.

turbaza ✪ Hut accommodation in a sort of low-tech holiday camp.

turbe ◇ Turkic term for a tomb tower (Ⅱ *Gonbad*) 11th-17th century, see pp65-6.

Türki ▲ A term used by writers such as Mirza Fatali Akhundov for the Azerbaijani language.

Turkmanchay Treaty ✪Ⅱ▲ The agreement that settled the Russo-Persian war of 1826-8 and was responsible for the permanent division of Azerbaijan and gave Russia control of Nakhchivan. Signed in Turkmenchay, today a small town in Iran.

UAZ Tough 4WD vehicle either styled like a WWII jeep or as a 'Wazik' mini-van.

Univermag/Universam ✪ (▲ MUM) Communist-era department stores.

Villa Petrolea Originally the home of the Nobels (now in Nizami Park, Black Town, eastern Baku). Villa Petrolea II in Bayil (south Baku) is BP's Baku HQ.

Xätirä Memorial

YPX Traffic police

Zhiguli The 'standard', indestructible Lada saloon car.

Zoroastrianism World's first monotheistic religion which became the unifying philosophy of Achaemanid Persia. Its prophet was Zarathustra who set about cleansing Persian religious life of its various animist rituals. At first the the Magi (Iranian priestly class) appeared to 'convert' to his new creed. But over time they reintroduced many of the pre-Zarathustran rituals including fire and water 'worship' which the prophet had considered inappropriate. Ironically, like Santa, chocolate eggs and Christmas trees in Christianity, these elements today are often better known than the religion's real philosophical message

APPENDIX D: WHO'S WHO

City streets across Azerbaijan are usually named after people. In the Soviet era these were often political or revolutionary leaders. Post independence, most are writers, painters and musicians. This section gives brief biographical sketches of some of the most important such Azeris and of other key historical figures in the region. You might be interested to compare my who's who with a more official version: 🖳 http://library.aliyev-heritage.org/en/6275267.html.

Key: ❖ Georgian; ▲ Azerbaijani; ✧ Greater Azerbaijan (including north Iran); ✪ Russian/other CIS; Ⅱ Persian/Iranian; ♠ Turkish; # Other nation; ☌ Popular during the communist era, now out of favour.

Abbas I (1571-1629) Ⅱ Great Persian Shah, contemporary of Suleiman the Magnificent (Turkey), Akbar the Great (Moghul India) and Elizabeth I (England). While his reign (1587-1629) did wonders for the tourist potential of Isfahan (Iran), it was devastating for parts of Azerbaijan and eastern Georgia. He destroyed Julfa (now Culfa, Nakhchivan, p311) in 1604, killed Queen Ketevan after his first trot around Georgia in 1614 and when he returned two years later he had around a quarter of the population of Kaheti killed. Many more Kahetians were deported to central Iran and culturally Georgian villages are still said to exist around Fereydun Shahr. More positively he ordered the building of the Juma Mosque in Gänjä.

Acami, Nakhchivani ▲ Leader of the 12th-century architectural renaissance and designer of the Momine Xatun Mausoleum in Nakhchivan city.

Agmashenabeli, David ❖ 'David the Builder' qv.

Ali, Imam # 4th Caliph (656-661) and most revered Shiite Imam – married Fatima, the daughter of the prophet Mohammed; buried at Najaf, Iraq.

Aliyev, Abulfaz ▲ See Elchibey.

Aliyev, Heydar Ali Rzaogli ('Heydar Baba') (1923-2003) ▲ Azerbaijan's father-figure, president 1992-2003. Also led Azerbaijan (1969-83) before becoming the 'first Turk' in the USSR Politburo. He was dropped in 1987, possibly because Gorbachev didn't want complaints as Russia started stirring up trouble in Nagorno Karabagh. Aliyev returned to Nakhchivan where he lived in relative austerity, became

Nakhchivan's leader and developed close Nakhchivan-Turkish relationships during the first months of Azerbaijan's independence. During Surat Husseinov's military putsch against the Elchibey government, Aliyev flew to Baku, lending a hand as a figure of authority to hold the country together. He was named speaker of parliament and deputy president. When Elchibey fled, Aliyev took over the reins of power and defused the military rebellion. After a referendum showed that the population no longer recognized Elchibey, new elections were held which overwhelmingly confirmed Aliyev as president. Aliyev was re-elected in 1998 and was initially a candidate in 2003. However, he collapsed during a televised speech shortly before his 80th birthday breaking some ribs as he fell. He never fully recovered and while his son Ilham, see below, won the summer 2003 election Heydar remained in hospital in the US amid much speculation that he had already passed away. Since his death his personality cult has snowballed with main streets, parks, and buildings all over the country named after him (and to a lesser extent his wife Zarifä Aliyeva).

Aliyev, Ilham (1961-) ▲ President of Azerbaijan (🖳 www.president.az). Once honoured by the world's press with the unlikely label 'playboy' (for his devil-may-care moustache?!) he was groomed for succession by his father, former president Heydar Aliyev.

Aliyev, Natiq ▲ Energy minister, former chairman of SOCAR

Aliyev, Rafiq (1967-) ▲ Former president of AzPetrol arrested under curious circumstances in October 2005. His brother

Farhad (🖳 http://faliyev.org/en), former minister of Economic Development was also incarcerated and the brothers' legal position has been the subject of a US congressional resolution (🖳 www.govtrack.us/congress/bill.xpd?bill=hc110-183).

Aliyeva, Mehriban (1964-) ▲ Wife of President Ilham Aliyev, Mehriban is widely considered by the Azeri press to be the world's most glamorous First Lady (🖳 www.mehriban-aliyeva.org). One of her crowd-pleasing jobs is to head the Heydar Aliyev foundation and thus she gets to give away large amounts of money to selected good causes. See also Pashayev, Mir Jalal (p368), her granddad.

Aliyeva, Zärifä (1923-85) ▲ Azerbaijan's most famous opthamologist was not uncoincidentally married to Heydar Aliyev and mother of president Ilham Aliyev. See 🖳 www.zarifa-aliyeva.az.

Amirani ❖ The Georgian mythical equivalent of Prometheus, Amirani was chained in a cave on Mt Kazbek.

Amirov, Fikrat (1922-84) ▲ Celebrated 20th-century composer of 'symphonic' muğam. Son of Mashadi Jamil Amirov.

Amirov, Mashadi Jamil (1875-1928) ▲ Shusha-born muğam musician, tar-player and composer. In 1915, Amirov's *Seyfal Muluk* gave Bül Bül (see p364) his first singing role.

Äsgerova, Salatyn (1961-91) ▲ Azeri journalist killed while covering the Karabagh war. One of very few women to have been declared a 'National Hero'.

Aslanov, Hazi (1910-45) ▲ WWII tank commander and Soviet hero of Stalingrad who remains a celebrated figure in his home town, Länkäran (p293).

Axmedoglu, Makki ▲ Golden Age geographer and astronomer from Bärdä.

Axundov, Mirzä-Fatali (1812-78) ▲ Writer, critic and philosopher, dubbed the 'Moslem Molière'. Although born in Shäki, his parents split up while he was young and he was brought up in various homes in Gänjä and Ardebil (now Iran). He gravitated to Tbilisi, then the capital of the Caucasus, where he was commissioned by governor Vorontsov to write a series of six comedies for the 'new' theatre.

Axundov, Shirali ▲ Bolshevik revolutionary who led the Soviet take-over of Länkäran, 3 May 1920. Victim of the Stalin purges in 1938.

Azimzade, Azim (1880-1943) ▲ Soviet cartoonist and realist painter. Modestly down-facing bust (p93, S10) amid fountains, house museum at 157 D Aliyev St, Baku (map p92, S5).

Azizbäyov, Meshadi (1876-1918) ▲ A Baku oil-workers' unionist of 1905 who became one of the 26 Commissars (pp96-7) and was shot in Turkmenistan.

Azizbekov Russified variant of Azizbäyov.

Babek, Khorramdin (795-838) ▲ Led the Khuramid anti-Arab uprising against Caliph Ismail Ibn Yasar (see p297 and p38).

Badalbeyli, Afrasiab (1907-76) ▲ Composer who worked with Bül Bül collecting/annotating Azeri folk songs.

Bağirov, Mir Jafar (1896-1956) ▲ Much reviled chief of the Azerbaijan communist party 1933-53, during which time he was an enthusiastic accomplice in the Stalin purges. Executed 1956.

Bagrat III (960-1014) ❖ Began the process of forming a unified Georgia, commemorating his victories by building cathedrals at Kutaisi (1003) and Nikortsminda (1014).

Bahlulzade, Sattar (1909-81) ▲ An archetypal artist who produced colourful pastel Van Gogh-esque landscape paintings which now form the backbone of the state collection of modern art. Grave and great statue in Ämircan (see p146).

Bakixanov, Abbas-Kuliaga (1794-1847) ▲ Controversial historian whose allegorical history of Azerbaijan, *Gulistan Iram*, traced the world's ethnicities back to the family tree of Noah. He supposedly spoke 29 languages and lived in Quba where the historical museum is now ensconced in his bedroom.

Bakixanov, Amad (1892-1973) ▲ Distinguished *tar* musician who founded a folk ensemble and instrument collection to ensure the continuity of traditional Azerbaijani music.

Behbutov, Rashid (1915-88) ▲ Hugely popular operatic tenor famed for his lyrical love songs.

Beria, Lavrenti (1899-1953) ❖◢ Stalin's infamous sidekick and possibly his eventual murderer. Installed as communist party secretary in Tbilisi when Stalin's ineptitude had brought the country to the brink of rebellion (1932). According to Krushchev 'Beria climbed the ladder to power up a mountain of corpses'. He fell off the top, nine months after Stalin's death, executed for treason.

Bicherakhov, Lazar (1882-1952) ○ An almost 'freelance' general who commanded former Tsarist Russian forces in Persia, operating in parallel with Dunsterville during 1918. To gain a foothold in Baku and help 'save' the city from invading Turks he tactically declared himself communist in June 1918. Emigrated to the UK in 1920 and moved to Germany in 1928.

Bül-Bül (Murtuza Rza Mammadov) (1897-1961) ▲ The most famous Azeri singer of all time. See pp96-7 for his house museum.

Cäfär Cabbarly (1899-1934) ▲ Writer born in a hovel near Xızı. Famous dramas include *Sevil* (1928) about women's liberation and *Firuza* (1934) about the changing face of Baku.

Cavid, Huseyn ▲ (1882-1944) Poet whose powerful drama *Sheikh Sanan* involves a love affair between a Muslim man and a Christian girl. Cavid was arrested in the 1937 purges when he refused to put a positive, uplifting communist slant on his tragedies. He died in Siberian exile but was posthumously rehabilitated by Heydar Aliyev. During the 1980s, Aliyev launched a campaign to bring back Cavid's bones to Azerbaijan, the eventual success of which was a celebrated token of Azeri nationalism during the Soviet era. The decision to build the Cavid mausoleum in Nakhchivan during 1993 at the height of the Armenian blockade was even more symbolic in asserting Nakhchivan's optimism in its darkest hour. There is a fine Cavid statue (map p101) near Elmar Akademasi metro, a Nakhchivan Mausoleum/house museum (p309), and a Baku House Museum (p89) across the hall from the Institute of Manuscripts.

Cheläbi, Khan Haji (ruled 1743-59) ▲ Fortified Shäki and declared his khanate independent from the Persian empire.

David the Builder, King (1073-1127) ✤ Ruled Georgia from 1089, broke away from Turkish rule and liberated Tbilisi after 400 years out of Georgian hands (1121). Founded Gelati monastery/college.

Denikin, Anton (1872-1947) ○ Civil war leader of the south Russian army of 'White Russians' (ie pro-Tsar, anti-Bolsheviks); survived the experience and died eventually in Ann Arbor, Michigan, USA.

Djaparidze, Prokopius (1880-1918) ✤ Georgian revolutionary who became chairman of the Baku Soviet in 1918 and was amongst the 26 Commissars who died in mysterious circumstances in Turkmenistan (box pp96-7).

Dumas, Alexandre (1802-70) # The famous French historical novelist (*The Three Musketeers*, *Count of Monte Cristo* etc) was also a great travel writer who visited the Caucasus in the 1850s.

Dunsterville, General Lionel (1865-1946) # Launched the British 'Dunsterforce' mission to hold Baku against the Turks in 1918 and was later British representative in Tiflis (Tbilisi).

Dzhugashvili, Iosep ✤ see Stalin.

DZHxxx – for other names beginning with the Russified spelling 'Dzh' see under 'J'.

Elchibey (real name **Abulfaz Aliyev**) (1939-2000) ▲ Elchibey means 'the messenger'. Teacher who rose to become Popular Front leader and was elected national president in 1992. Fled to his native Nakhchivan in 1993, preventing probable bloodshed of a showdown with the rebel army of Surat Husseinov.

Eldarov, Omar (1927-) Azerbaijan's foremost 20th-century sculptor. Masterworks include the Huseyn Cavid statue (p103), the endlessly expressive Bahlulzade statue at Ämircan (p146), the Mustafazade plaque beside Baku's Meridian Hotel (graphic p57) and numerous fine memorials in Faxri Xiyabani. More straightforward is the central 1955 Natavan (map p92, E3).

Eldegyz ▲ 12th-century lord of western Azerbaijan who developed an autonomous state of Atabeys based initially on Gänjä/Nakhchivan with a palace complex at Alinca (p311).

Fatali Khan (1736-89) ▲ Quba's best-known khan who tried to unify Azerbaijan but was undermined by growing Russian interference. His portrait is in Quba Museum.

Ferdowsi/Firdausi (Abu al Kasim Mansur (940-1020) Ⅱ Celebrated Persian poet whose works including Shahnameh

(*The Book of Kings*) were much studied/reworked by Azeri and Georgian scholars including Nizami.

Fizuli, Mohammad (1494-1556) ▲ Considered the 'father of Azerbaijani poetry' though usually resident in Baghdad, Fizuli's fame derives from his decision to write in the Azeri language. Previous greats such as Nizami and Xhagani had considered Persian was the language of poets. Most famously he rewrote the Firdowsi-Nizami Xamsa classics such as *Leyli and Majnun* in versions that have since proved very popular for operatic adaptation. Fizuli's use of Azeri was encouraged by Shah Ismail I (see Xatai).

G NB for contemporary Azeri 'G' names see under Q, for Russianized Gs see under H

Gajibekov ▲ (see Hajibǎyov).

Gamsakhurdia, Konstantin (1891-1975) ✢ Author of classic historical novels including *David the Builder* and *Abduction of the Moon*; father of Zviad, see below.

Gamsakhurdia, Zviad (1939-93) ✢ Long-term dissident during the USSR era and paranoid Georgian president following the 1991 elections. His stand-off with Russia in refusing to join the CIS led the country into a period of anarchic chaos. Violently ousted from power (1992-3) in battles that gutted much of central Tbilisi. He died in a failed attempt to force a comeback launched in Ajara.

Gatran, Tabrizi (1012-88) II▲ Early 11th-century poet who chronicled the wars of his era and wrote of the spherical world centuries before Copernicus was declared a mad heretic for believing in one. A contemporary critic flattered him thus 'All poets are drops in the ocean. Gatran is the ocean.'

Gazieva, Sevil ▲ The first Azeri woman to drive a cotton harvester, a feat which made her a true proletarian idol. Busts and streets still celebrate her in Baku and Zaqatala.

Gazvini, Zakaria (1203-83) II▲ Persian-Azeri geographer and town planner.

Gogol, Nikolai (1809-52) ✪ Novelist credited with 'modernizing' Russian writing.

Gorbachëv, Mikhail (1931-) ✪ Soviet leader famed in the West for his 'brave' introduction of perestroika and glasnost but widely loathed throughout most of the former Soviet Union. In Azerbaijan he is

blamed for the 20th January massacre in Baku and is commonly held responsible for stirring the Nagorno-Karabagh problem into an unnecessary war.

Gorgasali ✢ See Vakhtang Gorgasali.

Gorkii, Maksim (Alexey Peshkov) (1868-1936) ✪ Novelist and Soviet propagandist exiled 1905-14 to Italy. Major supporter of Stalin during the 1920-30s as President of the USSR Writers' Union.

Hacibayov **(Hajibayov, Hacibayli, Gajibekov), Üzeyir** ▲ (1885-1948) Azerbaijan's most celebrated composer. His opera version of Fizuli's *Leyli and Majnun* (1908) was the first truly Azerbaijani opera and remains a national favourite.

Hajinski, Isa-bey (1862-1918) ▲ Oil baron whose house on Baku Bulvar is arguably the most splendid of the era.

Hajinski, Mammad Hassan (died 1931) ▲ Politician and instigator of the plan for Baku's waterfront Bulvar, eventually arrested by Beria and died in a Tbilisi jail.

Herekle ✢ (see Irakli).

Hümbätov, Aliakram ▲ Tank commander who led the short-lived Talysh Mugam republic in 1993 (p280). In 1996 he was sentenced to life in jail for abuse of power, a sentence upheld in a 2003 retrial held at the request of the Council of Euroope who considered him to be a political prisoner.

Hussein, Imam (626-680) # 3rd Shiite Imam, son of Ali, grandson of the prophet Mohammed. His death at Kerbala (Iraq) is commemorated in the Ashura; days of self mortification and penance performed by more fanatical Shiites in Iran and Azerbaijan.

Hüsseinov, Surät (1959-) ▲ Army commander whose mutiny in 1993 brought down Elchibey's Popular Front government. Briefly prime minister, he reputedly backed the unsuccessful 1994 coup against Heydar Aliyev and was later jailed for treason. Pardoned in 2004.

Husseinzade, Alibey (1864-1941) ▲ Prominent 19th-century proponent of pan-Turkism, notably in his poem 'Turan'.

Husseinzade, Mehdi Hanifaogly 1918-44 ▲ Partisan agitator in Italy during WWII (see p104).

Ibrahimbǝyov, Rustam (aka Rustam Ibragimbekov/Ibrahimbǝyli, 1939-) ▲ Screenwriter of Oscar-nominated films *Close* *to Eden*, *Burnt by the Sun* (winner) and *East-West*. Also chairman of the Azerbaijan Cinematographic Union and the inspiration behind Baku's Ibrus Theatre (p123).

Iosseliani, Otar (1934-) ❖ Award-winning France-based Georgian film-maker. *Pastorale* (1976) is a character-based drama illuminating the Georgian character, *Brigands* is a hard-hitting glance at the Stalin era with cross references to modern Georgian mafiosi activities.

Irakli II (1720-98) ❖ Often written **Erekle** or **Herekle**, Irakli became King of Kaheti in 1734. He helped Persian armies attack India before annoying his erstwhile allies and reuniting Georgia in 1762 which he fought to maintain until finally capitulating in the epic battle of Tbilisi in 1795 thereafter retiring to Telavi.

Iskander # Turkic rendering of Alexander the Great (356-323BC).

Ismail I, Shah ▲ see Xatai.

Jafar Jabbarly see Cäfär Cabbarly

Javad Khan ▲ The last khan of Gänjä, 1786-1804. The distinctive purple and green silk flag with gold Islamic calligraphy with which he was buried is now in Gänjä Museum.

Javanshir (assassinated 669AD) ▲ Classic Mihranid-dynasty 'king' of Caucasian Albania who forged a pact with Byzantium in an attempt to resist the Arab invasions. Cavanshir Fortress at Talistan (p209).

Javidan (died 816) ▲ Pre-Babek leader of the Khuramid rebellion. An imaginary portrait in Qäbälä Museum depicts him as a nervous, wild-eyed, hairy Paul McCartney lookalike.

Jordania, Noe (1868-1953) ❖ Pre-WWI he was an outspoken Social Democrat. He read Georgia's declaration of independence on 26 May 1918 and was Georgia's prime minister before the Red Army takeover.

Kalinin, Mikhail (1875-1946) ☯❖ Peasant-born metal-worker who rose to be the formal USSR Head of State following the 1917 Russian revolution and retained the position almost continuously for 30 years, until his death. Real power was wielded by Stalin throughout the period.

Kamo (1882-1926) ❖ Pseudonym of ethnic Armenian revolutionary Semyon Ter-Petrossian who, along with Stalin, funded activities through blatant, brutal bank raids in Tbilisi. In a dramatic 1906 raid he stole 341,000 roubles from a carriage en route for the State Bank at Tbilisi and smuggled them in a hat box to Lenin in Moscow. The exposure of criminal funding caused an irrevocable split between Lenin and the milder wing of the Russian Socialists. Kamo was eventually killed in an 'accident', run down by a KGB car.

Kara Karaev see Qara Qaraev

Kasparov, 'Gary' ▲ (1963-) Born in Baku as Garry Vaynshteyn (Weinstein), Kasparov became the youngest-ever world chess champion at the age of 22. He's now a prominent opposition figure in Russian politics.

Kazbegi, Alexander (1848-93) ❖ Writer; born in Stepantsminda (since renamed Kazbegi in his honour). He lived as a shepherd for seven years and was famous for his tales of mountain folk and the Caucasian pastoral life. Died penniless and insane after four years in an asylum.

Ketevan, Queen of Kaheti (1565-1624) ❖ Overturned the Persian-inspired usurper of her husband's father's throne but was herself captured, tortured and eventually burnt by Persian Shah Abbas when she refused to join his Harem and convert to Islam.

Kh For names beginning with Kh look under X (Azeri rending of Kh)

Kirov, Sergei (1886-1934) ☾☯ Was a major player in bringing communist power to bear in the Caucasus especially Azerbaijan. He was assassinated on Stalin's orders when he appeared to be getting too popular, a deed covered up by simultaneously encouraging a posthumous Kirov personality cult. In Baku this was highlighted by the erection of an enormous bronze statue above a Kirov museum. The statue dominated the skyline until it was dismantled in 1991. A 1926 photo of Kirov in the Stalin Museum, Gori, bears an eerie resemblance to Arnold Schwarzenegger.

Koba ❖ Stalin's first pseudonym, based on a folk hero in an Alexander Kazbegi novel.

Koroğlu ▲ Azeri Robin Hood-style hero whose best friend was his horse 'Girat'. Instead of Sherwood Forest, he operated from Chanlibel in the Gädäbäy region.

Kostava, Merab (1939-89) ❖ Leading dissident; would have been a contender for the presidency of post-Soviet Georgia had he not been killed in a car 'accident'.

Kutkashenli, Ismailbey (1806-69) ▲ Born in Qäbälä; the first Azeri general in the Tsar's army, hero of battles in wars against Iran and Turkey.

Magomaev, Muslim (1885-1937) ▲ Celebrated opera singer and the composer of *Nargiz*.

Mähsäti ('Moon Face') Gänjävi ▲ 12th-century poetess, composer, artist and chessmaster. Biographical data is scanty but she appears to have been employed by the Seljuk/Attabek court. In one verse she declares that her bond to poetry is as sacred as the bond of marriage. Female writers were very rare at the time and over-politicized latter-day commentators have extrapolated such notions to portray Mäshäti as an early feminist, claiming she was persecuted for taking a stand against sexism in society/Islam. However, the poems which remain are simply words of encouragement to help people to live fully, thriftily and with love.

Mammadova, Shövkat (1897-1981) ▲ Azerbaijan's first great female opera star.

Mammadquluzade, Calil (1866-1932) ▲ Playwright known for *My brother's book* in which he plays off three brothers representing contrasting stereotypes: the still, intellectual Russified Rustam; the sheepskin-capped Persiaphile Mirza Mohammadali; and the Fez-topped, Istanbul-educated Ottoman Samad Vahid. Mammadquluzade was also editor of the famous satirical magazine *Molla Nasreddin* and inspired/encouraged Sabir (see p369).

Mammedaliyev, Yusif (1905-61) ▲ Prominent Azeri chemist.

Martov, L/Julius (1873-1923) ✪ Aka Yuliy Zederbaum, Martov was born in Istanbul but became leader of the Menshevik wing of the original Russian Social Democrats when the party split in 1903. Lenin controlled the other, Bolshevik, wing.

Marx, Karl (1818-83) # German historian and philosopher; organized the Communist League in London, where he also wrote *Das Kapital* attacking the state and religious organizations as instruments of oppression. Unlike Lenin, he advocated achieving communism gradually using capitalism to build the necessary social/educational framework.

Mehriban (see Aliyeva, Mehriban)

Mehmandarov, Samad-bey (1855-1931) ▲ Military hero in Russia's war against Japan who became defence minister in the 1918-20 independence period. He was initially arrested after the Red Army invasion but later released and became a military instructor for the new regime. Wow what a beard (see p89 & Baku plaque p86, φU6).

Melua, Katie (1984-) ✣ Although a naturalized Briton, this top-selling singer is possibly the best known Georgian in the west (after Stalin of course).

Memar Acami ▲ Literally 'Ajami the Architect' (see Acami Nakhchivani).

Mirian III, King (284-361) ✣ First ruler of Kartli/Iberia (basically Georgia) to be converted to Christianity (AD337). He was son of the Sassanian Shah of Persia.

Mir Jalal see Pashayev, Mir-Jalal

Mirjavad, Javad (1923-92) ▲ Artist whose bold, colourful canvasses drew inspiration from both Cézanne and African tribal art.

Murad/Murat, Haji (1797-1852) ✣ An 1843 recruit to Shamil's mountain guerrilla force whose fearless attacks caused terror amongst Russian troops. Immortalized by Tolstoy. Grave site p229.

Musabekov, Gazanfar (1888-1938) ▲ Communist leader in the 1920s and '30s. He died in the Stalin purges but for decades his bust remained the biggest in Baku until removed in 2008.

Mushviq, Mikayil (1908-38) ▲ Prolific Xızı-born poet with a colloquial twist. Born near the Candy Cane Mountains, died in Stalin's purges, rehabilitated in the 1960s.

Muslimov, Shirali (1805-1973) ▲ The world's oldest man? (see p299).

Mustafazadeh, Aziza (1969-) ▲ Daughter of Vagif; jazz pianist and 'scat' singer.

Mustafazadeh, Vagif (1940-79) ▲ Creator of the 'Jazz Muğam' musical style in the 1970s.

Mütällibov, Ayaz (1938-) ▲ Neo-communist first president of newly independent Azerbaijan (1991-2); resigned in March 1992. His later attempt to 'unresign' galvanized the Popular Front opposition.

Muxtarov, Murtuza (1855-1920) ▲ Baku oil-boom industrialist/millionaire (box p88).

Nadir Shah (1688-1747) # Afghan-Persian ruler who reversed late Safavid Persian decline, counter-attacked against the Ottomans and sacked Shamakha. Led an invasion of India in 1739. His death left a power vacuum in Persia.

Nağiyev, Musa (1849-1919) ▲ Turn-of-the-20th-century oil magnate who was infamously tight-fisted yet paid for the fabulous Ismayıllı Palace (p89) in memory of his son Ismail.

Naimi (1339-96) Ⅱ Real name Fazlallah Astarabadi, Naimi was an Iranian philosopher inspired by Rumi who lead the esoteric Hurufism movement. Seen as a threat to Islam by the despotic rulers of the day, Naimi was imprisoned at Alinca Castle (p311) then put to death on the orders of Timur's son Miran Shah. Naimi's pupil was the confusingly similarly named Nasimi.

Närimanov, Näriman (1870-1925) ▲ Idealistic communist and Azeri-nationalist, founder of the Azeri-language *Himmet* periodical in 1904. He became Soviet-Azerbaijan's leader immediately after the Red Army invasion which crushed Azeri independence, but fought courageously against Lenin to maintain Azerbaijan's pre-Soviet borders. His continuing intransigence with Stalin sealed his fate – he died in mysterious circumstances in Moscow. His body was swiftly cremated, against Islamic mores, before an autopsy could reveal the cause of death (probably poison). See p87.

Näsimi, Imadäddin (1369-1417) ▲ Shamakha-born philosopher-poet whose 'Hurufism heresy' was to postulate that 'God is in the heart' rather than a physical reality. For preaching this doctrine he was eventually arrested in Aleppo (now Haleb, Syria) and sentenced to death. Poorly informed executioners thought that he had claimed to be divine and taunted him 'If you are all powerful, why do you grow pale at the loss of your flesh?' He supposedly retorted 'I am the sun of love on eternity's horizon. The sun always grows pale at sunset'. Then they skinned him alive. Don't confuse him with Naimi nor Nizami.

Natavan, Khurshid Bahnu (1830-97) ▲ Progressive poetess and daughter of Ibrahim Khan who famously entertained Alexandre Dumas in Shusha and played him at chess.

Nevski, Alexander (1220-63) ✪ Sainted Russian prince, hero of battles defending his people against the Swedes and the Teutonic knights.

Nino, St (approx 296-340AD) ✧ Young saint who converted Georgia's king to Christianity. Although commonly referred to as a 'slave girl' she was nonetheless free enough to wander into Kartli from Christian Cappadocia to start her evangelizing. After assorted miracles (see Mtskheta, p344) she died peacefully at Bodbe (p330), much revered.

Nisharadze, Gayoz ✧ Pseudonym for Stalin during 1907 while in Baku.

Niyazi ▲(1912-84) In full Niyazi Zulfigar ogli Tagizade Hajibeyov, Niyazi was a celebrated Azeri conductor and composer.

'Nizami' Ganjavi (1141-1209) ▲ Born Ilias ibn Yusif, the pen name Nizami means 'stringer of syllables' – a professional praise-poet. For one piece of poetic obsequiousness he received, in lieu of a fee, a female slave who later became his wife. Nizami's mature work culminated in a collection of five epics collectively known as *Xamsa* for which he is now considered Azerbaijan's Shakespeare; each is a classic in its own right. You'll find Nizami statues, streets and cinemas in most Azeri towns.

Nobel, Robert, Ludwig and Alfred # 19th-century Swedish entrepreneur-brothers who were amongst the first to invest in the Baku oil fields (from 1874). Alfred's invention of powerful artificial explosives, as well as his Baku oil shares, earned the huge fortune and the sullied conscience that led him to sponsor the international peace prize and other awards which still bear his name.

Ordubadi, Mammad (1872-1950) ▲ Historical novelist, famed for the libretto to the opera, *Koroğlu*.

Panakh Khan (Panah-Ali Khan Javanshir) (1693-1761) Refounded the Khanate of Karabagh in 1747 and built Shusha which he rapidly developed as a musical and cultural centre.

Pashayev, Mir-Jälal (1908-78) ▲ Writer and critic whose 'Manifesto of a Young Man' is read by most school kids. Pashayev's work is being extensively rediscovered now that his grand-daughter Mehriban is first lady.

Pashayeva, Nargiz ▲ President's sister-in-law and owner of Baku's delightful Üns Theatre. She's the 'Nar' of Mobile and the 'Nargiz' after whom Baku's Fountains Square Mall (around McDonald's) is named.

Pushkin, Alexander (1799-1837) ☻ 'Russia's national poet' and author of the classic historical tragedy *Boris Godunov*. Made two visits to Tbilisi which he reputedly adored.

Qara Qarayev (1918-82) ▲ Composer of ballets, symphonies and the patriotic opera *Vatan* (Motherland). Set Nizami's *Seven Beauties* to music as a now classic ballet.

Qaşqäy, Ak Mir-Ali ▲ Celebrated Azeri geologist; see graphic below.

Rafibeyli, Nigar ▲ (1913-81) Wife of Rasul Rza and celebrated poet in her own right. Her father was shot by the Soviets in the 1920s; she narrowly escaped the gulags.

Rahimov, Suleyman (1900-83) Soviet-era parliamentarian and 'hack writer' who got a standing ovation from the Baku legislature for stating that 'God sent us his Son in the form of Gaidar Aliyev [Heydar Aliyev]'. Only the spellings have changed. See 🖥 www.bsos.umd.edu/gvpt/oppenheimer/ 100/remnicknyrb.html.

Rasulzade, Mammad Emin ▲ (1884-1955) The most celebrated figure from the brief democratic republic (1918-20) period. Arrested once the Soviet forces took over but eventually released and posted to Finland to make it easy for him to defect. Such leniency possibly reflects some gratitude from Stalin who had once been released from a Russian jail in Baku by Rasulzade.

Rostropovich, Mstislav ▲ (1927-2007) Globally acclaimed Baku-born cellist and conductor. Received Azeri 'Order of Glory'. House museum in Baku (p102, p101 πN7).

Rothschilds # Financiers of the French 'Caspian Black Sea Company' (founded in 1885) and major players in the development of the Baku oil boom though the family themselves didn't reside in Azerbaijan.

Mir Ali Qaşqäy fondling a red rock (Baku p92 ∂N1, beside Turkish Airlines)

Rüstäm, Suleyman (1906-89) ▲ Novxanı-born poet, translator, playwright and agitator for pan-Azeri awareness.

Rustaveli, Shota (1166-1216) ✤ Georgia's most celebrated poet.

Rza, Rasul (1910-81) ▲ Major literary figure in the Soviet era. 'Everyone needs a third eye' he once wrote, 'an eye to cry the tears and smile the smiles that the two physical eyes are not allowed to express'.

Sabir, Mirza Alekper 'Tairzade' (1862-1911) ▲ Widely celebrated anti-religious poet/satirist and usually pictured in his papax fez. House-museum in Shamakha.

Safarli, Islam (1923-) ▲ Nakhchivan poet.

Said, Gurban ▲ Pseudonym for the author of the must-read classic *Ali and Nino*. Said was probably Lev Nussimbaum, a Baku Jew who converted to Islam, emigrated to Berlin and later fled from the Nazis to Austria. His masterpiece was first published in German. Also wrote as Essad Bey.

Salahov, Tahir ▲ (1928-) Painter whose dark, brooding moods gave Soviet realism a brilliant new depth and hint of cynicism.

Sattar Khan (1868-1914) ♊ The 1908 leader of Iranian Azerbaijan's resistance to Shah Mohammad Ali when the latter crushed Iran's liberal new constitution and stormed parliament.

Shaiq, Abdulla (1881-1959) ▲ As an early socialist he used poetry to highlight the suffering of the oil workers during the boom years; became a teacher and celebrated writer of children's verse.

Shamil, Imam/Sheikh (1797-1871) ✤ Dağestan-born Sufi cleric turned Lezghian resistance fighter against the Russians (see boxes p237 and p232).

Shaumian, Stepan ☙ (1878-1918) Ethnic Armenian Bolshevik-era leader who led the first Baku commune. Now a despised figure considered at least partially responsible for the inter-communal massacres which occurred during his brief reign in 1918 (see 26 Commissars box pp96-7).

Shevardnadze, Eduard (1928-) ❖ Gorbachev's former sidekick as USSR foreign minister then Georgian President from 1992 till deposed in the peaceful 'Rose Revolution' in 2003. In February 1998 an attempted assassination by grenade attack was foiled by his German-donated, $2 million, armoured Mercedes; a replacement arrived within a week with a James Bond number-plate – AAA 007.

Shevchenko, Taras ✪ (1814-61) Ukraine's most celebrated poet, critical of the Tsarist regime and exiled 1847-57.

Stalin 'Man of Steel' (1878-1953) ❖ Born as Josep Dzhugashvili in Gori (p344) where statues and a museum to him remain, Stalin worked at Tbilisi Observatory while funding the Social Democrat Party – proto-Bolsheviks – through bank raids or 'expropriations'. Became thoroughly Russified and his purges, mass deportations of prisoners and reign of terror were unleashed perhaps even more fiercely in Georgia than elsewhere (80,000+ killed, 150,000 deported). Across the USSR perhaps 20 million perished as an indirect result of his rule, including his wife Nadezhda who shot herself in 1932. Stalin is buried in Moscow though some claim his body is actually now in the Georgian village of Akhalsopeli.

Sultanova, Ayna (1895-1938) Early Azeri female revolutionary

Tağiev, Haji Zeynallabdin (1838-1924) ▲ Tağiev developed a small manufacturing company and went on to find some of the richest oil sources beneath land he had bought with the profits. He reinvested in Baku's water-supply systems, sewers, schools, an orphanage and the city's first theatre (on the site of the new Theatre of Musical Comedy).

Tahirzade, Mirza-Alakbar see 'Sabir'.

Tamara, Queen (1154-1213) ❖ Granddaughter of David Agmashenabeli, she was the powerful Queen of Kartli (1184-1208) during the Golden Age (11th century) extending Georgian rule over most of the Caucasus. Her enlightened power-sharing agreement with the noble families has been likened to the Magna Carta. Her bewitching beauty reputedly inspired Rustaveli's classic epic poem *Knight in the Panther Skin*.

She bore her first child aged 40 but it was not Rustaveli's. There are at least two 'Tamara's Castles'.

Topchubashov, Alimardan-Bey (1862-1934) ▲ Tbilisi-born editor of the influential, Tağiyev-sponsored periodical *Kaspii*. Later became the Democratic Republic's foreign minister (1918) lobbying abroad for recognition of Azerbaijan's independence at the post WWI Versailles Conference.

Trotsky, Leon (pseudonym of Lev Bronstein, also nicknamed Pero [the pen]) (1879-1940) ✪ Ukrainian-Jewish revolutionary, President of the St Petersburg Soviet during the brief 1905 Russian revolution and Minister of War under Lenin's 1918 regime. He created the Red Army and regained secessionist parts of the former Russian empire to create a Russian-dominated USSR before falling from favour under Stalin in the 1920s. Fled to Mexico where he was infamously murdered with a Soviet ice pick. His goatee beard-moustache combination was a little more stylish than Lenin's.

Tsitsianov, Paul (1754-1806) ✪ Russian viceroy of the Caucasus 1803-6. Though of distant Georgian descent, Tsitsianov set out to reduce the notoriously independent area to a Russian province. Despite advice to the contrary, he accepted the Khan of Baku's invitation to dinner hoping to negotiate a peaceful handover to Russian power. For dessert the khan blew his head off.

Tusi, Nasruddin (1201-1274) Ⅱ Great Persian scientist, astronomer and mathematician (see box p314).

Usubbekov, Nasib (1881-1920) ▲ ADR finance minister and later prime minister (after Xoyski).

Vagabzade, Bakhtiyar (1925-) ▲ Poet who found beauty in ordinariness; quoted on p200.

Vagif, Mollah-Panah (1717-97) ▲ 'Love' poet, and Foreign Affairs minister in the court of the Karabagh Khan Ibrahim. When Khan Ibrahim was overthrown by his nephew in the wake of the 1795 Qajar-Persian invasion, Vagif was executed by being thrown off a cliff. His Shusha mausoleum is reputed to have been destroyed since 1991 by the Armenian occupation force.

Vahid, Aliaga (1895-1965) ▲ Little known in his life-time, his poetry was popularized after his death and praised for its wisdom and balance. Marvellously creative bust in Baku's Old City.

Vakhtang Gorgasali ✤ 5th-century king, founder of Tbilisi.

Väzirov, Äbdülrahman (1930-) ▲ Gorbachev's choice for leader of the Azeri Communist Party, forced to step down in response to the 20th January 1990 massacres.

Vidadi, Mollah Beli (1709-1809) ▲ Poet who moved from Qazax to the Georgian court of Irakli II to find work but spent most of the time writing about how homesick he was. A contemporary and friend of Vagif. The verses which they originally composed in mutual correspondence are now much celebrated as classic Azerbaijan literature. Ironically for a pessimist who said there was no such thing as a happy ending he lived to 100 years old.

Vorontsov, Prince Mikhael (1782-1856) ✪ As Tsar Nicholas I's viceroy of the Caucasus (1845-53) he commanded the Russian army against Imam Shamil but also built the first theatre in the Caucasus (in Tbilisi) and commissioned Axundov to write original works for it.

Vurğun, Samed (1906-56) ▲ Greatly celebrated Azeri poet/writer. In English translation it's hard to see the appeal of his simperingly Soviet verses, but don't voice your doubts too loudly. He's particularly adored in the Qazax region where his house-museum dominates his home village of Yukxhari Salahlı (see p274). Apartment museum (p91). Park and statue in Baku (p100).

Xaqani (Khagani='regal') Shirvani (1120-94 though some sources say 1126-99) ▲ The adopted son of the Shirvanshah's astronomer/doctor. Tired of writing meaningless praise-verse for his king he set out to see the world; *Tohvatul Irakein* was the resultant epic travelogue. Sickened by the ravages of wars he'd seen he wrote:

How many a tyrant this earth has embraced
Yet still she invites any despot to bed
And rouges her cheeks with the blood that
*   he sheds*

The shah was not happy and Xaqani was imprisoned for implied criticism but still managed to write many great works from the isolation of his dungeon at Shabran fortress (p166).

Xatai, Shah Ismail ▲ (1486-1524) Pen name of Shah Ismail I (p39), king of all Azerbaijan and indeed the Persian empire.

Xoyski, Fätäli-xan (1875-1920) ▲ Prime minister of the Gänjä-based Azeri government in 1918 while Baku was still in the hands of the Bolsheviks. Shot in the back by an assassin in 1920.

Yesenin, Sergey (1895-1925) ✪ Cult Russian poet, whose alcoholism and womanizing were as impressive as his direct, expressive writing. Initially pro-Bolshevik he famously married the American dancer Isadora Duncan in 1922. Not speaking a common language he swiftly jumped beds and remarried, this time picking a granddaughter of Tolstoy. Even a sojourn in Märdäkän (p149) wasn't enough to satisfy him and before he was 30 he'd hanged himself.

Zarathustra (or Zoroaster in Greek, Zarathushtra in Old Persian) ✦ The prophet of Zoroastrianism who came up with the curious notion of monotheism, later adopted by many best-selling religions. Some claim he was born in 588BC near Mt Savalan, in south Azerbaijan, ie Iran and that he spent a considerable period on the Absheron Peninsula though there's minimal proof.

Zarbadi, Hasanbey (1842-1907) Azeri enlightenment scholar and journalist.

Ziadkhanov, Adilxan (1878-1920) and **Ismailxan** (1876-1920) ▲ Gänjä-based brothers who led the initial declaration of the 1918 Azerbaijan Democratic Republic.

Zorge, Richard (1895-1944) # Ethnic German who spied for the USSR in Japan where he was eventually caught and hanged, see map p106 ('The Eyes').

Zoroaster – see Zarathustra.

Zubov, General VA ✪ Russian commander leading the abortive 1795 attack on Azerbaijan. Nicknamed 'Golden Leg' thanks to his shiny, gilded falsie.

APPENDIX E: USEFUL WORDS AND PHRASES

NB To make this section practical, I have used my own phonetic renderings rather than the 'correct' transliterated spellings which are sometimes misleading. Also note that I use the term 'Azeri' as a useful shorthand for the Azerbaijani language. Pedantic linguistics claim that this term is technically inappropriate because apparently there was once an obscure, unrelated Persian-family language called Azeri. The same linguists seem to have no trouble with two utterly unconnected languages called Albanian!

Key words	Azeri ▲	Russian ◐
Greeting	*Salam*	
How are you?	*Necäsän*	*Z dras {Z dras tvuy/tvuyte}*
	{or more formally, *Nicäsiniz*}	
(Very) good	*(Chok) Yakshi*	*Narmal/(Ochin) Kharrasho*
Bad	*Pis*	*Plakhoi*
Thank you (very much)	*(Chok) Saol*	*Spaseeba (Bolshoye)*
Please	*Zehmet olmasa*	*Pozhalsta*
Bon appétit	*Nush olsun*	*Priyatnava apetita*
Beautiful	*Güzel*	*Krasiva*
Delicious	*Dadli/Dad-lırdr*	*Vırkusna*
How much does it cost?	*Bu nechäyädırr*	*Skolka stoit* (numbers p373)
Yes	*Ha/bali*	*Da*
No	*Yok*	*Nyett*
Here/there	*Burda/orda*	*Tam*
This	*Bu nechayadır*	*Eta*
I	*Man*	*Ya*
You	*Siz {san}*	*Vı {Tı}*
He/she/it	*O*	*On/ona/ono*

Where is....?	*.....haradad`r?*	*Gdye.....?*
....hotel	*Mehmankhana*	*Gastinitsa*
....(cheap) restaurant	*Yemekhana*	*Stalovaya*
....toilet (men/women)	*Ayaq yolu (Kishi/Qadin)*	*Tualet (muzhchina/zhenshchina)*
....bath-house	*Hamam*	*Banya*
....(bus) station	*(Avtobus) vaghzalı*	*(Avto) vakzal*
....bus stop	*Avtobus dayanajaghı*	*Astanovka*
....left-luggage office	*Saxlama kamerasi*	*Kamera khraneniya*
....ticket office	*Kassa*	*Kassa*
....hospital	*Khastakhana*	*Balnitsa*
....(book) shop	*(Kitab) maghazası*	*(Knizhni) magazin*
....market	*Bazar*	*Rınok*
....post office	*Pochta*	*Pochta*
....embassy/consulate	*Safirlik/konsullug*	*Pasolstva/konsulstsva*

Transport		
Bus	*Avtobus*	*Avtobus*
Train	*Gatar*	*Poezd*
Which platform?	*Hansı platform-da?*	*Kakaya platforma?*
When does it leave?	*Nä vakht gedir?*	*Kagda atpravlyaetsa?*
When does it arrive?	*Nä vakht gelir?*	*Kagda pribıvayet?*
Does the ticket include sheets? (for overnight trains)	*Bilet doshak aghida dahildir?*	*Belyo verhodyit ver bil lett?*
Fill her up (ie petrol)	*Ağzına kimi*	*Polni*

Hotel — *Mehmankhana*

May I see a room?	*Otagha bakhmag olar?*	*Mozhna pasmatret kom natu?*
Is there....	*..... var?*	*Yest...?*
....a better room?	*Daha yakhshı otag*	*...komnata paluchsheh?*
....a bigger room?	*Daha böyük otag*	*...komnata pabolsheh?*
....a cheaper room?	*Daha ujuz otag*	*...komnata padeshevlyeh?*
....air-conditioning?	*Kondisioner*	*...skondisiyonerom?*
....an en suite bathroom?	*Vanna otagı*	*...swamnoi komnatoi?*
Is breakfast included?	*Sahar yemäyi*	*...zavtrak verkhodyit venomer?*

Restaurant — *Restoran*

Is there a menu?	*Menu var?*	*Yest oo vas menu?*
Is there a cover charge?	*Girish akıvar*	*vkhod platny?*
I'd like....	*.... isteyiram*	*Ya khatel bı...*
I don't want this	*Bunu istamiram*	*Ya nyeh hachoo etta*
Does that cost extra?	*Bunun bashga giymeti var?*	*Nuzhna lee daplata?*
Can I have the bill please	*Hesabı zekhmet olmasa*	*Pozhalsta shot*

Adjectives and adverbs

English		English	
Big	▲ *böyük* ✪ *balshoy*	Small	▲ *kichik* ✪ *malinki*
A lot	▲ *chokhlu* ✪ *mnoga*	A little	▲ *lazim* ✪ *ne-mnoga*
Interesting	▲ *maraglı* ✪ *interesni*	Expensive	▲ *baha* ✪ *daragoi*
Hot	▲ *isti* (eg bread, water)/*qaynar* ✪ *gariachi/zharka*		
Cold	▲ *sarin* (eg drinks)/*soyoq* ✪ *khalodni*		

Days

Day = ▲ *gün* ✪ *dyen*   week = ▲ *hafta* ✪ *nedelya*   month = ▲ *ay* ✪ *mesyats*

Monday	▲ *bazar ertasi*	✪ *panidelnik*
Tuesday	▲ *charshanba akhshamı*	✪ *ftornik*
Wednesday	▲ *charshanba gunu*	✪ *sreda*
Thursday	▲ *juma akhshamı*	✪ *chetverk*
Friday	▲ *juma gunu*	✪ *pyatnitsa*
Saturday	▲ *shanba*	✪ *subotta*
Sunday	▲ *bazar gunu*	✪ *vaskrisenye*
Today	▲ *bu gün*	✪ *sevodnya*
Tomorrow	▲ *sabah*	✪ *zavtra*
Yesterday	▲ *dünan*	✪ *vchera*

Numbers

Counting in Azeri is relatively easy and numbers are exactly the same as in Turkish, except for 1000 and an alternative form of 80. Russian is complicated by obscure grammatical rules which change the case of anything counted in a number ending 2, 3 or 4. Georgian and Xınalıqı both count up to 100 in base 20: ie 57 is constructed linguistically like 2x20+17; similarly 89 is linguistically 4x20+9. This logic should be easy for French speakers.

	Azerbaijani	Georgian	Russian	Xınalıqı	Udi	Talysh
1	*bir*	*erti*	*adin*	*sa*	*sa*	*ee*
2	*iki*	*ori*	*dva*	*ku*	*!pe*	*di*
3	*üch*	*sami*	*tri*	*pshwa / kchir*	*khib*	*se*
4	*dört*	*otkhi*	*chetiri*	*ong*	*bip*	*cho*
5	*besh*	*khuti*	*pyat*	*pwuh*	*ko*	*pench*
6	*altı*	*ekvsi*	*shest*	*zek*	*uk*	*shash*
7	*yeddi*	*shvidi*	*syem*	*yik*	*vrkh*	*haft*

	Azerbaijani	Georgian	Russian	Xınalıqı	Udi	Talysh
8	sakkis	hrva	vosiem	ink	murgh	hasht
9	doqquz	tshra	devyet	yohz	vwi	nav
10	on	ati	dyesit	yaz	vit	do
11	on bir	tertmeti	adin-natset	ya-a-sa	satse	yunza
12	on iki	tormeti	dve-natset	ya-as-ku	patse	dunza
13	on üch	sameti	tri-natset	ya-as-pshwa	khibets	senza
14	on dört	totkhmeti	chetir-natset	yas-as-ong	bibetse	chorda
15	on besh	tkhutmeti	pyat-natset	yas-as-pwuh	kotse	punza
16	on altı	tekvsmeti	shes-natset	yas-as-zek	ukse	shunza
17	on yeddi	chvideti	syem-natset	yas-as-yik	vrkhse	havda
18	on sekkis	tvramedi	vosiem-natset	yas-as-ink	murghse	hazhda
19	on doqquz	tskhramedi	devyet-natset	yas-as-yohz	vwise	nizda
20	yirmi	otsi	dvartset	!kan	!ga	bist
21	yirmi bir	otsda-erti	dvartset-adin	!kan-sa		bisto-ee
22	yirmi iki	otsda-ohri	dvartset-dva			bisto-di
	etc	etc	etc	etc		etc
30	otuz	uz-dat	tritset	!kan-yaz	atuz	
31	otuz bir	tsda-tertmedi	tritset-adin			
40	girkh (qirx)	urmutz	sorok	!ku-ne-kan (2 x 20)		
50	elli	urmutz-dat	pyat-desyat	!ku-ne-kan-yaz (2 x 20 + 10)		
60	altmısh	samutz	shest-desyat	kchir-ne-kan		
70	yetmısh	samutz-dat	syem-desyat	etc		

❑ Place name element guide

Azeri = ▲, Farsi = Ⅱ, Georgian = ✛, Russian = ☉, Turkish = ♠

Name element	Approximate English meaning	Name element	Approximate English meaning
...abad	▲Ⅱ ...ville (often named after someone)	djvari	✛ cross
		duz	▲ salt
adasi	▲ island	düz	▲ flat
ag, ak, aq	♠▲ white	dzveli	✛ new
akhal.../akhali	✛ new	gala/galasi	▲ castle
ashağı	▲ lower	gamziri	✛ avenue
azadlyq	✛ freedom	gora	☉ mountain
bağ	♠✛▲Ⅱ garden	gorod	☉ town
bash/bağ	▲ main/head	göy	▲ blue
batan	▲ get stuck	gül	▲ flower
birinci	▲ first/#1	gülüstan	▲ paradise
böyük	▲ big/greater	gyraq	▲ see qirax
bulaq	▲ spring	haci/haji	▲ pilgrim
...çay/chai	♠▲ tea/river	ikinci	▲ second/#2
çinar/chinar	♠▲ (plane) tree	istisu	▲ hot water (usually a mineral spring resort)
çuxur/chukhur	▲ beneath the hill		
cöl	▲ field	juma/cuma	▲☉ Friday/the main mosque
...dağ	♠▲ Mt...		
dağları	♠▲ mountain range	känd/kändi	♠▲ town
dahma	▲ tower of silence	kara	♠ black
dähna	▲ canyon	kasan	▲ cut
daş/dash	▲ rock/stone	kalaki	✛ town
däniz	♠▲ sea	Kavkaz	☉ Caucasus

	Azerbaijani	**Georgian**	**Russian**	**Xınalıqı**
80	heshtdadt (seksen)	otrhr-motz	vosiem-desyat	
90	dokhsan	otrhr-motz-dat	devinosta	
100	yüz	asi	sto	pan
101	yüz bir	as-erti	sto adin	
102	yüz iki	as-ohri	sto-dva	
etc	etc	etc	etc	
200	iki yüz	or-asi	dve-sti	!ku-ne-pan
300	uch yüz	sam-asi	tri-sto	pshwa-ne-pan
400	dört yüz	otkh-asi	chtiri-sto	
500	besh yüz	khut-asi	pyat-sot	
600	altı yüz	ekvs-asi	shes-sot	
700	yeddi yüz	shvid-asi	syem-sot	
800	sekkis yüz	rva-asi	vosiem-sot	
900	doqquz yüz	skhra-asi	devyet-sot	
1000	min (bin in Turkish)	atasi	tisichi	azr
2000	iki min	ori-atasi	dve-tisichi	- !ku-azr (pronounced ìkwazrî)
10,000	on min	ati atasi	dyesyat-tisichi	
100,000	yüz min	asi atasi	sto-tisichi	
Million	milyon	milion	milion	

> ❏ **!k and !g**
> !k and !g are a half-choked glottal sound

Name element	Approximate English meaning	Name element	Approximate English meaning
kedi	❖ mountains	qirax/qırakh	▲ by the river
kızıl	♠/▲ red/gold	qishlaq	▲ winter pasture
köhna	▲ old	qoyunlu	▲ sheep
kolkhoz	⊙ collective farm	rayon/raion	⊙❖▲ county/province/region
körfesi	▲ bay		
köshku	▲ summer pasture	Sameba	❖ holy trinity
köy	♠ blue	selo	⊙ village
küçäsi	▲ street	shirin	▲ sweet
Lenin	You've got an old map	Sioni	❖ Zion
mikrorayon	⊙❖▲ tower-block suburb	sovkhoz	⊙ collective farm
		soyuk	▲ cold
more	⊙ sea	...su/suu	♠▲ water/river/lake
nakrdzali	❖ reserve	taza	▲ new
neft...	♠▲ oil	tba	❖ lake
nov/novy	⊙ new	tepe/täpä	♠▲ hill
padar	▲ place of nomad cattlemen	tsikhe	❖ fortress
		tsiteli	❖ bridge
per	⊙ ... (mountain) pass	...tskhali	❖ water/stream
peri	▲ fairy (suggests inaccessibility)	...tsopeli	❖ village
		ulitsa	⊙ street
pir	▲ holy place	yaylaq	▲ summer pasture
Prospect/Pr	⊙ avenue/boulevard	yeni	♠▲ new
qala/qalasi	▲ castle	...yurd/yurt	♠▲ settlement
qara	▲ black	yuxarı/yukhari	▲ upper

APPENDIX F: NAMES

Personal names

In the pre-Russian era there were no family names as such. Thus famous individuals such as the great poet Nizami are often labelled with their place of birth (he was from Gänjä, hence Nizami Gänjävi). During the Russian era people typically took family names by adding *ov* (*ova* for women) to their father's name or title (eg Akhund, religious scholar, becomes Akhundov or, by contemporary spelling, Axundov). Those of higher social rank, the 'bey' landowners took the Russianized ending *-bekov* or *-begov*. Since independence some *-ov* family names have been rewritten in their Turkic form *-zade/zadeh* or *-li*. Curiously many *-bekov*s have been only partly Turkified to *-bäyov*. **Examples**: Akhundov = Akhundzade, Khasmammadov = Hasmehmetli; Rustambekov = Rustambeyov = Rustambäyli. The middle (patronymic) name is usually taken from the father's first name followed by *-oğlu* though sometimes oğlu is used as a surname (eg Aghayev = Agaoğlu). When a surname ends ev/ov the equivalent woman's surname will take the form eva/ova as in Russian.

● Note that *-zade* names are very likely to be Azeri in contrast to *-adze* which is almost always Georgian. Other specifically Georgian names end *-idze* or *-ashvili* (son of).

First names In Russian, the name Alexander, common to many first-born sons, is shortened to 'Sasha' in a contraction as predictable as William = Bill in English. Magomed was a Russianized form of Mohammad, itself commonly shortened in Azeri to Mammäd or sometimes Mehmet. The 'translation' was used in compound names too so that, for example, Magomedli and Mammädli are one and the same.

Place names

Once you know a few of the basic building blocks, you'll soon notice that town names are simpler to learn than they seem at first glance. Village names are most commonly formed from basic geographical features (eg white rock – *ağdash*), water sources (*göy göl* – ▲ blue lake, ▲ *soyukbulaq* – cold spring) or human constructions (*Akhaltsikhe* – ❖ new castle, *Tazakand* – ▲ new village). See box pp374-375 for more place-name elements.

Azeri names often end in ...*lı/lü*. this means it is the place founded by, enriched by or named in honour of a certain person or group – eg Hajialili – the village of Haji (ie pilgrim) Ali; ...*lar* is a plural equivalent so Hajilarli is the village of pilgrims; ...*abad/känd* is also possible or you may find Russified/partially Russified versions eg ...*ka/ov/ovka/bekov/bayov*.

Identically named villages are often clumped nearby and might be differentiated by such terms as upper and lower, new and old, or less imaginatively as first and second (▲ birinci/ikinci).

Deciphering an address

Addresses are written starting with the country then region, town, street and finally name – family first, then given name and finally the patronymic (XXX-*ovich* in Russian, XXX-*oğly* in Azeri). This is a logical way to run a postal system but to English speakers it seems back to front.

A potential confusion in Azerbaijan is that, with few exceptions, the *rayon* (province) carries the same name as the major town thereof. Make sure you check which of these is denoted in an address as a *rayon* can be very large. There are several other factors worth noting when given a street address:

● **a)** What is the **apartment** (*kvartiera*) **number**? In the cities, the vast majority of people live in tower blocks and a simple street address like 142 Azadliq will only get you to the doors of a concrete monster where you'll be lucky to find anyone who knows your friend's room number. You may also need the block (*korpus*) number.

● **b)** The vast majority of **streets are named after people**. Confusingly there may be several streets named after people with the same family name so the initial is more than a formality. Also bear in mind that there are Russian and local variants of family names which may at first glance look quite different but are in fact the same. Thus Ak Azizbekov and Ak Äzizbäyov are the same but are quite different from M Azizbäyov. Similarly S Rähimov street is the same as S Ragimov but quite different from Ş Rähimov.

● **c)** Some street names commemorate triumphal **dates**. Be careful when given addresses such as 28th May St 27 to denote the house number with a # to prevent future confusion eg 28th May St #27. Occasionally these streets have their names written out in full just to catch out the unwary: thus 1 May St is the same as Birincimay küçäsi (Azeri) AND Ul Pervomayskaya (Russian).

● **d)** What **district** of town? Streets of the same name sometimes occur more than once within big cities if they are in different city districts.

● **e)** Is it the **old or new name** for the street? Politics has brought a great confusion to street naming. Older people, especially in the provinces, tend to use the old, Soviet-era names, while official documents refer to the present name if one has been decided upon. Some town names have also changed: notably in 2008 Xanlar became Göygöl and Äli Bayramli was renamed Şirvan.

● **f)** If you're planning to post mail to Azerbaijan check whether the recipient has a post office box (safer than street delivery which is almost non-existent). Try to include the postal **index** number (post code).

INDEX

Notes <u>underline</u> = there's a map of that place, **bold** = boxed text, *italic* = the place in question is marked on a map here, ( ) = minor reference, C = photo number. Page references are arranged according to degree of importance rather than chronologically.

TRAILBLAZER GUIDES – TITLE LIST

Adventure Cycle-Touring Handbook	2nd edn Feb 2010
Adventure Motorcycling Handbook	5th edn out now
Australia by Rail	5th edn out now
Australia's Great Ocean Road	1st edn out now
Azerbaijan	4th edn out now
Coast to Coast (British Walking Guide)	3rd edn out now
Cornwall Coast Path (British Walking Guide)	3rd edn out now
Corsica Trekking – GR20	1st edn out now
Cotswold Way (British Walking Guide)	1st edn out now
Dolomites Trekking – AV1 & AV2	2nd edn out now
Inca Trail, Cusco & Machu Picchu	4th edn Jan 2010
Indian Rail Handbook	1st edn mid 2010
Hadrian's Wall Path (British Walking Guide)	2nd edn out now
Himalaya by Bike – a route and planning guide	1st edn out now
Japan by Rail	2nd edn out now
Kilimanjaro – the trekking guide (includes Mt Meru)	3rd edn Jan 2010
Mediterranean Handbook	1st edn out now
Morocco Overland (4WD/motorcycle/mountainbike)	1st edn out now
Moroccan Atlas – The Trekking Guide	1st edn mid 2010
Nepal Mountaineering Guide	1st edn mid 2010
Nepal Trekking & The Great Himalaya Trail	1st edn mid 2010
New Zealand – The Great Walks	2nd edn out now
North Downs Way (British Walking Guide)	1st edn out now
Norway's Arctic Highway	1st edn out now
Offa's Dyke Path (British Walking Guide)	2nd edn out now
Overlanders' Handbook – worldwide driving guide	1st edn mid 2010
Pembrokeshire Coast Path (British Walking Guide)	3rd edn out now
Pennine Way (British Walking Guide)	2nd edn out now
The Ridgeway (British Walking Guide)	2nd edn out now
The Silk Roads – a route and planning guide	2nd edn out now
Sahara Overland – a route and planning guide	2nd edn out now
Scottish Highlands – The Hillwalking Guide	2nd edn out now
South Downs Way (British Walking Guide)	3rd edn out now
Tibet Overland – mountain biking & jeep touring	1st edn out now
Tour du Mont Blanc	1st edn out now
Trans-Canada Rail Guide	4th edn out now
Trans-Siberian Handbook	7th edn out now
Trekking in the Annapurna Region	4th edn out now
Trekking in the Everest Region	5th edn out now
Trekking in Ladakh	3rd edn out now
Trekking in the Pyrenees	3rd edn out now
The Walker's Haute Route – Mont Blanc to Matterhorn	1st edn out now
West Highland Way (British Walking Guide)	3rd edn out now

www.trailblazer-guides.com

Key

LINE TYPES
Border; Cease-fire Line (cannot cross); PETROL STATION with 95 OCTANE; GATE; Roads; CHECK POINT; Tram route; Track; Walking path; Railway; BRIDGE; STEPS; Wall; River

FOOD & DRINK
Better local restaurant; Mid-range restaurant; Other local eatery; Upmarket Café; International food; Fast food/Döner; GEO Georgian; T Turkish; Ch Chinese/Oriental; I Indian; It Italian; Mex Mexican; R Russian/Ukrainian; Upmarket Tea-House; Çayxana; Terrace/Local Bar; Expat Pub; Bakery; Supermarket

Symbols and abbreviations
Dbl = double or twin room, sgl = Single, pp = per person, AZN=Manat, Sta = station, ⊞ = atmospheric, ✶ = recommended, ▲ = Azeri ÷ = Georgian ✿ = Russian ♠ = Turkish

AROUND TOWN
Airline Office; ATM cash machine; Bank; Moneychanger; Bookshop; Bath-house; Carpets; CDs; Embassy; Flowers; Hats; Hair cut; Internet; Laundry; Key cutting; Musical Instruments; Perfume; Photos; Post Office; Pharmacy; Shoe Repair; Stationery; Souvenirs; Telephone; Town Hall; Travel Agent; Wedding Palace

ACCOMMODATION
Top of the range; OK en-suite rooms; Basic but cheap; Turbaza/Huts

ATTRACTIONS
Archaeological Site; Castle, Fort; Palace; Caravanserai; Cave; Fire Temple or phenomenon; Ferris Wheel; Gallery; Hamam, historic bath-house; Museum; House Museum; Statue, Bust, Monument; Theatre; Cinema; Concert Hall, live music or disco; Mosque/Muslim Shrine; Church/Monastery; Synagogue; Viewpoint

TRANSPORT
Main bus station; Bus stand, bus stop; Turkish bus office; Rail station; Airport; Car Hire; METRO STATION

SHADING
Park; Market/Bazaar; Water; Marsh; Open area/car park

❏ **Baku map finder**

Colour section (following pages)

● **C1 Baku**: Statues of Azerbaijan's great poet Nizami are common across the country but few are finer than this one in central Baku (p90).

● **C2 Baku – Top (left)**: The mysterious Maiden's Tower (p80). **Top (right)**: The Philharmonia (p85). **Bottom**: Fountains Square (p90) the green heart of a desert city.

● **C3 Baku – Top**: Stylish new lighting brings an elegant extra dimension to central Baku's cityscape: the junction of Behbutov and 28th May streets (map p93, O12). **Bottom**: Typical night's entertainment in the Muğam Club restaurant (p114).

● **C4 Top (left)**: Fortress tower at Märdäkan (p149). **Top (right)**: Fascinating mud volcanoes (p64) suffer varying degrees of flammable flatulence. **Bottom (left)**: The 'Ateshgah' fire temple at Suraxanı (p154). **Bottom (right)**: Dusk at Yanar Dağ (p155) where a small area of hillside is permanently on fire.

● **C5 Top**: The Yeddi Gumbaz tombs (p198) survey the city of Shamakha. **Bottom (left)**: The 'Candy Cane Mountains' (p161). **Bottom (right)**: Mollah atop Mt Besh Barmaq where local Islam takes a particularly animistic guise.

● **C6-7**: Laza (p189-190) has the most glorious setting of any Azerbaijani mountain village.

● **C8 Top**: Xinaliq (p181) remains Azerbaijan's most magical mountain village though since this photo was taken some of the buildings shown have been altered or collapsed. **Bottom**: While Baku is awash with fancy top-range cars, in the countryside you can still occasionally find Soviet era Volgas as here near Alpan (p186). On the horizon is Mt Shahdağ.

● **C9 Bottom (right)**: Above Cloudcatcher Canyon (p179). **Bottom (left)**: Stark desert landscapes near Janji (map p193). **Top**: Bucolic scenery near Sumaqallı just two hours' drive further west along the same road. What a contrast!

● **C10**: The facade of Shäki's Xan Saray (Khan's Palace, p222).

● **C11 Top**: Shäki offers a unique opportunity to sleep in a genuine old Caravanserai (p225). **Bottom (left)**: Portraits of Imam Ali (p362), nazir-sweets and the 'Hand of Fatima' symbol (p48, box) are all typical features in Azerbaijan's Shiite mosques. **Bottom (right)**: Lenin as a plaything, in Yevlax (p248).

● **C12 Top (left)**: Shälälä waterfall (p289) en route to Yardımlı. **Top (right)**: Springtime at Heydar Bulaqi (map p218) between Kärimli and Xaldan. **Bottom (left)**: Batabat's floating islands (p314) sound more exotic than they actually look. **Bottom (right)**: Nakhchivan's Momine Xatun (p307) is Azerbaijan's most impressive medieval tomb tower.

● **C13 Top (left)**: At Yanar Bulaq in Archivan (p302) you can watch water 'burn'. There are other examples near Qäsämänli (p271-2) and at Yanardağ (p288) where you can set a whole river alight. **Top (right)**: Typical WWII memorial, Agdash (p246). **Bottom (left)**: Former president Heydar Aliyev died in 2003 but statues and museums in his honour have been multiplying ever since. This one's in Neftchala (p284). **Bottom (right)**: The seasonal shepherd-village of Durja (p214).

● **C14** (*clockwise from top left*) **1**: Dine in idyllic isolation at Javran Bulaq near Yardımlı (p290). **2**: Shäki 'halva'. **3**: Tum seller in the Shäki fortress complex. **4**: Hi-tech fruit and veg transport. **5**: Tea is considered a special treat when made with water that's been laboriously boiled in a wood-fired samovar. **6**: Decant hot tea into the saucer if you're in a hurry to get supping. **7**: Typical bazaar. **8**: If you order chicken in a rural restaurant you shouldn't be in a hurry. They'll probably need to pluck a whole bird for you.

● **C15** (*clockwise from top left*) **1**: Making düşbärä (p353) is incredibly fiddly and time-consuming. **2**: Vampire-repelling, garlic-overloaded kalapacha (p353) requires animal parts other dishes cannot reach. Before cooking blowtorch unwanted facial hair. Serve with vodka. **3**: Grilling lüle kebab in Oğuz. **4**: Tea is typically served in armudi ('pear') glasses, often from pots that have more lives than a proverbial cat (here held-together with pieces of recycled aluminium can). **5**: Shäki 'halva' is in reality more like paxlava.

● **C16 Top**: Autumnal Sighnaghi (Georgia, p330) viewed from the city walls above Chavchavadze St. **Bottom**: The spire-filled skyline of Tbilisi (Georgia) as seen from the rooftop of Hotel Sharden (p337).

C1

C3

C5

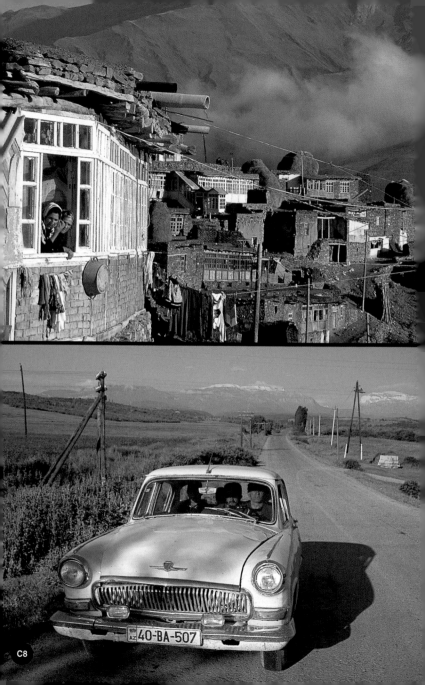

C9

C10

C11

C13

C14

C15

, C16